The Cambridge Handbook of Stakeholder Theory

In the decades since R. Edward Freeman first described stakeholder theory, which views firms in terms of their relationships to a broad set of partners, the stakeholder approach has drawn increasing attention as a model for ethical business. Edited by Freeman alongside other leading scholars in stakeholder theory and strategic management, this handbook provides a comprehensive foundation for study in the field, with 18 chapters covering some of the most important topics in stakeholder theory written by respected and highly cited experts. The chapters contain an overview of the topic, an examination of the most important research on the topic to date, an evaluation of that research, and suggestions for future directions. Given the pace of new scholarship in the field, this handbook will provide an essential reference on both foundational topics as well as new applications of stakeholder theory to entrepreneurship, sustainable business, corporate responsibility, and beyond.

JEFFREY S. HARRISON is a University Distinguished Educator and the W. David Robbins Chair of Strategic Management at the Robins School of Business, University of Richmond.

JAY B. BARNEY is a Presidential Professor of Strategic Management and the Pierre Lassonde Chair of Social Entrepreneurship at the Eccles School of Business at the University of Utah.

R. EDWARD FREEMAN is University Professor and Olsson Professor of Business Administration at the Darden School of the University of Virginia.

ROBERT A. PHILLIPS is Professor of Strategic Management and Public Policy and the George R. Gardiner Professor in Business Ethics at the Schulich School of Business, York University, Canada.

The Cambridge Handbook of Stakeholder Theory

Edited by

JEFFREY S. HARRISON
University of Richmond

JAY B. BARNEY
University of Utah

R. EDWARD FREEMAN
University of Virginia

ROBERT A. PHILLIPS
York University

CAMBRIDGE
UNIVERSITY PRESS

CAMBRIDGE
UNIVERSITY PRESS

University Printing House, Cambridge CB2 8BS, United Kingdom

One Liberty Plaza, 20th Floor, New York, NY 10006, USA

477 Williamstown Road, Port Melbourne, VIC 3207, Australia

314–321, 3rd Floor, Plot 3, Splendor Forum, Jasola District Centre, New Delhi – 110025, India

79 Anson Road, #06–04/06, Singapore 079906

Cambridge University Press is part of the University of Cambridge.

It furthers the University's mission by disseminating knowledge in the pursuit of education, learning, and research at the highest international levels of excellence.

www.cambridge.org
Information on this title: www.cambridge.org/9781107191464
DOI: 10.1017/9781108123495

First published 2019

Printed in the United Kingdom by TJ International Ltd. Padstow Cornwall

A catalogue record for this publication is available from the British Library.

Library of Congress Cataloging-in-Publication Data
Names: Harrison, Jeffrey S., editor.
Title: The Cambridge handbook of stakeholder theory / edited by Jeffrey S. Harrison [and three others].
Description: Cambridge, United Kingdom ; New York, NY : Cambridge University Press, 2019.
Identifiers: LCCN 2019003150 | ISBN 9781107191464 (hardback)
Subjects: LCSH: Management. | Organizational sociology. | Corporate governance.
Classification: LCC HD31 .C326 2019 | DDC 302.3/5–dc23
LC record available at https://lccn.loc.gov/2019003150

ISBN 978-1-107-19146-4 Hardback
ISBN 978-1-316-64204-7 Paperback

Contents

Contributors

Jay B. Barney is Presidential Professor of Strategic Management and the Pierre Lassonde Chair of Social Entrepreneurship at the Eccles School of Business at the University of Utah. He previously served as a Professor of Management and held the Chase Chair for Excellence in Corporate Strategy at the Max M. Fisher College of Business, The Ohio State University. Much of his research focuses on the relationship between costly-to-copy firm skills and capabilities and sustained competitive advantage. He has served as an officer of both the Business Policy and Strategy Division of the Academy of Management and the Strategic Management Society, and has served as an associate editor at the *Journal of Management*, senior editor for *Organization Science*, and co-editor at the *Strategic Entrepreneurship Journal*. He currently serves as the editor-in-chief of the *Academy of Management Review*. His work has been published in numerous leading outlets, including *Strategic Management Journal, Academy of Management Review, Academy of Management Journal*, and *Management Science*, and is among the most cited work in the fields of strategic management and entrepreneurship. Jay Barney is an SMS Fellow as well as a fellow of the Academy of Management.

CB Bhattacharya is the H.J. Zoffer Chair in Sustainability and Ethics at the Katz Graduate School of Business, University of Pittsburgh. He is a world-renowned expert in business strategy innovation aimed at increasing both business and social value. Professor Bhattacharya has published over 100 articles, is co-author of the book *Leveraging Corporate Responsibility: The Stakeholder Route to Maximizing Business and Social Value* (2011) and co-editor of the book *Global Challenges in Responsible Business* (2010) both published by Cambridge University Press. He

has served on the editorial review boards and served as editor of special issues of many leading international publications. He is the founder of the Center for Sustainable Business as well as the ESMT Sustainable Business Roundtable, a forum with more than twenty-five multinational members. In 2007, he started the Stakeholder Marketing Consortium with support from the Aspen Institute. Professor Bhattacharya is part of a select group of faculty that has been named twice to Business Week's Outstanding Faculty list. He has won several best paper awards, teaching awards and research prizes, including the Emory Williams Distinguished Teaching Award.

Douglas A. Bosse is Professor of Strategic Management and the David Meade White Jr. Chair in Business at the Robins School of Business, University of Richmond. His research examines how firms manage key stakeholder relationships to improve firm-level performance. Doug's work appears in *Academy of Management Review, Strategic Management Journal, Journal of Management Studies, Journal of Business Venturing, Strategic Entrepreneurship Journal*, and *Technovation*, among others. He is a two-time winner of The International Association for Business and Society's Best Paper Published Award and on the editorial board of *Long Range Planning*. Doug is a past chair and founding member of the Stakeholder Strategy Interest Group at the Strategic Management Society. He is a University Distinguished Educator, Chair of the Management Department, and Past-President of Richmond's Faculty Senate. Doug often facilitates strategic planning and leadership alignment activities for executive teams.

Jonathan Bundy is Assistant Professor of Management in the W. P. Carey School of

Business at Arizona State University. He received his PhD from the University of Georgia. His research investigates the social and cognitive forces that shape organizational behavior, with a focus on social evaluations, crisis management, stakeholder management, and corporate governance. His research has been featured in *Academy of Management Review, Administrative Science Quarterly, Journal of Management, Personnel Psychology*, and *Strategic Management Journal*. He has also served in leadership for the Stakeholder Strategy Interest Group at the Strategic Management Society.

Donal Crilly is Associate Professor of Strategy and Entrepreneurship at the London Business School. His research focuses on how managers make sense of corporate purpose and stakeholder pressures, as well as how they balance requirements for short- and long-term performance. In his research, he uses textual analysis, configurational analysis, and experiments. He serves as associate editor at the *Strategic Management Journal* and sits on multiple editorial boards. His work has been published in journals such as the *Strategic Management Journal, Academy of Management Journal, Organization Science*, and *Journal of International Business Studies*. He holds a PhD from INSEAD in strategy and a second PhD from University College London in comparative linguistics.

Sergiy Dmytriyev is a Doctoral Candidate in Management, specializing in Strategy and Business Ethics, at the University of Virginia–Darden School of Business. As of Fall 2019, he will be Assistant Professor at James Madison University. His research focuses on stakeholder theory and supererogation (going beyond duty) in organizations and he has published over ten articles, books, and book chapters on these topics. His last co-edited book was on *Research Approaches to Business Ethics and Corporate Responsibility* (2017) by Cambridge University Press. He also holds an MA in Economics from Michigan State University and an MBA from IESE Business School. Prior to joining Darden, Sergiy worked for Procter & Gamble, Bain & Company, and Bayer/Monsanto.

Sinziana Dorobantu is Assistant Professor of Management and Organizations at the Leonard N. Stern School of Business of New York University. Her research spans the areas of nonmarket strategy, stakeholder governance, and global strategy, and focuses on understanding the financial value and evolution of stakeholder engagement strategies, particularly in energy and infrastructure industries. Her research has been published in *Administrative Science Quarterly, Journal of Corporate Finance, Strategic Management Journal*, and *Strategy Science*. Prior to joining Stern, she completed a PhD at Duke University and a two-year postdoctoral fellowship at The Wharton School of University of Pennsylvania.

F.A. Elmore is a J.D./M.B.A. candidate at the University of Virginia, where he serves as the review editor of the *Virginia Law & Business Review*. Prior to his graduate studies, he worked as a senior research associate at Hanover Research, providing clients with strategic advice including best practices in stakeholder engagement.

R. Edward Freeman is University Professor and Olsson Professor of Business Administration; Academic Director of the Business Roundtable Institute for Corporate Ethics; and an Academic Director of the Institute for Business in Society at the Darden School, University of Virginia. He is also Adjunct Professor of Stakeholder Management at the Copenhagen Business School in Denmark, Visiting Professor at Nyenrode Business School (Netherlands), Adjunct Professor of Management at Monash University (Melbourne) and Visiting Professor at the International Center for Corporate Social Responsibility at Nottingham University. Professor Freeman is the author or editor of over twenty volumes and one hundred articles in the areas of stakeholder management, business strategy, and business ethics. He is perhaps best known for his award-winning book, *Strategic Management: A Stakeholder Approach* (Cambridge, 2010), originally published in 1984. Among his many awards, he has received Lifetime Achievement Awards from the World Resources Institute and Aspen Institute, the Humboldt University Conference on Corporate Social

Responsibility, and the Society for Business Ethics. He currently serves as co-editor-in-chief at *Journal of Business Ethics*. In addition, Professor Freeman was recently awarded an honorary doctorate (DHC) in economics from Comillas University in Madrid, The Hanken School of Economics in Helsinki, and an honorary doctorate in Management Science from Radboud University in Nijmegen, Netherlands, for his work on stakeholder theory and business ethics.

Paul C. Godfrey currently serves as the William and Roceil Low Professor of Business Strategy in the Marriott School of Management at Brigham Young University. Paul has long focused on the social impact of business organizations. His research has appeared in *Academy of Management Review, Strategic Management Journal, Journal of Business Ethics*, and *Journal of Management Inquiry*. Paul's most recent book, *Management, Society, and the Informal Economy* (2015), collects essays and research from top management scholars working to understand the role of the informal economy in global poverty reduction. He received his MBA and PhD degrees from the University of Washington and a Bachelor of Science in Political Science from the University of Utah.

Michelle R. Greenwood is Associate Professor in the Department of Management at Monash University. Her research focus is, broadly speaking, critical business ethics. In this context she has developed critical and ethical approaches to a number of distinct areas: ethics and HRM (critiquing ideology and consensus in HRM); stakeholder theory (developing critical and relational understandings of stakeholder theory); CSR (developing political approaches to nexus between CSR and employment); and corporate accountability (analyzing CSR reporting and visual rhetoric in corporate reports). She also has an ongoing interest in publication ethics. Her research has been published in a variety of high-quality outlets, including *Journal of Business Ethics, Journal of Management Studies*, and *Organizational Research Methods*. Michelle is active in critical management studies and business ethics scholarly communities, and works to build links between these fields of scholarship. She

currently serves as co-editor-in-chief at *Journal of Business Ethics*.

Jeffrey S. Harrison is a University Distinguished Educator and the W. David Robbins Chair of Strategic Management at the Robins School of Business, University of Richmond. Prior to his current appointment, he served as the Fred G. Peelen Professor of Global Hospitality Strategy at Cornell University. Dr. Harrison's research interests include stakeholder theory and strategic management. Much of his work has been published in high-impact journals such as *Strategic Management Journal, Business Ethics Quarterly, Journal of Business Ethics, Academy of Management Review*, and *Academy of Management Journal*. He has published eleven books with a variety of co-authors, including *Managing for Stakeholders: Survival, Reputation and Success* (2007); *Stakeholder Theory: The State of the Art* (Cambridge, 2010); and *Foundations of Strategic Management* (2014). Professor Harrison currently serves on the editorial boards at *Strategic Management Journal, Academy of Management Review*, and *Business Ethics Quarterly*. He is also a section editor at *Journal of Business Ethics*. He has served as chair of the Stakeholder Strategy Interest Group at the Strategic Management Society, a group he helped organize.

Irene Henriques is Professor of Sustainability and Economics at the Schulich School of Business, York University in Toronto, Distinguished Visiting Star Professor at the EGADE Business School, Tecnologico de Monterrey, Mexico, and co-editor of *Business & Society*. Her research interests span economics, stakeholder management and sustainability. She has published numerous articles in leading economic and management journals including *American Economic Review, Academy of Management Journal, Strategic Management Journal*, and *Journal of Management Studies*. Irene has served as chair of the Organizations and the Natural Environment Division of the Academy of Management and the Strategy Division of Administrative Sciences Association of Canada. She has also served as chair of the Joint Public Advisory Committee to the US, Canadian, and Mexican Environment Ministers under NAFTA (the Commission for Environmental Cooperation).

Jacob Hörisch holds the Junior-Professorship for Sustainability Economics and Management at the Centre for Sustainability Management, Leuphana University Lüneburg. His main research interests are in the fields of stakeholder theory, sustainability management, sustainable entrepreneurship and sustainability economics. He has published various articles on these topics in internationally renowned journals, including *Business Strategy and the Environment, Ecological Economics, Journal of Business Ethics, Organization and Environment*, and *Small Business Economics*. He was awarded with best-paper awards at international conferences, the Leuphana Best Young Researcher Award, and the Schöller Fellowship of the Dr. Theo and Friedl Schöller Research Center for Business and Society.

David Jonas is a policy analyst who conducted this research as an assistant at the University of Virginia-Darden School of Business. David holds a Master of Public Policy degree from the University of California-Berkeley and a Bachelor of Arts in Creative Writing from Macalester College. David has served as an economic policy aide to Senator Al Franken, an ethics reform aide to Governor Terry McAuliffe, and a policy director to former Congressman Tom Perriello during his run for Governor in 2017.

Thomas M. Jones retired in 2014 as the Boeing Professor of Business Management at the University of Washington's Foster School of Business. His PhD is from the University of California–Berkeley. His current research interests include stakeholder theory, alternative objective functions for corporations, and business ethics. He has published in *Academy of Management Review, Academy of Management Journal, Organization Science*, and *Business Ethics Quarterly*. He was the Connelly Visiting Scholar at Georgetown University in 1999 and the Rust Visiting Professor at the Darden School–University of Virginia in 2010. He won the UW Dean's Research Award in 2000 and the Dean's Citizenship Award in 2003. He won the 2007 Best Paper Award from the

International Association for Business and Society (IABS). In 2005, he received the Sumner Marcus Award, a "lifetime achievement" award, from the Social Issues in Management Division of the Academy of Management.

Daniel Korschun is an Associate Professor of Marketing at Drexel University's LeBow College of Business and a fellow of both the Center for Corporate Reputation Management and the Center for Corporate Governance at LeBow. His research examines employee and consumer reactions to companies that take controversial political stands. His research on stakeholder responses to corporate social responsibility is published in premier journals such as *Journal of Marketing, Academy of Management Review, MIT-Sloan Management Review, Journal of the Academy of Marketing Science, Journal of Public Policy & Marketing, Journal of Business Research*, and *Journal of Business Ethics*. He is co-author of two books: *We Are Market Basket* (2015) and *Leveraging Corporate Responsibility: The Stakeholder Route to Business and Social Value* (Cambridge University Press, 2011). He works with companies to develop innovative CSR practices that generate value for both the company and society.

Johanna Kujala is Professor of Management and Organization at the Tampere University. She is a docent of Business Administration (Stakeholder Management and Business Ethics) and a director of the RESPMAN (Responsible Management) Research Group. Her research focuses on stakeholder engagement and value creation, ethical decision-making, and case studies on corporate responsibility and sustainability. She has published over fifty scholarly articles in international peer-reviewed journals and volumes. She has acted as a visiting scholar at the University of Virginia and the University of Chieti and Pescara, and served as a member of the Executive Committee of the European Business Ethics Network (EBEN). She currently serves as a member of the review boards of *Journal of Business Ethics* and *Business Ethics: A European Review*. She has directed several research projects and is currently a PI of the Academy of Finland project Business to Nature: Stakeholder driven value creation in ecosystem services.

Jae Hwan Lee earned a PhD from Texas Tech University and is currently an assistant professor of management at Hamline University in Saint Paul, Minnesota. He takes a stakeholder approach to strategic management. He is specifically interested in stakeholder work and corporate citizenship. His work has been published in various management journals, including *Journal of Business Ethics* and *Business & Society*. He is an active member of the Social Issues of Management Division, and currently serves as the co-editor of the Division's newsletter (The SIMian).

Ben W. Lewis is Assistant Professor of Strategy in the Department of Management at the Brigham Young University Marriott School of Business. Ben's research explores how firms strategically manage their reputation, particularly within the domains of corporate social and environmental responsibility. His recent projects have addressed how corporations strategically respond to social evaluations such certifications, ratings, and rankings. His work has been published in leading management journals, including *Administrative Science Quarterly* and the *Strategic Management Journal*. In 2017, he received the William H. Newman Award, a prestigious recognition from the Academy of Management for solo-authored work based on a dissertation. Ben received his PhD in Management from the Johnson College of Business at Cornell University in 2013, and a MAcc and BS in Accounting and Economics from Brigham Young University in 2008.

Raza Mir is the Seymour Hyman Professor of Management at William Paterson University, USA. He is the co-editor of the journal *Organization*, and of *The Routledge Companion to Philosophy in Organization Studies* (2015). His research primarily deals with the transfer of knowledge across national boundaries in multinational corporations, issues relating to power and exploitation in organizational settings and their link to broader social and economic regimes. He is also interested in poetry, and is the author of *The Taste of Words: An Introduction to Urdu Poetry* (2014).

Samantha V. Miles is Associate Professor in Accounting and Finance, at the Oxford Brookes Business School, Oxford Brookes University, UK. She is the co-author of *Stakeholders: Theory and Practice* (2006) and has published widely in the areas of stakeholder management, stakeholder theory, corporate social responsibility reporting, socially responsible (ethical) investment and how SMEs deal with environmental challenges. Her articles have been published in high-ranking journals such as the *Journal of Management Studies, Journal of Finance and Accounting, Journal of Business Ethics, British Accounting Review, Accounting Forum* and *Business Strategy and the Environment*. Pedagogically, she specializes in post graduate and doctoral education.

Ronald K. Mitchell earned his PhD from the University of Utah and is currently Professor of Entrepreneurship and holds the JA Bagley Regents Chair in Management in the Jerry S. Rawls College of Business at Texas Tech University. He is also a Wheatley Institution Fellow at BYU, and a Distinguished Visiting Professor and Distinguished Educator at the University of Victoria, BC, Canada. His research interests include both stakeholder theory and entrepreneurship. His articles have appeared in such journals as *Academy of Management Journal, Academy of Management Review, Business & Society, Business Ethics Quarterly, Entrepreneurship Theory & Practice, Journal of the Academy of Marketing Sciences, Journal of Business Ethics, Journal of Business Venturing, Journal of Management Studies, Journal of Small Business Management*, and *Strategic Entrepreneurship Journal*. His academic mission focuses on problems and possibilities in opportunity emergence: understanding the core systems and institutions of society that enable greater human capacity. He researches, consults, and lectures worldwide.

Lite Nartey is Assistant Professor of International Business in the Sonoco International Business Department at the Darla Moore School of Business, University of South Carolina. Her research focuses on various aspects of stakeholder engagement, and examines the relationships, contingencies, and dynamics among multinational firms, multilaterals, governments, and civil society actors, and the implications of these dynamics on both firm performance and societal value. She is especially interested in stakeholder engagement in unique contexts, specifically within the extractive industries (oil, gas and mining) in developing country/emerging market environments, and draws insights and lessons for her research and teaching from in-depth field studies. Dr. Nartey's work has been published in leading outlets including *Administrative Science Quarterly, Strategic Management Journal*, and *Strategy Science*. She received her PhD in management from The Wharton School, University of Pennsylvania.

Robert A. Phillips is George R. Gardiner Professor in Business Ethics and Professor of Strategic Management and Public Policy at the York University's Schulich School of Business. Prior to joining Schulich, he held faculty positions at the University of Richmond, Cheung Kong Graduate School of Business (Shanghai), University of San Diego, The Wharton School, and Georgetown University. He was also the Gourlay Professor of Ethics in Business, at Trinity College, University of Melbourne. His research interests include stakeholder theory, historic corporate responsibility, and ethics in network organizations. He is the author of *Stakeholder Theory and Organizational Ethics* (2003). His work has also appeared in *Business Ethics Quarterly, Strategic Management Journal*, and *Academy of Management Review*, among others. He is special issues editor at *Journal of Business Ethics* and was previously associate editor at *Business & Society*. He has held leadership positions in the Academy of Management, the Strategic Management Society, the International Association for Business and Society, and is past president of the Society for Business Ethics. He was awarded the title of Master Teacher in Ethics by The Wheatley Institution at Brigham Young University.

David Rönnegard is a philosopher and economist (PhD, London School of Economics), affiliated with INSEAD and the University of Gothenburg. David specializes on corporate social responsibility (CSR), with a focus on political, moral, and strategic justifications for CSR. His current research concerns financial ethics, in particular the moral responsibilities of investors. He is the author of *The Fallacy of Corporate Moral Agency* (2015), as well as several journal articles.

Sybille Sachs (Dr. oec. publ. habil., University of Zurich) is founder and head of the Institute for Strategic Management: Stakeholder View at the HWZ University of Applied Sciences in Business Administration in Zurich (Switzerland) and is Adjunct Professor at the University of Zurich (Switzerland) and the University of Southern Queensland (Australia). Her research interests are in strategic management and stakeholder theory. She is the author or co-author of several books on stakeholder management in publishing houses such as Cambridge University Press, and has published over thirty scholarly articles in international peer-reviewed journals. Also, she currently serves on the editorial board at *Business & Society*, helped to organize the Stakeholder Strategy Interest Group at the Strategic Management Society, and served in the leadership group of the Social Issues in Management Division at the Academy of Management.

Stefan Schaltegger, PhD, is Professor for Sustainability Management and head of the Centre for Sustainability Management and the MBA Sustainability Management at Leuphana University Lüneburg. His main research interests are in the fields of sustainability management, stakeholder theory, sustainability accounting and reporting, and sustainable entrepreneurship. Professor Schaltegger's highly cited work covers more than 450 articles and books, including in leading management, sustainability, interdisciplinary, and accounting journals. He serves as associate editor and member of editorial boards of sixteen international journals.

N. Craig Smith is the INSEAD Chaired Professor of Ethics and Social Responsibility at INSEAD, France. He was previously on the faculties of London Business School, Georgetown University, and Harvard Business School. His research is at the intersection of business and society, encompassing business ethics, corporate social responsibility, and sustainability. As well as a broad interest in organizational or managerial good and bad conduct, at the core of much of his research is a focus on developing understanding of corporate accountability. His current research examines the purpose of the firm, social contract theory, corporate governance and sustainability, stakeholder theory and stakeholder value, marketing ethics, and strategic drivers of CSR/sustainability. He is the author, co-author or co-editor of eight books and forty journal articles. His latest books are *The Moral Responsibility of Firms* (with Eric Orts; 2017) and *Managing Sustainable Business* (with Gilbert Lenssen, 2018).

Trey Sutton is Assistant Professor of Management in the Robins School of Business at the University of Richmond. His research examines how firms interact with, and are affected by, influential stakeholders, especially non-market stakeholders such as governments and social movement organizations. His work has been published in *Academy of Management Perspectives* and *Long Range Planning*, among other outlets. Trey is currently serving on the editorial review board for *Africa Journal of Management*. He teaches strategic management and environmental management at the University of Richmond. Prior to his academic career, Trey worked as a management consultant, leading projects related to post-merger integration, performance management, and process change.

Sankaran Venkataraman ("Venkat") is the MasterCard Professor of Business Administration and the Senior Associate Dean for Faculty & Research at the Darden School, University of Virginia. He teaches MBA and executive level courses in strategy, entrepreneurship, and ethics.

He is an internationally renowned scholar and educator in the field of entrepreneurship. He has published extensively and has lectured around the world. He has earned the "Outstanding Faculty Award" at Darden. The Academy of Management, the largest professional body of management educators in the world, has recognized his research by awarding him the inaugural IDEA award for Foundational Research in entrepreneurship and in 2010, *Academy of Management Review*, a leading journal of the academy, cited one of his papers as the most influential in the past decade from among the papers published in that journal.

Andrew C. Wicks is the Ruffin Professor of Business Administration at Darden. His leadership roles across the school include director of the Olsson Center for Applied Ethics, academic director of the Institute for Business in Society, academic advisor for the Business Roundtable Institute for Corporate Ethics, and director of Darden's Doctoral Program. Wicks is a member of the leadership track for the Academy of Management, serving in a variety of leadership roles, including program chair of the Social Issues in Management (SIM) Division. Co-author of five books, Wicks has published extensively in journals in business ethics, management, health care, and the humanities, and served as guest editor of *Business Ethics Quarterly* and *Journal of Management, Spirituality and Religion*. He has received awards for both his research and teaching, and is frequently quoted in mainstream media such as *Bloomberg Businessweek, Financial Times, Fortune*, NPR, *Poets & Quants, Time Magazine*, and *The Washington Post*.

Chapter Summaries

Prepared by SERGIY DMTRIYEV[1]

Chapter 1

The first chapter in this *Handbook*, written by co-editors Robert Phillips, Jay Barney, Edward Freeman and Jeffrey Harrison, sets the stage for the stakeholder work to come, both in this volume and beyond. They examine some of the most important lingering questions found in the stakeholder literature. The first deals with implications regarding the boundaries of the firm. Stakeholder scholars often assume their existence, and use terms such as "internal" and "external " without really accounting for how boundaries are defined. How boundaries are conceived plays a significant, even determinative, role in what is measured and reported in accounting statements, and also have profound behavioral consequences. The role of norms, values, and ethics in stakeholder theory, as well as its pragmatic side, are also discussed. Moving forward, fruitful research topics also include stakeholder-oriented objective functions, multinational comparisons, interdisciplinary work, and integration of behavioral theory. The editors also provide advice regarding empirical stakeholder work and a list of interesting research questions.

Chapter 2

In Chapter 2, Paul Godfrey and Ben Lewis explore the moral foundations of stakeholder theory. Five main trends (or temporal phases) in the development of stakeholder theory scholarship are identified over the last thirty years. Early works tended to examine stakeholder theory from an instrumental (utilitarian) and/or normative (deontological) perspective, while the recent growing body of literature tends to look at stakeholder theory from a descriptive, practical perspective. The emphasis on descriptive stakeholder theory has its ground in the moral premises of pragmatism and pluralism. Contemporary moral philosophy challenges the presence of objective sources of morality as the world is too complex to be governed by universal moral rules, which leads to comprehending the domain of morality as intersubjective. As such, pragmatic and pluralistic perspectives on moral decision-making are the necessary underpinnings for stakeholder theory. At their very core, pragmatism and pluralism aim at achieving individual and societal flourishing, and stakeholder theory helps advance the desired outcomes by enabling constructive and sustainable relationships among stakeholders.

Chapter 3

Michelle Greenwood and Raza Mir take a critical look at stakeholder theory in Chapter 3, arguing that it has become overly conservative over the years such that it does not reflect some of the recent trends in business and society. Among other things, stakeholder theory needs to consider how race, class, culture, and gender shape individuals' decisions and behaviors. Stakeholder theory can be improved by better describing how business functions and how it interacts with our lives. Four key tenets of critical management studies are relevant: the salience of economic class, the power of non-class identity formations, the imperialist nature of global relations, and the intersubjective constituency. Although these tenets pose structuralist challenges for stakeholder theory that might prove to be insurmountable, their humanist challenges hold much promise for stakeholder theory to address many of its limitations by embracing the political and intersubjective constitution of relationships in society. Rethinking capital and property, stakeholder identification, stakeholder engagement, stakeholder governance, and stakeholder relationships could make stakeholder theory more engaged, more analytic, and more emancipatory.

Chapter 4

In Chapter 4, Ronald Mitchell and Jae Lee argue that stakeholder identification is a key element of "stakeholder work" – a system of value creation. Five consequential phases in stakeholder work are identified: from stakeholder awareness work, to stakeholder identification, to stakeholder understanding, to stakeholder prioritization, and, as a culminating outcome of the successful accomplishment previous stages, to stakeholder engagement. The chapter explains in detail how stakeholder identification contributes to the creation of value, namely, through the consonance (mutual support) of stakeholder identification with other phases of stakeholder work. As such, value becomes created only if there are dynamic and inter-supportive interactions across all phases of stakeholder work.

Chapter 5

Chapter 5 explores the role of corporations in society. Thomas Jones and Jeffrey Harrison examine whether, and under what conditions, it might be reasonable for corporations to establish an objective that simultaneously enhances social welfare and increases shareholder wealth, thus leading to sustainable wealth creation in society. First, the origins and key pillars of instrumental stakeholder theory are examined. Then, the authors question the common assumption that corporate profit maximization inevitably leads to maximum social welfare, and demonstrate that a single-valued corporate objective (total shareholder returns) is not the right goal from a societal perspective. Furthermore, aggregate social wealth creation should prevail over shareholder returns if these two goals come into conflict. The authors also propose a solution to resolve this tension: the

corporate objective should be to increase shareholder wealth without making any other stakeholders worse off, which can be achieved by applying Kaldor improvements with compensation. In doing so, it is important to distinguish between wealth creation and wealth transfer, where the latter should either involve compensation to offset the losses of some stakeholders or be avoided.

Chapter 6

Chapter 6 is devoted to investigating the interconnection between stakeholder theory and the disciplines of law and public policy. Andrew Wicks, F. A. Elmore, and David Jonas explore opportunities to deepen and make more overt the connections with stakeholder theory in those fields, aiming to strengthen the quality of their scholarly discussion on the relevant topics, for instance, in corporate governance or government programs. Currently, the law and public policy fields stand at a crossroads and further research developments in both fields could either embrace the ideas of stakeholder theory or discourage their adoption. In their review of the law literature, the authors focus on the areas of corporate governance (including board of directors, management, fiduciary duties, and the business judgment rule), corporate constituency statues and non-shareholder rights, and benefit corporations. In the survey of the public policy scholarship, the authors pay a special attention to such areas as new governance theory, participatory democracy, and public-private partnerships.

Chapter 7

Chapter 7 provides another perspective on stakeholder theory and the law. David Rönnegard and Craig Smith discredit the common belief that shareholder primacy is a legally binding norm in the USA and UK, and suggest that managers can largely run their businesses according to the principles of stakeholder theory without significant legal constraints. At the same time, their analysis shows that corporate law favors shareholders when it comes to corporate governance since shareholders enjoy sole voting rights on corporate boards. In practice, this makes business executives believe they are accountable mainly to shareholders. The authors also demonstrate that shareholder primacy is a strong social norm taught in business schools and popularized among managers. To correct the imbalance between shareholder interests and the interests of other stakeholders, they suggest two solutions: strive for a more inclusive governance structure by granting voting rights to other stakeholders and emphasizing that managers' fiduciary duties extend beyond shareholders, and include other stakeholders as well.

Chapter 8

Jacob Hörisch and Stefan Schaltegger apply a stakeholder perspective to an interdisciplinary body of literature dealing with natural environment and sustainability in Chapter 8. They explain why the natural environment is essential to the successful application of stakeholder theory and then they explore in detail two alternative but profoundly different possibilities for adding the natural environment to the theory. The first approach for integrating the environment into stakeholder theory is to make it an additional stakeholder. The second approach makes the environment an important shared concern among human stakeholders. They analyze pros and cons for both alternatives, bringing up supporting arguments from the literature and those of their own. This chapter also explores how a stakeholder perspective can contribute to solving environmental problems. In turn, stakeholder theory can benefit from developments in sustainability management such as understanding that business is embedded in ecological systems and putting more of an emphasis on future stakeholders.

Chapter 9

In Chapter 9, CB Bhattacharya and Daniel Korschun integrate stakeholder theory with developments in the area of marketing. They explain that the quality of engagement between employees and other stakeholders is largely dependent on the quality of the relationships between the employees and the company they work in. The key to understanding when, why, and how positive interactions between internal and external stakeholders take place lies in the nature of benefits that the company provides to its employees: transactional benefits (gaining attractive job features: role requirements, incentives, supervisor support, etc.) and ideological benefits (applying a stakeholder approach in company's marketing practices). The more prosocial motivation employees have, the more stakeholder-based ideological benefits resonate with them. Furthermore, ideological benefits play a major role in employees' willingness to exhibit cooperative behaviors toward other firm's stakeholders and a broader society.

Chapter 10

This chapter investigates the relationship between stakeholder theory and entrepreneurship. Sankaran Venkataraman argues that the fields of entrepreneurship and business ethics, though they have been developing mainly independently, have much to gain from each other. Stakeholder theory is a link that has the potential to bridge both fields. Stakeholder theory can provide a perspective of the firm as an equilibrating system by promoting fairness and efficiency. Three alternative mechanisms for doing so are the moral manager, the bargaining process, and the visible hand. Also, the entrepreneurial discovery process can help reconcile conflicting stakeholder claims. In addition, the weak and strong equilibrating forces in the marketplace are analyzed, resulting in important implications for both entrepreneurship and stakeholder theory scholarship.

Chapter 11

In Chapter 11, Samantha Miles analyzes how stakeholder theory has been used in the accounting literature, focusing on management accounting, financial accounting, and sustainability reporting. Based on the survey of twenty-eight accounting and special issue journals, she found out that accounting is behind other fields in embracing innovative ideas of stakeholder theory. Use in accounting is mainly limited to explaining firm's voluntary disclosure and exploring how reporting can help fulfill stakeholder needs. Lack of attention to stakeholder theory may be explained by the dominance of the shareholder primacy paradigm and the sociocultural characteristics of accounting. Accounting is focused on direct business operations and mostly ignores medium- and long-term indirect impacts on various firm's stakeholders, ecosystems, and society at large. The current challenges associated with embracing the tenets of stakeholder theory in accounting represent an opportunity for much-needed scholarship in the field.

Chapter 12

In Chapter 12, Douglas Bosse and Trey Sutton describe the results of a detailed search of premier management journals to identify a representative set of research articles that address the intersection of stakeholder theory and strategic management. Seventy-one articles were divided into an organizing framework by grouping the papers based on the construct relationships each attempted to explain. Our understanding of stakeholder management has improved with the numerous recent applications of stakeholder theory to strategic management. However, there are opportunities to broaden our collective understanding in important areas. Many constructs that are found in the strategy literature have not yet been given adequate attention through a stakeholder lens, such as the nature of knowledge, firm capabilities, competitive context, organizational form and the boundaries of organizations, and institutional and legal regimes. As more strategic management scholars begin to explore the potential of stakeholder theory to address their research questions, more of these construct categories should be utilized.

Chapter 13

Chapter 13 brings stakeholder theory into the classroom. Irene Henriques explores the methods

and techniques used to teach stakeholder theory in management courses. The chapter outlines some interesting practices that stakeholder scholars have employed in management education to challenge future business leaders to develop creative solutions and understand business issues from a more holistic perspective. Teaching of stakeholder theory to business students resonates well with the concept of "stakeholder work" described in detail in Chapter 4 of this *Handbook* (e.g., stakeholder awareness, identification, understanding, prioritization, and engagement). Methods for bringing stakeholder theory to life in the classroom include video cases, stakeholder negotiation exercises, social protest novels, and issue-based stakeholder town hall exercises. Exercises can enhance learning about stakeholder theory, such as embracing our biases, broadening a notion of value, filtering large arrays of incoming information, understanding the role of social media in amplifying stakeholder influence, and dealing with conflicts between social actors and companies. The chapter also outlines support materials that could serve as helpful resources for teaching stakeholder theory to future business leaders.

Chapter 14

In Chapter 14, Johanna Kujala and Sybille Sachs investigate how the ideas of stakeholder theory are practiced in the real world by specifically looking at stakeholder engagement. The authors review and structure the recent stakeholder engagement literature, the large part of which is based on clinical (real life) case studies, by applying a general framework. The framework, developed jointly with Edward Freeman, consists of four themes: examining stakeholder relations, communicating with stakeholders, learning with and from stakeholders, and integrative stakeholder engagement. Several important issues are identified in each of the four themes. Insights are offered to help advance stakeholder engagement scholarship and identify opportunities for further research on the subject.

Chapter 15

In Chapter 15, Jonathan Bundy examines stakeholder management through topics such as human cognition, emotion, and behavior, based on the premise that all businesses are comprised of humans, and humans are complex. Stakeholder-centered research is helpful in understanding the complexity of human nature on organizational outcomes. For example, in the wake of an expectancy violation, it may be important to consider not only how stakeholders are influenced by their own expectations (based on prior perceptions and experiences with the firm), but also how they are influenced by other stakeholders' expectations (based on how other stakeholders react to the violation). Considering such factors not only extends our behavioral understanding of firm–stakeholder relationships, but also considers the role of social context. Another critical behavioral topic for researchers to consider is the role of affect and emotions in stakeholder relationships. Future research might also address how the degree of emotional arousal (so called "hot" versus "cold" emotions) influences stakeholder reactions, perhaps in response to issues of fairness and trust. In addition, research might consider how firm leaders' emotional intelligence influences the depth and breadth of their stakeholder engagement.

Chapter 16

Donal Crilly, in Chapter 16, also examines stakeholder theory through the prism of behavioral research, which aims to bring realistic assumptions about human behaviors, emotions and cognition to understanding how to manage stakeholders. Although a broad stakeholder orientation – engaging with numerous stakeholders in the social-political environment – is associated with positive outcomes for firms in the form of increased collaboration and reduced conflict with actors in their sociopolitical environments, companies are constrained with limited resources. Looking inside the firm, particularly at how interdependencies and trade-offs across stakeholders are viewed and managed, helps to explain why some firms attend

to the interests of more stakeholders than others. Also, efforts to appeal to some stakeholders often fail to create value for firms. Behavioral research in stakeholder theory can address two overarching themes: how executives interpret their environment and devise appropriate responses (thus, accounting for heterogeneity across firms) and how stakeholders make sense of corporate data and difficult-to-observe corporate practices (thus, accounting for heterogeneity across outcomes).

Chapter 17

Sinziana Dorobantu observes in Chapter 17 that, although the literature on stakeholder theory provides many innovative ideas for successful stakeholder management, advancements in stakeholder research have opened up more new questions than they have answered. Three areas provide ripe opportunities for future stakeholder theory scholarship. The first is exploring mechanisms (contractual vs. relational), arrangements (dyadic vs. collective), and time horizons for stakeholder governance. The second involves examining the stakeholder landscape in full, especially interactions among stakeholders themselves, and how their differences (e.g., in values, norms, and access to information and skills) influence stakeholder management effectiveness. The third is investigating how broader institutional and physical environments enable or constrain stakeholder interactions. There is a need for a broadening of the scope of stakeholder research beyond its traditional unit of analysis – firm–stakeholder interactions – by studying relationships among stakeholder groups themselves within a broader environment.

Chapter 18

In Chapter 18, Lite Nartey argues that rather than pursuing generalizability, stakeholder scholars may instead consider focusing on contextual richness, especially in those situations where a deeper and more nuanced understanding of stakeholders and their environments is needed. Value creation is arguably *the* primary outcome sought from stakeholder engagement strategies by firms and a diverse set of other actors, such as governments, multilaterals, and nonprofit organizations. In addition to variation by actor type, the value created or sought by stakeholders will differ based on political, social, economic, and cultural situational and temporal factors. Value gained or created must also be shared among diverse stakeholders and how that value is shared (e.g., equitably, equally, by actor attribute) will also differ by actor type and situational and temporal factors. Value created may fundamentally change over time and the destruction of value may also depend on time and place. To develop new practice- and policy-relevant stakeholder engagement scholarly work, careful integration of contextual factors within scholarly research design is critical.

Notes

1. Sergiy Dmtriyev is a doctoral student at the Darden Graduate School of Business, University of Virginia.

PART I

Theoretical Foundations of Stakeholder Theory

Stakeholder Theory[*]

ROBERT A. PHILLIPS
York University

JAY B. BARNEY
University of Utah

R. EDWARD FREEMAN
University of Virginia

JEFFREY S. HARRISON
University of Richmond

Though there is clearly a "family resemblance" to the work that is typically done under its bailiwick, stakeholder theory continues to resist precise circumscription. Like the organizations it attempts to understand, the boundaries of the theory remain contentious. While various attempts have been made to clearly define the parameters of stakeholder theory (i.e., Clarkson Center for Business Ethics, 1999; Donaldson & Preston, 1995; Freeman, et al., 2010; Jones & Wicks, 1999; Phillips, 2003; Phillips, Freeman & Wicks, 2003), none of these efforts have gained universal acceptance. The following, which combines ideas from a variety of well-known sources (Freeman, 1984; Freeman, et al., 2010; Freeman, 2017), conveys the ideas that tie together stakeholder thinking:

> Business is a set of value-creating relationships among groups that have a legitimate interest in the activities and outcomes of the firm and upon whom the firm depends to achieve its objectives. It is about how customers, suppliers, employees, financiers (stockholders, bondholders, banks, etc.), communities, and management work cooperatively to create value. Understanding a business means understanding how these relationships work. The manager's job is to shape and direct these relationships.

With these ideas in common, stakeholder theory has struck a chord with scholars across a myriad of academic disciplines (Laplume, Sonpar, & Litz, 2008). Particularly in the current age of organizational complexity characterized by subcontracting, outsourcing, joint ventures, "doing business as"

(DBA), the "gig economy," etc., clear thinking about the organization of stakeholders and their cooperative role in value creation is needed more now than ever. By way of setting the stage for the work to come (both within this volume and beyond), below we will examine what we see as the important lingering questions for stakeholder theory.

Boundaries of the Firm

Perhaps the most fundamental question about stakeholder theory for management scholars is defining the boundaries of an organization. To some this is the defining challenge to stakeholder theory. Until the theory can define the boundaries of the firm, there is no "inside" that distinguishes the firm from the market. And because stakeholder theory includes actors that are typically seen as outside the boundaries of the firm (e.g., suppliers, customers, local communities), it is thought necessary that stakeholder theory present some principled way to re-define the boundaries. Critics maintain that until stakeholder theory provides a simple, elegant, binary, and parsimonious definition of the firm, it must itself remain outside the mainstream of economics and strategic management. However, rather than the defining challenge *to* stakeholder theory, we argue that firm boundaries are the defining challenge *of* stakeholder theory. That is, stakeholder theory invites us to reevaluate both what constitutes a firm boundary and what it means to be inside or outside.

At least since Coase, one of the most closely examined questions in management and economics scholarship has been why some economic interactions take place in firms rather than markets (recent reviews include Gibbons, 2005; Santos and Eisenhardt, 2005; Zenger, et al., 2011). Often taking the market as the default arena for economic value creation and trade, scholars seek to explain the conditions under which some transactions take place within the centralized, hierarchical, managerially controlled sphere of the firm. These theories include explanations of when and why markets may fail to maximize efficiency (e.g., transaction costs, complex coordination, knowledge sharing, etc.) and how collecting these activities under the control of a central hierarchy can improve efficiency.

Alternatively, these theories must also provide some answer to why there are many firms rather than simply one very large one – that is, what are the limits to efficiency gains from moving value creation inside the boundaries of the firm? According to extant scholarship, firm boundaries affect the degree of authority and control, shape social identity, influence informal organization and knowledge exchange, and permit activity coordination (Zenger, et al., 2011) and have been defended based on efficiency, power, competence, and identity (Santos and Eisenhardt, 2005).

Notwithstanding this remarkable wealth of scholarly insight, many of these questions remain under-addressed within the ambit of stakeholder theory. Indeed, for many stakeholder scholars, something called "the firm" (or the corporation, or the organization, etc.) is more or less assumed to exist and the boundaries are more or less taken for granted. This notwithstanding, the fact is that stakeholder theory's *raison d'etre* is to understand managerial behavior regarding actors typically seen as outside the firm's direct control and the implications of these behaviors. How one thinks about the question of organizational boundaries has implications across a myriad of stakeholder theoretic concerns.

For the most part, stakeholder studies make unstated, perhaps even unrecognized, assumptions about boundaries between actors. Terms such as primary and secondary or internal and external stakeholders are used, and their implications expounded with little or no justification given for drawing the distinction. For many organization scholars, this represents a significant gap in stakeholder theorizing. There are several reasons why this gap may matter, including, but not limited to, what processes and activities can and should be measured and how the actors involved think about themselves, others, and their relationships.

The effects of boundaries on accounting measures – It is a well-recognized difficulty for stakeholder theory that standard metrics of firm success are inadequate to capture total value created by the organization (Coff, 1999; Garcia-Castro and Aguilera, 2015). For example, some financial investments in stakeholders are considered expenses for the purposes of standard financial accounting and profitability measurement. Employee salaries are the most obvious case of stakeholders receiving (appropriating) funds that might otherwise be counted as profit. R&D and customer support are investments in customer utility that are nevertheless considered expenses, as are financial outlays for improving local communities (Hatherly, et al., 2018). Whether each of these stakeholders is considered inside the organization or outside (e.g., private contractor) will have different implications for recorded accounting profits and total value creation and the perceived difference between the two.

Speaking to the relationship between organizational boundaries and accounting, Miles (Chapter 11) writes,

> The boundary of reporting is based on ownership, control and significant influence within the definition of the legal entity. This determines what is, and, is not considered to be part of the organization and therefore what activities are reasonable to expect an organization to report on.

We can see from this quote that how boundaries are conceived plays a significant, even determinative, role in what is measured and reported in accounting statements. Work is well underway in the management and accounting disciplines to adapt accounting measures to the needs of stakeholders (Harrison and van der Laan Smith, 2015), but greater refinement is needed.

We would hasten to add that we are in the early stages of this stakeholder accounting process and that the early days of financial accounting were fraught with questions of accuracy, consistency, validity, reliability, and comparability. Eventually, those with some use for financial accounting reports came to agree – in general – on the proper metrics, but even today controversies remain both within and across financial accounting regimes.

It is also important to remember that accounting measures originally emerged to answer specific, typically financial, questions (e.g., comparability across time periods and between firms). In some ways, the demands of comparability from financial stakeholders and regulatory actors "outside" the firm precipitated the emergence of financial accounting. Managerial and cost accounting within the firm emulates this model. Measures designed for reporting on the *outcomes* of value creation processes became goals (*objective functions*) in their own right. The apparent accuracy, precision, and immediacy of the measures allowed them to emerge – and in some cases supplant – seemingly more nebulous firm purposes and sources of value. The mirage of measurability (methodolatry) and the power imputed by modern society to mathematical quantification is both an opportunity and a danger to managers.

As accountants and practitioners continue to refine their definitions of the firm – and perhaps even more so after agreement is reached on stakeholder metrics – managers and scholars would be well-advised to question what role accounting (and legal) definitions of the firm play in their own thinking. With an explicit and critical emphasis on values, stakeholder theory seeks to correct the psychological tendency toward "*displacement of goals* whereby 'an instrumental value becomes a terminal value'" (Merton, 1957/1968: 253 – emphasis in original). More below on terminal values and the role of purpose in stakeholder theory, but first there is more to say about the psychology of firm boundaries.

The effects of boundaries on actors' psychological processes – In addition to their influence on what is reported in financial documents, perceptions of organizational boundaries have profound psychological impacts. At the most fundamental level, ideas about who is inside and who is outside these boundaries affect who is and who is not considered a stakeholder as well as their relative managerial salience. This assessment, in turn, affects how actors interact. Miles writes, "Accounting also serves as a bonding mechanism designed to increase goal congruence through the construction of contracts tied to accounting ratios" (Chapter 11). In-group bias, perceptions of equity, fairness and reciprocity, social identity, and who does and does not "fit" within these boundaries are all influenced by where one draws the lines around a firm.

Much of this is familiar in some forms to management scholars (e.g., Ashforth and Mael, 1989; Blau and Scott, 1962; Ouchi, 1980), and has emerged as among the most influential directions in recent stakeholder scholarship (Bosse, Phillips, and Harrison; 2009; Brickson, 2005, 2007; Bridoux & Stoelhorst, 2014, 2016; Bundy, Vogel, & Zachary, 2018; Bundy, Shropshire, & Buchholtz, 2013; Crane and Ruebottom, 2011; Harrison, Bosse & Phillips, 2010; Korschun, 2015; Nason, Bacq & Gras, 2018). Work nevertheless remains to more precisely, holistically, and critically capture the influence of perceived boundaries on actors' psychological conceptions of their place in networks of value creation.

The prospects for behaviorally informed stakeholder theory is a common refrain within this volume as well. Bhattacharya and Korschun (Chapter 9) consider, among other contributions from marketing, the role of boundary-spanning employees. The boundary being spanned by these employees is that between internal and external stakeholders – the boundary itself is assumed. Similarly, Crilly (Chapter 16) concludes that, "The stakeholder problem is as much one of managing attention *within* the firm as it is one of managing external demands upon the firm" (emphasis original). Bosse and Sutton (Chapter 12) and Bundy (Chapter 15) join the call for an increased role for behavioral and cognitive science in the future of stakeholder scholarship.

The potential contributions will depend a great deal on the continuing viability of, and justification for, where and how to draw firm boundaries. Indeed, the want of such justifications and rationales has led some to conclude that we should abandon the search for firm boundaries. As we elaborate below, the question of boundaries – indeed all stakeholder questions – should be examined from a pragmatic perspective with boundaries being ultimately justified by their practical, managerial relevance. Pragmatism also informs our perspective on the role of values, norms, and ethics in stakeholder theory to which we now turn.

Values, Norms, and Ethics in Stakeholder Theory

The emphasis on the "legal entity" in the Miles quote above suggests a role for law in defining the boundaries of the firm. This is consistent with influential theories of firm boundaries emphasizing efficiency. Santos and Eisenhardt (2005) write, "Focusing on minimizing governance costs, the efficiency conception asks whether a transaction should be governed by a market or organization. This conception is grounded in a *legal* understanding of organizations as governance mechanisms distinct from markets." (2005: 492 – emphasis original). However, upon close examination, the legal status of firm boundaries is itself a complex question.

In Chapter 7, Rönnegard and Smith address the firm as an Anglo-American legal entity (see also Heminway, 2017). They conclude that even if there is no legal requirement to maximize shareholder wealth, the normative belief that shareholder wealth is the right and proper objective function of management has become such a pervasive norm that the legal requirement may be irrelevant. In fact, the shareholder primacy norm (SPN) determines, in part, how managers are evaluated and compensated through stock grants and options. Much work remains in assessing and adapting legal regimes and public policy to the realities of global commerce (see Wicks, et al., Chapter 6), but what is clear is that normative considerations also play a prominent role in understanding organizational boundaries.

The role of norms, values, and ethics have been fundamental to stakeholder theory from the earliest days. In his original elaboration, Freeman writes,

Every manager knows that value judgements are a primary ingredient of a successful strategy. Not only must values be taken into consideration when formulating strategy, but if the strategy is to be implemented the values of those affected by it must also be factored into the equation. When values are shared throughout an organization, implementation or strategy execution is relatively simple. (1984: 89 f)

The role of ethics in stakeholder theory became a more prominent – and contentious – element of the theory in subsequent decades. In perhaps the most influential stakeholder theoretic journal article to date, Donaldson and Preston (1995) write that, "stakeholder theory is fundamentally normative" (1995: 86) and "the ultimate justification for the stakeholder theory is to be found in its normative base" (1995: 87 f).[1] Similarly, Jones and Wicks (1999) write of their "convergent" stakeholder theory that its "normative foundation ('core') is explicitly and unabashedly moral and has to be explicitly defended in moral terms" (1999: 215). As the commentaries that accompany the Jones and Wicks article attest (Freeman, 1999; Gioia, 1999; Trevino and Weaver, 1999), the place of normative concepts within stakeholder theory has been hotly debated.

Why the role of norms, values, and ethics in stakeholder theory has been such lightning rod for debate is itself a point of contention. Some maintain that including normative considerations has no place in positive ("empirical") scientific inquiry (Treviño and Weaver, 1999). This objection seems to ignore the fact that norms are clearly amenable to empirical observation. Entire fields of study (e.g., sociology, anthropology) are premised on the ability to observe social and cultural norms. While it is true that there is a metaphysically dependent way of looking at ethics as valid only *a priori* and some prominent stakeholder scholars (many trained as moral philosophers) have reinforced this narrow, disciplinarily specific perspective, this is far from the only way to think about ethics. American Pragmatism vigorously defends ethics as an altogether empirical phenomenon. We return to the role of pragmatism below.

Norms and Contracts – Many of the above questions are thought to be rendered moot by the existence of contracts (or "complete contingent claims contracts"). The boundaries of the organization are contractually defined. Measurement and performance are defined in reference to these contractual terms and the underlying psychology of the actors is thought to be largely irrelevant to contracts and their enforcement. A nexus of contracts understanding of the firm has provided innumerable insights, but also suffers from severe shortcomings. Indeed, Barney (2018) argues that it is only because contracts evidence a measure of uncertainty, information asymmetry, and resource co-specialization that economic profits are even possible. He concludes that resource-based theory must adopt a stakeholder perspective. In addition to this logic, other theoretical gaps can be filled with a more nuanced and explicit consideration of empirical norms.

We are far from the first to point out this potential. Others have argued that " ... detailed negotiated contracts can get in the way of creating good exchange relations" and "legalistic remedies can erode the interpersonal foundations of relationship-[s]" (quoted in Zenger et al., 2011). Stakeholder theory seeks to bring these managerial issues to the fore. Norms are particularly relevant in the event of *ex post* contractual holdup opportunities by one of the parties. Parties create contracts to coordinate their future transactions, but in many cases one or both parties inaccurately predicts the surplus created (Barney, 1986) through the transaction and seeks to "re-negotiate" or even "efficiently breach" the contract when the inaccuracy becomes manifest. In still other instances, one of the actors is simply more powerful and can impose new terms on the less powerful transaction partners. Two things are interesting in such cases for our purposes.

In the former context – that of good faith misapprehension of future surplus – norms of fairness will pervade this new round (Bosse & Sutton, Chapter 12). And perceptions of the fairness of the newly renegotiated terms will influence the likelihood of future contracts between the parties. These perceptions may also affect the terms of future contracts between the parties and others not directly involved through the process of "generalized reciprocity." The advantaged party in this re-negotiation would handicap their future opportunities by failing to recognize the role of fairness norms.

The latter context includes cases of powerful customers who contract with suppliers, perhaps inducing relationally specific investments, then opportunistically take advantage of these investments by altering the terms to the benefit of the more powerful party. Increasingly common, however, are cases where firms demand terms of their contractual partners based on societal calls for responsible business practices. Contractual demands of this sort (e.g., supplier codes of conduct) include stipulations involving how and where raw materials are sourced, how supplier or subcontractor employees are treated, environmental and ecological practices and similar issues relating to the contract partners' own stakeholders further down the value chain.

Such matters have historically been considered within the discretionary purview of each contracting party. The increasing prevalence of outsourcing, independent contracting, sharing economy, and other creative arrangements of economic activity make claims of arm's length contracts increasingly difficult to sustain and are substantially altering the managerial landscape. In these cases, the boundaries of the firm are blurred. The ability to control and direct how personnel and resources are combined and deployed are among the defining characteristics of being "inside" the firm. Where "market contracts" contain clauses that permit the fiat direction of employment conditions, raw materials acquisition, selection of other business partners, and a myriad of other matters, it is unclear what "outside" or "market" mean.

Determining which people and processes to bring inside the boundaries of the organization (make or buy) has been central to strategic management scholarship for decades. Practicing managers, meanwhile, have been working hard to find innovative forms of organization that largely ignore these very boundaries. "Though hybrids are commonly framed as 'intermediate' forms, manager's real objective is not crafting governance that is intermediate to markets and hierarchies, but rather crafting governance that enjoys the virtues of both markets and hierarchies." (Zenger, et al., 2011: 115)

Critical and explicit examination of operative norms is among the avenues of greatest potential of stakeholder theory. We opened this discussion of values, norms, and ethics in stakeholder theory by reference to the role of shareholder primacy as a norm rather than a legal requirement (Rönnegard and Smith, Chapter 7). If shareholder wealth maximization is not a legally mandated objective function of for-profit firms, then what is the firm's proper objective function? In the complex world of stakeholder relationships, is the concept of an objective function functional?

Stakeholder Theory and Objective Functions

How to understand a firm's objective function from a stakeholder theoretic perspective is a matter of great interest among stakeholder scholars. Consistent with the preceding, much of this interest has been framed by normative concerns. Even where the objective function is implied or even taken for granted, there must be some underlying normative justification. Prominent examples of normative justifications include the obligations of stakeholder fairness (Phillips, 2003), the power of contracts and consent (above) and property rights (Asher, Mahoney, and Mahoney, 2005). As Donaldson and Preston write, "Even Friedman's (1970) famous attack on the concept of corporate social responsibility was cast in normative terms." (1995: 71).

Jones and Harrison (Chapter 5) take up this challenge of critically examining the role of firms in promoting social welfare and introduce what we will call "Jones Optimality" (cf., Pareto and Kaldor/Hicks optimality). Jones and Harrison write, "*how* a firm generates additional profits matters a great deal with respect to enhancing social welfare." (Chapter 5 – emphasis theirs). They go on to write:

We premise our discussion of alternative corporate objectives on three fundamental principles. First, aggregate wealth must never be destroyed in the "wealth creation" process; profit should not be pursued in cases where social/economic welfare, including effects on all corporate stakeholders, is reduced. Second, the baseline

condition for comparison purposes must be the set of existing entitlements of current normatively legitimate stakeholders[2] of the firm ... Third, the profit motive must be retained. The economic incentive provided to those who seek to gain from the creation of new wealth should not be replaced. (footnote original)

... an appropriate corporate objective is that the firm should increase the wealth of its shareholders without reducing (and presumably increasing) the aggregate wealth of its other stakeholder groups.

Relating the firm's objective function to broader societal well-being is echoed among other stakeholder scholars. Greenwood and Mir (Chapter 3) present a deep critical challenge to what they see as the narrowly constricted and simplistic view presented by much extant stakeholder scholarship, writing, "The simple idea of a claim or investment, which brings with it exposure to risk, when interpreted in the broadest sense, might take us some distance to making us think differently about the purpose of the firm and its relations with those who affect or are affected by it." How broadly to define the scope of stakeholders (i.e., broad vs. narrow interpretations, see Phillips, 2003) has been among the more persistent questions for stakeholder theory and continues in these pages.

Referring to it as "the question, at the core of a theory of the firm" Freeman (1994: 67) framed the relationship between stakeholder identification and objective functions more than two decades ago asking, "for whose benefit and at whose expense should the firm be managed?" Mitchell and Lee (Chapter 4) describe stakeholder identification as a fundamental element of "stakeholder work." Hörisch & Schaltegger (Chapter 8) examine the prospects and perils of how the natural environment might be explicitly included as a stakeholder. A case can be made that the concept of an objective function is inextricably intertwined with the question of "for whose benefit and at whose expense should the firm be managed?" returning the question of firm boundaries to the fore.

Venkataraman (Chapter 10) provocatively resists this interpretation writing,

From an entrepreneurship perspective, the central question of stakeholder theory, namely, "for whose benefit and at whose expense should the firm be managed?" is moot. The central assertion of the entrepreneurial process is that, even if the fiduciary duty of the manager is to the stockholder, the process of entrepreneurial discovery and exploitation will ensure that the corporation will be managed as if for the benefit of all the stakeholders to the enterprise.

Clearly more work is required on the question of firm objective functions in stakeholder theory, including whether or not the concept of "objective function" could be usefully replaced by the idea of firm purpose. Purpose may contain multiple objectives potentially responding to Mitchell and Lee's (Chapter 4) call for more "pluralistic-objective decision making and stakeholder inclusiveness." It is even possible that one implication of stakeholder theory is that both objective functions and firm boundaries are no longer necessary to describe and prescribe the stakeholder firm. Perhaps what is needed is a firm defined by value creation and values alignment. Your authors/editors disagree on the relative usefulness of these questions, suggesting a ripe space for future research.

Pragmatism and Managerial Stakeholder Theory

One widely recognized feature of stakeholder theory is that it draws on disciplines that some find quite distinct – perhaps even opposed or "essentially contested" (Miles, 2012). Prominent contributions to stakeholder theory have drawn on strategic management, economics, psychology, moral philosophy, sociology, ecology, etc. For some, this represents a promiscuous dilettantism. For others, managing the complexity of twenty-first century firms requires command of as many tools as cognition, judgment and technology permit. We maintain that this disciplinary cross-fertilization, though a challenge, is a source of strength of stakeholder theory. It is a challenge because it requires scholars and practitioners to use ideas outside their normal zones of comfort and familiarity. The difficulties of adjusting sense-making frames are legion and widely studied – so too are the potential advantages of the effort.

Rather than retreating to the relative comfort and heuristics of disciplinary training, we and others recommend theory based on the principles of pragmatism (see also Godfrey and Lewis, Chapter 2). Pragmatism allows scholars, analysts, and practitioners to think about boundaries according to the needs of the question being asked. Consider again the question of boundaries. Pragmatism sees boundaries – both around the firm and between disciplines – in terms of what these boundaries allow us to do. Pragmatism demands that we take account of the implications of drawing the boundaries one way rather than another. While boundaries help us see some elements more clearly, other features are obfuscated or, by design, ignored entirely.

One stakeholder corollary to pragmatism is the claim that the theory is *managerial* (Donaldson & Preston, 1994). The idea that stakeholder theory can be either descriptive, instrumental, or normative has been extraordinarily influential among stakeholder scholars. A closer reading of Donaldson and Preston's seminal article reveals a fourth element: stakeholder theory is **managerial**. Arriving at a similar conclusion from a different direction, Barney (2018) writes, "firm managers and entrepreneurs often have a special role to play in a resource-based theory that explicitly incorporates a stakeholder perspective."

Though there is more to say about what this fourth element of the taxonomy means, one pragmatist conclusion is that if the answer makes no difference to managerial practice, then the question is irrelevant. Managerial stakeholder theory, on our interpretation, echoes William James's conclusions from 1907:

> The pragmatic method in such cases is to try to interpret each notion by tracing its respective practical consequences. What difference would it practically make to any one if this notion rather than that notion were true? If no practical difference whatever can be traced, then the alternatives mean practically the same thing and all dispute is idle. Whenever a dispute is serious, we ought to be able to show some practical difference that must follow from one side or the other's being right. (1907: 26)

In fact, scholars have debated the pragmatic value of Donaldson and Preston's tripartite distinction itself. Reacting to Jones & Wicks's "convergent stakeholder theory," Freeman writes, "if we drop the tripartite typology of Donaldson and Preston, then plainly there is no need for anything like convergent stakeholder theory" (Freeman, 1999: 234; see also, Phillips, 2003, esp. pp. 67ff).

For current purposes, we would also like to re-emphasize that pragmatism is fundamentally empirical – if not always quantitative. Given the preceding discussion of the (empirical) role of values, norms, and ethics in stakeholder theory, we may still ask if the descriptive-instrumental-normative distinction itself is managerial. Even this extraordinarily influential taxonomy is not beyond the critical reach of pragmatic contingency. Again, we take this capacity for contingency and contest as essential to pragmatic, managerial stakeholder theory.

There remain challenges to a multi-disciplinary approach (Berman and Johnson-Cramer, 2017). Any path that crosses boundaries is destined to be fraught with peril including different languages, currencies, and guardians of the faith. But we need not make the trip blind. In the next sections, we describe the "traps" that have plagued stakeholder theory in the past and lie in wait still for the unsuspecting traveler.

Theoretical Traps

Though an exciting time in the development of theory and practice around stakeholder management, this period of ambiguity brings with it the potential for theoretical traps. Here we will mention three that merit particular attention for stakeholder scholars. The first trap is a "not invented here" (NIH) trap. Though generally intelligent, curious, and critical, scholars may also suffer from a need to fit phenomena into the categories they have found successful in the past. Occasionally, when we seek to understand something like managing stakeholder relationships, we feel compelled to define the phenomenon, to build boundaries around it, and to defend our interpretation as superior to all comers. This can mean shaping the phenomenon into well-worn channels (Ketokivi & Mahoney, 2016). For others it can mean a (more or less fundamental)

change to how preferred theories are understood (e.g., Barney, 2018; Hill & Jones, 1992; Williamson & Bercovitz, 1996).

The NIH trap manifests in at least two ways. The first is that much early theorizing was largely of the big-picture theory variety. It sought general principles and axioms that would apply to all (or nearly all) business organizations. This makes sense if one sees prior theories as having, like Athena, sprung fully grown from the head of their originators. More often, however, these scholars and fellow-travelers worked on more narrow and specific elements before rendering their broader theory. We believe that work is now underway (including within this volume) to backfill some of this foundation. Because disagreement remains on the precise definition and boundaries of stakeholder theory, avoiding this part of the NIH trap involves identifying an important research question – one that matters to managers' efforts at value creation – and then building on a particular stakeholder foundation to explore it. This foundation can be built on any useful way of thinking about stakeholder theory, as long as we clearly explain it and correctly cite any work upon which it is based.

Which brings us to the second manifestation of the NIH trap – reinventing the wheel. Because important contributions to stakeholder theory have arisen from groups of people who have not necessarily read the same books nor been influenced by the same ideas, there is a tendency to neglect or even dismiss scholarship outside a particular stream. Above we discussed the perceived challenges of engaging with normative stakeholder theory. We have witnessed otherwise excellent stakeholder scholarship forced into contortions of rhetoric to avoid the perceived challenges (e.g., calling a theory "instrumental" in order to avoid hard questions of norms, values, and ethics). It is our duty as scholars to understand influential ideas as comprehensively as possible irrespective of what journal published the articles. There are more than enough interesting new questions remaining in stakeholder theory to intentionally re-slog previously well-mapped terrain.

The second trap is "what we think we know" – as in "the only thing more dangerous than what we don't know is what we think we know that's wrong." It is common in many academic disciplines but seems to particularly afflict stakeholder theory. Scholars tend to learn from other scholars. This can be efficient but can also be problematic, not least when a scholar cites someone's work incorrectly, and then others, in a game of bibliographic telephone, use the same citation incorrectly in their own work and so on. This mistake is repeated until the original misconception is treated as fact. Much of the perceived lack of theoretical agreement within stakeholder theory can be traced to spurious quotations and "courtesy cites" being repeated until taken for true. Even prior to its 2010 reissue, Freeman's 1984 book was cited thousands of times more than there are copies of the book in print (Elms, et al., 2011).

Much has been attributed to Freeman (1984) – and stakeholder theory more generally – that represents neither the original work nor what most would consider the theory's mainstream. Perhaps most prominently, Freeman (1984) is frequently cited in the corporate social responsibility (CSR) literature (cf., Elms, et al., 2011). Stakeholder theory and CSR have some common elements leading many to see the two as synonymous (see also Phillips, et al., 2003). This misperceived synonymity has prevented, and continues to prevent, many management scholars from embracing stakeholder theory.

In an exemplary case of NOT falling into the "what we think we know" trap, Walsh reviewed three books of stakeholder scholarship for *Academy of Management Review* (2005). After admirably close readings of the three works (*viz.,* Freeman, 1984; Post, Preston & Sauter-Sachs, 2002; Phillips, 2003), Walsh expressed explicit surprise at what he found there no fewer than three times, including writing, "Many readers may be surprised to learn that the father of stakeholder theory draws such a clear distinction between 'real' strategic issues and social responsibility issues" (2005: 429). Likewise, based on careful readings of their own, Greenwood and Mir (Chapter 3) and others (e.g., Henriques, Chapter 13) would like to see a more socially and environmentally ambitious stakeholder theory than what they found. Others will disagree for other

reasons – our plea is that these reasons be informed by careful readings of extant scholarship rather than stylized and impressionistic cherry-picking and bibliographic telephone games.

The third trap is the obsession with trying to prove that managing for stakeholders is more profitable than other management approaches – the "business case" trap. In talking to other scholars about stakeholder theory, especially in the strategic management domain, we are often told that the evidence regarding stakeholder theory is inconclusive. When we dig deeper, we find that they often base their conclusion on studies testing the relationship between CSR and financial performance (see Margolis and Walsh, 2001; Orlitzky, Schmidt, & Rynes, 2003). Most studies of CSR include variables dealing with the environment or social phenomena such as the nature of the industry in which a firm competes (i.e., tobacco, gambling). A study based more specifically on a stakeholder theory of creating value through relationships may not necessarily include those variables. Misunderstanding regarding stakeholder management and performance is closely related with the misconception that stakeholder theory and CSR are essentially the same. As Hillman and Keim (2001) demonstrated, they are not, nor do they have the same influence on firm financial performance.

There is, in fact, substantial evidence of a positive relationship between practicing the principles found in the stakeholder management literature and firm financial performance across a wide range of companies and industries (i.e., Berman, et al., 1999; Choi & Wang, 2009; de Luque, et al., 2008; Henisz, Dorobantu, & Nartey, 2014; Ogden & Watson, 1999; Preston & Sapienza, 1990; Sisodia, Wolfe, & Sheth, 2007). There is also recent evidence that context matters (Garcia-Castro & Francoeur, 2016).

We cite this evidence for the convenience of the readers of this volume but would also hasten to add that financial performance is not the only – nor the most – interesting dependent variable. As we have mentioned elsewhere, and will address in a later section, what is needed most in the stakeholder literature is a broadening of the dependent variable in stakeholder-based studies to include more dimensions of the value that is both created and destroyed. Stakeholders get much more than financial value through their relationships with a firm and may also lose value in many forms through these relationships.

Future Directions

The authors of the chapters in this volume have provided excellent advice about promising research questions within their topic areas. We also have at various times and contexts written regarding stakeholder topics that need further attention (i.e., Barney & Harrison, 2018; Freeman, 2017; Freeman, et al., 2010; Wicks & Harrison, 2017). We will not repeat all these suggestions here. Instead, we would like to focus on a limited number of the topics that we believe are most essential to the advancement of stakeholder theory at this time. We will then discuss some measurement issues facing the field.

High potential research topics – Because of social, political, and economic differences, we do not believe that stakeholder management practices are likely to be equally successful across various regions of the world. For example, distributive and procedural justice (Harrison, et al., 2010) are likely to have much different interpretations for stakeholders in China, India, Europe, or Central America. We cannot simply assume that stakeholder management practices that work in the USA or some other country will work elsewhere. This idea suggests a need for cross-border comparative studies of stakeholder management philosophies and practices of the sort envisioned by Nartey in Chapter 18. What can Western firms learn from Eastern firms and vice versa in terms of creating more value through stakeholder management? Also, Devinney, McGahan, and Zollo (2013) suggest that a global perspective means not only examining stakeholder management at various locations across the globe, but multinationals as truly global stakeholders.

Second, there is a need for more work that engages with other important management theories, such as transaction cost economics (Williamson, 1975), the resource-based perspective (Barney, 1991), industrial organization economics (Porter, 1985), evolutionary theory of economic change (Nelson & Winter, 1982), or upper echelons theory (Hambrick & Mason, 1984). This work may seek to integrate stakeholder theory with other theories or new theorizing may deploy the findings from these theories for new and novel uses. Stakeholder theory takes a comprehensive view of the firm that is very complex, and therefore accommodates a wide range of theoretical perspectives.

Third, as demonstrated in our "New Voices" section (Bundy, Chapter 10; Crilly, Chapter 11), there is widespread interest in stakeholders as people, with all that implies. We believe that this stream of micro/behavioral research is vital to understanding how to manage stakeholder relationships to enhance the creation of value. Important research streams that stakeholder scholars can tap into include, but are not limited to, expectancy theory (Vroom, 1964), escalating commitment (Staw, 1976), cognition (Tversky & Kahneman, 1974), sense making (Weick, 1995), exchange rules (Meeker, 1971), and goal setting (Locke & Latham, 1990). Ideas from these streams have already found their way into some of the stakeholder research, but there is much more to be done.

Fourth, measurement of firm outcomes continues to be a vital issue. One issue around which all stakeholder scholars seem to agree is that what a firm does influences outcomes for more than just financial stakeholders such as shareholders, and that other stakeholders matter. Furthermore, as mentioned previously, stakeholders receive much more than purely economic value through their relationships and interactions with firms. However, much of the stakeholder research continues to adopt financial returns as the primary dependent variable. We need both better theory and better data to help define the value a firm creates (or destroys) in much broader stakeholder terms (Freeman, 2017; Harrison & van der Laan Smith, 2015; Harrison & Wicks, 2013; Mitchell, et al., 2015; Priem, 2007). Phillips, et al. (2010 &

2011) use work from upper-echelons theory to propose a stakeholder model using managerial discretion as a dependent variable. Jones and Felps (2013) consider stakeholder happiness as a candidate variable. We suspect there are other non-financial measures of interest deriving from previous scholarship that could be of great interest.

Measurement – Continuing with the theme of the last paragraph, it is one thing to conceptualize value more broadly and quite another thing to measure it. The most commonly used database in stakeholder research is what is known (though under other names as ownership and stewardship has changed) as the Kinder, Lydenberg, Domini (KLD) social ratings database (for a review, see Mattingly, 2017). In our experience, most other large databases compiled by private companies (and not academic researchers) are very similar (i.e., Asset4, Just Capital). The data are compiled based on publicly available information about a firm's activities related to social performance, as well as direct contact with the firms that are being rated. The data are not collected to support academic research. They are collected largely to help client firms such as mutual fund managers or investment advisors (partially explaining, perhaps, how financial returns continue to be the dominant dependent variable) screen companies based on social criteria. The advantage is that the data collectors are not biased by a specific research objective (beyond their interest in financial outcomes) as an academic researcher might be.

Though rather easily available from these private companies, there remain weaknesses with ratings data as they pertain to stakeholder-theoretic research. First, continuing the theme, they are oriented towards social performance rather than stakeholders. This means that there is a lot of valuable information in these databases, but much of it is better suited to CSR studies than stakeholder studies (i.e., environmental policy and performance, participation in "sin" industries, governance data such as the composition of the board). Indeed, MSCI (owner of the KLD data at the time) made substantial changes to its database in 2010 to make it even more CSR oriented. If that type of data is collapsed into the measurement of what is supposed to be a stakeholder construct – such as adding environmental dimensions to the product dimensions to come up with a measure of customer performance – then the result is a measure that is far from its theoretical counterpart. Often the KLD data are combined into a single measure of what is called "stakeholder performance" (cf. Rowley and Berman, 2000). Nor does KLD contain measures relating to firm-supplier relations.[3] It is no wonder, then, that findings regarding stakeholder performance and financial performance are mixed.

There is also a larger problem in many of these studies. To explain, we will use a specific example using human relations, which is probably the most comprehensive and stakeholder-oriented category in the KLD database. Firms are rated on:

- strong union relations
- cash profit sharing
- participation through means such as stock options or ownership
- strong health and safety programs
- strong record on human rights in their supply chain
- other (a miscellaneous category)

These are scored as 0,1 variables, which are then summed for a total employee score. This score and scores in other areas are summed, and then typically used as the independent variable measuring stakeholder performance, with the dependent variable some version of financial performance. But isn't this variable really measuring value distributed to stakeholders? Isn't it an outcome variable? If stakeholder theory is really about relationships with stakeholders, is that what is being measured? We suspect that returns to future study of these databases for stakeholder theoretic uses is limited.

As difficult as it may be, quantitative studies will be better specified when collecting their own data for stakeholder theoretic questions. Henisz, Dorobantu, and Nartey (2014) coded over 50,000 stakeholder events from media reports to determine the levels of cooperation or conflict gold mining companies have with their stakeholders. Large-scale collection of survey data also has promise. De Luque and colleagues (2008) analyzed data from 520 firms in seventeen countries to assess the role of stakeholder values on perceptions of visionary leadership. Case studies may also have potential, as long as they are conducted using rigorous methods (Eisenhardt, 1989; Langley & Abdallah, 2011; Yin, 2009).

Here is a short list of potentially interesting questions that would lend themselves to a variety of different research methods:

1) To what extent do stakeholders make decisions about engaging with a firm based on how the firm treats other types of stakeholders (suppliers, customers, communities, employees) or is economic value the principal driver for these decisions? What are the stakeholder and contextual characteristics that determine these types of choices?
2) How are a firm's operations influenced if it applies the same values and/or decisions rules when engaging with different types of stakeholders vs. if it treats various stakeholders differently?
3) What are some of the ways a stakeholder-oriented global company can successfully convey its stakeholder culture and values to subsidiaries in other nations?
4) What are best practices for stakeholder management in various national contexts and to what extent can these best practices be applied elsewhere?
5) Are entrepreneurs that focus on building a stakeholder-oriented culture early in the process more successful in engaging new stakeholders in their ventures?
6) When firms harm stakeholders (inadvertently or knowingly), what are the factors that influence how they respond?

Different Questions – The preceding may well lead one to some radical conclusions. At the extreme, one potential conclusion is that firm boundaries no longer matter. Ink has been spilled and Nobel Prizes awarded, but the bright-line distinctions between firm and market apply to a time that has passed. The days of lifetime employment, robust intellectual property protections, stable financial investments, and company towns have gone the way of the pre-Darwinian "essentialism" clearing the way for outsourcing, subcontracting, and the network economy. One could conclude that the corporate form was a useful fiction whose usefulness has waned. This seems too strong. The continued value-creating utility of enduring, trusting, reciprocal relationships – within and between organizations – and the norms, values, and ethics that underlie, inform, and facilitate these relationships is evident. The slightly less radical conclusion is that strategy, law, accounting, and ethics all need a new definition of the firm to match the world of commerce as we find it today: a value-creation theory of the firm.

Scholars have long recognized the porous nature of organizational boundaries, but nevertheless persisted in the search for such boundaries as well as their antecedents and implications. Indeed, most management scholars would agree with Granovetter (1985) that the way forward in understanding economic organization will cross legacy disciplinary lines. Stakeholder theory provides an opportunity to disaggregate these antecedents and implications and break down the conceptual silos that currently create artificial barriers to insight.

Notes

* Thanks to Heather Elms, Michael Johnson-Cramer, and Thomas Jones for helpful comments.
1. According to Google Scholar (accessed via Harzing's Publish or Perish 24 May 2018), the Donaldson and Preston article has been cited 11,769 times. The other contender for most influential peer-reviewed stakeholder article is Mitchell, et al., 1997 with 11,414 cites. They are the 8th and 9th most cited in AMR history. Of note, Dyer and Singh (1998) – occasionally cited in the context of stakeholder research – has been cited 12,990 times, but it does not use the word stakeholder.
2. See Phillips (2003) for a definitive discussion of normative (and derivative) legitimacy.
3. Thanks to Thomas Jones for pointing this out.

References

Asher, C., Mahoney, J. M., & Mahoney, J. T. (2005). Toward a property rights foundation for a stakeholder theory of the firm. *Journal of Management and Governance, 9*(1): 5–32.

Ashforth, B. E., & Mael, F. (1989). Social identity theory and the organization. *Academy of Management Review, 14*(1): 20–39.

Barney, J. B. (1986). Strategic factor markets: Expectations, luck, and business strategy. *Management Science, 32*(10): 1231–1241.

Barney, J. B. (1991). Firm resources and sustained competitive advantage. *Journal of Management, 17*(1): 99–118.

Barney, J. B. (2018). Why resource-based theory's model of profit appropriation must incorporate a stakeholder perspective. *Strategic Management Journal, 39*: 3305–3325.

Barney, J. B. & Harrison, J. S. (2018). Stakeholder theory at the crossroads. *Business & Society*, forthcoming.

Berman, S. L., & Johnson-Cramer, M. E. (2017). Stakeholder theory: Seeing the field through the forest. *Business & Society*.

Berman, S. L., Wicks, A. C., Kotha, S., & Jones, T. M. (1999). Does stakeholder orientation matter? The relationship between stakeholder management models and firm financial performance. *Academy of Management Journal, 42*(5): 488–506.

Blau, P. M., & Scott, W. R. (1962). *Formal organizations: A comparative approach*. San Francisco: Scott, Foreman.

Bosse, D. A., Phillips, R. A., & Harrison, J. S. (2009). Stakeholders, reciprocity, and firm performance. *Strategic Management Journal, 30*(4): 447–456.

Brickson, S. L. (2007). Organizational identity orientation: The genesis of the role of the firm and distinct forms of social value. *Academy of Management Review, 32*(3): 864–888.

Brickson, S. L. (2005). Organizational identity orientation: Forging a link between organizational identity and organizations' relations with stakeholders. *Administrative Science Quarterly, 50*(4): 576–609.

Bridoux, F. & Stoelhorst, J. W. (2014). Microfoundations for stakeholder theory: Managing stakeholders with heterogeneous motives. *Strategic Management Journal, 35*(1): 107–125.

Bridoux, F. & Stoelhorst, J. W. (2016). Stakeholder relationships and social welfare: A behavioral theory of contributions to joint value creation. *Academy of Management Review, 41*(2): 229–251.

Bundy, J., Vogel, R., & Zachary, M. (2018). Organization-stakeholder fit: A dynamic theory of cooperation, compromise, and conflict between an organization and its stakeholders. *Strategic Management Journal, 39*: 476–501.

Bundy, J., Shropshire, C., & Buchholtz, A. K. (2013). Strategic cognition and issue salience: Toward an explanation of firm responsiveness to stakeholder concerns. *Academy of Management Review, 38*(3): 352–376.

Choi, J., & Wang, H. (2009). Stakeholder relations and the persistence of corporate financial performance. *Strategic Management Journal, 30*(8): 895–907.

Clarkson Centre for Business Ethics. (1999). Principles of Stakeholder Management. Toronto: University of Toronto. Reproduced in 2002, *Business Ethics Quarterly, 12*(1): 256–264.

Coff, R. W. (1999). When competitive advantage doesn't lead to performance: The resource-based view and stakeholder bargaining power. *Organization Science 10*(2): 119–133.

Crane, A., and Ruebottom, T. (2011). Stakeholder theory and social identity: Rethinking stakeholder identification. *Journal of Business Ethics, 102*(1).

Devinney, T. M., McGahan, A. M., & Zollo, M. (2013). A research agenda for global stakeholder strategy. *Global Strategy Journal, 3*: 325–337.

Donaldson, T., & Preston, L. E. (1995). The stakeholder theory of the corporation: Concepts, evidence, and implications. *Academy of Management Review, 20*(1): 65–91.

de Luque, M. S., Washburn, N. T., Waldman, D. A., & House, R. J. (2008). Unrequited profit: How stakeholder and economic values relate to subordinate perceptions of leadership and firm performance. *Administrative Science Quarterly 53*: 626–654.

Dyer, J. H., & Singh, H. (1998). The relational view: Cooperative strategy and sources of interorganizational competitive advantage. *Academy of Management Review, 23*(4): 660–679.

Eisenhardt, K. M. (1989). Building theories from case study research. *Academy of Management Review, 14*: 532–550.

Elms, H., Johnson-Cramer, M. E., & Berman, S. L. (2011). Bounding the world's miseries: Corporate responsibility and Freeman's stakeholder theory. In R. A. Phillips, ed., *Stakeholder theory: Impact and prospects*, pp.1–53. Cheltenham, UK: Edward Elgar.

Freeman, R. E. (1984). *Strategic management: A stakeholder approach*. Marshfield, MA: Pitman.

Freeman, R. E. (1994). A stakeholder theory of the modern corporation. In T. L. Beauchamp & N. E. Bowie, eds., *Ethical Theory and Business*, pp. 66–67. Engelwood Cliffs, NJ: Prentice-Hall.

Freeman, R. E. (1999). Divergent stakeholder theory. *Academy of Management Review*, 24(2): 233–236.

Freeman, R. E. (2017). Five challenges to stakeholder theory: A report on research in progress. In D. M. Wasieleski & J. Weber, eds., *Stakeholder management*, pp. 1–20. United Kingdom: Emerald Publishing.

Freeman, R. E., Harrison, J. S., Wicks, A. C., Parmar, B., & de Colle, S. (2010). *Stakeholder theory: The state of the art*. Cambridge, UK: Cambridge University Press.

Garcia-Castro, R. and Aguilera, R. V. (2015). Incremental value creation and appropriation in a world with multiple stakeholders. *Strategic Management Journal*, 36: 137–147.

Garcia-Castro, R., & Francoeur, C. (2016). When more is not better: Complementaries, costs and contingencies in stakeholder management. *Strategic Management Journal*, 37: 406–424.

Gibbons, R. (2005). Four formal (izable) theories of the firm? *Journal of Economic Behavior & Organization*, 58(2): 200–245.

Gioia, D. A. (1999). Practicability, paradigms, and problems in stakeholder theorizing. *Academy of Management Review*, 24(2): 228–232.

Granovetter, M. (1985). Economic action and social structure: The problem of embeddedness. *American Journal of Sociology*, 91(3): 481–510.

Hambrick, D. C., & Mason, P. A. (1984). Upper echelons: The organization as a reflection of its top managers. *Academy of Management Review*, 9: 193–206.

Harrison, J. S., Bosse, D. A., & Phillips, R. A. (2010). Managing for stakeholders, stakeholder utility functions, and competitive advantage. *Strategic Management Journal*, 31(1): 58–74.

Harrison, J. S., & Wicks, A. C. (2013). Stakeholder theory, value, and firm performance. *Business Ethics Quarterly*, 23(1): 97–124.

Harrison, J. S., & van der Laan Smith, J. (2015). Responsible accounting for stakeholders. *Journal of Management Studies*, 52: 935–960.

Hatherly, D., Mitchell, R. K., Mitchell, J. R., & Lee, J. H. (2018). Reimagining profits and stakeholder capital to address tensions among stakeholders. *Business & Society*. Published online December 14, 2017.

Heminway, J. M. (2017). Shareholder wealth maximization as a function of statutes, decisional law, and organic documents. *Washington & Lee Law Review*, 74, 939.

Henisz, W. J., Dorobantu, S., & Nartey, L. J. (2014). Spinning gold: The financial returns to stakeholder engagement. *Strategic Management Journal*, 35(12): 1727–1748.

Hill, C. W., & Jones, T. M. (1992). Stakeholder-agency theory. *Journal of Management Studies*, 29(2): 131–154.

Hillman, A. J., & Keim, G. D. (2001). Shareholder value, stakeholder management, and social issues: what's the bottom line? *Strategic Management Journal*, 22(2): 125–139.

James, W. (1907/1981). *Pragmatism*, B. Kuklick, ed. Indianapolis: Hackett Publishing.

Jones, T. M., & Felps, W. (2013). Stakeholder happiness enhancement: A neo-utilitarian objective for the modern corporation. *Business Ethics Quarterly*, 23(3): 349–379.

Jones, T. M., & Wicks, A. C. (1999). Convergent stakeholder theory. *Academy of Management Review*, 24(2): 206–222.

Ketokivi, M & Mahoney, J. T. (2016). Transaction Cost Economics As a Constructive Stakeholder Theory, *Academy of Management Learning & Education*, 15(1): 123–138.

Korschun, D. (2015). Boundary-spanning employees and relationships with external stakeholders: A social identity approach. *Academy of Management Review*, 40(4): 611–629.

Langley, A., & Abdallah, C. (2011). Templates and turns in qualitative studies of strategy and management. *Research Methodology in Strategy and Management*, 6: 105–140.

Laplume, A. O., Sonpar, K., & Litz, R. A. (2008). Stakeholder theory: Reviewing a theory that moves us. *Journal of Management*, 34(6): 1152–1189.

Locke, E. A., & Latham, G. P. (1990). *A theory of goal setting and task performance*. Englewood Cliffs, N.J.: Prentice Hall.

Margolis, J. D., & Walsh, J. P. (2001). *People and profits?: The search for a link between a company's social and financial performance*. New York: Psychology Press.

Mattingly, J. E. (2017). Corporate social performance: A review of empirical research examining the corporation-society relationship using Kinder, Lydenberg, Domini Social Ratings Data. *Business & Society, 56*: 796–839.

Meeker, B. F. (1971). Decisions and exchange. *American Sociological Review, 36*: 485–495.

Merton, R. K. (1957/1968). *Social theory and social structure*. New York: Simon and Schuster.

Miles, S. (2012). Stakeholder: essentially contested or just confused? *Journal of Business Ethics, 108*(3): 285–298.

Mitchell, R. K., Van Buren III, H. J., Greenwood, M., & Freeman, R. E. (2015). Stakeholder inclusion and accounting for stakeholders. *Journal of Management Studies, 52*(7): 851–877.

Nason, R. S., S. Bacq, & D. Gras. (2018). A Behavioral Theory of Social Performance: Social Identity and Stakeholder Expectations, *Academy of Management Review, 43*(2): 259–283.

Nelson, R. R., & Winter, S. G. (1982). *Evolutionary theory of economic change*. London: Harvard University Press.

Ogden, S., and R. Watson. (1999). Corporate performance and stakeholder management: Balancing shareholder and customer interests in the U.K. privatized water industry. *Academy of Management Journal 42*(5): 526–536.

Orlitzky, M., Schmidt, F. L., and Rynes, S. L. (2003). Corporate social and financial performance: A meta-analysis. *Organization Studies 24*(3): 403–441.

Ouchi, W. G. (1980). Markets, bureaucracies, and clans. *Administrative Science Quarterly*, 129–141.

Phillips, R. (2003). *Stakeholder theory and organizational ethics*. San Francisco: Berrett-Koehler Publishers.

Phillips, R., Berman, S., Elms, H., & Johnson-Cramer, M. (2010). Strategy, stakeholders and managerial discretion. *Strategic Organization, 8*(2): 176–83.

Phillips, R., Berman, S., Elms, H., & Johnson-Cramer, M. (2011). Stakeholder orientation, managerial discretion and Nexus rents. In R. Phillips, ed., *Stakeholder Theory: Impact and Prospects*. Cheltenham, UK: Edward Elgar.

Phillips, R., Freeman, R. E., and Wicks, A. C. (2003). What stakeholder theory is not. *Business Ethics Quarterly, 13*(4): 479–502.

Porter, M. (1985). *Competitive Advantage*. New York: The Free Press.

Post, J. E., Preston, L. E., & Sauter-Sachs, S. (2002). *Redefining the corporation: Stakeholder management and organizational wealth*. Stanford, CA: Stanford University Press.

Preston, L. E., and Sapienza, H. J. (1990). Stakeholder management and corporate performance. *Journal of Behavioral Economics, 19*(4): 361–375.

Priem, R. (2007). A consumer perspective on value creation. *Academy of Management Review, 32*: 219–235.

Rowley, T., & Berman, S. (2000). A brand new brand of corporate social performance. *Business & Society, 39*(4): 397–418.

Santos, F. M., & Eisenhardt, K. M. (2005). Organizational boundaries and theories of organization. *Organization Science, 16*(5): 491–508.

Sisodia, R., Wolfe, D. B., & Sheth, J. (2007). *Firms of endearment: How world-class companies profit from passion and purpose*. Upper Saddle River, NJ: Wharton School Publishing.

Staw, B. M. (1976). Knee deep in the big muddy: A study of escalating commitment to a chosen course of action. *Organizational Behavior and Human Performance, 16*: 27–44.

Treviño, L. K., & Weaver, G. R. (1999). The stakeholder research tradition: Converging theorists – not convergent theory. *Academy of Management Review, 24*(2): 222–227.

Tversky, A., & Kahneman, D. (1974). Judgment under uncertainty: Heuristics and biases. *Science, 185*: 1124–1131.

Vroom, V. H. (1964). *Work and motivation*. New York: John Wiley & Sons.

Walsh, J. P. (2005). Book review essay: Taking stock of stakeholder management. *Academy of Management Review, 30*(2): 426–438.

Weick, K. E. (1995). *Sensemaking in organizations*. Thousand Oaks, CA: Sage Publications.

Wicks, A. C., and Harrison, J. S. (2017). Toward a more productive dialogue between stakeholder theory and strategic management. In D. M. Wasieleski & J. Weber, eds., *Stakeholder management*, pp. 249–274. United Kingdom: Emerald Publishing.

Williamson, O. E. (1975). *Markets and hierarchies: Analysis and antitrust implications*. New York: The Free Press.

Williamson, O. E., & Bercovitz, J. (1996). The modern corporation as an efficiency instrument: The comparative contracting perspective. In C. Kaysen, ed., *The American Corporation Today*, pp. 327–359. New York: Oxford University Press.

Yin, R. K. (2009). *Case study research*. Thousand Oaks, CA: Sage Publications.

Zenger, T. R., Felin, T., & Bigelow, L. (2011). Theories of the firm–market boundary. *Academy of Management Annals*, *5*(1): 89–133.

Pragmatism and Pluralism

A Moral Foundation for Stakeholder Theory in the Twenty-First Century

PAUL C. GODFREY

Brigham Young University

BEN LEWIS

Brigham Young University

In their now-classic mapping of the field, Donaldson and Preston (1995) grouped questions of interest in stakeholder theory into distinct groups known as the "three pillars": descriptive, instrumental, or normative. The descriptive pillar takes up questions about what managers *actually do* in their interactions with stakeholders, while instrumental and normative pillars consider what managers *should do* to benefit their organizations and affected stakeholder groups. The imperative of should, or what managers ought to do, in the instrumental and normative pillars connected stakeholder theory to two foundational moral theories: utilitarianism and deontology. These moral foundations gave stakeholder models a set of prescriptive imperatives that connected beneficent actions toward stakeholders with moral outcomes, either in terms of greater utility or a world protective of stakeholder rights. Over time, utilitarianism and deontology became the dominant moral paradigms of stakeholder theory (see Hill and Jones, 1992 and Bosse, Phillips, and Harrison, 2009 for the instrumental view; Logsdon and Wood, 2002, and Phillips, 2003 for the deontological argument).

Utilitarianism and deontology provided a foundation that could not stand the test of time, nor could they morally ground stakeholder research based on the descriptive pillar. Most lay people, and many scholars, see utilitarianism and deontology as contrasting, even contradictory, ethical systems; however, the two philosophies share a common origin – the Enlightenment – and employ the philosophical assumptions of the eighteenth century: epistemological objectivity and ontological unity. Eighteenth century foundations prove ill-fitted for a twenty-first-century world grounded in philosophical inter-subjectivity. The premise of an objective world where a single, universally recognizable moral imperative guided action encountered withering critique during the post-modern linguistic turn in the twentieth century (Levinas & Nemo, 1985; Rorty, 1992). Philosophers abandoned objective sources of morality, such as a God or transcendent natural principles, and focused instead on an inter-subjective social and moral sphere where iterative, reasoned discourse provided moral actors with the tools and frameworks that would guide decision-making (Heidigger, 2002/1926). No candidate principle holds a pre-eminent position as the unitary, or unifying, morality in this post-modern world. As the twenty-first century proceeds, contests and conflicts about the definition of moral action abound, and as societal evolution continues to expand and modify notions of the good life, the philosophical footings of the instrumental and normative pillars continue to erode.

Can we ground stakeholder theory in a moral paradigm that acknowledges, and perhaps embraces, the inter-subjective, fluid nature of post-modern morality? In this chapter, we answer Yes! The answer, for us, lies in the forgotten third pillar of stakeholder theory: pragmatism and its cousin, political pluralism. Pragmatism, the notion that moral action is that which meets people's desires, goes beyond the mere hedonism that underpins utilitarianism and includes a process of moral inquiry that accommodates multiple desires and differing views of morally appropriate action. Pragmatist morality deals at the level of individuals, but John Rawls's *A Theory of Justice* (1971) employs the fundamental moral tools of pragmatism to construct a societal, political philosophy: pluralism. Pluralism envisions a world of actors each seeking the morally good life, what the ancient Greeks referred to as eudemonia, but following moral precepts that sometimes resonate with those of others, but sometimes stand in conflict. In what follows, we argue that pragmatism, pluralism, and eudemonia provide a stronger moral foundation for stakeholder theory in a complex and inter-subjective moral world. We also show how stakeholder theory offers a compelling recipe for moral problem solving in a pragmatic, pluralistic world.

Our argument proceeds as follows. We first provide a unique review of the stakeholder literature to illustrate the evolution of stakeholder theory from its foundations, through a phase where instrumental questions dominated work, and now toward more descriptive, pragmatic concerns. We then describe the core arguments of pragmatism, pluralism, and eudemonia. The remainder of our chapter considers the intersection between stakeholder theory and this new moral grounding.

Literature Review

Unlike other literature reviews that systematically survey hundreds of articles at a time, in this chapter we seek to provide a high-level overview of the evolution of stakeholder theory within the broader of field of management. To accomplish this objective, we utilize a bibliometric methodology known as Main Path Analysis (MPA). MPA is a form of citation analysis used to identify and trace the evolution of research within a particular research domain (Hummon & Dereian, 1989; Hummon, Doreian, & Freeman, 1990). While other citation analysis tools have been used to quantify the impact of individual articles or identify cohesive sub-groups, MPA focuses on the connections between articles rather than the articles themselves. Implicit in this objective is an assumption that the accumulation of scholarly knowledge flows through citations and that "a citation that is needed in paths between many articles is more crucial than a citation that is hardly needed for linking articles" (de Nooy, Mrvar, and Batagelj, 2011: 281). MPA thus provides a concise way of visualizing incremental advances

along the most commonly traversed path (i.e., the main path) helping scholars to identify important scholarly contributions as well as the likely direction and trajectory of future work within the focal research domain.

Main Path Analysis

To begin our MPA of the stakeholder literature, we identified a set of source articles and books from which we could generate a citation network. Seeking to be as objective as possible, we utilized a list of ten journal articles and five books that were identified by members of the Stakeholder Strategy Interest Group of the Strategic Management Society to be "classic works" within stakeholder literature.[1] These articles and books are listed in Table 2.1.

From this initial source list, we utilized the ISI Web of Science database to identify and download all articles (and their corresponding reference lists) that cited at least one article or book on the source list. This step generated an initial list of 14,327

Table 2.1 Foundational works in stakeholder theory

Author (s)	Year
Articles	
Carroll	1991
Donaldson and Preston	1995
Clarkson	1995
Jones	1995
Mitchell etal.	1997
Rowley	1997
Frooman	1999
Berman et al.	1999
Hillman and Keim	2001
Jensen	2002
Books	
Freeman	1984
Post, Preston, and Sachs	2002
Friedman and Miles	2006
Freeman et al.	2007
Freeman et al.	2010

Source: Stakeholder Strategy Interest Group Summer 2016 Newsletter (see www.strategicmanagement.net/ig-stake holder-strategy/publications)

publications and 114,356 citations. To ensure that the final citation network included only relevant articles (and to reduce the risk of ceremonial citations), we excluded all articles that had less than three direct citations to the source list utilizing CitNetExplorer, a free software tool for visualizing and analyzing citation networks.[2] This procedure reduced the overall network size to 909 articles and 8,964 citations.

We then uploaded this citation network into Pajek 5.01, a free software program used to perform the MPA. The underlying objective of MPA is to "calculate the extent to which a particular citation is need for linking articles" (de Nooy et al., 2011: 282). This calculation is known as the traversal weight and is performed for each citation link between the "source" and "sink" vertices. Every citation network contains a set of source vertices (early or foundational articles or publications) that do not cite other articles within the network and set of sink vertices (recent articles) that are not cited by other articles in network. While there exist a variety of algorithms for calculating the traversal weight of a citation, we utilize an algorithm known as the Search Path Count (SPC) which reduces bias in the transversal weights for early and later articles (Batagelj, 2003; de Nooy et al., 2011).

Once the traversal weight for each citation was calculated, we then determined the global key route path within the citation network which ensures that the citation link with the largest transversal count is included on the main path and that the determined main path is path with the overall highest sum of transversal weights in the network (Liu and Lu, 2012). We display the resulting main path in Figure 2.1 and Table 2.2 illustrates its trajectory.

Results

Our main path analysis reveals a stream of work that can be categorized into five distinct phases of theoretical and empirical development. Articles represented within each phase, while important contributions in their own right, should be not be construed as the only significant scholarly contributions within each category, but rather as exemplary works that highlight the flow of knowledge within the stakeholder literature. Furthermore, the phases we review should not be interpreted as having specific start and end points but rather trends in scholarly conversations that wax and wane over time.

Phase 1. Foundations. The first phase begins with Freeman's (1984) seminal book and is then followed by a series of theoretical articles, mostly published in *Academy of Management Review*,

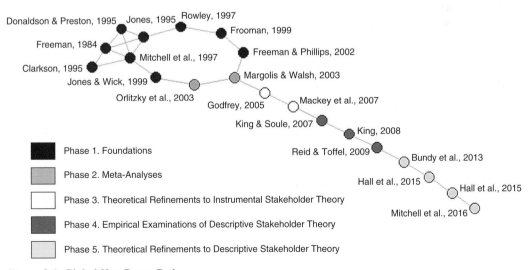

Donaldson & Preston, 1995   Jones, 1995   Rowley, 1997

Freeman, 1984

Clarkson, 1995

Jones & Wick, 1999

Orlitzky et al., 2003

Mitchell et al., 1997

Frooman, 1999

Freeman & Phillips, 2002

Margolis & Walsh, 2003

Godfrey, 2005

Mackey et al., 2007

King & Soule, 2007

King, 2008

Reid & Toffel, 2009

Bundy et al., 2013

Hall et al., 2015

Hall et al., 2015

Mitchell et al., 2016

Phase 1. Foundations

Phase 2. Meta-Analyses

Phase 3. Theoretical Refinements to Instrumental Stakeholder Theory

Phase 4. Empirical Examinations of Descriptive Stakeholder Theory

Phase 5. Theoretical Refinements to Descriptive Stakeholder Theory

Figure 2.1 Global Key Route Path

Table 2.2 List of Scholarly Publications on the Global Key Route Path and Phases of Theoretical Development

Author(s)	Year	Journal	Title
Phase 1. Foundations			
Freeman	1984	Book	*Strategic Management: A Stakeholder Approach*
Donaldson and Preston	1995	*Academy of Management Review*	The stakeholder theory of the corporation: Concepts, evidence, and implications
Clarkson	1995	*Academy of Management Review*	A stakeholder framework for analyzing and evaluating corporate social performance
Jones	1995	*Academy of Management Review*	Instrumental stakeholder theory: A synthesis of ethics and economics
Mitchell et al.	1997	*Academy of Management Review*	Toward a theory of stakeholder identification and salience: Defining the principle of who and what really counts
Rowley	1997	*Academy of Management Review*	Moving beyond dyadic ties: A network theory of stakeholder influences
Frooman	1999	*Academy of Management Review*	Stakeholder influence strategies
Jones and Wicks	1999	*Academy of Management Review*	Convergent stakeholder theory
Freeman and Phillips	2002	*Business Ethics Quarterly*	Stakeholder theory: A libertarian defense
Phase 2. Meta-Analyses			
Orlitzky et al.	2003	*Organization Studies*	Corporate social and financial performance: A meta-analysis
Margolis and Walsh	2003	*Administrative Science Quarterly*	Misery loves companies: Rethinking social initiatives by business
Phase 3. Theoretical Refinements to Instrumental Stakeholder Theory			
Godfrey	2005	*Academy of Management Review*	The relationship between corporate philanthropy and shareholder wealth: A risk management perspective
Mackey et al.	2007	*Academy of Management Review*	Corporate social responsibility and firm performance: Investor preferences and corporate strategies
Phase 4. Empirical Examinations of Descriptive Stakeholder Theory			
King and Soule	2007	*Administrative Science Quarterly*	Social movements as extra-institutional entrepreneurs: The effect of protests on stock price returns
King	2008	*Administrative Science Quarterly*	A political mediation model of corporate response to social movement activism
Reid and Toffel	2009	*Strategic Management Journal*	Responding to public and private politics: Corporate disclosure of climate change strategies
Phase 5. Theoretical Refinements to Descriptive Stakeholder Theory			
Bundy et al.	2013	*Academy of Management Review*	Strategic cognition and issue salience: Toward an explanation of firm responsiveness to stakeholder concerns
Hall et al.	2015	*Journal of Management Studies*	Who and what really counts? Stakeholder prioritization and accounting for social value
Mitchell et al.	2015	*Journal of Management Studies*	Stakeholder inclusion and accounting for stakeholders
Mitchell et al.	2016	*Academy of Management Review*	Stakeholder agency and social welfare: Pluralism and decision-making in the multi-objective corporation

which lay the conceptual foundation for stakeholder theory as we know it today. Unsurprisingly, we find that this phase includes seven of the nine "Classic Works" journal articles as identified by the Stakeholder Strategy Interest Group, providing strong face validity to our empirical approach. Donaldson and Preston's (1995) three pillars appears in this group of foundational works. In terms of the moral foundations of stakeholder theory, a close reading of Freeman's (1984) work reveals his strong pragmatist foundation. Within a decade, however, Donaldson and Preston had incorporated both a utilitarian/consequentialist (instrumental stakeholder theory) and a deontological/intentionalist (normative stakeholder theory) moral underpinning.

The development of the Clarkson Principles for stakeholder engagement in the late 1990's and codified in 2002 represents one of the few extensions of the normative pillar.[3] Each of the seven principles incorporates a "should" statement of moral authority; none of the seven principles allow managers to prioritize their own, or their organization's, financial rewards in considering how to approach issues regarding stakeholders. Perhaps because of their finality and authoritative content, or the lack of trained philosophers working in the field, business and society scholars have largely taken the normative position for granted and little work has been done in this area.

Phase 2. Meta-Analyses. With the emergence of stakeholder theory as a legitimate conceptual framework, scholars interested in exploring the instrumental outcomes of corporate responsibility now had a solid theoretical foundation to reference and build upon. Utilizing stakeholder theory as "theoretical lens" (Whetten, 2002), these works explained the disparate findings and justified the need for further scholarly inquiry. Margolis and Walsh (2003), in particular, suggested that scholars pursue a normative and descriptive research agenda untethered from instrumental concerns and embrace the apparent tension that exists between social and economic objectives rather than explain it away. Once again, we see Margolis and Walsh (2003) highlighting the limitations of consequentialist moral foundations on the types of questions stakeholder theorists could and should ask.

Phase 3. Theoretical Refinements to Instrumental Stakeholder Theory. Ironically, some of the most influential articles to follow Margolis and Walsh (2003) were nevertheless instrumental in their approach, despite their efforts' call to shift the focus from the instrumental to normative and descriptive perspectives. Godfrey (2005), for example, proposed that corporate philanthropy, and more generally corporate social responsibility, could be seen as a form of insurance that would preserve a firm's reputation after experiencing a negative event. A central assumption of his theory was the notion of pluralism, the idea that firms engage and interact with "multiple communities, each representing different ethical values and value systems" (2005: 779). While perhaps less direct in their approach, Mackey, Mackey, and Barney (2007) likewise drew upon the stakeholder literature to explain both why and when firms would engage in socially responsible activities even if those activities did little to increase the present value of a firm's cash flows.

Phase 4. Empirical Examinations of Descriptive Stakeholder Theory. Although scholarly interest in the instrumental perspective continued, the focus of this phase shifted away from justification (a normative perspective) to description; from what managers should do to what they actually do. In moral terms, the ship of stakeholder theory began to change course from a consequentialist direction and agenda and back toward stakeholder theory's pragmatist roots. Researchers worked to resolve the paradox that external stakeholders, seemingly powerless as individuals or diverse groups, could nevertheless bring about organizational change. King and Soule (2007), for example, examined the conditions under which a protest would influence a firm's stock price. While claims made by protesters were rarely urgent, the authors nevertheless explained how many of their claims were legitimate and how they could use the media as leverage to achieve their desired objectives. Following this study, King (2008) sought to explain when firms would concede to the demands of a social or environmental boycott. Central to his theory was the notion that firms experiencing declines in their reputation would be particularly susceptible to the demands of external stakeholders. Likewise, Reid and Toffel (2009) explored the conditions under which a firm would respond to direct appeals to management by concerned shareholders and found that direct appeals not only influenced the actions of the target firm, but could also influence other firms within the same institutional fields.

Phase 5. Theoretical Refinements to Descriptive Stakeholder Theory. Perhaps driven by a need to organize the burgeoning literature on firm responsiveness to stakeholders, Bundy, Shropshire, and Buchholtz (2013) developed a new framework for understanding how firms respond to stakeholder concerns. Central to their theory was the notion of issue salience and strategic cognition. Although prior work had acknowledged the importance of issue characteristics (Mitchell, Agle, and Wood, 1997; Reid and Toffel, 2009), scholars lacked a model for understanding how managers cognitively interpret issues and determine whether a stakeholder's concern is worthy of response. Building upon this work, a series of papers in a recent Special Issue of the *Journal of Management* highlighted the need for understanding how stakeholder issues are prioritized, accounted for, and reported (Hall, Millo, and Barman, 2015; Mitchell, et al., 2015). Understanding that the concept of social welfare is likely multidimensional and pluralistic, Mitchell and colleagues (2016) propose one plausible solution for understanding how firms prioritize potential trade-offs. Central to their theory is the notion that a firm and its stakeholders interact within an intra-corporate market where trade-offs among competing interests and actors can be "bought" and "sold" transparently. Such a market, the authors maintain, allows a multi-objective corporation to thrive in a world characterized by competing values and interests.

As we have shown above, the stakeholder literature has evolved substantially over the last thirty years. The foundational works gave scholars interested in stakeholder management a vocabulary and set of constructs upon which to build. While understanding what managers actually do in regard to

stakeholders has always been a key question within the literature (Donaldson and Preston, 1995; Parmar et al., 2010), work in stakeholder theory has only recently exhibited a renewed interest in understanding the practical nature of how managers decide to whom and to what issues they will respond and how they will manage the competing interests and values that they encounter. The empirical focus on the descriptive pillar in recent work invites an exploration of the moral foundation of the descriptive pillar, the topic to which we now turn.

The Three Ps: Pragmatism, Pluralism, And PERMA

As we noted at the beginning of this chapter, the instrumental and normative pillars rest on the foundations of epistemological objectivity – there is a real world "out there" that everyone can observe and agree upon – and ontological unity – competing prescriptions for moral action can be rank ordered, with the one listed first acting as the unitary, or unifying moral good. These Enlightenment assumptions fell out of favor with philosophers in the early to mid-twentieth century. Globalization, a latter-twentieth-century phenomenon, puts an exclamation point on the lack of objectivity and moral unity among social actors; we now live in a world with different, often competing, assumptions about the world "out there," and accompanying moral codes or rules. Utility maximization, or attention to rights and duties, become increasingly difficult moral groundings because, as the twenty-first century rolls on, debate and disagreement rages about what constitutes utility, or the nature of rights and duties, and which rights might take precedent.

In what follows, we outline the moral thinking of the American pragmatist philosophers, who present a moral theory unburdened by requirements for objectivity or rank-ordered moral principles or rules. We then identify linkages between an individual-level pragmatic moral system to a pluralistic social morality. The idea that individuals, and by extension groups, live a moral life when they flourish, or reach a state of eudemonia, acts as one tie that binds pragmatism and pluralism. The last part of this section describes the concept of eudemonia.

Pragmatism: Individual Moral Philosophy

James and individual moral groundings. William James articulated the first article of faith for pragmatists: "there is no such thing possible as an ethical philosophy dogmatically made up in advance" (James, 1891: 330). Morality and ethics begin with individuals, and individuals have desires or interests that motivate what people actually do. James presumes that people act with an eye toward meeting those desires and interests, which imbue those desires, for that individual, with the characters of goodness: "So far as he feels anything to be good, he *makes* it good. It is good, for him; and being good for him, is absolutely good, for he is the sole creator of values in that universe, and outside of his opinion things have no moral character at all" (James, 1891: 335).

A group of individuals, each with highly customized notions of the morally good, make up a society; because those individual moral goods are non-transferrable (your good may not be my good), and unless an external arbiter exists (e.g., God), then those non-transferrable moral goods each enjoy equal standing as a guide for action. This fact leads James to offer his only universal moral rule: "since everything which is demanded is by that fact a good, must not the guiding principle for ethical philosophy ... be simply to *satisfy at all times as many demands as we can?* That act must be the best act, accordingly, which makes for the *best whole*, in the sense of awakening the least sum of dissatisfactions" (Italics original; Talisse and Aiken, 2008: 112). Moral action is a tough business because individuals have multiple desires and demands that compete for attention. James (1891: 344) accepts the cost of the core principles of opportunity: that choosing to satisfy one demand leaves another unfilled. He explains:

> There is always a *pinch* between the ideal and the actual which can only be got through by leaving part of the ideal behind. There is hardly a good which we can imagine except as competing for the possession of the same bit of space and time with some other imagined good ... Some part of the ideal must be butchered, and he needs to know which part. It is a tragic situation, and no mere speculative conundrum, with which he has to deal.

Dewey and moral processes. If William James identified the difficulties of moral decision-making for a pragmatist, John Dewey provided a way out and a path to moral decision-making. Dewey agreed with James that, at the end of the day, a pragmatic view provides no easy or obvious right answer. He saw the world, in similar terms as James, as a set of individuals with their own moral codes; however, for Dewey those codes came from the influences of social upbringing and context as much as from the core self (Field, 2017). Moral decision-making invites actors to sort out and clarify moral priorities in a particular case and context, and the way individuals come to a knowledge of how to act entails the same process they use to come to knowledge of any other thing: ethical inquiry.

Ethical inquiry represents philosophy reinforced by history. Dewey (1859–1952) grew up during the civil war and spent the last of his days in the emerging Cold War; he lived through technological, economic, and social change on a scale and magnitude that few of us can imagine (Anderson, 2018 – *Stanford Encyclopedia of Philosophy*). Dewey witnessed increasing complexity in the physical and social world and that complexity led him, like James, to eschew any substantive rule to guide ethical action. Instead, ethical inquiry laid out a process for decision-making that mimicked scientific inquiry in the natural world. The only path to making the best decision, in a particular context, involved a deep examination of the problem at hand, collection of relevant facts (about antecedents, motivations, and potential outcomes), imagination of potential solutions, and the development of a plan of action (Field, 2017).

The acid test for moral action was, in the pragmatist tradition, whether a proposed course of action would solve the problem at hand. In the social and moral realm, problem solving means at least two things: enabling individuals to live together   in   productive   and   harmonious relationships with each other, and facilitating the development, flourishing, and growth of the individual. The first objective gives rise to political pluralism, the moral premise upon with John Rawls built his *Theory of Justice*. The focus on human flourishing connects pragmatism back to Aristotle, and his notion of eudemonia. We describe pluralism first.

Pluralism as a Political Morality

Pluralism, as envisioned by Rawls, takes two facts as axiomatic. First, individuals or collectives orient their lives according to sometimes irreconcilable visions of what constitutes moral goodness and the morally desirable life. Second, those individuals must live with each other in social groups and societies. Rawls and Kelly (2001: 3) articulates the core issue:

> A democratic society is not and cannot be a community, where by a community I mean a body of persons united in affirming the same comprehensive, or partially comprehensive, doctrine. The fact of reasonable pluralism which characterizes a society with free institutions makes this impossible. This is the fact of profound and irreconcilable differences in citizens' reasonable comprehensive religious and philosophical conceptions of the world, and in their views of the moral and aesthetic values to be sought in human life.

The reality of pluralism makes a simple homogenous community impossible, and requires a different plan of social organization than a monopoly of a unified moral code, or even a hegemony of the strongest among competing codes. In Rawls' work, the optimal organization of a pluralistic society arose from a set of moral actors creating social arrangements behind a veil of ignorance through a process of reflexive equilibrium (Rawls, 1971). An intelligent group of rational moral actors, equipped with a complete knowledge of the different pluralistic values and possible social outcomes, but without a knowledge of which value system or social position they would in fact occupy, would design a set of social and political systems that optimized the basket of potential social outcomes.

For Rawls (1971), decisions behind the veil of ignorance result in a polity organized around a set of processes, rights, and systems set up to protect the ability of each individual to pursue his or her foundational, inviolate moral principles and vision of the good life. These rights and systems, socially negotiated rather than transcendently given, would form the skeletal architecture of an actual political constitution. For Rawls, the interests of all should be looked after and the "whole strand is tied together;" the good society includes rather than excludes diverse beliefs and moral codes (1971: 129). Optimal social arrangements center on communication, cooperation, and coexistence rather than conversion, conflict, and conquest. The oft-used phrase "unity in essentials, liberty in non-essentials, charity in all" articulates the core principles of a pluralistic society.[4]

Rawls posits two concrete principles as essential: equality should serve as the default distributive principle, and any unequal distributions should protect the position of the least advantaged, broadly defined (Rawls, 1971). Sustainable social institutions leverage areas of agreement or joint concern, respect and accommodate areas of irreconcilable differences, and employ and promote an attitude of humility and equality rather than arrogance or domination. Social mechanisms should facilitate communication and exchange between and across groups to negotiate the innumerable transactions where moral visions overlap and may stand in conflict. Sustainable pluralistic societies need to create and institutionalize organizations and process that honor and perpetuate the two principles. These institutions and principles allow individuals and groups to pursue their interests and self-defined moral goods. The good society protects the rights of individuals against negative intrusion, but it also facilitates human welfare, well-being, flourishing, or eudemonia.

PERMA as a Desired Moral Outcome

Aristotle (1941) outlined the core concept of eudemonia in the *Nicomachean Ethics* when answering the question of what constitutes a moral life:

> Both the general run of men and people of superior refinement say that it is happiness, and identify

living well and doing well with being happy; but with regard to what happiness is they differ (bk 1, 4) ... any action [good] when it is performed in accordance with the appropriate excellence: if this is the case, human good turns out to be activity of soul in accordance with virtue, and if there are more than one virtue, in accordance with the best and most complete. But we must add "in a complete life" (bk 1, 7).

The good life, then, comes about both through a life of excellent action, but also a completely excellent life. An excellent life is eudemonia, interpreted today as flourishing. Individuals may flourish, but so might families, groups, or polities; the aim of the individuals behind the Rawlsian veil of ignorance lies in constructing a society where all can flourish according to their own definitions of what it means to flourish. Flourishing, or reaching one's full potential, represents, for Aristotle, an end in itself; no one hopes to flourish so they can earn more money, but earning more money may provide an individual with more opportunities to flourish.

In the late twentieth century, psychologist Martin Seligman (2011) defined flourishing as the purpose of positive psychology. He noted that extant psychological models and practice equated the eradication of mental challenges, neuroses, or problems with a happy life. Seligman saw these as merely the absence of unhappiness and his concept of positive psychology held that an individual needed positive, good things to occur in their life in order to be happy. The absence of disease did not equal health. As Seligman's work matured, the positive psychology movement came to describe flourishing, or eudemonia, as the presence and combination of five elements, captured under the acronym PERMA. We outline these below.

- **Positive emotion.** This is pleasure, a state of peace, well-being, or ease. Positive emotion captures what utilitarians and economist would classify as utility.
- **Engagement.** Engagement captures the notion of flow as defined by Mihaly Csikszentmihalyi. Flow occurs when individuals operate at the limit of competence, when they stretch in an activity, but not so much that they fail. There

must be some risk involved, but also a very reasonable chance of success. When in a state of flow, an individual feels absorbed by or "lost in" the activity itself. Positive emotion and engagement capture many elements of traditional utilitarian philosophy.
- **Relationships.** Living a life with others in deep and lasting relationships, leaning on, and learning from others represents an essential element of the good life. By focusing on relationships and their role in human excellence or flourishing, eudemonia goes beyond the selfish hedonism that utilitarianism may devolve into, and the self-righteous isolation that might arise from deontological reflection.
- **Meaning.** Eudemonia requires one to adopt a teleological orientation where life's activities lead to purposeful ends beyond sustenance or pleasure. To have meaning is to find a transcendent connection to one's life, to become involved with activities or causes larger than one's self or one's narrow interests. Eudemonia is as much about the process of finding personal meaning (both in isolation and with groups) as it is about reaching that end.
- **Achievement.** To flourish and attain excellences requires growth, the accrual of new skills and knowledge, the attainment of goals, and the nurturing of new and valuable elements of one's life. Achievement, like engagement and relationships, accepts that disutility must often be endured in the pursuit of larger goals. Achievement suggests a life lived beyond the mere performance of obligation and in pursuit of filling the measure of one's potential.

Pragmatism holds that the moral life for an individual involves fulfilling their unique individual desires. Pluralism extends that search to the larger social sphere and describes a set of social processes that provide the space and institutional context where individuals living with one another can pursue their own vision of the morally good life. PERMA and flourishing provides a framework for thinking about the activities individuals and groups actually engage in to live an excellent life. In what follows, we argue that these paradigms and theories provide the best moral foundation for stakeholder theory and that stakeholder theory, when put into practice, creates social structures and processes that encourage human flourishing.

Stakeholder Theory and the Three Ps

We begin our discussion with Table 2.3, which shows areas of convergence between stakeholder theory and the three Ps of pragmatism, pluralism, and PERMA. The rows capture the important dimensions of each of the Ps, and the columns describe each dimension in the different theories and provide examples of each dimension in

practice. We believe the table identifies clear and compelling overlaps and linkages between stakeholder theory and the three Ps, so rather than reviewing the elements of the table we focus here on some larger issues raised by this strong overlap.

The moral basis of stakeholder theory. Table 2.3 makes clear that stakeholder theory fits hand in glove with pragmatism's central ontological assumption that individual stakeholders hold heterogeneous desires. James's assertion that the moral imperative for a pragmatist lies in filling as many desires as possible resonates with stakeholder theory's *a priori* refusal to prioritize any

Table 2.3 Pragmatism, Pluralism, Eudemonia, and Stakeholder Theory

Pragmatism and Pluralism	Philosophical description, examples	Stakeholder theory interface	Stakeholder examples
Core premise			
Actors hold heterogeneous, non-hierarchical values	Individuals and groups bring different heritage, cultural norms, and value sets to society. Value sets cannot be ranked. *Religious denominations/ traditions*	Heterogeneity of backgrounds, interests, and needs at the core of Stakeholder Theory. Heterogeneity valued both instrumentally and intrinsically.	Goldman Sachs CEO criticizes 2017 Travel Ban on Foreign Nationals entering the USA, citing both human rights and business concerns.[1]
Key processes for moral living			
Leverage shared values	Social interactions build on common values to create structures for peaceable action and co-existence. *Interfaith projects for disaster/ hunger relief[2]*	Firms use their resources and position to serve as aggregators of stakeholder interests and serve as facilitators of exchange.	Real estate firm Redfin shares proprietary data with others to solve Seattle (and nationwide) housing crisis.[3]
Respect divergent values	Social actors and institutions create protected space for divergent values to co-exist and flourish. *Religious Freedom laws, ACLU Religious Liberty work[4]*	Organizations enact policies and procedures that recognize and protect fundamental needs and rights of stakeholders.	McDonald's adapts menus and supply chains to respect employee religious requirements, and certifications/constraints for food items across the world.[5]
Adopt an attitude of humility	Actors recognize limits of their own vision/values and accept the validity of other views. *Teaching tolerance project[6]*	Companies admit mistakes and work to rectify stakeholder concerns and issues.	Jet Blue's admission of poor customer service leads to passenger bill of rights.[7]
Communicate in meaningful ways	Social actors and institutions facilitate open dialogue between different groups. *Cois Tine, Irish interfaith group emphasizing communication for societal integration[8]*	Firms establish formal stakeholder communication processes that bring parties and factions together for dialogue.	Coca-Cola engages local community, business, and NGO partners as part of its source water protection plans in bottling operations.[9]

Element	Description, *examples*	Stakeholder theory interface	*Stakeholder examples*
Eudemonia (Flourishing)			
Positive emotion	Pleasant emotional state, described most often as contentment, happiness, or satisfaction. *The feeling after eating a favorite meal, seeing a great movie, or viewing a beautiful sunset*	Organizational policies, products, or processes that improve the quality of life for stakeholders.	EMC creates a suite of HR practices to combine learning, challenge, productivity, and fun in the workplace.[10]
Engagement and flow	A feeling of complete immersion in an activity, forgetting the self, being "in the zone." *A great day skiing, writing, or reading an excellent novel*	Formal activities and strategies that facilitate stakeholder engagement with a company's products or processes.	Lego invites customers to co-design Mindstorm® products, providing them with tools to maximize their creativity.[11]
Positive relationships	Sustained interactions with other individuals or groups that benefit all. *Marriage or other intimate partnerships, friendships, acquaintances*	Companies encourage and promote strong relationships with stakeholders, but also between stakeholders.	Google's cafeteria design provides space and time for employees to interact, create, and strengthen relationships.[12]
Meaning	Affiliation with something larger than mere self-interest. May be a cause, ideology, or organization. *Religious affiliation, membership in service group such as Rotary*	Firms provide opportunities and platforms for employees, customers, and other stakeholders to affiliate with a cause or transcendent meaning.	Better World Books allows students and others to donate books for resale as well as projects to promote literacy in the developing world.[13]
Achievement	Reaching goals, obtaining mastery, winning, succeeding in endeavors *Obtaining a PhD degree, earning a Michelin Star*	Companies facilitate stakeholder growth through mastery of new knowledge and skills.	CodeEval creates app building and programming competitions that allow programmers to develop/exhibit mastery.[14]

1. Goldman CEO takes lead on Wall Street in slamming Trump travel ban, Reuters, 30 Jan 2017. Retrieved February 1, 2017, from www.reuters.com/article/us-usa-trump-immigration-companies-goldm-idUSKBN15E1H2.
2. Mujahld, A. M. (2015). Katrina: Where faith and interfaith groups picked up as federal government failed. Huffington Post, 27 August. Retrieved January 27, 2017, from www.huffingtonpost.com/abdul-malik-mujahid/katrina-faith-interfaith_b_8046454.html.
3. John Whitley, Redfin Recap: State of the Seattle Real Estate Market, Redfin Real Time. Retrieved February 1, 2017, from www.redfin.com/blog/2016/10/redfin-recap-state-of-the-seattle-real-estate-market.html.
4. For more information, see www.aclu.org/issues/religious-liberty.
5. McDonald's the innovator: Fast food and cultural sensitivity, The Economist, 16 June 2011, Retrieved February 1, 2017, from www.economist.com/blogs/schumpeter/2011/06/fast-food-and-cultural-sensitivity.
6. Teaching tolerance project is run by the Southern Poverty Law Center, see tolerance.org/.
7. Matthew Jaffe, JetBlue offers passengers bill of rights. 20 Feb, 2007. ABC News. Retrieved February 1, 2017, from abcnews.go.com/Politics/story?id=2889582.
8. For more information, see www.coistine.ie/about-cois-tine
9. For more information, see www.coca-colacompany.com/stories/stakeholder-engagement, accessed February 6, 2016.
10. Jacquelyn Smith, 10 Companies with the happiest young professionals. Forbes, 08 May 2013. Retrieved February 2, 2017, from www.forbes.com/sites/jacquelynsmith/2013/05/08/the-10-companies-with-the-happiest-young-professionals/#7c85fd2576b3.
11. Patty Seybold, Customer led innovation at Lego and National Instruments, Outside Innovation, 09 March, 2006. Retrieved February 2, 2017, from http://outsideinnovation.blogs.com/pseybold/2006/03/customerled_inn.html.
12. Geoff Colvin, How to build the perfect workplace. Fortune, 05 March 2015. Retrieved February 2, 2017, from http://fortune.com/2015/03/05/perfect-workplace/.
13. See www.betterworldbooks.com/ for more information.
14. See http://blog.codeeval.com/about/ for more information.

group's interest; both theories support the belief that managers should include as many stakeholders as necessary in each issue that touches their interests (Freeman, 1984; Freeman, et al., 2010). Freeman, Harrison, and Wicks (2007) go so far as to argue that managers should consider the interests and desires of individual stakeholders (individuals or organizations) rather than defining interests by groups, such as customers or suppliers. We believe James would approve of such a prescription in order to identify the concrete desires at stake in any decision. Importantly, neither pragmatism nor stakeholder theory offers moral actors an easy way out of difficult decision-making by offering decision-makers a preset ranking of the moral worth of any particular desire or interest,

James's notion of the "pinch," or the reality that any decision involving conflicting demands will fall short of the ideal of satisfying all interests, helps resolve a key puzzle for stakeholder theorists: how to resolve trade-off conflicts between various stakeholder interests. The pinch reminds us that in *most* cases *all* stakeholders won't walk away completely satisfied, but if interests are earnestly weighed within the particular context of the decision to be made, then "doing the best one can" under the circumstances leaves the *most* stakeholders with *some* degree of their desires met. James's pinch provides a reality check for managers that attunes them to the difficulty of the decisions they face, but also some comfort in arguing that, in many cases, the nature of the situation and the interests involved preclude an ideal solution where all needs get met.

The pinch highlights the important role of Dewey's process of ethical inquiry in making ethical choices as well as effectively managing stakeholder relationships. Unlike utilitarianism, which places the morality of an action exclusively on its consequences, or deontology, where morality depends solely on the actor's intent, pragmatic stakeholder theory seats the morality of the action in the process of decision-making as well as the eventual outcomes or motivational inputs. Stakeholder theory justifies its final decisions on

the grounds of procedural, if not distributive, justice (Kim and Mauborgne, 1998).

Stakeholder theory as organization-level moral pragmatism. As we noted earlier, pragmatism provides guidance for individuals making moral decisions in a complex world and pluralism extends that moral logic to the societal level. Neither theory, however, addresses the moral challenges facing actors within organizations, driven by their own competing desires but also forced to factor in the competing desires and interests of their organization's stakeholders. An organizational-level account of moral action matters for two reasons. First, organizational decision-making involves more than the mere summation of the moral arithmetic employed by the various individuals who constitute a decision-making group, for instance a top management team. Optimal organizational decision-making accounts for the organization as a whole, a distinct social entity that has its own unique desires and interests. Some interests may converge cleanly with those of its individual members, such as a desire for greater revenues and wages; however, those interests may also diverge. For example, translating all revenue gains into wage gains (the desires of employees) jeopardizes the organization's viability by leaving no reserve for future contingencies (a desire of bondholders and shareholders).

Second, most people spend a substantial number of hours in settings impacted by organizations. We all spend the majority of our day playing roles in various organizations, from our families to our jobs to organized leisure activities such as sporting organizations, charitable work, or being a part of the PTA. As citizens and consumers, we live in an institutional environment defined by organizational decision-making (e.g., the political regulatory environment), and we use products and services that came about through processes of organizational decision-making. Pragmatists such as James, Dewey, and Freeman would all note that each of those organizational decisions, ones that accounted for and considered interests and desires of at least some stakeholder groups, constitute moral decisions.

Whether as consumers, employees, or affiliates, we all face moral decisions in our organizational roles and we all accept the assumption of organizational membership that when making moral decisions that affect the organization, we should not merely decide on our personal desires and interests. The notion of organizational citizenship demands that we place the demands of the organization above our own, for good or for ill (Umpress, Bingham, and Mitchell, 2010). Models of stakeholder engagement that build upon the foundations of Dewey's process of ethical inquiry provide organizational actors with a framework and system for effectively enacting their moral duties as organizational citizens (Noland and Phillips, 2010).

Stakeholder theory as dynamic pluralism. Rawls (1971) emphasized the role of social institutions, processes, and structures in protecting pluralistic visions of moral action and the morally desirable life. The two principles of equality, if properly implemented, work to assure that differing versions of the good do not result in social inequities of opportunity or outcomes. The two principles serve as anchors, or static foundations, upon which the institutions of daily life can build; however, that foundation fails to account for dynamic changes, either through the exogenous impact of interaction with other social groups or the endogenous evolution of interests within a social group. The process of globalization that increases the number of actors holding differing moral codes within a social group provides an example of exogenous changes; the evolution of concepts such as equality and liberty illustrate endogenous change (Fukayama, 1996; Wilson, 1997).

Processes such as stakeholder identification and engagement that build on these pluralistic foundations provide a recipe for organizational adaptation in the face of dynamically changing moral codes and prescriptions (Mitchell, Agle, and Wood, 1997; Greenwood, 2007). If Rawls presents a system of protection against coercion and conflict, stakeholder theory offers one of possible cooperation and coordination. A vibrant social life requires both a set of negative moral prescriptions (e.g., don't violate the rights or norms of diverse groups) and positive ones (e.g., seek out and leverage areas of common interest). To the

extent that stakeholder theory focuses on finding areas of cooperation, we believe it extends the moral reach of Rawlsian pluralism and, in this sense, offers a more powerful moral anchor than the preservation of differences. Stakeholder theory offers managers more than a mere moral justification for finding opportunities for positive engagement, it gives them a set of tools to implement that moral vision in everyday decisions.

Unfortunately, the fundamental irreconcilability of moral paradigms leads to conflict, sometimes intermittent and sometimes chronic. Cooperation between stakeholders may prove the exception rather than the rule (Godfrey and Hatch, 2006). What becomes of pluralism and its operating principles in the face of such conflict? We believe that pluralism, rather than consequentialist or intentional moral foundations, provides a better way forward. Instrumentalism allows organizational leaders to retreat during conflict to a position of "at the end of day, we have to look out for ourselves." Intentionalism, on the other hand, provides little actual guidance for resolving conflict other than treating others as we'd like to be treated. Pragmatism, as advocated by Dewey, reminds managers that conflict, like all moral choices, involves a process of moral resolution: Listening, discussion, and lively disagreement are the foundations of such a process. Pluralism reminds us that there will be no ultimate vanquishing victory for our side and that tomorrow we'll all be linked in the same social situation.

A stakeholder focus encourages eudemonia. The pragmatic, and stakeholder-theory, imperative to meet as many desires as possible brings about positive emotion, as stakeholders realize the satisfaction of met needs. If it provided nothing more, then stakeholder theory would devolve to a focused form of utilitarian consequentialism. A pragmatically grounded stakeholder theory, however, extends its reach far beyond the view of positive emotional outcomes as eudemonia. The emphasis on stakeholder engagement acts as more than an accidental linguistic overlap. As managers and stakeholders work together to find solutions to issues, often thorny and enduring ones such as environmental pollution or economic inequality, they push beyond the comfort zone of known recipes. They establish a foundation for eudemonistic engagement, or creating a state of flow, even if the sought-after solutions fail to appear. The process of stakeholder engagement and dialogue represents its own form of flow.

If either managers or stakeholders cling to positions that preclude any joint solution, then stakeholder engagement breaks down and eudemonistic engagement never occurs. If, however, both stakeholders and managers remember "the pinch" and that any practical, workable outcome will fall short of the ideal, then the exit from the comfort zone of known solutions may reveal new approaches to old problems and a deepened sense of commitment by all parties to implement that solution. That emotional commitment certainly increases the likelihood that concerned stakeholder groups, including organizational leaders, will continue to work in concert to achieve better outcomes.

Concerted effort requires, but also strengthens, positive relationships among stakeholder groups and between stakeholders and firms. Those positive relationships contribute to eudemonia for all. Differences in moral visions may never disappear and parallel lines will never meet; however, effective processes of stakeholder engagement can lead to relationships of mutual respect, open communication, and even admiration between diverse, and potential divisive, stakeholders. Positive relationships help produce better instrumental outcomes as trust and respect allow parties to identify areas where joint action may produce results. Relationships of trust also encourage each party to make the sometimes-risky investments needed to realize those results.

Finally, a pragmatically grounded stakeholder theory improves the odds that stakeholders, as individuals, will find a sense of transcendent meaning. That meaning comes as all stakeholders see the possibilities for satisfying desires and interests beyond the merely material or monetary. For example, when stakeholder groups and firms work to together to combat environmental degradation or improve social conditions in their home communities, everyone involved connects to something beyond, and larger than, themselves. Effective stakeholder engagement processes can help business produce more than just widgets and profits; organizations, and their members can contribute to causes with impacts beyond product and financial markets. Working together with their stakeholders, business, employees, and managers can contribute to a better world.

Conclusion

Stakeholder theory has moved from the margins to the mainstream of business conversations, both among academics and practitioners. As the reach of stakeholder theory increases, we see a distinctive turn in theory, research, and practice to the pragmatic and practical issues of effective stakeholder management such as how managers clearly identify stakeholders, engage with them, and work through the challenges of organizations operating with multiple decision criteria. We applaud this return to the descriptive pillar of the theory. Our goal in this chapter has been to show that a focus on descriptive stakeholder theory has its own moral underpinning in the moral theory of American pragmatism. We believe that moral underpinning results in a stronger, more robust version of stakeholder theory that can help managers and other organizational leaders effectively navigate in an increasingly pluralistic world.

Notes

1. The methodology for identifying these articles and books is outlined in the Stakeholder Strategy Interest Group Summer 2016 Newsletter (see www.strategicmanagement.net/ig-stakeholder-strategy/publications).
2. See http://www.citnetexplorer.nl/
3. These principles can be found at http://www.cauxroundtable.org/index.cfm?menuid=61, accessed July 5, 2017.
4. The origins of this phrase date back to early seventeenth-century Europe, a continent plagued by the schisms of the Reformation and the warfare of budding nation states. The exact origin of the statement is subject to debate, which readers will find available at http://faculty.georgetown.edu/jod/augustine/quote.html (accessed Feb 21, 2017).

References

Anderson, E. (2018). Dewey's Moral Philosophy. In E. N. Zalta, ed., The Stanford Encyclopedia of Philosophy (Fall Edition). Retrieved from https://plato.stanford.edu/archives/fall2018/entries/dewey-moral/.

Aristotle. (1941). *Nicomachean Ethics*. New York: Random House.

Batagelj, V. (2003). Efficient algorithms for citation network analysis. *arXiv Preprint cs/0309023*. Retrieved from https://arxiv.org/abs/cs/0309023

Berman, S. L., Wicks, A. C., Kotha, S., & Jones, T. M. (1999). Does stakeholder orientation matter? The relationship between stakeholder management models and firm financial performance. *Academy of Management Journal, 42*(5): 488–506.

Bosse, D. A., Phillips, R. A., & Harrison, J. S. (2009). Stakeholders, reciprocity, and firm performance. *Strategic Management Journal, 30*(4): 447–456.

Bundy, J., Shropshire, C., & Buchholtz, A. K. (2013). Strategic cognition and issue salience: Toward an explanation of firm responsiveness to stakeholder concerns. *Academy of Management Review, 38*(3): 352–376.

Carroll, A. B. (1991). The pyramid of corporate social responsibility: Toward the moral management of organizational stakeholders. *Business Horizons, 34* (4): 39–48.

Clarkson, M. B. E. (1995). A Stakeholder Framework for Analyzing and Evaluating Corporate Social Performance. *Academy of Management Review, 20*(1): 92–117.

de Nooy, W., Mrvar, A., & Batagelj, V. (2011). *Structural Analysis in the Social Sciences: Exploratory Social Network Analysis with Pajek*. New York: Cambridge University Press.

Donaldson, T., & Preston, L. E. (1995). The stakeholder theory of the corporation: Concepts, evidence, and implications. *Academy of Management Review, 20* (1): 65–91.

Field, R. (2017). John Dewey. *The Internet Encyclopedia of Philosophy (Peer Reviewed)*. Retrieved from http://www.iep.utm.edu.

Freeman, R. E. (1984). *Strategic management: A stakeholder approach*. Boston: Pitman.

Freeman, R. E., Harrison, J. S., & Wicks, A. C. (2007). *Managing for stakeholders: Survival, reputation, and success*. New Haven: Yale University Press.

Freeman, R. E., Harrison, J. S., Wicks, A. C., Parmar, B. L., & Colle, S. de. (2010). *Stakeholder theory: The state of the art*. Cambridge: Cambridge University Press.

Freeman, R. E., & Phillips, R. A. (2002). Stakeholder theory: A libertarian defense. *Business Ethics Quarterly, 12*(3): 331–349.

Friedman, A. L., & Miles, S. (2006). *Stakeholders: Theory and practice*. Oxford; New York: Oxford University Press.

Frooman, J. (1999). Stakeholder influence strategies. *Academy of Management Review, 24*(2): 191–205.

Fukuyama, F. (1996). *Trust: Human nature and the reconstitution of social order*. New York: Simon and Schuster.

Godfrey, P. C. (2005). The relationship between corporate philanthropy and shareholder wealth: A risk management perspective. *Academy of Management Review, 30*(4): 777–798.

Godfrey, P. C., & Hatch, N. W. (2006). Researching corporate social responsibility: An agenda for the 21st Century. *Journal of Business Ethics, 70*(1): 87–98.

Greenwood, M. (2007). Stakeholder engagement: Beyond the myth of corporate responsibility. *Journal of Business Ethics, 74*(4): 315–327.

Hall, M., Millo, Y., & Barman, E. (2015). Who and what really counts? Stakeholder prioritization and accounting for social value. *Journal of Management Studies, 52*(7): 907–934.

Heidegger, M. (2002). *Being and time*. New York: HarperSanFrancisco.

Hill, C. W. L., & Jones, T. M. (1992). Stakeholder agency theory. *Journal of Management Studies, 29*, 131–154.

Hillman, A. J., & Keim, G. D. (2001). Shareholder value, stakeholder management, and social issues: What's the bottom line? *Strategic Management Journal, 22*(2): 125–139.

Hummon, N. P., & Dereian, P. (1989). Connectivity in a citation network: The development of DNA theory. *Social Networks, 11*(1): 39–63.

Hummon, N. P., Dorian, P., & Freeman, L. C. (1990). Analyzing the structure of the centrality-productivity literature created between 1948 and 1979. *Knowledge, 11*(4): 459–480.

James, W. (1891). The moral philosopher and the moral life. *The International Journal of Ethics, 1* (3): 330–354.

Jensen, M. C. (2002). Value maximization, stakeholder theory, and the corporate objective function. *Business Ethics Quarterly, 12*(2): 235–256.

Jones, T. M. (1995). Instrumental stakeholder theory: A synthesis of ethics and economics. *Academy of Management Review, 20*(2): 404–437.

Jones, T. M., & Wicks, A. C. (1999). Convergent stakeholder theory. *Academy of Management Review*, *24*(2): 206–221.

Kim, C. W., & Mauborgne, R. (1998). Procedural justice, strategic decision making, and the knowledge economy. *Strategic Management Journal*, *19*(4): 323–338.

King, B. (2008). A social movement perspective of stakeholder collective action and influence. *Business and Society*, *47*, 21–49.

King, B. G., & Soule, S. A. (2007). Social movements as extra-institutional entrepreneurs: The effect of protests on stock price returns. *Administrative Science Quarterly*, *52*(3): 413–442.

Lévinas, E., & Nemo, P. (1985). *Ethics and infinity*. Lancaster, UK: Gazelle Book Services.

Liu, J. S., & Lu, L. Y. (2012). An integrated approach for main path analysis: Development of the Hirsch index as an example. *Journal of the American Society for Information Science and Technology*, *63*(3): 528–542.

Mackey, A., Mackey, T. B., & Barney, J. B. (2007). Corporate social responsibility and firm performance: Investor preferences and corporate strategies. *Academy of Management Review*, *32*, 817–835.

Margolis, J. D., & Walsh, J. P. (2003). Misery loves companies: Rethinking social initiatives by business. *Administrative Science Quarterly*, *48*(2): 268–305.

Mitchell, R. K., Agle, B. R., & Wood, D. J. (1997). Toward a theory of stakeholder identification and salience: Defining the principle of who and what really counts. *Academy of Management Review*, *22*(4): 853–886.

Mitchell, R. K., Van Buren, H. J., Greenwood, M., & Freeman, R. E. (2015). Stakeholder inclusion and accounting for stakeholders. *Journal of Management Studies*, *52*(7): 851–877.

Mitchell, R. K., Weaver, G. R., Agle, B. R., Bailey, A. D., & Carlson, J. (2016). Stakeholder agency and social welfare: Pluralism and decision making in the multi-objective corporation. *Academy of Management Review*, *41*(2): 252–275.

Noland, J., & Phillips, R. (2010). Stakeholder engagement, discourse ethics and strategic management. *International Journal of Management Reviews*, *12*(1): 39–49.

Parmar, B. L., Freeman, R. E., Harrison, J. S., Wicks, A. C., Purnell, L., & de Colle, S. (2010). Stakeholder theory: The state of the art. *Academy of Management Annals*, 4(0), 403.

Phillips, R. (2003). *Stakeholder theory and organizational ethics*. San Francisco: Berrett-Koehler.

Post, J. E., Preston, L. E., & Sachs, S. (2002). *Redefining the corporation: Stakeholder management and organizational wealth*. Palo Alto: Stanford University Press.

Rawls, J. (1971). *A Theory of Justice*. Harvard University Press.

Rawls, J., & Kelly, E. (2001). *Justice as fairness: A restatement*. Harvard University Press.

Reid, E. M., & Toffel, M. W. (2009). Responding to public and private politics: Corporate disclosure of climate change strategies. *Strategic Management Journal*, *30*(11): 1157–1178.

Rorty, R. (1992). *The linguistic turn: Essays in philosophical method*. Chicago: University of Chicago Press.

Rowley, T. J. (1997). Moving beyond dyadic ties: A network theory of stakeholder influences. *Academy of Management Review*, *22*(4): 887–910.

Seligman, M. E. P. (2011). *Flourish: A visionary new understanding of happiness and well-being*. New York: Free Press.

Talisse, R. B., & Aikin, S. F. (2008). *Pragmatism: A guide for the perplexed*. London; New York: Continuum.

Umphress, E. E., Bingham, J. B., & Mitchell, M. S. (2010). Unethical behavior in the name of the company: the moderating effect of organizational identification and positive reciprocity beliefs on unethical pro-organizational behavior. *Journal of Applied Psychology*, *95*(4): 769.

Whetten, D. A. (2002). Modelling-as-theorizing: A systematic methodology for theory development. In D. Partington, ed., *Essential skills for management research*, 2nd ed., pp. 45–71. Thousand Oaks, CA: SAGE Publications.

Wilson, J. Q. (1997). *The moral sense*. New York: Free Press Paperback.

Wood, D. J., & Logsdon, J. M. (2002). Business citizenship: From individuals to organizations. *Business Ethics Quarterly*, *12*, 59–94.

Critical Management Studies and Stakeholder Theory

Possibilities for a Critical Stakeholder Theory

MICHELLE GREENWOOD

Monash University

RAZA MIR

William Paterson University

Despite being labeled as fearfully radical in its early days, stakeholder theory has grown up to be remarkably conservative. Cries such as "thinly veiled socialism" (noted by Phillips, Freeman, & Wicks, 2003: 491) and "incompatible with business" (Sternberg, 1997: 4), voiced as warnings against a stakeholder conception of the firm, abounded at the turn of the century. These were promptly and roundly rebuffed by a "libertarian defense" of the stakeholder idea in the form of a "controlled burn" that argued that stakeholder theory was not about challenging the ownership of capital nor a social level doctrine (Freeman & Phillips, 2002: 331; Phillips et al., 2003: 479). Indeed, in the intervening decades, the versions of stakeholder theory that have gained greatest purchase have been the most transactional, the most strategic, the most managerialist (Jones, 1995; Mitchell, Agle, & Wood, 1997). Notwithstanding this history, we would argue, the seeds of transformation remain dormant in stakeholder theory waiting to be ignited.

To this end, we will embark on an unusual endeavor, to develop critical stakeholder theory. We will engage the proposition that *stakeholder theory can be made more meaningful if examined through a critical lens.* By critical, we mean "a willingness to explore the underlying assumptions of theory and practice, a questioning of key terms and definitions, and a thorough interrogation of the role of race, class, culture and gender in the development of our ideas" (Freeman & Gilbert, 1992: 15). By meaningful, we identify an aim to "redescribe business in ways that may well be liberating,

that enables us to live differently and better" (Freeman & Gilbert, 1992: 13). For purposes of our analysis, we draw explicitly on the scholarly oeuvre of critical management studies (CMS). We are not the first to be critical of stakeholder theory from this perspective (e.g., Banerjee, 2000), but we are the first, we believe, to invoke this critique to make stakeholder theory better rather than dismiss or destroy it.

This chapter will be organized into five sections. (1) We commence with a brief and provisional history of CMS, assuming that not all readers are conversant with this paradigmatic stance. (2) This will be followed by a necessarily fraught undertaking, a contingent mapping of the domain of CMS including the naming of four themes. (3) From these we generalize four tenets, drawing out their structuralist and humanist dimensions. (4) These themes will then be used as analytics for our reading of the problematics of stakeholder theory. (5) Finally, openings for the advancement of a more critical stakeholder theory will be outlined.

A Provisional History of Critical Management Studies

Moses led his people against the exploitative depredations of the Pharaoh's organizing practices. Gandhi organized the Indians against the oppressive bureaucracy of the British colonial empire. Marx theorized ways in which an organized proletariat could overthrow the regime of capitalism. In their own way, these figures could be considered critical management theorists, for their ideas about how to lead and organize, and how to resist and transform, have animated people over time, and continue to be invoked by the "wretched of the earth" as templates for freedom. Of course, we are academically conditioned to look askance at such assertions, but perhaps it is good to use these provocations to foreground our brief analysis of what constitutes "critical management studies" (CMS).

It could be argued that the sub-discipline of CMS has been around as long as management has been a discipline. In some respect, one could argue that CMS even predates management concepts. For example, take the case where the critique of cor-poratism in the 1930s following the Great Depression, as espoused most paradigmatically by Adolf Berle and Gardiner Means in their 1932 treatise *The Modern Corporation and Private Property,* produced a response that ultimately became enshrined as "corporate social responsibil-ity" (Berle and Means, 1991). Of course CSR as an idea did not come pre-named; its tenets were initi-ally articulated by industry leaders like Chester Barnard, whose 1938 treatise *The Functions of the Executive* (Barnard, 1968) was formulated to counter calls for more state oversight of corporate activity (Perrow, 1972: 62–68). Barnard and his CEO peers at the US Chamber of Commerce were doing their best to minimize talk of intra-organizational conflict, focusing instead on shared ideas and labor, independent of hierarchy. The idea of managers as potential servants of society, rather than individualistic profit maximizers, was even-tually formalized in 1953 with that name by Howard Bowen (2013).

To take such as approach, which appropriates Berle and Means as critical management scholars, might provoke further debate. Such debate is wel-come, for it highlights the reality that to chart the emergence of critical management studies is itself a fraught task, full of political pitfalls and contra-dictions. The progression between various avatars of CMS is a continuous one, and to break that continuity into a temporal taxonomy is an act of social construction that is neither helpful nor pro-ductive. For our purposes, we should swiftly move the discussion to the point where the discipline of

management was being formalized in the mid-twentieth century, by economists and behavioral psychologists, and being contested primarily by those scholars who belonged to the Marxist tradition.

The emergence of post-Marxist tradition, in the wake of Louis Althusser and Michel Foucault (Aktouf, 1992; Burrell, 1988), began to liberate cultural categories such as gender and race from the confines of the base-superstructure determinism of Marxist theory. Critical management scholars began to turn their attention toward a critique, not only of intra-organizational discrimination, but also of the tendency of mainstream management scho-lars to develop unreflective categories (e.g., "diversity") to paper over these structural schisms. A critique of the linguistic traditions of management from the "traditions of the post" began to gain traction, legitimacy and at times hegemony, leading to trenchant internal critiques as well (Clegg, 2015). Currently, CMS occupies a happily anarchic space, defined loosely as an opposition to the ideological tendencies to view organizational interests from the point of view of powerful and dominant classes and subjectivities. It has been "disciplined" into a category that occupies the big tent of management theory as evidenced by the fact that the academic disci-pline has formed a division of the Academy of Management, conducts its own conferences, has a number of journals that espouse an explicitly critical orientation, has its own PhD programs, and is critiqued by its interlocutors for having strayed from its own mandate (e.g., Tatli, 2012).[1]

Mapping Critical Management Studies

Notwithstanding the difficulties involved in devel-oping a taxonomy of CMS, we may divide the scholarship into four categories, reflecting the main focus of the corpus of work each represents: class-based analytics, feminist approaches, postco-lonial research and subjectivity-oriented studies. Needless to say, all four categories overlap and inform one another, and this taxonomy is vulner-able to critique on grounds of reductiveness.

Notwithstanding, we present these categories as a way to map the field, hopefully as a stepping-stone to more refined idiosyncratic taxonomies, to the point where the need for taxonomies is itself transcended.

Class-Based Analytics

The earliest critiques of management theory, such as Harry Braverman's 1974 analysis of the labor process (Braverman, 1998), Kenneth Benson's presentation of organizational theory as a dialectic (Benson, 1977), Katherine Stone's empirical analysis of the emergence of structure in the US steel industry (Stone, 1974) and Walter Nord's critique of humanistic psychology (Nord, 1977), tended to use the Marxian template to contest capitalism.[2] Other, non-Marxist critiques such as Charles Perrow's magisterial historicization of organizational theory (Perrow, 1972), tended to use historical analytic traditions that were close to the Marxist analytic.

Harry Braverman's foundational analysis of deskilling as the fundamental driver of the industrial labor process (Braverman, 1974) may be considered a polestar that Marxist and neo-Marxist organizational theorists used to navigate their way through the terrain of organizational exploitation. Braverman argued, following Marx, that the capitalist project as articulated within firms staked its survival and well-being on its ability to manage the "labor process," also referred to as "work organization." Braverman, a metal worker himself before he became a prominent theorist and journalist, developed a sharp critique of the regimes of scientific management and the assembly line, and in the process, defined the ways in which workers resisted the attempts by capitalists to view them as mere adjuncts to machines, and eventually to replace them with machines. He also suggested that absent avenues of organized actions such as strikes, workers articulated their dissent (and enacted their humanity) through acts of passive resistance, including work slowdowns, minor acts of sabotage, or mere incivility, and that researchers needed to dignify these acts of resistance by theorizing them, rather than dismissing them as mere instances of "resistance to change."

Studies of class-based paradigm in organizational theory have continued to animate discussions about exploitation and ideology into the 1990s (Smith & Willmott, 1991), and into the new century (Maclean, Harvey, & Kling, 2014). Scholars have applied Marx to the study of corporate behavior (Adler, 2007), technological changes in the workplace (Marquetti, 2003), learning and knowledge management (Ingvaldsen, 2015), and business process reengineering (Sanders, 1997), to name a few.

Scholars who study class conflicts in an organization setting are sharply critical of stakeholder theory (e.g., Marens, 2016), suggesting that it provides an illusion of access to disenfranchised groups while maintaining the control of the means of production for capitalists through the corporate route. In the context of the employment relations, for instance, stakeholder theory has been aligned with a "pluralist frame of reference" (Greenwood & Freeman, 2011; Stoney & Winstanley, 2001), and thus considered as differentiated from and incommensurable with a "radical/Marxist frame of reference" (Fox, 1974). Whilst a theory of the firm that demands consideration of stakeholders might broaden the corporate focus beyond shareholders and corporate purpose beyond profit, such that employment and work, for example, might be structured differently within the organization, it does not address the structural factors as a societal level that may be seen lead to illegitimate power and control (Budd & Bhave, 2008). To that extent, it is difficult to produce pathways for a productive conversation between this strand of CMS and stakeholder theories.

Feminist Approaches

Feminist scholarship in organizational theories emerged in the late 1970s and followed several trajectories, moving from liberal pleas for understanding organizations from women's point of view (Kanter, 1977) to radical rejections of the female sex role in the workplace (Koen, 1984), psychological critiques of the male referents that rendered women abnormal in workplaces (Benhabib, 1985), linguistic deconstruction of management texts using the post-structuralist tradition (Calás and Smircich, 1991), and Marxist analysis of gender as a special case of class divisions (Delphy, 1984).

Feminism as a construct has had a long history in social theory, dating back to the eighteenth century, principally the publication of Mary Wollstonecraft's 1792 book *A Vindication of the Rights of Woman* (Wollstonecraft, 1999). However, it was the so-named "second wave" of feminist theory that formalized gender studies as an important element in a variety of social sciences. The ringing statement of Simone de Beauvoir that "one is not born, but rather becomes, a woman" (de Beauvoir, 1988 [1953]: 295) brought into sharp relief the idea of gender as a social construction.

Organizational theory was slower to adopt feminist theory as a legitimate (see Calás, Smircich, & Holvino, 2014, for a comprehensive analysis of feminist theorizing, both in social theory and in organizational studies). Gender studies within organizational theory have mostly been critical, perhaps by compulsion, for the reality is that women who labor in organizations have always had to struggle for equality vis-à-vis their male counterparts. The earliest form of gender-based theorizing was classified as "women in management" literature, and tended to follow the tenets of liberal feminism, which argued for greater representation of women in organizational spaces (e.g., Valian, 1999). Practitioners like Sheryl Sandberg, who provide roadmaps for women to "lean in" and take on the glass ceiling in twenty-first-century organizations, can also be seen as a part of this conversation (Sandberg, 2013). Although the conversation is ongoing and fruitful in its own way, it can be critiqued for its reluctance to examine the structural determinants of such exclusion, and an insufficient critique of patriarchy (Calás & Smircich, 2006). Liberal feminism gave way to radical feminism, a movement that was predicated on developing a radical separation of sexes, to offer women a critical space of gender solidarity unencumbered by male referents. Kathy Ferguson's book *The Radical Case Against Bureaucracy* embodies this spirit best, and provides an argument for viewing all organizations as inherently patriarchal (Ferguson, 1984). In contingent solidarity with class-based critiques of organizing, socialist feminism attempted to view the subordination of women as a case of class-based oppression that had escaped the notice even of Marxist and class-antagonistic theorists (Acker, 2006). In the process of understanding the cycle of oppression, feminists necessarily began to analyze the way in which patriarchy functioned to produce the masculine as "normal" and the feminine as "different" or "other."

Feminist praxis then became a matter not just of making sure that women were represented in different social strata, but also that the "feminine" became a legitimate mode of analysis and articulation. For example, psychoanalytic feminism (Gilligan, 1982) attempted to view gender as a category that had been written out of psychological theory (e.g., critiques of Kohlberg's theory of moral development). As feminist approaches became more legitimate in social theory, it necessarily spawned intra-feminist conversations about who controlled the boundaries of the feminist agenda. For instance, postcolonial feminists argued that non-Western women faced a double disadvantage, and were destined to operate "under Western eyes," both in patriarchal and feminist spaces (Mohanty, 1988). In short, feminism as a category provides multiple ways to look at gender, and argues that its subsumption under other categories is not just a generalization, but is theoretical laziness.

Stakeholder theory and feminist approaches, especially of the liberal kind, have a number of areas of potential commensurability. These include a potential acknowledgment that women subjects are special organizational stakeholders, that patriarchy potentially erodes the stakeholder rights of organizational subjects, and that work-life balance impacts female stakeholders disproportionately.

Postcolonial Research

Corporations have long been implicated in the furtherance of colonialism and imperialism. For example, India was colonized in the eighteenth century, not by the British crown, but by the East India Company, a joint-stock corporation (Bowen,

2005). Likewise, sugar-colonialism in Haiti (Stinchcombe, 1995), oil colonialism in the Middle East (Prashad 2008), current regimes of metal neo-colonialism in Africa (Erlichman, 2010), and Halliburton's role in furthering and sustaining the war in twenty-first-century Iraq (Klein, 2007), all point to a nexus between state actors and corporate players, in a self-sustaining dance of exploitation and imperialism.

Critical organization scholars have analyzed this phenomenon in multiple ways. For example, post-colonial theorists began to analyze how non-Western activism was represented as an artifact of an archaic "culture" rather than being accorded the dignity of being theorized. Postcolonial theories emerged in organizational discourse in the late 1990s (Prasad, 1997a), but their efforts can be related to earlier critiques of Eurocentrism (Boyacigiller & Adler, 1991), postmodern theory (Radhakrishnan, 1994), and corporate interventions in the third world (Mir, Calás, & Smircich, 1999). Postcolonial theorists like Prasad (1997b: 91) attempted to critique "Europe's claim to universality as its problematic, and to contend that any serious attempt to reorganize the past and/or the future must subvert the European appropriation of the universal." In so doing, they invoke the idea of *orientalism* developed by Edward Said (1978), who claimed that the idea of the Orient was essentially an act of production by the west, rather than a representation of the East. The act of representing non-Western subjects as somehow underdeveloped – not just a matter of theoretical oversight but a necessary tool of statecraft – was intended to legitimize the processes of imperialism, which may be defined as a specific case of exploitation, where the surplus value generated in one part of the world is appropriated for use in a geographically distant land. Colonialism, therefore, is a special case of imperialism, where the ruling group settles in the native land, but continues to identify with, and work for the furtherance of, the colonizing state.

This research approach has generated a myriad of conceptual heuristics, such as *strategic essentialism,* a term that has developed a high level of valence in postcolonial theory. Articulated first by Gayatri Chakravorty Spivak (1988), the idea of strategic essentialism is to identify a space of

activism for non-Western subjectivities that, while acknowledging the political nature of all meta-narratives, advocates a subject position (say nationalism or feminism) and is assumed to open up a space for activism, despite the acknowledgement of the constructed and contested nature of such a subject position. For example, a woman can feel free to speak for *women*, despite the understanding that the category "woman" is far too heterogeneous for any single person to represent it. This perspective, despite acknowledging the hierarchical relations between various subjectivities such as race, gender, and class, chooses definite subject positions as an attempt to confront the ethnocentricity imbedded in various discourses. It allows people the latitude to practice *identity politics* in the short term. However, the goal of this identity politics is to transcend the very subject position it has chosen for itself, and render that position unremarkable. For example, even when we know that a term like "race" is socially constructed, we can organize around it to fight racism. Despite knowing that "nation" is a constructed term, it can be used as a strategic category to fight colonialism. The final task of the principled theorist/activist is that when the political goal is achieved, they must transcend the term. So if racial equality is achieved in society, the category of "race" can be dismantled. Until then, this category is indispensable to the racial minority, even if it is a constructed category.

Postcoloniality continues to find resonance among organizational scholars, as exemplified by recent special issues of journals (Banerjee & Prasad, 2008; Jack et al., 2011). These theories enable critiques of regimes of imperialism including interrogations of organizational change (Mir & Mir, 2012), professional service firms (Boussebaa, 2015), diversity (Mir, Mir, & Wong, 2006), and a variety of organizational constructs.

Subjectivity-Based Studies

As the previous sections have shown, critical management studies is preoccupied not only with the actions that are performed by organizations in the service of the elite and at the expense of the disadvantaged, but also by the way in which language, representative practices, and regimes of institutionalization are brought to bear in legitimizing these actions. Such an approach essentially takes issue with Marxist analytics, which had suggested that the sociocultural "superstructure" was essentially nothing but a representation of the economic "base." For example, Marxist theory is predicated upon the assumption that the economic base drives all social change, and sociocultural issues constitute a superstructure, where autonomous change is not possible. Changes in the superstructure are nothing but reflections of the changes that occur in the base. In contrast, theorists of subjectivity argue that the superstructure has far more autonomy than Marxist approaches give it credit for, and may sometimes even upend economic class relations.

According to these theorists, one of the most important representative acts performed by elite groups is the act of "changing the subject" (Radhakrishnan, 1996), whereby either the victims of exploitation are deemed worthy of such treatment, or sometimes the act of exploitation is deemed a part of some civilizing or normalizing mission. Theorists who have analyzed this phenomenon include Michel Foucault who analyzed how population-level representation created an understanding of what was normal/abnormal, Jacques Derrida who analyzed texts as being repositories of both presence and absence (Derrida, 1976), Ernesto Laclau and Chantal Mouffe who studied the fluidity of class identity (Laclau & Moffe, 1985), Luc Boltanski and Eve Chiapello who analyzed newer forms of capitalist organization (Boltanski & Chiapello, 2005), Homi Bhabha who analyzed invocation of mimicry and hybridity (Bhabha, 2012), and several others.

Subjectivity-based approaches have been used extensively by organizational scholars, as evidenced by Foucauldian analyses of organizational practice (Mennicken & Miller, 2014), textual deployment of Derridean deconstruction (Weitzner, 2007), Lacanian psychoanalytics (Kenny, 2009), Laclau and Mouffe's concept of articulatory practice (Bridgman, 2007), the application of Boltanski, and Chiapello's formulation of the "new spirit of capitalism" (Kazmi, Leca, & Naccache, 2016), or Bhabha's notion of "hybridity" (McKenna, 2011).

In the interest of space, we briefly analyze only the last concept.

Homi Bhabha's formulation of hybridity as an aspect of subjectivity allows the researcher to move past a simple Marxian dialectic of labor/capital and explore ways in which disadvantaged organizational actors use hybridity and mimicry-based tools to find a way to articulate their specific problems and issues. The idea is that when the power differential between the ruler and the ruled (the colonizer and the colonized, or in the organizational case, the management and the worker) are far too great for traditional forms of resistance to be enacted, resistance takes on a more sly aspect. One aspect could the deployment by the subject of the traditions of the master to secure advantages for themselves. The adoption of cricket in the British colonies, albeit with a particular local flavor (James, 1983) is a good example of hybridity. The cricketers from the West Indies played the same game as the British, but with a joy that was their own, and when they beat England in an international test, it felt as if a boundary of power had been breached. Likewise, when a multinational corporation headquartered in the West seeks to manage its subsidiary in a different nation, the relationship begins to acquire the same colonial relationship, where the accommodations by the subsidiary take on an ambiguous character, and shift the terrain of power infinitesimally toward the subsidiary. Scholars studying intra-organizational capability transfer (Frenkel, 2008) have theorized a similar space of hybridity, where the power of traditional managerialist discourse is reduced by the invocation of and by local specificities.

Subjectivity-based approaches draw into question some of the most basic aspects of stakeholder theory. We might begin with issues such as who is identified as a stakeholder (who is in and who is out, who is core and who is periphery), who gets to do the identifying (who has power over the discourse), and what does it mean to be classified as a stakeholder (how the utterance is performative) (Greenwood & Anderson, 2009). However, subjectivity-based approaches traverse the knowledge assumptions (Mir, Calás, & Smircich, 1999) upon which these "problems" are founded by attending to the inbuilt subjectification in these acts of identity, representation, and boundaries, that is the very recognition of ourselves as subjects.

Generalizing from Critical Management Studies

Overall, CMS is a big tent, but it is safe to generalize that the various strands emerge from dissatisfaction with the status quo in the socioeconomic realm, and a desire to correct unequal relationships therein. Based on the aforenamed approaches, one can identify four broad tenets that separate it from mainstream organizational approaches. Within that, we can make two broad distinctions based on the philosophical position assumed by the researcher. Those critical scholars who see oppressive social relations as being fixed and immutable have been referred to as *radical structuralists*, while those who see them as socially constructed and open to interpretation have been termed *radical humanists* (Burrell & Morgan, 1979).

Critical approaches recognize the salience of economic class as a category. This category creates powerful barriers to entry for disenfranchised groups, and CMS scholars argue that mainstream organizational theorists do not recognize the power of this barrier, thereby excluding a large swath of organizational actors from their purview. From a structuralist perspective, critical scholars attempt to examine ways in which institutional structures work to sustain the hegemony of elite class positions over subaltern class identities. From a humanist perspective, critical scholars focus on oppressed groups, and the impact of class exploitation on their personal life, their well-being, and their dignity as human subjects.

Critical theorists also recognize the power of non-class identity formations like gender and ethnicity, subsuming them under other categories, and thereby marginalizing a variety of identity groups. On a structural level, they study ways in which non-class identities are constructed, enacted, and sedimented over time, space, and context. At a humanistic level, they study ways in which women, minorities, and other groups' identities are performed and particularities are marginalized, and how connections of solidarity can be formed to oppose the oppression that is imposed on them by social practices.

Critical theorists see global relations as often being governed by regimes of imperialism. Imperialism is a specific form of exploitation, where labor and resources from a particular geographic region are deployed for the benefit of other geographies. Again, structuralist analyses focus on imperialism as a special case of exploitation made distinct by the geographic separation of the exploiter and the exploited, while humanistic analyses focus on how the subjects of imperialist exploitation experience a double separation from the mainstream, both economically and culturally.

Finally, critical theorists see their role as legitimizing the actions of disadvantaged subjectivities as they contest capitalist regimes and firms. Mainstream organizational theory is not predisposed to accord resistive acts by many subaltern subjects the status of theory, often undermining it by calling it "resistance to change" or "culture." By producing a counter-theory of sorts, critical theorists attempt to rebalance this power divide in the world of ideas, seeing it as an act of representation (or re-presentation), however contingent this may be. This tenet lends itself mostly to humanist analysis.

Thinking Critically about Stakeholder Theory

The lens of critical management studies is vital to developing a more engaged, a more analytic and a more emancipatory stakeholder theory. We return to the four critically inspired analytics– class, feminism, anti-imperialism, and subjectivism – to consider what provocations might arise from their application to stakeholder theory. Distinguishing between radical structuralism and radical humanism reminds us that to take a critical view of the nature of society (as political and contested) does not necessitate foreclosing on a specific view of the nature of social science (as either objectively determined by structure or subjectively constructed through agency) (Burrell & Morgan, 1979). However, as discussed earlier with regard to class-based conflict, elements of radical structuralism and stakeholder theory are deeply discordant. Hence, we rely primarily upon the humanist side of the four tenets to create a bridge between CMS and stakeholder theory

Class based analytics hold least joy for the future of stakeholder theories, being broadly incommensurable with scope and assumptions of many stakeholder approaches. However, some rapprochement might be possible in the arena of environmentalism. Scholars have applied Marx to the study of organizations and the environment. It is an indisputable truism that despite the persistence of class, environmental disasters have a secular effect on human beings regardless of geographies and social class. Of course, in the short term, the disastrous effects of macro phenomena like climate change fall disproportionately on the poor. However, despite the persistence of a few naysayers, a global consensus is taking shape that we ignore the effects of climate change at our own peril as a species (Beck, 2016). Critical scholars analyzing this phenomenon through a Marxist and post-Marxist lens have articulated the hope that the recognition of this crisis might convince a variety of hitherto reluctant actors to come on board and consider a radical shift in the manner in which social products are created, appropriated, and distributed (Klein, 2007). While critical scholars have applied Marx to the study of organizations and the environment (e.g., Foster & Burkett, 2001), and mainstream stakeholder theorists have weighed in explicitly on the matter of climate change (e.g., Haigh & Griffiths, 2009), they have hitherto been ships that pass by in the theoretical night. It is perhaps in the recognition of this mutual threat that true conversations can begin between critical scholars and theorists of stakeholder value.

Feminist approaches demand of us to consider heterogeneity and particularity, and the experience of being Other. From a stakeholder point of view, an important question to be asked is, are women a specific category of organizational stakeholders? Put differently, can stakeholder theory develop a specific granularity to see that the perspective of others in the organization cannot be subsumed under broader categories? What might a gender lens offer to our ontological understanding of stakeholders and our epistemological performativity of

stakeholder theory? Stakeholder theorists have occasionally argued that feminism has many rich insights to offer their field (e.g., Wicks, et al., 1994), but it is safe to say that there is still a lot of room for conversations in which feminism can inform stakeholder theory. For example, the gendered nature of work in the global apparel industry adds a vital layer of ethical concern and analytic richness rarely considered when thinking about a generic "sweatshop worker." More broadly, feminist ontology and feminist ethics (Benhabib, 1985; Nelson, 2003) have much to offer the new relational turn in stakeholder theory, including exploration of the ethics of alterity, the particularity and situatedness of lived experience, and the socio-materiality of organizational and economic life.

Postcolonial research forms a critique of management and organization scholarship on account of its inadequate analysis of imperialism, and stakeholder theory is no exception (e.g., Parsons, 2008). However, in an interesting inversion, native people across the world have been articulating their "stake" in various organizational spaces to demand redress for earlier imperialist practices. In particular, indigenous groups that rise up against corporations with mining interest over sacred lands present interesting challenges and possibilities for stakeholder theory (Banerjee, 2000). Postcolonial theories of subjectivity could be fruitfully employed to explore the lived experiences of often-overlooked subaltern stakeholder groups. Furthermore, concepts about subaltern subjectivities and activism, such as strategic essentialism outlined earlier, might overcome ontological impasses around stakeholder categorization and engagement, and advance more nuanced approaches to stakeholder influence and power.

Subjectivity-based studies have enormous potential to address many limitations and inadequacies of stakeholder theory. To begin, such perspectives recognize that the heterogeneity of identities impacted by organizations demands a far more sophisticated analytical schema than is provided by the relatively aggregated analytics of current approaches. For example, a Foucauldian analysis of organizational strategy (McKinlay, et al., 2010) can offer a more nuanced understanding of stakeholders as subjectivities rather than mere population groups. Further, stakeholder approaches infused with subjectivity theories and conceptualizations (e.g., governmentality, performativity, intersubjectivity, reflexivity) could open new thinking in areas such as governance, decision-making, organizational identity, accountability, and consumption *inter alia*. For instance, relational stakeholder theories could speak deeply to new forms of economy that are increasingly built at their core on social relationships, wherein value is derived from free social production or the ability "to transform weak ties into affectively significant strong ones" (Arvidsson, 2009: 13; 2010)

Many seeds of the core tenets of critical management studies are already embedded in early works in stakeholder theory. However, in the main, these works rely on weak versions of these concepts. In order to fundamentally advance stakeholder theory, to make it more meaningful, it is necessary to undertake a paradigmatic shift in thinking. Firstly, one needs to embrace the world as political, human experience as historic and situated, institutions as contested. Second, one needs to embrace an understanding of the world as non-entitic, as intersubjectively constituted, wherein relationality is seen as a unit of reality rather than merely a unit of analysis.[3] This chapter has expounded the thesis that political and philosophical commitments to radical forms of structuralism or humanism are needed to develop strong forms of critical stakeholder thinking and make stakeholder theory more meaningful.

Possibilities for a Critical Stakeholder Theory

In order to explore the radical future stakeholder theory, we find ourselves returning to some of the earliest ideas and concerns in the field. From the outset, a set of questions – what is a stake, who is a stakeholder, how might stakeholder governance be practiced, and what is the nature of the stakeholder relationship – dominated the stakeholder literature, with many pundits declaring these issues to be the core to understanding a stakeholder theory of the firm. We revisit these conundra with a distinctly critical edge.

What is Stake? Rethinking Capital and Property

If the word stakeholder is a shameless play on the words stockholder or shareholder, then what does this make a stake? The simple idea of a claim or investment, which brings with it exposure to risk, when interpreted in the broadest sense, might take us some distance to making us think differently about the purpose of the firm and its relations with those who affect or are affected by it.

This leads to an early radical claim that the organization and its managers owe a fiduciary obligation to a broad range of stakeholders (referred to by some as multi-fiduciary stakeholder theory, e.g. Goodpaster, 1991). That is, as an extension of the idea that corporate powers are held in trust for the entire community and not just shareholders, managers might hold direct and perfect obligations to non-owners.

> Perhaps the most important area of future research is the issue of whether or not a theory of management can be constructed that uses the stakeholder concept to enrich "managerial capitalism," that is, can the notion that managers bear a fiduciary relationship to stockholders or the owners of the firm, be replaced by a concept of management whereby the manager must act in the interests of the stakeholders in the organization? (Freeman, 1984: 249)

Thus, in the penultimate paragraph of his 1984 classic book, Freeman throws this bombshell that has the capacity to not just explode how we understand the firm and its responsibilities, but how we understand the nature of capitalism and structure its institutions.

Pushed one step further, we can think differently about property and capital. A broadened concept of property is also fundamental to rethinking the nature of claims and rights in organization-stakeholder relations. Rather than stakeholder theory driving us to think differently about property and property rights, the reverse can be argued; that an enlightened view of contracts as both explicit and *implicit*, and thus by their nature *incomplete*, shifts us to think differently about the firm and to imagine it as a nexus of stakeholders (Asher, Mahoney, & Mahoney, 2005). Such a view suggests a conceptualization of property beyond the concrete and private, which incorporates intangibles (e.g., intellectual property) and collective or widely held property.

One potential place where there could be a meeting of minds is the recognition that those who labor against the arbitrary imposition of property rights on collective lands are to be accorded a fair hearing by the owners of corporate capital. Nevertheless, such broader conceptualizations of ownership rights are based on neo-liberal views of society (e.g., Donaldson & Preston, 1995). Furthermore, they rely on a view of ownership as something that can be definitively identified and attributed and, as such, legally protected.

The limitations of this extended conceptualization are highlighted by the example of land subject to customary ownership by indigenous communities. General recognition of customary rights is available in some common law, but is often held to specific acts (e.g., Native Title in Australia; Australian Law Reform Commission, 1986). Hence, a legal process, which has potential to be based on a different way of thinking about property that is responsive to particular community beliefs, is evidently bound and specified such that it becomes a further recognition of imperative of legislated ownership.

Extended heuristics of capital that encompass enlargements of the concept beyond financial capital, namely social capital, human capital, symbolic capital, have been developed both within and beyond stakeholder theory. Phillips (1997) and Van Buren (2001) both provide arguments for principles of fairness in organization-stakeholder relations that recognize stakeholder contributions and sacrifices. However, capital implies that something is held or owned, and has capacity to yield returns; it almost demands for exchanges to be based on transactions. As noted by Van Buren (2016), even ideas such as social capital that purport to bring social relationships into the analysis of value production do so in a manner that propagates the financialization and co-optation of stakeholder contributions. The possibilities that any alternative understanding of property or capital might impact the experiences of those who have neither, but are nevertheless fully exposed to the risks inherent in corporatization of their lives, in the absence of significant change to political economy, at a minimum to existing ownership and control structures, appear negligible.

Who is a Stakeholder? Stakeholder Identification and Engagement as Process and Becoming

Who is in and who is out has been an obsession of stakeholder theorists from the outset (see Mitchell et al., 1997). In 1999, the word was described "stakeholder" as just coming into its "prime" and needing to take on "some serious responsibility" (Slinger, 1999: 136). Those scholars who worked with this promising young concept, like the analogous teenager, drilled deeper and deeper, and drew harder and firmer boundaries, in search of certainty in membership and identification. The difficulties and limitations involved in this quest have been both acknowledged and compounded by more and more sophisticated models for stakeholder identification. For instance, Crane and Ruebottom's (2011: 78) response to the problem that "stakeholder identification and mapping is too fragmented and superficial to be able to make meaningful assessments of the bases on which groups form, interpret, and act in relation to the firm" is to develop more sophisticated mapping, that is, to replace "traditional stakeholder roles" with another set of categories called "social identities."

To challenge and develop the categorical criteria for stakeholder identification is a fraught project from a critical structuralist's point of view. The identification of a "dependent stakeholder," one that had "low power" but "high legitimacy" and "high urgency," such as sweatshop workers (Mitchell et al., 1997), is not meaningful unless it is understood in the context of economic class and the material and other resources that this entails. Who gets to decide who or what is legitimate? In the case of Indigenous communities negotiating with mining communities in Australia, Banerjee (2000: 25) makes an important observation:

> [A]lthough Aboriginal stakeholders are positioned as legitimate stakeholders whose needs will be

"constructively addressed," the stakes that are involved for Aboriginal communities affected by mining are somehow positioned as "illegitimate" or "against national interest."

When understood as managerial prerogative, stakeholder recognition and engagement in the absence of structural change at a societal level (e.g., governance structures, see previous) are unlikely to lead to any form of self-determination for these stakeholders or betterment for society (Greenwood, 2007).

If authentic stakeholder engagement is impossible under structural conditions where the relative power and concomitant rhetorical skills of the parties predetermine the outcome, it is necessary for us to reconsider the rules of engagement. A line of scholarship in CSR has sought to apply Habermasian discourse ethics to the conceptualization of organization-stakeholder relations on the grounds that the corporation, as a political actor, should be subject to public expectations regarding discourse, transparency, and accountably (Noland & Phillips, 2010; Scherer & Palazzo, 2007). These arguments promote the establishment of conditions for deliberative discourse under which corporations, government, and civil society can reach intersubjective agreement about the firms and about various parties' obligations, duties, or rights. Rather than aim for unattainable ideal discourse conditions of engagement, which demand that power imbalances are removed from the interaction, a pragmatic approach "that narrows the gap between the actual practice of political decision making and the theoretical purity of ethical discourses" is advocated (Scherer & Palazzo, 2007: 1107).

In contrast, critical humanist perspective opens stakeholder thinking to many descriptive and analytic possibilities. By giving primacy to becoming, rather than being or having, we open a range of possibilities for stakeholder research. Stakeholder identities and subject positions are not seen as bestowed or predetermined, but rather constituted through discourses, processes, and practices. One might ask how CSR practices (e.g., as corporate social reporting) constitute employee identity, or for that matter how CEO identity is determined and

how this is experienced by those constituted as Other (Morsing, 2006).

Stakeholder Governance and Decision-Making

The idea of incorporating stakeholders into organizational governance and decision-making was an aspect of early stakeholder theories that attracted much controversy. Early versions of stakeholder theory were predicated on giving stakeholders formal, binding control over the corporation, in particular, over its board of directors (Freeman, 1994). Cries of subversion and socialism from neoliberals (Sternberg, 1997) were met with a "libertarian defense" of stakeholder theory (Freeman & Phillips, 2002), and a shift in commitment from these more radical positions to being agnostic about the value of change in the structure of governance (Moriarty, 2014).

Questions of corporate governance, however, "only become interesting when one refrains from thinking of firms as unified entities that make decisions and carry them out like individual agents" (Heath & Norman, 2004: 252). Focusing on the interconnectivity between stakeholders shifts us from our thinking about organizations as bounded entities with an "external" environment. Depicting stakeholders in a network of relationships has led researchers to theorize about the structural characteristics of an organization's network of relationships (Rowley, 1997); indirect stakeholder influence (e.g., low wage workers being represented by first world consumers (Frooman, 1999); and multi-stakeholder initiatives (Roloff, 2008).

Recognition of the political role of the firm, the alignment between corporate interests and government interest, and the failure of nation states to protect (often local and/or indigenous) communities (Scherer and Palazzo, 2007) leads to more radical ideas about structural arrangements. If the corporation is understood beyond traditional boundaries, then so should corporate governance be recognized as not just restricted to the board of directors. Governance becomes something that "spills out beyond the boundaries of the board, or even the corporation . . . to a more sprawling set of governmental institutions" that are distributed across industry, business, or the broader economy (Spicer & Banerjee, 2016: 408). Stakeholder participation in organizational decision-making at the board level needs to be supported by wider social institutions (Van Buren & Greenwood, 2009). From a critical structuralist perspective, Spicer and Banerjee (2016) argue that in order for marginalized and vulnerable stakeholders to exercise their common and customary property rights, corporations need to be subject to a variety of explicit regimes of accountability (in contrast with implicit responsibilities).

Rather than think about organizations as having or being in stakeholder networks, what if we thought about organizations as being a stakeholder network, as being constituted by stakeholders in multiple fluid relationships? Understanding the organization as made up of stakeholders, rather as a separate entity in relationship with stakeholders, cuts through many assumptions about governance and decision-making-based fixed structures and purposes. For example, the long-standing criticism that consideration of responsibilities to stakeholders diluted corporate purpose and divided accountability (Sternberg, 1997) is rendered absurd if the firm and its stakeholders are understood as inseparable. What if governance was understood as a critical humanist might; as in-the-making, as processes or practices that constitute organization-stakeholder relationships, as how within those relationships power is experienced and negotiated?

Stakeholder Relationships as a Call to Moral Entwinement

Developing a "more relational view" of stakeholder theory was an explicit goal of many early theorists (Buchholz & Rosenthal, 2005: 137; McVea & Freeman, 2005; Wicks, et al., 1994). For example, Buchholz and Rosenthal (2005: 147) draw on theories of American Pragmatism to fault atomistic versions of stakeholder theory and build an argument that the corporation is "in fact constituted by the multiple relationships in which it is embedded and which give it its very being." However, these authors uphold what could be

characterized as a weak relational perspective with their stance that ongoing growth "requires that a corporation internalize the perspectives of the stakeholders" (2005: 147). In contrast, a strong relational view – one that conceptualizes the firm as intersubjectively constituted by the interactions, processes, or practices of the stakeholders – has a myriad of implications for exploring how we understand reciprocity, trust, power, decision-making, value creation, or any number of key features explored through stakeholder theory.

The very idea of conceptualizing of humans as stakeholders, whether in theory or in practice, seems intrinsically at risk of universalizing, simplifying, and institutionalizing human interaction. Consider, for example, moves toward the stakeholder measurement and accounting (e.g., the Global Reporting Initiative); transactions based on reciprocity and justice (e.g., the "fairness principle," Phillips, 1997); organizational practices based on fairness and neutrality (e.g., equal employment opportunity); codified legal and risk management compliance regimes (e.g., company-based and industry-based codes of ethics). Indeed the "impulse to create a stakeholder tradition with a strong preference for the particular and local" present in some of Freeman's early work (Freeman, 1984; McVea & Freeman, 2005) "gravitates somewhat against the desire for generalizable theory in management" and remains only partially realized (Elms, Johnson-Cramer, & Berman, 2011: 23).

Overcoming the problem of the faceless stakeholder is vital to overcoming the problem of faceless responsibility and faceless accountability (Moriceaux, 2005), and critical to overcoming the institutionalization of responsibility and evacuation of human moral impulse (Bauman, 1993). For Bauman, and for Levinas on whose ideas Bauman built, the sort of rational calculation and universalizing involved in much stakeholder thinking is "inherently irresponsible" (Bevan & Werhane 2011: 53) and that, in contrast, we are called to responsibility through face-to-face encounter with an unknowable, complex and particular Other.

Relational views of stakeholder theory especially open up a rethinking of business ethics by placing morality squarely in relationships between subjects.

A neo-Marxist reinterpretation of stakeholder theory would visualize the validation of alternative organizational arrangements, especially those that go beyond denunciations of neoliberal capitalism, and visualize alternate economic arrangements that are non-capitalist in nature (Gibson-Graham, 2008). These arrangements include firms that engage with the overarching capitalist structure (making parts for automobile firms, for example), but practice non-hierarchical relations of production and ownership, and potentially seed the capitalist terrain with their ideas and possibilities. Arrangements of this nature, for example, have existed in the Mondragon, a federation of cooperatives that existed in the Basque region of Spain over half a century ago (Whyte & Whyte, 1991). Exemplars of this kind help produce the possibility of non-exploitative stakeholder relationships, however infrequent and tenuous.

Likewise, a feminist interpretation of stakeholder theory "places [stakeholder] relationships at the heart of what organisations do and, concretely rather than abstractly, promotes a personal connection to relationships" (Antonacopoulou & Méric, 2005: 30; Wicks et al., 1994). Yuthas and Dillard (1999: 48) propose a stakeholder theory that takes "an affirmative postmodern perspective, being able to understand the interests and concerns of others, being in face-to-face interaction with others, and being able to experience others as part of 'us' allows us to empathize with those Others." It is the last of these points that takes up the ontological challenge of relationality; that is, the idea that we are constituted by our relationships with others and, in opening ourselves to the Other, we are necessarily drawn into a moral entwinement.

Anti-colonial relations of production similarly compel democratic stakeholder arrangements as the Marxist and feminist ones, albeit at a different unit of analysis. Immigrant workers, contract laborers from the Global South producing goods for consumption in the affluent nations of the world, especially those from the lowest rungs of the human supply chain, can visualize stakeholder theory as a case of the emergence of "political society," a new formulation that has emerged as a contrast to "civil society" (Chatterjee 2004). The argument here is that we inhabit a world where institutions of civil society such as NGOs have become "the closed association of modern elite groups, sequestered from the wider popular life of the communities, walled up within enclaves of civic freedom and rational law" (Chatterjee 2004: 4). In contrast, political society includes large sections of the fragments of the nation who do not relate to the nation in the same way as the middle classes. They lack the citizenship rights that are the hallmark of civil society, but rather make their claims on nations through unstable arrangements arrived at through direct political negotiations. Political society is the realm of populations, of instrumental alliances between marginalized groups, and an attempt to wrest some concessions from a society where the status of its constituents is beyond the pale of legality. It is through their sheer presence, numbers, and the acknowledgment of their role in the production cycles of the world, that they are recognized as "stakeholders" in our economy, and in our theory (Mir, Marens, & Mir, 2008).

By way of a conclusion, we would like to recall the four tenets we have presented that underscored a possible relationship between CMS and stakeholder theory. We noted that three of the tenets – a recognition of the salience of economic class, a similar acknowledgment of the power of non-class identity formations, and that of the imperialist nature of global relations – posed particular structuralist challenges for stakeholder theory. However the fourth tenet – a recognition of the manner in which we are intersubjectively constituted – lends itself mostly to humanist analysis. Such an analysis suggests that while disadvantaged subjectivities contest capitalist regimes and firms, mainstream organizational theory is not predisposed to accord it the status of theory, often undermining it by calling it "resistance to change" or "culture." It underscores that mainstream theory *anthropologizes* resistance, while *theorizing* the mainstream. To combat this, a critical scholar must perform the reverse, by theorizing the resistance and anthropologizing the mainstream, in an effort to bring parity to the playing field. We believe that a critical stakeholder theory, one that conceptualizes a myriad of deeply intersubjective relationships embedded in political society, can in some measure accomplish this task.

Notes

1. The CMS division began as workshops at AOM in 1998 to provide "a unique forum for researchers with an interest in critical approaches (broadly defined) to present research on management and management education." The group became a special interest group (SIG) in 2001 and became a full Division of AOM in 2008. Membership is highly international, comprising over 700 scholars working in over forty-five countries. See http://cms.aom.org/. The first Biennial Critical Management Studies Conference was held in 1999, and the tenth will be held in July 2017 at Liverpool. See www.edgehill.ac.uk/business/cms2017/. Journals include, but are not limited to, *Organization*, a journal that began in 1993 with an explicit critical orientation, *Critical Perspectives on International Business, Ephemera*, a web-based journal on theory and politics, and several others. Moreover, several journals have devoted special issues to CMS-related issues, and the *Journal of Business Ethics* has developed a section examining the intersection between business ethics and CMS. Schools with PhD programs include Lund University, and indirectly, several universities in the United Kingdom as well as the University of Massachusetts at Boston.

2. It is not our intention in this chapter to provide an exhaustive literature review of CMS. Several such reviews exist, the most recent being Prasad et al.'s (2015) exhaustive mapping of the field. Other primers include Tadajewski et al. (2011) and Alvesson, Bridgman, and Willmott (2009).

3. The very neat but rarely used concept of "unit of reality" has been associated with the Process Philosopher Alfred Whitehead, who is said to have taken the "throb of experience" as the "actual entity" of reality (Nelson, 2003: 113).

References

Acker, J. (2006). Inequality regimes: Gender, class, and race in organizations. *Gender & Society, 20*(4): 441–464.

Adler, P. S. (2007). The future of critical management studies: A paleo-Marxist critique of labour process theory. *Organization Studies, 28*(9): 1313–1345.

Aktouf, O. (1992). Management and theories of organizations in the 1990s: Toward a critical radical humanism? *Academy of Management Review*, 17(3): 407–431.

Alvesson, M., Bridgman, T., & Willmott, H. (2009). *The Oxford handbook of critical management studies*. Oxford: Oxford University Press.

Antonacopoulou, E. P., & Méric, J. (2005). A critique of stake-holder theory: Management science or a sophisticated ideology of control? *Corporate Governance: The International Journal of Business in Society, 5*(2): 22–33.

Arvidsson, A. (2009). The ethical economy: Towards a post-capitalist theory of value. *Capital & Class, 33*(1): 13–29. doi: 10.1177/030981680909700102.

Arvidsson, A. (2010). Speaking out: The ethical economy: New forms of value in the information society? *Organization, 17*(5): 637–644. doi: 10.1177/1350508410372512.

Asher, C. C., Mahoney, J. M., & Mahoney, J. T. (2005). Towards a property rights foundation for a stakeholder theory of the firm. *Journal of Management & Governance, 9*(1): 5–32.

Australian Law Reform Commission. (1986). Recognition of Aboriginal Customary Laws at Common Law. www.alrc.gov.au/publications/report-31

Banerjee, S. B. (2000). Whose land is it anyway? National interest, indigenous stakeholders and colonial discourses: The case of the Jabiluka uranium mine. *Organization & Environment, 13*(1): 3–38.

Banerjee, S. B., & Prasad, A. (2008). Introduction to the special issue on "Critical reflections on management and organizations: A postcolonial perspective." *Critical Perspectives on International Business, 4*(2/3): 90–98.

Barnard, C. I. (1968). *The functions of the executive.* Cambridge, MA: Harvard university press.

Bauman, Z. (1993). *Postmodern ethics.* London: Routledge.

Benson, J. K. (1977). Organizations: A dialectical view. *Administrative Science Quarterly*, 22 (1): 1–21.

Benhabib, S. (1985). The generalized and the concrete other: The Kohlberg-Gilligan controversy and feminist theory. *Praxis International, 5*(4): 402–424.

Berle, A. A., & Means, G. G. C. (1991). *The modern corporation and private property.* New York: Transaction Publishers.

Beck, C. (2016). Earth hour: Do we still need the lights-out protest? *The Christian Science Monitor*, March 19, A2.

Bevan, D., & Werhane, P. (2011). Stakeholder theory. In M. Painter-Morland & R. ten Bos, eds., *Business ethics and continental philosophy*, pp. 37–60. Cambridge: Cambridge University Press.

Bhabha, H. K. (2012). *The location of culture*. London: Routledge.

Boltanski, L. & Chiapello, E. (2005). *The new spirit of capitalism*, trans. Gregory Elliott. London: Verso.

Boussebaa, M. (2015). Professional service firms, globalisation and the new imperialism. *Accounting, Auditing & Accountability Journal*, 28(8): 1217–1233.

Bowen, H. W. (2005). The business of empire: The East India Company and imperial Britain, 1756–1833. Cambridge: Cambridge University Press.

Bowen, H. R. (2013). *Social responsibilities of the businessman*. Iowa City: University of Iowa Press.

Boyacigiller, N., & Adler, N. (1991). The parochial dinosaur: Organization science in a global context. *Academy of Management Review*, 16: 262–290.

Braverman, H. (1998). *Labor and monopoly capital: The degradation of work in the twentieth century*. New York: New York University Press.

Bridgman, T. (2007). Reconstituting relevance: Exploring possibilities for management educators' critical engagement with the public. *Management Learning*, 38(4): 425–439.

Buchholz, R. A., & Rosenthal, S. B. (2005). Toward a contemporary conceptual framework for stakeholder theory. *Journal of Business Ethics*, 58(3): 137–148.

Budd, J. W., & Bhave, D. (2008). Values, ideologies, and frames of reference in industrial relations. In N. Bacon, E. Heery, J. Fiorito, & P. Blyton, eds., *The Sage Handbook of Industrial Relations*, pp. 92–112. London: Sage.

Burrell, G. (1988). Modernism, post modernism and organizational analysis: The contribution of Michel Foucault. *Organization Studies*, 9(2): 221–235.

Burrell, G., & Morgan, G. (1979). *Sociological paradigms and organizational analysis*. London: Heinemann.

Calás, M. B., & Smircich, L. (1991). Voicing seduction to silence leadership. *Organization Studies*, 12 (4): 567–601.

Calás, M. B., Smircich, L., & Holvino, E. (2014). Theorizing gender-and-organization: changing times . . . changing theories? In *The Oxford handbook of gender and organizations*, pp. 53–75. Oxford: Oxford University Press.

Chatterjee, P. (2004). *The politics of the governed: Reflections on popular politics in most of the world*. New York; Columbia University Press.

Clegg, S. (2015). Foreword. In A. Prasad, P. Prasad, A. J. Mills, & J. H. Mills, eds., *The Routledge companion to critical management studies*, pp. xiii-xiv. London: Routledge.

Crane, A., & Ruebottom, T. (2011). Stakeholder theory and social identity: Rethinking stakeholder identification. *Journal of Business Ethics*, 102(1): 77–87.

De Beauvoir, S. (1988). *The second sex*. New York: Random House.

Delphy, C. (1984). *Close to home: A materialist analysis of women's oppression*. London, Hutchinson.

Derrida, J. (1976). *Of grammatology*. Baltimore: Johns Hopkins University Press.

Donaldson, T., & Preston, L. E. (1995). The stakeholder theory of the corporation: Concepts, evidence and implications. *Academy of Management Review*, 20(1): 65–91.

Elms, H., Johnson-Cramer, M. E., & Berman, S. L. (2011). Bounding the world's miseries: Corporate responsibility and Freeman's stakeholder theory. In *Stakeholder theory: Impact and prospects*, 1–38. Cheltenham, UK: Edward Elgar.

Erlichman, H. J. (2010). *Conquest, tribute, and trade: The quest for precious metals and the birth of globalization*. New York: Prometheus Books.

Ferguson, K. (1984). *The feminist case against bureaucracy*. Philadelphia: Temple University Press.

Fox, A. (1974). *Beyond contract: Work, power and trust relations*. London: Faber.

Foster, J. B., & Burkett, P. (2001). Marx and the dialectic of organic/inorganic relations: A rejoinder to Salleh and Clark. *Organization & Environment*, 14(4): 451–462.

Frenkel, M. (2008). The multinational corporation as a third space: Rethinking international management discourse on knowledge transfer through Homi Bhabha. *Academy of Management Review*, 33(4): 924–942.

Freeman, R. E. (1984). *Strategic management: A stakeholder approach*. Boston: Pitman.

Freeman, R. E. (1994). The politics of stakeholder theory: Some future directions. *Business Ethics Quarterly*, 4(4), 409–421.

Freeman, R. E., & Gilbert, D. R. (1992). Business, Ethics and Society: A Critical Agenda. Business & Society, 31(1): 9–17.

Freeman, R. E., & Phillips, R. A. (2002). Stakeholder theory: A libertarian defense. *Business Ethics Quarterly*, 12(3): 331–349.

Frooman, J. (1999). Stakeholder influence strategies. *Academy of Management Review*, 24(2): 191–205.

Gibson-Graham, J. K. (2008) Diverse economies: Performative practices for "other worlds," *Progress in Human Geography* 32(5): 613–32.

Gilligan, C. (1982). *In a different voice*. Cambridge, MA: Harvard University Press.

Goodpaster, K. E. (1991). Business ethics and stakeholder analysis. *Business Ethics Quarterly*, 1(1): 53–73.

Greenwood, M. (2007). Stakeholder engagement: Beyond the myth of corporate responsibility. *Journal of Business Ethics*, 74(4): 315–327.

Greenwood, M., & Anderson, E. (2009). "I used to be an employee but now I am a stakeholder" Implications of labelling employees as stakeholders. *Asia Pacific Human Resource Journal*, 47(2): 186–200.

Greenwood, M., & Freeman, R. E. (2011). Ethics and HRM: The contribution of stakeholder theory. *Business and Professional Ethics Journal*, 30(3/4): 269–292.

Haigh, N., & Griffiths, A. (2009). The natural environment as a primary stakeholder: The case of climate change. *Business Strategy and the Environment*, 18(6): 347–371.

Heath, J., & Norman, W. (2004). Stakeholder theory, corporate governance and public management: What can the history of State-Run Enterprises teach us in the post-Enron era? *Journal of Business Ethics*, 53(3): 247–265. doi: 10.1023/B:BUSI.0000039418.75103.ed

Ingvaldsen, J. A. (2015). Organizational learning: Bringing the forces of production back in. *Organization Studies*, 36(4): 423–443.

Jack, G., Westwood, R., Srinivas, N., & Sardar, Z. (2011). Deepening, broadening and re-asserting a postcolonial interrogative space in organization studies. *Organization* 18(3): 275–302.

James, C. L. R. (1983). *Beyond a boundary*. New York: Pantheon.

Jones, T. M. (1995). Instrumental stakeholder theory: A synthesis of ethics and economics. *Academy of Management Review*, 20(2): 404–437.

Kanter, R. M. (1977). *Men and women of the corporation*. New York: Basic Books.

Kazmi, B. A., Leca, B., & Naccache, P. (2016). Is corporate social responsibility a new spirit of capitalism? *Organization*, 23(5): 742–762.

Kenny, K. (2009). Heeding the stains: Lacan and organizational change. *Journal of Organizational Change Management*, 22(2): 214–228.

Klein, N. (2007). *The shock doctrine: The rise of disaster capitalism*. London: Macmillan.

Koen, S. (1984). Feminist workplaces: Alternative models for the organization of work. PhD dissertation, Union for Experimenting Colleges, University of Michigan Dissertation Information Service.

Laclau, E. & Mouffe, C. (1985). *Hegemony and socialist strategy: Towards a radical democratic politics*. London/New York: Verso.

McVea, J. F., & Freeman, R. E. (2005). A names-and-faces approach to stakeholder management: How focusing on stakeholders as individuals can bring ethics and entrepreneurial strategy together. *Journal of Management Inquiry*, 14(1): 57–69.

Maclean, M., Harvey, C., & Kling, G. (2014). Pathways to power: Class, hyper-agency and the French corporate elite. *Organization Studies*, 35(6): 825–855.

Marens, R. (2016). Giving the devils their due: What Marxian historiography can contribute to management history. In *Academy of Management Proceedings* (vol. 2016, no. 1, p. 10142). Academy of Management.

Marquetti, A. A. (2003). Analyzing historical and regional patterns of technical change from a classical-Marxian perspective. *Journal of Economic Behavior & Organization*, 52(2): 191–200.

McKenna, S. (2011). A critical analysis of North American business leaders' neocolonial discourse: Global fears and local consequences, *Organization*, 18(3): 387–399.

McKinlay, A., Carter, C., Pezet, E., & Clegg, S. (2010). Using Foucault to make strategy. *Accounting, Auditing & Accountability Journal*, 23(8): 1012–1031.

Mennicken, A., & Miller, P. (2014). *Michel Foucault and the administering of lives*. Oxford: Oxford University Press.

Mir, R., Calás, M., & Smircich, L. (1999). Global technoscapes and silent voices: Challenges to theorizing global cooperation. In D. Cooperrider & J. Dutton, eds., *Organizational Dimensions of Global Change*, pp. 270–290. London: Sage Publications.

Mir, R. Marens, R., & Mir, A. (2008). The corporation and its fragments: Corporate citizenship and the legacies of imperialism. In A. Scherer & G. Palazzo, eds., *The handbook of corporate citizenship*, pp. 819–852. London: Edward Elgar Press.

Mir, R & Mir, A. (2012). Organizational change as imperialism. In D. Boje, B. Burnes, & J. Hassard, eds., *Routledge companion to organizational change*, pp. 425–439. London: Routledge.

Mir, R., Mir, A., & Wong, D. (2006). Diversity: The cultural logic of global capital? In A. Konrad, P. Prasad, & J. Pringle, eds., *Handbook of workplace diversity*, pp.167–188. London: Sage.

Mitchell, R. K., Agle, B. R., & Wood, D. J. (1997). Towards a theory of stakeholder identification and salience: Defining the principle of who and what really counts. *Academy of Management Review*, *22*(4): 853–886.

Mohanty, C. T. (1988). Under Western eyes: Feminist scholarship and colonial discourses. *Feminist Review*, (30): 61–88.

Moriceau, J.-L. (2005). Faceless figures: Is a socially responsible decision possible? In M. Bonnafous-Boucher & Y. Pesqueux, eds., *Stakeholder theory: A European perspective*, (pp. 89–103). Basingstoke, UK: Palgrave

Moriarty, J. (2014). The connection between stakeholder theory and stakeholder democracy. *Business & Society*, *53*(6): 820–852.

Morsing, M. (2006). Corporate social responsibility as strategic auto-communication: On the role of external stakeholders for member identification. *Business Ethics: A European Review*, *15*(2): 171–182.

Nelson, J. (2003). Once more, with feeling: Feminist economics and the ontological question. *Feminist Economics*, 9 (1): 109–118.

Noland, J., & Phillips, R. (2010). Stakeholder engagement, discourse ethics and strategic management. *International Journal of Management Reviews*, *12* (1): 39–49.

Nord, W. (1977). A Marxist critique of humanistic psychology. *Journal of Humanistic Psychology*, 17 (1): 75–83.

Parsons, R. (2008). We are all stakeholders now. *Critical Perspectives on International Business*, *4*(2): 99–126.

Perrow, C. (1972). *Complex organizations: A critical essay*. Glenview, IL: Scott, Foresman.

Phillips, R. (1997). Stakeholder theory and a principle of fairness. *Business Ethics Quarterly*, *7*(1): 51–66.

Phillips, R., Freeman, R. E., & Wicks, A. C. (2003). What stakeholder theory is not. *Business Ethics Quarterly*, *13*(4): 479–502.

Prasad, A. (1997a). The colonizing consciousness and representation of the Other: A postcolonial critique of the discourse of oil. In P. Prasad, A. Mills, M. Elmes, & A. Prasad, eds., *Managing the organizational melting pot: Dilemmas of workplace diversity*, pp. 285–311. Thousand Oaks, CA: Sage.

Prasad, A. (1997b). Provincializing Europe: Towards a post-colonial reconstruction: A critique of Baconian science as the last strand of imperialism. *Studies in Cultures, Organizations and Societies* 3: 91–117.

Prasad, A., Prasad, P., Mills, A. J., & Mills, J. H. (2015). *The Routledge companion to critical management studies*. London: Routledge.

Prashad, V. (2008). *The darker nations: A people's history of the Third World*. New York: The New Press.

Radhakrishnan, R (1994). Postmodernism and the rest of the world. *Organization*, 1(2): 305–340.

Radhakrishnan, R. (1996). The changing subject and the politics of theory. In *Diasporic mediations: Between home and location*, (pp. 68–92). Minneapolis: University of Minnesota Press.

Roloff, J. (2008). A life cycle model of multi-stakeholder networks. *Business Ethics: A European Review*, *17*(3): 311–325.

Rowley, T. J. (1997). Moving beyond dyadic ties: A network of stakeholder influences. *Academy of Management Review*, *22*(4): 887–910.

Said, E. (1978). *Orientalism*. New York: Vintage.

Sandberg, S. (2013). *Lean in: Women, work, and the will to lead*. New York: Random House.

Sanders, R. L. (1997). If Marx had been a business process reengineer … *Information Management*, *31*(2): 58–72.

Scherer, A. G., & Palazzo, G. (2007). Toward a political conception of corporate responsibility: Business and society seen from a Habermasian perspective. *Academy of Management Review*, *32*(4): 1096–1120.

Slinger, G. (1999). Spanning the gap: The theoretical principles that connect stakeholder policies to business performance. *Corporate Governance: An International Review*, 7: 136–151.

Smith, C. & Willmott. H. (1991). The new middle class and the labour process. In C. R. Smith & H. Willmott, eds., *White-collar work: The non-manual labour process*, pp. 13–34. London: Springer.

Spicer, A., & Banerjee, S. (2016). Governance: Changing conceptions of the corporation. In R. Mir, H. Willmott, & M. Greenwood, eds., *The Routledge companion to philosophy in organization studies*, (pp. 403–411). London: Routledge.

Spivak, G. (1988). Can the subaltern speak? In C. Nelson & L. Grossberg, eds., *Marxism and the interpretation of culture*, pp. 271–313. Urbana: University of Illinois Press.

Sternberg, E. (1997). The defects of stakeholder theory. *Corporate Governance: An International Review*, *5*(1): 3–10.

Stinchcombe, A. L. (1995). *Sugar island slavery in the age of Enlightenment: The political economy of the Caribbean world*. Princeton, NJ: Princeton University Press.

Stone, K. (1974). The origins of job structures in the steel industry. *Review of Radical Political Economics*, 6(2): 113–73.

Stoney, C., & Winstanley, D. (2001). Stakeholding: Confusion or utopia? Mapping the conceptual terrain. *The Journal of Management Studies*, 38 (5): 603–626.

Tadajewski, M., Maclaran, P., & Parsons, E. (Eds.). (2011). *Key concepts in critical management studies*. London: Sage.

Tatli, A. (2012). On the power and poverty of critical (self) reflection in critical management studies: A comment on Ford, Harding and Learmonth. *British Journal of Management*, 23 (1): 22–30.

Valian, V. (1999). *Why so slow? The advancement of women*. Cambridge, MA: MIT Press.

Van Buren III, H. (2001). If fairness is the problem, is consent the solution? Integrating ISCT and stakeholder theory. *Business Ethics Quarterly*, 11(3): 481–499.

Van Buren III, H. (2016). Capital as a neglected, yet essential, topic for organization studies. In R. Mir, H. Willmott, & M. Greenwood, eds., *The Routledge companion to philosophy in organization studies*, (pp. 293–300). London: Routledge.

Van Buren III, H. & Greenwood, M. (2009). Stakeholder voice: A problem, a solution, and a challenge for managers and academics. *Philosophy of Management*, 8(3): 15–23.

Weitzner, D. (2007). Deconstruction revisited: Implications of theory over methodology. *Journal of Management Inquiry*, 16(1): 43–54.

Wicks, A. C., Gilbert, J., Daniel R., & Freeman, R. E. (1994). A feminist reinterpretation of the stakeholder concept. *Business Ethics Quarterly*, 4(4): 475.

Whyte, W. F., & Whyte, K. K. (1991). *Making Mondragon: The growth and dynamics of the worker cooperative complex*. Ithaca, NY: Cornell University Press.

Wollstonecraft, M. (1999). *A vindication of the rights of woman*. Boston: Thomas and Andrews Press.

Yuthas, K., & Dillard, J. F. (1999). Ethical development of advanced technology: A postmodern stakeholder perspective. Journal of Business Ethics, 19(1), 35–49.

Stakeholder Identification and Its Importance in the Value Creating System of Stakeholder Work

RONALD K. MITCHELL

Professor, and Jean Austin Bagley Regents Chair Texas Tech University

JAE HWAN LEE

Assistant Professor, Hamline University

Due to the economic importance of stakeholders in creating and distributing value (Freeman et al., 2010; Mitchell et al., 2015; Venkataraman, 2002), there is growing interest in theories that help to identify an organization's stakeholders.[1] Currently, the research conversation concerns various means whereby economic-impact stakeholders may be identified consistently and reliably. Such identification is important both to improve explanations of value creation generally, and of economic profit creation specifically (e.g., Barney, 2018). However, to date, the study of stakeholder identification to connect it explicitly to value creation (Freeman et al., 2010; Freeman, Harrison, & Wicks, 2007; Harrison & Wicks, 2014) has begun, but is unfinished.

For example, one suggested approach to stakeholder identification with economic ramifications has been to focus on distinguishing "secondary" stakeholders from "primary" stakeholders – those without whose participation the enterprise would cease to exist (Clarkson, 1995). However, this approach focuses stakeholder identification research more on explaining stakeholder importance to firm survival, and less on the objective of value creation. Another commonly accepted approach, in this case toward more general stakeholder identification, has been to study the relational attributes of stakeholders: for example, their levels of power, legitimacy, and urgency in stakeholder relationships (Mitchell, Agle, & Wood, 1997). But, similarly, this attributes-based approach does not readily explain how the

stakeholder types that result from this analysis (e.g., definitive, dominant, dependent, etc.) connect to value creation.

Our third example occurs within the strategic management conversation. Here stakeholder groups beyond shareholders (such as employees, suppliers, customers, and debtholders) are suggested to be important strategically because they provide resources to a firm in return for some compensation and are therefore entitled to some distribution of expected economic profits (Barney, 2018). In our view, this more recent explanation moves closer to research connecting stakeholder identification to creating value. Nevertheless, a gap in the literature remains, because there exists no theoretical explanation for how stakeholder identification is value creating. We therefore build on this idea to explore the research question: How can the identification of stakeholders in value creation be better conceptualized to further stakeholder identification and value creation research?

We suggest that a helpful next step is to set stakeholder identification research within a more comprehensive and fundamental framework: one that links such identification to the economic work that is to be accomplished by and with stakeholders overall. We argue that what seems to be assorted, distinct stakeholder research streams are, in fact, parts of a comprehensive system of stakeholder work that leads to value creation. We therefore undertake to situate the stakeholder identification task in creating value, within the overall stakeholder research literature, by proposing that the specific work of stakeholder identification is but a part, a subsystem – albeit an important one – within the more comprehensive general system of stakeholder work (Lee, 2015). Lee suggests that five stakeholder-centric work domains follow each other roughly in sequence: (1) stakeholder awareness work, (2) stakeholder identification work, (3) stakeholder understanding work, and (4) stakeholder prioritization work, which culminate in (5) stakeholder engagement work. Thus, we cast stakeholder identification as a task that is necessary but insufficient for creating value, an undertaking that requires assistance from each phase of the stakeholder-work system.

In the first section of this chapter, we summarize the stakeholder identification literature chronologically to note some of the influential scholarly research as a foundation for our later analysis of *stakeholder identification work.* In the second section, we provide a high-level précis of the relatively new notion of stakeholder work with its five temporally derived phases. In the third section, we suggest a possible mechanism through which the stakeholder work system creates value: *consonance across phases,* by which we mean: *all elements of the stakeholder work system function effectively together.* And in the final section of the chapter we discuss the contributions, strengths, shortcomings, and potential of stakeholder identification research. In short, through articulating the broader lens of the stakeholder work system, we seek to develop new possibilities for research on stakeholder identification work in the important economic work of value creation.

Stakeholder Identification

The definition of a stakeholder, as the term is used currently in the literature, first appeared in the Stanford Memo (1963), which identified stakeholders as "those groups without whose support the organization would cease to exist" (see reference in Mitchell et al., 1997: 858). Scholars have since proposed various definitions of stakeholder identification. Table 4.1 provides a chronology of selected works to date on stakeholder identification.

Additionally, Mitchell et al. (1997) synthesized twenty-seven studies examining definitions used to identify stakeholders and classified them by integrating the stakeholder attributes of power, urgency, and legitimacy. They proposed an eight-part typology: dormant, demanding, discretionary, dominant, dangerous, dependent, definitive, and non-stakeholders (Mitchell et al., 1997). The resulting *theory of stakeholder identification and salience* helped to address the longstanding problem with stakeholder identification work: deciding which stakeholders – among a virtually unbounded set – necessitate managerial attention given their attributes. Several other approaches to stakeholder identification are listed in Table 4.1, and are further analyzed in Table 4.2. However, most identification mechanisms do not, in themselves, explain what leads to value creation. We therefore develop an argument to suggest that stakeholder identification work is an important phase in creating value – one step of several that comprise the overall system of stakeholder work.

Stakeholder Work

The stakeholder work system – which we argue is both comprehensive *and* fundamental – includes five distinct phases or subsystems. These phases correspond to the temporal phases in stakeholder relationships that lead to value creation: (1) stakeholder awareness work, (2) stakeholder identification work, (3) stakeholder understanding work, and (4) stakeholder prioritization work; that ultimately results in (5) stakeholder engagement work (Lee, 2015). Recently, it has been argued that these five *phases* of stakeholder work are inter-supportive *types* within the larger stakeholder work system, and thereby are mutually influential in explaining a variety of stakeholder/firm relations, especially stakeholder salience (Mitchell, Lee, & Agle, 2017).

This logic parallels the stakeholder attribute cumulation approach to the assessment of stakeholder salience pioneered by Mitchell et al. (1997). However, as it may apply to creating value, the specific mechanism whereby *inter-supportive* stakeholder work phases create value has been more implicit than

Table 4.1 Chronology of Stakeholder Identification Research (Representing Stakeholder Identification Work)

Author(s)	Year	Key Ideas / Definitions	Narrative
Stanford memo	1963	"those groups without whose support the organization would cease to exist" (Freeman & Reed, 1983, and Freeman, 1984)	Firms' dependence on stakeholders was suggested as a rationale for stakeholder identification
Rhenman	1964	"are depending on the firm in order to achieve their personal goals and on whom the firm is depending for its existence" (Näsi, 1995)	Mutual dependence between firms and stakeholders was proposed as another rationale for stakeholder identification
Ahlstedt & Jahnukainen	1971	"driven by their own interests and goals are participants in a firm, and thus depending on it and whom for its sake the firm is depending" (Näsi, 1995)	The same view was reemphasized in the literature
Freeman & Reed	1983	Narrow: "on which the organization is dependent for its continued survival" (p. 91)	Firms' dependence on stakeholders reappeared in the literature, suggesting the importance of this idea
Freeman & Reed	1983	Wide: "can affect the achievement of an organization's objectives or who is affected by the achievement of an organization's objectives" (p. 91)	Stakeholders' influence upon firms was suggested as a rationale for stakeholder identification
Freeman	1984	"can affect or is affected by the achievement of the organization's objectives" (p. 46)	The same relationship above was reemphasized
Freeman & Gilbert	1987	"can affect or is affected by a business" (p. 397)	The same relationship above continued to receive acceptance, highlighting the importance of power
Cornell & Shapiro	1987	"claimants" who have "contracts" (p. 5)	The contract relationship between firms and stakeholders as a basis for legitimacy was examined as a rationale for stakeholder identification
Evan & Freeman	1988	"have a stake in or claim on the firm" (p. 75–76)	Stakeholders' claims as a basis for legitimacy was introduced as a rationale for stakeholder identification
Evan & Freeman	1988	"benefit from or are harmed by, and whose rights are violated or respected by, corporate actions" (p. 79)	Stakeholder as a moral claimant was suggested, further refining the characteristic of a claimant
Bowie	1988	"without whose support the organization would cease to exist" (p. 112, note 2)	Firms' dependence on stakeholders was reemphasized, suggesting continued interest in this idea
Alkhafaji	1989	"groups to whom the corporation is responsible" (p. 36)	Stakeholder as a claimant reemphasized, suggesting the importance of the legitimacy basis
Carroll	1989	"asserts to have one or more of these kinds of stakes" – "ranging from an interest to a right (legal or moral) to ownership or legal title to the company's assets or property" (p. 57)	Stakeholder as a legitimate claimant was further detailed in terms of a right to ownership
Freeman & Evan	1990	"Contract holders" (cited in Mitchell et al., 1997: 858, table 1)	The contract relationship between firms and stakeholders as a rationale for stakeholder identification reappeared in the literature
Thompson et al.	1991	in "relationship with an organization" (p. 209)	The relationship view reappeared in the literature, competing with other views
Savage et al.	1991	"have an interest in the actions of an organization and . . . the ability to influence it" (p. 61)	Stakeholders' influence upon firms reappeared in the literature, reemphasizing power as a basis for stakeholder identification

Table 4.1 (*cont.*)

Author(s)	Year	Key Ideas / Definitions	Narrative
Hill & Jones	1992	"constituents who have a legitimate claim on the firm … established through the existence of an exchange relationship" who supply "the firm with critical resources (contributions) and in exchange each expects its interests to be satisfied (by inducements)" (p. 133)	Stakeholder as a legitimate claimant was explored in terms of an exchange relationship between the firms and stakeholders
Brenner	1993	"having some legitimate, non-trivial relationship with an organization (such as) exchange transactions, action impacts, and moral responsibilities" (p. 205)	The relationship view was further reemphasized in terms of legitimacy
Carroll	1993	"asserts to have one or more of the kinds of stakes in business"; may be affected or affect (p. 60)	Stakeholders' influence upon firms was reemphasized, demonstrating the continued popularity of power
Freeman	1994	participants in "the human process of joint value creation" (p. 415)	Stakeholders as joint value creation participants emerged, suggesting a new rationale for stakeholder identification
Wicks et al.	1994	"interact with and give meaning and definition to the corporation" (p. 483)	Firms' dependence upon stakeholders resurfaced in terms of organizational existence
Langtry	1994	"the firm is significantly responsible for their well-being, or they hold a moral or legal claim on the firm" (p. 433)	Stakeholder as a legitimate claimant was reemphasized
Starik	1994	"can and are making their actual stakes known"; "are or might be influenced by, or are or potentially are influencers of, some organization" (p. 90)	Stakeholders as influencers resurfaced in the literature, emphasizing the power attribute
Clarkson	1994	"bear some form of risk as a result of having invested some form of capital, human or financial, something of value, in a firm" or "are placed at risk as a result of a firm's activities" (p. 5)	A risk-taking stakeholder idea was suggested in the literature as a rationale for stakeholder identification
Clarkson	1995	"have, or claim, ownership, rights, or interests in a corporation and its activities" (p. 106)	The stakeholder as a legitimate claimant was reemphasized, demonstrating continued interest in legitimacy
Näsi	1995	"interact with the firm and thus make its operation possible" (p. 19)	Firms' dependence on stakeholders was reemphasized, affirming the stakeholder dominance perspective
Brenner	1995	"are or which could impact or be impacted by the firm/ organization" (p. 76, note 1)	Stakeholders' influence on firms continued to receive attention, affirming the popularity of power
Donaldson & Preston	1995	"persons or groups with legitimate interests in procedural and/or substantive aspects of corporate activity" (p. 85)	Stakeholders as legitimate claimants were refined in terms of corporate activity
Kaler	2002	"It is argued that for the purposes of business ethics, stakeholders are claimants towards whom businesses owe perfect or imperfect moral duties beyond those generally owed to people at large." (p. 91)	Stakeholders as claimants are reemphasized, contributing the influencer vs. claimant debate
Cragg & Greenbaum	2002	"Anyone with a material interest in the proposed project was a stakeholder. More specifically, they distinguished three main nested categories of stakeholders: first, the general public; second, local communities in general; and third, local Aboriginal communities in particular." (p. 322)	A material interest is proposed as a criterion of stakeholder identification
Phillips	2003	"Normative stakeholders are those stakeholders to whom the organization has a moral obligation …	Normative and derivative stakeholders are theorized, suggesting a new research area

Table 4.1 (cont.)

Author(s)	Year	Key Ideas / Definitions	Narrative
		Derivative stakeholders are those groups whose actions and claims must be accounted for by managers due to their potential effects upon the organization and its normative stakeholders." (p. 30–31)	
Driscoll & Starik	2004	"The authors also critique and expand the stakeholder identification and salience model developed by Mitchell, Agle, and Wood (1997) by recognizing the stakeholder attributes of power, legitimacy, and urgency, as well as by developing a fourth stakeholder attribute: proximity. The authors provide a stronger basis for arguing for the salience of the natural environment as the primary and primordial stakeholder of the firm." (p. 55)	The natural environment is argued as a stakeholder, adding to the class of primary stakeholders
Schwartz	2006	"This paper will make the argument that God both is and should be considered a managerial stakeholder for those businesspeople and business firms that accept that God exists and can affect the world." (p. 291)	God is conceptualized as a stakeholder, extending the broad stakeholder view
Fassin	2009	"An attempt is made to clarify the categorizations and classifications by introducing new terminology with a distinction between stakeholders, stakewatchers and stakekeepers." (p. 113)	Stakeholders are distinguished from stakewatchers and stakekeepers, suggesting a new research area
Barraquier	2013	"The analysis reveals that attributes shared with clannish stakeholders gradually replace attributes of a claimed identity, and that, when confronting hostile stakeholders, organizations act in solidarity with clannish stakeholders." (p. 45)	A new concept of clannish stakeholder is suggested, refining the scope of stakeholder identification
Bridoux & Stoelhorst	2014	"We propose that a fairness approach is more effective in attracting, retaining, and motivating reciprocal stakeholders to create value, while an arms-length approach is more effective in motivating self-regarding stakeholders and in attracting and retaining self-regarding stakeholders with high bargaining power." (p. 107)	Stakeholders are further differentiated as reciprocal stakeholders or self-regarding stakeholders

explicit. Therefore, as one possibility for such a mechanism, we suggest that *consonance of stakeholder work across phases* is value creating. We argue that only *consonance* within the system of stakeholder work provides both necessary and sufficient conditions for value creation. That is, value is created when, and only when, *all elements of the stakeholder work system function effectively together*.

We take as our definition of value creation the following:

Business [value creation] is about making sure that products and services actually do what you say they are going to do, doing business with suppliers who want to make you better, having employees who are engaged in their work, and being good citizens in the community, all of which may well be in the long-run (or even possibly the short-run) interest of a corporation. (Freeman et al., 2010: 11)

In this section, we therefore explore briefly the attributes of each phase of stakeholder work. To proceed with this discussion, we now provide the following: (1) a summary of the literature on work in organizations, in order to set our analysis within the context of the literature on organizations, (2) the definition of stakeholder work itself, to bind the analysis, and (3) a summary of the five sequential subsystem phases that together constitute the stakeholder work system. This groundwork will support our approach to answering our research question: How can the identification of stakeholders in value creation be better conceptualized to further stakeholder identification and value creation research?

Work in Organizations

At the 2013 International Association for Business and Society (IABS) Annual Meeting in Portland, Oregon, USA, we proposed (Lee & Mitchell, 2013) the idea of stakeholder work as a more comprehensive lens for interpreting the stakeholder literature. At the time, our aim was to suggest that work – conceptualized as the ongoing patterns of action that comprise productive human activity – could provide a lens through which to view the research literature related to organizations. Following Barley and Kunda (2001), we hoped that a focus on work itself might suggest templates for better understanding the structures of organizing. We expected that through such templates, scholars might assess the strengths and weaknesses of a given research literature relative to explaining a phenomenon. We based our analysis on a foundation of ideas that were part of the literature that was developed from studies on work in organizations.

Beginning with Taylor (1911), continuing in the Hawthorne studies (Roethlisberger & Dickson, 1939), and through the industrial sociology research of the 1950s (e.g., Weber's theory of bureaucracy), the study of work in organizations entailed situated observations of routine human productive activity. Thereafter, the study of work in organizations was ignored for several decades (Barley & Kunda, 2001). Recently, however, to make sense of post-bureaucratic organizing, scholars have revived the notion of work as a research construct. These newer conceptualizations of work view both individuals and organizations as expending effort purposefully and strategically, in their attempts to affect their social-symbolic context (Phillips & Lawrence, 2012).

The organization science literature now includes many organizational-work-focused sub-streams, a few examples of which include: boundary work, as suggested by Gieryn (1983) and Kreiner, Hollensbe, and Sheep (2009); identity work, including Ibarra and Barbulescu (2010) as well as Snow and Anderson (1987); and institutional work, as developed by Lawrence and Suddaby (2006). In each instance, an underlying temporal structure is evident to us; and therefore, when temporality is applied to stakeholder work, five phases of stakeholder work can be distinguished: awareness, identification, understanding, prioritization, and engagement. Drawing upon the logic implied within this temporal structure, Lee (2015) categorized research on stakeholder-centric activities into the foregoing inter-supportive work-types, under the broad umbrella of stakeholder work.

Stakeholder Work: Definition

Stakeholder work is defined to be *the purposive processes of organization aimed at being aware of, identifying, understanding, prioritizing, and engaging stakeholders* (Lee, 2015: 12). As noted, these five stakeholder-centric work domains follow each other roughly in sequence. This temporal progression suggests a higher-order, more comprehensive system of stakeholder-centric work may occur as an organization's stakeholder engagement relationships develop. By sorting stakeholder research streams into these temporal phases, we can assess stakeholder identification and its importance in value creation from a more targeted (work-focused) but also a more wide-scope (systematic) vantage point (Lee, 2015; Lee & Mitchell, 2013).

The Five Phases of the Stakeholder Work System

In this section, we summarize how each type of stakeholder work is represented within the management literature. In the section following, we offer a more detailed analysis of stakeholder identification work.

Stakeholder Awareness Work. Defined to be: *organizing activities aimed at evaluating stakeholders' action and/or potential action toward a given organization* (Lee, 2015). Stakeholder awareness work requires attention to the social environment. This work reflects at least in part Freeman's (1984) idea that stakeholders include all entities who are affected by and who affect the organization; that is, a broad-environment notion of stakeholder theory (e.g., Mitchell et al., 1997). Two elements of stakeholder awareness work are suggested in the literature. First, managers pay attention to the socioeconomic environment surrounding the organization, seeking to understand the competitive landscape and gathering information about potential and actual stakeholders (Daft, Sormunen, & Parks, 1988). Second, managers study how stakeholders exert influence on the organization itself (Frooman, 1999; Frooman & Murrell, 2005; Hendry, 2005; Sharma & Henriques, 2005). Thus, stakeholder awareness work as a category captures the portion of the literature addressing how stakeholder work often begins. But awareness is only a beginning. Becoming aware of potential stakeholders sets the stage for the more rigorous task of identifying the stakeholders who matter most.

Stakeholder Identification Work. Stakeholder identification work, as specifically defined for the purposes of this chapter, entails *organizing activities aimed at recognizing stakeholders who matter (to value creation) for a given organization* (Lee, 2015). In other words, stakeholder identification work concentrates managers' attention on the stakeholders who will be included in the work of value creation. Agle, Mitchell, and Sonnenfeld (1999: 509) describe elements that may contribute to stakeholders being identified as relationally important:

> social salience depends upon: (1) attentional tasks, such as stimulus "domination" of the visual field, (2) prior knowledge or expectations, which prompt individual notice of "unusual" or "differential" aspects of behavior, and/or (3) the immediate context, through which individuals experience "figural/novel" elements, which contribute to the overall salience notion, "selectivity." (Fiske & Taylor, 1984: 184–187)

Without narrowing the field of stakeholders through stakeholder identification work, focus would be diffused and energy wasted. Thus arises the idea that we develop further below, that stakeholder identification work enables social actors to begin to enact *consonance* across the temporal work-phases of the stakeholder engagement process. This creates value by recognizing from among the awareness pool, stakeholders who matter to the value creation activities of a given organization.

Stakeholder Understanding Work. Defined to include *organizing activities aimed at knowing the needs and desires of stakeholders of a given organization* (Lee, 2015), stakeholder understanding work broadly encompasses research on corporate responsibility to stakeholders, such as corporate social responsibility (CSR) (e.g., Carroll, 1979) and corporate citizenship (e.g., Logsdon & Wood, 2002; Matten & Crane, 2005; Scherer & Palazzo, 2011). CSR research emphasizes the expectation that stakeholders require business persons to comply with a societal mandate; and that they assume social responsibilities commensurate with their social power according to, for example, Davis' "Iron Law of Responsibility" (Davis, 1960). The literature on CSR argues that managers fulfill the obligation to "pursue those policies, to make those decisions, or to follow those lines of action which are desirable in terms of the objectives and values of our society" (Bowen, 1953: 6), or to make decisions and take actions "for reasons at least partially beyond the firm's direct economic or technical interest" (Davis, 1960: 70–71). Such conceptualizations of CSR later were integrated by Carroll (1979: 500) suggesting CSR as "the social responsibility of businesses encompassing the economic, legal, ethical, and discretionary expectations that society has of organizations at a given point in time."

Traditionally, the literature on CSR has specified explicitly or has implied that organizations fulfill those broad responsibilities desired by stakeholders (Freeman et al., 2010). However, the literature on corporate citizenship argues that an organization becomes a good citizen, as desired by stakeholders, not only through implementing its responsibilities but also exercising its rights (e.g., Logsdon & Wood, 2002) or even by playing the political roles as a government-like entity (e.g., Matten & Crane, 2005; Scherer & Palazzo, 2011).

Both research on CSR and research on corporate citizenship imply that stakeholder understanding work – if it is to be value adding – requires that managers attend closely to, and manage well, the potential gap between what stakeholders need and what an organization delivers (Deegan & Rankin, 1999). Addressing this gap often requires tough calls about prioritizing, which we address next.

Stakeholder Prioritization Work. Stakeholder prioritization work is defined to be *organizing activities aimed at prioritizing competing stakeholder claims with respect to a given organization* (Lee, 2015). To date, the primary stakeholder prioritization construct in the literature comes from Mitchell et al.'s (1997) seminal article on stakeholder identification and salience. They described salience as "the degree to which managers give priority to competing stakeholder claims" (1997: 854) and argued that stakeholder salience will be positively related to the cumulative number of stakeholder attributes – power, legitimacy, and urgency – that managers perceive to be present. They tested and supported this assertion in the case of Fortune 500 CEOs (Agle et al., 1999).

Subsequently, scholars have focused on examining additional stakeholder attributes associated with stakeholder prioritization, such as proximity (Driscoll & Starik, 2004), various types of power (e.g., Eesley & Lenox, 2006), or powerlessness and illegitimacy (Weitzner & Deutsch, 2015). Such analysis of stakeholder prioritization work has extended theory and provided analysis from which research may be developed further (Mitchell et al., 2017). Then, after managers become aware of potential stakeholders, identify those who are most important to value creation, understand those stakeholders' needs and expectations, and decide which of their claims to prioritize, it is time to act. This action takes the form of stakeholder engagement work that depends for its effectiveness on the collective consonance of the previously (or perhaps simultaneously) occurring phases of stakeholder work.

Stakeholder Engagement Work. Stakeholder engagement work is the culmination of the work accomplished in the preceding four phases, and is defined as *organizing activities aimed at taking action with respect to the stakeholders of a given organization* (Lee, 2015). Stakeholder engagement work leads to value creation via support from stakeholders, which the literature suggests may be gained through a variety of actions. Jones (1995) argues that organizations can gain stakeholders' support by building trust rather than treating stakeholders opportunistically (see similar arguments by Calton & Lad, 1995; Heugens, van den Bosch, & van Riel, 2002; Hosmer & Kiewitz, 2005; Husted, 1998). Others argue that stakeholder support may be garnered through the charitable efforts of the organization (Adams & Hardwick, 1998; Brammer & Millington, 2003a, 2003b; Godfrey, 2005). Still other scholars suggest that organizations can win stakeholder support through employee stock option programs (Marens & Wicks, 1999), reputation management, impression management, rhetoric, and the strategic use of images (Carter, 2006; Snider, Hill, & Martin, 2003; Ulmer & Sellnow, 2000). Notably, Scott and Lane (2000) proposed that organizations gain stakeholder support through more effective identification of stakeholders by the organization.

However, until Lee (2015), theoretical explanations of value creation through stakeholder engagement (see Freeman, 1984, 1994; Freeman et al., 2007, 2010; Freeman, Wicks, & Parmar, 2004; Harrison, Bosse, & Phillips, 2010; Mitchell et al., 2015) had not been completely operationalized in the strategic management context. Recently, Barney (2016) made an even stronger case for stakeholder engagement, suggesting that the field of strategy *must* adopt the stakeholder perspective to properly recognize value creation, including for those persons or entities who contribute to the residual of the firm. These developments suggest that stakeholder engagement work is central to management research; and we therefore argue that stakeholder engagement work is the culminating objective of stakeholder work. By conceptualizing stakeholder engagement work as the culminating phase in a stakeholder-focused value creation process, we are then enabled to address directly our research question: How can the identification of stakeholders in value creation be better conceptualized to further stakeholder identification and value creation research?

Consonance in Stakeholder Work and Value Creation

In this section, we pursue in more detail the idea that the five phases of stakeholder work support each other within the larger stakeholder work system to result in value creation. We term this mutual support *consonance*, which earlier we suggested involves *all elements of the stakeholder work system functioning effectively together.* We therefore define *stakeholder work consonance* to be: *the ongoing adjustment among the various temporal phases/subsystems of stakeholder work to enable the inclusion and integration of the stakeholders necessary for value creation.* In other words, value only emerges when there is dynamic and inter-supportive interplay among various phases of stakeholder work.

Returning to the Freeman et al. (2010) definition of value creation that we have adopted for use in our analysis, we therefore propose that value creation by firms specifically comprises at least the following:

- *Quality and customer service*: "making sure that products and services actually do what you say they are going to do";
- *Supplier relationships*: "doing business with suppliers who want to make you better";
- *Employee enrichment*: "having employees who are engaged in their work";
- *Community benefit*: "being good citizens in the community"; and
- *Stockholder reward*: "efforts that in the long-run (or even possibly the short-run) are in the interest of the corporation" (2010: 11)

Value creation thus involves many of the organization's stakeholders and encompasses most of the organization's tasks. Because organizational elements do not stand alone, but rather are nested and configured with one another (Black & Boal, 1994), consonance is not only inherent within market-based exchange-relationship systems, but is also essential for the accomplishment of value creation in organizations (as suggested earlier by Lawrence and Lorsch, 1967).

Our use of consonance logic parallels configuration theory, which suggests that the effectiveness of a process can be explained better when viewed as interconnected vs. in isolation (Fiss, 2007). Specifically, the strategic management literature has long noted that certain organizational elements tend to appear together (Meyer, Tsui, & Hinings, 1993; Miller, 1986; Mintzberg, 1980). Configurational logic suggests that relationships manifesting an underlying order, such as sequential appearance together or consonance across phases (as is typical in precedence relationships), are expected to be causal (Fiss, 2007). Therefore, the better the fit among ordered components – such as the first four phases of stakeholder work – and the contingent factor – meaning the fifth phase, effectiveness of stakeholder engagement – the greater the viability of the system (e.g., Galunic & Eisenhardt, 1994).

This point has been argued, and more rigorously developed, as an extension of value creation stakeholder theory by Mitchell et al. (2015). They suggested four stakeholder value-creation premises that require consonance:

> We take note that as the foregoing four premises are considered as a whole, the process of value creation becomes more explicit: as a sequential risk-sharing process of stakeholder organization (from activities to alignment, to interaction, to reciprocity) toward the end of value creation. (2015: 858)

	Phase 1	Phase 2	Phase 3	Phase 4
Value Creation Premises	Activities Premise	Alignment Premise	Interaction Premise	Reciprocity Premise
Stakeholder Work	*Stakeholder Awareness Work*	*Stakeholder Identification Work*	*Stakeholder Understanding Work*	*Stakeholder Prioritization Work*

Stakeholder Engagement Work **(Phase 5)**

Figure 4.1 Toward Stakeholder Engagement: The Stakeholder Work Value Creation System
Adapted from Mitchell et al. (2015: 855)

Similarly, in the present analysis, we argue that consonance across stakeholder work phases can increase the effectiveness of stakeholder engagement. As illustrated in Figure 4.1, the phases of stakeholder work proposed by Lee (2015) can be mapped on the value creation process as articulated by Mitchell et al. (2015).

Specific to this chapter, we note that effective stakeholder identification work (Phase 2) – joined with effectiveness in Phases 1, 3, and 4 – helps to enable effective stakeholder engagement work (Phase 5). In turn, effective engagement results in value creation and, ideally, distribution of value back to the stakeholders identified in Phase 2 (see also Mitchell et al.'s [2016] discussion of distributions via intra-corporate markets). In this manner, we provide a rich context within which we can discuss a refined and more explicit role for stakeholder identification work in the value-creating task of the stakeholder work system specifically, as well as for the identification and importance of stakeholders more generally.

Value Creating Stakeholder Engagement, Stakeholder Identification Work, and Value Creation

Given the foregoing groundwork, we now ask: What is it about the stakeholder engagement work of value creation that depends so crucially upon stakeholder identification work? In this section, we suggest the following answer: that stakeholder identification work is necessary because it enables social actors to enact otherwise-unlikely consonance across temporal work phases in service of a value-creating stakeholder work system; but, that sufficiency for purposes of value creation requires consonance across the entire stakeholder work system. We therefore address two subsequent questions: (1) What is value creating stakeholder engagement? and (2) How does effective stakeholder identification work enable value creating stakeholder engagement?

Value Creating Stakeholder Engagement

Research has demonstrated various factors that prompt firms to engage stakeholders. Such factors include instrumental motivations (Bansal & Roth,

2000), normative rationales (Bansal & Roth, 2000), sense of stewardship (Davis, Schoorman, & Donaldson, 1997), firm mission and values (Bansal, 2003; Maignan, Ferrell, & Hult, 1999), long-term institutional stewardship (Neubaum & Zahra, 2006), top management equity (Johnson & Greening, 1999), and corporate governance structure (Johnson & Greening, 1999), among others. How do these motivations comport with the idea of value creation – particularly in an increasingly turbulent and globalized business environment?

Over the last several decades, scholars have begun to develop what might be called "value creation stakeholder theory" (Freeman, 1984, 1994; Freeman et al., 2004, 2007, 2010; Harrison et al., 2010; Mitchell et al., 2015) to explain how stakeholders are involved in value creation. These theorists point out that assumptions of equilibrium (Weber, 1968), which may have been appropriate for more stabilized and localized businesses (Freeman et al., 2010), fall short when addressing value creation by businesses in the twenty-first century. Compared to Weberian-era corporations, present-day firms face substantial additional dynamism within their environment, such as the rise of globalization, the increasing dominance of information technology, the liberalization of states, and increased awareness of the societal impact on communities and nations (Freeman et al., 2010).

Value creation stakeholder theory therefore is built upon notions of stakeholder cooperation, engagement, and responsibility. Embracing principles of complexity, continuous creation, and emergent competition, this theory leads to the idea that "to successfully create, trade, and sustain value, a business must engage its stakeholders" (Freeman et al., 2010: 282). Freeman (1984), who originally outlined this principle of stakeholder engagement, and has since continued to develop it (e.g., Freeman et al., 2004, 2007, 2010), asserts that stakeholder theory begins with the assumption that value is necessarily and explicitly a part of doing business (Freeman, 1984; Freeman et al., 2004, 2007, 2010). Drawing upon the literature on value creation stakeholder theory, we therefore define value creating stakeholder engagement to be *the pursuit of value-creation activities with stakeholders.*

Using this definition has conceptual implications for our analysis. From its early development, stakeholder theory has emphasized effective management of a broad group of stakeholders as more than simply being a social responsibility (Freeman, 1984; Freeman et al., 2010). Rather, stakeholder theory is about managing a firm effectively through creating value for stakeholders, including society (Freeman et al., 2007; Harrison et al., 2010). Here we have built our explanations on the conceptual foundations offered by value creation stakeholder theory (Freeman, 1984, 1994; Freeman et al., 2004, 2007, 2010; Harrison et al., 2010; Mitchell et al., 2015). How, then, does stakeholder identification work provide the means to serve the value creating ends of stakeholder engagement? We address this question next.

Stakeholder Identification Work and Value Creation Stakeholder Engagement

As we asserted earlier in this chapter, the approaches to stakeholder identification are many and varied. In total, we suggest, however, that they comprise the essence of stakeholder identification work. We argue that without this identification work, value creating stakeholder engagement is compromised, and correspondingly, that the stakeholder-work system of value creation is less effective. Table 4.2 summarizes many of these definitions, approaches, and even techniques, as well as outlining some possible applications of stakeholder identification work to better facilitate stakeholder engagement work. We offer Table 4.2 as the embodiment of what we mean by "consonance," that value is created *because* the stakeholder identification work – the necessary work that precedes, but also enables, stakeholder engagement work – has been accomplished effectively.

Stakeholder identification work therefore effectuates the alignment premise of value creation (Mitchell et al., 2015: 857): "to create optimal value, stakeholder activities should be arranged such that stakeholder interests are aligned (that when organizational managers make primary stakeholder A better off, they also tend to make primary stakeholders B, C, D ... *n* better off)" (see also Tantalo & Priem, 2016).

Importantly, the concept of stakeholder identification work thus enables previous definitions used for stakeholder identification (e.g., primary/secondary, definitive, dependent, dominant, dormant, etc., see also Table 4.2) to be pressed into service in the value creation task; that is, to ascertain the identity of stakeholders A, B, C, D ... *n*. Through the stakeholder identification work that supports stakeholder engagement work, "questions such as how value creation and value distribution can be more effectively reconciled" (Mitchell, 2002; Venkataraman, 2002), and "risk-sharing value-creating relationships through aligning value distribution with value creation can be enabled" (Mitchell et al., 2015: 857). Thus, in the "consonance" sense – where effective stakeholder identification enables alignment in value creation – stakeholder identification work supports stakeholder engagement, and more effective value creation is expected to result.

Discussion

Our task in this chapter has been to address the identification and importance of stakeholders as viewed through the twin lenses of value creation and the stakeholder work that enables it. In the previous sections, we have situated stakeholder identification work within the larger system of the stakeholder-centric work that relates to organizations. In this section, we comment on the strengths and contributions of the stakeholder identification literature, consider some of its shortcomings, and proceed to suggest possibilities offered by this research approach.

Strengths and Contributions

Stakeholder identification work took a clarifying step forward with the introduction of the relationship-based approach to stakeholder identification as proposed by Mitchell et al. (1997). This typology helped researchers build a better understanding of the work of stakeholder identification. Indeed, the large body of scholarly work that draws upon this framework attests to its applicability. For example, scholars have used the typology to explain phenomena based on stakeholder relationships in the family business context (e.g.,

Table 4.2 Definitions, Approaches, and Techniques Suggested for Stakeholder Identification Work

Author(s)	Year	Definition, Approach, or Technique	Application of Stakeholder ID Work: *recognizing stakeholders that matter [to value creation] for a given organization* **to Stakeholder Engagement Work:** *the extent to which a firm pursues value-creation activities with stakeholders*
Stanford memo	1963	"those groups without whose support the organization would cease to exist" (cited in Freeman & Reed, 1983, and Freeman, 1984)	Focuses attention on those groups to whom value creation will matter in terms of gaining and retaining support
Freeman	1984	"can affect or is affected by the achievement of the organization's objectives" (p. 46)	Creates a common-purpose conceptualization among and legitimizes value creation effects among a broad scope of relational actors
Savage et al.	1991	"potential to threaten or to cooperate with the organization, managers may identify supportive, mixed blessing, non-supportive, and marginal stakeholders" (p. 61)	Provides an early creation of theoretically driven categorization and label-assigning typologies designed to more precisely specify the attention function of managers toward stakeholders, and concurrently to communicate value creation expectations with respect to such labels
Clarkson	1995	"primary and secondary stakeholders … with primary stakeholder groups typically comprised of shareholders and investors, employees, customers, suppliers, governments, and communities" (pp. 105–106)	Suggests (textually/sub-textually), that prioritization of stakeholders might somehow adhere to their identification, thereby providing a foundation for later combinations implicating both identification and salience in theory building
Mitchell et al.	1997	"We first lay out the stakeholder types that emerge from various combinations of the attributes: power, legitimacy, and urgency. Logically and conceptually, seven types are examined – three possessing only one attribute, three possessing two attributes, and one possessing all three attributes. We propose that stakeholders' possession of these attributes, upon further methodological and empirical work, can be measured reliably. This analysis allows and justifies identification of entities that should be considered stakeholders of the firm" (p. 874)	Extends earlier work in the creation of theoretically driven categorization and label-assigning typologies that, in this case, enable managers not only to identify a given stakeholder; but coincident with identification to apprehend immediately the requirements/challenges for stakeholder engagement associated with each type
Mitchell et al.	1997	"a relationship exists between the firm and stakeholder" (pp. 860–862, table 2)	Recognizes the social basis for stake-holding
Mitchell et al.	1997	"power dependence dominated by stakeholders" (pp. 860–862, table 2)	Explicitly relates previous attention rationales (e.g., "to exist," "objectives," and "cooperation") to identification on dependence grounds
Mitchell et al.	1997	"power dependence dominated by the firm" (pp. 860–862, table 2)	Examines alternative identification rationales where domination vs. value creation may prompt firm pursuits
Mitchell et al.	1997	"the firm and the stakeholder have mutual power-dependence relationship" (pp. 860–862, table 2)	Acknowledges early reciprocal notions as relevant in the identification of stakeholders for mutually beneficial (e.g., value creation) reasons
Mitchell et al.	1997	"based on legitimacy in relationships, including contracts, claims, risk, and moral claims" (pp. 860–862, table 2)	Accentuates and confirms the idea that legitimacy justifies recognition; and suggests the notion that economic *and* moral grounds support value creation through stakeholder identification
Mitchell et al.	1997	"grounded in the notion that the stakeholder has an interest in the firm (with legitimacy not implied)" (pp. 860–862, table 2)	Recognizes the financial/legal realities of the institutional context within which stakeholders who are owners (or at least value-creation claimants) may have economic rights to the firm residual

Table 4.2 (*cont.*)

Author(s)	Year	Definition, Approach, or Technique	Application of Stakeholder ID Work: *recognizing stakeholders that matter [to value creation] for a given organization* to Stakeholder Engagement Work: *the extent to which a firm pursues value-creation activities with stakeholders*
Cragg & Greenbaum	2002	"anyone with a material interest in the firm" (p. 322)	Concentrates stakeholder identification on tangible attribution
Phillips	2003	"differentiates derivative from normative stakeholders: derivative stakeholders – those groups or individuals who can either harm or benefit the organization but to whom the organization has no direct moral obligation as stakeholders; normative stakeholders – those to whom the organization has a moral obligation." (pp. 30–31)	Consolidates and establishes philosophical justification for stakeholder identification across broad-spectrum moral criteria, thereby enabling stakeholder-engagement explanations that comport with reciprocal expectations as the moral standard for stakeholder identification
Driscoll & Starik	2004	"the natural environment as the primary and primordial stakeholder of the firm" (p. 55)	Expands the identification criteria set, motivating theoretical explanations that consider both positive and negative externalities attendant to value creation through broad-scope stakeholder engagement
Schwartz	2006	"God both is and should be considered a managerial stakeholder" (p. 291)	Also expands the identification criteria set to suggest stakeholder engagement in value creation based upon spiritually linked inclusion
Dunham et al.	2006	"two new variants of community – the virtual advocacy group and the community of practice" (p. 23).	Specifies explicitly additional stakeholder identification sets that are (or can be) relevant to value creation stakeholder engagement
Pajunen	2006	"stakeholders having the needed resources and able to control the interaction and resource flows in the network most likely have a strong influence on an organization's survival" (p. 1263).	In some respects, duplicates earlier work on power (see Mitchell, et al.'s 1997 discussion of Etzioni's [1988] coercive, utilitarian, and normative power)
Fassin	2009	"distinguished stakeholders from stakewatchers – who act on behalf of stakeholders, and stakekeepers – who impose constraints on how the firm tackles its relations with the stakeholders" (p. 83)	Imposes additional normative criteria for explaining second-order (e.g., scrutiny "once-removed"; indirect non-stakeholder engagement) stakeholder identification influence in first-order stakeholder engagement processes.

Mitchell et al., 2011), in the workplace spirituality context (e.g., Mitchell et al., 2013), and within the ethnic business context (Marin, Mitchell, & Lee, 2015).

In the teaching realm, the power, legitimacy, and urgency framework for stakeholder identification (Mitchell et al., 1997) often appears in coursework and in textbooks (e.g., Carroll & Buchholtz, 2015; Lawrence & Weber, 2016) as a critical skill for management students. Additionally, the applicability of the framework to practice has been chronicled in governmental organizations (e.g., Matty, 2011), non-governmental organizations (e.g., Reed et al., 2009), and in many other businesses large and small (e.g., Kochan, & Rubinstein, 2000; Slack & Parent, 2006).

Stakeholder identification work, using the Mitchell et al. (1997) model, is thus firmly woven within the scholarly fabric of research, teaching, and service.

We note that this relationships-based approach to stakeholder identification work complements and is complemented by the many other definitions, approaches, and techniques that have developed to better illuminate and to make more effective the task of stakeholder identification, as noted in Table 4.2. But notwithstanding the prominence and usefulness of the relationship-focused approach to stakeholder identification and other important works to date, we also note that the need for a more comprehensive approach to stakeholder identification work has been increasingly evident, as may be seen by some of the remaining shortcomings that we now identify within the literature.

Shortcomings

Without wishing to undermine the usefulness or viability of the relational stakeholder identification model, we nevertheless hope that constructive criticism of the extant literature might serve to further exploration and development of explanations that focus on stakeholder identification work. Recent scholarship and thinking suggest to us three areas of present concern: (1) economic assumptions, (2) inclusiveness, and (3) research gaps.

Economic Assumption Concerns. The economic assumption concerns that have surfaced in our review center primarily on the idea of value creation given tradeoffs. In explaining the Alignment Premise for value creation in their article, Mitchell et al. (2015: 857) have suggested that "of course, in the real world there must inevitably be tradeoffs . . . but [value creation stakeholder theory] maintains that managers will do well to try and minimize the value destruction from 'trading off,' since trading off at least partially disables risk sharing and it sacrifices the benefits of managing paradox (Cameron, 1986; Mitchell et al., 2016)." In some circumstances, however, the identification of stakeholders and the alignment of their interests may not require managers to engage in trading off (Tantalo & Priem, 2016). Here, other economic mechanisms may apply. Arthur (1994, 1996), for instance, suggests the existence of "increasing returns" situations where momentum, not trading off, is critical. In these situations, a bandwagon effect is possible (Arthur, 1994; Sherif, 1936), and economic momentum may make tradeoffs unnecessary. Stakeholder identification research has not hitherto addressed such situations. Furthermore, current stakeholder identification models do not, as a primary output of their application, account for pre-aligned identification of stakeholders who coalesce in coproduction, for example, in producing information goods (e.g., Rumelt, 1987). Stakeholder identification models to date may also conflict with notions that

organized stakeholders represent a nexus of contracts (Hill & Jones, 1992; Mitchell et al., 2016), as represented by, for example, an implicit "value-creation stakeholder partnership" (Mitchell et al., 2015: 856, 868–870).

Inclusiveness Concerns. One general shortcoming of business-focused scholarship is its implicit or explicit dismissal of normative standards for stakeholder inclusiveness (Agle et al., 2008; Mitchell et al., 2015; Mitchell et al., 2016). Effective identification of stakeholders relies upon the idea that all stakeholders who participate in value creation should be identified to enable distribution of value to those who helped to create it. However, the task of identifying and then "managing" stakeholders may at times be used to justify dismissing them. Such exclusion can occur particularly where managers use the stakeholder identification tools, provided, in theory, to support a single-objective-function-based (Jensen, 2002) conceptualization of their organization, rather than a pluralistic conceptualization.

Although the stakeholder identification model suggested by Mitchell et al. (1997) does not explicitly call for pluralism, Mitchell et al. (2016) have advocated strongly for value pluralism in organizations, and have proposed an intra-corporate marketplace as a mechanism for enabling both pluralistic-objective decision-making and stakeholder inclusiveness. So far, scant research explores situations in which the stakeholder identification model, rather than being helpful, might entice managers away from the demanding task of stakeholder inclusion. In this instance, the simplicity of the stakeholder identification model – which has been and continues to be its strength – might also emerge as a weakness. We call for additional research to further evaluate this potential shortcoming.

Research Gaps. In addition to economic and inclusiveness considerations, we see an opportunity for scholars to pursue further theoretical integration of stakeholder identification work with other kinds of stakeholder work. Earlier, we argued that the stakeholder literature might be organized into an integrated whole under the umbrella system of stakeholder work. Because we assume stakeholder awareness work as a pre- or at least concurrent condition for stakeholder identification work, we call for further research to examine more closely the remaining three phases: stakeholder understanding work, stakeholder prioritization work, and stakeholder engagement work. Is there precedence, concurrence, or even rearrangement of these phases that we have asserted are temporally ordered? How might operationalization of the stakeholder work system as necessary in its components, and sufficient in its totality, be accomplished effectively? We hope that, as investigators within a field of research, our becoming more explicit about potential inter-supportive overlaps will help scholars derive more comprehensive stakeholder-work-system-based explanations of the processes that lead from stakeholder awareness and identification work, to the work of understanding, prioritizing and engaging stakeholders in the value creation process. In this regard, Mitchell et al. (2017) reported no integrative research to date that incorporates stakeholder understanding work into the body of the literature that we have characterized as stakeholder-work-focused research. Thus, it appears that there is room in this research space for interested colleagues to respond to our invitation.

Possibilities

As we view the research work that has focused on the identification and importance of stakeholders, we note the need for deeper analyses that can systematize the literature based on the inter-supportive nature of the stakeholder work concept. Mitchell et al. (2017) have called for more extensive use of systems theory to develop a unifying rationale; and, they suggested Wood (1991) as an exemplar of deeper analysis that has helped scholars more easily comprehend an extensive literature stream (in Wood's case, CSR).

Within the Mitchell et al. (1997) model, stakeholder dynamism – when and how stakeholders move from being one type of stakeholder to another – represents another research opportunity. Mitchell et al. (2017) used the work of the Think Tank on Native Economic Development (Mitchell, 2003) to illustrate possibilities for dynamism

within the stakeholder salience model, and we suggest that this extension might be apt in the stakeholder identification case as well. We agree with their assertion that "such extensions – despite the possible shortcomings of the model – offer hope for greater stakeholder awareness, understanding, and engagement work in theory and in practice" (Mitchell et al., 2017: 148).

We further observe an emerging linkage between stakeholder work research and strategic management research (Barney, 2018). As an important and integrative development within both the stakeholder and strategy research streams, this new linkage may also reveal additional problems with stakeholder inclusion that need further research attention. We particularly note the restriction that Barney (2016) places upon the definition of what or who is to be identified as a stakeholder of the firm: those who contribute to expected profits. Mitchell et al. (2017) describe our concern:

> . . . beginning [his paper] with the Freeman (1984) definition, *anyone with an interest in how a firm is managed*, Barney [2016] paradoxically include[s] only employees, suppliers, customers, debtholders, and shareholders in his conceptualization, [and has] argued that these groups provide resources to a firm in return for some compensation, and thereby can be considered residual claimants [and argues for the exclusion of] other previously accepted or asserted primary stakeholders, such as governments, communities (e.g., Clarkson, 1995), and the natural environment (e.g., Driscoll & Starik, 2004). These groups, he reason[s], are only stakeholders as a matter of convenience. (Mitchell et al., 2017: 148)

Because strategic inclusion, and value creation-based inclusion, have not been well enacted in the past or present, additional research, understanding, and further theory development and explanation appear to be warranted.

In asserting the foregoing possibilities, we offer the stakeholder work lens as a promising tool. The focus of Lee (2015) on stakeholder awareness, identification, understanding, prioritization, and engagement is one that permits a much more systematic look at how stakeholder identification contributes to the overall system of stakeholder work and, thereby, to value creation through stakeholder engagement.

Conclusion

In this chapter, we have examined stakeholder identification research as seen through the new lens of stakeholder work to surface its importance to those whose affecting or being affected by firms brings them together to create value. In doing so, we have advanced a rationale for a work-focused and stakeholder-centric view of the stakeholder literature that casts stakeholder identification work as a necessary and integral part of a larger value-creating system. This permits us to close the gap in the stakeholder literature, which has not yet explained how stakeholder identification influences value creation.

In this regard, we have summarized the literature to date on stakeholder identification work, represented primarily by the stakeholder identification model (Mitchell et al., 1997) as complemented and further illuminated by other definitions, approaches, and techniques for accomplishing stakeholder identification work. We have asserted that value creation is amplified through the consonance of stakeholder identification work within the temporal phases of stakeholder work as they are likely to proceed: from stakeholder awareness, to identification, to understanding, to prioritization, and then to engagement work. We have then outlined contributions, shortcomings, and possibilities for future stakeholder identification research. We anticipate the stakeholder work lens to become ever-more productive in enabling both the consolidation and interpretation of a wide range of stakeholder-related explanations, especially those that concern the importance and identification of stakeholders in creating value.

Notes

1. While in this chapter we bound our analysis by economic considerations, we invite the reader to see also the chapter in this volume called "A Moral Foundation for Stakeholder Theory," wherein the normative importance of stakeholder identification is discussed.

References

Adams, M., & Hardwick, P. (1998). An analysis of corporate donations: UK evidence. *Journal of Management Studies, 35*(5): 641–654.

Agle, B. R., Donaldson, T., Freeman, E., Jensen M., Mitchell, R. K., & Wood, D. J. (2008). Dialogue: Toward superior stakeholder theory. *Business Ethics Quarterly, 18*(2): 153–190.

Agle, B. R., Mitchell, R. K., & Sonnenfeld, J. A. (1999). Who matters to CEOs? An investigation of stakeholder attributes and salience, corporate performance, and CEO values. *Academy of Management Journal, 42*(5): 507–525.

Ahlstedt, L., & Jahnukainen, I. (1971). *Yritysorganisaatio Yhteistoiminnan Ohjausjaerjestel maenae.* Helsinki: Weilin + Goeoes.

Alkhafaji, A. F. (1989). *A Stakeholder Approach to Corporate Governance: Managing in a Dynamic Environment,* New York: Quorum Books.

Arthur, W. B. (1994). *Increasing Returns and Path Dependence in the Economy,* Ann Arbor: University of Michigan Press.

Arthur, W. B. (1996). Increasing returns and the two worlds of business. *Harvard Business Review, 74* (4): 100–109

Bansal, P. (2003). From issues to actions: The importance of individual concerns and organizational values in responding to natural environmental issues. *Organization Science, 14*(5): 510–527.

Bansal, P., & Roth, K. (2000). Why companies go green: A model of ecological responsiveness. *Academy of Management Journal, 43*(4): 717–736.

Barley, S. R., & Kunda, G. (2001). Bringing work back in. *Organization Science, 12*(1): 76–95.

Barney, J. B. (2016). Why strategic management scholars must adopt a stakeholder perspective. Unpublished manuscript presented at the *2016 International Association for Business and Society Annual Meeting,* Park City, UT, June 17, 2016. Earlier versions of this paper were presented at the Indian School of Business, the Hong Kong University of Science and Technology, the 2016 BYU-University of Utah Winter Strategy Conference, the University of Tennessee, the

University of Southern California, The University of California at Irvine, Baruch College, The Strategic Management Society's 2015 "Stakeholder Theory at a Crossroads" conference held at Zion's National Park, and at the 2015 Academy of Management Meetings.

Barney, J. B. (2018). Why resource-based theory must adopt a stakeholder perspective. Strategic Management Journal, forthcoming. Retrieved from https://sites.insead.edu/facultyresearch/research/file.cfm?fid=59440.

Barraquier, A. (2013). A group identity analysis of organizations and their stakeholders: Porosity of identity and mobility of attributes. *Journal of Business Ethics, 115*(1): 45–62.

Black, J. A., & Boal, K. (1994). Strategic resources: Traits, configurations and paths to sustainable competitive advantage. *Strategic Management Journal, 15*(S2): 131–148.

Bowen, H. (1953). *Social Responsibilities of the Businessman*, New York: Harper.

Bowie, N. (1988). The moral obligations of multinational corporations. In S. Luper-Foy, ed., *Problems of International Justice*, pp. 97–113. Boulder, CO: Westview Press.

Brammer, S., & Millington, A. I. (2003a). The effect of stakeholder preferences, organizational structure and industry type on corporate community involvement. *Journal of Business Ethics, 45*(3): 213–226.

Brammer, S., & Millington, A. I. (2003b). The evolution of corporate charitable contributions in the UK between 1989 and 1999: Industry structure and stakeholder influences. *Business Ethics: A European Review, 12*(3): 216–228.

Brenner, S. N. (1993). The stakeholder theory of the firm and organizational decision making: Some propositions and a model. In J. Pasquero & D. Collins, eds., *Proceedings of the Fourth Annual Meeting of the International Association for Business and Society*, pp. 205–210. San Diego: International Association for Business and Society.

Brenner, S. N. (1995). Stakeholder theory of the firm: Its consistency with current management techniques. In J. Näsi, ed., *Understanding stakeholder thinking*, pp. 19–31. Helsinki: LSR-Jukaisut Oy.

Bridoux, F., & Stoelhorst, J. W. (2014). Microfoundations for stakeholder theory: Managing stakeholders with heterogeneous motives. *Strategic Management Journal, 35*(1): 107–125.

Calton, J. M., & Lad, L. J. (1995). Social contracting as a trust-building process of network governance. *Business Ethics Quarterly, 5*(2): 271–295.

Cameron, K. S. (1986). Effectiveness as paradox: Consensus and conflict in conceptions of organizational effectiveness. *Management Science, 32*(5): 539–553.

Carroll, A. B. (1979). A three-dimensional model of corporate performance. *Academy of Management Review, 4*, 497–505.

Carroll, A. B (1989). *Business and Society: Ethics and Stakeholder Management*. Cincinnati: South-Western.

Carroll, A. B. (1993). *Business and Society: Ethics and Stakeholder Management*, 2nd edn. Cincinnati: South-Western.

Carroll, A. B., & Buchholtz, A. K. (2015). *Business and Society: Ethics, Sustainability, and Stakeholder Management*, 9th edn. Stamford, CT: Cengage Learning.

Carter, S. M. (2006). The interaction of top management group, stakeholder, and situational factors on certain corporate reputation management activities. *Journal of Management Studies, 43*(5): 1145–1176.

Clarkson, M. B. E. (1994). A risk based model of stakeholder theory. *Proceedings of the Second Toronto Conference on Stakeholder Theory*. Toronto: Centre for Corporate Social Performance & Ethics, University of Toronto.

Clarkson, M. B. E. (1995). A stakeholder framework for analyzing and evaluating corporate social performance. *Academy of Management Review, 20*(1): 92–117.

Cornell, B., & Shapiro, A. C. (1987). Corporate stakeholders and corporate finance. *Financial Management, 16*(1): 5–14.

Cragg, W., & Greenbaum, A. (2002). Reasoning about responsibilities: Mining company managers on what stakeholders are owed. *Journal of Business Ethics, 39*(3): 319–335.

Daft, R. L., Sormunen, J., & Parks, D. (1988). Chief executive scamming, environmental characteristics, and company performance: An empirical study. *Strategic Management Journal, 9*(2): 123–139.

Davis, J. H., Schoorman, F. D., & Donaldson, L. (1997). Toward a stewardship theory of management. *Academy of Management Review, 22*(1): 20–47.

Davis, K. (1960). Can business afford to ignore social responsibilities? *California Management Review*, 2, 70–76.

Deegan, C., & Rankin, M. (1999). The environmental reporting expectations gap: Australian evidence, *British Accounting Review*, 31(3): 313–346.

Donaldson, T., & Preston, L. E. (1995). The stakeholder theory of the corporation: Concepts, evidence, and implications. *Academy of Management Review*, 20(1): 65–91.

Driscoll, K., & Starik, M. (2004). The primordial stakeholder: Advancing the conceptual consideration of stakeholder status for the natural environment. *Journal of Business Ethics*, 49(1): 55–73.

Dunham, L. D., Freeman, R. E., & Liedtka, J. (2006). Enhanced stakeholder practice: A particularized exploration of community. *Business Ethics Quarterly*, 16(1): 23–42.

Eesley, C., & Lenox, M. J. (2006). Firm responses to secondary stakeholder action. *Strategic Management Journal*, 27(8): 765–781.

Evan, W. M., & Freeman, R. E. (1988). A stakeholder theory of the modern corporation: Kantian capitalism. In T. L. Beauchamp & N. Bowie, eds., *Ethical Theory and Business*, pp. 75–84. Englewood Cliffs, NJ: Prentice-Hall.

Etzioni, A. (1988). *The Moral Dimensions*. New York: Free Press.

Fassin, Y. (2009). The stakeholder model redefined. *Journal of Business Ethics*, 84(1): 113–135.

Fiske, S. T., & Taylor, S. E. (1984). *Social Cognition: From Brains to Culture*. Reading, MA: Addison-Wesley.

Fiss, P. C. (2007). A set-theoretic approach to organizational configurations. *Academy of Management Review*, 32(4): 1180–1198.

Freeman, R. E. (1984). *Strategic management: A stakeholder approach*. Boston: Pitman.

Freeman, R. E. (1994). The politics of stakeholder theory: Some future directions. *Business Ethics Quarterly*, 4(4): 409–421.

Freeman, R. E., & Evan, W. M. (1990). Corporate governance: A stakeholder interpretation. *Journal of Behavioral Economics*, 19: 337–359.

Freeman, R. E., & Gilbert, D. R. (1987). Managing stakeholder relationship. In S. P. Sethi & C. M. Falbe, eds., *Business and society: Dimensions of Conflict and Cooperation*, pp. 397–423. Lexington, MA: Lexington Books.

Freeman, R. E., Harrison, J. S., & Wicks, A. C. (2007). *Managing for stakeholders: Reputation, survival and success*, New Haven, CT: Yale University Press.

Freeman, R. E., Harrison, J. S., Wicks, A. C., Parmar, B. L., & de Colle, S. (2010). *Stakeholder theory: The state of the art*, New York: Cambridge University Press.

Freeman R. E., & Reed, D. L. (1983). Stockholders and stakeholders: A new perspective on corporate governance. *California Management Review*, 25(3): 93–94.

Freeman, R. E., Wicks, A. C., & Parmar, B. (2004). Stakeholder theory and the corporate objective revisited. *Organization Science*, 15(3): 364–369.

Frooman, J. (1999). Stakeholder influence strategies. *Academy of Management Review*, 24(2): 191–205.

Frooman, J., & Murrell, A. J. (2005). Stakeholder influence strategies: The roles of structural and demographic determinants. *Business & Society*, 44(1): 3–31.

Galunic, D. C., & Eisenhardt, K. M. (1994). Reviewing the strategy-structure-performance paradigm. *Research in Organizational Behavior*, 16: 215–255.

Gieryn, T. F. (1983). Boundary-work and demarcation of science from non-science: Strains and interests in professional ideologies of scientists. *American Sociological Review*, 48(6): 781–795.

Godfrey, P. C. (2005). The relationship between corporate philanthropy and shareholder wealth: A risk management perspective. *Academy of Management Review*, 30(4): 777–798.

Harrison, J. S., Bosse, D. A., & Phillips, R. A. (2010). Managing for stakeholders, stakeholder utility functions, and competitive advantage. *Strategic Management Journal*, 31(1): 58–74.

Harrison, J. S., & Wicks, A. C. (2014). Stakeholder theory, value and firm performance. *Business Ethics Quarterly*, 23(1): 97–124.

Hendry, J. (2005). Stakeholder influence strategies: An empirical exploration. *Journal of Business Ethics*, 61(1): 79–99.

Heugens, P., van den Bosch, F., & van Riel, C. (2002). Stakeholder integration: Building mutually enforcing relationships. *Business & Society*, 41(1): 36–60

Hill, C. W., & Jones, T. M. (1992). Stakeholder-agency theory. *Journal of Management Studies*, 29(2): 131–154.

Hosmer, L. T., & Kiewitz, C. K. (2005). Organizational justice: A behavioral science concept with critical implications for business ethics and stakeholder theory. *Business Ethics Quarterly, 15*(1): 67–91.

Husted, B. W. (1998). Organizational justice and the management of stakeholder relations. *Journal of Business Ethics, 17*(6): 643–651.

Ibarra, H., & Barbulescu, R. (2010). Identity as narrative: Prevalence, effectiveness, and consequences of narrative identity work in macro work role transitions. *Academy of Management Review, 35*(1): 135–154.

Jensen, M. C. (2002). Value maximization, stakeholder theory, and the corporate objective function. *Business Ethics Quarterly, 12*(2): 235–256.

Johnson, R. A., & Greening, D. W. (1999). The effects of corporate governance and institutional ownership types on corporate social performance. *Academy of Management Journal, 42*(5): 564–576.

Jones, T. M. (1995). Instrumental stakeholder theory: A synthesis of ethics and economics. *Academy of Management Review, 20*(2): 404–437.

Kaler, J. (2002). Morality and strategy in stakeholder identification. *Journal of Business Ethics, 39* (1):91–100.

Kochan, T. A., & Rubinstein, S. A. (2000). Toward a stakeholder theory of the firm: The Saturn partnership. *Organization Science, 11*(4): 367–386.

Kreiner, G. E., Hollensbe, E. C., & Sheep, M. L. (2009). Balancing borders and bridges: Negotiating the work-home interface via boundary work tactics. *Academy of Management Journal, 52* (4): 704–730.

Langtry, B. (1994). Stakeholders and the moral responsibilities of business. *Business Ethics Quarterly, 4*(4): 431–443.

Lawrence, A. T., & Weber, J. (2016). *Business and society: Stakeholders, ethics, public policy*, 15th edn. New York: McGraw-Hill Education.

Lawrence, P., & Lorsch, J. (1967). Differentiation and integration in complex organizations, *Administrative Science Quarterly, 12*: 1–47.

Lawrence, T. B., & Suddaby, R. (2006). Institutions and institutional work. In S. R. Clegg, C. Hardy, T. B. Lawrence, & W. R. Nord, eds., *Handbook of organization studies*, 2nd edn., pp. 215–254. London, UK: Sage Publications.

Lee, J. H. (2015). Stakeholder work and value creation stakeholder engagement: An integrative framework. Unpublished doctoral dissertation, Texas Tech University, Lubbock, Texas.

Lee, J. H., & Mitchell, R. K. (2013). Stakeholder work and stakeholder research. Presented at the 2013 International Association for Business Society Annual Meeting, Portland, Oregon.

Logsdon, J. M., & Wood, D. J. (2002). Business citizenship: From domestic to global level of analysis. *Business Ethics Quarterly, 12*(2): 155–187.

Maignan, I., Ferrell, O. C., & Hult, G. T. M. (1999). Corporate citizenship: Cultural antecedents and business benefits. *Journal of the Academy of Marketing Science, 27*: 455–469.

Marens, R., & Wicks, A. (1999). Getting real: Stakeholder theory, managerial practice, and the general irrelevance of fiduciary duties owed to shareholders. *Business Ethics Quarterly, 9*(2): 273–293

Marin, A., Mitchell, R. K., & Lee, J. H. (2015). The vulnerability and strength duality in ethnic business: A model of stakeholder salience and social capital. *Journal of Business Ethics, 130*(2): 271–289.

Matten, D., & Crane, A. (2005). Corporate citizenship: Toward an extended theoretical conceptualization. *Academy of Management Review, 30*(1): 166–179.

Matty, D. (2011). Enterprise architecture shapes stakeholder salience influence on enterprise value-creation. Unpublished doctoral dissertation, Massachusetts Institute of Technology, Cambridge, MA.

Meyer, A. D., Tsui, A. S., & Hinings, C. R. (1993). Configurational approaches to organizational analysis. *Academy of Management Journal, 36*(6): 1175–1195.

Miller, D. (1986). Configurations of strategy and structure: A synthesis. *Strategic Management Journal, 7*(3): 233–249.

Mintzberg, H. (1980). Structures in 5's: A synthesis of the research on organization design. *Management Science, 26*(3): 322–341.

Mitchell, R. K. (2002). Entrepreneurship and stakeholder theory. *The Ruffin Series of the Business Ethics Quarterly, 3*: 175–196.

Mitchell, R. K. (2003). Assessing stakeholder interests in prosperity and cultural well-being – Appendix A. In C. Nyce, ed., *Masters in Our Own House: The Path to Prosperity and Cultural Well-being*, pp. 163–182. Terrace, BC: Skeena Native Development Society.

Mitchell, R. K., Agle, B. R., Chrisman, J. J., & Spence, L. J. (2011). Toward a theory of stakeholder salience in family firms. *Business Ethics Quarterly*, *21*(2): 235–255.

Mitchell, R. K., Agle, B. R., & Wood, D. J. (1997). Towards a theory of stakeholder identification and salience: Defining the principle of who and what really counts. *Academy of Management Review*, *22*(4): 853–886.

Mitchell, R. K., Lee J. H., & Agle, B. R. (2017). Stakeholder prioritization work: The role of stakeholder salience in stakeholder research. In J. Weber & D. Wasieleski, eds., *Business and Society 360 Book Series on Stakeholder Management*, vol. 1, pp. 123–157. Bingley, UK: Emerald Publishing.

Mitchell, R. K., Robinson, R. E., Marin, A., Lee, J. H., & Randolph, A. F. (2013). Spiritual identity, stakeholder attributes, and family business workplace spirituality stakeholder salience. *Journal of Management, Spirituality and Religion*, *10*(3): 215–252.

Mitchell, R. K., Van Buren, H. J. III, Greenwood, M., Freeman, R. E. (2015). Stakeholder inclusion and accounting for stakeholders. *Journal of Management Studies*, *52*(7): 851–877.

Mitchell, R. K., Weaver, G. R., Agle, B. R., Bailey, A. D., & Carlson, J. (2016). Stakeholder agency and social welfare: Pluralism and decision making in the multi-objective corporation. *Academy of Management Review*, *41*(2): 252–275.

Näsi, J. (1995). What is stakeholder thinking? A snapshot of a social theory of the firm. In J. Näsi, ed., *Understanding Stakeholder Thinking*, pp. 19–32. Helsinki: LSR-Julkaisut Oy.

Neubaum, D. O., & Zahra, S. A. (2006). Institutional ownership and corporate social performance: The moderating effects of investment horizon, activism, and coordination. *Journal of Management*, *32*(1): 108–131.

Pajunen, K. (2006). Stakeholder influences in organizational survival. *Journal of Management Studies*, *43*(6): 1261–1288.

Phillips, N., & Lawrence, T. B. (2012). The turn to work in organization and management theory: Some implications for strategic organization. *Strategic Organization*, *10*(3): 223–230.

Phillips, R. A. (2003). Stakeholder legitimacy. *Business Ethics Quarterly*, *7*(1): 51–66.

Reed, M. S., Graves, A., Dandy, N., Posthumus, H., Hubacek, K., Morris, J., & Stringer, L. C. (2009). Who's in and why? A typology of stakeholder analysis methods for natural resource management. *Journal of Environmental Management*, **90**(5): 1933–1949.

Rhenman, E. (1964). *Foeretagsdemokrati och Foeretagsorganisation*, Stockholm: Thule.

Roethlisberger, F. J., & Dickson, W. J. (1939). *Management and the worker*, Cambridge, MA: Harvard University Press.

Rumelt, R. P. (1987). Theory, strategy, and entrepreneurship. In D. Teece, ed., *The competitive challenge*, pp. 137–158. Boston: Ballinger.

Savage, G. T., Nix, T. H., Whitehead, C. J., & Blair, J. D. (1991). Strategies for assessing and managing organizational stakeholders. *Academy of Management Executive*, *5*(2): 61–75.

Scherer, A. G., & Palazzo, G. (2011). The new political role of business in a globalized world: A review of a new perspective on CSR and its implications for the firm, governance, and democracy. *Journal of Management Studies*, *48*(4): 899–931.

Schwartz, M. S. (2006). God as a managerial stakeholder? *Journal of Business Ethics*, *66*(2–3): 291–306.

Scott, S. G., & Lane, V. R. (2000). A stakeholder approach to organizational identity. *Academy of Management Review*, *25*(1): 43–62.

Sharma, S., & Henriques, I. 2005. Stakeholder influences on sustainability practices in the Canadian forest services industry. *Strategic Management Journal*, *26*(2): 159–180.

Sherif, M. (1936). *The psychology of social norms*. New York: Harper Collins.

Slack, T., & Parent, M. M. (2006). *Understanding sport organizations: The application of organization theory*, 2nd edn. Champaign, IL: Human Kinetics.

Snider, J., Hill, R. P., & Martin, D. (2003). Corporate social responsibility in the 21st century: A view from the world's most successful firms. *Journal of Business Ethics*, *48*(2): 175–187.

Snow, D. A., & Anderson, L. (1987). Identity work among the homeless: The verbal construction and avowal of personal identities. *American Journal of Sociology*, *92*(6): 1336–1371.

Stanford memo. (1963). Stanford Research Institute (SRI) internal memorandum as cited in Freeman and Reed (1983) and Freeman (1984, pp. 31–33).

Starik, M. (1994). Essay by Mark Starik. pp. 89–95 of the Toronto conference: Reflections on stakeholder theory. *Business & Society*, *33*(1): 82–131.

Tantalo, C., & Priem, R. L. (2016). Value creation through stakeholder synergy. *Strategic Management Journal*, *37*(2): 314–329.

Taylor, F. W. (1911). *The principles of scientific management*. New York: Harper and Bros.

Thompson, J. K., Wartick, S. L., & Smith, H. L. (1991). Integrating corporate social performance and stakeholder management: Implications for a research agenda in small business. *Research in Corporate Social Performance and Policy, 12*(1): 207–230.

Ulmer, R. R., & Sellnow, T. L. (2000). Consistent questions of ambiguity in organizational crisis communication: Jack in the box as a case study. *Journal of Business Ethics, 25*(2): 143–155.

Venkataraman, S. (2002). Stakeholder value equilibration and the entrepreneurial process. *The Ruffin Series of the Society of Business Ethics Quarterly, 3*: 45–58.

Weber, M. (1968). *Economy and society*, Los Angeles: University of California Press.

Weitzner, D., & Deutsch, Y. (2015). Understanding motivation and social influence in stakeholder prioritization. *Organization Studies, 36*(10): 1337–1360.

Wicks, A. C., Gilbert, D. R. Jr., & Freeman, R. E. (1994). Toward a substantive definition of the corporate issue construct: A review and synthesis of the literature. *Business and Society, 33*(3): 293–311.

Wood, D. J. (1991). Corporate social performance revisited. *Academy of Management Review, 16*(4): 691–718.

PART II

Stakeholder Theory and Society

Sustainable Wealth Creation

Applying Instrumental Stakeholder Theory to the Improvement of Social Welfare

THOMAS M. JONES

University of Washington

JEFFREY S. HARRISON

University of Richmond

This chapter briefly reviews core ideas and research results in the existing instrumental stakeholder theory (IST) literature and then applies the IST concept to the simultaneous pursuit of two objectives – advancing social welfare, the presumed goal of morally legitimate social systems in general, and preserving the key elements of shareholder wealth enhancement, the traditional goal of the corporation.[1] In so doing, we expand the range of ethical approaches to IST beyond deontological principles (e.g., treat stakeholders fairly; be trustworthy in dealing with stakeholders) present in extant versions of IST, to a consequentialist focus (i.e., a utilitarian concern for "the greatest good for the greatest number"). Our analysis leads to a suggestion for a modified corporate objective and lays out several research questions as a starting point for a new research agenda.

Instrumental Stakeholder Theory as Originally Envisioned

Donaldson and Preston (1995) suggested that stakeholder theory has three interrelated but distinct perspectives. The descriptive/empirical perspective provides accounts of how firms, their managers, and their stakeholders actually behave. Normative theory deals with the moral aspects of this behavior – i.e., how firms/managers/stakeholders *should* behave. Instrumental stakeholder theory (hereafter IST) proposes theoretical connections between particular stakeholder management practices and resulting end states. Specifically, IST suggests that firms that treat their stakeholders ethically will enjoy higher profit

performance (and presumably higher returns for shareholders) than firms that do not. Although examining a theory from multiple perspectives may be a useful intellectual exercise, the normative implications of stakeholder theory are foundational to all forms of the theory (Donaldson & Preston, 1995; Jones, 1995). The normative aspects of IST most clearly differentiate it from other possible management approaches – it is based on ethical treatment, and consideration of what is or is not ethical, in the stakeholder context, is obviously a normative exercise.

Core Elements of Instrumental Stakeholder Theory

Ethical management principles upon which extant IST is based include the notion that firms should conform to widely accepted rules of society, but also include principles such as fairness, trustworthiness, respect, loyalty, care, and cooperation (Greenwood & Van Buren, 2010; Hendry, 2001; Jones, 1995; Phillips, 2003). Jones (1995) developed a strong rationale to support the notion that ethical treatment of stakeholders reduces contracting costs between firms and stakeholders. First, from an agency cost perspective (Jensen & Meckling, 1976), ethical treatment can reduce monitoring costs because the actors can trust that the basic terms of the agreement will be satisfied. Second, bonding costs will be reduced because actors do not have to worry about opportunistic behavior; that is, taking actions that harm the other party. Third, residual losses will be reduced because monitoring and bonding may not completely address the interests of both parties. Similarly, from a transactions cost perspective (Williamson, 1975), ethical treatment can reduce costs associated with searching for an adequate trading partner, lengthy negotiation processes, high levels of monitoring, costly enforcement mechanisms, and, again, residual losses. Ethical treatment also addresses moral hazard, or the risk that one of the parties may shirk their responsibilities (Alchian & Demsetz, 1972), as well as hold up problems stemming from a reluctance of one of the parties to make specialized investments, which could impede progress.

Along these same lines, Bridoux and Stoelhorst (2016) argue that communal sharing relationships between firms and stakeholders provide a highly efficient production model. These types of relationships are characterized by high levels of trust, shared goals, willingness to share even proprietary information, a high level of cooperation, and an emphasis on relational (as opposed to arms-length formal) contracts. These relational characteristics increase efficiency by reducing contracting costs, making maximum use of information available anywhere in the production system, reducing or eliminating enforcement costs, and increasing the motivation and loyalty of stakeholders. These sorts of benefits would seem to be sufficient to motivate a large proportion of firms to pursue strategies that result in communal sharing relationships with stakeholders, yet they tend to be somewhat rare. Jones, Harrison, and Felps (2018) explain that this is because they are difficult to execute successfully and also very hard to imitate. However, it is these very characteristics – rarity and inimitability – that gives them the potential to lead to a sustainable competitive advantage. Also, there is a wealth of theory that suggests that there are economic benefits to ethical treatment of stakeholders, even short of full communal-like treatment (Freeman, et al., 2010). As the next section will demonstrate, the empirical evidence tends to support the idea that, on average, the performance advantages of IST-oriented treatment of stakeholders outweigh the costs.

In addition to the arguments put forth by Jones (1995), and further developed by Bridoux and Stoelhorst (2016) and Jones, et al. (2018), ethical treatment of stakeholders can reduce costs associated with negative stakeholder actions such as boycotts, walkouts, strikes, adverse regulation, bad press, and legal suits (Cornell & Shapiro, 1987; Harrison & St. John, 1996; Shane & Spicer, 1983). This also makes a firm less risky for investors, which can enhance the value of its securities (Graves & Waddock, 1994). In addition, reduced risk makes a firm a more attractive investment partner, whether the investments are in the form of cash invested by stockholders or financiers, suppliers entering into new contracts, or specific investments made by employees in the firm (Wang, Barney, & Reuer, 2003). As firms develop ethical reputations, stakeholders will want to engage with them, customers will want to buy their products, more people will want to become their employees, governments will be less likely to closely scrutinize and regulate them, and communities will find them more attractive as local partners (Hosmer, 1994; Jones, 1995; Post, Preston, & Sachs, 2002; Roberts & Dowling, 2002). The surplus of desirable and willing stakeholders with whom to engage can enhance a firm's ability to acquire and develop resources leading to competitive advantage (Post, et al., 2002), and its ability to coordinate multiple contracts simultaneously (Freeman & Evan, 1990). The firm will also have a greater ability to discover ways to produce stakeholder synergy, the simultaneous creation of value for multiple stakeholders through one decision or action (Tantalo & Priem, 2016).

Organizational justice considerations also suggest a positive relationship between ethical stakeholder treatment and firm performance (Harrison, Bosse, & Phillips, 2010). A firm that exhibits distributional justice will allocate value fairly to the stakeholders that helped to create it. Procedural and interactional justice help stakeholders feel valued, and can reduce the possibility of negative actions. All of these forms of justice can result in reciprocity in the form of higher levels of stakeholder motivation, loyalty, and cooperation (Bosse, Phillips & Harrison, 2009). Also, organizational justice increases trust, and thus the willingness of stakeholders to share information about their own utility functions with the firm. The firm can use this stakeholder utility information to create more appealing value propositions, to generate higher levels of efficiency and productivity, and to guide innovation efforts (Harrison, et al., 2010). As an additive effect, as a firm treats a particular stakeholder well, other stakeholders who are aware of the treatment may also reciprocate toward the firm, a phenomenon called generalized exchange (Ekeh, 1974).

Of course, the sort of stakeholder treatment discussed in this section is not without incremental costs. Some of these costs include a generous allocation of value to stakeholders, the risk that stakeholders may not reciprocate, the cost of holding onto stakeholders that no longer provide adequate value to the value creating process, the additional time and other resources that must be devoted to managing relationships with stakeholders, and higher information management costs resulting from the additional information acquired from stakeholders and required to manage relationships with them effectively (Bridoux & Stoelhorst, 2016; Garcia-Castro & Francoeur, 2016; Harrison & Bosse, 2013; Jones, et al., 2018; Sisodia, Wolfe & Sheth, 2007). In fact, it is probable that some firms experience higher performance because they take advantage of a strong bargaining position in their interactions with stakeholders (Bridoux & Stoelhorst, 2014), a cost in lost opportunities to firms that eschew the use of bargaining advantages. Along these same lines, heterogeneity among stakeholders with regard to their preferences regarding equity and the extent to which they reciprocate mean that the benefits stemming from excellent treatment of stakeholders may not exceed the costs of doing so (Hayibor, 2017).

Because of cost factors, managers need to be careful not to "give away the store" in their efforts to please stakeholders. Harrison and Bosse (2013) provide theory that suggests when firms may be over- or under-allocating value to stakeholders, from a firm performance perspective. Also, Jones, et al. (2018) suggest that the benefits associated with IST-based stakeholder treatment are more likely to exceed the costs in high-velocity industries, knowledge-intensive industries, and in contexts in which there is high task and outcome interdependence.

The Empirical Evidence

A large body of evidence demonstrates that firms that practice IST principles tend to have higher financial performance. Freeman, et al. (2010) provided an extensive review of the empirical evidence on the performance of firms that practice IST principles up to the date their book went to press. Among the most compelling of the studies they reviewed was an early study by Preston and Sapienza (1990), who found that firms that serve the interests of multiple stakeholders (shareholders, employees, community, and customers) had ten-year rates of return that were positively correlated with each of their stakeholder variables. Also important, Berman, Wicks, Kotha, and Jones (1999) examined whether it is an instrumental motive (treating stakeholders well enhances performance) or an intrinsic motive (all stakeholders have inherent worth) that tends to drive financial importance. They found some evidence to support the IST motive and no support for the intrinsic motive. In addition, Hillman and Keim (2001) distinguished between stakeholder management attributes and social attributes (dimensions associated with socially desirable behaviors), and found that the stakeholder management attributes had a positive effect on shareholder value creation. Finally, Sisodia, Wolfe, and Sheth (2007) conducted an exhaustive study in which they identified firms that were universally admired by a broad group of their stakeholders, and found that these firms also had high financial performance over a variety of time frames. Studies that examined the relationship between financial performance and the salience given to particular stakeholders by management have been less conclusive (i.e., Agle, Mitchell, & Sonnenfeld, 1999).

More recently, additional empirical evidence has established a strong link between stakeholder-based management and financial performance. Choi and Wang (2009), using a very large sample, found support for the idea that good stakeholder relations have a positive effect on persistent superior performance. In addition, they discovered that such relations can help a firm recover from inferior performance. In another important study set in the gold mining industry, Henisz, Dorobantu, and Nartey (2014) found support for the notion that financial markets take stakeholder relations into account when determining the value of increases in resource evaluations (or the expected increase in resource evaluations) of different mines, providing evidence that good stakeholder relations can enhance firm efficiency and reduce operating risk, and that market participants observe and react to the quality of relations between a firm and its stakeholders.

As mentioned previously, generalized exchange is an important assumption of IST. That is, the way a firm treats one stakeholder can influence the way other stakeholders respond to the firm. Cording, Harrison, Hoskisson, and Jonsen (2014) found support for this assumption in a post-merger context, a time when organizations are in tumult, implicit contracts are at risk of being violated, and stakeholders are likely to feel vulnerable. Finally, and consistent with the notion that there are both benefits and costs to IST-based stakeholder management, Garcia-Castro and Francoeur (2016) examined the notion that there are rational limits to the size of investments firms make in stakeholder relations. Among their important findings, they concluded that stakeholder investments are more effective when they are done simultaneously across a firm's high priority stakeholders and when no single stakeholder group is provided with a disproportionately high investment. In addition, they discovered that there are lower bounds for stakeholder investments for firms with very high performance, evidence that neglect of even one important stakeholder can hold back performance. They also found contextual effects associated with different types of strategies and national settings.

Adding the findings from these four studies to previous empirical work, we continue to see evidence for a positive relationship between IST-based management and firm performance, and for the existence of a generalized exchange effect. There is also evidence that context matters, and that there are situations in which stakeholder management based on IST principles may actually reduce firm performance, or at least that over-investment in stakeholder relations can suppress performance. There is, of course, variance in performance for firms that practice IST in their relations with

stakeholders, and the field is only beginning to explain this variance.

One interesting, but not fully explored concept, is that because IST is built on a foundation that encourages ethical treatment of a broad group of a firm's stakeholders, and discourages behavior that destroys value for any of its stakeholders, a management approach based on IST may offer the potential to genuinely increase social welfare (Jones, et al., 2016). In other words, a stakeholder perspective may offer the potential to enhance shareholder welfare and social welfare simultaneously. This notion will be explored in the rest of this chapter.

Shareholder Welfare and Social Welfare

Originally based on work dating back centuries (Smith, 1776/1937), reinforced at the dawn of managerial capitalism (Berle & Means, 1932), famously and stoutly defended by a Nobel Laureate (Friedman, 1970), and more recently reformulated (Jensen, 2002; Jensen & Meckling, 1976), the primary objective of the corporation has been the maximization of profit (more recently, shareholder wealth). This objective has the advantages of being clearly stated, theoretically achievable since it is single-valued, considered to be morally grounded in utilitarian moral philosophy, and backed by the imperatives of equity investors – "Wall Street."[2] Unfortunately, achieving shareholder wealth maximization is far more complicated than describing it (Freeman, Wicks, & Parmar, 2004). While there are many ways to increase shareholder wealth, no single formula exists for maximizing it.[3]

Importantly, although some may consider shareholder wealth maximization an appropriate objective of the firm, it is not the objective of society as a whole. Rather, it is a part of an economic system – market capitalism – intended to advance social welfare. Put differently, it is one of the *means* by which the *end* – social welfare – is pursued. In fact, existing in parallel to the conclusion that the primary objective of the firm is to maximize shareholder welfare is a widely accepted view that the advancement of social welfare, through wealth creation, is the defining function of business in a market capitalist system (Barney, 1991; Jensen, 2002; Wallman, 1998). Walsh, Weber, and Margolis (2003) make an explicit claim regarding the central importance of social welfare in management research, calling the economic and social objectives of business the *raison d'être* of corporations. Indeed, the role of profit seeking/maximization in the advancement of social welfare appears in statements by two prominent economic thinkers – Adam Smith and Michael Jensen. In his discussion of the *invisible hand* of the market, wherein *individual* self-interested behavior leads to *socially* beneficial outcomes, Smith famously wrote:

> It is not from the benevolence of the butcher, the brewer, or the baker, that we can expect our dinner, but from their regard to their own interest ... He is in this, as in many other cases, led by an invisible hand to promote an end which was no part of his intention. Nor is it always the worse for the society that it was no part of it. By pursuing his own interest he frequently promotes that of the society more effectually than when he really intends to promote it. (1776/1937: 488–489)

Contemporary expressions of this relationship, specifically involving the *maximization* of shareholder wealth, are represented in the words of Michael Jensen:

> Two hundred years of work in economics and finance implies that in the absence of externalities and monopoly (and when all goods are priced), social welfare is maximized when each firm in an economy maximizes its total market value. (2002: 239)

Both Smith and Jensen make it clear that profit seeking (Smith)[4] and market value maximization (Jensen)[5] are means to a larger end – social welfare.[6]

With these two important objectives in mind, we now consider whether they can be maximized simultaneously. Traditionally, in accordance with neo-classical microeconomic theory, profit maximization on the part of firms was thought to assure that social welfare was also maximized. Unfortunately, recent work in stakeholder theory

(e.g., Jones & Felps, 2013a; Jones, et al., 2016; Mitchell, et al., 2016; Freeman, et al., 2004) has thoroughly debunked the notion that corporate profit maximization inevitably leads to maximal social welfare. Indeed, in some cases, this objective may lead to *decreases* in social welfare. If profit maximization (leading to high shareholder returns) as a corporate objective is an unreliable path to maximal social welfare, is there an alternative single-valued objective that could serve the end of maximal social welfare? One proposed alternative – stakeholder happiness enhancement (Jones & Felps, 2013b), while also grounded in utilitarian precepts, presents some thorny measurement problems and has garnered little scholarly traction. Indeed, the search for a single-valued corporate objective that will (at least in theory) produce maximal social welfare remains an elusive goal. Therefore, even when social welfare is viewed exclusively in terms of economic value, its pursuit is highly contingent. This conclusion is greatly amplified by the observation that social welfare cannot realistically be viewed in economic terms alone. Concerns about stability and justice (Marti & Scherer, 2016) and several other dimensions of welfare (Mitchell, et al., 2016) are also legitimate considerations in any discussion of social welfare. To sum up, maximal social welfare cannot be achieved through the application of a single-valued objective, like maximizing shareholder returns; enhancing social welfare is a highly contingent undertaking.

Which Objective Should Prevail?

Given that the profit maximization objective of the firm and the wealth creation function of business in the economy will sometimes work at cross-purposes, which of the two goals should take precedence? We posit that when profit maximization leading to high shareholder returns and aggregate wealth creation for all stakeholders (including shareholders) come into conflict, the latter should prevail. Policies intended to create wealth for one stakeholder group, shareholders in this case, should not destroy wealth overall. In our view, the fundamental purpose of business in a market capitalist economy – i.e., creating wealth for society as a whole – should be preserved irrespective of the imperatives of individual businesses. Why? First, business, as an institution, is instrumental – a means to an end (Smith, 1776/1937; Jensen, 2002; Wallman, 1998). The end of business activity is the improvement of social welfare in general and of economic welfare in particular.[7] If the appropriate end of business activity is social welfare, and profit maximization leading to high shareholder returns is only a means to that end, when the two objectives conflict, social welfare through total wealth creation should supersede profit maximization that is intended to maximize shareholder returns.

Furthermore, it is almost an axiom of social theory that social institutions must be supported by some legitimating moral logic or society will no longer permit them to exist. In other words, social institutions must have a purpose that is not simply the perpetuation of the institution itself or the advancement of the interests of the beneficiaries of its existence. For example, democratic political institutions in general are legitimized by their reliance on the consent of the governed, not by their ability to bestow benefits on a few favored groups. Similarly, legal institutions are legitimized by their quest to produce a substantial measure of justice – protecting the citizenry in general as well as those accused of transgressions – not by their ability to enrich attorneys or employ other legal functionaries (e.g., judges, bailiffs, and court reporters). Economic institutions, by an analogous logic, are legitimized by their ability to produce economic wealth for society writ large, not just for shareholders or top executives. Although this logic can take many forms, it must be compelling to at least a significant majority of those affected by the institution in question.

Another perspective on legitimacy is also relevant to the choice of economic objectives – in this case, shareholder wealth vs. aggregate wealth creation/social welfare. In a classic analysis of corporate legitimacy, Hurst (1970) posited the existence of two possible foundations for the legitimacy of social institutions – utility and responsibility. Of the two, utility is most relevant to this discussion. Underlying this analysis, and much economic theorizing in general, is the moral concept of utilitarianism – the improvement (ideally *maximization*) of social welfare/utility, popularly (but imprecisely) described as "the greatest good for the greatest number" (Mill, 1863; Bentham, 1823/1907; Sidgwick, 1879). A social institution has utility if it promotes an end valuable to society. Economic welfare is such an end. Most US citizens would endorse the social usefulness of promoting economic welfare. The same cannot be said for shareholder wealth maximization *per se*. A social institution dedicated solely to increasing the wealth of those who own shares in corporations would not be regarded as legitimate by many citizens. Therefore, we conclude that economic welfare should always be preserved as corporate policies focus on maximizing (or increasing) shareholder wealth. This is not the same as concluding that corporations should pursue policies that advance social welfare at the expense of shareholders. Corporations are not charities and their viability would be jeopardized if they acted like charities. However, retarding social welfare in the interests of shareholders is not appropriate.

This conclusion allows us to offer a general statement of what we believe corporations should strive to achieve: the objective of the firm should be to "maximize" the wealth of corporate shareholders without making any other stakeholders worse off. In other words, they should strive for social welfare improvements (as expanded on below) with shareholders being the primary beneficiaries and other stakeholders either benefitting or, at minimum, being held harmless. Nonetheless, corporate profitability leading to high shareholder returns and social welfare gains can be achieved (albeit not optimized) simultaneously. The next section expands on this conclusion.

Achieving Shareholder Wealth and Social Welfare Simultaneously

Rather than reinvent the wheel, we adopt as premises a number of conclusions drawn from recent contributions to the literature as well as a few assumptions that seem noncontroversial. Many of these premises are derived from the introduction to a recent Special Topic Forum on Management

Theory and Social Welfare in the *Academy of Management Review* that addressed the issue of improving social welfare in the context of profit-seeking corporations (Jones et al., 2016). We aim to modify and expand on this recent treatise on the topic of social welfare in a profit-driven economy in which shareholder returns still persist as a predominant objective. As such, our analysis is built on the following already established foundation:

1) Stakeholder theory, with its fundamental normative principle that the interests of all corporate stakeholders have intrinsic value, is essential to our analysis. Employing stakeholder analysis has the side benefit of obviating a discussion of negative externalities. Those negatively affected by corporate actions *are* stakeholders (Freeman, 1984) and the negative effects are incorporated into the stakeholder analysis.

2) Social welfare is defined broadly as "the well-being of a society as a whole, encompassing economic, social, physical, and spiritual health" (Jones, et al., 2016: 220). Importantly, stability and justice, in addition to efficiency, are elements of economic welfare (Marti & Scherer, 2016).

3) "In theory, there is an array of net benefits – benefits less costs for each individual – that is socially optimal" (Jones, et al., 2016: 221). However, the achievement of such an optimum is all but impossible for two reasons: (a) the economic dimensions of this calculus alone are beyond our cognitive capacity, especially in a dynamic economy; and (b) although the non-economic dimensions of social welfare are certainly legitimate concerns, the metrics employed to measure them are incommensurable with each other as well as with economic measures.

4) Therefore, we cannot optimize social welfare, but we can employ a criterion that can be definitively tied to a particular form of welfare improvements. From the welfare economics literature, Pareto improvements – wherein someone is made better off without making anyone else worse off – emerge as a credible

standard for assuring that social welfare improves as corporations pursue profits so as to increase shareholder returns. Indeed, the Pareto criterion can be applied to the non-economic facets of social welfare as well as to the economic facets, rendering the incommensurability of measures far less problematic (Jones, et al., 2016). Therefore, one route to unambiguous social welfare improvements for profit seeking corporations is decisions that increase profits without harming any of the firm's stakeholders.

5) Outcomes for which no stakeholder group is made worse off, however, probably make up a small proportion of corporate decisions. To consider a much more extensive range of corporate policy decisions, we must consider tradeoffs, making sure that social welfare is assured in the process.

6) Kaldor (1939) proposed that since tradeoffs, with winners *and losers*, were often necessary in policy decisions, social welfare could still be improved if it was possible (in theory) for the winners to compensate the losers without exhausting their gains. Jones and colleagues (2016) point out that, while the Kaldor criterion does indeed meet the utilitarian standard of a net gain in social welfare, it fails any reasonable standard of distributive justice (because no actual compensation is paid) and procedural justice (because the losses are not voluntarily accepted). Nonetheless, this position requires further elaboration, as does a supplement to Kaldor's position provided by Hicks (1939).

We now turn to a more detailed analysis of the three options alleged to enhance social welfare – Pareto improvements, Kaldor improvements, and Hicks improvements – including an approach mentioned by Jones and colleagues (2016) as "an intriguing line of inquiry for future exploration" (2016: 225) – *Kaldor improvements with compensation*. In this analysis, we elaborate on two considerations – surplus transfers and "tragedy of the commons" problems – that we believe are essential to understanding the relationship between the corporate quest for profits and social welfare. Based on the following analysis, we propose/defend a new corporate objective that meets important criteria for social welfare improvement.

Social Welfare According to Pareto, Kaldor, and Hicks

Pareto Improvements

As noted above, the term Pareto improvements applies to exchanges wherein one (or more) parties is (are) made better off without making any other party (parties) worse off. Because one party's gain does not involve another party's loss, there is always a net gain, resulting in unambiguous improvements in social welfare. As outlined by Jones and colleagues (2016), and with reference to Figure 5.1a, firms have three ways of increasing profits. They can: (1) increase/reduce price while holding economic value and input costs constant; (2) increase economic value and price while holding input costs constant; or (3) reduce input costs while holding economic value and prices constant.[8]

Surplus Transfers

Under condition set 1, although the price/quantity relationship of its product may allow a firm to increase its profits either by increasing or decreasing its prices, price increases will result only in surplus transfers (Shleifer & Summers, 1990), thus apparently failing the Pareto test.[9] Under condition set 2, raising prices more than the incremental economic value added also results only in surplus transfers from customers to the producer, another apparent failure of the Pareto test. Under condition set 3, if the firm, using market power made possible by disequilibrium conditions, forces price reductions on its suppliers or appropriates more than the incremental surplus generated by production efficiencies or transaction costs efficiencies, it will only be transferring surplus value from its suppliers to itself, another apparent Pareto test failure. If, however, firms avoid these practices in their quest for greater profits, the Pareto criterion for social welfare will be met. In other words, increasing profits to benefit shareholders and enhancing social welfare simultaneously is

a highly contingent enterprise: *how* a firm generates additional profits matters a great deal with respect to enhancing social welfare.

A few examples of Pareto improvements should help illustrate our points. Firms that develop new products/services or improve existing products/services and appropriate no more than the incremental surplus meet the Pareto improvement standard. In addition, Priem (2007) highlights ways that firms can grow the "top line." As long as the firm raises prices no more than the incremental value added, social welfare will be improved. Pareto improvements can also be achieved by firms with market power reducing their prices, as described above, thus increasing the consumer surplus of existing customers and adding new customers. Assuming that the price reduction actually improves the firm's profits, Pareto improvements accrue. Similarly, reductions in input costs that result from transaction costs efficiencies can result in Pareto improvements as long as the focal firm does not appropriate more than the savings created. Because Pareto improvements unambiguously enhance social welfare, they are a desirable element in our modified corporate objective.

Kaldor Improvements

Since Pareto improvements are unlikely to be possible over a large range of potential corporate decisions, we must consider situations in which cost/benefit tradeoffs are required. If the "winners" can (in theory) compensate the "losers" for their losses and remain "winners," a Kaldor improvement in social welfare can be made. In the preceding discussion, we were careful to use the term *surplus* rather than *wealth* and add the adjective *apparent* because, as we consider Kaldor improvements, the choice of wording is important and substantial. Surpluses transferred between non-shareholder stakeholders are transferred on a roughly one-to-one basis. A price concession extracted from a supplier and passed in its entirety on to customers in the form of reduced prices results in no net change in total surpluses. However, when *producer* surpluses are involved in the transfer, those surpluses are translated into shareholder wealth at a rate roughly equal to the price/earnings ratio that the firm's stock commands on the stock market. Using the very conservative 10–1 ratio suggested by Jones and colleagues (2016), $1 of surplus transferred from, say, employees to the producer (the firm) results in a roughly $10 increase in shareholder wealth.[10] Thus, a firm that shifts $1 million of health care costs from the company to its employees could expect to realize roughly $10 million in increased market value. Therefore, in many cases, surplus transfers from non-shareholder stakeholders do indeed increase aggregate wealth, a Kaldor improvement in social (economic) welfare, at least in the short run.

In spite of the apparent improvements in aggregate welfare from Kaldor improvements, the actual wealth reduction for employees will probably extend beyond one year and the actual aggregate wealth created over the longer term will be a function of not only the expected duration of the benefit reduction, but also the P/E ratio of the firm. For companies with low P/E ratios, the wealth lost by employees could exceed the wealth gained by shareholders in a few years, resulting in an aggregate wealth reduction and a violation of our rule that aggregate wealth should never be destroyed. Thus, social welfare improvements resulting from corporate profit seeking, while virtually certain in the short run, are highly contingent over longer time periods.

Another threat to longer-term social welfare enhancement is discussed in detail below.

It appears that, through applications of the aggregate wealth creation criterion in the short run, corporations would be justified in cutting (ideally *minimizing*) their costs in any number of ways – e.g., eliminating not only "extraneous" employees, but also the benefits of remaining employees (vacations, retirement plans, sick leave, day care services, subsidized cafeterias, and health care insurance, etc.) as well as cutting wages until employee attrition becomes too costly. Cost savings involving other stakeholders could result in cutting supplier prices to the bone, reducing customer service as far as market forces would allow, forcing local governments to reduce taxes under threat of moving to another locale, eliminating community involvement programs, and so on. In other words, a corporate objective of shareholder wealth maximization could be justified, in Kaldor improvement terms, to force payments to these stakeholders down to their reservation prices (see Figure 5.1b).[11] In aggregate economic welfare terms, policies that convert non-shareholder stakeholder wealth to shareholder wealth would almost always result in net welfare gains in the short run – gains to shareholders routinely exceeding losses to other stakeholders – thereby meeting a utilitarian

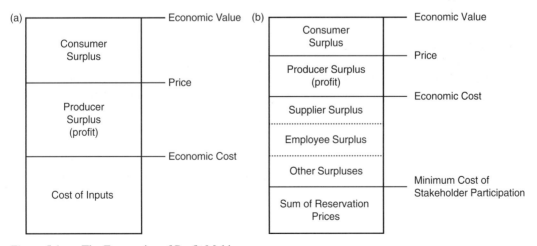

Figure 5.1a – The Economics of Profit Making
Figure 5.1b – The Components of Economic Value

(aggregate social welfare) ethical standard as well.

Under this decision criterion, aggregate economic wealth would certainly be increased in the short run, but with non-shareholder stakeholders consistently sacrificing wealth in favor of (greater) wealth for shareholders, the economic sustainability of the system as a whole is called into question. At the firm level, Ghemawat and Costa (1993) make a similar distinction between *static efficiency* and *dynamic efficiency,* where static efficiency refers to earning the greatest profit possible in the short term, while dynamic efficiency involves positioning the firm to produce and sell competitive products/services into the foreseeable future.

In addition, while the wealth transfers associated with the pursuit of profit maximization could increase (static) efficiency – i.e., Kaldor improvements – in the economy very substantially, they would fail our expanded Pareto test because of substantial increases in income/wealth inequality – i.e., a setback for distributive justice. Of course, the coercive aspects of transfers of this type would remain.

In fact, the economic history of the USA over many years is highly consistent with an analysis based on Kaldor improvements. Aggregate income and wealth seem to grow at consistent, if not always spectacular, rates even as income and wealth grow ever-more concentrated in the hands of a small proportion of the population. Simply put, the country keeps getting collectively richer, but also more and more unequal (Piketty, 2013). Furthermore, if this means of improving aggregate social welfare continues into the future, the USA could see income/wealth disparities even greater than those currently observed. However, as we argue in the next section, a regime of Kaldor improvements could present an even greater threat in the long term.

A "Tragedy of the Commons" Economy?

Originally associated with the grazing of cattle on commonly owned pastures, the "tragedy of the commons" has come to represent situations in which firms, acting rationally in their self-interest, can severely deplete resources held in common, sometimes to the point of economic ruin for firms in a particular market.[12] The frequently used example of fishing grounds makes this point quite clear. For a given fishery, the best way for an individual boat owner to maximize his/her profits is to maximize his/her catch; catching as many fish as possible in the shortest possible time maximizes the profits of the individual boat. For the fishery as a whole, however, this strategy, if employed by all boats, can lead to disaster. Left unchecked, this strategy will deplete the stock of fish, perhaps totally, and all boats will be out of business. Even if some boats drop out of the market, the incentives will remain the same for the remaining boats. Furthermore, when the price of fish rises with declining catches, the incentive to catch more fish merely grows larger. Examples on a larger scale include environmental pollution and global climate change. In all cases of the tragedy of the commons, the pursuit of maximum profits by individual firms creates wealth and expands social welfare only in the short term. How does this parable apply to social welfare under a regime of Kaldor improvements?

Applying the Kaldor criterion, corporations create greater net wealth by increasing shareholder wealth – i.e., rising share prices – at the expense of the wealth of other stakeholders. Absent other changes, non-shareholder stakeholders would become less and less prosperous.[13] While an increasing concentration of wealth is normally not a concern in a utilitarian (aggregate social welfare) moral logic, it can become a significant concern over the long term due to a dynamic analogous to the tragedy of the commons.

This analogy makes sense if one thinks of the consuming (buying) power of the population as "the commons." That is, the ability and willingness of people to consume the output of economic producers is a resource available to all producers and, like many resources, it can be depleted and, in extreme cases, nearly destroyed. Importantly, this consuming power is essential to the perpetuation of a healthy market economy since about 70 percent of the US gross domestic product is consumer spending. To be sure, those becoming increasingly wealthy are also consumers, but they *invest* a far greater proportion of their income/wealth than do those less well off. And, of course, the wealthy make up a small proportion of the total population.

The "tragedy" is that individual firms, acting in an economically rational manner – i.e., maximizing profits – will implement decisions that marginally diminish the buying power of large segments of the population. If the wealth of non-shareholder stakeholders is regularly being transferred to shareholders, these stakeholders, *as consumers*, become less able to purchase the output of the corporate sector. If employees earn less, pay for their own insurance, pensions, and other benefits, and become less numerous; if suppliers operate increasingly marginal businesses (and, presumably, drive down the wages paid to their employees and prices paid to their suppliers); if customers pay higher prices and experience reduced customer service; if local governments increasingly are unable to provide and maintain infrastructure (as firms are given tax breaks); and if companies become increasingly separated from the communities in which they operate, then the continuing pursuit of shareholder prosperity is likely to be unsustainable. Collectively, there is a potential for shrinking markets for many products and a downward spiral in the economy as a whole. In other words, a *tragedy of the commons economy* could emerge.[14] In short, an ongoing quest for Kaldor improvements as the criterion for enhanced social welfare could be disastrous for social welfare in the longer term.[15]

Kant's Universalizability Criterion

Although our analysis thus far has been couched in terms of social welfare (i.e., a utilitarian approach), which stresses an optimal balance of favorable and unfavorable consequences, we recognize that elements of deontological ethics are relevant as well. According to the deontological perspective, certain moral principles are morally binding regardless of the consequences that may result. More specifically, Kant's notion of universalizability comes into play. Universalizability means that, in order for a principle to be morally binding, it must be acceptable for everyone to adopt it; in simpler terms, no one should be able to play by their own

moral rules. A classic application of universalizability involves promises. Although it sometimes becomes expedient for an agent to renege on a promise, the moral acceptability of doing so rests on whether reneging on promises would be acceptable for everyone who could benefit from doing so. However, if everyone were to regard the commitments that underlie promises as binding only if honoring them were in the promisor's interests, the concept of promises would cease to have any meaning and their value in human interactions would be virtually nil.

With respect to our "tragedy of the commons economy" analogy, universalizability applies when an individual firm marginally reduces the consuming power of the populace by transferring wealth from non-shareholder stakeholders to shareholders by, for example, cutting health care benefits to employees or extracting price concessions from suppliers. In our example, total wealth almost certainly increases in the short run because shareholder wealth increases at (about) 10 times the rate that stakeholder wealth (surplus) decreases. However, if it were morally acceptable for *all firms* to transfer wealth from non-shareholder stakeholders to shareholders, theoretically reaching the reservation prices of stakeholders, the consuming power of the economy as a whole would collapse – a "tragedy of the commons" outcome. Thus, although wealth transfers from non-shareholder stakeholders to shareholders are acceptable under the Kaldor improvement criterion, they would be prohibited under Kant's universalizability criterion.

Regardless of the perspective one takes, an economy operating under criteria that allow profit maximizing wealth transfers from non-shareholder stakeholders to shareholders could lead to a near-Hobbesian world in which life for many people could be "solitary, poore, nasty, brutish, and short." On the other hand, an economy populated with firms: (1) striving for *dynamic* efficiency; (2) trying to avoid an economic tragedy of the commons; and (3) concerned about the universalizability of their actions, should be able to maintain a high level of economic/social welfare, the ultimate end of economic systems founded on utilitarian principles.

Although negative externalities are largely subsumed under "harms to non-shareholder stakeholders" in our analysis, the use of some common resources is inevitable in most economic activities. Given this situation, we note that many "tragedy of the commons" problems cannot be solved by individual firms; they almost always require allocation decisions made by political entities. Under such circumstances, firms can make Pareto or Kaldor improvements by drawing on the common resource – e.g., fishing grounds, acceptably clean air or water, the earth's ability to dissipate heat – only to the extent permitted by public policy.

The apparent magnitude of the efficiency gains through applications of the Kaldor criterion for social welfare enhancement suggest not only a major problem with profit seeking by corporations under these conditions, as discussed in the previous section, but also a plausible solution. We now address this possible solution.

Hicks Improvements

Jones and colleagues (2016) mention an addendum to Kaldor's insight by Hicks (1939) – in situations requiring tradeoffs, social welfare gains can also be assured if the potential losers could (in theory) pay the focal decision-maker not to proceed with the proposed action. However, as in the case of Kaldor improvements, no actual payments were contemplated, so the distributive aspects of the Hicks addendum are clearly negative. Potential losers are still losers and, even though net social welfare in efficiency terms may be improved, our expanded Pareto criterion is not met. Efficiency is enhanced at the expense of distributive justice. Also, the coercion of losers violates our sense of procedural justice. Indeed, given the relationship between shareholder wealth increases and non-shareholder stakeholder surplus decreases, the Hicks criterion becomes absurd. Shareholders would (in theory) demand payments based on the potential increase in the value of their stock at our assumed 10 to 1 ratio to the potential losses of non-shareholder stakeholders, such payments would be irrational in the extreme, not to mention unaffordable to many of these potential "losers." Thus, any application of the Hicks addendum in the context of

shareholder/non-shareholder stakeholder tradeoffs is a nonstarter, regardless of whether it would lead to greater aggregate economic wealth.

A Modified Corporate Objective

Given the analysis of the preceding sections, the central question becomes: what corporate objective would best serve to enhance social welfare? Recall that we are asking our version of IST to be instrumental in two ways. We seek to find ethically appropriate means of: (1) helping firms achieve improved profitability so as to provide high shareholder returns; and (2) simultaneously enhance social welfare through their economic activities. In other words, we seek means of achieving sustainable wealth creation. We premise our discussion of alternative corporate objectives on three fundamental principles. First, aggregate wealth must never be destroyed in the "wealth creation" process; profit should not be pursued in cases where social/economic welfare, including effects on all corporate stakeholders, is reduced. Second, the baseline condition for comparison purposes must be the set of existing entitlements of current normatively legitimate stakeholders of the firm.[16] While this principle is bound to be controversial, we know of no other way to avoid advocating a truly massive and disruptive (and hence unrealistic) redistribution of wealth in society.[17] These existing entitlements include jobs, employee benefits, contracts with suppliers and customers, debt covenants, commitments to communities, etc. Third, the profit motive must be retained. The economic incentive provided to those who seek to gain from the creation of new wealth should not be replaced.

These three premises suggest that an appropriate corporate objective is that the firm should increase the wealth of its shareholders without reducing (and presumably increasing) the aggregate wealth of its other stakeholder groups. One means of achieving this objective is through seeking improved profitability by making Pareto improvements, an approach examined in adequate detail in the previous section. In addition, based on the previous analysis, we reject the conclusion that companies should *always* make profit-enhancing tradeoffs because they enhance economic welfare in the short run. Instead, we argue that firms should do so only if they *actually* compensate stakeholders for their losses.

Kaldor Improvements with Compensation

Based on the discussion in the previous section, we propose that *actual* compensation be paid to stakeholders harmed by policies intended to increase shareholder wealth, a position we call *Kaldor improvements with compensation*. Actual compensation would assure that wealth is not destroyed in the "wealth creation" process. If those harmed by corporate policies are actually compensated for their losses – i.e., "made whole" – and if profits increase anyway, we can be assured that utilitarian (social/economic welfare) ends are served.

Given the substantial difference between shareholder gains ($10 million, in our example) and the annual losses of other stakeholders ($1 million), it would seem an easy task to compensate stakeholders for their losses. However, although firms have some control over decisions regarding the allocation of surpluses between the company (producer surplus) and, for example, employees (employee surplus), once improved earnings are reported, the gains are no longer within the control of company executives; that is, share values may have increased, but the shares belong to the shareholders. What can be done?

One solution is to compensate stakeholders who are harmed by shareholder wealth maximizing policies *with company stock* to mitigate their losses. In theory, these stakeholders should be given stock *equivalent* to their losses, but since these losses often cannot easily be determined, we use the term *mitigate*. However, with P/E ratios historically around 15 and currently around 25, firms should have the resources – in shareholder equity – to substantially ease the pain of stakeholder losses. To extend our example, employees who, in total, suffered annual losses of $1 million in company-paid insurance premiums could be given company stock with a value equivalent to a year or two of their losses without seriously undermining the gains of shareholders.[18] In other

words, those harmed by wealth tradeoffs made at a ratio of 1/1 (producer surplus/employee surplus) could be compensated for their losses at a wealth ratio of 10/1 (in our example), resulting in a net gain in social/economic welfare and, by extension, a policy acceptable by utilitarian (Pareto or Kaldor) standards.

To be sure, the aggregate value of shareholder wealth increases would be diluted by the number of shares given to employees in compensation for their losses and, in some cases, additional shares would have to be issued, but the effects of this dilution would, in most cases, be modest in comparison to share price gains. In other words, shareholders would be required to give up some gains made at the expense of other stakeholders, but the amounts they would be required to give up are subject to the share price/employee surplus ratio (10/1) rather than the producer surplus/employee surplus ratio (1/1). In this way, shareholder wealth can be increased without harming other stakeholders, in accordance with the standards of Pareto improvements in social welfare. Furthermore, because the tragedy of the commons can be mitigated in this way, the application of Kaldor improvements with compensation paid *in company stock* to stakeholders harmed by profit-enhancing corporate actions will allow the resulting wealth creation to be much more sustainable.

The Social Welfare Proposal Summarized

A detailed summary of the Pareto Improvements, Kaldor Improvements, and Kaldor Improvements with Compensation decision criteria is presented in Table 5.1.

Table 5.1 clarifies the meaning of our stated corporate objective in more specific terms. First, policies that cause shareholder wealth to decline (Column C) are never appropriate, regardless of their effect on aggregate economic welfare. The quest for profits motivates corporate behavior and we see no reason to advocate financially irrational policies, especially since they fail the Pareto improvement criterion. Nor do we advocate corporate engagement in "socially responsible" practices that are purely altruistic (Cell C1) since they fail not only the Pareto criterion but, assuming P/E

Table 5.1 Wealth Effects on Shareholders vs. Wealth Effects on Other Stakeholders

Wealth effects on other stakeholders	Wealth effect on shareholders		
	A – Increase	B – Neutral	C – Decrease
1 – **Increase**	Desirable policies	Beneficent policies (not required)	Irrational policies
2 – **Neutral**	Desirable policies (Pareto improvement)	Status quo	Irrational policies
3 – **Decrease**	Policies acceptable only under conditions described herein (Kaldor improvement with compensation)	Vindictive policies (irrational)	Irrational policies

ratios greater than 1, the Kaldor test as well. Second, policies with no effect on shareholder wealth (Column B) are never required, but could be adopted in the interest of beneficence, the moral principle that commends acts that benefit others at no (or little) cost to the agent. Finally, and most relevant to our analysis, policies that increase shareholder wealth (Column A) are desirable/acceptable according to more detailed criteria.

Cell 1A represents ideal policies, those likely to elicit little argument. Shareholder wealth, as well as the wealth of other stakeholders, is increased. Cell 2A also represents desirable policies, those that enhance shareholder wealth without decreasing the wealth of other stakeholders. These policies meet the Pareto criterion and have clear positive economic welfare implications. Cell 3A represents situations in which shareholder wealth is increased at the expense of other stakeholders and are described above under "Kaldor Improvements with Compensation." As long as corporate actions/policies meet one of the requirements of Column A (or B1), social welfare will rise as corporations seek increased profits.

Institutional Accommodations

Although the adoption of a sustainable wealth creation standard for managers would involve some significant changes in the way that corporations are governed, there seem to be few formal institutional barriers to the changes that we propose. First,

as Stout (2012) and others have made abundantly clear, the existing law of corporations could accommodate such changes. Although corporate directors owe duties of loyalty and care to the corporation, nothing requires them to regard maximizing the wealth of shareholders as their only responsibility. Indeed, the *business judgment rule,* wherein courts defer to the judgment of those with expertise in business, grants corporate boards a great deal of latitude in terms of what they consider to be the best interests of the firm. Stout sums up her analysis by stating that "American corporate law [. . .] fiercely protects directors' power to sacrifice shareholder value in the pursuit of other corporate goals" (2012: 32). Nonetheless, because appropriate business judgment is determined by courts, the resulting uncertainty causes many boards to err on the side of shareholder interests to avoid litigation (Cormac & Haney, 2012). In addition, the pressure from financial markets to produce impressive quarterly returns keeps profitability front and center in the minds of corporate managers and directors (Cormac & Haney, 2012; Reiser, 2011).

Another legal mechanism that could potentially serve to support sustainable wealth creation is the existence of *other constituency* or *stakeholder* statutes in several states. These laws, which allow, but do not require, corporate managers and directors to take the interests of non-shareholder stakeholders into account in their deliberations, are now on the books in a majority of states. On the surface, these statutes seem to acknowledge the legitimacy of stakeholder interests in corporate decision-making. However, a closer look reveals another motive. Most of these statutes were passed in the midst of a wave of takeover attempts – actual and threatened – that would involve substantial layoffs of employees of target firms. The new statutes allowed corporate officers to actively resist such takeovers, which would clearly benefit share-holders, under the banner of protecting employee interests. While deterring the layoff of local job-holders is certainly a noble goal, the protection provided for incumbent managers, who would pre-sumably be replaced after a takeover, cannot be ignored. Indeed, a number of states specifically allow the consideration of stakeholder interests *only* in the event of a potential "change of control," strongly suggesting that the second motive domi-nated the first in the passage of many stakeholder statutes. Reiser has gone so far as to call these statutes "anti-takeover legislation" (2011: 599). Regardless of their intent, stakeholder laws clearly give corporate managers and directors additional latitude with respect to their pursuit of values other than shareholder wealth maximization.

Nonetheless, public policy makers seem to have anticipated changes of the general nature of our proposal in the very recent past. More specifically, several states, beginning with Maryland in 2010, have passed *benefit corporation* statutes that, in addition to generating profit for shareholders, require firms to provide a general benefit to society (Reiser, 2011). Although statutory provisions vary from state to state, they have some common fea-tures that would facilitate the establishment of firms devoted to sustainable wealth creation. First, dual missions are required. Firms must pro-vide a material, positive benefit (general or speci-fic) for society along with profits for shareholders. Second, they impose fiduciary duties on directors to include the interests of non-shareholder stakeholders, in addition to those of shareholders, in their decision-making processes.[19] Third, they stress accountability by requiring reporting of the firm's social and/or environmental performance to an independent third party.

Benefit corporation statutes also eliminate the threat of lawsuits based on conventional, single-purpose views of the corporate objective – i.e., profit maximization. Therefore, benefit corpora-tions should be able to pursue their social mis-sions without the institutional restrictions that inspire other firms to focus exclusively on the bottom line. In addition, the formal designation "benefit corporation" should allow firms that truly have a social mission to distinguish themselves from conventionally chartered firms that wrap themselves in the cloak of social or environmental responsibility even as they continue their exclu-sive pursuit of profit. Put differently, the designa-tion "benefit corporation" should help interested parties – customers, employees, etc. – to separate rhetoric from reality (Reiser, 2011). To sum up, while this part of our chapter attempts to create a compelling normative case for sustainable wealth creation, a growing number of states have created institutional mechanisms through which this form of wealth creation could gain a practical foothold.

An Agenda for Future Research

A proposal as broad and as foundational as the one presented here necessarily leaves a significant num-ber of questions unanswered and, as a result, leaves the underlying normative theory vulnerable to claims that it is underdeveloped. However, it would be counterproductive to judge a new normative theory negatively because it fails to meet the standards of development and refinement set by a theory that has been subjected to over 230 years of scrutiny, devel-opment, and refinement – i.e., since Adam Smith's *Wealth of Nations* (1776) – and still leaves some questions unanswered – e.g., unequal distributions of income and wealth; externalities. Therefore, in the interest of beginning a scholarly discussion of these issues, we offer a short list of general questions to start the conversation.

1) If stakeholders harmed by shareholder wealth-enhancing corporate actions are to be compen-sated, a definitive list of eligible stakeholders will need to be established. For example, should governmental units be compensated for lost tax

revenues when terminated employees are no longer paying taxes? A discussion of this issue could begin with the definition of *normatively legitimate* stakeholders articulated by Phillips (2003).

2) If stakeholders harmed by profit-enhancing corporate actions are to be compensated for their losses in corporate shares, how much stock should they receive? In the case of terminated employees, shares worth a lifetime's wages would clearly be too much, while shares equivalent to a two-week severance package would be too little. Key considerations in such a calculation would involve fairness, perhaps based on years of service, the market for the employees' services, incentives to return to the workforce sooner rather than later, and the effect on the consuming/buying power of the economy as a whole.

3) How should stakeholders whose wealth *per se* is not reduced but whose well-being is harmed – e.g., surviving employees who have to absorb the work of their terminated former co-workers – be compensated?

4) How are critical lines to be drawn between situations that warrant compensation and those that do not? For example, sometimes the survival of a firm will depend on the layoff of a significant number of employees while at other times a layoff of similar magnitude will be undertaken simply to make the firm "lean and mean." In the former case, compensation would make little sense while in the latter case it would. But, given that there will be cases in between these two extremes, where should the line be drawn?

We have no illusions about the difficulties involved in answering these and related questions. However, human beings and the institutions that surround them are capable of substantially improving the quality of their decisions, even those with no clear guidelines, over time. In particular, we have faith in the ability of talented managers and scholars to come up with increasingly workable solutions given appropriate incentives to do so. The alternative is to continue to allow the harms done in the pursuit of corporate profits to be borne entirely by non-shareholder stakeholders, with all the negative distributive effects

associated with that outcome, and to risk the emergence of a "tragedy of the commons" situation within the economy as a whole.

Summary and Conclusions

This chapter began with a brief examination of, and empirical support for, IST as originally envisioned. We found that there is strong reason to believe that companies that practice management based on IST principles, on average, can also enhance their profit performance, thus satisfying the widely accepted notion that enhancing profit performance to increase shareholder returns is one of the most important (some would say *the* most important) objectives of a corporate manager. We then enlarged the discussion to consider the domain of social welfare in general, arguing that there is an important point of tension between objectives within modern market capitalism, and that management scholars should recognize it and address it in a direct way. One objective – corporate profit maximization to increase shareholder returns – is not always compatible with the other – wealth creation at the societal level – a foundational objective of economic activity in general. The continuing quest by strategy scholars to identify practices that result in sustainable competitive advantage so as to maximize shareholder returns will sometimes, but not always, result in social welfare increases. Scholars who engage in sustainable competitive advantage research should also assess the sustainability of the practice in question for the economy as a whole if all firms engaged in similar practices. The goal of integrating social welfare concerns into our research agendas was advocated by Walsh, et al. (2003) over a decade ago. These authors, after providing evidence that "performance and welfare work at the societal level of analysis seems to be the least appreciated work of all" in the management literature, suggest that it is time to "rekindle the debate about the purposes of the firm and about the place of the corporation in society" (862; 877).

Unfortunately, a distressingly large number of corporate managers seem to pursue greater corporate financial performance without regard for harm done to stakeholders other than shareholders. This chapter is also a call for strategy scholars to engage in research that carefully discriminates between corporate policies that result in actual wealth creation and those that result only in wealth transfers, encouraging managers to avoid the latter *unless* the losses of non-shareholder stakeholders are appropriately compensated. The development of methods of determining appropriate compensation for such losses should also be on the agenda. The proposed changes in the corporate objective represent the *direct* creation of economic wealth with respect to discrete decisions, as advocated by Quinn and Jones (1995), rather than reliance on the assumption that increasing the wealth of shareholders alone will unerringly enhance social/economic welfare over time.

To some extent, the two strategy research agendas – traditional and proposed – will overlap; there are certainly shareholder wealth enhancing policies that do not harm, and may help, other stakeholders (e.g., Jones, et al., 2018). Indeed, as demonstrated by the research examined in the first section of this paper, there is substantial evidence that firms that manage for stakeholders also have high profits leading to increased shareholder wealth. However, there are several categories of policies that result in gains for shareholders but also losses for other stakeholders, and we must be assured that the losses incurred by these other stakeholders are substantially mitigated in order to keep the economy sustainable. Managers should also be attuned to this new agenda. If they take the broad wealth creation charter of business seriously, they must take the wealth of all their stakeholders into account.

Notes

1. Parts of this chapter are drawn from an unpublished manuscript by Thomas M. Jones and R. Edward Freeman. Gary Weaver provided useful comments on this unpublished manuscript.
2. The protection of property rights, the meeting of contractual obligations, and the advancement of economic freedom have also been offered as elements of the moral grounding of the market capitalist system in which profit maximization is a prominent part.
3. Strategic management scholars have instead focused on identifying sources of *sustainable competitive advantage*.
4. Smith, a moral philosopher as well as an economic thinker, recognized the importance of limits to the quest for profit as well as the centrality of moral concepts such as justice. Nonetheless, extensions of the logic of the invisible hand have been used to justify profit maximization.
5. Although market value can be increased by means other than increased profits – e.g., changes in capital structure – increasing profit is the primary means of increasing firm value. Furthermore, we focus on profit *maximization*, rather than profit seeking, because it reflects the contemporary view of the purpose of the corporation as well as reflecting a reasonable approximation of the behavioral intentions of many managers.
6. Two prominent strategic management scholars recognize the importance of social welfare in competitive markets. According to Peteraf and Barney, sustainable competitive advantage involves creating "more economic value than the marginal (breakeven) competitor in its product market," where economic value can "enhance the welfare of all of its [the firm's] stakeholders" (2003: 314).
7. We recognize that social welfare and economic welfare are not identical concepts. However, since strategy scholarship is concerned with economic value and since differentiating between the two concepts would needlessly complicate the analysis, we do not address the issue in this paper. We focus on the economic welfare of society as a whole.
8. The following analysis is based on the assumption that relevant markets are not in equilibrium. That is, firms are not price takers; they have the power to raise/lower their prices, presumably to increase profits and depending on the price/quantity relationship for their products/services.
9. We realize that price reductions can increase sales volume, thus leading to higher total producer surplus; however, for simplicity we make the assumption that volume remains constant. A more complete analysis with supply and demand curves results in the same conclusion, but requires a highly detailed discussion that space requirements preclude.

10. P/E ratios for S & P listed firms averaged over 15 over several decades up to the present. As of February 6, 2017, the average P/E ratio was over 25 and soared to over 123 in May of 2009 (multpl.com/shiller-pe/ – downloaded February 6, 2017).
11. Reservation prices are either the highest price a buyer is willing to pay or the lowest price a seller is willing to accept for a good or service. Since voluntary exchanges virtually always involve prices between these limits, both the buyer and the seller receive surplus value and social welfare is increased. However, corporate profit-seeking policies are rarely voluntary. Those that reduce a seller's reservation price or increase a buyer's reservation price create wealth. Conversely, profit-enhancing actions that move either a seller or a buyer closer to its reservation price do not create wealth, but merely transfer wealth from non-shareholder stakeholders to shareholders. Increased profits and aggregate wealth need not rise and fall together; either can move up or down with changes – positive or negative – in the other.
12. Some scholars regard the tragedy of the commons to be an extension of the problem of externalities. While we are agnostic on this issue, we feel that the tragedy of the commons perspective deserves separate treatment.
13. For the purposes of simplification and as a concession to current U.S. political realities, we do not consider the possibility of massive governmental transfer payments intended to correct any of the resulting imbalances discussed below.
14. Some commentators would argue that this process is already well underway (e.g., Hartman, 2006; Smith, 2012). The distributions of income and wealth in the United States have become increasingly unequal in recent decades. While the upper reaches of the income spectrum have improved their economic lot substantially in recent decades, and the poor have remained poor, the middle class – mostly employees and former employees of corporations – has suffered significant losses and, at least statistically, has shrunk substantially.
15. Despite some similarities, this is not a Marxian analysis. Our focus is on the declining buying power of *all* non-shareholder stakeholders, not the exploitation of the working class.
16. See Phillips (2003) for a definitive discussion of normative (and derivative) legitimacy.
17. Our use of this principle is not without precedent. In his classic work on distributive justice, *Anarchy, State, and Utopia* (TS Please link.), Robert Nozick is unable to deal with the effects of historical injustice in a satisfactory manner.
18. Presumably, the tax effects of this compensation plan would be taken into account as well.
19. References to shareholders, employees, customers, suppliers, communities, and the environment are common in these statutes.

References

Agle, B. R., Mitchell, R. K., & Sonnenfeld, J. A. (1999). Who matters to CEOs? An investigation of stakeholder attributes and salience, corporate performance, and CEO values. *Academy of Management Journal*, 42(5): 507–525.
Alchian, A. A. & Demsetz, H. (1972). Production, information costs, and economic organization. *The American Management Review*, 62, 777–795.
Barney, J. (1991). Firm resources and sustained competitive advantage. *Journal of Management*, 17(1): 99–118.
Bentham, J. (1823/1907). *Introduction to the Principles of Morals and Legislation*, (2nd edn.) Oxford: Clarendon Press.
Berle, A. A. & Means, G. C. (1932). *The Modern Corporation and Private Property*. New York: Macmillan.
Berman, S. L., Wicks, A. C., Kotha, S., & Jones, T. M. (1999). Does stakeholder orientation matter? The relationship between stakeholder management models and firm financial performance. *Academy of Management Journal*, 42(5): 488–506.
Bosse, D. A., Phillips, R. A., & Harrison, J. S. (2009). Stakeholders, reciprocity and firm performance. *Strategic Management Journal*, 30: 447–456.
Bridoux, F., & Stoelhorst, J.-W. (2014). Microfoundations for stakeholder theory: Managing stakeholders with heterogeneous motives. *Strategic Management Journal*, 35: 107–125.
Bridoux, F., & Stoelhorst, J.-W. (2016). Stakeholder relationships and social welfare: A behavioral theory of contributions to joint value creation. *Academy of Management Review*, 41(2): 229–251.
Choi, J., & Wang, H. (2009). Stakeholder relations and the persistence of corporate financial

performance. *Strategic Management Journal, 30*(8): 895–907.

Cording, M., Harrison, J. S., Hoskisson, R. E., & Jonsen, K. (2014). Walking the talk: A multi-stakeholder exploration of organizational authenticity, employee productivity and post-merger performance. *Academy of Management Perspectives*, 28(1): 38–56.

Cornell, B., & Shapiro, A. C. (1987). Corporate stakeholders and corporate finance. *Financial Management*, 16(1): 5–14.

Cormac, S. M. & Haney, H. (2012). New corporate forms: One viable solution to advancing environmental sustainability. *Journal of Applied Corporate Finance*, 24(2): 49–56.

Donaldson, T., & Preston, L. E. (1995). The stakeholder theory of the corporation: Concepts, evidence, and implications. *Academy of Management Review*, 20(1): 65–91.

Ekeh P. P. (1974). *Social Exchange Theory*. Cambridge, MA: Harvard University Press.

Freeman, R. E. (1984). *Strategic Management: A Stakeholder Approach*, Boston: Pitman.

Freeman, R. E., & Evan. W. (1990). Corporate governance: a stakeholder interpretation. *The Journal of Behavioral Economics*, 19(4): 337–59.

Freeman, R. E., Harrison, J. S., Wicks, A. C., Parmar, B., & de Colle, S. (2010). *Stakeholder Theory: The State of the Art*,. Cambridge: Cambridge University Press.

Freeman, R. E., Wicks, A. C., & Parmar, B. (2004). Stakeholder theory and "The corporate objective revisited." *Organization Science*, 15: 364–369.

Friedman, M. (1970). The social responsibility of business is to increase its profits. *New York Times Magazine* (September 13).

Garcia-Castro, R., & Francoeur, C. (2016). When more is not better: Complementaries, costs and contingencies in stakeholder management. *Strategic Management Journal*, 37: 406–424.

Ghemawat, P., & Costa, J. E. R. I. (1993). The organizational tension between static and dynamic efficiency. *Strategic Management Journal*, 14: 59–73.

Graves, S. B., & Waddock, S. A. (1994). Institutional owners and corporate social performance. *Academy of Management Journal*, 37: 1034–1046.

Greenwood, M., & Van Buren, H. J. III. (2010). Trust and stakeholder theory: Trustworthiness in the organisation-stakeholder relationship. *Journal of Business Ethics*, 95(3): 425–438.

Harrison, J. S., and St. John, C. H. (1996). Managing and partnering with external stakeholders. *Academy of Management Executive*, 10(2): 46–60.

Harrison, J. S., Bosse, D. A., & Phillips, R. A. (2010). Managing for stakeholders, stakeholder utility functions, and competitive advantage. *Strategic Management Journal*, 31(1): 58–74.

Harrison, J. S., & Bosse, D. A. (2013). How much is too much? The limits to generous treatment of stakeholders. *Business Horizons*, 56(3): 313–322.

Hartman T. (2006). *Screwed: The Undeclared War Against the Middle Class*. San Francisco: Berrett-Koehler Publishers.

Hayibor, S. (2017). Is fair treatment enough? Augmenting the fairness-based perspective on stakeholder behavior. *Journal of Business Ethics, 140*: 43–64.

Hendry, J. (2001). Economic contacts versus social relationships as a foundation for normative stakeholder theory. *Business Ethics: A European Review*, 10(3): 223–232.

Henisz, W. J., Dorobantu, S., & Nartey, L. J. (2014). Spinning gold: The financial returns to stakeholder engagement. *Strategic Management Journal, 35*(12): 1727–1748.

Hicks, J. (1939). The foundations of welfare economics. *Economic Journal*, 49(196): 696–712.

Hillman, A. J., & Keim, G. D. (2001). Shareholder value, stakeholder management, and social issues: What's the bottom line? *Strategic Management Journal*, 22(2): 125–139.

Hosmer, L.T. (1994). Strategic planning as if ethics mattered. *Strategic Management Journal, 15*: 17–34.

Hurst, J. W. (1970). *The Legitimacy of the Business Corporation in the Law of the United States*, Charlottesville: University of Virginia Press.

Jensen, M. C. (2002). Value maximization, stakeholder theory and the corporate objective. *Business Ethics Quarterly*, 12: 235–256.

Jensen, M. C., & Meckling, W. H. (1976). Theory of the firm: Managerial behavior, agency costs and ownership structure. *Journal of Financial Economics*, 3: 305–360.

Jones, T. M. (1995). Instrumental Stakeholder Theory: A synthesis of ethics and economics. *Academy of Management Review*, 20(2): 404–437.

Jones, T. M., Donaldson, T., Freeman, R. E., Harrison, J. S., Leana, C., Mahoney, J. T., & Pearce, J. (2016). Management theory and social welfare: Contributions and challenges. *Academy of Management Review*, *41*(2): 216–228.

Jones, T. M., & Felps, W. (2013a). Shareholder wealth maximization and social welfare: A utilitarian critique. *Business Ethics Quarterly*, *23*(2): 207–238.

Jones, T. M., & Felps, W. (2013b). Stakeholder happiness enhancement: A neo-utilitarian objective for the modern corporation. *Business Ethics Quarterly*, *23*(3): 349–379.

Jones, T. M., Harrison, J. S., & Felps, W. (2018). How applying instrumental stakeholder theory can provide sustainable competitive advantage. *Academy of Management Review*, *43*(3): 349–370.

Kaldor, N. (1939). Welfare propositions in economics and interpersonal comparisons of utility. *Economic Journal*, *49*(195): 549–552.

Marti, E., & Scherer, A. G. (2016). Financial regulation and social welfare: The critical contribution of management theory. *Academy of Management Review*, *41*(2): 298–323.

Mill, J. S. (1863). *Utilitarianism*. London: Parker, Son, and Bourn.

Mitchell, R. K., Weaver, G. R., Agle, B. R., Bailey, A. D., & Carlson, J. (2016). Stakeholder agency and social welfare: Pluralism and decision making in the multi-objective corporation. *Academy of Management Review*, *41*(2): 252–275.

Nozick, R. (1974). *Anarchy, State and Utopia*. New York: Basic Books.

Peteraf, M. A., & Barney, J. B. (2003). Unraveling the resource-based tangle. *Managerial and Decision Economics*, *24*: 309–323.

Phillips, R. (2003). *Stakeholder Theory and Organizational Ethics*. San Francisco: Berrett-Koehler.

Piketty, T. (2013). Capital in the Twenty-First Century. Trans. A. Goldhammer and published in English by Harvard University Press in 2014.

Post, J., Preston, L., & Sachs, S. (2002). *Redefining the Corporation: Stakeholder Management and Organizational Wealth*, Stanford, CA: Stanford University Press.

Preston, L. E., & Sapienza, H. J. (1990). Stakeholder management and corporate performance. *Journal of Behavioral Economics*, *19*(4): 361–375.

Priem, R. L. (2007). A consumer perspective on value creation. *Academy of Management Review*, *32*(1): 219–235.

Quinn, D., & Jones, T. M. (1995). An agent morality view of business policy. *Academy of Management Review*, *20*: 22–42.

Reiser, D. B. (2011). Benefit corporations: A sustainable form of organization? *Wake Forest Law Review*, *46*: 591–625.

Roberts, P. W., & Dowling, G. R. (2002). Corporate reputation and sustained superior performance. *Strategic Management Journal*, *23*: 1077–1093.

Shane, P. B., & Spicer, B. H. (1983). Market response to environmental information produced outside the firm. *Accounting Review*, *58*(3): 521–536.

Shleifer, A., & Summers, L. H. (1990). The noise trader approach to finance. *Journal of Economic Perspectives*, *4*(2): 19–33.

Sidgwick, H. (1879). The establishment of ethical first principles. *Mind*, *4*(13): 106–111.

Sisodia, R., Wolfe, D. B., & Sheth, J. (2007). *Firms of Endearment: How World-Class Companies Profit from Passion and Purpose*, Upper Saddle River, NJ: Wharton School Publishing.

Smith, A. (1776/1937). *The Wealth of Nations*. New York: Modern Library Edition.

Smith, H. (2012). *Who Stole the American Dream?* New York: Random House.

Stout, L. (2012). *The Shareholder Value Myth: How Putting Shareholders First Harms Investors, Corporations, and the Public*, San Francisco: Berrett-Koehler Publishers.

Tantalo, C., & Priem, R. L. (2016). Value creation through stakeholder synergy. *Strategic Management Journal*, *37*(2): 314–329.

Wallman, S. M. H. (1998). Understanding the purpose of a corporation: An introduction. *Journal of Corporation Law*, *24*: 807–818.

Walsh, J. P., Weber, K., & Margolis, J. D. (2003). Social issues and management: Our lost cause found. *Journal of Management*, *29*(6): 859–881.

Wang, H., Barney, J. B., and Reuer, J. J. (2003). Stimulating firm-specific investment through risk management. *Long Range Planning*, *36*(1): 49–58.

Williamson, O. E. (1975). *Markets and Hierarchies: Analysis and Antitrust Implications*, New York: The Free Press.

Connecting Stakeholder Theory to the Law and Public Policy

ANDREW C. WICKS
University of Virginia

F.A. ELMORE
University of Virginia

DAVID JONAS
University of Virginia

Introduction

Stakeholder theory was developed as a theory about business (Freeman, 1984; Phillips, Freeman, & Wicks, 2003) to reflect how it works and to theorize about how it should operate. It has, however, had an impact well beyond the scholarship in business ethics and strategy in American business schools. The ideas at the heart of stakeholder theory, and the larger narrative it enables, make stakeholder theory a powerful source for thinking about how people come together to cooperate and create value in a wide array of settings. Stakeholder theory has not only influenced other disciplines, but has itself been shaped by ideas, rules, and structures that form the landscape of how businesses operate in particular communities and social contexts.

In this chapter, we devote our attention to two areas where this reciprocal relationship has been very important and where it will continue to be vital to the development of the field: the law and public policy.[1] While a thorough and exhaustive review of the linkages between stakeholder theory and these two domains is beyond the scope of this chapter, we will try to highlight some of the main points of connection. Our focus will not only be to note where stakeholder theory (or stakeholder theory-related themes) show up in these literatures and how they relate to existing conversations in stakeholder theory, but to identify opportunities to deepen these connections in ways that can be mutually beneficial. Our contention is that stakeholder theory can be enriched by developments in

law and public policy, and some of the ideas advanced by stakeholder theory can beneficially contribute to the "real world" through new mindsets, policies, and institutional contexts. We see value in discussing both topics in one chapter because both literatures speak to the interface between business and society – particularly the relevant rules, regulations, and procedures for generating standards – as well as the larger values operating within society that shape this interface. Both fields can develop in ways that either enable and encourage the practice of stakeholder theory (and stakeholder-style cooperation) or inhibit and discourage it. A survey of leading journals in both fields reveals few references and little systematic discussion of stakeholder theory, with some notable deviations from this theme. We see opportunities to expand these linkages and deepen the connections between the law and public policy. Thus, our goal is not simply to provide a history of the literature so far, we want to inspire scholars to become more intentional in connecting them – particularly when doing so can enrich the conversation and add value within each of these disciplines.

We would like to note an over-arching theme from the outset: one of the principal debates that gave life and focus to stakeholder theory as a distinct field of inquiry has both a philosophical and legal dimension. That is, the debate between stakeholder theory (e.g., Ed Freeman) and "shareholder" theory (e.g., Milton Friedman) touched on claims about how firms should be run as well as what the law allows or requires of managers leading publicly traded firms. Friedman, as well as many others who follow him, claims that US law requires managers to prioritize the interests of shareholders in a manner that undercuts the core narrative of stakeholder theory (Friedman, 1970). Freeman and others in the stakeholder literature argue that the law does not require the kind of differential privileging of interests claimed by shareholder theorists, and that practicing stakeholder theory is entirely consistent with US law (Freeman, 1994; Marens & Wicks, 1999; Stout, 2012). This theme will recur through the chapter, both in the law and public policy, and we will try to cast further light on where this debate stands in the contemporary conversation.

Finally, we would like to note that as we discuss these two fields, we are focused primarily on the US legal and policy context. Even with this limitation, covering this terrain in one chapter is a tall order; doing so globally would require a far more elaborate, lengthy, and complicated discussion.

Part I: Stakeholder Theory and the Law

The debate over corporate purpose within the law – including the status of shareholders and stakeholders and how their interests fit into the larger purpose of the firm – has been explicit since the days of Berle and Means (1932). This debate persists to the present in both the scholarly legal literature and court cases. The work in this field has far-reaching implications and is being used to shape the legal structures society creates to govern firms as well as the larger theories and norms taught in schools about how managers ought to run companies.

We noted earlier that there has been limited explicit discussion of stakeholder theory within the legal literature. That statement is subject to a few caveats. First, as noted above, the debate about corporate purpose (e.g., corporate governance) is explicit and ongoing within the law. While the term "stakeholder theory" may not always be used (e.g., Blair & Stout, 1999, talk about "team production," which has many similarities to stakeholder theory), questions about the purpose of the firm and the status of shareholders versus other stakeholders is frequently discussed. Second, many scholars active in the fields of

business ethics and strategy also write on legal topics and publish in law journals, and one can see traces of this link in their scholarship (e.g., Boatright, 1994; 2000; Fort, 1997; Hasnas, 1998; Jennings & Happel, 2003; Orts, 1992; Windsor, 2000). Third, there are some underlying affinities that make an overlap between disciplines not only important but unavoidable. Legal rules and norms provide both constraints and imperatives that speak directly to what purposes they serve, how firms operate, and how they treat stakeholders. Indeed, many accounts of stakeholder theory draw upon elements of the law to make the case for their view or discuss implications of their interpretation of the law (see e.g., Johnson, 2013; Macey, 2008). Finally, there is considerable debate about what stakeholder theory is (e.g., a single "theory" or a "genre of theories"), which has significance for legal scholarship (Freeman, 1994). If one wanted to create legal structures and governance mechanisms that were more conducive to stakeholder theory, what changes would that entail, if any? Just how different would laws need to be if one started with a stakeholder account of the firm? Given the range of different views on stakeholder theory, how might legal scholars (and lawmakers) constructively engage with normative theorists who argue about how firms should operate? We do not propose answers to these questions – we only note their significance for both stakeholder theory and the law.

We begin our section on the law with an overview of the corporate governance status quo, and how company structure affects the efficacy of various normative and descriptive theories of corporate purpose. The remainder of the section highlights several areas and/or topics in the legal literature that relate to the dialectic between shareholder theory advocates and stakeholder theory advocates, including corporate constituency statutes, legislation responding to recent corporate scandals, recent legal scholarship, and the advent of benefit corporations. We conclude with speculations about the future of stakeholder theory in the law.

The Law and Corporate Governance

Corporate governance has been defined as "the systems of laws, rules and factors that control operations at a company" (Gillan & Starks, 2003: 5). It provides the terms under which society allows a firm to come into existence and the parameters within which it must operate.

Legal and public policy scholars interested in corporate governance have long debated the purpose of the corporation and the efficacy of different governance theories on achieving that purpose. By definition, corporate governance is subject to the rules imposed on it by legislatures, regulators, and other non-shareholders. As a result, legal scholars not only use stakeholder and shareholder theory as tools for describing different systems of corporate governance, they use them to inform their proposals around the aim of proposed reforms – namely, the underlying "ought" that should shape where future regulation goes and what interests should be given greater prominence. Thus, our discussion will focus on how the literature interprets what existing rules and laws say about what is allowed and required in the law (i.e., descriptive analysis, including descriptive stakeholder theory), as well as the normative theories (i.e., normative analysis, including normative stakeholder theory) different scholars bring to their analysis of existing law along with their suggestions for improving it.

Our discussion of corporate governance begins by noting several foundational considerations. First, corporate governance and stakeholder theory embody sets of social values – including fairness, property rights, duties of loyalty, individual freedom, voluntary cooperation, and internalization of the costs of business, among others – although each theory may prioritize those values differently (see e.g., Macey, 2008; Strine, 2012). Second, both corporate governance and stakeholder theory attempt to structure governance mechanisms so that businesses can maximize value to society (see e.g., Friedman, 1970; Strine, 2012). Corporate governance prioritizes efficiency and low costs to reduce the obstacles to running a valuable business profitably. Similarly, stakeholder theory focuses on how stakeholder cooperation can enhance value creation. Third, governance structures are designed to enable cooperation among the stakeholders who make the firm a going concern (see e.g., Macey, 2008; Strine, 2012). Recognizing that there may be structural

problems and agency costs that can impede sustained cooperation, both corporate governance and stakeholder theory attempt to incentivize both efficiency and a long-term value horizon amongst interested parties (see e.g., Siebecker, 2010).

With our larger topic in mind, we want to highlight the following themes within corporate governance that recur in legal scholarship and pertain to the role of stakeholder theory in the law: the Board of Directors, Management, Shareholders and Fiduciary Duties, and the Business Judgment Rule.

Board of Directors (BOD): The BOD play a critical role in the firm and how it is governed. When firms come into existence, a BOD is created to ensure the firm operates within the legal and ethical parameters set by society. The literature is full of discussions about what exactly is required of members of the BOD and what objectives they should have while overseeing firms. The BOD in publicly traded firms is typically responsible for hiring (and firing), overseeing, and advising the management team of the firm. As we will explore below, the debate about the duties of the BOD focuses on whose interests they should serve.

Shareholder advocates emphasize that BODs were created to serve the interests of shareholders, particularly since the modern firm is characterized by professional managers and the separation of ownership and control (Bebchuck, 2005; Dougherty, 2016; Jensen, 2001). The BOD is, on this view, a critical governance innovation that enables firms to function and retain their focus on serving the interests of owners, rather than running amok and lacking any kind of accountability. Much as owners of private companies can be their own advocates in the structure and operation of the firm, shareholders can enjoy a similar form of protection and assurance that the firm will be run properly if the BOD is there to protect their interests.

Critics of the shareholder view, including those who invoke stakeholder theory-like arguments, note that the BOD was created to serve the interests of the company, not the shareholders (Bebchuck, 2005; Jensen, 2001; Johnson, 2013). As such, their function is not simply to make choices solely based on financial returns, but to take a larger view of what is good for the company in both the short and the long term. Doing so requires judgment that may go beyond specific financial projections or metrics and consider a wide array of stakeholders, particularly those groups whose interests are closely tied to the firm (e.g., so-called "primary" stakeholders; see Freeman et al., 2010).

Management: Since the days of the separation of ownership and control, the potential differences in interest between shareholders and managers makes keeping management focused on the larger company objectives a critical challenge for any BOD. The famous debates between Berle and Means explored this tension (e.g., Berle and Means, 1932), as well as the larger objectives of the firm in a world where firms were growing larger, more complex, and more the province of a class of people trained to run companies (i.e., professional managers). The potential for managers to become more focused on their own interests than those of their owners is one critical challenge for how modern firms operate, since their position, power, and knowledge of insider information can be used to benefit themselves as well, or instead of, the firm and its stakeholders (see e.g., Bebchuck, 2005).

Advocates for shareholder theory, particularly from economic and legal scholars who draw upon game theory and agency theory, emphasize the fundamental nature of the challenge of policing management and how critical it is to adequate governance. Unless there are clear and simple metrics for performance, and systems in place to both oversee the performance of managers and punish them for failure to perform (e.g., by reducing their pay or firing them), then firms are likely to see significant "shirking" or outright self-dealing (e.g., Bebchuk, 2005; Jensen, 2001).

Critics of shareholder theory agree that the worry about management loyalty is an issue, but insist that it is not as problematic as shareholder theorists maintain. Indeed, they are concerned that so much focus on defeating managerial self-dealing has skewed structures of corporate governance, making them too simplistic, too focused on shareholders, and susceptible to short-term pressures rather than focusing on the good of the firm overall (e.g., Elhauge, 2005; Marens and Wicks, 1999; Stout, 2012).

Shareholders and Fiduciary Duties: The existence of shareholders who can exchange shares in open markets is a critical element of corporate governance for publicly traded firms. Legal debates about corporate governance include disputes about what exactly shareholders own and the rights or privileges to which they are entitled. Some have argued that shareholders "own the company" (e.g., Friedman, 1970; Hansmann & Kraakman, 2001; Jensen, 1989), while others maintain that they merely own a piece of paper that entitles them to certain (largely residual) benefits (e.g., Donaldson & Preston, 1995; Marens & Wicks, 1999; Stout, 2012).

The fiduciary duties that the BOD and management owe to shareholders are another critical feature of corporate governance. No other stakeholder group has a similar status. The exact meaning and the implications of this duty is a central topic of discussion. Some advocates of shareholder theory use the existence of fiduciary duties to argue that the purpose of the firm – and the duty of managers – is to maximize profits for shareholders (e.g., Friedman, 1970).

Critics, including those from within the world of finance and law, point out that the claims made by these shareholder advocates are disputable, as is the larger inference they draw in putting them together (e.g., Marens & Wicks, 1999; Stout, 2012; Zingales, 2012). Not only does the term "shareholders" over-simplify a complex array of individuals and institutions, it masks important differences across this category – including the time horizon of the investor (e.g., day-trader, short-term investor, medium-term, long-term), and the variety of interests they may have (e.g., beyond a concern with simple financial returns). As a result, "maximizing" becomes an extremely complex and untenable goal unless one makes a series of other normative judgments about which interests to prioritize. On this view, rather than being an obvious and indisputable truth about the nature of business, the theory of "maximize profits for shareholders" is best seen as a contingent ideology that needs to be described and defended as such.

The Business Judgment Rule (BJR): The final theme of corporate governance we wish to note is the existence of the BJR. It can be succinctly defined as "a statutory or judicial presumption that protects directors from liability for action taken by them if they act on an informed basis in good faith, and in a manner they reasonably believe to be in the best interests of the corporations' shareholders" (Dougherty, 2016). This rule provides parameters and flexibility to both BOD and management in running the company, such that shareholders and courts have limited ability to second-guess management's decisions, by providing fairly widespread discretion to make choices that serve the larger interests of the corporation. Exactly how much discretion is a subject of debate.

Advocates of the shareholder view maintain that the business judgment rule's main function is to ensure proper separation of shareholders from the board and management (Strine, 2012). While shareholder advocates want management to feel pressure to perform, and to increase that pressure when management fails to do so, they also recognize there are limits to how much shareholders should be involved in the operations of the modern firm. Management is there for a reason, and if they are not given freedom to lead, develop, and implement strategies with the confidence of their employees, it becomes difficult for any management team to succeed. Additionally, shareholders frequently lack the time, expertise, and vision to step in and run the company, which is why managers are hired in the first place.

Critics of the shareholder view put far more emphasis on the BJR, particularly on how much freedom or discretion it gives to BODs and managers to make decisions that serve the interests of the firm (e.g., Elhauge, 2005; Stout, 2012). Far from mandating that profits be maximized or that shareholders have exclusive and dominant status in the corporate hierarchy, this rule makes clear it is the firm – not shareholders – that takes precedence (Marens & Wicks, 1999; Stout, 2012). Managers should prioritize the stakeholders and interests that are most conducive to the health of the firm, not just shareholders or maximizing the stock price.

Corporate Constituency Statutes and Non-Shareholder Rights

Corporate Constituency Statutes (CCSs) are another area of corporate governance that has been subject to significant debate between theorists (Freeman, et al., 2010). CCSs are state laws that explicitly either allow, or require, corporate managers to consider constituency groups besides shareholders when making strategic decisions. For advocates of stakeholder theory, CCSs represent one of the major ways in which stakeholder theory has been operationalized and can (legally) be internalized by board directors. In response to their adoption by many state legislatures, legal critics ranging from academics to judges posit that CCSs merely give cover to board directors who want to insulate themselves from their fiduciary demands to shareholders. These critics think board directors use CCSs to structure "poison pills" (also sometimes referred to as shareholder rights plans) into their charters as a precaution against takeover attempts and other maneuvers by forces outside management that desire to change the corporation.

Thus, many legal scholars have used the development of CCSs as a context to evaluate and apply stakeholder theory to corporate governance. In this academic literature, defining the proper role of the corporation and its ultimate purpose in society is perhaps the most common theme (Fort, 1997). Beyond that debate, the development of managerial philosophies that place greater responsibility in taking customer, employee, and even local community claims into account often invokes stakeholder theory as a major influence (Orts, 1992). Some of the legal literature perceives CCSs as fairly radical policy shifts that move the law in a very pro-stakeholder direction. Millon (1991), for example, sees CCSs as critical reforms that cut to the core of how we understand corporate law and allow managers to have fiduciary duties to stakeholders, not just shareholders. Others see CCSs as confusing and either useless or dangerous (e.g., American Bar Association, 1990). In their view, these statutes make little sense given the existing body of law and precedent and should be used in only highly specialized cases that render them virtually meaningless. Orts (1992) argues for a more middle-of-the-road view. He notes the consistency of these statutes as more explicit statements of what was already clear in existing law: managers have discretion to consider a wide array of stakeholder interests to promote the best interests of the firm. CCSs have some useful qualities, but they do not seem to be a particularly powerful tool to shift the balance of power in the dispute between stakeholder theory and shareholder theory advocates.

Recently, CCSs have led to lawsuits, as companies increasingly use CCSs to prevent takeover attempts. Legal scholars like Leo Strine (2012) – a former Delaware Court of Chancery judge – assert that corporate actions allowed by CCSs that run counter to shareholder profit maximization ought to be viewed hostilely by the courts. Strine dismisses corporate actions that attempt to operationalize stakeholder theory, arguing this runs counter to established Delaware and federal case law, and the social purpose of the corporation. Macey (2008: 179) believes that CCSs are best understood as mere tiebreakers, "allowing managers to take the interests of non-shareholder constituencies into account when doing so does not harm shareholders in any demonstrable way." Other critics contend that CCSs essentially replicate the federal government's "diffusion of power" among stakeholders and are thus inappropriate to apply to corporate boards (Hallett & Rogers, 1994). However, Kacperczyk (2009) offers empirical evidence that, on average, firms with substantial takeover protections attend to stakeholder considerations, benefitting the long-term health of the corporation more than corporations without takeover protections. He concludes that this result is due to board directors being "relieved" of some of the pressure to deliver short-term profits. Ultimately, the legal and policy scholarship contest the significance of CCSs for corporate governance.

Stakeholder Theory in an Age of Crisis and Failure

Many of the economic crises of the last two decades have resulted in legal scholars using stakeholder theory to analyze and advocate for changes to (or to support defenses of) the status quo on corporate governance. When corporations suffer failure because of misguided strategy or willful deception of shareholders, scholars have stepped up to suggest changes in the way corporate governance is structured, in the hopes of preventing similar failures in the future.

The latest application of stakeholder theory to corporate governance came as a result of the Enron, WorldCom, and Tyco scandals in the early 2000s. These scandals not only inspired the adoption of the Sarbanes-Oxley Act of 2002 – one of the most significant laws passed on corporate governance in a generation – but also an academic debate about how corporate managers can avoid the short-termism that incentivized overly risky and deceptive behavior. Bertus, Jahera and Yost (2008) used data from before and after the passage of Sarbanes-Oxley to determine what happened to the dividend policies of affected corporations, alluding to the need for corporations "to develop internal and external governance measures to allow a firm's stakeholders to more accurately monitor and measure its performance." Other prominent legal scholars like Stephen Bainbridge and Leo Strine (2008: 1081) saw Sarbanes-Oxley as a burdensome and irresponsible "crisis-inspired legislation." In other words, stakeholder theory gains caché in times of emergency and crisis.

Arguably, stakeholder theory's most significant application in the twenty-first century came in the development, passage, and continued debate over the Dodd-Frank Wall Street Reform and Consumer Protection Act of 2010. This act represents the most fundamental reform of the regulation of the banking system and corporate boards since the Great Depression, and the effects of stakeholder theory on policymakers and lawyers is discernible everywhere. Provisions on whistleblower protections, "say-on-pay," increased corporate governance on disclosures – these were all rooted in the idea that shareholders alone could not act as the proper counterweight against corporate managers engaged in systemically risky behaviors. Interestingly, stakeholder theory is invoked much more often by critics of Dodd-Frank than supporters. For stakeholder theory critics like Bainbridge (2011), Dodd-Frank represents a kind of "quack" nod to increasing stakeholder accountability while just benefitting industry players like institutional investors, attorneys, and other rentiers. Indeed, critics of stakeholder theory often decry the theory as a kind of motivated intellectual crutch that interested lobbies can use to steer changes in corporate governance toward their economic interests. In this sense, stakeholder theory becomes the language of the "mark" to hoodwink policymakers into furthering their own narrow interests.

Stakeholder theory's prominence in legal circles after 2008 is also evident in the field of crisis management. Alpaslan, Green, and Mitroff, (2009) argue that firms undergoing extreme duress are best served by abandoning the dominant corporate governance model and adopting one informed by the tenets of stakeholder theory, even temporarily. This is because twenty-first-century corporate crises almost inevitably involve the sudden elevation of once "dormant" stakeholders to "dominant" importance. Consider any natural disaster or liquidity crisis where forces that have no immediate shareholder connection immediately take on outsized importance: Alpaslan, et al. (2009) uses the example of Exxon's handling of an oil spill, where a decision to shortchange investments in safety (to maintain profit margins) led to a massive and expensive shift to replacing stakeholder value caused by environmental damage from the spill. They conclude: "Thus, it may be both fair and efficient for corporations to have multiple objectives, and to put emphasis on moral claimants, not only on 'explicit' residual claimants" (Alpaslan, et al., 2009: 47). In situations such as layoffs, relocations, mergers, acquisitions, or hostile takeovers, the stakeholder model may benefit both shareholders and stakeholders to a greater extent than the shareholder model (Alpaslan, et al., 2009). Thus, for some academics, stakeholder theory at the intersection of crisis prevention and management is used not only as a framework for analysis, but also as a foundation for proposing best practices and reforms to help corporate managers succeed.

Stakeholder Versus Shareholder Theory Debate in Recent Legal Research

A look at recent debates in the courts shows continued advocacy for shareholder theory in corporate case law. Landmark court cases in Delaware (such as *eBay Domestic Holding, Inc. v. Newmark* 2010, hereinafter "*eBay*") – and the ensuing analysis by prominent legal scholars – have affirmed the

centrality of shareholder theory in corporate law, making consideration of stakeholders a secondary concern and generally dependent upon the discretion of management (Johnson, 2013; Macey, 2008; Murray, 2013). However, in recent years, there has been a notable "counter-wave" by corporate legal scholars that seek to grant more flexibility to corporate directors in how they pursue profits. The approaches here vary from descriptive to normative, and they often disagree on whether giving corporate boards more or less control over decision-making ends up increasing stakeholder input. But they all largely share one tenet: that long-term value creation is a legitimate purpose of the corporation, and to deny corporations the legal ability to take in greater account of stakeholder concerns deprives both shareholders and stakeholders of potential long-term gains.

Shareholder theory came to be the dominant framework by which courts and corporate legal academics viewed the purpose of the corporation as the result of several different normative and descriptive approaches. Bainbridge (1993) defends shareholder theory by arguing that it most closely hews to actual human behavior, and that managers who take non-shareholder concerns into account have taken on a kind of conflict of interest by diluting efforts made on the behalf of shareholders. Strine (2012) says he is "weary of the naiveté" that corporations are somehow to be imbued with greater moral responsibility than simply to generate profits for shareholders. Strine cites Van Der Weide (1996) to argue that if stakeholders had any formal power on corporate boards, then managers could "reallocate the costs of the duty of loyalty among stakeholder groups," which would presumably make the corporation less competitive. Fisch (2006) does not advocate the norm herself, but as she points out, nearly every MBA curriculum in the United States uses the norm as one of its intellectual foundations in teaching the basics of corporate finance and structure.

While shareholder theory is the prevalent framework in legal academia, several authors have a counter-wave of scholarship proposing a more stakeholder-centric model of governance. Professor Lynn Stout of Cornell Law School is perhaps the most visible and prolific legal academic who is advocating against shareholder theory. In her article with Belinfanti (2017), they posit that managerial attitudes that afford corporate boards some flexibility in operating as larger social instructions within corporate law were purposively discarded in the 80s and 90s by motivated interests when executive compensation became more aligned with shareholder interests. Belinfanti and Stout (2017) identify three main arguments used by shareholder theorists, and then use aspects of stakeholder theory to respond to each: (i) The Ownership Justification (which we discussed earlier in this chapter under "Shareholders and Fiduciary Duties" – they challenge this idea by focusing on the limits of shareholder claims to own the firm, particularly that they own a piece of paper, not "the firm"; (ii) The Residual Claiming Justification (that being the residual claimant makes shareholders justified in demanding profit maximization) by focusing on the idea that companies, not shareholders, are the owners of residual claims; and (iii) The Necessary Metric Justification (that we must have a single metric, like profits or share price to "keep score" and hold management accountable) focusing on the challenge of the time horizon, and that as one pushes the time horizon out longer, the appropriate norm becomes more diffuse and closer to firm value and stakeholder theory.

Belinfanti and Stout (2017) end up advocating a systems-based model for evaluating corporate performance. In their view, shareholder profits only sometimes equate to shareholder value, and a systems theory approach (that considers how multiple inputs interact to create outputs) focused on the long-term health and survivability of a corporation more accurately measures the value shareholders are getting.

Cremers and Sepe (2016: 109) adopt an instrumental approach by examining staggered corporate board terms and show – contrary to much previous scholarly work – that they result in improved long-term value creation. By empowering boards vis-à-vis shareholders, such reforms would promote long-term value creation in the interest of shareholders and society as a whole.

Siebecker (2010) uses the *Citizens United* ruling (2010) to make a descriptive argument that greater shareholder control of corporate boards is important to increase stakeholder consideration in corporate activities. He advocates a new discourse theory, arguing that "as corporations evolve from simple investment vehicles" to full, if not dominant, participants in economic, social, and political life, a more dynamic view of the corporation is required (Siebecker, 2010: 164). According to Siebecker, shareholders need greater tools (such as proxy board director votes) so that they can bring greater stakeholder concerns to the attention of corporate boards.

Ciepley (2013) advances a normative case that the modern corporation is similar to a government and thus should be regulated as a hybrid public/private entity. He suggests that integrating stakeholders in corporate decisions is a difficult issue, but one that must be addressed: "How exactly corporations are to be brought to attend to broader stakeholder interests has always been a difficult question. Nevertheless, corporations' debt to public authority is a strong argument that they ought to, beyond what is expected of genuinely private actors" (Ciepley, 2013: 153).

Elhauge (2005) makes the descriptive argument that the business judgment rule confers broad powers on corporate managers to defer short-term interests for long-term ones. More importantly, "social and moral sanctions" are costs that are very real to corporations, even if they do not show up in ledger books. Thus, courts should defer to managers more than shareholders, because courts are fundamentally unable to evaluate whether a morally good action (such as a charitable donation) is being made for profitable purposes or not. Elhauge specifically nods to boards assuming greater responsibility for stakeholder concerns, arguing that they already must divvy up resources between employees, contractors, and creditors. Thus, the "too many masters" argument is invalid in Elhauge's analysis.

Law and Benefit Corporations

In response to the perceived exclusivity of the shareholder value theory and its ostensible role in the 2008 financial crisis, several states adopted statutes permitting the incorporation of explicitly formed social enterprises: businesses that seek to both produce profits and serve some social or environmental purpose (Johnson, 2013; Murray, 2013). The most well-known and widely adopted corporate form is a benefit corporation, but states have also created a low-profit limited liability company (or L3C) and a flexible purpose corporation.[2] Finally, California has also adopted a flexible purpose corporation statute (Americans for Community Development, n.d.; Johnson, 2013; Murphy; 2013).

Although the statutes differ slightly from state to state, most of their provisions are written along similar lines. Each state stipulates that benefit corporations do not need to maximize profits, and that their purposes must include the general public benefit. Specific public benefits may also be explicitly articulated in the corporation's charter, but such particular purposes are optional. Furthermore, the statutes typically require directors, as they attempt to act in the best interests of the corporation, to consider the effects of decisions on a variety of stakeholders (Johnson, 2013).

Some legal scholars question the effectiveness of these statutes at accomplishing their stated purposes. These critiques typically articulate the lack of unique advantages benefit corporations offer over regular corporate forms or a misalignment of the statutory provisions (Cummings, 2012; Johnson, 2013; Murray, 2013). With respect to the former, they note that "despite the common perception that corporate directors are legally bound to maximize shareholder wealth, existing law in many respects permits directors to take into account non-shareholder interests" (Cummings, 2012; Murray, 2013).

The latter critique – the misalignment of social enterprise statutory provisions – is interesting, however, because it suggests that benefit corporation and related legislation only partially adopts a stakeholder-centric view of corporate responsibility. Johnson (2013) suggests that the misalignment arises from "continuing confusion over three related subjects in corporate law: the corporation's best interests, corporate purpose, and fiduciary duties." Corporate statutes are "silent and agnostic" about corporate purpose so long as the corporation's stated purpose is

lawful, and cases like *Dodge v. Ford Motor Co.* (1919) ("*Dodge*") and *eBay* (in which courts expressly restrict managerial decisions because of shareholder interests) are infrequent and have limited effect on the statutory interpretation. Rather, those cases serve to illustrate the relationship between the remaining two subjects – the corporation's best interests and fiduciary duties. As a matter of convention, Johnson (2013) notes that "it is routinely stated that the 'best interests of the corporation' should be the directors' focus," which would suggest that managerial discretion can determine a range of legitimate interests, not simply profit maximization. *eBay* and similar cases limit that range of options by requiring that the "best interests" at least include improving the value of the corporation for the benefit of its shareholders (i.e., the fiduciary duties flow to shareholders, not just to the corporation; Johnson, 2013).

Benefit corporation statutes specify a narrower range of permissible purposes, and typically define the corporation's best interests as the achievement of its purposes – while considering effects on stakeholders – neatly aligning the business' purpose and stakeholder interests. However, (most of) the statutes do not change the benefit corporation directors' fiduciary relationships or grant any non-shareholder stakeholders standing to bring civil or enforcement claims against the corporation. Consequently, as Johnson (2013: 293) concludes, benefit corporations in most states are "hybrid vehicles" that combine "a novel mandatory consideration of stakeholders with the more traditional enforcement rights of directors and shareholders." So, benefit corporations only partially embody a stakeholder model of corporate governance.

In addition to the legal limitations of the benefit corporation form, significant uncertainty remains about the persistence, efficacy, and effects of benefit corporations and similar corporate forms on conceptions of corporate purpose and fiduciary duties. Since the corporate forms are legal innovations and comparatively few companies currently use them, there is little evidence about investor or consumer responses to for-profit companies formed with an explicit social purpose (Johnson,

2013). Cummings (2012) notes the difficulty social enterprises have in meeting either capital market expectations or the criteria to receive funding traditionally reserved for non-profits. In addition to the possibility that benefit corporations might not receive sufficient interest or support in capital and product markets to flourish, Cummings (2012) also suggests that the statutory third-party certification and disclosure requirements imposed on benefit corporations are insufficient to ensure compliance to the public interest purposes. To improve accountability, she suggests a more adaptable framework that utilizes stakeholders and industry self-regulation to craft individualized standards and assessments that focus on structures and practices rather than fixed inputs or outcomes without the threat of public sanctions. Finally, some scholars have noted that the mere existence of benefit corporations could sideline conversations and investment in corporate social responsibility in the general corporate context (e.g., "Social responsibility activity would then become a niche in the larger market rather than exist pervasively, if modestly, in many businesses"; Johnson, 2013: 296). Of course, there are also reasons to think that the sentiments and values that led to the creation of benefit corporations will continue to influence corporate values more generally (Johnson, 2013; Murray, 2013).

Future Directions for Stakeholder Theory and the Law

The renewed interest in applying the tenets of stakeholder theory to corporate governance reforms following the 2008 subprime mortgage crisis has led to new ground being broken on the theory. These range from novel attempts to gauge how widespread the adoption of stakeholder theory-inspired reforms are to attempts to steer stakeholder theory's application into new directions. In a study on Anglo-American attitudes about stakeholder theory in corporate governance, Keay (2011) points to a host of developments since the 1990s that suggest that the stakeholder model may one day become the dominant model used in corporate governance law in the United States, the United Kingdom, Canada, Australia,

and New Zealand. Keay details a litany of recent developments – Supreme Court decisions in Canada, empirical research in Australia, the bank failures of Lehman Brothers in the USA and Northern Rock in the United Kingdom, among others – that appear to show an emerging consensus on stakeholder primacy as at least being on par with shareholder primacy in the literature. For scholars like Keay, stakeholder theory is already one of the chief intellectual backbones of twenty-first-century corporate and commercial law, even if most academics and practitioners fail to realize it.

Other legal scholars question whether stakeholder theory itself has "sold out," particularly from a normative point of view. These legal scholars posit that stakeholder theorists have abandoned their roots by increasingly downplaying the need to give stakeholders "formal, binding control over the corporation" (Moriarty, 2012). In this view, corporate governance should advance an offshoot of stakeholder theory called "stakeholder democracy," which gives stakeholders the formal power to appoint the board (Matten & Crane, 2005). Regardless of the efficacy of such a proposal, this kind of approach speaks to the wide spectrum of ways stakeholder theory is interpreted and operationalized in academic discussions of corporate governance. Beyond these developments, stakeholder theorists need to pay increased attention to state and federal policymakers and their proposed reforms to corporate governance. As seen in the example of CCSs, new legal structures and powers given to boards of directors are one the chief forces shaping how (and whether) stakeholder theory is applied in the real world. These developments trickle down to legal practitioners and academics who in turn use them as lenses for discussing the proper role of the corporation in society.

Particularly since the financial crisis, stakeholder theorists can inject a new element into the long-standing discussion with shareholder purists – that "short-termism" imperils corporations and discounts the input and interests of other stakeholders. This kind of "preventative" application of stakeholder theory will likely have much greater caché, especially as the next generation of corporate managers, lawyers, and policymakers confront an even more interconnected, globalized economy (e.g., see Smith & Rönnegard, 2016, including a critique of teaching about shareholder primacy in business schools). Stout, the lead signatory on the "Modern Corporation Statement of Law" (a descriptive attempt to re-center the foundations of corporate law on the purpose of the corporation), argues alongside others that short-term profit maximization is, "usually a product not of legal obligation, but of the pressures imposed on them by financial markets, activist shareholders, the threat of a hostile takeover and/or stock-based compensation schemes" (Stout, Robé, et al., 2016: 2). Such sentiment shows how some legal scholars are normatively moving away from the shareholder theory-centric view dominant in the corporate legal field.

Additionally, as the economic downsides to short-termism become readily apparent through empirical work and instrumental approaches, policymakers will need legal tools to nudge corporate behavior toward greater long-term considerations. Undermining short-termism was a major focus for policymakers in Dodd-Frank in 2009–2010, but the legislation's effects on corporate behavior are still being evaluated. Normative approaches considering the roles of executive pay, quarterly earnings reports, and other outgrowths of short-termism are likely to become more regulated over time to avoid the pitfalls of short-term economic incentives. Such developments create an opening for stakeholder theorists to develop normative insights that could guide policymakers toward alternatives that better align with stakeholder theory and fit with larger social values around inclusion, voluntary cooperation, and the creation of more value for stakeholders (rather than a myopic focus on stock price and short-term shareholder value).

Part II: Public Policy and Stakeholder Theory

As we noted in the beginning of this chapter, most of the existing connections between stakeholder theory and public policy are merely descriptive: it focuses on both the language of stakeholders as a salient and empowering term and use of "stakeholder analysis" as a helpful tool to inform the process of policy formulation. The language of "stakeholder" has become the language of choice in much of the public policy literature: scholars have gravitated toward "stakeholder" as a resonant and important term that captures something critical about individuals/ groups who deserve some measure of consideration. This evolution is significant – and an indicator of both the challenge and opportunity in front of stakeholder scholars. Surprisingly, despite the popularity of the term stakeholder in the literature, systematic discussions of normative stakeholder theory in the public policy context are very rare. Indeed, there seems to be a reluctance to venture into this "normative" territory, even though many of the topics raised make such a conversation both relevant and important. How can this work be developed to enable scholars to go beyond merely using the term stakeholder to exploring the underlying normative conversations that such a term implies? What does it mean to be a stakeholder, why would I want to be one, and what are the larger purposes and norms that tie me to other stakeholders? Perhaps it is because scholars in public policy either assume a fairly settled answer to these questions or lack the training and/or disposition to do so, that they are not being asked more systematically in the literature.

In the remainder of the chapter we explore some of the more promising aspects of the public policy literature – topics where stakeholder theory is both discussed and may have the greatest opportunities to enrich the conversation. Before exploring these topics in more detail, we wish to begin by noting recent work that addresses some of the larger conceptual affinities between the descriptive and normative approaches. Brugha and Varvasovsky (2000), for example, note that public policy literature has long been focused on the need to be "aware of interest groups in the policy process; and the need to characterize and categorize levels of interest and power which influence, and therefore impact on, particular policies" (2000: 240). These affinities and common interests show up in a variety of places: works on the structure of power (e.g., Marxism, liberalism, professionalism, elitism, and pluralism), community and policy networks (Smith,

1993), and political mapping (Reich 1994). They also perceive both the policy process and stakeholder analysis as both focused on individuals and groups that are part of policy processes and on how making predictions about future behavior (given specific interests) will influence policy (Brugha & Varvasovsky, 2000; Reich, 1994; Smith, 1993).

Others, like Bryson (2004), openly support more direct interactions between the fields, noting the value of stakeholder mapping and other tools of stakeholder analysis. He even goes as far as to note the significance of how we talk about stakeholders – who gets counted as a stakeholder and how their interests are discussed – suggesting that for reasons of social justice we need to attend to normative considerations in talking about stakeholders in the policy process (Bryson, 2004: 22). While this aspiration is commendable, much of the rest of the work is focused on a range of specific tools to enhance the ability to map and predict stakeholder behaviors and create more positive outcomes in the policy process, rather than the normative considerations he lauds.

Finally, Freidman and Mason (2005) highlight some challenging contexts in public policy where stakeholder theory may add particular value. They focus on cases like professional sports franchises moving from one city to another (e.g., the Houston Oilers to the Tennessee Titans) as an occasion to do the kind of analysis that stakeholder theory invites. They hope to use stakeholder theory to inform and improve policy management to serve the larger public interest. In their analysis of Freeman's classic text on stakeholder theory (1984), the authors find great value in the tools for mapping and analyzing stakeholders, and concur that adhering to stakeholder principles is likely to be beneficial in creating outcomes that better satisfy core stakeholders. However, when it comes to the normative challenge of balancing stakeholder needs and deciding what to prioritize, the authors find Freeman (1984) less helpful, deferring instead to the model of stakeholder prioritization developed by Mitchell, Agle, and Wood (1997).

This work highlights the awareness of normative questions within the field. The literature can be characterized as aware of normative implications, but desirous of avoiding them in favor of a practical prioritization tool that helps resolve disputes. Perhaps this speaks to the discomfort of having open normative conversations with the field – raising the possibility scholars in the field see them either outside their expertise or as fundamentally unsolvable. If this conjecture is correct, then prioritization tools become an attractive alternative: a seemingly rigorous and objective way of deciding how to allocate resources and make hard choices without having to systematically analyze the normative dimensions.

The remainder of this section is divided into four parts. The first three parts discuss topics in public policy literature that have been enriched by stakeholder theory, specifically new governance theory, participatory democracy, and public-private partnerships. The final part explores future directions for stakeholder theory in the public policy literature.

Public Policy and New Governance Theory

"New governance theory" can be understood as a collection of approaches to governance in the public policy literature that emphasize innovation, grassroots involvement by policy stakeholders, and attempts to eliminate more traditional command-and-control approaches to policy (e.g., Jonas, 2016: 473). These approaches explicitly aim to be "open-textured, participatory, bottom-up, consensus oriented, contextual, flexible, integrative, and pragmatic" (Jonas, 2016: 474). New governance theory has been used to explore a wide array of contexts and challenges in policy, including the natural environment, efforts to reform and improve public schools, discrimination in the workplace, health care, equal protection issues, worker rights, the court system, and economic development (474).

This collection of research assumes a general consensus about the need to combine creativity and engagement at the local level with some element of larger norms and processes (e.g., at a state or federal level) in order to create accountability, consistency, and structure in governance. There is, however, considerable disagreement about how much emphasis to put on structure: many of these scholars want to emphasize process, participation, and emergent solutions as far superior to those created by policy experts sitting in a centralized office.

Some of the work in new governance theory, particularly on the natural environment, makes explicit ties to stakeholder theory. Theorists like Shutkin (2000) focus on empowering stakeholders and engaging them in the process to better serve them and their communities. He argues policy efforts should be about "empowering a diverse set of stakeholders to work to improve and protect our natural resources . . . while building social capital . . . and promoting sustainable economic development" (Shutkin, 2000: 14–15). This governance approach not only puts faith in the ability of individuals to engage and contribute to a process that serves the interests of many, it is keenly aware of the important concomitant effects of this process, like civic engagement, the formation of character, and ownership of problems.

While much of the new governance literature assumes that wider participation is better, some scholars have demonstrated the need for a more refined and contextual understanding of how to engage stakeholders in the policy process (Berner, Amos, & Morse, 2011). They note that the push for stakeholder participation is "rooted in normative theory" (2011: 129), and has both intrinsic and instrumental ends. So, they focus on understanding "effective" participation by reviewing both published literature and doing their own empirical work. One important theme to highlight from their literature review (focused here on Eran Vigoda's work) is a shift in the consensus from seeing citizens as "voters" and the government as a "trustee," toward a newer model where citizens are viewed as "customers" and government as a "manager who [is] responsive to the needs of citizen-clients" (2011: 133). The authors conclude, based on both results of their study and the literature, that conceptions of effective participation need to be more nuanced and contextual: "our normative definitions of effective participation may not work well in practical application because the real actors on the stage (the politicians, staff, and citizens) have different expectations and definitions" (2011: 158).

In conclusion, it is important to note another thread of commentary in the new governance literature related to the non-profit sector. While there

are good reasons to want to hold all organizations accountable for misdeeds, and there are important similarities across all types of organization (e.g., private sector businesses, public administration agencies, non-profit organizations), there are also important reasons for their differences. Mulligan (2007) argues that the efforts of many states to improve the governance of nonprofit organizations by simply applying the structure and set of assumptions of Sarbanes-Oxley to nonprofits will do little to improve governance, and may well create problems. At the core of his criticism is a "mistaken moral premise," namely, that policy makers used ideas and assumptions from shareholder theory rather than stakeholder theory. He argues, "As every nontrivial activity assumes a philosophical perspective, corporate governance reforms also presuppose a particular normative view, such as a stockholder or a stakeholder view. Sarbanes-Oxley is no exception. I contend that Congress employed a stockholder conception of business ethics when it passed the Act" (Mulligan, 2007: 2005). First, Mulligan notes the similarities in approach to governance between nonprofit organizations and stakeholder theory: they both serve many stakeholders and their interests, rather than just one. He also suggests important ways in which non-profit firms are fundamentally different from for-profit businesses, such as they "cannot protect stockholder interests" since they do not exist in that organizational form. Asking them to operate within that system presupposes an inappropriate set of norms and creates an imperative that is impossible to fulfill (Mulligan, 2007: 2006). Finally, he notes ways in which future regulation could be improved by using a stakeholder theory perspective – especially by bringing in a broader array of stakeholder perspectives into their process and fostering accountability (Mulligan, 2007: 2006–2007).

Public Policy and Participatory Democracy

The research on participatory democracy incorporates stakeholder theory into discussions of democratic experimentalism, local participatory budgeting (where members of the public directly get to decide how public funds are spent), and other areas. Although participatory democracy is often associated with new governance theory, we choose to treat it separately because of the significant and novel relationship to stakeholder theory.

One important strand within the participatory democracy literature involves "pragmatic experimentalism," a set of ideas traced back to John Dewey (Jonas, 2016: 483) that shares an affinity with the roots of stakeholder theory in Freeman's work (1984), but focuses on an open-ended search for approaches that "work" rather than following or evaluating ideologies (also Dorf & Fagan, 2003; Dorf & Sabel, 1998). While many authors do not explicitly mention stakeholder theory, the combination of stakeholder involvement and democratic experimentalism gives this body of work a distinctly stakeholder theory-style feel:

> democratic experimentalism, in which power is decentralized to enable citizens and other actors to utilize their local knowledge to fit solutions to their individual circumstances, but in which regional and national coordinating bodies require actors to share their knowledge with others facing similar problems... [this] both increases the efficiency of public administration by encouraging mutual learning among its parts and heightens its accountability through participation of citizens in the decisions that affect them. (Dorf & Sabel, 1998: 267)

Much of the participatory democracy literature is focused on the need to (i) do more to get stakeholders involved in the policy process, (ii) open new possibilities for organizational learning, (iii) support collaborative solutions, and (iv) increase civic engagement. The literature encourages a shift toward more modern impulses like localized systems that are self-implementing, sustainable, flexible, and dynamic, rather than centralized, elaborate rules and oversight from agencies the compel adherence to rules and regulations (Fiorino, 1999). Some scholars note that these concepts are spreading globally, especially alongside discussions about tackling difficult problems like the environment (Fiorino, 1999).

The ideas associated with participatory democracy are also being applied to exploring alternative dispute resolution vehicles, called "public policy dispute resolutions" (Stephens & Burner, 2011). Work in this domain speaks to the power of having stakeholders engaged in a conversation, a shared process, and a commitment toward creating solutions

that serve multiple stakeholders. Work by Innes (1998; Innes & Booher, 2004) shows the practical value of participation as a way to bring stakeholders together to get beyond what appear to be irreconcilable differences or impassable policy conflicts.

Other authors attempt to show how these approaches lead to "better" policies – meaning "greater perceived legitimacy of the decision based on involvement by stakeholders, open-minded consideration of diverse information and perspectives in the decision-making process, the opportunity for new proposals to be raised and considered in the process, and having the ultimate decision-maker acknowledge the input of the participants" (Stephens & Burner 2011: 2). While debate continues about the proper forms of participation and how to operationalize theory at scale, there is a growing interest in participatory democracy within the field, especially in negotiation, collaboration, and participation models (Stephens & Burner, 2011: 16; see also Carlson, 2007; Lukensmeyer & Torres, 2006; and O'Leary & Bingham, 2007).

Given the complex nature of environmental problems and their increasing pervasiveness in society, much of the recent participatory democracy work focuses on facilitating consensus regarding polices that affect the natural environment. In the context of ecological complexity, interdependencies between human and ecological contexts, uncertainty, and non-linearity, it is particularly important to have the capacities to adapt, to get feedback, and to include the perspective of local actors (e.g., Trimble & Lazaro, 2014). On this view, having stakeholder participation is critical to creating a dynamic and relevant set of policy tools that incorporate critical new capabilities to find solutions to specific environmental challenges.

While participation is understood as a fundamental element of this approach to policy, significant disagreement about how to structure participation within the policy process remains. Some of the issues here are functional and learning-based – participation leads to new discoveries or key insights – and others are about fostering the legitimacy of processes and outcomes, inspiring trust, and getting buy in from stakeholders (e.g., Fiorino, 1999; Trimble & Lazaro, 2014; Walker & Daniels, 2001). A few papers within this field try to systematically establish a process for developing the proper stakeholder participation (e.g., a "framework to implement stakeholder participation"; Luyet, et al., 2012). Much of this work presupposes that substantial stakeholder participation is essential, and, therefore, focuses more on the contextual trade-offs that may inform whether more or less participation is needed, when it should occur, and under what terms (e.g., Luyet, et al., 2012). These approaches have much in common with the Mitchell, Agle, and Wood (1997) paper about stakeholder theory, as well as less explicit discussions of the normative dimensions of stakeholder participation prevalent in the stakeholder theory literature.

Public Policy and Public-Private Partnerships

In the realm of public policy, the biggest development in the use of stakeholder theory is in public-private partnerships (PPPs). Both practitioners and academics are increasingly interested in how large public projects can strike the best balance between government, private, and stakeholder interests. Stakeholder theory is being applied to address this question in some fascinating ways. Scholars are using it as a framework for deciding (i) how to define project success, (ii) how to best structure and use public input, (iii) how to maintain peaceful relationships among players, and (iv) how to hold public and private actors accountable. This field promises to be a goldmine for stakeholder theorists who are interested in the scope for creative application of stakeholder theory in public policy. It appears to be a promising opportunity for incorporating real-world results into stakeholder theory's analytic work.

PPPs are defined as "working arrangements based on a mutual commitment (over and above that implied in any contract) between a public-sector organization with any organization outside of the public sector" (Bovaird 2004: 199). Many in public policy see PPPs as a promising vehicle that can deliver on key policy objectives while also fostering economic growth (Greiling and Halachmi, 2012: 137). Factors that include stakeholder input and participation to foster true collaboration are critical to their success. The biggest perceived threats come

in the form of opportunism from private-sector participants seeking profits.

PPPs have had both many successes and many failures. Rather than simply being a function of the gap between expectations of a stakeholder and the performance of the PPP, De Schepper and colleagues note that dissatisfaction with PPPs has much to do with "the imbalance of reactive and proactive stakeholder management approaches and an absence of any guidance on the responsibility and accountability issues surrounding the stakeholder management of PPP projects" (Dooms, & Haezendonck, 2014: 1210). As a result, finding ways to identify stakeholders, gather, incorporate their feedback, and create "appropriate stakeholder management processes" is critical to the long-term success of PPPs (2014: 1210).

One other factor that makes PPPs unique is their complexity: they are hybrids that combine different organizational forms and, thus, complicate some of the ideas embedded within stakeholder theory (De Schepper, et al., 2014: 1211). That said, the authors still find value in the insights of stakeholder theory, particularly with respect to identifying the interests and influence of different stakeholders (e.g., Mitchell, Agle, Wood, 1997).

Some scholars see PPPs as critical to creating policy successes. Leland and Read (2012) claim that PPPs have been commended for contributing to the resolution of challenging social problems, despite the criticism they face for insufficient stakeholder input and fears that the private sector participants may impose significant costs on the public sector partners through their oversized influence (2012: 312). The authors in this field see private sector partners as legitimate and valuable resources that offer ways of creatively addressing an array of social problems that might otherwise be difficult or impossible to resolve. Yet, private partners bring additional challenges, especially a profit-seeking posture and significant power in project negotiations. Chapin (2002) argues that municipalities have taken on a "capitalistic mindset" and have, therefore, demonstrated their comfort level in investing public funds into activities that are "speculative." Others, like Ghere (2001), see PPPs as governments giving up vital resources and values – including due process and accountability –

as a way to create more real-world benefits. Leland and Read, on the other hand, remain more optimistic about the potential of PPPs to create value and serve multiple stakeholders – particularly when policy advocates are well-trained and can fully understand the opportunistic tendencies of their private-sector partners (2012: 336).

Others note the complexity of PPPs and the challenge of creating theory and governance insights that can appropriately address them (e.g., Kabanda, 2014). Stakeholder theory has become a popular tool to select criteria for decision-making, to identify and assess different stakeholders, and to determine the appropriate balance of risks and rewards in existing PPPs themselves (Kabanda, 2014: 2). Kabanda (2014) notes that one of the big challenges associated with PPPs is not their initial design, but their ability to evolve in light of ongoing activities. In many cases, stakeholders may be ignored or neglected after PPPs are launched, even though their input and support may be vital to the project's ongoing success. After conducting a study on a PPP involving hydropower in Uganda, Kabanda (2014) concluded that PPPs *can* be powerful and effective vehicles that create value for all parties involved. Getting support from the private sector is increasingly critical to accomplishing policy goals in a global world where resources for the public sector are decreasing (Kabanda, 2014: 11). Additionally, he suggests the following factors should be considered in the creation of a successful PPP: (i) a readiness assessment; (ii) a clear understanding of the interests and expectations of the relevant stakeholders; (iii) the creation of trust within the PPP and among key partners; (iv) a strong risk-mitigation process tailored to the project; and (v) clarity around the relevant responsibilities and roles of both public and private sector participants (Akintoye, Beck, and Hardcastle, 2003; Kabanda, 2014: 12;).

We see PPPs as an exciting new context for the policy conversation, which holds great value, both as a way of deepening ties to stakeholder theory and as a way for policy to create more value for stakeholders. The hybrid and complex nature of PPPs makes questions of "purpose" critical subjects of discussion to ensure the long-term success of the project. Such conversations rely uniquely on normative stakeholder theory. Stakeholder theory, then, appears to be a prime resource that could enrich the policy dialogue on PPPs in terms of both content (i.e., a complex set of objectives that spans outcomes, values, and goals) and process (i.e., how to engage stakeholders in a process that clarifies and establishes purpose). Additionally, by blending concerns for purpose and core values with a desire to create positive outcomes for stakeholders, stakeholder theory provides a way for policy scholars to harness the power of business – particularly efficient and cost-effective operational processes – without losing focus on larger objectives. Given the complexity of PPPs, such conversations are critically important, and may be vital to aligning the interests of the diverse parties and achieving lasting success.

Future Directions in Public Policy

The policy domain appears to us to be one of the richest for strong connections with stakeholder theory. Important linkages already exist, particularly with the widespread use of stakeholder language, tools, and forms of analysis. Despite the notable examples listed above, scholarly policy work often lacks systematic discussion of normative issues such as questions of purpose, how to give due consideration to various constituencies, and how to serve the larger public good. This is surprising given how central normative questions are in public policy. However, since academics tend to confine themselves to the literatures and skills they have, such discourse may be alien to scholars operating in this field, or they may feel ill-equipped to address them. This may, therefore, be an opportunity for stakeholder theory scholars to spend more time writing about public policy, attend conferences, and help illustrate how normative thinking within this field could elevate scholarship and enhance existing work. New governance theory and PPPs provide rich new opportunities for building deeper connections between stakeholder theory and public policy, especially in terms of the normative dimensions of inquiry and exploring new ways for stakeholders to come together to jointly pursue their interests.

In the near future, we expect the public policy and stakeholder literature to contain a renewed focus on the corporate governance and public policy implications of automation and "disruptive" technology (such as driverless cars). In an age where people "own" less and "subscribe" more to quasi-public services and where machines, robots and big data are rapidly displacing human workers and ramping up the capacity to do more with less, we face a rapidly changing world where the pace and scale of change seems only to be increasing. When you combine those trends with shrinking resources and demands to do more with less, it is no surprise that people in policy are experimenting with new ways of organization, many of which involve engaging with stakeholders and bringing them more thoroughly into the policy process. Such efforts may go a long way toward re-enfranchising stakeholders as well as ensuring that policy mechanisms and choices can better deliver the value that stakeholders seek.

In an age where government is under pressure to innovate, to do more with fewer resources, and to be more accountable for delivering results, it is not a surprise to see the language of stakeholder theory (and that of business) show up with more frequency in the public policy literature as well. While we acknowledge the importance of retaining key disciplinary boundaries, we see room to enrich each field with insights derived from other disciplines. Stakeholder theory provides a focus on the notions of purpose and values that are central to policy discussions, yet also incorporates concern for delivering results and engaging with stakeholders to add mutual value. All of these factors make it a timely theory that may assist policy theorists to respond to calls for reform, change, and improvement. It also provides an attractive alternative to proposals that government become a "business," a theme that was prominent in the 2016 election and a common refrain among those who increasingly associate public policy with gridlock, division, and dysfunction.

Conclusion

In this chapter, we have focused on understanding the impact of stakeholder theory on law and public policy, particularly noting where it appears within the academic literature and has influenced the dialogue. We have also tried to explore ways in which these connections can be deepened and made more overt, particularly where doing so can enhance the quality of scholarship in the field.

Due to the long-standing and extensive ties between stakeholder theory and corporate law, a slight majority of the chapter focused on stakeholder theory and the law. The debates between stakeholder and shareholder theorists are long-standing, have profound implications for how corporate governance works and how managers run firms, and look likely to continue for the foreseeable future. From proposed policy reforms to corporate governance, to legal debates about shareholder and stakeholder rights and the evolution of benefit corporations, stakeholder theory is an established part of the dialogue in law and its influence appears to be growing.

Notes

1. Please note that in this chapter we rely extensively on a few published works, which are also great resources for this topic, particularly "Stakeholder theory in related disciplines" from *Stakeholder Theory: The State of the Art* (Freeman, et al., 2010) and *The Shareholder Value Myth* (2012) by Lynn Stout.
2. At least twelve states have adopted B-Corporation statutes, including Colorado, California, Hawaii, Louisiana, Maryland, Massachusetts, New Jersey, New York, Pennsylvania, South Carolina, Vermont, and Virginia. At the time of this writing, at least nine states and one federal territory have adopted L3C statutes, including Illinois, Louisiana, Maine, Michigan, North Carolina, Rhode Island, Utah, Vermont, Wyoming, and Puerto Rico.

Bibliography

Americans for Community Development. (n.d.). Laws. Retrieved April 29, 2017, from https://americansforcommunitydevelopment.org/laws/.

Akintoye, A., Beck, M., & Hardcastle, C. (2003). *Public-private partnerships: Managing risks and opportunities.* Oxford, UK: Blackwell Science.

Alpaslan, C. M., Green, S. E., & Mitroff, I. I. (2009). Corporate governance in a context of crises: Towards a stakeholder theory of crisis management. *Journal of Contingencies and Crisis Management, 17*(1): 38–49.

American Bar Association. (1990). Other constitution statutes: Potential for confusion. *The Business Lawyer, 45*(4): 2253–2271.

Bainbridge, S. M. (1993). Independent directors and the ALI corporate governance project. *George Washington Law Review, 61*: 1034–1083.

Bainbridge, S. M. (2011). Article: Dodd-Frank: Quack federal corporate governance round II. *Minnesota Law Review. 95*: 1779–1821.

Bebchuk, L. A. (2005). The case for increasing shareholder power. *Harvard Law Review, 115*(3): 833–914.

Belinfanti, T., & Stout, L. A. (2017). Contested visions: The value of systems theory for corporate law. Cornell Legal Studies Research Paper No. 17–17.

Berle, A.A. Jr., & Means, G. C. (1932).*The modern corporation and private property.* New York: Macmillan

Berner, M. M., Amos, J. M., & Morse, R. S. (2011). What constitutes effective citizen participation in local government views from city stakeholders. *Public Administration Quarterly, 35*(1): 128–63.

Bertus, M., Jahera Jr., J. S., & Yost, K. (2008). Sarbanes-Oxley, corporate governance, and strategic dividend decisions. Unpublished article, Auburn University.

Blair, M. M., & Stout, L. (1999). A team production theory of corporate law. *Virginia Law Review, 85*(2): 248–392.

Boatright, J. R. (1994). Fiduciary duties and the shareholder-management relation: Or, what's so special about shareholders? *Business Ethics Quarterly, 4*(4): 393–407.

Boatright, J. R. (2000).*Ethics and the conduct of business.* 3rd edn. Upper Saddle River, NJ: Prentice-Hall.

Bovaird, T. (2004). Public-private partnerships: From contested topics to prevalent practice. *International Review of Administrative Sciences, 70*(2): 199–215.

Brugha, R., & Varvasovsky, Z. (2000). Stakeholder analysis: A review. *Health Policy and Planning, 15*(3): 239–246.

Bryson, J. (2004). What to do when stakeholders matter. *Public Management Review, 6*(1): 21–53.

Carlson, C. *A practical guide to collaborative governance.* (2007). Portland, OR: Policy Consensus Initiative.

Ciepley, D. (2013). Beyond public and private: Toward a political theory of the corporation. *American Political Science Review, 107*(1): 139–158.

Citizens United v. FEC, 558 US 310 (2010).

Chapin, T. (2002). Beyond the Entrepreneurial City: Municipal Capitalism in San Diego. *Journal of Urban Affairs, 24*(5): 565–581.

Cremers, M., & Sepe, S. M. (2016). Article: The shareholder value of empowered boards. *Stanford Law Review, 68*: 67–148.

Cummings, B. (2012). Benefit corporations: How to enforce a mandate to promote the public interest. *Columbia Law Review, 112*(3): 578–627.

De Schepper, S., Dooms, M., & Haezendonck, E. (2014). Stakeholder dynamics and responsibilities in Public-Private Partnerships: A mixed experience. *International Journal of Project Management, 32*: 1210–1222.

Dodge v. Ford Motor Co., 204 Mich. 459 (1919).

Donaldson, C., & Preston, L. E. (1995). The stakeholder theory of the corporation: Concepts, evidence, and implications. *Academy of Management Review, 20* (1): 65–91.

Dorf, M. C., & Fagan, J. A. (2003). Problem solving courts: From innovation to institutionalization. *American Criminal Law Review, 40*: 1501–1511.

Dorf, M. C., & Sabel, C. F. (1998). A constitution of democratic experimentalism. *Columbia Law Review, 98*(2): 267–473.

Dougherty, T. J. (2016). *The director's handbook.* New Providence, NJ: Corporation Services Company.

eBay Domestic Holdings, Inc. v. Newmark. *16 A 3d 1* (2010).

Elhauge, E. (2005). Sacrificing corporate profits in the public interest. *New York University Law Review, 80* (3): 733–869.

Fiorino, D. J. (1999). Rethinking environmental regulation: Perspectives on law and governance. *Harvard Environmental Law Review, 23*: 441–469.

Fisch, J. E. (2006). Symposium: Robert Clark's corporate law: Twenty years of change: Measuring efficiency in corporate law: The role of shareholder primacy. *Iowa Journal of Corporate Law, 31*: 637–674.

Fort, T. (1997). The corporation as mediating institution: An efficacious synthesis of stakeholder theory and corporate constituency statutes. *Notre Dame Law Review, 73*(1): 173–203.

Freeman, R. E. (1984). *Strategic management: A stakeholder approach.* Boston: Pitman.

Freeman, R. E. (1994). The politics of stakeholder theory: Some future directions. *Business Ethics Quarterly, 4*(4): 409–421.

Freeman, R. E. (1999). Response: Divergent stakeholder theory. *Academy of Management Review* 24 (2): 233–36.

Freeman, R. E., Harrison, J. S., Wicks, A. C., Parmar, B. L., & De Colle, S. (2010). *Stakeholder theory: The state of the art.* New York: Cambridge University Press.

Friedman, M. (1970). The social responsibility of business is to increase its profits. *New York Times.* September 13: 33.

Friedman, M. T., & Mason, D. (2005). Stakeholder management and the public subsidization of Nashville's coliseum. *Journal of Urban Affairs, 27* (1): 93–118.

Ghere, R. K. (2001). Ethical futures and public-private partnerships: Peering far down the track. *Public Organization Review: A Global Journal, 1*: 303–319.

Gillan, S., & Starks, L. T. (2003). Corporate governance, corporate ownership, and the role of institutional investors: A global perspective. *Journal of Applied Finance, 13*(2): 4–22.

Greiling, D., & Halachmi, A. (2012). Introduction: Public private partnerships: Accountability and governance. *Public Administration Quarterly, 36*(2): 133–139.

Hallett, M. A. & Rogers, R. (1994). The push for "truth in sentencing": Evaluating competing stakeholder constructions: The case for contextual constructionism in evaluation research. *Evaluation and Program Planning, 17*(2): 187–196.

Hansmann, H. & Kraakman, R. (2001). Essay: The end of history for corporate law. *Georgetown Law Journal, 89*(2): 439–468.

Hasnas, J. (1998). The normative theories of business ethics. A guide for the perplexed. *Business Ethics Quarterly, 8*(1): 19–42.

Innes, J. E. (1998). Information in communicative planning. *Journal of the American Planning Association, 64*: 52–63.

Innes, J. E., & Booher, D. E. (2004). Reframing public participation: Strategies for the 21st century. *Planning Theory & Practice, 5*: 419–436.

Jennings, M. M., & Happel, S. (2003). The post-Enron era for stakeholder theory: A new look at corporate governance and the Coase Theorem. *Mercer Law Review, 54*; 873–938.

Jensen, M. C. (1989). The evidence speaks loud and clear. *Harvard Business Review, 67*(6): 186–188.

Jensen, M. C. (2001). Value maximization, stakeholder theory, and the corporate objective function. *European Financial Management, 7*(3): 297–317.

Johnson, L. (2013). Pluralism in corporate form: Corporate law and benefit corps. *Regent University Law Review. 25*(2): 269–298.

Jonas, C. (2016). Reply: "New governance" in legal thought and in the world: Some splitting as an antidote to overzealous lumping. *Minnesota Law Review, 89*: 471–495.

Kabanda, U. (2014). A Case Study of Bujagali Hydropower Public Private Partnership Project Between Uganda Government and Bujagali Energy Ltd in Electricity Generation in Africa. *American Scientific Research Journal for Engineering Technology, and Sciences, 8*(1): 1–13.

Kacperczyk, A. (2009). With greater power comes greater responsibility? Takeover protection and corporate attention to stakeholders. *Strategic Management Journal, 30*: 261–285.

Keay, A. (2011). *The corporate objective, corporations, globalization and the law.* Cheltenham: Edward Elgar Publishing.

Leland, S., & Read, D. (2012). Stimulating real estate development through public-private partnerships assessing the perceived opportunities and challenges. *Public Administration Quarterly, 36*(3): 311–340.

Lukensmeyer, C., & Torres, L. *Public deliberation: A manager's guide to citizen engagement.* (2006). Washington, DC: IBM Center for Business and Government.

Luyet, V., Schlaepfer, R., Parlange, M., & Buttler, A. (2012). A framework to implement stakeholder participation in environmental projects. *Journal of Environmental Management, 11*: 213–219.

Macey, J. R. (2008). Essay: A close read of an excellent commentary on *Dodge v. Ford. Virginia Law and Business Review, 3*; 177–90.

Marens, R., & Wicks, A. C. (1999). Getting real: Stakeholder theory, managerial practice, and the general irrelevance of fiduciary duties owed to shareholders. *Business Ethics Quarterly, 9*(2): 272–293.

Matten, D., & Crane, A. (2005). Corporate citizenship: Toward an extended theoretical conceptualization. *Academy of Management Review, 30*(1): 166–179.

Millon, D. (1991). Redefining corporate law. *Indiana Law Review, 24*(2): 223–277.

Mitchell, R., Agle, B. R., & Wood, D. J. (1997). Toward a theory of stakeholder identification and salience: Defining the principles of who and what really counts. *Academy of Management Review, 22*(4): 853–886.

Mulligan, L. N. (2007). What's good for the goose is not good for the gander: Sarbanes-Oxley-style nonprofit reforms. *Michigan Law Review, 105*(8): 1981–2009.

Moriarty, J. (2012). The connection between stakeholder theory and stakeholder democracy: An excavation and defense. *Business & Society, 53*(6): 820–852.

Murray, J. H. (2013). Choose your own master: Social enterprise, certifications, and benefit corporation status. *American University Business Law Review*, 2: 1–53.

O'Leary, R., & Bingham, L. B. (2007). *A manager's guide to resolving conflicts in collaborative networks*. Washington, DC: IBM Center for the Business of Government.

Orts, E.W. (1992). Beyond shareholders: Interpreting corporate constituency statutes. *George Washington Law Review. 61*(1): 14–135.

Phillips, R., Freeman, R. E., & Wicks, A. C. (2003). What stakeholder theory is not. *Business Ethics Quarterly. 13*(4): 479–502.

Reich, M. (1994). *Political mapping of health policy: A guide for managing the political dimension of health policy*. Boston, MA: Harvard School of Public Health.

Shutkin, W. A. (2000). *The land that could be: Environmentalism and democracy in the twenty-first century*. Cambridge, MA: The MIT Press.

Siebecker, M. R. (2010). A new discourse theory of the firm after *Citizens United. The George Washington Law Review, 79*(1): 161–231.

Smith, M. (1993). *Pressure, power and policy: State autonomy and policy networks in Britain and the United States*. Hemel Hempstead: Harvester Wheatsheaf.

Smith, N.C., & Rönnegard, D (2016). Shareholder primacy, corporate social responsibility, and the role of business schools. *Journal of Business Ethics. 134*(3): 463–478.

Stephens, J., & Berner, M. (2011). Learning from your neighbor: The value of public participation evaluation for public policy dispute resolution. *Journal of Public Deliberation, 7*(1), Article No. 10.

Stout, L. A. (2012). *The shareholder value myth*. San Francisco: Berrett-Koehler Publishers.

Stout, L. A., Robé, J., Ireland, P., et al. (2016). *The Modern Corporation Statement on Company Law*. Retrieved August 16, 2017, from https://papers.ssrn.com/sol3/papers.cfm?abstract_id=2848833.

Strine Jr., L. E. (2012). Our continuing struggle with the idea that for-profit corporations seek profit. *Wake Forest Law Review, 47*: 135–172.

Strine Jr., L. E. (2008). Breaking the corporate governance logjam in Washington: Some constructive thoughts on a responsible path forward. *The Business Lawyer, 63*(4): 1079–1107.

Trimble, M., & Lazaro, M. (2014). Evaluation criteria for participatory research: Insights from Coastal Uruguay. *Environmental Management, 54*: 122–137.

Van Der Weide, M. (1996). Against fiduciary duties to corporate stakeholders. *Delaware Journal of Corporate Law, 21*: 27–241.

Walker, G. & Daniels, S. (2001). Natural Resource Policy and the Paradox of Public Involvement: Bringing Scientists and Citizens Together. In G. Gray, M. Enzer, & J. Kusel, eds., *Understanding community-based ecosystem management*, pp. 253–269. New York: The Haworth Press,

Windsor, D. (2000). Moral activism and value harmonization in an integrating global economy. In Proceedings, 7th Annual International Conference Promoting Business Ethics, 2 vols. 1, 300–312.

Zingales, L. (2012). Do Business Schools Incubate Criminals? Bloomberg. July 16, 2012. Retrieved May 12, 2017, from www.bloomberg.com/view/articles/2012-07-16/do-business-schools-incubate-criminals-.

Shareholder Primacy vs. Stakeholder Theory

The Law as Constraint and Potential Enabler of Stakeholder Concern[*]

DAVID RÖNNEGARD
University of Gothenburg and INSEAD

N. CRAIG SMITH
INSEAD

Abstract

This chapter examines the Shareholder Primacy Norm (SPN) as a widely acknowledged impediment to corporate social responsibility (CSR), including how this relates to Stakeholder Theory. We start by explaining the SPN and then review its status under US and UK law and show that it is not a legal requirement, at least under the guise of shareholder value maximization. This is in contrast to the common assertion that managers are legally constrained from addressing CSR issues if doing so would be inconsistent with the economic interests of shareholders. Nonetheless, while the SPN might be muted as a legal norm, we show that it is certainly evident as a powerful social norm among managers and in business schools— reflective, in part, of the sole voting rights of shareholders on corporate boards and of the dominance of Shareholder Theory. We argue that this view of CSR is misguided, not least when associated with claims of a purported legally enforceable requirement to maximize shareholder value. We propose two ways by which the influence of the SPN among managers might be attenuated: extending voting rights to non-shareholder stakeholders or extending fiduciary duties of executives to non-shareholder stakeholders.

The "basic debate" in business ethics is often characterized as one between whether managers should focus primarily on the interests of shareholders and whether they should consider or balance the interests of a wider group of stakeholders (Agle & Mitchell, 2008; Boatright, 2002; Campbell, 2007; Freeman, 1984; Phillips, 1997). This has also become known as the "Friedman-Freeman debate," though it should be noted that Freeman himself rejects this characterization (Freeman, 2008).[1] Nonetheless, business ethics as an academic field has reacted disapprovingly to the managerial focus on shareholder interests of the so-called shareholder theory of Milton Friedman, who asserted that the social responsibility of business is "to use its resources and engage in activities designed to increase its profits so long as it stays within the rules of the game" (1962: 133). In contrast, Freeman's (1984) seminal formulation of stakeholder theory, while not denying that profitability should be a goal of corporations, sees the primary purpose of the corporation as being a vehicle to manage stakeholder interests. This has become one of the most prominent theories both within business ethics (Phillips, 2003) and the wider field of management, as well as a dominant paradigm for corporate social responsibility (CSR; McWilliams & Siegel, 2001).

The prescription that managers should focus primarily on shareholder interests has been closely tied to the shareholder primacy norm (SPN). The SPN is considered part of a manager's legal fiduciary duty that requires managers to make decisions on behalf of the corporation that further the interests of shareholders. It has been treated as a major obstacle to CSR, and by extension stakeholder theory, because it is said to hinder managers from considering the interests of other corporate stakeholders besides shareholders (Boatright, 1994; Campbell, 2007; Dodd, 1932, Evan & Freeman, 2003; Hinkley, 2002; Phillips, Freeman, & Wicks, 2003; Testy, 2002).

While there are many definitions of CSR, the EU has advanced a widely disseminated definition of CSR as: "a concept whereby companies integrate social and environmental concerns in their business operations and in their interaction with stakeholders on a voluntary basis. It is about enterprises deciding to go beyond the minimum legal requirements and obligations stemming from collective agreements in order to address societal needs" (COM/2006/0136/final). It is clear from this base definition that CSR can be at odds with the SPN, at least if managers act to meet obligations to non-shareholder stakeholders (beyond legal requirements and collective agreements) and in doing so are acting contrary to shareholders' interests. Accordingly, the legitimacy of the SPN is a major issue of debate in business ethics.

The SPN most typically finds expression in shareholder value maximization (SVM). If one starts from the assumption that the interests of shareholders lie in maximizing their return on investment, then this results in a prescription to managers to maximize shareholder value. This does not necessarily preclude CSR, but it does make it conditional on SVM. Accordingly, van Marrewijk (2003: 102) offers five distinct and specific interpretations of CSR, of which his "profit driven" interpretation is clearly the most compatible with the SVM: "the integration of social, ethical and ecological aspects into business operations and decision-making provided it contributes to the financial bottom line." In contrast, his "caring" interpretation of CSR "consists of balancing economic, social, and ecological concerns, which are all three important in themselves." Similarly, Garriga and Mele (2004: 53) identify four categories of CSR theories

(instrumental, political, integrative, and ethical), of which instrumental includes those theories under which SVM "is the supreme criterion to evaluate specific corporate social activity."

The SPN does not necessarily preclude attention to CSR that would not be maximizing shareholder value. If the interests of shareholders are primary, then their interests will decide what goal the corporation should pursue, whether it is SVM or something else. Nevertheless, the legitimacy of the SPN has an important bearing on the goal of the corporation and whether it should be a vehicle for the pursuit of shareholder interests (Friedman, 1970; Jensen, 2002) or for managing stakeholder interests (Freeman, Harrison, & Wicks, 2007; Freeman et al. 2010). Walsh (2004: 349) has highlighted the critical importance of this question: "Since the rise of the first corporations two thousand years ago, we have been trying to develop a theory of the firm that explains and guides firm behavior … This is arguably the most important theoretical and practical issue confronting us today."

Shareholder theory and stakeholder theory are not necessarily incompatible (Freeman et al., 2010). However, if SPN is a dominant norm among managers, this has implications for the shape that stakeholder theory can take, as well as for CSR. Descriptively, if shareholder primacy expressed as SVM (i.e., consistent with Friedman's shareholder theory) is the dominant model of practice, it is little surprising that CSR advocates are disappointed with corporate social performance and charge companies with "greenwashing" (e.g., *New Scientist*, 2010; Polaris Institute, 2007). To a large extent, we know already this model of shareholder primacy as SVM often predominates. Indeed, it seems that the view that the purpose of the firm is something other than maximizing shareholder value has yet to gain widespread acceptance within the academy, let alone within business (Jones, 2010; Stout, 2012).

In answer to the normative question, if the SPN expressed as SVM is the better, more legitimate model, this has profound implications for CSR. This need not be understood as a death blow to

CSR, but it does mean that CSR should be seen primarily from a strategic perspective rather than a moral perspective, and that CSR activities should be justified through "business case" reasoning (e.g., Porter & Kramer, 2006; 2011). Caring, synergistic, and holistic interpretations of CSR (van Marrewijk, 2003) would have little practical import in most business contexts. Nevertheless, it is not the aim of this chapter to answer whether SVM or its proposed alternatives are *normatively* preferable. The aim of this chapter is to examine the *descriptive* grounds for adherence to the SPN, with specific attention to its efficacy as a legal and social norm for management and the basis by which it can serve as an impediment to CSR, specifically in terms of stakeholder theory.

We start by exploring the descriptive grounds for the SPN and based on this descriptive understanding – and given the extensive criticism of the SPN – we move on to explore potential legal avenues for attenuating the SPN. We maintain that the SPN is mute as a legal norm while operative as a social norm, in part because shareholders are afforded sole voting rights regarding the board of directors. Several corporate governance suggestions are considered for addressing the primacy of shareholders and we suggest that extending managerial fiduciary duties beyond shareholders is the most promising.

Explanations for the Influence of the SPN

We first consider the SPN as a legal norm in the common law systems of the United States and the United Kingdom. We maintain that the SPN is not legally enforceable due to the business judgment rule as well as legal enactments that specifically allow managers to consider the interests of a wider group of stakeholders. Second, we consider the role of the SPN as a social norm among managers. We maintain that even though normative pressures are mounting on managers from non-shareholder constituencies, the SPN is still relied upon by managers because it is reinforced by the *structure* of corporate law (i.e., the sole voting rights of

shareholders) as well as systems of remuneration that tie managerial incentives to shareholder interests. We conclude that although the SPN has its origins in corporate law, the SPN today is not a legally enforceable norm, but it is still very much alive as a social norm among managers. Moreover, while managers are no longer legally prohibited from engaging in CSR that might be inconsistent with shareholder interests, the incentive structures that guide corporate behavior are still geared toward shareholder primacy, leading managers to favor shareholder interests over those of other stakeholders.

The SPN as a Legal Norm

Corporate law in the United States and the United Kingdom, comprising both common law and statutory law, is structured to ensure that corporations work in the interest of shareholders. However, this primacy of shareholders has not been formally identified in statutory law (Fisch, 2006). Thus the SPN is a development of common law and debate about its efficacy is as a norm stemming from judicial decisions. Common law provides the clearest articulation of shareholder primacy in the court cases specifying that managers and directors owe fiduciary duties to shareholders and must make decisions that are in their best interests (Smith, 1998). The most famous articulation of the norm comes from the 1919 case of *Dodge v. Ford Motor Co.*, wherein Chief Justice Ostrander said:

> A business corporation is organized and carried on primarily for the profit of the stockholders. The powers of the directors are to be employed for that end. The discretion of directors is to be exercised in the choice of means to attain that end, and does not extend to a change in the end itself, to the reduction of profits, or to the non-distribution of profits among shareholders in order to devote them to other purposes.

This fiduciary duty in part consists of a duty of loyalty and a duty of care to shareholders (Clark, 1985). "Loyalty" implies that managers should promote the interest of shareholders but also that they should not put themselves in a position where their interests might conflict with those of the shareholders. An example would be if a director stood to benefit directly from a corporate contract, or if a director were to put the interest of some third party ahead of shareholder interests. "Care" implies that managers are expected to make decisions that ordinary, prudent individuals in a similar position would make under similar circumstances for the benefit of shareholders (Clark, 1985; Paine, 2006). The primacy of shareholders is manifest in that they are, in the normal course of business, the sole corporate constituency to be granted fiduciary protection by the courts (Fisch, 2006).

Dodge v. Ford is often cited by advocates of shareholder primacy. However, Cornell law professor Lynn Stout (2012) suggests that it is widely misunderstood. First, it is not a case about a public corporation: "It was a case about the duty a controlling majority shareholder (Henry Ford) owed to the minority shareholders (Horace and John Dodge) in what was functionally a closely held company – a different legal animal altogether" (Stout, 2012: 26). Second, Justice Ostrander's remark was just that; as Stout (2012: 26) observes: "This remark … was what lawyers call 'mere dicta' – a tangential observation that the Michigan Supreme Court made in passing, that was unnecessary to reach the court's chosen outcome or 'holding'. It is holdings that matter in law and create binding precedent for future cases."

The judicial development of the SPN has a long history, dating back well before it became operative in the courts in the 1830s (Smith, 1998). Much current interest in the SPN stems from the flourishing advocacy of CSR, with progressive legal scholars, as well as business ethicists and corporate directors, viewing the SPN as a major impediment to managers including the interests of stakeholders other than shareholders in their decision-making (Testy, 2002). For much of the nineteenth century, this analysis was probably correct. However, with the subsequent development of the business judgment rule in common law and more recent statutory developments, managers today have significant discretion in addressing non-shareholder interests (Marens & Wicks, 1999; Stout, 2012). Thus Smith (1998: 280) concludes that "application of the

shareholder primacy norm to publicly traded corporations is muted by the business judgment rule."

Stout (2012: 30) suggests that the 1986 case, *Revlon, Inc. v. MacAndrews & Forbes Holdings,* is the only significant modern case "where a Delaware court has held an unconflicted board of directors liable for failing to maximize shareholder value." But she adds that this case ruling, while often cited by advocates of shareholder wealth maximization along with *Dodge v. Ford,* is also misunderstood, and is the exception that proves the rule. Revlon's Board planned to take Revlon private, thus "it is only when a public corporation is about to stop being a public corporation that directors lose the protection of the business judgment rule and must embrace shareholder wealth as their only goal" (Stout, 2012: 31). In contrast, Stout cites the 2011 case of *Air Products, Inc. v. Airgas, Inc.,* wherein the Delaware court ruled in favor of the Airgas board of directors, which had refused a takeover offer from Air Products at $70 a share when Airgas was trading at $40–50 a share. As a memorandum from law firm Skadden (2011: 3) explains, the judge "was 'constrained' to follow Delaware Supreme Court precedent, holding clearly that a law-trained Court must not substitute its business judgment for that of the board."

The business judgment rule is the presumption that directors have not breached their fiduciary duty of care, so-called because it relieves the court of any duty to make evaluations of the business judgment of a director. For example, if a board of directors decides to donate a million dollars of corporate resources to the Japanese Earthquake Relief Fund of the Red Cross, shareholders might try to sue the directors personally for using corporate funds in a manner that does not further shareholder interests. But the business judgment rule relieves the court from considering whether or not the donation is a good business decision (and it might be, if favorable publicity were to result) – evaluating the quality of business decisions is difficult and this is not the primary competence of the courts. In effect, the rule makes the fiduciary duty of care unenforceable because courts will not consider the quality of business decisions which would otherwise be the primary evidence for lack of care (Cohn, 1983).

Shareholders rarely succeed in derivative suits against directors on claims of a breach of care. It is generally only the duty of loyalty that courts will consider when derivative suits are brought against directors. However, evaluating whether directors acted in bad faith is also difficult to determine because most business decisions seen as unfavorable to shareholders can be rationalized to seem reasonable at the time they were made. Thus, courts primarily consider whether any self-dealing has occurred when evaluating breaches of loyalty. Heracleous and Lan (2010: 24) comment:

> ... when directors go against shareholder wishes – even when a loss in value is documented – courts side with directors the vast majority of the time. Shareholders seem to get this. They've tried to unseat directors through lawsuits just 24 times in large corporations over the past 20 years; they've succeeded only eight times. In short, directors are to a great extent autonomous.

Fiduciary duties developed in common law have been explicitly defined by the incorporation statutes of most states in the United States. For example, the Model Business Corporation Act (2002) prepared by the American Bar Association and adopted by twenty-four states (but not Delaware) says: "An officer, when performing in such capacity, shall act: 1) in good faith; 2) with the care that a person in a like position would reasonably exercise under similar circumstances; and 3) in a manner the officer reasonably believes to be in the best interests of the corporation" (section 8.42 Standards of Conduct for Officers).

Thus, item 1 states the duty of loyalty, item 2 states the duty of care, and item 3 can be interpreted as referring to something akin to the SPN. Whether or not "the best interests of the corporation" includes non-shareholder interests is not entirely clear. Millon (1991: 228) writes that "corporate law has avoided such puzzles by, for the most part, equating the duty to the corporation with a duty to act in the best interest of its shareholders." But this does not *per se* exclude directors from considering the interests of non-shareholders. In Delaware, where 56 percent of US corporations

are registered (Eisenberg, 2000), and which is generally considered to have the most shareholder friendly statutes, there is no explicit statutory requirement that managers should only consider the interests of shareholders in their decision-making.

Moreover, most states have adopted "non-shareholder constituency statutes" that explicitly allow managers to consider the interests of non-shareholder constituencies when making decisions (McDonnell, 2004; Orts, 1992). Pennsylvania was first to adopt such a statute in 1983; states such as New York and Nevada have followed suit (Delaware, however, has not). These statutes do not *require* managers to consider the interests of non-shareholders, but they make explicit that managers are not prohibited from doing so. As Orts (1992: 133) concludes:

> Some argue that the statutes do not go far enough – employees and other interests should be granted "codetermination" status with their own representatives on the board or standing to enforce independent claims against the corporation. Others respond that the statutes go too far, conferring to corporate management unaccountable power, removed from such necessary constraints as hostile takeovers. In any event, constituency statutes once again move the debate surrounding corporate governance beyond the interests of shareholders alone.

The American Law Institute's (1994: 55) *Principles of Corporate Governance* also provides considerable latitude for managers to act beyond the apparent dictates of the SPN. Section 2.01 states:

> Even if corporate profit and shareholder gain are not thereby enhanced, the corporation, in the conduct of its business: 1) Is obliged, to the same extent as a natural person, to act within the boundaries set by law; 2) May take into account ethical considerations that are reasonably regarded as appropriate to the responsible conduct of business; and, 3) May devote a reasonable amount of resources to public welfare, humanitarian, educational and philanthropic purposes.

This consensus document has been regularly cited and relied upon by US courts.

The United Kingdom has also seen the introduction of statutes that explicitly allow managers to consider the interests of multiple stakeholders. The 1985 Companies Act stated that directors must take into account the interests of employees when performing their functions for the company and that this is to be regarded as a fiduciary duty owed to the company. Under the 2006 Companies Act, directors are further required to take into account the interests of other stakeholders such as suppliers, customers, the community, and the environment. However, as in the USA, the act does not give non-shareholder stakeholders the right to challenge decisions of directors in court if they feel their interests have not been taken into account. While this suggests directors still only have fiduciary duties to shareholders, they are now also at liberty to take into consideration the interests of a wider constituency of stakeholders.

Thus, potential common law restrictions on managerial discretion for considering non-shareholder interests have largely disappeared; the SPN is muted by the business judgment rule and recent statutory provisions in most US states and the United Kingdom explicitly allow managers to consider non-shareholder constituencies in their decision making. Stout (2012: 31) observes as follows:

> The business judgment rule thus allows directors in public corporations that plan to stay public to enjoy a remarkably wide range of autonomy in deciding what to do with the corporation's earnings and assets. As long as they do not take those assets for themselves, they can give them to charity; spend them on raises and health care for employees; refuse to pay dividends so as to build up a cash cushion that benefits creditors; and pursue low-profit projects that benefit the community, society, or the environment. They can do all these things even if the result is to decrease – not increase – shareholder value.

We may then justifiably question the claim that managers are legally bound to disregard non-shareholder interests that conflict with those of shareholders. As Stout concludes, SVM is a managerial choice, not a managerial obligation. Progressive legal scholars and others are correct in pointing out the importance of the SPN, but not as a *legal* norm. There are good reasons to think that managers follow the SPN, not because they are

legally bound to do so, but because the SPN is a *social* norm in the business community.

The SPN as a Social Norm

Anderson (2000: 170) defines a social norm as "a standard of behavior shared by a social group, commonly understood by its members as authoritative or obligatory for them." Cialdini and Trost (1998: 152) specify that social norms "guide and/or constrain social behavior without the force of laws." We maintain that managers as a social group, both within and between corporations, are generally guided by a social norm of shareholder primacy.

Business schools teach as part of the "Theory of the Firm" that profit maximization is the purpose of the corporation in society and that it is the duty of managers to pursue this end on behalf of shareholders as their agents (Gentile, 2004; Ghoshal, 2005). West (2011) affirms that this is not only true of business schools but also law schools, and that many of these institutions have no required courses that explore alternative purposes of business. West (2011: 18) observes that "some law and business professors mistakenly are training future lawyers and corporate leaders that corporations have no authority to do good or benefit society other than its shareholders." Of course, these social norms can have profound effects: "what is taught in classes and how students internalize information have consequences for society, government, and business" (West 2011: 18; also see McDonald 2017).

Smith and Van Wassenhove (2010) write, "In most business schools, SVM is the leitmotif of finance teaching and implicit throughout the rest of the curriculum." Consequently, when their students get jobs in the corporate world they are working to an implicit assumption of shareholder primacy – an assumption often reinforced, at least for more senior executives, by compensation packages tied to the share price.[2] Dobson (1999: 69) suggests they "will have had drummed into them that the ultimate objective of all activity within the firm is the maximization of shareholder wealth." Diminished moral responsibility accompanies this, according to Ghoshal (2005). Various commentators (e.g., Gardiner, 2009; Holland, 2009; McDonald 2017) have suggested that a disproportionate focus on SVM by business schools was a contributory factor in the 2008 financial crisis.

There are signs of change. Four out of five executives surveyed by the consulting firm McKinsey (2006: 1) thought that "generating high returns for investors should be accompanied by broader contributions to the public good." However, almost 90 percent of respondents said they were motivated to champion social or environmental causes by profitability or improving public relations. Although many executives think that they should consider the interests of non-shareholder stakeholders, this appears to mostly hold true when they don't conflict with shareholder interests and in particular when both go hand in hand.

While the SPN is prevalent among managers there may be other, potentially countervailing norms. For example, championing CSR and environmental friendliness may be emerging as a social norm among managers in many corporations. Nonetheless, some surveys suggest that US managers believe the law requires them to maximize shareholder wealth and hinders them from pursuing interests that conflict with shareholder interests (Gentile, 2004; Rose, 2007). Managers may believe they are following a legal norm, but it would seem that they are following a social norm that they believe is legal because of its pervasiveness in business.[3] Nevertheless, we maintain that the social norm of shareholder primacy is also reinforced by the *structure* of corporate law that is geared towards shareholder primacy: shareholders exert control over the corporation primarily through their legal right to elect and dismiss directors.

The fiduciary duties imposed on managers in common law are due to early judicial depictions of their relationship with shareholders as one of trust (e.g. Berle, 1931; 1932). Managers were considered *trustees* for the shareholders who were the *owners* of the corporation. However, the corporation was legally separated from its shareholders in the mid-nineteenth century and considered to own

itself, whereas shareholders were considered to own shares as a separate form of property (Pickering, 1968). Despite the legal separation of the corporation from its shareholders in terms of ownership, important features of the structure of corporate law that came with the earlier depiction remained, both in terms of fiduciary duties and more importantly in terms of voting rights of shareholders.

Because shares generally confer voting rights to shareholders, which gives them the power to elect and dismiss the board of directors, there is a real sense in which the directors of the corporation act as agents representing the interests of the shareholders; quite simply, if they do not they may be dismissed (Kraakman et al., 2004). Shareholders may not have the type of direct control necessary for a legal characterization of a principal-agent relationship, but they do have sufficient indirect control for that characterization to be made more generally.[4] For example, the academic literature on agency costs typically describes managers as agents of the shareholders (Clark, 1985). Although the threat of dismissal/non-reelection to the board is real, it should be acknowledged that it rarely happens in practice in large public corporations (Benz & Frey, 2007). However, there are usually other incentive structures in place that aim to align shareholder interests with those of top management; for example, the issuing of shares or stock options and payment of bonuses tied to corporate financial performance. Voting rights matter even in this context because it is common practice for shareholders to approve top management's remuneration by voting. Thus the legal power of shareholders to vote for the board of directors and their remuneration helps perpetuate the SPN as a social norm, not as a principle of law likely to be upheld in court.

The preceding analysis of the SPN as a social norm suggests that, in practice, managers work in the primary pursuit of shareholder interests because: a) they believe it is their legal duty, if not a moral duty (Vermaelen, 2009); b) they fear being dismissed by the board if they do not; and, c) they are often incentivized by remuneration that is tied to shareholder interests. With this norm and the associated set of beliefs and incentives in place, it is not surprising that managers also believe that they should not engage in CSR that might be inconsistent with shareholder interests. With this established, we turn to exploring legal measures that might change the dominance of the SPN as a social norm. We will consider the possibility for change in the sole voting rights of shareholders as well as the possibility of extending fiduciary duties to a broader set of stakeholders. In this context we will also consider the merits of a new form of incorporation statutes called the Benefit Corporation and efforts to increase board diversity.

Extending Voting Rights and Fiduciary Duties of Executives to Non-Shareholder Stakeholders

Given our argument about the structure of corporate law underpinning managerial beliefs about shareholder primacy as a legal norm and reinforcing its status as a social norm, it is appropriate to consider first whether there might be changes in corporate governance such that non-shareholder stakeholders have a greater say, if not voting rights, at board level. In fact, numerous authors over the years have suggested consideration be given to non-shareholder stakeholders in corporate governance, particularly by the board of directors. However, the problem proves to be somewhat intractable.

The suggestions come in a variety of forms and with various justifications. Galai and Wiener (2008) suggest that management "allocation" of board seats to a broader group of stakeholders, primarily employees, can reduce agency costs for corporations. Chilosi and Damiani (2007) suggest that stakeholder representatives on the board may be chosen by employees or appointed by trade unions or government authorities. Bonnafous-Bocher (2005) presents a "proprietorialist" view where stakeholders are encouraged to buy shares and obtain voting rights as shareholders.[5] And Evan and Freeman (2003) suggest on normative grounds that stakeholders be given voting membership on the board, and furthermore, that stakeholders should demand voting membership on pragmatic

grounds in order to have their interests properly represented (Freeman & Evan, 1990). Common to all these conceptions of stakeholder consideration is that none of them articulate how non-shareholder stakeholders (beyond employees) are to be identified, nor how such stakeholders are to vote for their board representatives when such a view is advocated.[6]

The reason why no one has suggested how to appropriately operationalize stakeholder voting rights for board representation is that there are significant practical difficulties to be overcome. These difficulties come primarily in two forms. First, how do we identify who the relevant stakeholders are? Are we concerned with relevant stakeholder organizations, groups, or individuals? Are suppliers and customers relevant stakeholders if they make a single transaction or should they have a working relationship over time in order to have a relevant stake? Also, who is meant to represent "society" as a stakeholder? Second, how do stakeholders vote for their representatives on the board? Does each member of a stakeholder organization get to vote on board decisions or does only the organization as a whole get a vote? Is the size of the stakeholder organization important? Should all stakeholders' votes receive equal weight or do some groups have priority interests? Thus, in abstract, the idea of stakeholder representation on corporate boards is appealing; in practice, it is difficult to realize. Beyond the representation of employees (as we see in German corporate governance), it may be that stakeholder consideration at board level must rely on a broader conception of the role of the board.

Extending voting rights for the board beyond shareholders (and employees) is mired with so many difficulties as to seem infeasible in practice. One might thus instead consider removing the voting rights of shareholders. This too would put stakeholders on an equal footing by making all stakeholders equal with respect to lacking voting rights. This removes the primacy of shareholders and overcomes the problems of identifying relevant stakeholders to give equal voting rights to. However, the problem of who the "relevant stakeholders" are that management owes equal consideration to is still left opaque as well as creating the difficulty of who should appoint the board of directors if there are no voters that decide.

An alternative path suggested by several authors (e.g., Schrenk, 2006) is to extend the legal fiduciary duty of board members beyond shareholders to encompass a wider constituency of stakeholders (recognizing that boards already have obligations to employees). This seems like the most feasible augmentation to corporate governance for weakening the SPN (as a social norm) as it does not extend voting rights but only fiduciary duties to non-shareholder stakeholders. However, extending board fiduciary duties beyond shareholders only makes sense if non-shareholder stakeholders also obtain a legal right to challenge board decisions in court, like shareholders can. For example, the UK Companies Act 2006, requires directors to consider the interests of a wider group of stakeholders but does not provide stakeholders with a legal remedy by which to challenge board decisions.

Another avenue has been pursued by B Lab, an American non-profit organization that has created a certification standard for so-called B-Corporations. As we discuss further below, a business that wishes to be a B-Corporation is required to include stakeholder considerations in its incorporation statutes. By augmenting the incorporation statues in this way, it provides shareholders with the ability to seek legal redress if executives have not properly taken stakeholder interests into account. This allows shareholders to seek legal redress for the interests of stakeholders, but does not enable such rights for stakeholders themselves.

Charging directors with a duty without corresponding legal stakeholder rights calls into question whether stakeholders would have their interests represented in practice. Extending stakeholders' rights to legal remedy suffers from the same problem of identifying relevant stakeholder groups beyond shareholders. There is, however, an important difference. Decisions about how and to whom board voting rights should be extended needs to be done prior to such a scheme being implemented, while decisions regarding relevant beneficiaries of fiduciary duties can be delegated

to the courts to decide on a case-by-case basis. Courts in the common law system need not tackle the insurmountable problem of deciding who all stakeholders are with relevant stakes for all corporations, but can instead address each specific concern for each stakeholder, for each company, as they arise in court cases. In this manner, who the relevant stakeholders are and what their relevant concerns are will be settled as substantial case law is built up over time.

Marcoux (2003) has pointed out that extending fiduciary duties of directors to multiple stakeholders is both conceptually and practically impossible. It is conceptually impossible because the duty of loyalty can only be had in relation to one principal, and it is practically impossible because loyalty will be violated whenever stakeholder interests conflict. We see two potential avenues for addressing these concerns. Firstly, it can be up to the courts to decide for any given case which stakeholder is to be considered the relevant principal who is owed fiduciary duties, perhaps on the basis of which stakeholder group is considered most *vulnerable* (see, Marcoux, 2003: 5–16).[7] Second, one might stop short of literally extending fiduciary duties of directors to non-shareholder stakeholders, but merely extend director duties to take into account the interests of other stakeholders, like the UK Companies Act 2006, with the addition that stakeholders have a right to challenge directors' decisions in court if their interests are not taken into account.

Thus some expansion in stakeholder influence on boards and in courts is certainly conceivable, but it is far from a ready or easy solution to the problem of shareholder primacy. That said, this is a direction for further research.

Benefit Corporations

Clark and Babson (2012: 838) observe: "It is against the paradigm of shareholder primacy that benefit corporation statutes have been drafted."[8] Their article elaborates on this rationale and provides an account of the distinctive features of benefit corporations and how they are intended to operate in practice. There are three major provisions in benefit corporation legislation that are consistent from state to state and represent distinctive features of benefit corporations (Clark & Babson 2012: 838–839):

> A benefit corporation: (1) has the corporate purpose to create a material, positive impact on society and the environment; (2) expands fiduciary duty to require consideration of nonfinancial interests; and (3) reports on its overall social and environmental performance as assessed against a comprehensive, credible, independent, and transparent third-party standard.

They stress that benefit corporations are intended to make profits for shareholders, "but the way in which that profit is to be made is through the conduct of business in a socially and environmentally responsible way" (Clark and Babson 2012: 819). There are several benefits to being a benefit corporation beyond this explicit and validated commitment to a social and environmental purpose, including making the business more attractive to various stakeholders, especially customers and potential investors, by distinguishing the business as truly committed to social responsibility when many other companies might be suspected of greenwashing.[9]

Benefit corporation legislation does not extend voting rights to non-shareholder stakeholders. It does, however, *require* that these stakeholders are considered by the corporation and this is a designated fiduciary duty of its directors.[10] This is distinct from constituency statutes. As Clark and Babson (2012) observe, with constituency statutes consideration of stakeholders is permissive, while with benefit corporation legislation it is mandatory. They claim that this is an important difference because even if directors wish to give non-shareholder stakeholders attention, there is uncertainty with constituency statutes as to the extent to which they might do this in many contexts, as well as a potential risk of litigation.

Moreover, this attention to the concerns of non-shareholder stakeholders must also be reported on and relative to an independent, third-party standard.[11] Clark and Babson (2012: 843) write that "in many ways the third party standard is the heart of benefit corporation legislation." This is

because it is the basis for the benefit corporation's accountability relative to the social and environmental objectives it has established for itself. Non-shareholder stakeholders may not have voting rights and they may not even have had much influence over these objectives, but their interests are at least partially addressed through this provision.

Thus benefit corporations might be seen as a direct response to many of the challenges for CSR posed by SPN and, in this way, as a promising development. The first benefit corporation statute was introduced in 2010. As of 2017, benefit corporation legislation had been enacted in thirty-three states (including Delaware) and the District of Columbia and there were 2,221 registered benefit corporations in 130 industries in over fifty countries.[12] However, most are relatively small and privately held; Patagonia is perhaps the best-known example.[13] It remains to be seen whether many more firms will adopt benefit corporation status, particularly larger publicly traded corporations – Google would be an interesting potential example – and how this will be treated in the courts.

Board Diversity

Company boards are notoriously lacking in diversity. Despite claims from various quarters that more diverse boards are associated with greater board effectiveness (Adams and Ferreira 2009; Myatt 2013, Peregrine 2016), many are comprised largely, if not exclusively, of white males over fifty. Catalyst, an organization promoting gender diversity in the boardroom, found that in 2015 less than 20 percent of board positions in S&P 500 companies were held by women; rates of ethnic diversity are even lower (Higginbottom 2017). This might reflect the perceived talent pool of suitably qualified and experienced board candidates, but it inevitably also limits board perspective. We believe that greater board diversity – and not just in relation to demographic variables – would likely be an indirect way of strengthening board attention to company stakeholders.

The Institute of Chartered Secretaries and Administrators guide to corporate governance in the UK (ICSA 2005: 87) suggests that board nominating committees should "consider candidates for appointment from a wide range of backgrounds, and look beyond the 'usual suspects'." It also observes that, in practice, the nomination system is often not independent enough, with the chairman and CEO having too much influence, and that boards tend to feel comfortable with people they know, likely perpetuating the problem of insufficient diversity. We suggest that, at a minimum, board nominating committees take it upon themselves to assess the extent to which existing board members can speak effectively to the interests of the organization's primary stakeholders and be prepared to go outside the comfort zone in looking to address shortfalls in board composition when vacancies arise. Should board members be charged with a fiduciary duty to take into account stakeholder concerns, it further seems reasonable that board nominating committees be charged with a corresponding legal fiduciary duty to nominate board members that are competent to further multiple stakeholder concerns (individually or perhaps collectively).

Conclusion

This chapter has examined the SPN as a widely acknowledged impediment to CSR. In contrast to the common assertion that managers are legally constrained from addressing CSR issues if doing so would be inconsistent with the interests of shareholders, we have shown that this is no longer a legal constraint, if it ever has been. However, while the SPN might be muted as a legal norm, it is very much evident as a social norm among managers (and in business schools). This stems largely from the sole voting rights of shareholders on corporate boards. We have shown how this view of the SPN as an impediment to CSR and stakeholder theory is misguided when grounded in a purported legally enforceable requirement to maximize shareholder value.

Two avenues for change in the dominance of the SPN as a social norm have been examined. We looked at the possibility of extending voting rights to non-shareholder stakeholders and alternatively extending to them fiduciary duties. Extending voting rights presents a slew of stakeholder identification and weighting difficulties, while extending

fiduciary duties can overcome such difficulties within common law systems by deciding such issues on a case-by-case basis. We also considered how law enabling B Corporations is a promising development as well as the merits of increasing board diversity. In conclusion, although the law does not present an obstacle to stakeholder theory, extending executives' fiduciary duties to non-shareholder stakeholders, together with efforts to encourage boards to give more attention to all company stakeholders. could make it a facilitator.

Notes

* This chapter is based, in part, on N. Craig Smith and David Rönnegard, (2016), Shareholder primacy, corporate social responsibility and the role of business schools, *Journal of Business Ethics*, *134*(3): 463–478.

1. Freeman does not regard stakeholder theory as opposed to the satisfaction of shareholder interests; rather, he regards shareholder theory as encompassed by stakeholder theory (see Freeman, et. al., 2010). Freeman, Harrison, & Wicks (2007: 76) note that "even if you want to maximize value for shareholders, you still have to create value for stakeholders."

2. This was further reinforced in 1993 by a congressional change to the US tax code that capped the tax deductibility of top management compensation not qualified as "performance based" (primarily interpreted as profitability). The purpose was to limit executive compensation perceived as being "excessive," although research suggests that the law has had little effect on executive compensation in practice (Rose and Wolfram, 2002).

3. That managers *believe* that the SPN is legally enforceable might be interpreted as something more than a social norm. Although legal action against corporate management for breaching the SPN is unlikely to be successful, the threat of such action might act as a reinforcement of the SPN. This does not make the SPN a legal norm as such a managerial belief is based on a misinterpretation of the law. However, this misinterpretation reinforces the SPN as a *social norm* because managers *believe* that they are legally required to follow the SPN.

4. Long ago, Berle and Means (1932) argued that shareholders of public corporations with

dispersed shareholdings had lost their de facto control to corporate managers because of diluted voting power. More recent times have seen a return of more concentrated voting power of shareholders based primarily on three developments: (1) Since the days of Berle and Means the composition of ownership on the stock market has shifted from a majority ownership by individual shareholders to a majority ownership of institutional shareholders (Blume and Keim, 2012; Davis, 2008), which has led to more effective voting power when a greater concentration of a corporation's shares are held by an institution. (2) The rise of Institutional Shareholder Services (ISS), which is a proxy advisory firm for institutional investors advising how they should vote with their shares as well as often voting on their behalf. ISS dominates the market for such services and its rise has led to a greater concentration of shareholder voting power. (3) In 2010 the Securities and Exchange Commission (SEC) introduced a "proxy access" rule designed to make it easier for shareholders to get their own nominees onto corporate boards (although a Federal Appeals Court has since blocked the rule, and the SEC has yet to revive it).

5. This suggestion does not so much solve the problem as avoid it. For example, it implies that employees, who have a stake in the corporation qua employees, should become shareholders so that they can have their interests as employees considered qua shareholders. Also, there is no reason why employees' ability to obtain stock stands in any proportion to their stake qua employees.

6. German corporate law provides employees with board representation for corporations above a certain size (number of employees). This is made possible because employees are easily identifiable individuals while other stakeholder groups with more transactional relationships with the corporations do not lend themselves to such easy and relevant identification.

7. Marcoux (2003) argues that fiduciary duties are owed on the basis of control and information vulnerabilities of principals. Although he maintains that such vulnerabilities are generally greatest for shareholders as principals, we believe that there are circumstances where such vulnerabilities might be greater for other stakeholders.

8. Clark has drafted all of the benefit corporation legislation enacted or introduced, at least as of the publication of this 2012 article.

9. See Lankoski and Smith (2018) for an account of alternative objective functions for firms that may be adopted by benefit corporations and allow for different degrees of emphasis on profit and social welfare, in its various permutations.

10. Clark and Babson (2012: 839–840) provide the California legislation by way of illustration, observing: "The directors of benefit corporations, in considering the best interests of the corporation, [S]hall consider the effects of any action or decision not to act on: (i) The stockholders of the benefit corporation; (ii) The employees and workforce of the benefit corporation and the subsidiaries and suppliers of the benefit corporation; (iii) The interests of customers as beneficiaries of the general or specific public benefit purposes of the benefit corporation; (iv) Community and societal considerations, including those of any community in which offices or facilities of the benefit corporation or the subsidiaries or suppliers of the benefit corporation are located; and (v) The local and global environment ... "

11. However, under current legislation, benefit corporations are not required to have their benefit report certified or audited by a third party (Clark and Babson 2012).

12. Source is the B-Lab website: https://www.bcorporation.net (accessed 15 August 2017).

13. Patagonia is privately held. Its founders chose B-corp status to protect its commitment to a social mission, recognizing that this could not be assured as the business passed to future generations even with constituency statutes. Alterrus Systems Inc., an urban farming company, claimed in March 2013 to be the first publicly listed company to earn B-corp certification; see www.csrwire.com/press_releases/35379-Alterrus-Becomes-First-Publicly-Listed-Company-To-Earn-B-Corp-Certification-Indicating-Its-Commitment-To-A-Better-Way-Of-Growing (accessed 6 October 2014).

References

Adams, R. B., & Ferreira, D. (2009). Women in the boardroom and their impact on governance and performance. *Journal of Financial Economics, 94* (2): 291–309.

Agle, B. R., & Mitchell, R. K. (2008). Introduction: Recent research and new questions. In Dialogue: Towards superior stakeholder theory. *Business Ethics Quarterly*, *18*(2): 153–159.

Anderson, E. (2000). Beyond homo economics: New developments in theories of social norms. *Philosophy and Public Affairs*, *29*(2): 170–200.

American Law Institute. (1994). *Principles of corporate governance: Analysis and recommendations*. St. Paul, MN: American Law Institute Publishers.

Benz, M., & Frey, B. S. (2007). Corporate governance: What can we learn from public governance? *Academy of Management Review*, *32*: 92–104.

Berle, A. A. (1931). Corporate powers as powers of trust. *Harvard Law Review*, *44*: 1049–1074

Berle, A. A. (1932). For whom are corporate managers trustees: A note. *Harvard Law Review*, *45*(7): 1365–1372

Berle, A. A., & Means, G. (1932). *The modern corporation and private property*. New York: Macmillan.

Blume, M. E., & Keim, D. B. (2012). Institutional investors and market liquidity: Trends and relationships. Working paper, The Wharton School, University of Pennsylvania, USA.

Boatright, J. R. (1994). Fiduciary duties and the shareholder-management relation: Or, what's so special about shareholders? *Business Ethics Quarterly*, *4*(4): 393–407.

Boatright, J. R. (2002). Contractors as stakeholders: Reconciling stakeholder theory with the nexus-of-contracts firm. *Journal of Banking and Finance*, *26*: 1837–1852.

Bonnafous-Boucher, M. (2005). Some philosophical issues in corporate governance: The role of property in stakeholder theory. *Corporate Governance*, *5*(2): 34–47.

Campbell, J. L. (2007). Why would corporations behave in socially responsible ways? An institutional theory of corporate social responsibility. *Academy of Management Review*, *32*(3): 946–967.

Chilosi, A., & Damiani, M. (2007). Stakeholders vs. shareholders in corporate governance. *Journal of Corporate Governance*, *6*(4): 7–45.

Cialdini, R. B. & Trost, M. R. (1998). Social influence: Social norms, conformity and compliance. In D. T. Gilbert, S.T. Fiske, & G. Lindzey, eds., *The Handbook of Social Psychology*, vol. 2, pp. 151–92. New York: McGraw-Hill.

Clark, R. (1985). Agency costs versus fiduciary duties. In J. W. Pratt & R. J. Zeckhauser, eds., *Principals and Agents: The Structure of Business*, pp. 55–79. Boston: Harvard Business School Press.

Clark, W. H., Jr. & Babson, E. K. (2012). How benefit corporations are redefining the purpose of business corporations. *William Mitchell Law Review*, *38*(2): 817–851.

Cohn, S. R. (1983). Demise of the director's duty of care: Judicial avoidance of standards of sanctions through the business judgment rule. *Texas Law Review*, *62*(4): 591–613.

Davis, G. F. (2008). A new finance capitalism? Mutual funds and ownership re-concentration in the United States. *European Management Review*, *5*: 11–21.

Dobson, J. (1999). Is shareholder wealth maximization immoral? *Financial Analysts Journal*, *55*(5): 69–75.

Dodd, M. E. (1932). For whom are corporate managers trustees? *Harvard Law Review*, *45*: 1145–1163.

Eisenberg, M. A. (2000). *Corporations and other Business Organizations*. New York: Foundation Press.

Evan, W. M., & Freeman, R. E. (2003). A stakeholder theory of the modern corporation: Kantian capitalism. In T. L. Beauchamp & N. E. Bowie, eds., *Ethical theory and business*, pp. 97–106. London: Prentice Hall.

Fisch, J. E. (2006). Measuring efficiency in corporate law: The role of shareholder primacy. *The Journal of Corporation Law*, *31*: 637–674.

Freeman, R. E. (1984). Strategic management: A stakeholder approach. Boston: Harper Collins.

Freeman, R. E., & Evan, W. M. (1990). Corporate governance: A stakeholder approach. *Journal of Behavioral Economics*, *19*(4): 337–359.

Freeman, R. E., Harrison, J. S., Wicks, A. C., (2007). *Managing for stakeholders: Survival, reputation and success*. New Haven: Yale University Press.

Freeman, R. E., Harrison, J. S., Wicks, A. C., Parmar, B. L., & de Colle, S. (2010). *Stakeholder theory: The state of the art*. Cambridge: Cambridge University Press.

Friedman, M. (1962). *Capitalism and Freedom*. Chicago: University of Chicago Press.

Friedman, M. (1970). The social responsibility of business is to increase its profits. The New York Times Magazine, September 13.

Galai, D., & Wiener, Z. (2008). Stakeholders and the composition of the voting rights of the board of directors. *Journal of Corporate Finance*, *14*(2): 107–117.

Garriga, E. & Mele, D. (2004). Corporate social responsibility theories: Mapping the territory. *Journal of Business Ethics, 53*: 51–71.

Gardiner, B. (2009). B-schools rethink curricula amid crisis. *The Wall Street Journal Europe*, March 27: 10.

Gentile, M. C. (2004). *Corporate governance and accountability: What do we know and what do we teach future business leaders?* The Aspen Institute Business & Society Program.

Ghoshal, S. (2005). Bad management theories are destroying good management practices. *Academy of Management Learning & Education, 4*(1): 75–91.

Heracleous, L. & Lan, L. L. (2010). The myth of shareholder capitalism. Harvard Business Review, April: 24.

Higginbottom, K. (2017). Board diversity still unusual in a Fortune 500 firm. Forbes, 30 January. Retrieved August 15, 2017, from www.forbes.com/sites/karenhigginbottom/2017/01/30/board-diversity-still-unusual-in-a-fortune-500-firm/.

Hinkley, R. (2002). How corporate law inhibits social responsibility. *The Humanist, 62*(2): 26–28

Holland, Kelley. (2009). Is it time to retrain B-schools? *The New York Times*, March 15.

ICSA. (2005). *Corporate governance*. London: ICSA Publishing.

Jensen, M. C. (2002). Value maximization, stakeholder theory, and the corporate objective function. *Business Ethics Quarterly, 12*(2): 235–256.

Jones, T. M. (2010). The future of business ethics research: Reflections on the twentieth anniversary of *Business Ethics Quarterly. Business Ethics Quarterly, 20*(4): 746–747.

Kraakman, R. R., Davies, P., Hansmann, H., Hertig, G., Hopt, K. J., Kanda, H., & Rock, E. B. (2004). *The anatomy of corporate law: A comparative and functional approach.* New York: Oxford University Press.

Lankoski, L., & Smith, N. C. (2018). Alternative objective functions for firms. *Organization & Environment, 31*(3): 242–262.

Marens, R., & Wicks, A. (1999). Getting real: Stakeholder theory, Managerial practice, and the general irrelevance of fiduciary duties owed to shareholders. *Business Ethics Quarterly, 9*(2): 273–293.

Marcoux, A. M. (2003). A Fiduciary Argument Against Stakeholder Theory. *Business Ethics Quarterly, 13*(1): 1–24.

McDonald, D. (2017). Harvard Business School and the propagation of immoral profit strategies. *Newsweek*, 6 April. Retrieved August 15, 2017, from www.newsweek.com/2017/04/14/harvard-business-school-financial-crisis-economics-578378.html?amp=1&utm_content=bufferbb608&utm_medium=social&utm_source=facebook.com&utm_campaign=buffer.

McDonnell, B. H. (2004). Corporate constituency statutes and employee governance. *William Mitchell Law Review, 30*(4): 1227–1259.

McKinsey. (2006). Global survey of business executives: Business and society. *McKinsey Quarterly, 2*: 33–39.

McWilliams, A., & Siegel, D. (2001). Corporate social responsibility: A theory of the firm perspective. *Academy of Management Review, 26* (1): 117–127.

Millon, D. (1991). Redefining corporate law. *Indiana Law Review, 24*: 223–277.

Myatt, M. (2013). Top 10 reasons diversity is good for the boardroom. Forbes, 18 November. Retrieved August 15, 2017, from www.forbes.com/sites/mikemyatt/2013/11/18/top-10-reasons-diversity-is-good-for-the-boardroom/#1ab235001b90.

New Scientist. (2010). Editorial: Time for another green revolution; A fog of unreliable information and confusion is hampering efforts to weigh up eco-credibility. *New Scientist*, 20 February: 3.

Orts, E. W. (1992). Beyond shareholders: Interpreting corporate constituency statutes. *George Washington Law Review, 61*: 14–135.

Paine, L. S. (2006). The fiduciary relationship: A legal perspective. Note prepared for class discussion. Boston: Harvard Business School.

Peregrine, M. W. (2016). Corporate board diversity gets push from business leaders. *The New York Times*, 12 October. Retrieved August 15, 2017, from www.nytimes.com/2016/10/14/business/dealbook/corporate-board-diversity-gets-push-from-business-leaders.html.

Phillips, R. A. (1997). Stakeholder theory and a principle of fairness. *Business Ethics Quarterly, 7*(1): 51–66.

Phillips, R. (2003). *Stakeholder theory and organizational ethics*. San Francisco: Berrett-Koehler Publishers.

Phillips, R., Freeman, E. R., & Wicks, A. C. (2003). What stakeholder theory is not. *Business Ethics Quarterly, 13*(4): 479–502.

Pickering, M. A. (1968). Company as a separate legal entity. *Modern Law Review, 31*: 481–511.

Polaris Institute. (2007). Coca-Cola Company wins corporate greenwashing award. Polaris Institute.

Retrieved April 29, 2013, from www.polarisinsti
tute.org/coca_cola_company_wins_corporate_
greenwashing_award.

Porter, M. E., & Kramer, M. R. (2006). The link
between competitive advantage and corporate
social responsibility. *Harvard Business Review*,
84(12): 78–92.

Porter, M. E., & Kramer, M. R. (2011). Creating
shared value: Redefining capitalism and the role
of the corporation in society. *Harvard Business
Review*, *89*(1/2): 62–77.

Rose, J. M. (2007). Corporate directors and social
responsibility: Ethics versus shareholder value.
Journal of Business Ethics, *73*: 319–331.

Rose, N. L, & Wolfram, C. (2002). Regulating executive pay: Using the tax code to influence chief
executive compensation. *Journal of Labour
Economics*, *20*(2): 138–174.

Schrenk, L. P. (2006). Equity versus stakeholder and
corporate governance: Developing a market for
morality. *The Business Renaissance Quarterly*, *1*
(3): 81–90.

Skadden. (2011). Air Products & Chemicals, Inc.
v. Airgas, Inc. Skadden Newsletter, February 16.
Retrieved May 14, 2013, from www.skadden.com/
newsletters/Air_Products_Chemicals_Inc_v_
Airgas_Inc.pdf.

Smith, D. G. (1998). The shareholder primacy norm.
The Journal of Corporation Law, *23*: 277–323.

Smith, N. C., & Van Wassenhove, L. (2010). How
business schools lost their way. *BusinessWeek*,
January 11. Retrieved April 29, 2013, from www
.businessweek.com/bschools/content/jan2010/
bs20100111_383186.htm.

Stout, L. (2012). *The shareholder value myth: How
putting shareholders first harms investors, corporations and the public.* San Francisco: Berrett-
Koehler Publishers.

Testy, K. (2002). Linking progressive corporate law
with progressive social movements. *Tulane Law
Review*, *76*: 1227–1252.

van Marrewijk, M. (2003). Concepts and definitions
of CSR and corporate sustainability: Between
agency and communion. *Journal of Business
Ethics*, *44*: 95–105.

Vermaelen, T. (2009). Maximizing shareholder
value: An ethical responsibility? In N. C. Smith &
G. Lenssen, ed., *Mainstreaming corporate responsibility*. Chichester: Wiley.

Walsh, J. P. (2004). The corporate objective revisited.
Organization Science, *15*(3): 349.

West, D. M. (2011). The purpose of corporations in
business and law school curricula. Governance
Studies at Brookings.

CHAPTER
8

Business, the Natural Environment, and Sustainability

A Stakeholder Theory Perspective

JACOB HÖRISCH

Leuphana University Lüneburg

STEFAN SCHALTEGGER

Leuphana University Lüneburg

1 Why the Natural Environment Matters for Stakeholders

Stakeholder theory highlights that companies are embedded in, and established and maintained by, a network of internal and external stakeholders, on which they depend in order to achieve their goals (e.g., Freeman, 1984; Freeman, et al., 2010). The network of companies and their stakeholders is furthermore embedded in the natural environment (e.g., Starik & Kanashiro, 2013). The natural environment can be, and ultimately is, essential to secure existence and for achieving goals of a company and its stakeholders for various reasons, including the use of natural resources, the embedding into and dependence on ecosystems, and the intrinsic value of nature for stakeholders.

First, each stakeholder and each company depends on resources the natural environment delivers. This includes basic human needs such as unpolluted freshwater or clean air (Rockström, et al., 2009). No human existence and therefore also no existence of stakeholders or organizations is possible without vital natural resources. Furthermore, nature's resources include important production factors for business, for instance, the supply of renewable or non-renewable materials (e.g., rare earths, ores, wood). These resources build the basis of entire industries constituting a large part of the economy, such as agriculture, fishing, forestry, mining, oil drilling, or the electric, car, and airline industries, and shape entire societies (Starik, 1995). For example, the entire industry around modern communication is built on the use

of rare earths (Golev, et al., 2014), and as consequence the entire service industry also depends on natural resources. Coal-fired power stations provide electric power to a large part of the old economies, and although they need to be replaced to reduce global carbon emissions if sustainable development is to be achieved (United Nations, 2015), they will still use huge amounts of natural resources until the substitution is achieved. However, less polluting technologies such as hydro, solar, and wind power also require natural resources such as ores, siliceous, copper, etc. to build the infrastructure. Thus, old as well as modern technologies and businesses and their stakeholders depend on natural resources to fulfill their needs.

Second, all interactions between stakeholders take place within the setting of the natural environment (Driscoll & Starik, 2004) and rely on various ecosystem services (e.g., Daily, et al., 2009). In ecological economics, all stakeholder interactions are considered a subsystem of the natural environment, as stakeholders can transform the resources the natural environment delivers but are only able to do so within the limits of the natural environment (Boulding, 2013), or as Rockström, et al. (2009: 472) coin it, society, the economy and businesses are challenged to keep their activities in a "safe operating space of planetary boundaries." Wood (1990: 633) therefore concludes that "business necessarily exists and operates in an environment larger and more complex than itself." Thus, stakeholders can jointly create value, but this value creation always depends on the natural environment, is limited by the state of the natural environment and relies on ecosystem services. Based on this understanding, Starik (1995: 209) even considers nature "a relevant, perhaps *the* relevant, business environment." While this is clearly visible for industries like the multibillion business of tap and bottled drinking water (e.g., Daily, et al., 2009), where the functioning of watershed ecosystems is decisive for the quality and quantity of water production, other industries rely more indirectly on the natural environment and may have created largely artificial business environments. Hairdressing, banking, insurance, or gaming do not sell natural resources like water but are still dependent on energy based on the use of natural resources and influenced by the impact the natural environment has on its customers, employees, and further stakeholders (e.g., floods causing insurance damage).

Third, most individuals assign the natural environment an intrinsic value, also known as existence and option values. Environmental economists have been eager to monetize this value, in an attempt to make it comparable to other types of value that are more directly visible and measurable (e.g., Stevens, et al., 1991; Costanza, et al., 1997). While monetization attempts vary with regard to methodology and their political impact is critically debated (Kallis, Gómez-Baggethun, & Zografos, 2013; 2015; Gsottbauer, Logar, & van den Bergh, 2015), intrinsic as well as option values are of substantial practical relevance for many companies. The intrinsic value stakeholders assign to the natural environment becomes visible in the engagement of NGOs, media coverage, philanthropic activities, and regulations. Stakeholders even value nature and ecological issues that are not directly linked to human needs, business functioning, or survival, such as the preservation of unknown species or species most people will never be able to see (e.g., Brookshire, Eubanks, & Randall, 1983; Campos, 2002; Foster, 1997; More, Averill, & Stevens, 1996). To strengthen the intrinsic value stakeholders assign to the natural environment and to sensitize stakeholder appreciation of this value, Starik (1995: 211) advocates for the concept of environmental aesthetic, which implies an "ascription of beauty to or sensory appreciation of the natural environment" and allows the creation of emotional ties to nun-

human entities. Even though these approaches from environmental economics and environmental aesthetics use entirely different logics, both highlight that many stakeholders value the natural environment and that nature as such can serve to create value to stakeholders.

These three examples of why the natural environment matters to stakeholders and businesses do not imply that other kinds of value are unimportant for stakeholders. In contrast, research on utility functions from a stakeholder theory perspective (e.g., Harrison, Bosse, & Phillips, 2010) highlights that stakeholder utility can stem from various sources, such as monetary benefits, better products, increased safety, etc. This suggests that stakeholders facing dependencies and having a variety of different needs also have preferences, expectations, and demands directly related or indirectly linked to the natural environment, and that these preferences, expectations, and demands regarding the natural environment are of fundamental importance, as life cannot exist for long without staying in the ecological limits of planetary boundaries.

Fueled by the publication of the Brundtland-Report in 1987 (Brundtland, et al., 1987), the paradigm of sustainable development evolved and has gained increasing attention as an approach to overcoming trade-offs between the different economic, social, and environmental expectations and needs stakeholders have. Whereas in preceding decades, the debate on environmental protection centered around conflicts between environmental and economic aims, e.g. reflected in publications such as the "Limits to Growth" report (Meadows, 1972) or the United Nations Conference's "Only One Earth" (Ward & Dubos, 1972), the concept of sustainable development aims at simultaneously satisfying different environmental, social, and economic needs. To assess whether these needs are met at a societal level, the United Nations has developed the sustainable development goals (UN SDGs) and respective indicators in a broad process involving multiple stakeholders (UN, 2015). These allow assessing to what extent contributions to environmental, economic, and social goals are made and enable companies to evaluate their contributions to the satisfaction of specific sustainability needs as formulated by stakeholders involved in the UN process of creating the seventeen SDGs. The world's largest chemical company BASF, for example, uses the UN SDGs as a starting point to explore how its core business and its stakeholder interactions are linked to sustainability and to identify stakeholder interests that relate to the SDGs (BASF, 2017).

2 How to Consider the Natural Environment in Stakeholder Theory

Section 1 of this chapter argued that mankind depends on the natural environment and that nature matters for stakeholders. Freeman et al. (2010), therefore, acknowledge the need to recognize the natural environment in stakeholder theory. Based on earlier literature, two alternative and fundamentally different possibilities of introducing the natural environment in stakeholder thinking can be identified: As the natural environment plays such an important role for stakeholders, the maybe most obvious possibility is to introduce it as an additional stakeholder. Alternatively, in stakeholder theory the environment can be considered as a shared concern of various human stakeholders.

2.1 Considering the Natural Environment a Stakeholder?

The first possibility, i.e. introducing the natural environment as an additional stakeholder, has mainly been brought forward in the 1990s and early 2000s (e.g., Driscoll & Starik, 2004; Starik, 1995; Stead & Stead, 1996). It is based on the logic that the natural environment meets central criteria of what Stead and Stead (1996) call "stakeholderness," because it can be affected by an organization's objectives and is in turn also able to influence an organization, e.g. through natural disasters or by providing assets necessary for a particular business (Starik, 1995). The inclusion of the natural environment is usually motivated by the observation that nature is not adequately considered in many business decisions, as company managers often give the natural environment only low priority when they are confronted with trade-

offs between economic and environmental objectives (Driscoll & Starik, 2004; Starik, 1995).

Another reason for including the natural environment as a stakeholder is that nature, or various parts of it (resources, ecosystems, etc.), are part of the same network as organizations and an organization's stakeholders. Driscoll and Starik (2004) highlight these network links, drawing on the example of a coal power plant, which is in a network with species in the polar region, because a coal power plant's greenhouse gas emissions have consequences for the habitat of these species through the contribution to global warming and the melting of the polar ice caps. Similarly, many stakeholders are affected by the absence or presence of natural entities, as, for example, workers are laid off if coal runs out or jobs are created in recycling facilities (Driscoll & Starik, 2004).

Additionally, Starik (1995) argues that stakeholders can be understood as representatives of different business environments. He, for instance, considers consumers as representative of the market environment or regulators as representatives of the legal environment. As the natural environment is also an important aspect of the business environment, he concludes that nature should be recognized as a stakeholder representing the ecological aspects of the business environment. Starik (1995) even sees a historical development toward integrating ever more stakeholder groups who were initially neglected (such as indigenous minorities, slaves, and women) in the decision-making of organizations, and expects this broadening to finally also include non-human nature.

To better justify the inclusion of the natural environment as a stakeholder from a theoretical perspective, Driscoll and Starik (2004) review the criteria of stakeholderness developed by Mitchell, Agle and Wood, (1997), i.e. power, legitimacy, and urgency. They conclude that proximity should be considered a fourth criterion for stakeholderness. This implies that if an organization shares a physical space with another entity, this entity should be recognized as a stakeholder. In turn, since many environmental aspects of nature are proximate to organizations, these natural entities should be considered stakeholders of the respective organizations.

Similarly to Starik (1995), as well as Driscoll and Starik (2004), Stead and Stead (1996) argue for the inclusion of the natural environment as a stakeholder. However, their rationale differs slightly from the above, because they emphasize the power human stakeholders have in using their stakes on behalf of nature. They argue that it is, besides the above factors, "the power of its green stakeholders ... which make(s) the Earth a stakeholder" (Stead & Stead, 1996: 178).

Concluding from these reasons to consider the natural environment as a stakeholder, Driscoll and Starik (2004: 69) argue that the natural environment should be "the primordial and primary stakeholder of all firms." They continue that as multiple aspects of the environment can be affected or affect an organization, the natural environment is likely to constitute multiple stakeholders of a firm.

Starik (1995) expects that such recognition of stakeholder status for the natural environment would not only help to solve environmental problems, but also be beneficial for organizations. First, this would widen an organization's perspective. Second, considering nature a stakeholder would allow companies to prioritize their actions according to the importance of influences of the natural environment and to incorporate the natural environment in their policies and activities. Lastly, Starik (1995) postulates that including nature as a stakeholder would allow companies to particularize the specific aspects that constitute the relevant natural environment of an organization.

2.2 The Environment as a Shared Concern among Human Stakeholders?

The view that the natural environment should be considered a stakeholder has also received criticism and evoked alternative possibilities to introduce environmental concerns in stakeholder theory. First, Starik (1995), one of the most prominent proponents of the nature as a stakeholder approach, admits that if nature is considered a stakeholder, it still remains unclear what the particular stakes of nature are. Possible stakes could be habitat preservation or the continuation of evolution (Starik, 1995), but it would still be up to human stakeholders to decide which of these or

other stakes are declared nature's interest. This highlights a second problem of the nature as a stakeholder approach. The natural environment lacks a human and political voice, i.e. it is unable to articulate its stakes. Therefore, Phillips (2003) argues that it would have no effect if the natural environment was declared a stakeholder as managers would still have no guideline of how to deal with the natural environment. He therefore argues for considering the environment in stakeholder theory, but highlights that this is not the same as calling nature a stakeholder. Similarly, Phillips and Reichart (2000) apply the principle of fairness, as developed by John Rawls, to the question of how to identify stakeholders. They conclude that the natural environment does not meet this criterion, while there are other reasons to consider nature in business decisions.

In effect, a comparison of common definitions of the term stakeholder against the background of considering the natural environment a stakeholder, shows that nature does not match with common definitions of what a stakeholder is. Freeman et al. (2010) provide two widely recognized definitions of the term stakeholder consistent with other definitions of the concept, as well as with the concept's historical roots (Näsi, 1995). The broader definition describes stakeholders as "any *group or individual* that can affect or be affected by the realization of an organization's purpose" (Freeman et al., 2010: 26). According to the narrower definition, stakeholders are "those specific *individuals and groups* that (1) make the firm ... (2) ... contribute to its success ... and (3) bear the consequences of its activities" (Freeman et al., 2010: 260). This indicates that even broader definitions of the stakeholder concepts concentrate on *individuals and groups*. Therefore, by definition, natural entities such as (non-)renewable resources are not stakeholders, in contrast to groups and individuals who are able to articulate their stakes based on their perspectives and interpretations.

The lack of a human and political voice to articulate stakes highlights that acknowledging the importance of the environment as pointed out by Starik (1995) and others, it seems without effect to state that the natural environment is a stakeholder.

This perhaps becomes best visible in the example of the depletion of the ozone layer. Chlorofluorocarbons (CFCs) were diffused after the Second World War and used widely in various products such as spray cans and in many industrial processes because of the perceived health, environmental, and economic advantages (CFCs are neither toxic nor explosive and they are cheap). They had, however, already been causing huge environmental damage for many decades without mankind being aware of these problems (Mégie, 2006; Andersen et al., 1995). CFCs are a main cause of the destruction of the ozone layer protecting Earth's life from too-strong sun radiation. Nature was not able to articulate the problem and mankind was not aware of it. The destructive effect of CFCs on the ozone layer as a planetary boundary was first detected by researchers in the seventies (Mégie, 2006), and only became shared knowledge and relevant for stakeholder expectations and activities after a sufficient number of stakeholders accepted this knowledge. Today, CFCs are largely banned because stakeholders advocated for this ecological problem and politicians and businesses took action. This example illustrates that nature is only of stakeholder relevance when considered by human stakeholders and that environmental problems, even though existent and fundamental for human survival, can be without effect on human action prior to recognition by human stakeholders.

As a consequence, the example of the ozone layer destruction highlights the importance of environmentalism and sustainability being in the mindsets of human stakeholders, who are able and willing to articulate these issues and to develop strategies preventing ecological problems and disasters. The example furthermore reveals that considering the natural environment a stakeholder is not the only possible reaction to the insight that environmental concerns are currently often not sufficiently considered in corporate decisions. As Freeman et al. (2010) point out, stakeholders always interact around specific values or normative cores. Hörisch, Freeman, and Schaltegger, (2014) explore the possibilities for environmentalism and sustainability to be such a value around which stakeholders interact and negotiate.

The integration of environmentalism and sustainability in stakeholder theory as a shared valued of stakeholders, however, requires that stakeholders have respective interests. Stead and Stead (1996) investigate this prerequisite and identify numerous "green stakeholders," such as employees, environmental standard setters (including business associations), ethical investors, green consumers (including B2B consumers), interest groups, capital providers, insurance companies, and regulators.

Concerning employees, numerous authors (e.g., Ciocirlan, 2016; Dilchert & Ones, 2012; Norton, et al., 2015) point out the vast potential of employees engaging for environmental and related health interests within the firm (see also International Labour Organization, 2011). Similarly, explicitly ethical or sustainability oriented investors are gaining importance and environmental criteria are increasingly recognized by conventional investors as well (e.g., Iqbal & Molyneux, 2005; Ito, Managi, & Matsuda, 2013). Concerning external stakeholders, Cohen (2007) identifies a growing movement of LOHAS (Lifestyle of Health and Sustainability) consumers who make up a relevant share of the US end-consumer market (some estimate up to 30 percent; see Cohen, 2007). Additionally, Stead and Stead (1996) emphasize that not only end consumers can act as environmental stakeholders, but also business-to-business consumption may foster pro-environmental corporate activities. Through introducing labels, standard setters have increased the possible influence of environmentally oriented consumers. Additionally, further standards for company internal processes have been offered (Hörisch et al., 2014; Stead & Stead, 1996). Shrivastava and Hart (1995) as well as Bendell, Miller, and Wortmann (2011) highlight the growing engagement of regulators for environmental concerns. Last, but not least, environmental interest groups explicitly take the role of representing the interests of the natural environment and increasingly collaborate with businesses to consider their interests in corporate practice (van Tulder et al., 2016).

The fact that numerous stakeholders have particular environmental interests shows that there is a basis among (human) stakeholders that allows representing nature's interest. While a full and perfect representation of nature's interest by human stakeholders may be an illusion, in the era of the Anthropocene, environmental aspects cannot be considered well without stakeholder awareness, interest, and engagement. To acknowledge and use the interests of environmentally alert stakeholders effectively for the preservation of nature, it is important to empower these stakeholders, to strengthen their environmental interests, and to carve out that their respective environmental or sustainability interests are common interests among diverse stakeholders (Hörisch et al., 2014). To achieve these aims, Hörisch et al. (2014) suggest three key approaches: education, regulation, and value creation.

Education can help to strengthen the sustainability interests of stakeholders and to empower stakeholders to act as representatives of environmental interests (Shriberg et al., 2013; Siebenhüner, 2004). First steps in this direction have been the increasing recognition of sustainability in academic courses as well as the UN Decade of Education for Sustainable Development (Collins & Gannon, 2014; Starik & Turcotte, 2014). Regulation is challenged to install a framework with incentives for stakeholder collaboration to create sustainable value and transparency about the value created. For this purpose, the European Commission introduced the Eco-Management and Audit Scheme (EMAS) and sustainability reporting regulations (EU, 2014), and the Global Reporting Initiative (GRI) introduced a guideline, which not only set a framework for environmental management within a company and reporting of social and environmental issues, but also require companies to involve their stakeholders with regard to environmental (and social) issues (Hörisch et al., 2014). Lastly, the idea of value creation emphasizes that constellations need to be identified or created, in which different stakeholders benefit from the consideration of environmental interests. Such sustainability-based value creation for stakeholders is not restricted to financial gains, but can also be reflected in quality of life improvements, e.g. improved health or well-being (Hörisch et al., 2014). Creating sustainable value is rooted in the business model of a company and

often requires its transformation or innovation to consider sustainability effects of the business caused in supply chains and the consumption of the products offered (e.g., Schaltegger, Lüdeke-Freund, & Hansen, 2016). Different corporate but also political initiatives can be identified, which successfully aim at creating sustainability-based value for stakeholders.

Constance and Bonanno (2000), for example, discuss how Unilever collaborated with the WWF to establish the Marine Stewardship Council (MSC) for sustainable fishing. This collaboration also involved many further stakeholders including fisheries, consumer organizations, regulators, local communities, etc. Additional value is created not only for the natural environment but also for consumers who benefit from improved transparency and are better informed in their decision-making, for fisheries applying sustainable fishing practices, and retailers providing an improved offer of fish to their customers. By establishing MSC as an independent organization for auditing and certification of fishing companies, and the labeling of fish products, a new institutional arrangement was created that supports and enlarges the market for sustainable fishing.

The MSC example demonstrates that the particular environmental and sustainability interests of diverse stakeholders can indeed be used to create value for diverse groups of stakeholders. We therefore suggest that to introduce the environment in stakeholder theory in a way that effectively creates environmental improvements, it is the more promising path to introduce it as a shared value among human stakeholders and to strengthen this shared value, to empower human stakeholders to act on behalf of nature, and to identify or create constellations which allow mutual benefits based on environmental interests.

Onkila (2011) conducted a qualitative empirical study of stakeholder interactions in environmental management among twenty-five corporations. On the basis of analyzing environmental reports and conducting interviews, she identified four categories of businesses in terms of the way they included the environment in their stakeholder interactions. While Onkila (2011) found practical differences in how and to which extent companies actually consider environmental concerns in their stakeholder management, for all categories of stakeholder interactions, stakeholders are defined as *actors*. Her empirical observation thus reveals that even companies giving environmental issues a high priority do not, and do not have to, consider the natural environment a stakeholder. Thereby, the results provide empirical support for the argument brought forward by Phillips (2003) that managers do not consider it effective and feasible to treat the natural environment as a stakeholder, as such view cannot serve managers as a guideline when facing decisions that involve environmental aspects.

In sum, consideration of nature as a stakeholder has stimulated an important academic but also practically relevant debate and has contributed to an increased attention to the role nature plays in stakeholder theory. However, most of the conceptual and theoretical, as well as the practitioner oriented, empirical contributions to this debate speak against considering the natural environment a stakeholder, but highlight the necessity of considering it in stakeholder theory.

3 Why Stakeholder Theory Matters for the Environment

Numerous conceptual and empirical analyses demonstrate that business has an enormous impact on the environment (Heede, 2014; Shrivastava, 1995). Heede (2014), for example, reveals that two-thirds of the historic greenhouse gas emissions are caused by only ninety companies. This highlights the crucial importance of large corporations for successfully addressing environmental problems.

From an environmental perspective, this raises the question whether stakeholder theory and stakeholder management can assist in reducing the environmental impacts of companies. Based on a conceptual analysis of different management models, Ransom and Lober (1999) suggest that stakeholder theory is indeed able to explain how companies set environmental goals, as companies acting in accordance with this management approach react to pressure by stakeholders interested in the natural environment and aim at

increasing stakeholder satisfaction. Wagner (2011) highlights that stakeholders possess the power to effectively influence the environmental management of corporations. Similarly, Madsen and Ulhøi (2001) demonstrate that, based on a survey among Danish firms, many stakeholders can exert a great influence on corporate environmental performance. They find the highest potential to influence corporate environmental performance for regulators, financiers, employees, and customers. Lower potential is found for environmental pressure groups, which contrasts findings in other contexts (Fineman & Clarke, 1996; Hörisch & Windolph, 2014; Schaltegger, et al., 2014). Buysse and Verbeke (2003) confirm the power of consumers, financiers, employees, and suppliers have on corporate environmental management. In a survey among sustainability managers in eleven countries, Hörisch and Windolph (2014) find that non-governmental organizations, the media, and the general public, as well as international authorities, are promoting corporate sustainability the most. These findings on the influences of different stakeholders on sustainability or environmental management activities of companies firstly show that stakeholders indeed have a crucial part to play in reducing the negative environmental consequences of companies. Secondly, the differences observed with regard to the specific impacts of particular groups of stakeholders in different contexts suggest which stakeholder groups are most influential depends on contextual factors. Hörisch et al. (2017), for example, empirically find that national as well as international authorities have a stronger influence on corporate sustainability practices in countries with French code law legal systems, while the influence of these stakeholder groups is significantly lower in case and German code law countries. Additionally, conceptual and empirical analyses not only suggest that stakeholders can positively influence corporate sustainability and environmental management measures, but that comprehensive stakeholder management approaches of companies are likely to improve a company's environmental performance and simultaneously address stakeholder demands (e.g., Buysse & Verbeke, 2003; Hart, 1995;

Hörisch, Schaltegger, & Windolph, 2015; Ransom & Lober, 1999).

The above described rationale highlights that the stakeholder approach matters for the environment as its consideration can help to reduce negative environmental impacts of companies. Obviously, cases exist in which certain stakeholder interests and environmental requirements are in conflict with each other, as Phillips and Reichart (2000) argue to be likely for the context of developing countries. In some cases, such as in finance and services, the main environmental effect may not be directly caused by the company itself but by some of its stakeholders. While, for instance, the direct environmental effects of Deutsche Bank are rather limited, it has a significant indirect impact on the natural environment through its business customers depending on whether it provides loans to customers realizing environmentally harmful projects (such as the dissemination of genetically modified seeds) or, whether it does not serve these customers. The bank's investments in shares of polluting or green companies may influence their corporate strategies with regard to carbon emissions or other sustainability impacts. Furthermore, while the greenhouse gas emissions of Deutsche Bank itself may be limited, its employees can have a significant impact on emissions by commuting to work or on business trips.

The example of Deutsche Bank suggests that while there is a huge potential for synergies between stakeholder interests and environmental interests, these synergies may not always be recognized or difficult to achieve as they may not exist *ex ante* but need to be created. A key task for environmental and sustainability management is thus to transform possible trade-offs to synergies by bringing stakeholders with diverse interests together and arranging processes leading to innovative, effective sustainability solutions. This also becomes visible in the prominent definition of business sustainability Szekelny and Knirsch (2005: 628) provide. In their definition, they point out that business sustainability "also means adopting and pursuing ethical business practices, creating sustainable jobs, building value for all the company's stakeholders and attending to the needs of the underserved." As a consequence, the understanding of

the relationship between sustainability and business cases as well as the role of stakeholders in creating business cases for sustainability is different, if a conflict view or a collaborative view is perceived and pursued (Schaltegger & Burritt, 2015; Schaltegger, Hörisch, & Freeman, 2017). Conflicting views oppose financial and societal stakeholders whereas a collaborative perspective of a business case for sustainability is based on involving stakeholders to create solutions to social and environmental problems, which also create economic value.

The example of the company Tesla demonstrates that such an understanding can indeed help to create value for many stakeholders involved by creating a product that contributes to the solution of environmental problems. To develop its business, Tesla has motivated stakeholders to invest in a venture with substantial potential to transform the existing car market, suppliers to engage in new technology, and further stakeholders to report on the vision of large-scale electric mobility. Similarly, car-sharing companies are engaging new supplier groups such as software companies producing apps to assist customers in finding nearby cars in urban areas as well as public authorities, municipalities, and NGOs to support the realization of new forms of individual mobility. These examples, as well as the above academic investigations, point out that a stakeholder theory perspective can indeed help to create contributions to the solution of environmental problems by creating value for stakeholders (e.g., Schaltegger et al., 2017).

4 Why Stakeholder Theory Matters in Environmental and Sustainability Management Research – and Vice Versa

In their widely recognized article, Starik and Kanashiro (2013) develop fundamentals of a distinct theory of sustainability management. Their approach aims at developing a theoretical framework that specifically allows analyzing phenomena of sustainability management. While the idea of setting up a separate sustainability management theory certainly has its merits, the approach has also received critical resonance (e.g., Hörisch, et al., 2014), because a specific sustainability management theory runs the risk of separating the sustainability discourse from conventional business studies rather than integrating it to the core discipline. Hörisch et al. (2014) therefore highlight the benefits of applying a theory established in business studies and develop a framework for systematically applying stakeholder theory in sustainability management. They highlight that the sustainability management discourse and stakeholder theory share many basic assumptions and perspectives. Firstly, both concepts consider the purpose of business as not restricted to increasing profits for shareholders. Instead, in both concepts, value creation in a broader sense, i.e. not only monetary value, is regarded as the purpose of business. Furthermore, sustainability management as well as stakeholder theory aim at locating this value creation process in the core business of a company (e.g., & Burritt, 2015). Consequently, in opposition to the idea of residual CSR, value should not be created by compensating, e.g. via philanthropy or sponsoring, value destruction in the core business, but by value creation for stakeholders in the first place.

These general similarities in the fundamentals of both concepts demonstrate that stakeholder theory can serve as a theoretical framework in sustainability management. A stakeholder theory perspective in sustainability management can thereby help to identify all actors and groups of actors who need to get involved in order to create sustainable value and which actors are most likely to get involved.

In turn, we believe that a sustainability perspective can also be beneficial for stakeholder theory (cf. Hörisch et al., 2014). It highlights that organizations are not only embedded in a network of stakeholders, but also act within ecological systems. Furthermore, the idea of sustainability can help to broaden the stakeholder theory perspective to the dimension of time and durability. Consequently, new questions that arise from the recognition of sustainability in stakeholder theory include how mutual benefits for different stakeholders can be maintained over time, recognizing the children of our generation and the children of today's children as future stakeholders.

These stimulations of stakeholder theory to sustainability management and vice versa provide promising avenues for further research. Firstly, whereas the link between environmental and financial performance has received vast attention in prior research (e.g., King & Lenox, 2001; Wagner, 2010; Wagner & Schaltegger, 2004), possible synergies between a stakeholder management approach and environmental benefits have not yet been investigated sufficiently in empirical research. Secondly, transdisciplinary research, a research approach originating from sustainability sciences, emphasizes the relevance of stakeholder collaboration for corporate management from a different perspective (Schaltegger, Beckmann, & Hansen, 2013). To address complex environmental problems effectively and to find lasting, effective solutions requires that sustainability phenomena are analyzed and solutions developed from the perspectives of (and thus involving stakeholders from) various disciplines and corporate practice as no single scientific discipline can cover the whole range of influences and dependencies related to complex environmental and social problems such as climate change or loss of biodiversity. Stakeholder theory can inform transdisciplinary sustainability management research in multiple ways. It can, for instance assist in identifying which stakeholders need to be considered or which practical outcomes are desired from a stakeholder perspective.

References

Andersen, S. O., Halberstadt, M. L., & Borgford-Parnell, N. (1995). Stratospheric ozone, global warming, and the principle of unintended consequences: An ongoing science and policy success story. *Journal of the Air & Waste Management Association, 63*: 607–647.

BASF. (2017). UN Sustainable Development Goals. Retrieved February 17, 2017, from www.basf.com/de/company/sustainability/employees-and-society/goals.html.

Bendell, J., Miller, A., & Wortmann, K. (2011). Public policies for scaling corporate responsibility standards: Expanding collaborative governance for sustainable development. *Sustainability Accounting, Management and Policy Journal, 2*: 263–293.

Boulding, K. E. (2013). The economics of the coming spaceship Earth. In H. Jarrett, ed., *Environmental* quality in a growing economy: Essays from the sixth RFF Forum, pp. 3–14. New York; London: Routledge.

Brookshire, D. S., Eubanks, L. S., & Randall, A. (1983). Estimating option prices and existence values for wildlife resources. Land Economics, 59: 1.

Brundtlandt, G. H., Khalid, M., Agnelli, S., Al-Athel, S. A., Chidzero, B., Fadika, L. M., Hauff, V., . . . Strong, M. (1987). Our common future. Oxford/ New York: Oxford University Press.

Buysse, K., & Verbeke, A. (2003). Proactive environmental strategies: A stakeholder management perspective. Strategic Management Journal, 24: 453.

Campos, D. G. (2002). Assessing the value of nature: A transactional approach. Environmental Ethics: An Interdisciplinary Journal Dedicated to the Philosophical Aspects of Environmental Problems, 24: 57–74.

Ciocirlan, C. E. (2016). Environmental workplace behaviors definition matters. Organization & Environment, Online First: doi: 10.1177/1086026615628036.

Cohen, M. J. (2007). Consumer credit, household financial management, and sustainable consumption. International Journal of Consumer Studies, 31: 57–65.

Collins, D. & Gannon, A. (2014) Walking the eco-talk movement: Higher education institutions as sustainability incubators. Organization & Environment, 27: 16–24.

Constance, D. H. & Bonanno, A. (2000). Regulating the global fisheries. The World Wildlife Fund, Unilever, and the Marine Stewardship Council. Agriculture and Human Values, 17: 125–139.

Costanza, R., d'Arge, R., Groot, R. de, Farber, S., Grasso, M., Hannon, B., Limburg, K., . . . van den Belt, M. (1997). The value of the world's ecosystem services and natural capital. Nature, 387: 253–260.

Daily, G., Polasky, S., Goldstein, J., Kareiva, P., Mooney, H., Pejchar, L., Ricketts, T., Salzman, T., & Shallenberger, R. (2009). Ecosystem services in decision making: Time to deliver. Frontiers in Ecology and the Environment, 7: 21–28.

Dilchert, S., & Ones, D. S. (2012). Environmental sustainability in and of organizations. Industrial and Organizational Psychology, 5: 503–511.

Driscoll, C., & Starik, M. (2004). The primordial stakeholder: Advancing the conceptual consideration of stakeholder status for the natural environment. Journal of Business Ethics, 49; 55–73.

EU (European Union). (2014). Directive 2014/95/EU and of the Council of 22 October 2014 amending Directive 2013/34/EU as regards disclosure of non-financial and diversity information by certain large undertakings and groups. Official Journal of the European Union, L330, 1–9.

Fineman, S., & Clarke, K. (1996). Green stakeholders: Industry interpretations and response. Journal of Management Studies, 33: 715–730.

Foster, J. (1997). Valuing nature? Ethics, economics and the environment, London/New York: Routledge.

Freeman, R. E. (1984). Strategic management: A stakeholder approach, Boston: Pitman.

Freeman, R. E., Harrison, J. S., Wicks, A. C., Parmar, B. L., & de Colle, S. (2010). Stakeholder theory: The state of the art, Cambridge/New York: Cambridge University Press.

Golev, A., Scott, M., Erskine, P. D., Ali, S. H., & Ballantyne, G. R. (2014). Rare earths supply chains: Current status, constraints and opportunities, Resources Policy: 41, 52–59.

Gsottbauer, E., Logar, I., & van den Bergh, J. (2015). Towards a fair, constructive and consistent criticism of all valuation languages: Comment on Kallis et al. (2013). Ecological Economics, 112: 164–169.

Harrison, J. S., Bosse, D. A., & Phillips, R. A. (2010). Managing for stakeholders, stakeholder utility functions, and competitive advantage. Strategic Management Journal, 31: 58–74.

Hart, S. L. (1995). A natural-resource-based view of the firm. The Academy of Management Review, 20: 986–1014.

Heede, R. (2014). Tracing anthropogenic carbon dioxide and methane emissions to fossil fuel and cement producers, 1854–2010. Climatic Change, 122: 229–241.

Hörisch, J., Burritt, R., Christ, K., & Schaltegger, S. (2017). Legal Systems, Internatio-nalization and Corporate Sustainability. An empirical analysis of the influence of national and international authorities. Corporate Governance, 17(5): 861–875.

Hörisch, J., Freeman, R. E., & Schaltegger, S. (2014). Applying stakeholder theory in sustainability management: Links, similarities, dissimilarities, and a conceptual framework. Organization & Environment, 27: 328–346.

Hörisch, J., Schaltegger, S., & Windolph, S. (2015). Linking sustainability-related stakeholder feedback to corporate sustainability performance. An empirical analysis of stakeholder dialogues, *International Journal of Business Environment*, 7: 200–218.

Hörisch, J., & Windolph, S. E. (2014). Overview of the aggregate results of the international corporate sustainability barometer. In S. Schaltegger, S. E. Windolph, D. Harms, & J. Hörisch, eds., *Corporate sustainability in international comparison: State of practice, opportunities and challenges*, pp. 21–33. Heidelberg; New York; Berlin: Springer,.

International Labour Organization. (2011). *Assessing green job potential in developing countries*. Geneva: International Labour Organization.

Iqbal, M., & Molyneux, P. (2005). *Thirty years of Islamic banking: History, performance, and prospects*, Houndmills/New York: Palgrave Macmillan.

Ito, Y., Managi, S., & Matsuda, A. (2013). Performances of socially responsible investment and environmentally friendly funds. *Journal of the Operational Research Society*, 64: 1583–1594.

Kallis, G., Gómez-Baggethun, E., & Zografos, C. (2013). To value or not to value? That is not the question. *Ecological Economics*, 94: 97–105.

Kallis, G., Gomez-Baggethun, E., & Zografos, C. (2015). The limits of monetization in valuing the environment: Reply. *Ecological Economics*, 112: 170–173.

King, A. A., & Lenox, M. J. (2001). Does it really pay to be green?: An empirical study of firm environmental and financial performance. *Journal of Industrial Ecology*, 5: 105–116.

Madsen, H., & Ulhøi, J. P. (2001). Integrating environmental and stakeholder management. *Business Strategy & the Environment*, 10: 77–88.

Meadows, D., Meadows, D., Randers, J., & Behrens, W. (1972). *The limits to growth: A report for the Club of Rome's project on the predicament of mankind*. New York: Potomac Associates Books/Universe Books.

Mégie, G. (2006). From stratospheric ozone to climate change: Historical perspective on precaution and scientific responsibility. *Science And Engineering Ethics*, 12: 596–606.

Mitchell, R. K., Agle, B. R., & Wood, D. J. (1997). Toward a theory of stakeholder identification and salience: Defining the principle of who and what really counts. *Academy of Management Review*, 22: 853–886.

More, T. A., Averill, J. R., & Stevens, T. H. (1996). Values and economics in environmental management: A perspective and critique. *Journal of Environmental Management*, 48: 397–409.

Näsi, J. (1995). *Understanding stakeholder thinking*, Helsinki: LSR-Julkaisut Oy.

Norton, T. A., Parker, S. L., Zacher, H., & Ashkanasy, N. M. (2015). Employee green behavior: A theoretical framework, multilevel review, and future research agenda. *Organization & Environment*, 28: 103–125.

Onkila, T. (2011). Multiple forms of stakeholder interaction in environmental management: business arguments regarding differences in stakeholder relationships. *Business Strategy & the Environment*, 20: 379–393.

Phillips, R. (2003). *Stakeholder theory and organizational ethics*, San Francisco: Berrett-Koehler Publishers.

Phillips, R. A., & Reichart, J. (2000). The environment as a stakeholder? A fairness-based approach. *Journal of Business Ethics*, 23: 185–197.

Ransom, P., & Lober, D. J. (1999). Why do firms set environmental performance goals?: Some evidence from organizational theory. *Business Strategy & the Environment*, 8: 1–13.

Rockstrom, J., Steffen, W., Noone, K., Persson, A., Chapin, F. S., Lambin, E. F., Lenton, T. M., ... Foley, J. A. (2009). A safe operating space for humanity. *Nature*, 461: 472–475.

Schaltegger, S., Beckmann, M., & Hansen, E. (2013). Transdisciplinarity in corporate sustainability. Mapping the field. *Business Strategy and the Environment*, 22: 219–229.

Schaltegger, S., & Burritt, R. (2015). Business cases and corporate engagement with sustainability. differentiating ethical motivations. Journal of Business Ethics, *147*(2): 241–259.

Schaltegger, S., Hörisch, J., & Freeman, E. (2017, forthcoming). Business cases for sustainability. a stakeholder theory perspective. Organization & Environment. DOI: 10.1177/1086026617722882.

Schaltegger, S., Lüdeke-Freund, F. & Hansen, E. (2016). Business models for sustainability: A co-evolutionary analysis of sustainable entrepreneurship, innovation, and transformation. *Organization & Environment*, 29(3): 264–289.

Schaltegger, S., Windolph, S.E., Harms, D., & Hörisch, J. (2014). *Corporate sustainability in international comparison: State of practice, opportunities and challenges*, Dordrecht: Springer.

Shriberg, M., Schwimmer, S., & MacDonald, L. (2013). University of Michigan's Sustainability

Scholars Program: Empowering Leaders. *Sustainability: The Journal of Record*, 6: 259–264.

Shrivastava, P. (1995). The role of corporations in achieving ecological sustainability. *Academy of Management Review*, 20: 936–60.

Shrivastava, P. & Hart, S. L. (1995). Creating Sustainable Corporations. *Business Strategy and the Environment*, 4: 154–165.

Siebenhüner, B. (2004). Social learning and sustainability science: Which role can stakeholder participation play? *International Journal of Sustainable Development*, 7: 146–63.

Starik, M. (1995). Should trees have managerial standing? Toward stakeholder status for non-human nature. *Journal of Business Ethics*, 14: 207–217.

Starik, M., & Kanashiro, P. (2013). Toward a theory of sustainability management: Uncovering and integrating the nearly obvious. *Organization & Environment*, 26: 7–30.

Starik, M., & Turcotte, M.-F. (2014). With a little (urgent) help from our friends: Management academic leadership for a sustainable future. *Organization & Environment*, 27: 3–9.

Stead, W. E., & Stead, J. G. (1996). *Management for a small planet*. Thousand Oaks/London/New Delhi: Sage Publications.

Stevens, T. H., Echeverria, J., Glass, R. J., Hager, T., & More, T. A. (1991). Measuring the existence value of wildlife: What do CVM estimates really show? *Land Economics*, 67: 390–400.

Székely, F., & Knirsch, M. (2005). Responsible leadership and corporate social responsibility: Metrics for sustainable performance. *European Management Journal*, 23(6): 628–647.

UN (United Nations). (2015). Transforming our world: The 2030 Agenda for Sustainable Development, Resolution adopted by the General Assembly on 25 September 2015, New York, United Nations.

van Tulder, R., Seitanidi, M. M., Crane, A., & Brammer, S. (2016). Enhancing the impact of cross-sector partnerships. *Journal of Business Ethics*, 135: 1–17.

Wagner, M. (2010). The role of corporate sustainability performance for economic performance: A firm-level analysis of moderation effects. *Ecological Economics*, 69: 1553–1560.

Wagner, M. (2011). Corporate performance implications of extended stakeholder management: New insights on mediation and moderation effects. *Ecological Economics*, 70: 942–950.

Wagner, J., & Schaltegger, S. (2004). The effect of corporate environmental strategy choice and environmental performance on competitiveness and economic performance: An empirical study of EU manufacturing. *European Management Journal*, 22: 557–572.

Ward, B., & Dubos, R. (1972). *Only one earth: The care and maintenance of a small planet*. New York: Norton & Company.

Wood, D. J. (1990). *Business and society*, Glenview: Scott, Foresman & Co.

PART III

Stakeholder Theory in the Business Disciplines

CHAPTER 9

Motivating Boundary-Spanning Employees to Engage External Stakeholders

Insights from Stakeholder Marketing

CB BHATTACHARYA
University of Pittsburgh

DANIEL KORSCHUN
Drexel University

A fundamental objective of stakeholder theory is to better understand how companies interact with the world around them (Freeman, 1984). To achieve that objective, theorists have focused on understanding the complex and far-reaching relationships that companies have with their stakeholders (e.g., Whetten, Rands, & Godfrey, 2002). Those stakeholder relationships are so central to stakeholder theory that some theorists define the organization in part by the very relationships it forms with a diffuse nexus of stakeholders (Post, Preston, & Sachs, 2002). Stakeholders provide resources so that the organization can enhance wealth and achieve its objectives; in return, those stakeholders make claims on the organization's future wealth (Bosse, Phillips, & Harrison, 2009). Such reciprocal stakes and claims have led theorists to place a spotlight on the quality of relationships with stakeholders. Indeed, a central tenet of stakeholder theory is that, in order to survive in the long-term, firms must form relationships that provide benefits to the wider network of stakeholders, not just the firm's investors (Freeman 1984).

But how does a firm develop relationships with those stakeholders? For most firms, a distinct set of employees serves as the conduit to the external environment. Those boundary-spanning employees are tasked with negotiating the terms of the relationship and with delivering on the implicit promise to reciprocate stakes by providing benefits to stakeholders. Thus, a corporate imperative is to motivate employees, especially boundary-spanning employees, to

create mutually beneficial relationships with external stakeholders (Bhattacharya, Korschun, & Sen, 2009).

Notwithstanding the importance of boundary-spanning employees forging strong and enduring relationships with external stakeholders, companies often struggle to orient employees to achieve that aim. Despite the best efforts of companies, boundary-spanning employees can behave idiosyncratically. While some employees seek to collaborate with external stakeholders for joint gain (Vivek, Beatty, & Morgan, 2012), others withhold information from a customer, supplier, or other external stakeholder in order to close a deal (Fandt & Ferris, 1990). Prior research documents such heterogeneity even within the same work group where supervisors are the same, and incentive structures are uniform (Grizzle, et al., 2009). Thus, in practice, there is considerable heterogeneity in whether, and how much, individual employees serve those beyond the traditional confines of the firm (Korschun, 2015).

There is thus a need for frameworks that (a) examine how firms interact with external stakeholders, including society at large, and (b) acknowledge the considerable heterogeneity among boundary-spanning employees who interact with external stakeholders. Perhaps unfortunately, the modal approach in the literature has been to use the organization or stakeholder group as the unit of analysis. While such an approach has been valuable in examining tensions *between* one stakeholder group and another, the heterogeneity *within* groups suggests that additional value can materialize if one disaggregates the analysis, perhaps down to the individual level. Such an approach would be consistent with McVea and Freeman's (2005) call for research that takes a "names and faces" approach.

The burgeoning literature on *stakeholder marketing*, which seeks to apply and expand marketing theory to examine relationships between companies and society, may be uniquely equipped to address these challenges (Bhattacharya & Korschun, 2008; Hult, et al., 2011; Hillebrand, Driesen, & Oliver, 2015). First, stakeholder marketing draws from a long tradition of marketing theory on how companies create, communicate, and deliver value for customers, a key external stakeholder. For example, extant marketing theory addresses how to motivate employees by appealing to both their extrinsic (e.g., commissions; Anderson & Oliver, 1987) and intrinsic motivations (e.g., ideological rewards of the job; Du, Bhattacharya, & Sen, 2015). Stakeholder marketing extends that literature and seeks to understand how inputs from employees and other multiple stakeholders combine to improve relationships with customers (e.g., Vargo & Lusch, 2004). Second, and just as important, stakeholder marketing emphasizes how a company's marketing actions impact external stakeholders and the wider environment. Thus, it is not only concerned with the immediate impact of marketing actions, but also the second-order "ripple" effects of those actions on a wider network of stakeholders. For example, scholars have long been interested in how price collusion, price discrimination, and price confusion can affect social welfare both directly and indirectly (Grewal & Compeau, 1999).

Stakeholder marketing is a promising platform to build theory on when and why boundary-spanning employees will seek to create quality relationships with members of the company's external environment. In this chapter, we integrate stakeholder theory with advanced thought in marketing to build a framework for understanding when and why employees will engage other stakeholders in ways that improve relations between the firm and the external environment in which it operates. Thus, we examine why, when, and how internal stakeholders will interact with external stakeholders.

Our central premise is that the extent to which a boundary-spanning employee reaches beyond the organizational boundary to positively impact others is driven by the quality of the relationship the employee has with the company, and that the quality of the relationship is a function of the benefits the company provides to such employees. Moreover, we detail two complementary routes through which this occurs. One route is based on a more traditional logic where features of the job provide transactional benefits to the employee. However, the other, complementary route, is more novel. In that second route, a company can provide ideological benefits to its employees by applying the tenets of stakeholder marketing into its day-to-day marketing practices; these benefits are most likely to be derived by those employees with a prosocial motivation. To the extent that employees derive either type of benefit from their employer, they will cooperate with traditional organizational members; however, we argue that ideological benefits are more likely to trigger cooperative behaviors with external stakeholders and society at large.

In the next section, we review the conceptual foundations for our approach. We then outline our full framework. Finally, we discuss implications of the framework.

Conceptual Foundations

The Ascendance of Stakeholder Marketing

The marketing function is "the company's prime mechanism for connecting with external players" (Chakravorti, 2010). Yet, traditional marketing thought has tended to be firm-centric, and driven by a classical input-output approach, with profit maximization as the primary objective of the firm. Under this traditional view, a company is "a commercial entity seeking to satisfy short-term, material needs through consumption behaviors" (Smith, Drumwright, & Gentile, 2010: 4). However, such a view of marketing is partly to blame for companies that sell dangerous products such as cigarettes, include processes that may harm the environment such as the use of plastic shopping bags, or encourage consumption habits that are socially or environmentally unsustainable such as predatory lending or high CO_2 emissions automobiles. The same myopic view may also be responsible for companies not recognizing opportunities to develop new practices (e.g., micro-lending), processes (e.g., inclusive hiring practices), or technologies (e.g., energy-efficient products) such as reducing waste. In short, marketing researchers have too often overlooked the varied ways that a company's marketing actions can affect society at large.

Recognizing the limitations of such marketing thought, some theorists are devoting more attention to the interconnected sets of stakeholders that affect and are affected by marketing actions. The emergent approach, falling under the umbrella of stakeholder marketing, promotes a shift from firms as centers of control to ones of more dispersed control (Chakravorti, 2010). Stakeholder marketing has been described as "a radical and . . . socially beneficial revision of how most marketing practitioners currently perceive the purpose of their firms with respect to stakeholders" (Laczniak & Murphy, 2012). It keeps marketing's broad topical foci such as communications, distribution, consumer choice, and employee motivation. However, it places special emphasis on societal outcomes and on how a wide range of stakeholders respond to company actions. The boundaries of stakeholder marketing are still being developed, but it can be described as doing the following (Bhattacharya, 2010): (a) it considers the interests of a range of stakeholders, (b) it considers the full impact of not just immediate stakeholders but also society and the environment, (c) it studies the relations among and between stakeholders, and (d) it helps marketers deal with potential conflicts in stakeholder interests.

Hult, Mena, Ferrell, and Ferrell (2011) define stakeholder marketing as "activities within a system of social institutions and processes for facilitating and maintaining value through exchange relationships with multiple stakeholders." This definition is intended to reflect the fact that companies must manage relationships with multiple sets of stakeholders, not merely customers. Stakeholders are not only parties to an exchange of value with the company (as in customers

receiving value; Sheth & Uslay, 2007; Lusch & Vargo, 2006), but also key players in the creation of that value for customers. Employees, shareholders, regulators, suppliers, and community members are all cocreators of value, which, in turn, drives marketing performance. These relationships are founded on a set of shared values among multiple groups of stakeholders, not just customers.

Stakeholder marketing is perhaps best thought of as an offshoot of stakeholder theory; it draws from the tenets of stakeholder theory, yet focuses on somewhat different phenomena. Like stakeholder theory, stakeholder marketing has descriptive, instrumental, and normative elements (Donaldson & Preston, 1995); that is, it describes how companies and stakeholders behave, it reveals connections between actions and desired outcomes (e.g., profit maximization, consumer welfare), and it prescribes improvements to current practice. To achieve these aims, stakeholder marketing tends to draw from different theoretical bases, such as social psychology, decision-making, attitude, the service profit chain, organizational behavior, and marketing and public policy.

Interestingly, Hult et al. (2011: 14) explain explicitly that they do not address effects on "society at large" in their definition because it is "difficult to operationalize, and does not capture the systems networks, and real world complexity of marketing activities related to decision making." In contrast, other scholars have begun to explore some of the ways by which companies can affect society at large through their supply chains or other means; and some of these outcomes are sparked originally by consumer purchase (Smith, Palazzo, & Bhattacharya, 2010). Thus, while there is some disagreement as to how far to extend the focus of stakeholder-marketing research, scholars appear to agree that such second-order effects are possible. As we clarify when presenting our framework, we contend that broader effects of the firm on society can be understood and measured. Moreover, they can be detected at the individual level of analysis where individual-to-individual relationships between employees and external stakeholders can be observed. These employee–external-stakeholder relationships are perhaps the most fruitful area for stakeholder marketing to contribute to the broader literature on stakeholder theory.

Boundary Spanning Relationships with External Stakeholders

A recurring theme in both stakeholder theory and stakeholder marketing is that companies need to form relationships with an array of external stakeholders. Marketers have long viewed relationship building as actions that promote successful exchange between two or more parties over time (e.g., Morgan & Hunt, 1994). In general terms, the value that is exchanged between a company and its external stakeholders involves the stakeholder putting something at risk (i.e., a stake) in anticipation of a benefit or claim on the company's wealth (Post, et al., 2002). Such an exchange of stakes for claims could be misconstrued as a simple exchange of monetary value. It is true, of course, that these exchanges frequently involve spot transactions, motivated purely by self-interest, and comprised of tangible financial rewards. But there is emerging consensus in both stakeholder theory and stakeholder marketing that relationships between firms and their stakeholders can go well beyond the transactional, and be based on more than simple self-interest. They can also be very highly personal and value laden (Freeman & Velamuri, 2008).

Exchange can incorporate both tangible and intangible elements, and we contend that any individual relationship may contain a combination of both. This follows a long tradition in marketing that has sought to untangle value that customers derive from tangible products, but also the more intangible elements that emerge from service delivery. For example, Levitt (1981) noted that companies marketing either intangible products or intangible qualities of products need to behave more relationally, by continually communicating and adjusting to the expectations of customers. This not only alters expectations of service, but also invites customers to cocreate the value they receive through interactions with the company. Because customers do not derive benefits from a product or service until they consume it, customers are *always* cocreators of value (Vargo and Lusch

2004). As a result, successful companies must develop employees who are customer oriented and focused on forging quality relationships with customers that maximize the value that customers are able to cocreate.

One key way that companies communicate the value that they can provide to external stakeholders is the way they define the organization's identity (Brown, et al., 2006). Stakeholders interpret the behaviors, communications, and symbolism (van Riel & Balmer, 1997) of a company in order to construct their understanding of the company's history, strategy, and values. For example, a company may become endeared to its customers or other stakeholders when they learn of its corporate social responsibility initiatives, because such initiatives may be construed as communicating the underlying values of the company (Sen, Bhattacharya, & Korschun, 2006). To the extent that such an assessment leads a stakeholder to believe that the company can provide value, they may engage the company. Such an idea is consistent with the marketing notion of relationship quality, or the ''overall assessment of the strength of a relationship, conceptualized as a composite or multidimensional construct capturing the different but related facets of a relationship'' (De Wulf, Odekerken-Schroder, & Iacobucci, 2001: 36).

But another way that companies communicate the value that they can provide to external stakeholders is through the actions of boundary-spanning employees. It is boundary-spanning employees involved in the marketing of complex services, who often perform the role of relationship manager (Lawrence, Evans, & Cowles, 1990). Of course, those employees, just as customers, have their own, potentially idiosyncratic motivations. Thus, motivating employees to serve customers often involves first creating a package of benefits that will be valued by those employees (George 1990). Such a package is sometimes referred to as the "job-product" because the features of the job provide benefits to employees just as features of a product provide benefits to customers. A properly configured job-product, with features such as flexible work hours, work related perks (Berry 2002), or community volunteering opportunities (Bhattacharya, Sen, & Korschun, 2008) that deliver valued benefits, can make employees more satisfied in their job, which, in turn, can influence their interactions with customers (Homburg & Stock, 2004).

Just as companies can foster relationships with external stakeholders, so too can they foster quality relationships with internal stakeholders (i.e., employees). We extend the relationship quality construct to employees, defining employee-company relationship quality as an employee's multi-faceted assessment of the overall strength of their relationship with the focal company. Relationship quality can range from strong to weak and take various forms as the bonds of the relationship are strengthened. For example, relationship quality that is still forming may manifest itself as job satisfaction (e.g., Crosby, et al., 1990; Garbarino & Johnson, 1999), which reflects the degree to which an employee's job expectations are met or exceeded. However, as relationship quality strengthens, an employee may begin to identify with the company, integrating their sense of self with their sense of what the company stands for. Since this chapter is concerned with how a company engages its external environment, we focus on the relationship between boundary-spanning employees and the company; however, our conceptualization could apply equally to employees with no direct contact with external stakeholders.

The relational approach which is present – whether implicitly or explicitly – in so much of the marketing literature places greater onus on boundary-spanning employees. Yet, motivating boundary-spanning employees to collaborate with external stakeholders is a less than straightforward exercise. In fact, the marketing literature on this question has produced a rather large body of research, much of it falling under the moniker of internal marketing; that is, applying marketing principles to motivate employees to reach sales and service targets and to improve customer satisfaction. The literature borrows the notion that products have features that provide benefits to customers. Marketing scholars interested in motivating employees to serve customers utilize this train of thought in describing the job-product. The job-product concept suggests that one's job has features of its own and that, if configured correctly, those features can motivate employees to behave in ways that align with the company's goals (Ahmed & Rafiq, 2003). For example, sales commissions provide an extrinsic reward that can encourage employees to exert maximal effort to make sales.

However, others point out that besides traditional job-product features, there may be additional motivations for serving those beyond the corporate boundary. "Most of us do what we do because we are self-interested and interested in others," observe Freeman and Velamuri (2006: 17); "business works in part because of our urge to create things with others and for others." The fundamental job of business leaders is to "instill into followers a sense of oneness with the organization" that in turn influences behaviors toward others both inside and outside the organization (Wieseke, et al., 2009: 123). This suggests that researchers interested in understanding when and why boundary-spanning employees will serve other stakeholders must account for a complex multi-faceted set of motivations. In the next section, we present a framework that integrates stakeholder theory and stakeholder marketing, and which explains boundary-spanning employee behavior toward others.

A Framework for Understanding Boundary-Spanning Behaviors toward Stakeholders

Figure 9.1 depicts our conceptual approach. In essence, we propose that an employee will engage in society-oriented, external-stakeholder-oriented, and internal-stakeholder-oriented behaviors to the extent that they maintain a high-quality relationship with the company. That relationship is driven by the extent to which the company provides transactional benefits (by creating a compelling job-product), and ideological benefits (by engaging in stakeholder-marketing practices).

Thus, we detail two complementary routes. The first is the more traditional route, in which features of the job such as role requirements, incentives, and supervisor support provide transactional benefits, which also enhance the employee-company relationship. The second, and perhaps more compelling route, is that which emanates from

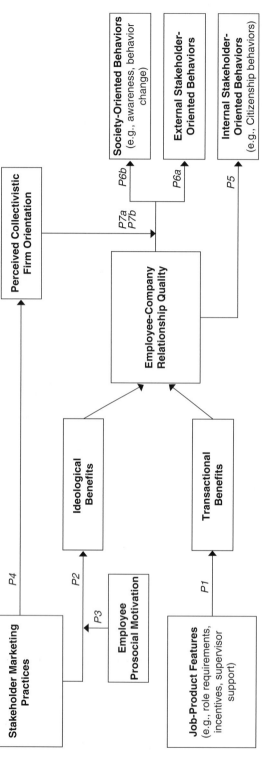

Figure 9.1. A Framework for Understanding Boundary-Spanning Employee Responses to Stakeholder-Marketing Practices and the Job-Product

stakeholder-marketing practices. The more a firm defines itself through its stakeholder marketing, the more this will enhance many employee-company relationships, because it will provide ideological benefits to those employees who already define themselves in similar terms; these ideological benefits will be particularly consequential for those employees who crave prosocial elements in their job. The employee–company relationship then drives (a) collaborative behaviors toward external stakeholders, and (b) personal behavior change, effects which are magnified to the extent that the employee perceives the company to have a collectivistic identity orientation (Brickson, 2007).

Overall, we contend that in order to motivate employees to act in ways that maximize benefits for internal stakeholders, external stakeholders, and society at large, firms need to move beyond traditional features of the job. Rather, we explain how corporate-level stakeholder-marketing practices can spill over from the organizational level to individual behaviors of boundary-spanning employees, behaviors which can have a profound impact on the wider stakeholder environment.

The Job-Product Path to Employee–Company Relationship Quality

Researchers in the marketing literature have extended the marketing concept to employees (e.g., George 1990; Ahmed & Rafiq 2003). This research stream, sometimes appearing under the moniker "internal marketing," extends the marketing notion that customers derive benefits from products based on the distinct configurations of each product's features. The internal marketing literature depicts the company as having an internal market of employees (Foreman & Money, 1995). Analogously, research on internal marketing holds that the design of the job can be thought of as having features that provide benefits to employees (Berry, 2002). For example, job training can provide benefits of career advancement, and incentives for salespeople can provide more sizable paychecks. Proper configurations of the job-product can meet expectations of the employee and therefore lead to employee job satisfaction, one expression of employee–company relationship

quality. Thus, these appeals to the employee's self-interest can improve the relationship between an employee and the employer company (Ballantyne, 2003). Based on this literature, we expect that features of the job-product will enhance employee–company relationship quality and that this will occur to the extent that the job-product features provide the employee with transactional benefits. These benefits involve an explicit exchange where the company provides features such as good compensation, clear direction, or supportive supervisors, in exchange for employee behaviors such as effort, and adherence to the company's policies and procedures. The employee can derive transactional benefits related to the job to the extent that this exchange is satisfying to them. And when such exchange is satisfying over the term of the employee–company relationship, the employee will consider the relationship to be of high quality. In all, we suggest that the mechanism that connects features of the job-product to employee–customer relationship quality is the extent to which the job-product provides transactional benefits to the employee.

Proposition 1: Features of the job-product contribute to employee–customer relationship quality to the extent that they provide transactional benefits to the boundary-spanning employee.

The Stakeholder-Marketing Practices Path to Employee–Company Relationship Quality

While the traditional job-product path has proven a powerful means to predict employee behavior, burgeoning thinking on stakeholder marketing suggests a parallel path that may be just as consequential. We contend that employee–company relationships may also be enhanced when stakeholder-marketing practices are enacted by the company. Drawing from conceptualizations in the stakeholder marketing literature, stakeholder-marketing practices are those that facilitate and maintain value through exchange relationships with multiple stakeholders (Hult, et al., 2011). In short, "stakeholder marketing [practices] helps a firm better recognize the symbiotic relationship of its marketing-related actions with the workings of society" (Gundlach & Wilkie, 2010: 90). A company that adopts stakeholder-marketing practices considers the interests of a range of stakeholders, both internal and external, and both primary stakeholders and the broader society (Bhattacharya, 2010). It seeks to share both risks and benefits with stakeholders (Sachs & Maurer, 2009), and attempts to minimize negative externalities while maximizing positive externalities. Thus, stakeholder-marketing practices elevate the needs of other entities, not just the company. In contrast, a company that does not espouse such practices bases decisions, policies, and procedures only on the interests of the corporation – or its most immediate stakeholders. It will seek to shift risks to stakeholders while maximizing benefits for the firm with consideration to neither negative nor positive externalities.

Decades of research documents that organizational-level factors can influence individual behaviors of organizational members by how those members interpret the central, enduring, and distinctive characteristics of the organization (e.g., Albert & Whetten, 1985). Organizational-level practices can suggest the motives of the company and communicate norms for individual behavior. Prior research in the stakeholder literature has examined these practices, and to some extent how those practices are interpreted by employees and customers, but our understanding of why, how, and when such practices encourage boundary-spanning employees to become more stakeholder oriented is still underdeveloped. We now delineate this complementary path connecting stakeholder-marketing practices to individual employee responses.

Stakeholder-Marketing Practices and Employee–Company Relationship

The stakeholder-marketing literature suggests that defining a company by a broader stakeholder-driven purpose can enhance performance and benefit society. As Bartlett and Ghoshal explain (1994: 79) rather than focus on industry or product strategy, companies adopting a stakeholder-marketing approach stand to simultaneously gain market advantage and serve the public good benefit by "shap[ing] a shared institutional purpose" around

those practices. To cite one example, Ellsworth (2002: 11) argues that maintaining a "customer-focused corporate purpose provides the key to outstanding performance and to enhancing the lives of those the company serves and of those who serve it."

Yet, despite this contention, it remains unclear through what mechanism this would occur. We argue that the responses of employees, and boundary-spanning employees in particular, represent such a mechanism. By embedding the *raison d'être* of the company in terms of its impact on stakeholders and society, employees are better able to construe the values of the company. Since altruism and prosocial behaviors tend to be socially desirable values, the employee may derive ideological benefits by working for a company engaged in stakeholder-marketing practices. These benefits involve psychological rewards from working for, associating with, or representing a company with distinct core values that may align with their own. The benefits are ideological because stakeholder-marketing practices inculcate issues of altruism, social justice, ethics, and welfare; they draw on a system of ideas or ideals, which relate to how the company fits in the larger economic or even political landscape (Korschun, et al., 2017). By framing the business as a means to reach a societal aim, the employee may begin to psychologically connect aspects of their job with those objectives. They may view their individual job as a means to serve others, rather than simply as a means to earn a paycheck. They may feel free to express their personal ideology during their work routines. This is consistent with prior work which finds that corporate social responsibility (CSR) programs can fulfill employees' ideological needs (Du, et al., 2015), and that employees can view their job more as a calling than an occupation (Glavas & Godwin, 2013).

To the extent that an employee derives these benefits, we predict that they will perceive an overlap in values with the company. Such a prediction is based on research from the CSR and social identity literatures. Both those literatures suggest that psychological benefits can make a company an attractive target for identification by consumers (Bhattacharya & Sen, 2003) and employees

(Greening & Turban, 2000). For example, many employees at the supermarket chain Market Basket are highly motivated by the notion that, via the company they work for, they are able to give low-income families access to affordable groceries; a shared understanding that explains, in part, their almost cultish devotion to the company (Korschun & Welker, 2015). Thus, we predict that stakeholder-marketing practices can improve the employee–customer relationship because it provides ideological benefits.

Proposition 2: Stakeholder-marketing practices contribute to employee-customer relationship quality to the extent that it provides ideological benefits to the boundary-spanning employee.

The Influence of Employee Prosocial Motivation

We do not expect that engaging in stakeholder-marketing practices will engender uniformly strong and positive relationships with boundary-spanning employees. There may be considerable variance in how much employees seek to work with a company that values other entities and stakeholders in its wider network. One particularly relevant individual difference is boundary-spanning employees' prosocial motivation, or their desire to protect and promote the well-being of others (Grant & Berg 2011). Whereas some employees may choose to mainly pursue their independent interests (Miller, 1999; Meglino & Korsgaard, 2004), others may be more interested in promoting the interests of others (Batson, et al., 2008).

We propose that employees with a prosocial motivation at work will be especially receptive to stakeholder-marketing practices. Prosocial motivation can alter the way that employees interpret the world around them (Grant 2008). Stakeholder-marketing practices accentuate more collectivistic norms and expectations, and, therefore, should provide self-confirming benefits such as altruism to those employees. Such practices may also underscore the task significance of one's work, further enhancing ideological benefits. Thus, employees with a prosocial motivation will derive considerable ideological benefit from such practices and develop a strong relationship with the company.

For example, outdoor retailer Patagonia describes itself as being an "activist company"; it frequently advocates for people affected by climate change and also considers the environment itself to be a key stakeholder. We expect that an employee for whom benefiting others is an important value will respond more positively to Patagonia's concern for its network of stakeholders. It will suggest to the employee that the company shares the employee's concern for others. Overall, this path will be particularly relevant for those employees with a prosocial motivation.

Proposition 3: The extent to which stakeholder-marketing practices provide ideological benefits is moderated by the employee's prosocial motivation. Employees with a prosocial motivation at work will derive more ideological benefits from stakeholder-marketing practices than peers without a prosocial motivation.

Stakeholder-Marketing Practices and Perceived Collectivistic Identity Orientation

Companies can approach the world around them in myriad ways. One useful taxonomy for how companies engage their external constituents is their organizational identity orientation (Brickson, 2007). Brickson defines organizational identity orientation as "the nature of assumed relations between an organization and its stakeholders as perceived by members." These perceptions may be that the company is individualistic, relational or collectivistic. An individualistic company is believed to act based primarily on its organizational self-interest. Such a company would assess its performance based on market share compared to competitors. A relational identity orientation is believed by organization members to be concerned with a particular other's benefit, and would assess its performance largely by how much it is contributing to the relationship with that partner. Finally, a collectivistic identity orientation is based on the belief that the company is concerned with improving the welfare of a greater collective.

This collectivistic orientation is of greatest relevance to the present discussion. We propose that the more a company engages in stakeholder-marketing practices, the more likely a boundary-spanning employee will perceive it to have a collectivistic identity orientation. It is well established that employees – as well as external stakeholders – attend to the actions and statements of companies as they construe its motivations and aims. Stakeholder-marketing practices are likely to provide a foundation upon which an individual will view the company as concerned with its place in society as much as its own welfare. This assertion is consistent with Brickson's (2000) finding that *group-based* organizational structure, tasks, and reward structures suggest a collectivistic identity orientation, while atomistic structures and tasks suggest an individualistic identity orientation. Thus, the extent to which a company engages in stakeholder-marketing practices will alter the way that boundary-spanning employees perceive it in relation to its stakeholder base and broader society.

Proposition 4: Stakeholder-marketing practices lead boundary-spanning employees to perceive the company as having a collectivistic orientation.

Outcomes of Employee–Company Relationship Quality

Employee behavior can be predicted in part by the employee's relationship quality with the company. Much of the literature to date has focused on a rather limited set of behavioral consequences, for example, behaviors toward coworkers. However, the stakeholder-marketing approach suggests that the relationship quality felt by individual employees may lead to behaviors toward a wider array of audiences than generally noted in the literature. In this section, we argue that strong employee-company relationships can affect behaviors toward internal stakeholders, external stakeholders, and society at large.

Relationship Quality and Internal Stakeholder-Oriented Behaviors

Evidence from the literature strongly implies that an employee will be more likely to engage in helping behaviors toward internal stakeholders to the extent that the employee–company relationship quality is strong (Dukerich, Golden, & Shortell,

2002; Riketta, 2005; van Knippenberg, & Sleebos, 2006). By internal stakeholders we refer to coworkers, supervisors, upper-management, or others who work within the traditional confines of the organization (Harrison & St. John 1996). This proposition is based on research showing that employees who are committed to, or identify with, the company are those most likely to engage in organizational citizenship behaviors. These citizenship behaviors include helping, civic virtue, sportsmanship, organizational loyalty, organizational compliance, and individual initiative. For example, MacKenzie, Podsakoff, and Ahearne (1998) find job satisfaction and organizational commitment drive organizational citizenship behaviors and other extra-role behaviors, while van Dick et al. (2006) find that organizational identification, another indicator of relationship quality, is an antecedent of citizenship toward internal stakeholders. It is worth noting that organizational citizenship behaviors are also linked to higher-level outcomes such as unit performance (Podsakoff, et al., 2009). The underlying logic of these effects is that the positive affect and improved morale that these employees feel carries over to their daily interactions with fellow employees. In addition, when an employee has a quality relationship with the company, they may be more willing to help the organization reach its goals by contributing to shared objectives. As a result, one should expect a linkage between employee–company relationship quality and internal-stakeholder-oriented behaviors.

Proposition 5: The greater the employee–company relationship quality, the more the employee will engage in internal-stakeholder-oriented behaviors.

Relationship Quality and External-Stakeholder-Oriented Behaviors

Stakeholder theory suggests that a key contributor to company performance is how the company engages stakeholders in the external environment. Our approach examines this phenomenon at the individual level. We seek to predict when an employee will engage in behaviors that provide value to external stakeholders. We call these external-stakeholder-oriented behaviors. As an illustrative example, an employee can engage in information sharing and trusting behaviors with suppliers, as opposed to an employee withholding information or seeking ways to get suppliers to compete among themselves for business with the employee's company. Similarly, with customers, an employee might serve the customer by directing them to products and services that will provide the most value for them, as opposed to an employee who directs customers to products and services that improve the financial performance of the company even if at the expense of the customer's welfare.

We contend that a key factor in predicting such engagement at the individual level is the extent to which there is a quality relationship between the employee and the company. An employee who senses a high-quality relationship with the company, may psychologically connect the satisfaction of the stakeholder to the long-term performance of the company. The employee may therefore view service to external stakeholders as a means to reciprocate the quality relationship that the company fostered in the employee. Furthermore, we argue that this effect will be particularly potent when the company is believed to have a collectivistic identity orientation. Such a collectivistic identity orientation may redefine the boundaries of the corporation to the employee. While some employees may view organizational members as only those who are traditionally defined as internal (e.g., employees), a collectivistic identity orientation suggests a more extended enterprise that includes external stakeholders as well, to the extent that the employee views some external stakeholders as part of the network of actors that make up the organization and contribute to its success. Since a collectivistic identity orientation suggests to the employee that the organization is concerned with the welfare of its wider network of actors (Brickson & Brewer, 2001), the employee may view cooperation with those partners as an additional avenue to contribute to the organization. Overall, we contend that employee-relationship quality will lead to external-stakeholder-oriented behaviors and that this effect will become stronger to the extent that the employee believes that the company has a collectivistic identity orientation.

Proposition 6a: The more that employee–company relationship quality is based upon ideological benefits, the more the employee will engage in external-stakeholder-oriented behaviors.

Proposition 7a: The effect in P6a is moderated by perceived collectivistic firm orientation. The effect of employee–company relationship quality on external stakeholders will be stronger when the company is perceived to have a collectivistic orientation.

Relationship Quality and Society-Oriented Behaviors

So far, we have argued that when employee–company relationship quality is high, it can lead to collaborative behaviors toward both internal and external stakeholders. But we also argue that, under the right circumstances, relationship quality can also encourage behaviors that benefit others beyond the traditional reach of the company. We call these society-oriented behaviors, which we define as employee actions that are intended to improve the welfare of people in society at large, regardless of their affiliation with the company. There are ample opportunities for employees to take action as an official representative of the company. For example, they may recycle at work, even when they are not required to do so by company policy or supervisor direction. Or they may design operations processes to waste fewer resources or consume less energy.

But unlike the other behaviors in propositions 6a and 7a, these behaviors also have the potential to extend beyond the traditional domain of work. Specifically, they may occur at home or in other spheres of the employee's life. For example, an employee may try to influence macro-level discussions of public policy by participating in town halls, social media, or other platforms where there is public discourse. In this way, they may increase awareness of an issue among the general public, or persuade others to consider their own position. Similarly, an employee may change their personal behaviors in ways that have broader benefits for society. The literature on such behavior change has examined changes such as increased donating behavior, exercise, recycling, or decreases in AIDS-risk behaviors or smoking.

Overall, such society-oriented behaviors can be distinguished in large part from other employee outcomes in that they can encompass multiple spheres of an employee's life. These behaviors also have the potential – and in fact are intended to – affect the lives of a broad swath of the population.

We predict that employee–company relationship quality will drive these society-oriented behaviors when the company is perceived to have a collectivistic identity orientation. This is because, when there is a strong relationship with the company, the employee will engage in behaviors that serve the goals and mission of the company. When the company's identity is collectivistic in nature, the employee will be more likely to believe that the company measures its performance in part by how much it contributes positively to social and environmental issues. Thus, the employee may be reminded of a moral and ideological responsibility to engage in society-oriented behaviors, because the employee may ascribe those responsibilities to the company as well. This can serve as an impetus to benefit a broader collective, rather than merely those considered to be the primary stakeholders of the firm.

Proposition 6b: The more the employee-company relationship quality is based upon ideological benefits, the more the employee will engage in society-oriented behaviors.

Proposition 7b: The effect in P6b is moderated by perceived collectivistic firm orientation. The effect of the employee-company relationship quality on society-oriented behaviors will be stronger when the company is perceived to have a collectivistic orientation.

Discussion/Implications

In this chapter, we applied a marketing approach to address an urgent question facing stakeholder theorists. The resulting framework explains that a key to motivating a boundary-spanning employee to serve fellow employees, external stakeholders, and the broader society is the quality of the relationship that the company forms with the employee. We contend that the job-product and the corporate identity each contribute to relationship quality, but that they do so by providing distinct types of benefits: tangible benefits for the job-product and ideological benefits for the corporate identity. This relationship quality will motivate employees to work toward the company's goals, and, to the extent that those goals are perceived to be collectivistic, the employee will be especially likely to serve external stakeholders and society at large.

Our analysis is at the individual rather than group or organizational level. This enables a deeper examination of the underlying psychology behind boundary spanners' thoughts and behaviors in multiple work, and non-work domains. In doing so, our approach has a number of contributions to the literature.

Multiple Benefits Drive Relationship Quality

Our framework distinguishes between two types of benefits that boundary-spanning employees can derive from their job and the company: transactional and ideological. Furthermore, we suggest that the primary drivers of these benefits are features of the job-product and the corporate identity, respectively. Such a notion unifies two largely disparate literature streams and thereby expands our understanding of how employees interpret their job in terms of their broader relationship with the company.

An objective of this chapter is therefore to encourage scholars (and managers) to consider multiple ways that companies can enhance relationships with employees. The immediate job requirements, rewards, and responsibilities play an important role, but employees can also react to the way that the company defines itself. Thus, an important theoretical implication is that employees may be quite active interpreters of their work environment. Such a notion is consistent with some management research on how employees engage in sense making when confronting ethical issues at work (Sonenshein, 2007). This invites future research on how employees might reconcile conflicts between job incentives and the way that a company defines itself. For a high-profile example of such a conflict, one might examine the case of Wells Fargo, which has been very active in community development, yet, until 2016, placed so much pressure on sales employees that thousands fraudulently opened new accounts on behalf of unwitting customers.

Content of the Organizational Identity

Another proposal in our framework is that relationship quality can manifest itself in distinct orientations, depending on employee perceptions of the firm's identity orientation. When the orientation of the company is believed to be collectivistic, this informs the employee of the extent to which the culture of the company values engagement with the broader society. Our analysis suggests that those values can create social norms which employees will use as a guide for their behaviors toward others on the other side of the organizational boundary.

Our framework focuses on the construct of collectivistic identity orientation. However, corporate identity is a multifaceted concept that can take many forms, depending on the stakeholder perceiving it (Albert & Whetten, 1985). Moreover, it is negotiated over time, based on interactions between a company and stakeholders (Scott & Lane, 2000). This suggests that relationship quality could lead to very different outcomes depending on other dimensions of an organization's identity. For example, one might reason that a company that is perceived to be aggressive and individualistic (as opposed to collectivistic) could encourage employees to behave opportunistically toward external stakeholders. Analogously, employees with a high-quality relationship with a publicly held company with a relatively short-term perspective may sense very different expectations than another employee with an equally high-quality relationship with a company that is privately held and has a longer-term focus; the former employee may only facilitate exchange with stakeholders when return on that investment is expected to be swift, whereas the latter employee may facilitate exchange where returns on investment require more patience. Since an organization's identity resides in the mind of employees and other stakeholders, and since it is negotiated over time, future research may wish to examine how boundary-spanning employees and external stakeholders interact based on their shared

or divergent understandings. Future research may also investigate under which conditions a company and its stakeholder base will perform better under a collectivistic orientation (Harrison, Bosse, & Phillips, 2010), and under which conditions an individualistic orientation might be preferable.

Array of Downstream Outcomes

Stakeholder theory, and stakeholder marketing, are not only interested in the direct impacts that a company can have on the wider societal environment, but also the indirect effects of those actions. Our framework is consistent with this notion as it predicts employee behaviors toward a wide range of organizational stakeholders, both internal and external to the organization. Some of these behaviors are indirect, in that they are not dictated by the organization; rather, they are enacted voluntarily through the employees' behaviors that contribute to awareness of societal issues, or through behavior change of their own that may benefit people who ordinarily would not be in contact with the company.

Our approach thus portrays boundary-spanning employees as potentially expanding the ways in which organizations interact with society. To our knowledge, there is no research on how such behaviors might change the perceptions of those distant stakeholders. Thus, if the organization should really be thought of as an extended enterprise, such a marketing-based and individual-level view could provide insight on where the boundary of that organization is and how people interact on the very margins of the organization.

References

Ahmed, P. K., and Mohammed R. (2003). Internal marketing issues and challenges. *European Journal of Marketing*, *37*(9): 1177–1186.

Anderson, E., and R. L. Oliver. (1987). Perspectives on behavior-based versus outcome-based salesforce control systems. *The Journal of Marketing*: 76–88.

Albert, S., & D, A. Whetten. (1985). Organizational identity. Research in Organizational Behavior.

Ballantyne, D. (2003). A relationship-mediated theory of internal marketing. *European Journal of Marketing*, *37*(9): 1242–1260.

Bartlett, C. A., & S. Ghoshal. (1994). Changing the role of top management: Beyond strategy to purpose. *Harvard Business Review*, 72(6): 79–88.

Batson, C. D., N. Ahmad, A. A. Powell, E. L. Stocks, J. Shah, & W. Gardner. (2008). Prosocial motivation. In *Handbook of motivation science*: 135–149. New York: Guilford Press.

Berry, L. L. (2002). Relationship marketing of services perspectives from 1983 and 2000. *Journal of relationship marketing*, 1(1): 59–77.

Bhattacharya, C. B. (2010). Introduction to the special section on stakeholder marketing. *Journal of Public Policy & Marketing*, 29(1): 1–3.

Bhattacharya, C. B., D. Korschun, &. S. Sen. (2009). Strengthening stakeholder–company relationships through mutually beneficial corporate social responsibility initiatives. Journal of Business Ethics, 85(2): 257–272.

Bhattacharya, C. B., & D. Korschun. (2008). Stakeholder marketing: Beyond the four Ps and the customer. *Journal of Public Policy & Marketing*, 27(1): 113–116.

Bhattacharya, C. B., & S. Sen. (2003). Consumer-company identification: A framework for understanding consumers' relationships with companies. *Journal of Marketing*, 67(2): 76–88.

Bhattacharya, C. B., S. Sen, & D. Korschun. (2008). Using corporate social responsibility to win the war for talent. MIT Sloan Management Review, 49(2).

Bosse, D. A., R. A. Phillips, & J. S. Harrison. (2009). Stakeholders, reciprocity, and firm performance. *Strategic Management Journal*, 30(4): 447–456.

Brickson, S. (2000). The impact of identity orientation on individual and organizational outcomes in demographically diverse settings. *Academy of Management Review*, 25(1): 82–101.

Brickson, S. L. (2007). Organizational identity orientation: The genesis of the role of the firm and distinct forms of social value. *Academy of Management Review*, 32(3): 864–888.

Brickson, S., & M. B. Brewer. (2001). Identity orientation and intergroup relations in organizations. *Social Identity Processes in Organizational Contexts*, 49: 49–66.

Brown, T. J., P. A. Dacin, M. G. Pratt, & D. A. Whetten. (2006). Identity, intended image, construed image, and reputation: An interdisciplinary framework and suggested terminology. *Journal of the Academy of Marketing Science*, 34(2): 99–106.

Chakravorti, B. (2010). Stakeholder marketing 2.0. *Journal of Public Policy & Marketing*, 29(1): 97–102.

Crosby, L. A., K. R. Evans, & D. Cowles. (1990). Relationship quality in services selling: An interpersonal influence perspective. *The Journal of Marketing*: 68–81.

De Wulf, K., G. Odekerken-Schroder, & D. Iacobucci. (2001). Investments in consumer relationships: A cross country and cross-industry exploration. *Journal of Marketing*, 65(October): 33.

Donaldson, T., & L. E. Preston. (1995). The stakeholder theory of the corporation: Concepts, evidence, and implications. *Academy of management Review*, 20(1): 65–91.

Du, S., C. B. Bhattacharya, & S. Sen. (2015). Corporate social responsibility, multi-faceted job-products, and employee outcomes. *Journal of Business Ethics*, 131(2): 319–335.

Dukerich, J. M., B. R. Golden, & S. M. Shortell. (2002). Beauty is in the eye of the beholder: The impact of organizational identification, identity, and image on the cooperative behaviors of physicians. *Administrative Science Quarterly*, 47(3): 507–533.

Ellsworth, R. R. (2002). *Leading with purpose: The new corporate realities*. Stanford University Press.

Fandt, P. M., & G. R. Ferris. (1990). The management of information and impressions: When employees behave opportunistically. *Organizational Behavior and Human Decision Processes*, 45(1): 140–158.

Foreman, S. K., & A. H. Money. (1995). Internal marketing: Concepts, measurement and application. *Journal of Marketing Management*, 11(8): 755–768.

Freeman, R. E. (1984). Strategic management: A stakeholder approach. Marshfield, MA: Pitman.

Freeman, R. E., & Velamuri, S. R. (2006). A new approach to CSR: Company stakeholder responsibility. In Corporate social responsibility, pp. 9–23. London: Palgrave Macmillan.

Garbarino, E. & M. S. Johnson. (1999). The Different Roles of Satisfaction, Trust, and Commitment in Customer Relationships. *Journal of Marketing*, 63(2): 70–87.

George, W. R. (1990). Internal marketing and organizational behavior: A partnership in developing customer-conscious employees at every level. *Journal of Business Research*, 20(1): 63–70.

Glavas A., Godwin L. (2013). Is the perception of "goodness" good enough? Exploring the relationship between perceived corporate social responsibility and employee organizational identification. *Journal of Business Ethics*, 114: 15–27.

Grant, A. M. (2008). Does intrinsic motivation fuel the prosocial fire? Motivational synergy in predicting persistence, performance, and productivity. *Journal of Applied Psychology*, *93*(1): 48–58.

Grant, A. M., & J. M. Berg. (2011). Prosocial motivation at work. In G. M. Spreitzer & K. S. Cameron, eds., *The Oxford handbook of positive organizational scholarship.* Oxford: Oxford University Press.

Greening, D. W., & D. B. Turban. (2000). Corporate social performance as a competitive advantage in attracting a quality workforce. Business & Society, *39*(3): 254–280.

Grewal, D., & L. D. Compeau. (1999). Pricing and public policy: A research agenda and an overview of the special issue. *Journal of Public Policy & Marketing*: 3–10.

Grizzle, J. W., A. R. Zablah, T. J. Brown, J. C. Mowen, & J. M. Lee. (2009). Employee customer orientation in context: How the environment moderates the influence of customer orientation on performance outcomes. *Journal of Applied Psychology*, *94*(5): 1227–1242.

Gundlach, G. T., & W. L. Wilkie. (2010). Stakeholder marketing: Why stakeholder was omitted from the American Marketing Association's official 2007 definition of marketing and why the future is bright for stakeholder marketing. *Journal of Public Policy & Marketing*, *29*(1): 89–92.

Harrison, J. S., D. A. Bosse, & R. A. Phillips. (2010). Managing for stakeholders, stakeholder utility functions, and competitive advantage. *Strategic Management Journal*, *31*(1): 58–74.

Harrison, J. S., & C. H. St John. (1996). Managing and partnering with external stakeholders. *The Academy of Management Executive*, *10*(2): 46–60.

Hillebrand, B., P. H. Driessen, & O. Koll. (2015). Stakeholder marketing: theoretical foundations and required capabilities. *Journal of the Academy of Marketing Science*, *43*(4): 411–428.

Homburg, C., & R. M. Stock. (2004). The link between salespeople's job satisfaction and customer satisfaction in a business-to-business context: A dyadic analysis. *Journal of the Academy of Marketing Science*, *32*(2): 144–158.

Hult, G., M. Tomas, J. A. Mena, O. C. Ferrell, & L. Ferrell. (2011). Stakeholder marketing: A definition and conceptual framework. *AMS Review*, *1*(1): 44–65.

Korschun, D. (2015). Boundary-spanning employees and relationships with external stakeholders: A social identity approach. Academy of Management Review, *40*(4): 611–629.

Korschun, D., H. Rafieian, A. Aggarwal, & S. D. Swain. (2017). Taking a Stand: Consumer Responses When Companies Get Political, working paper, LeBow College of Business.

Korschun, D., & G. Welker. (2015). We are Market Basket: The story of the unlikely grassroots movement that saved a beloved business. New York: Amacom.

Laczniak, G. R., & P. E. Murphy. (2012). Stakeholder theory and marketing: Moving from a firm-centric to a societal perspective. Journal of Public Policy & Marketing, *31*(2): 284–292.

Levitt, T. (1981). Marketing intangible products and product intangibles. *Harvard Business Review, 59* (May- June): 95–102.

Lusch, R. F., & Vargo S. L. (2006). Service-dominant logic: Reactions, reflections and refinements. Marketing Theory, *6*(3): 281–288.

MacKenzie, S. B., P. M. Podsakoff, & M. Ahearne. (1998). Some possible antecedents and consequences of in-role and extra-role salesperson performance. *Journal of Marketing*, *62*(3): 87–98. doi:10.2307/1251745.

McVea, J. F., & R. E. Freeman. (2005). A names-and-faces approach to stakeholder management how focusing on stakeholders as individuals can bring ethics and entrepreneurial strategy together. *Journal of Management Inquiry*, *14* (1): 57–69.

Miller, D. T. (1999). The norm of self-interest. *American Psychologist*, 54: 1053–1060.

Meglino, B. M., & Korsgaard, M. A. (2004). Considering rational self-interest as a disposition: Organizational implications of other orientation. *Journal of Applied Psychology*, 89: 946–959.

Morgan, R. M., & Hunt, S. D. (1994). The commitment-trust theory of relationship marketing. *The Journal of Marketing*: 20–38.

Podsakoff, N. P., S. W. Whiting, P. M. Podsakoff, & B. D. Blume. (2009) Individual-and organizational-level consequences of organizational citizenship behaviors: A meta-analysis. Journal of applied Psychology, *94*(1): 122.

Post, J. E., L. E. Preston, & S. Sauter-Sachs. (2002). *Redefining the corporation: Stakeholder management and organizational wealth.* Stanford: Stanford University Press,

Riketta, M. (2005). Organizational identification: A meta-analysis. *Journal of Vocational Behavior, 66* (2): 358–384.

Sachs, S., & M. Maurer. (2009). Toward dynamic corporate stakeholder responsibility. *Journal of Business Ethics*, 85: 535–544.

Scott, S. G., & V. R. Lane. (2000). A Stakeholder Approach to Organizational Identity. *The Academy of Management Review*, *25*(1): 43–62.

Sen, S., C. B. Bhattacharya, & D. Korschun. (2006). The role of corporate social responsibility in strengthening multiple stakeholder relationships: A field experiment. *Journal of the Academy of Marketing Science*, *34*(2): 158–166.

Sheth, J. N., & C. Uslay. (2007). Implications of the revised definition of marketing: From exchange to value creation. Journal of Public Policy & Marketing, *26*(2): 302–307.

Smith, N. C., M. E. Drumwright, & M. C. Gentile. (2010). The new marketing myopia. Journal of Public Policy & Marketing, *29*(1): 4–11.

Smith, N. C., G. Palazzo, & C. B. Bhattacharya. (2010). Marketing's consequences: Stakeholder marketing and supply chain corporate social responsibility issues. *Business Ethics Quarterly*, *20*(4): 617–641.

Sonenshein, S. (2007).The role of construction, intuition, and justification in responding to ethical issues at work: The sensemaking-intuition model. *Academy of Management Review*, *32*(4): 1022–1040.

van Dick, R., M. W. Grojean, O. Christ, & J. Wieseke. (2006).Identity and the extra mile: Relationships between organizational identification and organizational citizenship behaviour. *British Journal of Management*, *17*(4): 283–301.

van Riel, C. B., & Balmer, J. M. (1997). Corporate identity: The concept, its measurement and management. *European Journal of Marketing*, 31(5/6): 340–355.

van Knippenberg, D., & E. Sleebos. (2006). Organizational identification versus organizational commitment: Self-definition, social exchange, and job attitudes. *Journal of Organizational Behavior*, *27*(5): 571–584.

Vargo, S. L., & R. F. Lusch. (2004). Evolving to a new dominant logic for marketing. *Journal of Marketing*, *68*(1): 1–17.

Vivek, S. D., S. E. Beatty, & R. M. Morgan. (2012). Customer engagement: Exploring customer relationships beyond purchase. *Journal of Marketing Theory and Practice*, *20*(2): 122–146.

Whetten, D. A., G. Rands, & P. Godfrey. (2002). What are the responsibilities of business to society. In A. Pettigrew, H. Thomas, & R. Whittington, eds., *Handbook of strategy and management*: 373–408. London: Sage.

Wieseke, J., M., Ahearne, S. K. Lam, & R. van Dick. (2009). The role of leaders in internal marketing. *Journal of Marketing*, *73*(2): 123–145.

Stakeholder Value Equilibration and the Entrepreneurial Process

S. VENKATARAMAN

University of Virginia

In this chapter, I wish to explore the possibility of a useful dialogue between the fields of entrepreneurship and business ethics for mutual benefit.[1] Although these two fields have much to offer, they have developed largely independent of each other. I wish to argue that entrepreneurship has a role to play in stakeholder theory and, relatedly, that stakeholder theory enriches our understanding of the entrepreneurial process.

The scholarly field of study in the domain of entrepreneurship is defined around the construct of opportunity. Entrepreneurship, as I have previously argued (Venkataraman, 1997), "seeks to understand how opportunities to bring into existence 'future' goods and services are discovered, created, and exploited, by whom, and with what consequences." Davidsson (2015) has since found about 210 articles in leading journals that mention the word opportunity but shows that the construct itself is understood and used differently in these papers. A predominant line of enquiry asks whether these opportunities to create value are subjectively imagined by the entrepreneur or objectively discovered by them as market imperfections that can be exploited (Alvarez & Barney, 2007; Alvarez, et al., 2017; Shane & Venkataraman, 2000,). More recent research theorizes that opportunities are propensities waiting to be actualized by creative entrepreneurs (Ramoglou & Tsang, 2016). In an attempt to offer a middle ground, scholars suggest that opportunities require the exercise of entrepreneurial judgment (Foss & Klein, 2017), and others argue elsewhere that opportunities are intersubjective and require a focus on the action and interaction between entrepreneurs and their stakeholders (Venkataraman, et al., 2012). A focus on the intersubjective requires that the notion of entrepreneurial opportunity examine the interactions between entrepreneurs and their stakeholders in the pursuit of value creation for everyone concerned and is therefore the most useful for our purposes here. Starting with the premise that opportunities are intersubjective, I suggest that to the extent value is embodied in products and services, entrepreneurship is concerned with how the opportunity to create "value" in society is discovered and acted upon by some individuals.

The field of business ethics, on the other hand, I think, is concerned with the "methods" used to create this "value," and the ensuing distribution of the value among various stakeholders to the enterprise. For a fuller explanation of this perspective on business ethics, refer to Freeman, Harrison, and Wicks (2007) and Freeman, Wicks, and Parmar (2004). Thus, if we understand entrepreneurship and ethics as the fields that together seek to describe, explain, predict, and prescribe how value is discovered, created, distributed, and perhaps destroyed, then there is not only much that we can learn from each other, but together we represent two sides of the same coin: the coin of value creation and sharing.

A preoccupation of the stakeholder literature within business ethics has been on the purpose and role of the widely held corporation. The central question seems to be "for whose benefit and at whose expense should the firm be managed?" (Freeman, 1997). But the essence of the corporation is the competitive claims made of it by diverse stakeholders. It is a fact of business life that different stakeholders have different and often conflicting expectations of a corporation. Indeed, the firm itself can be said to be an invention to allow such conflict to be discovered, surfaced, and resolved, because conflicting claims have to be discovered and methods for resolution executed. We expand on this view in Dew, Velamuri, and Venkataraman (2004).

This inherent conflict is a feature not only of the established giant corporation, but also of the very act of creation of the productive enterprise. Rarely do giant corporations begin their life as widely held joint-stock companies. All corporations can be traced back to entrepreneurial beginnings or to the gleam in the eye of an entrepreneur and to the efforts of these individuals at creating a firm. Entrepreneurship involves joint production where several different stakeholders have to be brought together to create the new product or service (Shane & Venkataraman, 2000). The creative task of the entrepreneur is to identify, assemble, and institutionalize the joint production function in a way that meaningful surplus is created.

In a typical scenario, the entrepreneur does not own or control all the resources required to develop the market, establish the value-chain infrastructure, and eventually profit from his or her particular knowledge. Most of these resources have to come from other people or institutions. Thus, the entrepreneur has to assemble, organize, and execute the market development and value-chain infrastructure before potential profits can be realized and conjectures proven to be "insights." The process of creating products and markets implies that much of the information required by potential stakeholders – for example, technology, price, quantity, tastes, supplier networks, distributor networks, and strategy – are not reliably available. Relevant information will only exist once the market has been successfully created (Arrow, 1974). Potential stakeholders thus have to rely on the entrepreneur for information, but without the benefit of the entrepreneur's "insight." Thus, decisions about all aspects of the firm, its future and stakeholders participation have to be made behind the classic "veil of ignorance" (Rawls, 2009).

The seeds of potential conflicts between stakeholders are sown right at the inception of the firm, at the very forging of the joint production function. It could be argued that without fundamentally different expectations and interpretations about the future, there is no need or opportunity for the firm to exist in the first place. The firm owes its very existence, at least in large part, to the differing information bases and expectations of the stakeholders.

A major insight of stakeholder theory is that the firm is an equilibrating mechanism and not a governance mechanism.[2] It deflects attention from a coordinating role for the manager to that of an arbitrator. There is a subtle but significant difference to viewing the firm and its decision-makers as responsible for equilibration rather than governing. The skills, mind-set, and character required of a governor are as different from that required of an equilibrator, as the skills, mind-set, and character required of an attorney representing a client are different from a judge adjudicating between the rights and claims of competing agents (and their principals).

If indeed, the firm is an equilibrating mechanism, then questions such as "what are the properties of a fair and efficient equilibrating mechanism" and "what alternative mechanisms would render the firm an effective reconciler of competing claims," become crucial within the theory. I interpret the stakeholder literature to offer three alternative mechanisms to ensure a fair and efficient equilibrating system. One is embodied in a person (the moral manager), one is embodied in a process (the bargaining process), and one is embodied in an external (to the firm) institution (the visible hand of law and government). To these three, I add a fourth mechanism from an entrepreneurship perspective.

1 The Moral Manager

The argument here is that since the manager or decision-maker is responsible for adjudicating current and potential conflicts rather than interpreting and enforcing a pre-existing, well-established set of rules and routines, the necessary qualifications for the reconciler is strong moral character. Carroll (1995) captures the essential requirement for such a moral manager thus: they are

> exemplars of "good guys." Moral managers employ and adhere to ethical norms, which reflect high standards of right behavior. Moral managers not only conform to accepted high levels of professional conduct, they also frequently exhibit ethical leadership ... Moral managers strive to operate well above and beyond what the law

mandates. Sound moral principles such as justice, rights, utilitarianism and the Golden Rule are employed for decision-making and conduct ... [Moral managers consider] stakeholders maximally because stakeholders possess intrinsic worth in and of themselves; that is, they are *ends* and not *means.*" (Carroll, 1995).

The odds that a firm will act as a fair equilibrator increase considerably because (1) the morality of top managers will be reflected in the system of incentives and sanctions employed by the firm; (2) the firm will be populated by moral managers through a process of imitation, learning and self-modeling; and finally (3) self-selection (Clinard, 1983; Jones, 1995; Lee & Mitchell, 1994).

2 The Bargaining Process

Central to the process view is the conception of the "value-creation activity as a contractual process among those parties affected" (Freeman, 1997). Thus, the firm is a nexus of multilateral contracts where equilibration occurs over time through a process of bargaining among the various resource owners and stakeholders in the firm. In this respect, the firm can be seen as a clearinghouse for potentially conflicting stakeholder claims, and the story of the evolution of the firm is the evolution of stakes (where participants make risky investments) and the evolution of claims.[3] The bargaining process is a dynamic one of give and take over time, all occurring within a mutually accepted framework of reconciliation rules. For, at the coordinating node is a set of reconciliation rules that are developed behind a Rawlsian "veil-of-ignorance" and embody legal notions of "fair contract" (Freeman & Evan, 1990).

Conflicts, especially about ex-post distributions, are an integral part of the value-creation process. Thus, emphasis is placed on the procedural aspects of multiple stakeholder coordination rather than upon the results of value-creating activity itself or upon the specific outcomes of the bargaining process (Donaldson & Preston, 1995). The odds that a firm will act as a fair equilibrator increases considerably because each stakeholder has equal rights to bargain and is protected equally under the

system. However, *crucial to the working of the process view is the replacement of the very purpose of the firm from serving stockholder interest to serving stakeholder interests.* Unless a change in the worldview comes about, neither will the "separation thesis" be abandoned nor will the institutions of law embrace the role of the firm as an equilibrator rather than a governor in the interest of the stockholder. I am personally skeptical that reconciliation rules idea will be widely accepted as a practical solution. However, I sense that many in the field believe (and indeed some have taken up the onerous task) that this change in worldview can be brought about "plank by plank" through an intellectual "rebuilding of the corporate ship, while it remains afloat." Freeman, Harrison, and Wicks (2007) and Freeman, Harrison et al. (2010) are very promising efforts in this direction.

3 The Visible Hand

The argument for a visible hand is an old and familiar one, and so I do not wish to spend much time on it. In the event that the moral manager and/or the bargaining process do not satisfactorily perform the job of equilibration, there is need for a countervailing force, in the form of an external visible hand.[4] While Freeman and Evan (1990) require a moral manager to avoid stakeholder problems, this view augments management with an external creator and enforcer of laws to overcome problems that may arise due to information asymmetries, moral hazards, and negative externalities, even if actions were taken in good faith (Hill & Jones, 1992). Thus, we would have reporting requirements, monitoring agencies, enforcement agencies, etc., overseeing the activities of the central coordinators of the firm.

Together, these three mechanisms will ensure that the firm is a fair and efficient equilibrating institution, where no party is used as a means to some other party's ends. The corporation would be managed for the benefit and at the expense of all stakeholders to the enterprise. There continues to be a debate in the literature over the exact qualification to be a stakeholder (see Mitchell, Agle, and Wood, (1997) for a survey and Phillips (1997),

Freeman and McVea (2001), and Friedman and Miles (2002) for more recent developments about how to frame the debate around the legitimacy of stakeholders), and whether the prescribed mechanisms indeed lead to fair and efficient resolution to stakeholder problems. At least one pair of writers has argued that the stakeholder arguments are generally biased towards fairness at the expense of efficiency (Donaldson & Preston 1995). In my own view, these are largely empirical questions to be settled with more careful argumentation and accumulating evidence. The greater challenge for proponents of stakeholder theory is to show that the prescribed forms can come into existence, do indeed come into existence, and are evolutionarily robust, that is, they can survive and flourish in a competitive market place of alternative forms. Otherwise, the theory runs the risk of being of merely academic interest.

A major contribution of the stakeholder theory to entrepreneurship is the broadening of the reason for the existence of a firm. It deflects attention from the firm merely meeting narrow, conventional economic and financial criteria of the founding entrepreneurs to a broader one of satisfying multiple stakeholder interests.[5] Meeting a broader social charter would constitute the ultimate test of firm performance. I have myself argued elsewhere (Venkataraman, 1997) that a preoccupation of entrepreneurship researchers with financial success of individual entrepreneurs and firms misses the point of the very existence of entrepreneurship. Entrepreneurship is concerned with the discovery and exploitation of profitable opportunities for private wealth accumulation and, as a consequence, for social wealth creation as well. Therefore, the relevant benchmarks for entrepreneurship are (1) the absolute level of economic performance that provides a return for enterprising effort, and (2) the social contribution of the individual's effort.

Both Schumpeter and Adam Smith (much earlier) drew a profound connection between the personal profit motive and social wealth. Entrepreneurship is particularly productive from a social welfare perspective when, even in the process of pursuing selfish ends, entrepreneurs also enhance social wealth by creating new markets, new industries, new technology, new institutional forms, new jobs, higher

standards of living, and net increases in real productivity.[6] Arguably, were it not for the social surplus generated by private wealth seeking, the privilege and freedom to pursue selfish ends may not be accorded by societies to individuals at all. For this reason, in entrepreneurship we need a measure of performance that is able to capture, simultaneously, the economic performance at the individual or firm level as well as social performance. This construct would be the most relevant, legitimate, and distinctive performance variable for entrepreneurship research. Indeed, I would go so far as to claim that explaining the behavior of this construct is the very *raison d'être* of the field (Venkataraman, 1997).

Ideas within stakeholder theory offer a promising start in this direction and open up fruitful areas of collaboration between us. Concepts and constructs, such as balanced scorecards, multiple bottom lines, corporate social performance, stakeholder satisfaction indices, etc., offer relevant meaningful benchmarks for the field of entrepreneurship. For an excellent review and survey see Wood and Jones (1995). Also refer to Orlitzky, Schmidt, & Rynes, (2003) for a meta-analysis on the link between corporate social performance and corporate financial performance; Henriques and Richardson (2013) for a summary of what we know about the triple bottom line; and Hoque (2014) for a review of twenty years of research on the balanced score card.

The field of entrepreneurship, in turn, has some insights to offer stakeholder theory. If indeed equilibration is a major role of the firm, then stakeholder theory has neglected one powerful source of such equilibration, namely, the entrepreneurial discovery process. The very process of entrepreneurial discovery serves as a fair and efficient mechanism to reconcile conflicting stakeholder claims.

4 The Entrepreneurial Process Perspective

From an entrepreneurship perspective, the central question of stakeholder theory, namely, "for whose benefit and at whose expense should the firm be managed?" is moot.[7] The central assertion of the entrepreneurial process is that, *even if* the fiduciary duty of the manager is to the stockholder, the process of entrepreneurial discovery and exploitation will ensure that the corporation will be managed *as if* for the benefit of all the stakeholders to the enterprise.[8] Firms, which are not so managed, will, over time, be selected out of the business (and, therefore, social) landscape. While this process may not happen instantaneously, or even in some direct fashion, the process of entrepreneurial discovery and exploitation will eventually force fair and efficient reconciliation of competing stakeholder claims in firms in general and in each firm in question.

This equilibration process works in two ways: by equilibrating the value anomaly stakeholder by stakeholder and by bringing about a fundamental change in a complete system of stakeholders. I call these, respectively, the weak equilibrating process and the strong equilibrating process. The strong equilibrating process overcomes some of the limitations of the weak process. The weak equilibrating process holds that whenever a stakeholder justifiably believes that the value supplied by him or her to a firm is more than the value received, the entrepreneurial process will redeploy the resources of the "victimized" stakeholder to a use where value supplied and received will be equilibrated. The strong equilibrating process holds that if the redeployment of individual stakeholders does not work freely and efficiently, and serious value anomalies accumulate within firms and societies, the entrepreneurial process will destroy the value anomalies by fundamental rearrangements in how resources and stakeholders are combined.[9]

4.1 Weak Equilibrating Force

In an important paper called "The Use of Knowledge in Society," Hayek (1945) pointed out that in any collective, equilibration has to be brought about under circumstances where the knowledge required to equilibrate exists neither concentrated in some integrated form nor is "given" to a single mind. Rather such knowledge exists as "dispersed bits of incomplete and frequently contradictory knowledge which all the separate individuals possess" (Hayek 1945: 519).

The dispersion of information among different people who do not have access to the same observations, interpretations, or experiences has two fundamental implications for the firm as an equilibrating mechanism. First, it is physically impossible for the value of all resources in a firm to be in balance at any given time, that is, exist in a state of equilibrium. Thus, in most firms, most of the time, some resource owners will not get their due.[10] Second, the existence of these inefficiencies is a known source of profit for those alert individuals who can discover and eliminate value inequities.

Value inequities or anomalies represent entrepreneurial opportunities for individuals. By definition, whenever there is an asymmetry in beliefs about the value of a resource (say between the value supplier and those who receive it, i.e., the firm) there exists inefficiency. Inefficiencies are a major incentive for alert individuals seeking to profit from them, and the central feature of a free market system is the abundant supply of such alert profit-seeking entrepreneurs (Kirzner, 1979).

I define, for this purpose, an entrepreneur as one who realizes or conjectures (either through genuine insight and knowledge, or through mere luck) that some resources are underutilized in their current occupation and recombines them into potentially a more useful and fruitful combination. Such redeployment goes on all the time in a market economy and plays three important roles from a stakeholder theory perspective. First, they provide important information about the competitive value of alternative resources. Value inequities or anomalies can often be discovered only in reference to some external benchmark, and the entrepreneurial process provides this important information to the stakeholders, from which they can recognize the presence of inequities. Second, the competition for resources from opportunity-seeking entrepreneurs potentially forces managers to act as if each stakeholder is an end unto himself or herself and not a means to others' ends. Third, the entrepreneurial process can provide a viable exit route for victimized stakeholders. The first principle that (Freeman, 1997) postulates for a fair bargaining process within the firm is the principle of entry and exit. According to Freeman, clearly defined exit conditions are vital to a fair contract entered into behind a Rawlsian "veil of ignorance."

This notion of exit has a long history in economics and liberal political philosophy. Hirschman (1970) argues that when organizations decline, individuals can have three different responses: loyalty to the declining organization, exercising voice to change the organization, or exit to a new organization. Exit represents a discontinuity in the individual's life and is therefore the most "costly" option (Borchers & Vitikainen 2012). Liberal political philosophy considers the right to exit the bedrock of freedom: individuals can and will leave groups and associations that they do not want to be a part of. The plain or minimal exit principle is "nothing more or less than the right to repudiate authority," and arises from the "no-right" of coercion of authority to remain in particular associations (Kukathas, 2003). Whereas the right to exit is fundamental to freedom, the ability to exit, who provides these exit options, and what to exit to is not automatically clear. Without an explanation of what to exit to, where these options come from, and who provides these options, the idea of exit is meaningless. Entrepreneurship is fundamental in building these viable alternatives to exit to and understanding entrepreneurial processes is important in this regard.

4.2 Strong Equilibrating Force

The weak equilibrating force is a necessary but not sufficient condition for solving stakeholder anomalies in firms. Hayek's insight about the dispersion of information in any collective suggests that ignorance, error, and more importantly, ignorance about one's ignorance, is part of the system itself. The "manager of a firm, like any individual in the market, will be ignorant of his/her own ignorance with respect to opportunities" and problems in the firm – the double Hayekian knowledge problem (Sautet & Foss, 1999). The presence of ignorance has two other important implications: (1) there is scope for genuine novelty in the marketplace, or as Sautet and Foss (1999) express it, the economy is open-ended; and (2) individuals can imagine a future and act to make it happen. The presence of ignorance, error, novelty, and genuine surprise

means that the system will only *tend towards equilibrium* and never really attain perfect equilibrium (Kirzner, 1979; 1997). In other words, there will always be some individuals or groups who will be used as means to someone else's ends.

Indeed, it may not even be desirable to have perfect stakeholder equilibration. (Schumpeter, 2008: 83) forcefully argued, "[a] system – any system, economic or other – that at every point of time fully utilizes its possibilities to the best advantage may yet in the long run be inferior to a system that does so at no given point in time, because the latter's failure to do so may be a condition for the level or speed of long-run performance." Schumpeter is referring to our ability to leap frog to a qualitatively superior quality of life for all. Brenner (1983) has offered the provocative hypothesis that grave inequalities (and perhaps inequities) in a system is potentially a great motivator, for the only human way in which those at the bottom of society can rise is to take extraordinary gambles. This in turn may be good for society because extraordinary leaps are possible in social, technical, and economic development.

Historically, people in many societies have accepted significant disparities in fortunes and wealth, especially in free and democratic societies where people are confident that the disparities are outcomes of a fair process, *a la* Rawls. But often, there are systematic local problems, both in outcomes and in the working of the weak equilibrating force. Stakeholder inequities in some sections of the economy (e.g., the giant widely held corporation) may accumulate and may be spread over a large spectrum of stakeholders. Moreover, such inequities may persist for non-trivial periods. The sources of such accumulation and persistence may be several. First, because the weak force harbors errors and ignorance, stakeholder inequities may never be discovered in the first place. Second, even if these inequities are discovered, the affected group may be fragmented, or cannot coalesce into a concentrated power capable of changing the current order. Third, even if the victimized stakeholder groups are concentrated, there may be significant asymmetry in relative power and so they are powerless to alter the status quo. Fourth, even if power is not an issue, the stakeholders may be so dispersed that their problems are economically unattractive for the entrepreneurial process to solve. Fifth, there may be conflicts of interests, lack of fairness, and a lack of ethics in those that are aware of and can correct the inequities. Finally, there may be willful desire to do harm on the part of some.

The persistence of accumulated inequities calls not for incremental change through the weak force, but for a fundamental qualitative change of the kind Schumpeter envisioned – a revolutionary change in economic order through a process of creative destruction. But who or what brings about such a change? Of all the sources of such change, including wars and revolutions, Schumpeter highlighted the unfailing power of innovation in goods and services. And the agent of this innovation, he argued, is the entrepreneur.[11] The "fundamental impulse that sets and keeps" in motion such systemic change "comes from the new consumer goods, the new methods of production or transportation, the new markets, and the new forms of industrial organization" (Schumpeter, 2008: 83). The history of business is littered with such entrepreneurially introduced innovations. Each succeeding innovation has altered the economic, political, and social landscape and, for our purposes, has brought about a fundamental qualitative change in relative stakeholder power.

It is important to appreciate here that while this process has been incessant, the innovations themselves occur in what Schumpeter (2008) calls *discrete rushes,* or what we know as business cycles. Schumpeter's observation calls for patience and recommends giving the evolutionary process of entrepreneurship and innovation a chance to make changes from *within* rather than rushing to make changes from *without* by resorting to some form of visible hand.[12] In short, if the giant, widely held corporation truly represents an unfair and/or inefficient organizational form, then business history suggests that somewhere, somehow, some entrepreneurs will arise to introduce innovative products, methods, and forms that will inevitably destroy this form by creatively replacing it with a qualitatively superior form. When we are dealing with an organic process, analysis of what happens in any particular

part of it – say in the giant corporation – or even at a particular time period – say the post-World War II period – may indeed clarify details of the mechanism but is inconclusive beyond that. "Every piece of business strategy acquires true significance only against the background of that process and within the situation created by it" (Schumpeter 2008: 83–84).

The weak and strong equilibrating forces have several implications for both stakeholder theory and entrepreneurship research. First, stakeholder theory needs to consider the entrepreneurial process as a legitimate method of bringing about stakeholder equilibration. The repertoire of the theory must be increased to include (in addition to the moral manager, the fair bargaining process, and the visible hand) the weak and strong entrepreneurial equilibrating forces. Without these forces within its framework, the theory is simply incomplete. Similarly, entrepreneurship theory must consider stakeholder equilibration explicitly. Entrepreneurship research is, in turn, incomplete without this consideration.

Second, we need to undertake the challenging task of understanding the specific ways in which the weak and strong forces bring about equilibration, both in theory and in practice. Many of the arguments for the competitive entrepreneurial process remain theoretical speculations, ideological assertions, or rhetorical orations. The challenging empirical work is yet to be undertaken in a systematic and persuasive manner. Third, if we are persuaded by the arguments for the entrepreneurial process in bringing about stakeholder equilibration, then more systematic work is required to understand and implement the institutions, the conditions, and the rules of the games that promote such entrepreneurship. To borrow a phrase from the late Mancur Olson, the need is for *entrepreneurship augmenting* firms, governments, and societies (Arrow, Kamien, et al., 1999). Finally, not all entrepreneurship is good. Enterprising individuals may devote their energy, time, and attention to productive, unproductive, and criminal (where some get richer necessarily at the expense of others) entrepreneurship (Baumol, 1990). It is necessary to understand "what determines, and how do we influence, the level of demand and supply of enterprising individuals in society?" (Venkataraman, 1997: 135). But it is even more important to understand what determines the allocation of enterprising talent into rent-seeking (or parasitical) activities and productive activities? Both entrepreneurship and business ethics have a deep and mutual interest in these questions and they hold profitable collaborative opportunities.

I would like to close by pointing out a more compelling collaborative opportunity between the proponents of stakeholder theory and the entrepreneurial process. In my judgment, recasting the central purpose of the firm as serving the interests of stockholders to one where it serves the stakeholders is an innovation in organizational form of Schumpeterian proportions. Designing a corporation with such intent requires changes in managerial (and even non-managerial) mind-sets, changes in the law, revising financial market expectations, to name a few changes. How will such systemic changes come about? I submit, that it is the entrepreneurs that can internalize the stakeholder idea, design organizations founded on the principles contained in this idea, bring them into existence, and create a competitive marketplace where all stakeholders can flourish. This empirical demonstration of the validity of the stakeholder idea by life-and-blood entrepreneurs is perhaps the most efficient and effective way of diffusing the stakeholder innovation, for nothing diffuses as quickly as success. To paraphrase Freeman (1997) the weakly equilibrating entrepreneur has the potential to rebuild the ship of stakeholders, plank by plank, while it still remains afloat.[13] When the efforts of this entrepreneur is inadequate, if we give the entrepreneurial process its time and chance to act, a "gale force of creative destruction," unleashed by an innovating entrepreneur, will sink the unfair and inefficient corporate ship while evacuating all stakeholders to the safety of a new vessel. A new vessel that is better than the old, until new anomalies are created and experienced ... and the cycle continues ...

Notes

1. This chapter is an updated version of the Ruffin Lecture delivered in 2000, and published in *Business Ethics Quarterly: The Ruffin Series,* Special Issue # 3: 45–58. I thank Anusha Ramesh for her assistance in updating from the earlier version of this paper.
2. Although Coase, (1937) postulated the firm as an alternative to the price system as an equilibrating mechanism in an economy, Williamson's (1975) transaction cost theory and agency theory narrowed its role to one of mere governance. Stakeholder theory is attempting to rescue the firm from this confinement.
3. While I separate the bargaining process as a distinct mechanism, this mechanism subsumes the moral manager. Indeed, effective operation of the process might well require a moral manager. In this sense, the bargaining process is additive.
4. The visible hand mechanism is not necessarily in conflict with the other two mechanisms. It may be seen as an addition to the other two. Ideally, the process view would argue that a well-designed bargaining process, run by moral managers who do not subscribe to the "separation thesis," would be effective independent of the existence of a countervailing external force (Freeman, 1994).
5. The firm is an essential organizational form for the entrepreneur because it is through the firm that the opportunity-pursuing entrepreneur can coalesce and keep the myriad stakeholders together.
6. I hasten to add that I am using the word selfish in all its meanings intended by Adam Smith, including greed, other regarding, and prudence (Werhane, 1991).
7. I am deliberately using the phrase entrepreneurial process rather than market process because I wish to contrast my use of the process from the more mainstream conception of the perfectly competitive market process. I refer to a process where it is at best tending towards equilibrium and never really there. It is a world filled with actors who are liable to make errors, are sometimes ignorant, sometimes ignorant about their ignorance, sometimes brilliant, but mostly prosaic, sometimes knowingly deceitful, but mostly well intentioned, and most important of all, boundedly rational. The process has scope for genuine discovery, genuine disappointment, or pleasant surprise.

This is in stark contrast to the "equilibrium-always approach" with instantaneously optimizing actors, who are exceptionally well informed and never commit an error, operating in instantly clearing markets.

8. I am aware that there is a current debate in the stakeholder field about instrumental vs. normative views of stakeholder theory. Although I find this distinction convenient, I think it is unnecessary.

9. Such recombination may occur through invention of new products, new organizational forms, new processes of production, transportation, and communication, new markets, and new ways of organizing life in societies. Both the weak and strong processes may operate with some lag because value anomalies have to be discovered and are not always given. The strong process may operate with significant lag because anomalies have to accumulate to a significant threshold level before innovation becomes a worthwhile endeavor.

10. The source of this value asymmetry, whether willful or good faith, is irrelevant from the alert entrepreneur's point of view. Both are sources of profits and profit-seeking entrepreneurs can potentially eliminate both.

11. Such entrepreneurs can come from within the firm or without, can operate within the firm or without. They may be lone entrepreneurs, but are more likely to include several. Finally, following Hayek, the innovations may be a product of numerous interacting individuals in the markets. I owe this last insight to Nick Dew and we have developed on this insight in Dew, Velamuri and Venkataraman (2004).

12. This is not to say a visible hand is not required, only that its use must be very carefully considered. There are numerous instances (especially where transaction costs of using the market processes are high) where the visible hand of law and government or some other countervailing force may be the best alternative.

13. The original quote is rightly attributed to Neurath.

References

Alvarez, S. A., & Barney, J. B. (2007). Discovery and creation: Alternative theories of entrepreneurial action. *Strategic Entrepreneurship Journal*, *1*(1-2): 11–26.

Alvarez, S. A., Barney, J. B., McBride, R., & Wuebker, R. (2017). On opportunities: Philosophical and empirical implications. *Academy of Management Review*, *42*(4): 726–730.

Arrow, K. J. (1974). Limited knowledge and economic analysis. *The American Economic Review*, *64*(1): 1–10.

Arrow, K., Kamien, M., Olson, M., Sexton, D., Simon, H., & Venkataraman, S. (1999). Report on the seminar on research perspectives in entrepreneurship. *Journal of Business Venturing*, *15*(1): 1–57.

Baumol, W. J. (1990). Entrepreneurship: Productive, unproductive, and destructive. *Journal of Political Economy*, *98*(5, Part 1): 893–921.

Borchers, D., & A. Vitikainen (2012). *On exit: Interdisciplinary perspectives on the right of exit in liberal multicultural societies*. Berlin: Walter de Gruyter.

Brenner, R. (1983). *History: The human gamble*. London: Institute of Philosophy.

Carroll, A. B. (1995). Stakeholder thinking in three models of management morality: a perspective with strategic implications. In J. Nasi, eds., *Understanding stakeholder thinking*, pp. 47–74. Helsinki: LSR-Publications.

Clinard, M. B. (1983). *Corporate ethics and crime: The role of middle management*. Beverly Hills: Sage Publications.

Coase, R. H. (1937). The nature of the firm. *Economica*, *4*(16): 386–405.

Davidsson, P. (2015). Entrepreneurial opportunities and the entrepreneurship nexus: A re-conceptualization. *Journal of Business Venturing*, *30*(5): 674–695.

Dew, N., Velamuri, S. R., & Venkataraman, S. (2004). Dispersed knowledge and an entrepreneurial theory of the firm. *Journal of business venturing*, *19*(5): 659–679.

Donaldson, T., & Preston, L. E. (1995). The stakeholder theory of the corporation: Concepts, evidence, and implications. *Academy of management Review*, *20*(1): 65–91.

Foss, N. J., & Klein, P. G. (2017). Entrepreneurial discovery or creation? In search of the middle ground. *Academy of Management Review*, *42*(4): 733–736.

Freeman, R. E. (1997). A stakeholder theory of the modern corporation. In T. L. Beauchamp & N. E. Bowie, eds., *Ethical Theory and Business*, pp. 144–146 Englewood Cliffs, NJ: Prentice-Hall.

Freeman, R. E., & Evan, W. M. (1990). Corporate governance: A stakeholder interpretation. *Journal of behavioral economics*, *19*(4): 337–359.

Freeman, R. E., Harrison, & Wicks, A. C. (2007). *Managing for stakeholders: Survival, reputation, and success*. New Haven, CT: Yale University Press.

Freeman, R. E., Harrison, J. S., Wicks, A. C., Parmar, B. L., & De Colle, S. (2010). *Stakeholder theory: The state of the art*. Cambridge: Cambridge University Press.

Freeman, R. E., & McVea, J. (2001). A stakeholder approach to strategic management. Darden Business School Working Paper No. 01-02. University of Virginia, Charlottesville.

Freeman, R. E., Wicks, A. C., & Parmar, B. (2004). Stakeholder theory and "the corporate objective revisited." *Organization science, 15*(3): 364–369.

Friedman, A. L., & Miles, S. (2002). Developing stakeholder theory. *Journal of Management Studies, 39*(1): 1–21.

Hayek, F. A. (1945). The use of knowledge in society. *The American Economic Review:* 519–530.

Henriques, A., & Richardson, J. (2013). The triple bottom line: Does it all add up? London: Routledge.

Hill, C. W., & Jones, T. M. (1992). Stakeholder-agency theory. *Journal of Management Studies, 29*(2): 131–154.

Hirschman, A. O. (1970). *Exit, voice, and loyalty: Responses to decline in firms, organizations, and states*. Cambridge, MA: Harvard University Press.

Hoque, Z. (2014). 20 years of studies on the balanced scorecard: Trends, accomplishments, gaps and opportunities for future research. *The British Accounting Review, 46*(1): 33–59.

Jones, T. M. (1995). Instrumental stakeholder theory: A synthesis of ethics and economics. *Academy of Management Review, 20*(2): 404–437.

Kirzner, I. M. (1979). Perception, Opportunity, and Profit. Chicago: University of Chicago Press.

Kirzner, I. M. (1997). Entrepreneurial discovery and the competitive market process: An Austrian approach. *Journal of Economic Literature, 35*(1): 60–85.

Kukathas, C. (2003). *The liberal archipelago: A theory of diversity and freedom*. Oxford: Oxford University Press.

Lee, T. W., & Mitchell, T. R. (1994). An alternative approach: The unfolding model of voluntary employee turnover. *Academy of Management Review, 19*(1): 51–89.

Mitchell, R. K., Agle, B. R. & Wood, D. J. (1997). Toward a theory of stakeholder identification and salience: Defining the principle of who and what really counts. *Academy of Management Review, 22* (4): 853–886.

Orlitzky, M., Schmidt, F. L. & Rynes, S. L. (2003). Corporate social and financial performance: A meta-analysis. *Organization Studies, 24*(3): 403–441.

Phillips, R. A. (1997). Stakeholder theory and a principle of fairness. *Business Ethics Quarterly, 7*(1): 51–66.

Ramoglou, S., & Tsang, E. W. (2016). A realist perspective of entrepreneurship: Opportunities as propensities. *Academy of Management Review, 41* (3): 410–434.

Rawls, J. (2009). *A theory of justice*. Cambridge, MA: Harvard University Press.

Sautet, F. E., & Foss, N. J. (1999). The organization of large, complex firms: An Austrian view. Unpublished working paper presented at the Austrian Economics Seminar at New York University and at Peter Boettke's Seminar George Mason University.

Schumpeter, J. A. (2008). Capitalism, socialism and democracy, 3rd edn. New York: Harper Perennial Modern Thought.

Shane, S., & Venkataraman, S. (2000). The promise of entrepreneurship as a field of research. *Academy of Management Review, 25*(1): 217–226.

Venkataraman, S. (1997). The distinctive domain of entrepreneurship research. *Advances in Entrepreneurship, Firm Emergence and Growth, 3*(1): 119–138.

Venkataraman, S., Sarasvathy, S. D., Dew, N., & Forster, W. R. (2012). Reflections on the 2010 AMR decade award: Whither the promise? Moving forward with entrepreneurship as a science of the artificial. *Academy of Management Review, 37*(1): 21–33.

Werhane, P. (1991). *Adam Smith and his legacy for modern capitalism*. New York: Oxford University Press.

Williamson, O. E. (1975). *Markets and hierarchies*. New York: Free Press.

Wood, D. J., & Jones, R. E. (1995). Stakeholder mismatching: A theoretical problem in empirical research on corporate social performance. *The International Journal of Organizational Analysis, 3*(3): 229–267.

Stakeholder Theory and Accounting

SAMANTHA MILES

Oxford Brookes University

This chapter reviews the extent to which stakeholder theory has been applied to, and adopted within, the academic accounting literature. The influence of stakeholder theory on accounting is growing but lags behind other business disciplines. This is due to the prevailing dominance of the shareholder primacy paradigm and a lack of convergence between the epistemological structure and socio-cultural characteristics of accounting, with university and professional education lagging behind contemporary thinking. This chapter starts with a discussion of these factors to provide context.

The academic field of accounting is vast, and spans various distinct, yet overlapping, fields. This review is based on three sub-disciplines: management accounting (internal control and decision-making), financial accounting (reporting to external stakeholders) and sustainability reporting. Finance, auditing and corporate governance are not included. The review is restricted to the twenty-seven accounting journals identified as 3* or 4* in the Chartered Association of Business Schools *Academic Journal Guide* (2018) and the *Journal of Management Studies* special issue (52:7) on accounting for stakeholder value. The review is organized by sub-discipline and structured around prevailing themes.

Considering the widespread appeal of stakeholder theory there is surprisingly little application to accounting research. The majority of research identified focused on two applications of stakeholder theory: (i) as an explanation for reporting content of financial statements or sustainability reporting; (ii) as a means of widening the remit of the accounting function beyond shareholder primacy. For the majority of papers reviewed, however, the research is framed within stakeholder terminology and discourse but does not adhere to the tenets of stakeholder theory. Conclusions suggest that there exists a strong opportunity to

advance accounting through more novel, and more in-depth, applications of stakeholder theory. Accounting directly impacts stakeholders through the manner in which claims are recognized, recorded, and prioritized. Influencing accounting to report on ways that are more relevant to stakeholders presents a clear opportunity for mainstreaming stakeholder theory and for enhancing the usefulness of the accounting function.

The Socio-Cultural Characteristics of Accounting

Accounting is a cultural artifact which serves an important social welfare function in wealth distribution. Perry and Nölke (2006: 560) argued, "Accounting impacts the lives of everyone in society, even (or perhaps especially) those who know very little about the subject and have never set eyes on a financial statement." Accounting policy choice has economic consequences as accounting numbers determine, to varying extents, the price paid for goods by consumers, wage rises, bonuses and investments in staff, corporate taxation contributions to society, shareholder returns, and pension actuary rates. The impact of accounting choice can be widespread. For example, fair value accounting (FAS157), enacted in 2006 by FASB in the USA which updated asset and liability values for banks, was highlighted by Laux and Leuz (2009) as a key determinant in the 2008 financial crisis.

Anglo-American accounting is predominantly self-regulated by the accountancy profession. Standard-setting bodies retain independence but are subject to significant political pressure from the vested interests inherent. The corporate and investor voice are the dominant pressures, as shareholders have historically provided the prevailing source of corporate finance. This influences the nature of standards issued and the objective of reporting, which is skewed toward meeting the needs of "investors, lenders and other creditors in making decisions about providing resources to the entity" (IASB, 2010: OB2). The needs of other stakeholders are either ignored or assumed to be included within this objective. This extends to sustainability reporting, despite the perception of this information being aimed at a wider audience, as evident in the Integrated Reporting Framework and the Sustainability Accounting Standards Board standards which focus on "providers of financial capital" and "investors" respectively (Ringham & Miles, 2018).

Hines (1988) advocated that the social influence of accounting is so strong that accountants "create reality" (of what is accepted as valuable in business) by constructing the reality of what is recognized, measured, and accounted for. For financial accounting, this is restricted to those items in which a monetary value can be assessed with a reasonable degree of certainty. The boundary of reporting is based on ownership, control, and significant influence within the definition of the legal entity. This determines what is, and is not, considered to be part of the organization and therefore what activities are reasonable to expect an organization to report on. This limits reporting to significant direct impacts of operations over which the organization has control (including subsidiaries), but excludes medium and long-term indirect impacts on ecosystems and society, which may be of interest to a wider stakeholder audience. To exacerbate this issue Archel, Fernández, and Larrinaga (2008) argued that the financial reporting boundary is generally adopted within sustainability reporting. Alternative forms of investment, such as social, environmental, or human capital are ignored, together with any return on capital derived, or associated distribution of value. This is considered poor strategic management (Freeman, et al., 2010) and leads to inequity in the distribution of value.

Despite dramatic changes in the business world and "a barrage of business scandals" leading to "a crisis of legitimacy" for the accounting profession (Fisher, Swanson, & Schmidt, 2007), accounting education has not progressed (Albrecht & Sack,

2000). Moral development is considered to be poor for both accounting students (Gray, Bebbinton, & McPhail, 1994) and professional accountants (Armstrong, 1987). Many accounting firms have experienced detrimental consequences for their involvement in accounting frauds, the most high profile being the collapse of Arthur Andersen LLP in 2001 following the fraudulent handing of the Enron audit. Whilst the fallout of scandals and corporate collapses has damaging financial impacts on shareholders, it is often the wider groups of stakeholders that are most seriously affected, both at the individual (psychologically, socially, and financially) and societal levels (increased unemployment and social benefits bill).

Albrecht and Sack (2000) suggested that there is a greater need to take account of the interests of different stakeholders across academic and professional accounting education. The solution to date has not, however, emerged. Accounting bodies have a long history of accrediting higher education programmes whereby the syllabi is tailored to the syllabi of professional exams in exchange for offering professional exam exemptions to students. This affords the accounting bodies a substantial amount of power over shaping module content, which is significantly pronounced compared to other disciplines. Furthermore, the extent to which the syllabi of the major accounting bodies embrace the stakeholder approach is weak, reflecting the dominant political pressures. This is, consequently, reflected throughout many degree programmes.

The Epistemological Origins of Accounting

Accounting is a sub-discipline of economics with the origins of its epistemological elements traced to the neo-classical economic framework. Historically, accounting was created to record the financial aspects of organizations, but within the Anglo-American system soon developed into a corporate monitoring mechanism to protect capital providers against managerial self-interest, abuse, and fraud. Accounting also serves as a bonding mechanism designed to increase goal congruence through the construction of contracts tied to accounting ratios. For example, corporate debt covenants tied to leverage levels and managerial bonuses and share plans determined by profit, earnings per share, or total shareholder return.

Traditional Anglo-American accounting theory reflects corporate law and is based on the theory of property rights and the maximization of shareholder wealth, presumed to be synonymous with the maximization of the value of the firm (Clarke, 2014). Little consideration is given to stakeholder interests beyond their impact on shareholder wealth or to elements (assets, liabilities, capital, revenues, and expenses) that cannot be measured in monetary terms. This contrasts sharply with, for example, accounting in Finland, which is seen as a means of providing information to satisfy the needs of a wide range of stakeholders (Näsi & Näsi, 1996). The work of Rhenman has heavily influenced Finnish university education in accounting, which draws on the capital circulation and stakeholder models and incorporates social, environmental, public sector, and not-for-profit disclosure as part of the mainstream accounting function.

Anglo-American accounting research has focused on the development of shareholder-centric models resulting from the intricate power relations that enshrine the importance of shareholders over other groups in society. "The theoretical underpinnings of the subject are restricted to only one 'subset' of ethical reasoning: financial utilitarianism ... which is, in a sense, 'indoctrination'" (Ferguson, et al., 2005: 24). Parker (2007) argued that the historic influence from economics and finance-based positivism has led to accounting research being largely uncritical of the role of accounting in (i) accepting the demands of the financial markets, (ii) questioning the need to engage in reform via addressing major policy questions, and (iii) reporting for a broader range of stakeholders. Cooper and Owen (2007) called for legal reform toward a pluralistic form of governance to remove the one-dimensional power afforded to shareholders. Further lobbying of the profession is also warranted. Hawley (1991) argued that if shareholder wealth maximization is continually prioritized as the superordinate goal, accounting academics are abdicating their responsibility to encourage corporate managers to recognize and deal with stakeholder inclusiveness effectively.

Whilst shareholder primacy remains the predominant paradigm, there have been various attempts in accounting research that have questioned this, and it is to this subject that the discussion now turns. Partial reviews of the application of stakeholder theory to accounting exist (e.g., Roberts & Mahoney, 2004; Freeman, et al., 2010; Brown & Jones, 2015), but there is further scope for a comprehensive, systematic review in this area.

Financial Accounting

Considering the widespread appeal of stakeholder theory, there is surprisingly little research that has focused on a stakeholder-theory approach to financial accounting. The majority of research within this stream relates to the exploration of stakeholder influence on financial disclosure and stakeholder information needs. There is also some exploratory research on stakeholder-oriented accounting systems. These will be considered in turn.

(i) Stakeholder Influence on Accounting Information

Accounting disclosure is determined in the first instance by regulators, such as standard setters and, in the second instance by corporate management. Anglo-American accounting studies recognize that standard setting is a mixed-power system with stakeholders viewed as external social and political forces which pressurize standard setters and organizations to select accounting policies that satisfy their interests (Kwok & Sharp, 2005). This was illustrated by Nobes (1991): Upward force for tighter regulation, stemming from government, international influences, the profession and the media, are countered by demonstrable downward pressures for flexible standards from corporations.

Stakeholder theory has been used as a framework to explain corporate earnings management, particularly with respect to earnings quality (the selection of more conservative accounting policy choices) and the timing of earnings announcement under management discretion. Thomson (1993) provided an early example through an analysis of stakeholder power during the pre- and post-privatization of the UK electricity industry. Pre-privatization focus of primary stakeholder groups (government, consumers, competitors) was on rates of return which incentivized management to minimize profits to avoid price-capping, whereas post-privatization, profit-maximizing accounting choices were selected, as management were incentivized by newly constructed bonus and share option contracts to align their interests with those of the recently created shareholders. In a similar vein, Bowen, DuCharme, and Shores (1995) found that implicit claims between an organization and its customers, suppliers, employees, and short-term creditors act as incentives for management to use long-run income-increasing accounting choices in relation to depreciation and inventory. The use of a socio-economic perspective to evaluate accounting policy choice, as explored in such studies, provides a richer, more inclusive explanation of behaviour than reference to economic theories alone (Mangos & Lewis, 1995).

Scott, McKinnon, and Harrison (2003) examined the historical assessment (1857–1975) of stakeholder influence on the "cash-based versus accruals" accounting choice at two Australian hospitals. Stakeholder influence was found to be a determinant of accounting choice if stakeholders possessed power to exert influence and an incentive to exercise that power. Earnings management practices were found to differ between stakeholder-oriented countries and shareholder-orientated countries, with individuals from the former being less tolerant of earnings management due to the perceived impact on multiple stakeholder groups (Geiger & van der Laan Smith, 2010).

Mattingly, Harrast, and Olsen (2009) argued that stakeholder management is an effective process for governing organizations as it is associated with higher levels of accountability and higher earnings quality. Their findings clearly indicated that companies with more effective stakeholder management followed more conservative accounting choices and had more transparent financial disclosure, thereby meeting a wider range of stakeholders' needs. Likewise, Hui, Klasa, and Yeung (2012) illustrated that suppliers and customers with a bargaining advantage influence the selection of more conservative accounting policies. Such stakeholders bear significant downside risks if an organization fails but gain little from strong corporate performance.

A "stakeholder hypothesis" was developed by Bowen, et al. (1992) to explain how organizations may benefit from timing the earnings announcement. The conceptualization of stakeholder theory was taken from the accounting and finance literature (citing Cornell & Shapiro, 1987). They argued that managers have an incentive to minimize the adverse reaction of stakeholders to bad news by delaying related earnings announcements. Building on this, Burgstahler and Dichev (1997) argued that firms with higher earnings face lower transaction costs: consumers will pay a premium for assurance that warranties will be honored, and suppliers/lenders offer better terms if repayment is more certain. They reasoned that implicit claims act as incentives for management to select accounting choices that maximize profits/minimize losses.

Drawing on the "proactive-accommodative-defensive-reaction" organizational strategy model and the life-cycle model (citing Jawahar & Mclaughlin, 2001), Camara, Chamorro, and Moreno (2009) examined how the amount and type of financial information in the annual reports of the tobacco industry varied over the period 1887–1986 depending on the interests and power of key stakeholders (the State, employees, and society).

One area where stakeholder theory is repeatedly used (in conjunction with legitimacy theory and agency theory) is within the voluntary disclosure of intellectual capital (see, for example, Leuz & Verrecchia, 2000; Yongvanich & Guthrie, 2005; Alcaniz, Gomez-Bezares, & Roslender, 2011; Castilla-Polo & Gallardo-Vázquez, 2016). Disclosure is dealt with within traditional balance sheet measures but can be supported by non-financial metrics and narrative, as, for example, developed in the Danish Intellectual Capital Statement (Nielsen, Roslender, & Schaper, 2017). Beattie and Thomson (2007) and Beattie and Smith (2012) offered a managerial stakeholder perspective (disclosure driven by demands of primary stakeholders) and ethical stakeholder theory perspective (responsibility-driven disclosure) to explain motives for voluntary disclosure. They concluded that whilst the needs of financial market participants were paramount, the media and consumers were influential in disclosure decisions, especially disclosures that aimed to avoid scrutiny from stakeholder groups.

(ii) Accounting Information Needs of Stakeholders

The objective of financial reporting, closely associated with user information needs, has been heavily contested by the accounting profession. Two objectives have dominated this debate: economic decision-making (aligned to shareholder primacy) and stewardship (more aligned to stakeholder theory). Early regulation (e.g., US Securities Act, 1933; US Securities Exchange Act, 1934; UK Corporate Report, 1975), mandated the provision of reports for stewardship in the first instance and economic decision-usefulness information as a secondary objective. The current international conceptual framework (IASB, 2010) has regressed. Stewardship has been replaced by economic decision-making, thereby reinforcing the shareholder primacy paradigm (Harrison & van der Laan Smith, 2015).

There is widespread criticism of the nature of financial reporting for reinforcing shareholder primacy and failing to meet stakeholder needs. Murphy, O'Connell, and Ó hÓgartaigh (2013), for example, contended that stewardship is central to the "living law" of accounting and is fundamental to encouraging corporate decision-makers to broaden their responsibilities. Barsky, Hussein, and Jablonsky (1999) also called for richer disclosure to encompass a societal balanced-scorecard approach. A "wheel of stakeholder interests" was presented and stakeholder theory was discussed (citing Woodward, et al., 1996 and Langtry, 1994). They argued that financial reporting practices contributed to the selection of a poor downsizing strategy at United Technologies Corporation that favored shareholders over other stakeholder groups.

A stewardship approach to reporting will result in greater levels of disclosure as transparency is fundamental in discharging stewardship. This is particularly important for public sector reporting and several papers have explored this area from a stakeholder theory perspective. Goddard and Powell (1994) criticized the usefulness of public sector accounting systems in improving services due to a misalignment between the shareholder wealth-creation model followed in the reporting of public goods (determined by financial and legal probity) and lack of consideration of the plurality of stakeholder claims, concerns, issues, values, and needs. Their "naturalistic stakeholder evaluation" concluded that greater levels of stakeholder consultation were needed to understand how stakeholders use accounting information. This sentiment was echoed by Ellwood (2009) and Tooley, Hooks, and Basman (2010). Ellwood (2009) applied the ladder of stakeholder engagement (Friedman & Miles, 2006) to analyze public healthcare in the United Kingdom. Tooley, et al., (2010) highlighted the need to balance the multiple interests of stakeholders. They observed differences between the perceptions of internal and external stakeholders on the relative importance of disclosure items in the public sector reports.

The stakeholder salience model (Mitchell, Agle, & Wood, 1997) has also been applied to explore financial reporting user needs (e.g., Kamal, Brown, Sivabalan, & Sundin, 2015). Specific applications included analysis of the response of the accounting profession to a crisis of credibility following an embezzlement scandal in New Zealand (Baskerville-Morley, 2004) and to assess public perception of profits during a period when the social reputation of the Canadian banking industry was sullied (Breton & Côté, 2006).

(iii) Alternative financial reporting systems

Current financial reporting systems are considered deficient with regard to stakeholder inclusiveness (Mitchell, Van Burren, Greenwood, & Freeman, 2015). This impedes the adoption of stakeholder theory within management practice and has led to calls for the reconceptualization of the accounting function. A special issue of the Journal of

Management Studies, dedicated to accounting for stakeholder value, addresses such concerns. In it, Harrison and van der Laan Smith (2015) criticized the approach adopted by standard setters, calling for a reversal of the narrowing of the accounting function to widen the objectives toward accountability and stewardship. Brown and Dillard (2015) proposed a governance-focused solution that advocated a move beyond the managerial ethos to reflect a more pluralistic dialogue within accounting. For the remaining contributors, the solution recommended was less radical. Hall, Millo, and Barman (2015) supported the calculation of a stakeholder-orientated social return on investment whilst both Crane, Graham, and Himick (2015) and Andon, Baxter, and Chua (2015) proposed adaptation of the current system. Crane, et al. (2015) argued that pension accounting already provides metrics needed to coordinate stakeholder claims, through the accommodation of the time, security, and priority aspects of the claims of pension beneficiaries. Shaoul (1998) provided a much earlier illustration of how financial reports can be used to assess the distribution of value to consumers, employees, industry, and the public. The guest editors (Mitchell, et al., 2015) detailed a pragmatic stakeholder value-creation accounting model that required a conscious shift away from the organization-centric entity concept of financial reporting to a proprietary concept model to capture value creation and risk sharing through the recording of exchange activities. They acknowledged that their ideas represented a sketch of a complex process, calling for further research in this emerging area.

In summary, the financial accounting research stream has acknowledged that stakeholder theory provides a richer, more inclusive explanation of behaviour compared to economic theories in examining stakeholders' influence on standard setting, earnings management and voluntary disclosure. Stakeholder theory provides convincing explanations of management incentives to manage stakeholder pressure, minimize information asymmetry, decrease transaction costs, reduce unwanted scrutiny from stakeholders, and legitimize actions following reputation breaches. Research indicates that the adoption of a strategic stakeholder orientation results in greater levels of accountability,

higher earnings quality, higher levels of voluntary disclosure, and the adoption of more conservative accounting policies. The resulting increase in predictability and reliability of earnings has palpable societal benefits for stakeholders.

There remains, however, significant scope to explore financial reporting from a stakeholder theory perspective. Relatively little is known about how stakeholders influence accounting disclosure, particularly outside the public sector. Whilst most papers within this research stream view the organization as a nexus of stakeholder contracts, stakeholder models are rarely adopted or tested, offering potential avenues for future research. Opportunities also exist to develop alternative financial accounting systems, along the lines of Mitchell, et al., (2015), which aim to question the fundamental structure of existing financial reporting provision. Further research is therefore required to make stronger theoretical connections between stakeholder inclusiveness and the reporting function.

Management Accounting

Studies that examine the influence of stakeholder theory in management accounting are focused in the area of control and performance management. Kaplan and Norton (2001) are very clear that the balanced scorecard (BSC) is not a stakeholder scorecard aligned to corporate strategy. They claimed that a focus on stakeholder interests fails to reflect the causal relations between strategic areas and that the "balance" relates to the balancing of outcomes, not stakeholder interests. Nevertheless there have been a number of articles that have evaluated the BSC from a stakeholder theory approach. Sundin, Granlund, and Brown (2010) questioned Kaplan and Norton's assertion that stakeholder and strategy scorecards are mutually exclusive in a capitalist system. The BSC was revised to a "balancing scorecard" which started with a systematic identification of multiple stakeholders' interests before implementing a traditional BSC analysis of the perceived cause-and-effect relationships and trade-offs between objectives and measures. The challenges that a stakeholder theory approach raises for resource allocation, performance measurement, and achieving an equitable balance of interests were acknowledged by Sundin, et al. (2010) but their conclusions clearly supported a focus on the balancing process to achieve procedural justice.

Stakeholder analysis was also considered beneficial in understanding the dynamic influences of the external and internal environments on the formulation of objectives and strategy in a study by Li and Tang (2009). They provided empirical support for Jensen's (2001) enlightened stakeholder theory with respect to the application of a BSC. Axa and Bjørnenak (2005) found that Swedish corporations clearly implemented the BSC in a stakeholder-orientation manner that aligned with the Swedish stakeholder capitalism model. This form of capitalism recognizes implicit long-term bonds with stakeholders and is based on a system of mutual trust and cooperation.

The influence of stakeholder theory on management control research was not evident until the publication of Norris and O'Dwyer (2004). Stakeholders are increasingly concerned with how corporate social and environmental issues are measured, monitored, and reported, suggesting the need for management to consider and weigh stakeholders' concerns when selecting key performance indicators (KPIs) (Dillard & Roslender, 2011). Combining stakeholder theory with resource dependency theory, Länsiluoto, Järvenpää, and Krumwiede (2013) found that buy-in was more achievable if goal congruence between stakeholders and resource providers was achieved in setting stakeholder objectives. This requires the explicit identification of stakeholder expectations and the subsequent translation of these expectations into specific accounting performance indicators. They found evidence of stakeholder influence in the selection of KPIs. This reflected the findings from Brignall and Ballantine (2004): stakeholders negotiate proposals for change and use power and conflict to influence managerial choice of performance measures.

Durden (2008) presented case evidence to demonstrate that a management control system that explicitly considered stakeholder goals would clearly differentiate management's efforts to operate in a socially responsible manner from public relations exercises. Stakeholder influence on the selection of environmental KPIs was also investigated by Rodrigue, Magnan, and Boulianne (2013). Stakeholder influence ranged from (i) mediated influence on environmental strategy, (ii) indirect influence from explicit stakeholder pressures on environmental KPIs selection, (iii) shared influence arising from a common mind-set for environmental improvement, and (iv) environmental benchmarking influence, stemming from a comparison of performance by stakeholders to corporate peers.

Other papers referred to the stakeholder model but did not base the analysis undertaken around it (e.g., Carlsson-Wall, Kraus, & Messner, 2016). Merchant (2006) explicitly rejected stakeholder theory as a framework but recognized that there could be some benefit if applied in a stakeholder-oriented not-for-profit setting. There is very limited research that investigates management accounting problems from a stakeholder theory perspective, providing clear opportunities for future research.

Sustainability Reporting

Within the sustainability reporting literature, stakeholder theory is viewed as an overlapping, complementary theory to legitimacy theory, set within a political economy framework (Gray, Kouhy, & Lavers, 1995). This overlap is frequently mentioned (e.g., Cormier, Magnan, & Van Velthoven, 2004), supported (e.g., Thorne, Mahoney, & Manetti, 2014), but rarely questioned (e.g., Tilling & Tilt, 2010). The predominant stakeholder perspective adopted is a strategic, instrumental theory approach.

Gray, Dey, Owen, Evans, & Zadek, (1997) contended that stakeholder theory has only limited use as a lens for evaluating motives for disclosure, in so far as it helps to define which stakeholder groups management deem important, and in doing so identifies the boundaries of responsibility that organizations are willing to accept. They argued that the stakeholder perspective, being organization-centric, assumes that stakeholder interests are subsumed within the interest of management and therefore results in flawed, partial, and biased reporting. This sentiment was echoed by Adams and Whelan (2009) and Parker (2005) who likened instrumental stakeholder theory to corporate enlightened self-interest driven by corporate strategic aims.

Normative stakeholder theory, which is often referred to as the accountability variant of stakeholder theory within the accounting literature, is considered to have little descriptive power within a sustainability-reporting context (Gray, Owen, & Adams, 1996). The ongoing discussion in the stakeholder theory literature on the validity of the separation of ethics from actions that implies that instrumental (strategic) stakeholder theory can be applied separately from normative (ethical) stakeholder theory is largely ignored in the accounting literature as most researchers accept separation (Oriji, 2010).

There have, nevertheless, been some attempts at looking at wider accountability within a stakeholder perspective (e.g., O'Dwyer, Unerman, & Bradley, 2005). Williams and Adams (2013) proposed an "intrinsic" stakeholder approach, likened to that adopted in the AccountAbility AA1000 series and based on inclusivity, materiality, and responsiveness. This framework combined normative stakeholder theory with the theories of legitimacy, political economy, and the role of language and rhetoric in order to consider the moral responsibilities corporations have to employees, including the discharge of accountability evident in sustainability reporting.

Most sustainability reporting research is organisation-centric and focused on economic stakeholders such suppliers, customers, lenders, competitors, and investors (Islam & Deegan, 2008; Mahadeo, Oogarah-Hanumana, & Soobaroyen, 2011). Few authors, such as Momin (2013), focused on a stakeholder-centric perspective, or a wider range of non-commercial stakeholders, despite the concern that it is important for research to capture marginal voices. Notable exceptions are Tilt (1994), O'Dwyer, Unerman and Hession (2004; 2005), O'Dwyer, et al., (2005), Deegan and Blomquist (2006), and Unerman and O'Dwyer (2006), who examined NGOs, and Grosser and Moon (2008) who explored gender equality reporting.

Research can be categorized into two streams, which are now discussed in turn: (i) stakeholder theory as an explanation for voluntary disclosure; (ii) stakeholder engagement in the sustainability reporting process.

(i) Voluntary Disclosure

Stakeholder theory was first suggested as a framework for explaining voluntary disclosure by Ullmann (1985). The logic is straightforward: stakeholders demand sustainability information, and those with power to influence the corporation, derived from their control of critical resources, are more likely to have their demands met. Subsequent disclosure is the mechanism by which conformance to stakeholder expectations is demonstrated (Moneva & Llena, 2000). Ullmann (1985) cited the seminal contribution of Freeman's (1984) generic stakeholder strategies and Pfeffer and Salancik's (1978) discussion on power and resource dependency. These theories were combined in the development of a three-dimensional "contingency framework" for implementing sustainability issues that considered stakeholder power, strategic posture, and economic performance. This framework has empirical support in the accounting literature (e.g., Magness, 2006; Prado-Lorenzo, Gallego-Alvarez, & Garcia-Sanchez, 2009). Roberts (1992) found significant relationships between stakeholder power, strategic posture, economic performance, and levels of disclosure across 130 major corporations, particularly with respect to government and creditor relationship management. More recently, Herbohn, Walker, and Loo (2014) found sustainability reporting was significantly associated with media coverage, disposable resources, and heightened exposure to environmental costs, thereby concluding that Ullmann's framework remains relevant in explaining voluntary disclosure.

Closely related to the issues of resource dependency and power is the notion of stakeholder salience. Researchers have provided empirical support for the proposition that the level and quality of sustainability reporting is positively correlated to stakeholder salience (see Soobaroyen & Ntim, 2013; Dong, Burritt, & Qan, 2014). Orij (2010) and van der Laan Smith, Adhikari, and Tondkar (2005) also found that power, legitimacy, and urgency attributes of stakeholders are more pronounced in an international context and that stakeholder theory offers plausible explanations for variations in sustainability disclosure across countries. Van der Laan Smith, et al. (2005) explored institutional and cultural differences between American and Norwegian/Danish organizations operating in the electric power generation industry. Their proposition that stakeholder theory provides a useful explanation for observed international differences was further tested by van der Laan Smith, Adhikari, Tondkar, and Andrews (2011) through the creation of a six-point stakeholder scale to determine stakeholder/shareholder orientation. This tool captured issues such as perceptions of corporate social responsibility (CSR), the willingness to sacrifice return for improved CSR performance, and perceptions of the corporate objective function. They confirmed the earlier finding that stakeholder theory provided a proficient lens to evaluate and explain the systematic cross-national differences in investor responses to sustainability reporting.

Pérez, López, and García-De los Salmones (2017) also supported the explanatory powers of the salience model in their empirical application to Spanish companies and recommended the establishment of regular stakeholder salience-monitoring mechanisms as part of the reporting process. Brennan and Merkl-Davies (2014) adapted the salience model to incorporate the role of rhetoric skill in achieving conflict resolution in sustainability reporting. Rhetoric skill in harnessing stakeholder support from environmental activists, consumers, the general public, and the media, was considered to be more effective in attaining power than direct control of financial resources. They tested their model on the interaction between Greenpeace and six sportswear/fashion firms over the elimination of hazardous chemicals within supply chains. Greenpeace's success in this endeavor was attributed to its rhetoric skills in coalition-building and political action.

Accounting research examining stakeholder influences on voluntary sustainability reporting has been fairly limited (e.g., Deegan & Blomquist, 2006 and Leisen, Hoepner, Patten, & Figge, 2015). Elijido-Ten (2008) fully embraced stakeholder theory in an application of Frooman's

stakeholder influencing strategy framework to the issue of how stakeholder demands for sustainability reporting are attended to. The inconclusive results were considered to be a consequence of a lack of urgency in the focal event studied, leading to a subsequent re-examination in the context of an urgent issue which had potential significant negative stakeholder impacts (Elijido-Ten, Kloot, & Clarkson, 2010). They concluded that stakeholder theory is useful in understanding both stakeholder and managerial behaviour with respect to sustainability reporting.

Elijido-Ten (2011) also applied Freeman's stakeholder strategy framework to voluntary sustainability reporting decisions. Her analysis juxtaposed the potential of a comprehensive range of stakeholders (consumers, media, government agencies, suppliers, shareholders, creditors, competitors, environmentalists, and employees) to cooperate, against their potential to threaten organization process. She identified real and significant opportunities for some groups (government and consumers) to pressure corporations into addressing environmental concerns and disclosing impact.

Leisen, et al. (2015) provided an extensive empirical study of greenhouse gas (GHG) emissions disclosure using a stakeholder theory framework. They established alternative hypotheses to explain GHG emission disclosures of 431 companies. The first hypothesis suggested stakeholder-driven disclosure, given the increased importance assigned to GHG emissions for climate change and associated stakeholder pressure to conform. The second hypothesis was based on disclosure as a legitimating strategy, given that GHG disclosure is largely voluntary and subject to managerial capture and manipulation. They found support for both arguments and evidenced stakeholder influence on GHG emission reporting.

(ii) Stakeholder Engagement

There are a multitude of papers that explore the role of stakeholder engagement in the sustainability reporting process (e.g., Tilt, 1994; Deegan & Rankin, 1997). Stakeholder engagement offers increased accountability to powerless and marginalized stakeholders and is linked to good governance, increased long-term value, and reduced reputational and operational risks (Miles, Hammond, & Friedman, 2002; Barone, Ranamagar, & Solomon, 2013). Stakeholder engagement is a means of managing disclosure and it dominates the professional sustainability-reporting arena, such as the Global Reporting Initiative and AccountAbility AA1000 series.

Most contributors adopt stakeholder terminology but do not rigorously base their analysis on stakeholder theory (see Calabrese, Costa, & Rosati, 2015). Boesso and Kumar (2009), Connolly, Hyndman, and McConville (2013), and Manetti and Bellucci (2016) are all examples of papers that do place stakeholder theory explicitly within their analysis. Boesso and Kumar (2009) investigated the stakeholder prioritization and engagement process, associated with stakeholder salience (Mitchell, et al., 1997), through an empirical assessment of US and Italian practice. Their findings highlighted the practical difficulties and limitations involved in meeting the needs of multiple stakeholder groups, despite managerial desires to address stakeholder demands. Despite astronomic increases in social media use, Manetti and Bellucci (2016) found that only a small minority of the 332 corporations examined actively used social media for stakeholder engagement and that the level of interaction was low. Social media can be effective in providing a voice to a wide range of stakeholders, but Manetti and Bellucci (2016) warned that this may be deceptive if the democratic process is not embedded. Connolly, et al. (2013) highlighted the problems of involving stakeholder groups meaningfully in a consultation process and, like Manetti and Bellucci (2016), highlighted the danger of quasi-consultation being undertaken to generate buy in rather than to genuinely involve stakeholders and address their needs within the context of UK charity accounting standard-setting process. They concluded that although funders were identified as legitimate primary stakeholders, their influence was fairly negligible in determining content and disclosure.

In summary, the largest impact that stakeholder theory has had on accounting research has been in the area of sustainability reporting (Gray, et al., 1995). This research is predominantly organisation-centric. There remains significant scope to engage with stakeholder theory in a more robust way as the majority of research whilst framed within stakeholder terminology and discourse lacks systematic application (Spence, Husillos, & Correa-Ruiz, 2010).

Conclusions

This review has outlined a growing body of accounting research that embraces stakeholder theory. There are two dominant areas in which stakeholder theory has been used as a frame of reference. Firstly, as an explanatory theory for accounting choice and voluntary disclosure, the implicit claims of powerful stakeholders are considered. This enriches understanding by providing plausible explanations for anomalies that cannot be explained through traditional economic theories, such as agency theory. Stakeholder theory is also applied in exploring stakeholder influence, focusing on the identification of stakeholders needs, and addressing how reporting can best fulfill these needs (or not).

Significant future research opportunities still exist. Firstly, researchers can learn from the application of stakeholder theory in other disciplines. Whilst there are some exceptions, for example, the multiple applications of the salience model (Mitchell, et al., 1997), there is generally a notable lack of acknowledgement of seminal stakeholder theory contributions originating from outside the accounting literature. This indicates that further interdisciplinary research could provide useful insights into accounting problems and enhance understanding of management behaviour regarding the accounting function.

Secondly, more robust and explicit theoretical analysis is needed. The majority of accounting papers reviewed use stakeholder theory as a notional guide or a point of reference devoid of particular content. There is therefore significant scope to develop stronger theoretical connections between stakeholder inclusiveness and accounting theory and practice.

Thirdly, stakeholder theory is not a common frame of reference within the management accounting literature, which remains dominated by the corporate objective to maximize shareholder wealth. The shareholder–stakeholder orientation affects both the content of strategy and the strategic management accounting process, which is central to financial decision-making in business. Nixon and Burns (2012) argued that, in an environment of anti-business sentiment, corporate governance failures, and the recent financial crisis, adherence to the classical strategic management accounting perspective, which assumes a stable and predictable environment, is questionable. A significant majority of the stakeholder theory informed management accounting papers are post-2003. Research indicates a growing awareness of the need to reassess traditional models of performance measurement, however, other management accounting theories and models, such as strategic management accounting techniques, capital investment appraisal and costing, would also benefit from being re-examined from a stakeholder theory perspective, highlighting an important area for future research. This is also an important area for management accounting education, which at best pays lip service to stakeholder theory, thereby reinforcing the shareholder primacy model in the minds of future managers.

Fourthly, there is evidence of a call for broader narratives that engage accounting with a questioning of the status quo of shareholder primacy to widen accountability. The accounting profession has a significant role to play in advancing this issue, given the power and influence that it has over professional and academic qualifications as well as corporate disclosure. A clearer understanding of stakeholder strategies deployed to influence accounting decision-makers (standard setters, the profession, academia, and corporate management) is needed in order to change managerial mind-set and expectations placed on the profession through the delivery of reports that are more useful and relevant to managers and stakeholders.

Finally, there is further scope for the critical school to develop novel ways of recording and prioritizing stakeholder claims that capture value creation and risk. This is a complex step-wise process that will require researchers to question:

1. the basic objectives, assumptions, concepts, and principles and qualitative characteristics adopted in accounting; 2. the reporting boundary of what should, and should not, be reported on, which extends beyond the principles of ownership and control to encompass impact and implicit claims; 3. recognition principles that are capable of including stakeholder claims and value exchange activities; 4. Measurement techniques and metrics that go beyond monetary representation of transactions to capture impacts and value creation; and 5. disclosure practices which enhance, not hinder, stakeholder communication and engagement.

This research agenda is multifaceted, challenging, and thought provoking. Accounting researchers are in a strong position to promote stakeholder theory in practice, as well as being in a privileged position to develop better ways of recognizing and fulfilling stakeholder rights.

References

Adams, C. A., & Whelan, G. (2009). Conceptualising future change in corporate sustainability reporting. *Accounting, Auditing & Accountability Journal, 22* (1): 118–143.

Albrecht, W. S., & Sack, R. J. (2000). *Accounting Education: Charting the Course through a Perilous Future.* Accounting Education Series, vol. 16, American Accounting Association.

Alcaniz, L. Gomez-Bezares. F., & Roslender, F. (2011). Theoretical perspectives on intellectual capital: A backward look and a proposal for going forward, *Accounting Forum, 35*(2): 104–117.

Andon, P., Baxter, J. & Chua, W. F. (2015). Accounting for stakeholders and making accounting useful. *Journal of Management Studies, 52*(7): 986–1002.

Archel, P., Fernández, M., & Larrinaga, C. (2008). The organizational and operational boundaries of triple bottom line reporting: a survey. *Environmental Management, 41*: 106–117.

Armstrong, M. B. (1987). Moral development and accounting education. *Journal of Accounting Education, 5*: 27–43.

Axa, C., & Bjørnenak, T. (2005). Bundling and diffusion of management accounting innovations: The case of the balanced scorecard in Sweden. *Management Accounting Research, 16*: 1–20.

Barone, E. Ranamagar, N., & Solomon, J. F. (2013). A Habermasian model of stakeholder (non) engagement and corporate (ir) responsibility reporting. *Accounting Forum*, *37*(3): 163–181.

Barsky, N. P., Hussein, M. E., & Jablonsky, S. F. (1999). Shareholder and stakeholder value in corporate downsizing: The case of United Technologies Corporation. *Accounting, Auditing & Accountability Journal*, *12*(5): 583–604

Baskerville-Morley, R. F. (2004). Dangerous, Dominant, Dependent, or Definitive: Stakeholder Identification When the Profession Faces Major Transgressions. *Accounting and the Public Interest*, *4*(1): 24–42.

Beattie, V., & Smith, S. J. (2012). Evaluating disclosure theory using the views of UK finance directors in the intellectual capital context. *Accounting and Business Research*, *42*(5): 471–394.

Beattie, V., & Thomson, S. J. (2007). Lifting the lid on the use of content analysis to investigate intellectual capital disclosures. *Accounting Forum*, *31*(2): 129–163.

Boesso, G., & Kumar, K. (2009). Stakeholder prioritization and reporting: Evidence from Italy and the US. *Accounting Forum*, *33*(2): 165–175.

Bowen, R. M. DuCharme, L., & Shores, D. (1995). Stakeholders' implicit claims and accounting method choice. *Journal of Accounting and Economics*, *20*(3): 255–295.

Bowen, R. M., Johnson, M. F., Shevlin, T., & Shores, D. (1992). Determinants of the timing of quarterly earnings announcement. *Journal of Accounting, Auditing and Finance*, *7*(4): 395–422.

Brennan, N. M., & Merkl-Davies, D. M. (2014). Rhetoric and argument in social and environmental reporting: The Dirty Laundry case. *Accounting, Auditing & Accountability Journal*, *27*(4): 602–633.

Breton, G., & Côté, L. (2006). Profit and the legitimacy of the Canadian banking industry. *Accounting, Auditing & Accountability Journal*, *19*(4): 512–539.

Brignall, S., & Ballantine, J. (2004). Strategic enterprise management systems: New directions for research. *Management Accounting Research*, *15*(2): 225–240.

Brown, R., & Dillard, J. (2015). Dialogic accountings for stakeholders: On opening up and closing down participatory governance. Journal of Management Studies, *52*(7): 961–985.

Brown, R., & Jones, M. (2015). Mapping and exploring the topography of contemporary financial accounting research. *The British Accounting Review*, *47*(3): 237–261.

Burgstahler, D., & Dichev, I. (1997). Earnings management to avoid earnings decreases and losses. *Journal of Accounting and Economics*, *24*(1): 99–126.

Calabrese, A. Costa, R., & Rosati, F. (2015). A feedback-based model for CSR assessment and materiality analysis. *Accounting Forum*, *39*(4): 312–327.

Camara, M., Chamorro, E., & Moreno, A. (2009). Stakeholder reporting: The Spanish tobacco monopoly (1887–1986). *European Accounting Review*, *18*(4): 697–717.

Carlsson-Wall, M., Kraus, K., & Messner, M. (2016). Performance measurement systems and the enactment of different institutional logics: insights from a football organization. *Management Accounting Research*, *32*(September): 45–61.

Chartered Association of Business Schools. (2018). Academic Journal Guide 2018 Retrieved October 23, 2018, from https://charteredabs.org/academic-journal-guide-2018/.

Connolly, C., Hyndman, N., & McConville, D. (2013). UK charity accounting: An exercise in widening stakeholder engagement. *The British Accounting Review*, *45*(1): 58–69.

Cooper, S. M., & Owen, D. L. (2007). Corporate social reporting and stakeholder accountability: The missing link. *Accounting, Organizations and Society*, *32*(7–8): 649–667.

Cormier, D., Magnan, M., & Van Velthoven, B. (2004). Environmental disclosure quality in large German companies: Economic incentives, public pressures or institutional conditions? *European Accounting Review*, *14*(1): 3–39.

Crane, A., Graham, C. & Himick, D. (2015). Financializing stakeholder claims. *Journal of Management Studies*, *52*(7): 878–906.

Deegan, C., & Blomquist, C. (2006). Stakeholder influence on corporate reporting: an exploration of the interaction between WWF-Australia and the Australian minerals industry. *Accounting, Organizations and Society*, *31*: 343–72.

Deegan, C., & Rankin, M. (1997). The materiality of environmental information to users of annual reports. *Accounting, Auditing & Accountability Journal*, *10*(4): 562–583.

Dillard, J., & Roslender, R. (2011). Taking pluralism seriously: embedded moralities in management accounting and control systems. *Critical Perspectives on Accounting*, *22*(2): 135–147.

Dong, S., Burritt, R., & Qan, W. (2014). Salient stakeholders in corporate social responsibility reporting by Chinese mining and minerals companies. *Journal of Cleaner Production, 84*(1): 59–69.

Durden, C. (2008). Towards a socially responsible management control system. *Accounting, Auditing & Accountability Journal, 21*(5): 671–694.

Elijido-Ten, E. O. (2008). The case for reporting pro-active environmental initiatives: a Malaysian experiment on stakeholder influence strategies. *Issues in Social and Environmental Accounting, 2* (1): 36–60.

Elijido-Ten, E. O. (2011). Media coverage and voluntary environmental disclosures: A developing country exploratory experiment. *Accounting Forum, 35*(3): 139–157.

Elijido-Ten, E. O., Kloot, L., & Clarkson, P. (2010). Extending the application of stakeholder influence strategies to environmental disclosures: An exploratory study from a developing country. *Accounting, Auditing & Accountability Journal, 23* (8): 1032–1059.

Ellwood, S. (2009). Accounting for (a) public good: public healthcare in England. *Financial Accountability & Management, 25*(4): 411–433.

Ferguson, J., Collison, D. J., Power, D. M., & Stevenson, L. A. (2005). What are recommended accounting textbooks teaching students about corporate stakeholders? *British Accounting Review, 37*, 23–46.

Fisher, D. G., Swanson, D. L., & Schmidt, J. J. (2007). Accounting education lags CPE ethics requirements: Implications for the profession and a call to action. *Accounting Education: An International Journal, 16*(4): 345–363.

Freeman, R. E., Harrison, J. S., Wicks, A. C., Parmar, B., & de Colle, S. (2010). *Stakeholder theory: The State of The Art*. Cambridge: Cambridge University Press.

Freeman, R. E. (1984). *Strategic management: A stakeholder approach*. Boston: Pitman.

Friedman, A. L., & Miles, S. (2006). *Stakeholders: Theory and practice*. Oxford: Oxford University Press.

Castilla-Polo, F., & Gallardo-Vázquez, D. (2016). The main topics of research on disclosures of intangible assets: A critical review. *Accounting, Auditing & Accountability Journal, 29*(2): 323–356.

Clarke, T. (2014). The impact of financialisation on international corporate governance: The role of agency theory and maximising shareholder value. *Law and Financial Markets Review*, March: 39–51.

Geiger, M., & van der Laan Smith, J. (2010). The effect of institutional and cultural factors on the perceptions of earnings management. *Journal of International Accounting Research, 9*(2): 21–43.

Goddard, A., & Powell, J. (1994). Accountability and accounting: Using naturalistic methodology to enhance organizational control: A case study. *Accounting, Auditing & Accountability Journal, 7* (2): 50–69.

Gray, R. H., Bebbington, J., & McPhail, K. (1994). Teaching ethics and the ethics of teaching: Educating for immorality and a possible case for social and environmental accounting. Accounting Education: *An International Journal, 3*(1): 51–75.

Gray, R. Dey, C., Owen, D., Evans, R., & Zadek, S. (1997). Struggling with the praxis of social accounting: Stakeholders, accountability, audits and procedures. *Accounting, Auditing & Accountability, 10*(3): 325–364.

Gray, R., Kouhy, R., & Lavers, S. (1995). Corporate social and environmental reporting: A review of the literature and a longitudinal study of UK disclosure. *Accounting, Auditing & Accountability Journal, 8*(2): 47–77.

Gray, R., Owen, D., & Adams, C. A. (1996). *Accounting and accountability: Changes and challenges in corporate social and environmental reporting*. London, Prentice Hall.

Grosser, K., & Moon, J. (2008). Developments in company reporting on workplace gender equality? A corporate social responsibility perspective. *Accounting Forum, 32*: 179–98.

Hall, M., Millo, Y., & Barman, E. (2015). Who and what really counts? Stakeholder prioritization and accounting for social value. *Journal of Management Studies, 52*(7): 907–934.

Harrison, J. S., & van der Laan Smith, J. (2015). Responsible Accounting for Stakeholders. *Journal of Management Studies, 52*(7): 935–960.

Hawley, D. (1991). Business ethics and social responsibility in finance instruction: An abdication of responsibility. *Journal of Business Ethics, 10*: 711–721.

Herbohn, K. Walker, J., & Loo, H. Y. M. (2014). Corporate social responsibility: The link between sustainability disclosure and sustainability performance. *Abacus, 50*(4): 422–459.

Hines, R. D. (1988). Financial accounting: In communicating reality, we construct reality. *Accounting, Organizations and Society, 13*(3): 251–261.

Hui, K. W., Klasa, S., & Yeung, P.E. (2012). Corporate suppliers and customers and accounting conservatism. *Journal of Accounting and Economics*, *53*: 115–135.

IASB. (2010). *The Conceptual Framework for Financial Reporting*. London: IASB.

Islam, M. A., & Deegan, C. (2008). Motivations for an organisation within a developing country to report social responsibility information: Evidence from Bangladesh. *Accounting, Auditing & Accountability Journal*, *21*(6): 850–874.

Jensen, M.C. (2001). Value maximization, stakeholder theory, and the corporate objective function. *Journal of Applied Corporate Finance*, *14*(3): 8–21.

Kamal, O., Brown, D., Sivabalan, P., & Sundin, H. (2015) Accounting information and shifting stakeholder salience: an industry level approach. *Qualitative Research in Accounting & Management*, *12*(2): 172–200.

Kaplan, R. S., & Norton, D. P. (2001). Transforming the balanced scorecard from performance measurement to strategic management: Part I. *Accounting Horizons*, *15*(1): 87–104.

Kwok, W. C. C., & Sharp, D. (2005). Power and international accounting standard setting: Evidence from segment reporting and intangible assets projects. *Accounting, Auditing & Accountability Journal*, *18*(1): 74–99.

Länsiluoto, A. Järvenpää, M., & Krumwiede, K. (2013). Conflicting interests but filtered key targets: Stakeholder and resource-dependency analyses at a University of Applied Sciences. *Management Accounting*, *24*(3): 228–245.

Laux, C., & Leuz, C. (2009). The crisis of fair-value accounting: Making sense of the recent debate. *Accounting, Organisations and Society*, *34*, 826–834.

Leisen, A, Hoepner, A. G., Patten, D. M., & Figge, F. (2015). Does stakeholder pressure influence corporate GHG emissions reporting? Empirical evidence from Europe. *Accounting, Auditing & Accountability Journal*, *28*(7): 1047–1074.

Leuz, C., & Verrecchia, R E. (2000). The economic consequences of increased disclosure. Journal of Accounting Research, *38*(Supplement): 91–124.

Li, P., & Tang, G. (2009). Performance measurement design within its organisational context: Evidence from China. *Management Accounting Research*, *20* (3): 193–207.

Magness, V. (2006). Strategic posture, financial performance and environmental disclosure: An empirical test of legitimacy theory. *Accounting, Auditing & Accountability Journal*, *19*(4): 540–563.

Mahadeo, J. D., Oogarah-Hanumana, V., & Soobaroyen, T. (2011). Changes in social and environmental reporting practices in an emerging economy (2004–2007): Exploring the relevance of stakeholder and legitimacy theories. *Accounting Forum*, *35*(3): 158–175

Giacomo Manetti, G., & Bellucci, M. (2016). The use of social media for engaging stakeholders in sustainability reporting. *Accounting, Auditing & Accountability Journal*, *29*(6): 985–1011.

Mangos, N. C., & Lewis, N. R. (1995). A socio-economic paradigm for analysing managers' accounting choice behavior. *Accounting, Auditing & Accountability Journal*, *8*(1): 38–62.

Mattingly, J. E., Harrast, S. A., & Olsen, L. (2009). Governance implications of the effects of stakeholder management on financial reporting. *Corporate Governance: The International Journal of Business in Society*, *9*(3): 271–282.

Merchant, K. A. (2006). Measuring general managers' performances: Market, accounting and combination-of-measures systems. *Accounting, Auditing & Accountability Journal*, *19*(6): 893–917.

Miles, S., Hammond, K., & Friedman, A. L. (2002). *Social and Environmental Reporting and Ethical Investment*, ACCA Research Report 77: Certified Accountants Educational Trust, London.

Mitchell, R. K., Agle, B. R., & Wood, D. J. (1997). Towards a theory of stakeholder identification and salience: Defining the principle of who and what really counts. *Academy of Management Review*, *22*: 853–86.

Mitchell, R. K., Van Burren II, H., Greenwood, M., & Freeman, R. E. (2015). Stakeholder inclusion and accounting for stakeholders. *Journal of Management Studies*, *52*(7): 851–877.

Momin, M. A. (2013). Social and environmental NGOs' perceptions of corporate social disclosures: The case of Bangladesh. *Accounting Forum*, *37*(2): 150–161.

Moneva, J. M., & Llena, F. (2000). Environmental disclosures in the annual reports of large companies in Spain. *European Accounting Review*, *9* (1): 7–29.

Murphy, T., O'Connell, V., & Ó hÓgartaigh, C. (2013). Discourses surrounding the evolution of the IASB/FASB Conceptual Framework: What they reveal about the "living law" of accounting. *Accounting, Organizations and Society*, *38*(1): 72–91.

Näsi, S., & Näsi, J. (1996). Accounting and business economics traditions in Finland: From a practical discipline into a scientific subject and field of research. *European Accounting Review, 6*(2): 199–229.

Nielsen, C., Roslender, R., & Schaper, S. (2017). Explaining the demise of the intellectual capital statement in Denmark. *Accounting, Auditing & Accountability Journal, 30*(1): 38–64.

Nixon, B., & Burns, J. (2012). The paradox of strategic management accounting. *Management Accounting Research, 23*(4): 229–244.

Nobes, C. W. (1991). Cycles in UK standard setting. *Accounting and Business Research, 21*(83): 265–274.

Norris, G., & O'Dwyer, B. (2004). Motivating socially responsive decision making: The operation of management controls in a socially responsive organisation, *The British Accounting Review, 36*(2): 173–196.

O'Dwyer, B., Unerman, J., & Bradley, J. (2005). Perceptions on the emergence and future development of corporate social disclosure in Ireland: Engaging the voices of nongovernmental organisations. *Accounting, Auditing & Accountability Journal, 18* (1): 14–43.

O'Dwyer, B., Unerman, J., & Hession, E. (2005). User needs in sustainability reporting: perspective of stakeholders in Ireland. *European Accounting Review, 14*(4): 759–787.

O'Dwyer, B., Unerman, J., & Hession, E. (2004). The emergence and future development of corporate social disclosure in Ireland: The perspectives of non-governmental organisations. *Accounting, Auditing & Accountability Journal, 18*(1): 14–43.

Orij, R. (2010). Corporate social disclosures in the context of national cultures and stakeholder theory. *Accounting, Auditing & Accountability Journal, 23* (7): 868–889.

Parker, L. D. (2005). Social and environmental accountability research: A view from the commentary box. *Accounting, Auditing & Accountability Journal, 18*(6): 842–860.

Parker, L. D. (2007). A Commentary on professionalizing claims and the state of UK professional accounting education: Some evidence. *Accounting Education: An International Journal, 16*(1): 43–46.

Pérez, A., López, C., & del García-De los Salmones, M. (2017). An empirical exploration of the link between reporting to stakeholders and corporate social responsibility reputation in the Spanish context. *Accounting, Auditing & Accountability Journal, 30*(3): 668–698.

Perry, J., & Nölke, A. (2006). The political economy of International Accounting Standards. *Review of International Political Economy, 13*(4): 559–586.

Pfeffer, J. & Salancik, G. R. (1978). The *External Control of Organizations: A Resource Dependence Perspective*. New York: Harper and Row.

Prado-Lorenzo, J., Gallego-Alvarez, I., & Garcia-Sanchez, I. (2009). Stakeholder engagement and corporate social responsibility reporting: the ownership structure effect. *Corporate Social Responsibility and Environmental Management, 16*: 94–107.

Ringham, K., & Miles, S. (2018) The boundary of corporate social responsibility reporting: The case of the airline industry. *Journal of Sustainable Tourism, 26*(7): 1043–1062.

Roberts, R. W. (1992): Determinants of corporate social responsibility disclosure: An application of stakeholder theory. *Accounting, Organizations and Society, 17*(6): 595–612.

Roberts, R. W., & Mahoney, L. (2004). Stakeholder conceptions of the corporation: Their meaning and influence in accounting research. *Business Ethics Quarterly, 14*(3): 399–431.

Rodrigue, M., Magnan, M., & Boulianne, E. (2013). Stakeholders' influence on environmental strategy and performance indicators: A managerial perspective. *Management Accounting Research, 24*(4): 301–316.

Scott, J. E. M., McKinnon, J. L., & Harrison, G. L. (2003). Cash to accrual and cash to accrual: A case study of financial reporting in two NSW hospitals 1857 to post-1975. *Accounting, Auditing & Accountability Journal, 16*(1): 104–140.

Shaoul, J. (1998). Critical financial analysis and accounting for stakeholders. *Critical Perspectives on Accounting, 9*: 235–49.

Soobaroyen, T., & Ntim, C. G. (2013). Social and environmental accounting as symbolic and substantive means of legitimation: The case of HIV/AIDS reporting in South Africa. *Accounting Forum, 37*(2): 92–109.

Spence, C. Husillos, J., & Correa-Ruiz, C. (2010). Cargo cult science and the death of politics: A critical review of social and environmental accounting research. *Critical Perspectives on Accounting, 21*(1): 76–89.

Sundin, H., Granlund, M., & Brown, D. A. (2010). Balancing multiple competing objectives with a balanced scorecard. *European Accounting Review, 19*(2): 203–246.

Thomson, L. (1993). Reporting changes in the electricity supply industry and privatisation. *Financial Accountability & Management, 9*(2): 131–157.

Thorne, L., Mahoney, L. S., & Manetti, G. (2014). Motivations for issuing standalone CSR reports: A survey of Canadian firms. *Accounting, Auditing & Accountability Journal, 27*(4): 686–714.

Tilling, M. V., & Tilt, C. A. (2010). The edge of legitimacy. *Accounting, Auditing & Accountability Journal, 23*(1): 55–81.

Tilt, C. A. (1994). The influence of external pressure groups on corporate social disclosure: Some empirical evidence. *Accounting, Auditing & Accountability Journal, 7*(4): 47–72.

Tooley, S., Hooks, J., & Basnan, N. (2010). Performance reporting by Malaysian local authorities: Identifying stakeholder needs. *Financial Accountability & Management, 26*(2): 103–133

Ullmann, A. A. (1985). Data in search of a theory: A critical examination of the relationships among social performance, social disclosure, and economic performance of US Firms. *The Academy of Management Review, 10*(3): 540–557.

Unerman, J., & O'Dwyer, B. (2006). Theorising accountability for NGO advocacy. *Accounting, Auditing & Accountability Journal, 19*(3): 349–376.

Van der Laan Smith, J., Adhikari, A., & Tondkar, R. H. (2005). Exploring differences in social disclosures internationally: A stakeholder perspective. *Journal of Accounting and Public Policy, 24*(2): 123–151.

Van der Laan Smith, J., Adhikari, A., Tondkar, R. H., & Andrews, R. L. (2011). The impact of corporate social disclosure on investment behavior: A cross-national study. *Journal of Accounting and Public Policy, 29*(2): 177–192.

Williams, S. J., & Adams, C. A. (2013). Moral accounting? Employee disclosures from a stakeholder accountability perspective. *Accounting, Auditing & Accountability Journal, 26*(3): 449–495.

Yongvanich, K., & Guthrie, J. (2005). Extended performance reporting: An examination of the Australian mining industry. *Accounting Forum, 29*(1): 103–119.

The Stakeholder Perspective in Strategic Management

DOUGLAS A. BOSSE
University of Richmond

TREY SUTTON
University of Richmond

Strategic management scholars commonly define the field by its focus on explaining a firm's competitive advantage (e.g., Rumelt, Schendel, & Teece, 1994; Nag, Hambrick & Chen, 2007). Competitive advantage, in turn, is commonly conceived of and measured in terms of rent or the residual financial resources available to shareholders after all other claimants have been paid (e.g., Rumelt, 1987; Coff, 1999). Over the last four decades, a rich collection of theories (e.g., agency theory, resource-based theory, the positioning view) has developed to explain the behaviors of general managers as they attempt to maximize shareholder returns.

Ed Freeman wrote his 1984 book, the seminal work in stakeholder theory, for a strategy audience. The core ideas of this theory, however, have not been widely recognized in strategic management theory. Stakeholder theory takes a broad perspective on the processes and outcomes of businesses. It considers how general managers behave in dynamic settings where many different stakeholders affect the outcomes of the firm and are, at the same time, affected by the actions of the firm. One concept that distinguishes stakeholder theory is the explicit acknowledgement that general managers are responsible to a variety of the firm's stakeholders, not just its shareholders. General managers who perceive such a responsibility do not view stakeholders as just a means to someone else's end; they recognize stakeholders are important ends in themselves. Responsibility is not an easy concept to maximize or even to compare. Instead, the general manager's responsibility in a range of situations is contestable, and the resulting scholarship often intersects with individual and organizational ethical concepts such as rights and justice, values, norms, and moral principles.

As the other chapters in this Handbook explain, the core ideas of stakeholder theory have been cultivated and nurtured into a body of theories with tremendous influence in a wide range of fields and disciplines. This chapter explores the ways stakeholder theory has been used to address issues of interest to strategic management scholars and highlights some of the influence stakeholder theory has had on questions relevant to strategic management.

This exploration illuminates new insights about stakeholder theory, strategic management, and future research questions. For example, the stakeholder perspective in strategic management is breathing new life into the conversation about what it means to achieve better firm-level performance. Rather than defining firm performance in terms of changes in shareholder value, some are conceiving of and measuring it as the change in total economic value created and appropriated by all of the firm's primary stakeholders (e.g., Garcia-Castro & Aguilera, 2015; Lieberman, Garcia-Castro, & Balasubramanian, 2017). This perspective supports the view that firms do not just compete in product markets or factor markets in isolation, but are in constant, simultaneous competition for all of their stakeholders. We suggest this work will continue to challenge and provoke shifts in the boundaries of strategic management.

Our process for examining this intersection started with selecting a frame that would delineate the scholarship we would include. As we explain in more detail below, we searched the premier strategic management journals for published work that refers to the implications of managing for stakeholders on firm-level performance outcomes. We did not include every paper that mentions stakeholders in a cursory way. Instead, we attempted to review every paper that employs stakeholder theory to better understand firm-level performance drivers while acknowledging ethical implications in some way.

A different way to examine the intersection of stakeholder theory and strategic management would be to focus on how aspects of stakeholder theory have been or might be integrated into other strategic management theories.[1] Such a review would need to establish its sampling frame by first specifying precisely which aspects of stakeholder theory it would examine. For example, it might look at how concepts like bounded self-interest, justice, or stakeholder rights change these theories. Although our review was not centered on agency theory, resource-based theory, and the positioning view, near the end of this chapter we briefly discuss how consideration for a larger set of stakeholders and the ethical issues that raises can alter the implications of these three important theories in strategic management.

In the next section, we describe our methodology for reviewing the journal articles that we believe represent the application and development of stakeholder theory as a theory for addressing questions relevant to the field of strategic management. We then present a new framework for making sense of the many constructs and relationships in the research at this intersection. We categorize the papers in this literature based on the paths that represent the relationships between pairs of constructs. We provide critiques and future research ideas throughout the review, and conclude with a general discussion of broad implications for stakeholder theory and strategic management.

Methodology

We performed a detailed search of premier management journals to identify a representative set of research articles that address the intersection of stakeholder theory and strategic management. We began by identifying the journals we would search. Because they are known to publish strategic

management research and have consistently high impact factors, we focused our search on *Academy of Management Journal, Academy of Management Review, Academy of Management Annals, Administrative Science Quarterly, Journal of Management, Journal of Management Studies, Organization Science*, and *Strategic Management Journal.*

Scholars use a variety of terms to refer to stakeholder theory, including "stakeholder perspective," "stakeholder approach," and "stakeholder theory," among others. To avoid the omission of stakeholder theory articles that employ a unique term for the theory, we performed a broad search of these journals, using only the word "stakeholder" as our search term.

Due to our broad search, the results included a large number of articles that had to be removed because they do not address stakeholder theory and strategic management. Some of these articles focus on ethics and corporate social responsibility, both of which are the subject of other chapters in this Handbook. Other articles were removed because they use the term stakeholder as a label for actors but do not engage stakeholder theory. We also removed articles that mention stakeholder theory only in a superficial sense. After manually reviewing and filtering our search results, we were left with seventy-one articles at top rated journals that represent the intersection of stakeholder theory and strategic management. While our search was not limited to certain years, these seventy-one articles were all published between 1992 and 2016. Table 12.1 presents the distribution of these articles across the searched journals and categorizes them by the nature of the article (e.g., an empirical study, a conceptual article, etc.).

Our next step was to record important information about each article. We decided to record the dependent constructs, independent constructs, mediators and moderators, geography and industry settings, methodology (conceptual, quantitative, qualitative, review), data, analytical method, and major findings. Both authors recorded these characteristics for the same five articles in a pilot process to ensure that recording rules were clear and being followed consistently. The authors then recorded the remaining sixty-six articles.

Table 12.1 Articles at the Intersection of Stakeholder Theory and Strategic Management

Journal	Empirical	Conceptual	Dialogue	Review	Total
Academy of Management Annals	0	0	0	1	1
Academy of Management Journal	10	0	0	0	10
Academy of Management Review	0	14	5	0	19
Administrative Science Quarterly	2	0	0	0	2
Journal of Management	1	0	0	1	2
Journal of Management Studies	3	4	0	1	8
Organization Science	4	6	0	0	10
Strategic Management Journal	13	6	0	0	19
Total	33	30	5	3	71

Finally, we developed an organizing framework by grouping the papers according to the construct relationships each attempted to explain. To do so, we first identified common groups of constructs employed in the papers. For example, we grouped all constructs related to firm-level performance outcomes (e.g., profitability, sales growth, employment growth) under "firm performance." Another construct group represented in this literature is "stakeholder orientation, normative core, and general policies." After establishing all of the construct groups, we created a list of all the possible paths (i.e., relationships) between the groups. We then coded each paper to one or more of the paths. In total, these seventy-one articles represent seven paths among unique pairs of explanatory and dependent construct groups. For example, we identified one path leading from the firm's "stakeholder orientation, normative core, and general policies" as an explanatory construct group to "firm performance" as the dependent construct group. Figure 12.1 illustrates the seven paths in a comprehensive framework. Table 12.2 presents the constructs employed in each path with example variables for each construct and example papers that propose and explain the relationship in each path.

One of the challenges in organizing the literature is the considerable variance in the level of detail with which stakeholder management is explained. Some earlier studies invoke broad constructs such as multiple stakeholder orientation (Greenley &

Foxall, 1997). Though Greenley and Foxall (1997) discuss the various conceptual components of multiple stakeholder orientation, such as planning and firm mission, the study does not detail the relationships between actions within the firm (e.g., Does the firm's mission affect its inclusion of stakeholders in planning activities?).

More recent studies have begun to explain stakeholder management at a finer level. For example, de Luque, Washburn, and Waldman (2008) present a mediated model of the relationship between stakeholder values and firm performance. The authors posit a relationship between stakeholder values and visionary leadership, a relationship that corresponds to Path 2 in Figure 12.1. A firm's stakeholder values represent the normative core, and leadership style represents the firm's behavior in response to the values. Further, de Luque et al. (2008) propose relationships between visionary leadership and increased effort by employees (Path 6) and between increased employee effort and firm performance (Path 7).

de Luque et al. (2008) is important for its detailed analysis of causal relationships within the firm (e.g., the firm's stakeholder values lead to visionary leadership), which demonstrates the necessity of distinguishing a firm's normative core from its resulting treatment of stakeholders. The causal sequence is important if scholars are to distill the research for deeper understanding and developing actionable guidance for practitioners. For the purposes of our framework, we treat a firm's actions as responsive only

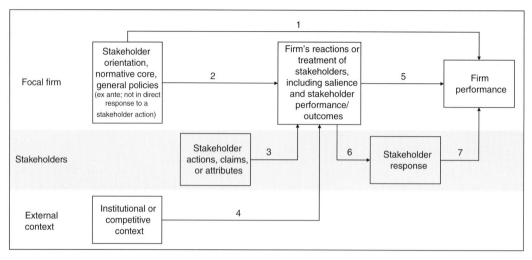

Figure 12.1 A framework for organizing the literature at intersection of stakeholder theory and strategic management

Table 12.2 Representative constructs and papers for each relationship in the framework

Independent Construct Group	Path Number	Dependent Construct Group	Example Papers
Stakeholder orientation, normative core, general policies Example variables – Sensitivity to stakeholder groups – Governance structures – Firm strategy – Stakeholder relations – Enterprise logic – Organizational architecture – Ethics training – Firm values	Path 1 Path 2	**Firm performance** Example variables – Profitability – Sales growth – Persistence of performance **Firm's reaction or treatment of stakeholders** Example variables – Attention to stakeholders – Application of ethics – Support for stakeholder groups – Perceived stakeholder salience – Firm response to activism	– Donaldson & Preston (1995) – Jones (1995) – Berman, et al. (1999) – Choi & Wang (2009) – Buysse & Verbeke (2003) – de Luque, Washburn, & Waldman (2008) – Adams, Licht, & Sagiv (2011) – Crilly & Sloan (2014)
Stakeholder actions, claims, or attributes Example variables – Stakeholder power, legitimacy, urgency – Stakeholder network characteristics – Stakeholder pressure	Path 3		– Hill & Jones (1992) – Mitchell, Agle, & Wood (1997) – Rowley (1997) – Eesley & Lenox (2006) – Darnall, Henriques, & Sadorsky (2010)
Institutional or competitive context Example variables – Industry regulation – Community characteristics	Path 4		– Luoma & Goodstein (1999) – Kassinis & Vafeas (2006)

Table 12.2 (cont.)

Independent Construct Group	Path Number	Dependent Construct Group	Example Papers
Firm's reaction or treatment of stakeholders Example variables – Customer service – Perceived salience of stakeholder groups – Announcement of withdrawal from conflict zone – Communication with stakeholders – Fairness vs. arms-length treatment of stakeholders – Monitoring of employees	Path 5 Path 6	**Firm performance** Example variables – Abnormal returns – Profitability – Social performance **Stakeholder response** Example variables – Likelihood of supporting a venture – Continuing support – Effort	– Meznar, Nigh & Kwok (1994) – Agle, Mitchell & Sonnenfeld (1999) – Ogden & Watson (1999) – Choi & Shepherd (2005) – Pajunen (2006) – Bridoux & Stoelhurst (2014)
Stakeholder response Example variables – Reciprocal reward/punishment – Effort – Information sharing – Stakeholder support	Path 7	**Firm performance** Example variables – Profitability – Abnormal returns	– King & Soule (2007) – Bosse, Phillips, & Harrison (2009) – Harrison, Bosse, & Phillips (2010) – Henisz, Dorobantu, & Nartey (2014)

when the paper makes the responsiveness clear, as in the case of de Luque et al. (2008) proposing that visionary leadership is an outcome of stakeholder values. We return to the case of within-firm cause-and-effect relationships in the discussion because we see this as an area in need of greater clarity.

In the following sections, we briefly address each of these relationships to make sense of the work that has been done so far.

Path 1: The Link between Stakeholder Orientation and Firm Performance

Path 1 is the most abstract path in this literature. The papers in this group explain the link between firm performance and the firm's *ex ante* stakeholder orientation, normative core, or general policies that are not in direct response to particular stakeholders. These papers provide some of the conceptual pillars of stakeholder theory – pillars that have made and continue to make the theory polemical. From this distance, it seems that

stakeholder theorists have been challenging the mainstream strategy conversation for over twenty years.

Conceptual, Theory-Building Work Directly Relevant to Strategic Management

Diving into the heart of strategic management literature, stakeholder theory contrasts with the overwhelmingly popular organizational economics theories on contracting (Jones, 1995). Agency theory, transaction cost theory, and team production theory each propose solutions to typical contracting problems that arise from tensions of mistrust and competition between transacting parties. Rather than writing more complete contracts to control the other party's *ex post* bad behavior, logic associated with stakeholder theory suggests contracting based on mutual trust and cooperation can substitute for contracting and ultimately provide competitive advantage (Jones, 1995). This thinking recalls earlier economists who pointed out that markets cannot form or operate reliably without trust and cooperation (e.g., Adam Smith, 1776).

Another idea takes direct aim at the contemporary core of strategy literature by stating that managers serve the firm rather than individual stockholders (Donaldson & Preston, 1995). Recognizing firms are autonomous economic actors in the eyes of the law and society, this theme that managers are responsible to more than just one group of stakeholders is foundational in stakeholder theory (Freeman, 1984). Donaldson and Preston go on to articulate how scholars can use stakeholder theory as a descriptive theory, an instrumental theory, and a normative theory. Of particular distinction among strategy theories, normative implications arise when stakeholders (1) are identified by their interest in the firm (rather than vice versa) and (2) have a right to be treated as ends in themselves rather than means to someone else's objective (Donaldson & Preston, 1995). This seemingly simple normative argument was, and remains, contentious in the strategy literature (e.g., Sundaram & Inkpen, 2004).

At least since Donaldson and Preston's (1995) taxonomy located normative considerations at the core of stakeholder theory, scholars have been developing applications of the normative core construct (Purnell & Freeman, 2012). A firm's normative core is an abstract account of its basic functions and its responsibilities to stakeholders (Freeman, 1994) and is, in practice, reflected in "the assumptions and values imbedded in the way managers talk about how value is created among stakeholders" (Purnell & Freeman, 2012: 109). Example normative cores discussed in the literature include Kantian capitalism (Evan & Freeman, 1993), personal projects (Freeman & Gilbert, 1988), ethics of care (Wicks, Freeman, & Gilbert, 1994), fairness (Phillips, 1997), and libertarian (Freeman & Phillips 2002).

Another conceptual pillar of stakeholder theory in the context of strategic management is that ethical firms can be viable and productive in competitive markets, a view that converges normative and instrumental perspectives (Jones & Wicks, 1999). One implication of this view is that measuring firm performance using conventional financial measures does not adequately recognize that all stakeholders have intrinsic value (e.g., human rights, dignity). A recurring theme in this literature is that traditional accounting and stock market measures of firm performance inadequately capture value created for all the relevant stakeholders.

As these ideas provoked some debate, one enduring argument arose called the integration thesis (Freeman, 1999). This thesis holds that facts and values are indistinguishable by both managers and scholars; there is no such thing as value-free or value-neutral theory. Therefore, any delineation of normative, descriptive, and instrumental theories is artificial. This view is not widely observable in the larger strategic management literature. The integration thesis notwithstanding, additions to the stakeholder literature still occasionally specify how they contribute to these three "branches" of the theory (e.g., Crilly, 2013).

Debating the Purposes of the Firm

Another volley of ideas at the intersection of stakeholder theory and strategic management involved the argument that the only purpose of a public corporation is to create wealth for shareholders (Sundaram & Inkpen, 2004). To simplify the job of explaining managerial decision-making, some scholars assume non-shareholder stakeholders have fixed claims and fully specified contracts. It is also common for these scholars to claim that managers cannot juggle multiple goals so they must prioritize the creation of residual claims for shareholders over all other stakeholders' interests (Sundaram & Inkpen, 2004). Bypassing these assumptions, the view that firms exist to enrich shareholders can be seen as a special case of stakeholder theory where firms attract and retain stakeholders who agree to prioritize the interests of one stakeholder group (shareholders) over all others (Freeman, Wicks, & Parmar, 2004). Freeman et al. ask, "How else could managers create shareholder value than by creating products and services that customers are willing to buy, offering jobs that employees are willing to fill, building relationships with suppliers that companies are eager to have, and being good citizens in the community?" (2004: 366). They then clarify that stakeholder theory allows for many possible answers to the questions "What is the purpose of our company?" and "What kinds of relationships will we need with our stakeholders to realize that purpose?" (2004: 368). Although some scholars argue this is a poorly formed debate (Freeman, et al., 2010), others continue arguing that shareholder value maximization is the only legitimate objective function for a firm (Smith & Rönnegard, 2014).

The conversation about corporate objectives has also recently dusted off and expanded the concept of enterprise-level strategy that Freeman (1984) used (Crilly, 2013). A concept actively addressed by early strategy scholars (e.g., Schendel & Hofer, 1979) but then largely ignored outside the stakeholder literature for thirty years, enterprise strategy is another bridge between mainstream strategy research and stakeholder management. Enterprise-level strategy draws attention to the firm's role in the broader economic, social, and political environments – and reminds us that firms are among the most powerful drivers of change in these three realms of society. Earlier generations of strategy scholars accepted the broader responsibilities this implies (Barnard, 1938; Drucker, 1954).

Empirical Work in Path 1

Over time, the empirical literature in Path 1 has grown increasingly sophisticated in both theory and methods. The early tests all find support for the general hypothesis that firms serving multiple stakeholder groups realize higher financial performance (e.g., Berman, et al., 1999). The strength of this relationship, however, can vary based on the level of competitive hostility in the industry (Greenley & Foxall, 1997). Firm-level success increases with the inclusion of stakeholders in key decision-making processes and the use of governance systems that can be adapted to specific stakeholder contributions (Kochan & Rubinstein, 2000).

Maintaining good relations with nonfinancial stakeholders helps firms sustain positive financial performance over time (measured as ROA and Tobin's Q), and these good relations are even more effective in turning around firms with poor financial performance (Choi & Wang, 2009).

Extending the argument further, corporate diversification strategies generate more rent for all stakeholders when the owners of the firm form close ties with the firm and hold onto their shares longer, but these same diversification strategies generate more rent for shareholders when the owners maintain more transactional, arms-length relationships with the firm (David, et al., 2010).

Discussion

This path serves as an ideal entry point for strategy scholars who are seeking to learn the basic conceptual foundations of stakeholder theory. The papers in this path provide the overarching arguments for why firms that attend to the interests of multiple stakeholders generate more overall value. In this way, this path helps to distinguish stakeholder theory from other strategic management theories. While a significant portion of the strategy literature focuses on ideal transaction governance designs between the firm and actors that can be recognized as stakeholders, stakeholder theory places more focus on the complex relationships between and among these parties. Trust and cooperation take a larger role than mistrust and competition. A related difference is the concept that the firm is itself an entity that can be served, rather than just a vehicle for creating wealth for its owners. The "firm" might be considered shorthand for the network of stakeholders it represents. A final distinction is that firms can demonstrate any one of a variety of ethical philosophies in the course of engaging their stakeholders while at the same time realizing high economic performance.

To the extent researchers choose to sustain the "shareholder vs. stakeholder" debate, we believe future arguments will benefit from precise articulations of firms' stakeholder orientation or normative core. Stakeholder theory does not advocate that all firms adopt the same type. We also hope to see more research about heterogeneity in enterprise-level strategy. More firms appear to be pursuing profit margin in order to achieve a larger mission for society, rather than as an end in itself (Leaf, 2017). To what extent are firms able to generate outcomes that are consistent with their enterprise strategies? Questions like this will help the field identify additional contingencies that affect the central proposition of Path 1.

Finally, before moving on to the other paths in our framework, we point out that much of the future work linking stakeholder management to firm performance will arguably be done using more granular explanatory concepts. The phenomena captured by stakeholder orientation, normative core, and general policies that are used independent of specific stakeholders have largely been drilled down another level to the firm's reactions to or treatment of specific stakeholders, as reflected in the remaining paths in Figure 1.

Path 2: The Link between Stakeholder Orientation and the Firm's Reactions to or Treatment of Stakeholders

Stakeholder theory calls attention to the fact that different firms can choose to have different kinds of relationships with their stakeholders (Freeman et al., 2004). The papers in Path 2 provide insights about how a firm's stakeholder orientation affects the way it treats its stakeholders. For example, managers prioritize various stakeholders' interests based on the firm's environmental management strategy and institutional context. Environmentally proactive firms perceive many stakeholder groups to be important, and environmentally reactive firms perceive only the media to be important (Henriques & Sadorsky, 1999). Among firms that use one of the three environmental strategies identified by Hart (1995) [reactive, pollution prevention, and environmental leadership], pollution preventers are more concerned with regulatory stakeholders than are firms using one of the other strategies (Buysse & Verbeke, 2003). Environmental leaders, on the other hand, seem to be concerned about a variety of stakeholders beyond regulators, and community stakeholder pressure positively affects environmental performance at the plant level (Buysse & Verbeke, 2003).

Other articles in this path explore the relationships between firm governance and stakeholder management as well as the effects of managers' individual differences on the firm's stakeholder management

practices. Governance choices can directly influence the firm's stakeholder management approach. Given the positive relationship between stakeholder management and firm financial performance, it is notable that boards of directors at large publicly traded firms do not typically reward CEOs for attending to a wide range of stakeholders' interests in the short term (Coombs & Gilley, 2005). This insight is ripe for further explanation. At a more granular level, directors' personal values help explain the decisions they make that affect stakeholders. Directors who value power, achievement, and self-direction tend to prioritize shareholders over other types of stakeholders (Adams, Licht, & Sagiv, 2011).

A common thread among these articles is the conclusion that strategy choices can drive a firm's approach to stakeholders. Noticing that much of the conventional thinking suggests characteristics of the external environment drive top management to focus on certain stakeholders, why do firms in similar environments engage with stakeholders differently? One hypothesis is that managerial cognition affects a firm's attention to stakeholders by influencing the firm's dominant stakeholder logic (Crilly & Sloan, 2012). Another construct used in this path is organizational architecture. A firm's organizational architecture helps explain how some firms get their middle managers to provide better attention to the stakeholders for whom they are responsible (Crilly & Sloan, 2014). A "cascaded control" architecture emphasizes standardization and control across managers who are stakeholder generalists. A "guided autonomy" architecture focuses each manager's attention on a narrow range of stakeholders most salient to their part of the business. Managers in the guided autonomy architecture are collectively more effective serving the firm's stakeholders as a matter of routine (Crilly & Sloan, 2014). Firms implement these organizational architectures, in part, by choosing the corporate governance mechanisms they will use. The board of directors, managerial incentives, threat of takeover, and legal context all play roles in helping resolve diverging interests of stakeholders and managers (Kock, Santalo, & Diestre, 2012).

Some firms have a code of ethics that represents their ex ante orientation toward stakeholders. However, what the firm says in its code of ethics and how the managers actually behave can be different things. Executives' decisions better reflect their official code of ethics when they feel more pressure from market stakeholders (e.g., suppliers, customers, shareholders), when they believe this behavior improves the firm's image to both internal and external stakeholders, and when the code has been spread widely through internal training (Stevens, et al., 2005). Interestingly, pressure from government actors does not seem to have a unique effect on the use of ethics codes in decision-making.

Another contribution to understanding how firms' ex ante orientation affects their stakeholders' outcomes builds on the concept of organizational identity orientation. Employees believe their firms are motivated to consistently treat stakeholders on an individualistic, relational, or collectivistic basis (Brickson, 2007). Each of these three organizational identity orientations is associated with a range of stakeholder outcomes such as level of wealth, innovative and low-priced products, level of personalization, understanding, empathy, social capital, and social change (Brickson, 2007). This idiosyncratic list of dependent variables shows the recurring challenge of measuring firm performance in ways relevant to managing for stakeholders.

In sum, researchers have tried to examine this path from a variety of perspectives and using a variety of constructs. Firms differ in many ways that affect how they manage their stakeholders. Some of these are strategies examined elsewhere in the strategy literature. The existing range of explanatory constructs in this path includes environmental strategy, governance choices, managerial cognition and dominant logic, organizational architecture, codes of ethics, and organizational identity orientation. We believe future research will also look at international strategies and alliance portfolio strategies, for example, as explanatory variables in this path. The range of dependent constructs is equally broad. We believe this path is ripe for more exploration and will eventually benefit from a consolidation or structured ordering of theoretical constructs.

Path 3: The Link between Stakeholder Actions, Claims, or Attributes and the Firm's Reactions to or Treatment of Stakeholders

Path 3 captures a large number of the articles at the intersection of stakeholder theory and strategic management. A significant portion of this literature focuses on determining which stakeholders are most salient under a range of conditions. Clearly, strategy is contextual and stakeholders are context, so it is important to clarify which stakeholder interests deserve the most attention at a given point in time.

It is common in the strategy literature to view value creation and distribution as a two-stage process (Brandenburger & Stuart, 1996). From that perspective, stakeholders' attributes can arguably affect how much of the firm's value they appropriate in the second stage. For example, stakeholders with great bargaining power may demand larger distributions so the firm's financial performance appears inferior even if it possesses a competitive advantage (Coff, 1999). Stakeholder bargaining power depends on such things as the ability of stakeholders to act collectively, their access to information, the cost of replacing the stakeholder, and the stakeholder's cost of exiting (Coff, 1999).

A different perspective on "who and what really counts" in stakeholder theory refers to the salience of stakeholders. Salience is the degree to which managers give priority to competing stakeholder claims. Much of the work in this path expands on the idea that salience is collectively determined by three factors: the stakeholder's power to influence the firm, the legitimacy of the stakeholder's relationship with the firm, and the urgency of the stakeholder's claim on the firm (Mitchell, Agle, & Wood, 1997). Subsequent tests found the perceived power, legitimacy, and urgency of a stakeholder group's claims are positively related to that stakeholder group's salience (e.g., Agle, Mitchell, & Sonnenfeld, 1999).

A more encompassing perspective on determining how managers prioritize stakeholders argues that it is not enough to look only at dyadic relationships between each stakeholder and the firm. Instead, stakeholder theory needs to consider the simultaneous influence of multiple stakeholders by incorporating insights from network theory to examine how the structure of a firm's stakeholder relationships affects its response to stakeholder pressures (Rowley, 1997). These arguments predict how a firm responds to the pressures of multiple stakeholders depending on the density of the firm's network and the firm's centrality in that network.

Another potential factor in determining stakeholder salience is how the firm's relationship with each of the primary stakeholder groups varies with the life-cycle stage of the firm (Jawahar & McLaughlin, 2001). Largely based on resource dependence logic, different types of stakeholders may be more critical to a firm depending on where it is in the organizational life cycle. This theory treats all of the stakeholders in a given category (e.g., customer, employee, etc.) that same; it does not account for differences among managers or individual stakeholders.

Empirical studies in this path find that firms are most likely to respond to stakeholders' requests for environmental change when some of the stakeholders employ a withholding strategy and others employ usage strategies (Sharma & Henriques, 2005); when activist secondary stakeholders are powerful and legitimate (Eesley & Lenox, 2006); when managers understand the issue and consider it urgent and manageable (Julian, Ofori-Dankwa, & Justis, 2008); and when a firm is rated poorly for its stakeholder treatment (Chatterji & Toffel, 2010). Managers who respond to stakeholders' requirements or expectations about the natural environment seem to attach the most importance to regulatory stakeholders and corporate governance stakeholders (managers, directors) (Murillo-Luna, Garces-Ayerbe, & Rivera-Torres, 2008). Firm size can also affect responsiveness to environmental pressures. As firm size increases, the positive impact that value chain, internal, and regulatory stakeholders have gets weaker. The explanation for this moderating effect includes smaller firms' limited resources, simplified decision-making processes, and greater innovation propensity (Darnal, Henriques, & Sadorsky, 2010). When there are competing stakeholder interests,

managers are more likely to figure out their responses as they go and as they test their own perceptions of the environment against those of their peers (Crilly, Zollo, & Hansen, 2012).

Parsimony can present a particular challenge for scholars who write at the intersection of stakeholder theory and strategic management because the theory calls for attending to the unique interests of specific stakeholders but strategic management is largely focused on the firm level of analysis. The role-primacy approach in the stakeholder literature assumes all the stakeholders in a particular role, such as customers or employees, have similar interests (Wolfe & Putler, 2002). However, like the recognition that firm rivalry within strategic groups can be stronger than between groups (Porter, 1980), two subgroups within different role-based stakeholder groups might have more similar priorities than either subgroup has with others in their group (Wolfe & Putler, 2002). One compromise is to group stakeholders that are relatively homogenous in their interests, like the way marketing scholars segment customers (Freeman, 1984).

In an example of research that considers stakeholder diversity, Kassinis and Vafeas (2006) ask how the internal heterogeneity of stakeholder groups affects the firm's response to stakeholder pressures, as measured by its toxic chemicals emissions. They show community factors (income, population density, pro-environmental preferences) are associated with decreased emissions, but regulatory factors, interestingly, are not. Although this study does not test for heterogeneity within each community, the authors conclude firms adjust their environmental practices based on many community stakeholder characteristics, including how dependent the firm is in that situation.

Considered together, paths 2 and 3 show that the extent to which certain stakeholders are salient and have their interests served is a function of both the firm's ex ante orientation or approach to stakeholders (broadly) and the stakeholders' actions, claims, or attributes. It is not one or the other, but both categories of constructs that matter. The strategic management literature on governance choice is also concerned with how firms interact with stakeholders, but uses different assumptions and constructs. Future research will likely create more bridges between literatures and theories that seek to explain similar dependent variables. The next path in our framework adds one more construct category: the external context.

Path 4: The Link between the Institutional or Competitive Context and the Firm's Reactions to or Treatment of Stakeholders

This path is distinguished from Path 3 because it explores the external influence of institutional or competitive context on the firm's treatment of stakeholders. Representative of this path, Luoma and Goodstein (1999) asks how institutional factors influence stakeholder representation on the board of directors at a sample of 224 NYSE traded firms over a ten-year period. Their results suggest the legal environment, industry regulation, and firm size all affect non-shareholder representation on the board, but do not affect non-shareholder representatives' board committee assignments. They also conclude the legal context and firm size both influence the formation of board committees to address stakeholder-oriented issues. We suggest additional research on the links between external context and stakeholder treatment may be particularly interesting to strategic management scholars.

In one sense, stakeholder theory challenges strategic management scholars to open up their field of view with respect to who and what really matters to a firm. In another sense, however, stakeholder theory's primary focus on parties that are already directly affecting or affected by the firm is a limiting view. The small number of studies in this path might signal an opportunity to broaden stakeholder theory in the context of strategic management by considering more carefully the role of the external environment. The chapter in this Handbook addressing the intersection of stakeholder theory and international business might point the reader to open questions in this domain.

Path 5: The Link between How the Firm Reacts to its Stakeholders and the Firm's Performance

Path 5 in Figure 12.1 corresponds to the direct effects of the firm's treatment of specific stakeholders on firm performance. Stakeholder theorists have long argued that firms can establish competitive advantage by creating trusting relationships with stakeholders instead of creating short-sighted, transactional, and opportunistic relationships (Freeman, 1984; Jones, 1995). However, Wicks, Berman, and Jones (1999) argue that instead of constantly striving for higher levels of trust, managers should aim to build "optimal" trust. The authors explain their term:

> Optimal trust exists when one creates (and maintains) prudent economic relationships biased by a willingness to trust. That is, agents need to have stable and ongoing commitments to trust so that they share affect-based belief in moral character sufficient to make a leap of faith, but they should also exercise care in determining whom to trust, to what extent, and in what capacity. (1999: 103)

Investing too much in trust can lead to opportunistic behavior by untrustworthy stakeholders, but underinvesting in trust may lead otherwise trustworthy stakeholders to be suspicious of the firm.

The work in this path has helped explain what happens to a firm's performance when it responds to stakeholder pressure. For example, social opposition to South Africa's apartheid system grew between the early 1970s and the early 1990s, so many publicly traded US firms withdrew from South Africa during that period. The announcement of a withdrawal from South Africa was associated with negative abnormal shareholder returns, and the effect was stronger for firms that announced early (Meznar, Nigh, & Kwok, 1994). Similarly, social issue participation is negatively related to shareholder value even though stakeholder management is positively related to shareholder value (Hillman & Keim, 2001). One takeaway from this path, then, is the importance of attending to the right stakeholders at the right time.

We suggest the papers in this path show the need for restraint in stakeholder management. Managing for stakeholders is beneficial, but attending to some stakeholder claims or trusting too much can harm the firm's market performance. Managers need to reassess the firm's priorities as stakeholder relationships change over time. We know relatively little about how stakeholder relationships and stakeholder management change over time. Therefore, we consider longitudinal exploration of stakeholder management to be an important area for future research.

Paths 6 and 7: The Links from How a Firm Treats Stakeholders to How Those Stakeholders React and the Impact on Firm Performance

The research discussed in the prior section attempts to establish links between a firm's actions and its performance. However, it seems this link must be mediated by the responses of those stakeholders most affected by the actions. For a managerial decision to improve performance, primary stakeholders (i.e., those who transact with the firm) must contribute more resources to the firm or extract fewer resources, *ceteris paribus*. A growing body of research explains how firm actions lead to beneficial stakeholder responses, which are the relationships represented by paths 6 and 7 in Figure 1.

Some research examines what firms do to increase the likelihood a stakeholder will support a new venture or remain engaged with a firm. A related question is how the resulting stakeholder engagement affects firm performance. One approach to exploring these questions borrows the concepts of perceived psychological bonds from social psychology. At least four types of perceived psychological relationship bonds can attach stakeholders to firms, and characteristics of those relationships can drive stakeholders to engage in pro-relationship behaviors that affect firm performance (Bosse & Coughlan, 2016). The empirical evidence shows that stakeholders are drawn to organizations by factors such as firm age, legitimacy, accountability, and strategic flexibility (Choi & Shepherd, 2005), and they remain engaged with the firm when management communicates

openly and frequently (Pajunen, 2006). Increased stakeholder engagement has market performance advantages (Henisz, Dorobantu, & Nartey, 2014).

As discussed above, stakeholder theorists have consistently argued that trust is critical to keeping stakeholders engaged (Jones, 1995). All stakeholders look for an alignment between the firm and the stakeholder's values, but beyond that similarity, different stakeholder groups look for different signals of trustworthiness (Pirson & Malhotra, 2011). Thus, managers should focus on driving stakeholder identification with the firm, but tailor the signals to each stakeholder group.

Scholars have reframed some of these questions to explain not just if stakeholders engage but *why* and *how* stakeholders react to firm behavior in ways that affect firm performance. Instead of assuming that stakeholders are purely self-interested, Bosse, Phillips, and Harrison (2009) build on research demonstrating that self-interest is bounded by norms of fairness and reciprocity (Jolls, Sunstein, & Thaler, 1998; Fehr & Gächter, 2000). A firm's treatment of stakeholders can trigger positive or negative reciprocity. Firms that treat stakeholders fairly (unfairly) generate increased (decreased) performance as stakeholders reward (punish) the firm for its behavior (Bosse et al., 2009). Stakeholders may reward the firm by sharing detailed information about their utility functions (Harrison, Bosse, & Phillips, 2010) or by increasing their effort (de Luque et al., 2008).

However, some firms appear to achieve high performance without adopting particularly fair or just stakeholder management practices. Bridoux and Stoelhurst (2014) address these cases, as well as the case of reciprocity, by relaxing the assumption that stakeholders are homogenous in terms of their perceived justice norms. Some stakeholders may prefer an arm's-length relationship characterized by bargaining power while others respond better to relationships characterized by fairness and justice. In this model, firm performance is improved when the firm matches its stakeholder interactions with its stakeholders' preferences.

As mentioned previously, viewing value creation and distribution separately supports the argument that firm performance is affected not just by the actions a firm takes, but also by the value that is appropriated by stakeholders (Coff, 1999). However, some research challenges the assumption that value creation and appropriation are unrelated. One taxonomy demonstrates how the value appropriated by a particular stakeholder may affect the total value *created* by the firm (Garcia-Castro & Aguilera, 2015). This framework supports some of the findings that show how firms can increase the value created for multiple stakeholders simultaneously (Ogden & Watson, 1999).

Implicit in the research discussed above is the idea that adversarial stakeholder interactions diminish firm performance, a phenomenon that has received attention in a few studies. Scholars have explained when and how stakeholders will mobilize, and have demonstrated the performance effects of contentious mobilization. Stakeholders mobilize when the firm violates their interests or threatens a stakeholder group's identity (Rowley & Moldoveanu, 2003). In situations where there is little interdependence between the firm and the stakeholder or when the stakeholders are powerful, stakeholders will tend to withhold resources from the firm (Frooman, 1999). Otherwise, the stakeholder will attempt to engage with the firm by making requests for the firm to change. These requests occasionally take the form of protests and boycotts, which tend to negatively affect a firm's market performance (King & Soule, 2007).

Clearly, stakeholders respond to how they are treated by the firm and how they see the firm treating other parties. We see the potential for significant future research in these paths to better understand the complex behaviors that affect the content and nature of human relationships that both create and destroy value. Stakeholders' expectations of ethics, duties, and norms surely differ in different industries, countries, and regions. This presents substantial challenges for multinational corporations, and therefore, interesting research questions for strategy scholars.

Critiques and Future Directions

Our understanding of stakeholder management has improved with the numerous recent applications of stakeholder theory to strategic management. Still,

we see opportunities to broaden our collective understanding in important areas. The framework in Figure 12.1 that emerged in the collection of papers we reviewed is as interesting for the categories of constructs it includes as for those that are missing. Categories of constructs in more mainstream strategy research include, for example, the nature of knowledge, firm capabilities, competitive context, organizational form and the boundaries of organizations, and institutional and legal regimes. As more strategic management scholars begin to explore the potential of stakeholder theory to address their research questions, we expect to see more of these construct categories in studies that acknowledge aspects of stakeholder theory. If we are correct, the literature ten years from now at this intersection will reveal a more complex framework of constructs and relationships than the one we found.

Adding complexity to a framework like this might reflect a natural progression of science. We mentioned earlier that some studies examined the effects of broadly conceived constructs such as "multiple stakeholder orientation." More recent research, such as de Luque et al. (2008), provide a detailed explanation of how the firm's values or normative core are translated into firm performance through various mediating mechanisms. Stakeholder values may lead to visionary leadership, which itself may lead to greater employee effort and ultimately to improved firm performance (de Luque, et al., 2008). We applaud this trend toward more a more granular explanation of causal relationships and encourage more work of this type. When managers act, they are typically triggering other actions by employees; actions that affect other stakeholders. What are those major actions and reactions that make stakeholder management successful?

Relatedly, a focus on the stakeholders themselves could contribute more to the study of strategic management. Firm actions are translated into firm performance by stakeholders, and stakeholders may respond in a variety of ways. For example, several conditions explain when stakeholders give greater effort to the firm or reveal important information to the firm, respectively (Bosse, et al., 2009; Harrison, et al., 2010;

Bridoux & Stoelhorst, 2014). The universe of possible stakeholder actions and the conditions that lead to them is clearly quite large.

As noted in an earlier section, stakeholder theorists often emphasize the long-term benefits of stakeholder management. However, what the literature does not yet seem to explain is how stakeholder relationships change over time. Behavioral theories may provide an effective toolkit for addressing this phenomenon. Research has consistently demonstrated, for example, that perceptions are dependent upon the reference used as a point of comparison (Kahneman & Tversky, 1979; Kahneman, 1992), perceptions of fairness can be influenced by framing (Kahneman, Knetsch, & Thaler, 1986), and reference points adjust with experience (Chen & Rao, 2002). Are firms rewarded for having a high level of fairness compared to competitors or for consistently increasing the level of fairness with which they treat their stakeholders? Stakeholder theorists will need to incorporate competitors more explicitly in their research to answer these questions, and they may need to rethink what defines a competitor. Competition for employees, for example, may be driven by geography as much as by product markets. Similarly, stakeholder evaluations about fairness and justice are based on information about the firm, which is ordinarily obtained gradually (Ambrose & Cropanzano, 2003). How do firms manage the flow of information to stakeholders over time to provide them with an accurate idea about the firm's behaviors?

Stakeholder theory also holds great promise for contributing to some of the phenomenologically driven research in strategic management, such as scholarship in diversification, mergers and acquisitions, and competitive dynamics, among others. The focal phenomena in these literatures involve numerous stakeholder interactions and could therefore be usefully explained with stakeholder theory. In a recent review of the literature on turnarounds, Trahms, Ndofor, and Sirmon (2013: 1294) explain the situation well:

> Preliminary evidence suggests that stakeholders play a key role in decline and turnaround scenarios. However, given the fragmented empirical examination of the stakeholders within the turnaround setting, this area of research could benefit

from the application of stakeholder theory to present a more robust understanding of how the divergent interests and claims of stakeholders are manifested and sorted during decline and how this process affects turnaround outcome."

The integration of stakeholder theory and nonmarket strategy may also yield important insights for firm performance. Nonmarket strategy is concerned with influencing political and social actors (Doh, Lawton, & Rajwani, 2012). That influence is often intended to shape "the rules of the game" (North, 1990), which partially shape a firm's interactions with its stakeholders. The removal of regulations, for example, may require stakeholders to transition from a monitoring-based relationship with the firm to a trust-based relationship. Such changes in stakeholder relationships are likely to have varying degrees of success and, thus, varying impacts on firm performance. Nonmarket strategy represents an indirect mechanism for managing stakeholders, and we need to understand more completely how it affects a firm's relationships with its stakeholders and a firm's performance.

Finally, stakeholder theory, and strategic management more broadly, are in need of better definitions and measures of firm performance. The widespread reliance on financial measures of performance ignores the fact that financial performance and competitive advantage are not perfectly correlated (Coff, 1999). Further, we need to heed Jones and Wicks' (1999) call to acknowledge stakeholders' intrinsic value when considering firm performance. Stakeholder theorists may need to refine what the "instrumental" in instrumental stakeholder theory represents and continue exploring new measures of performance accordingly.

Other Strategic Management Theories and the Stakeholder Perspective

How have aspects of stakeholder theory been integrated into other strategic management theories? In this section we provide a very brief discussion of recent and possible contributions to agency theory, resource-based theory, and the positioning view. Each of these theories can be reexamined and reimagined to align them more closely with stakeholder theory by working through the implications of a change in one or more of their assumptions.

Agency theory provides insights about how firms can design governance in ways that maximize shareholder value. One key assumption at the core of agency theory is that all economic actors are exclusively self-interested. The standard advice based on agency theory is that firms should design governance in ways that limit their agents' self-serving behavior. Changing just this one assumption so that it more closely aligns with the concepts underlying stakeholder theory results in a substantial insight about how to design governance (Bosse & Phillips, 2016). If actors are boundedly self-interested, instead of exclusively self-interested, they positively reciprocate toward the firm when they experience something better than they expected. However, they will negatively reciprocate when they experience an exchange with the firm that is worse than expected. The implication is that firms maximize value by designing governance in ways that initiate positive, and not negative, reciprocity from their agents (Bosse & Phillips, 2016). Future research might reexamine agency theory in other ways that align with stakeholder theory. For example, the agency theory assumption that social welfare is maximized when firms maximize shareholder value diverges from stakeholder theory logic.

Resource-based theory (RBT) has traditionally assumed that shareholders are a firm's only residual claimant. Changing that assumption to align with stakeholder theory would change RBT's explanation about how firms create competitive advantage. For example, a standard argument of RBT is that firms should exploit factor market imperfections by negotiating the lowest possible price required to access a resource of given quality from actors in the factor market. Assuming all stakeholders are residual claimants – and the related assumption that they provide varying levels of effort or quality ex post – leads to different logic (Bosse & Harrison, 2011). The firm might realize competitive advantage, all else equal, when it provides its factor market stakeholders with value propositions that exceed their reservation value proposition by a noticeable amount (Harrison & Bosse, 2013). This logic stretches the focus of the

theory from one or more spot transactions to the ongoing relationships it has with factor market stakeholders who, like shareholders, can help the firm reduce search costs by demonstrating their preference to remain engaged with the firm. Future research in the RBT tradition might explore the logical implications of other assumptions with ethical or moral theory foundations.

Finally, the positioning perspective seeks to explain firm performance in the context of the firm's bargaining power relative to a range of other parties including customers, suppliers, rivals, potential future rivals, and producers of substitute goods (Porter, 1980). The underlying argument of this perspective is that each of these other parties represents a threat to the firm's performance. Integrating stakeholder theory concepts would change this argument, at least as it regards customers and suppliers. Stakeholder theory does not advocate a perspective where customers and suppliers are viewed as competitors or threats. Yes, these parties can affect the firm negatively, but they can also affect the firm positively, and the firm is arguably responsible for how it affects their performance. Future research might explore conditions under which a firm behaves as though it is in competition *with* its stakeholders versus being in competition *for* its stakeholders.

Conclusion

This chapter reviews a bulk of the scholarship at the intersection of strategic management and stakeholder theory. For much of the last four decades, the stakeholder perspective in strategic management has been an outsider's perspective. The vast majority of strategy articles do not develop or test stakeholder theory. After conducting two careful studies designed to clarify the boundaries of strategic management as a field, Nag, Hambrick and Chen (2007: 951) conclude, "The consensus definition of the field appears to give primacy to financial shareholders ('owners') rather than to other stakeholders, such as customers or employees." Strategy, the field that explores firm-level heterogeneity, will surely learn to appreciate that firms differ in the salience of their stakeholders under different conditions. Perhaps within the *next* four decades we will see the majority of strategy scholars asking how firms can achieve high performance while serving a variety of stakeholder interests.

Notes

1. We thank the editorial team for pointing out this alternative approach.

References

Adams, R. B., Licht, A. N., & Sagiv, L. (2011). Shareholders and stakeholders: How do directors decide? *Strategic Management Journal*, *32*(12): 1331–1355.

Agle, B. R., Mitchell, R. K., & Sonnenfeld, J. A. (1999). Who matters to CEOs? An investigation of stakeholder attributes and salience, corporate performance, and CEO values. *Academy of Management Journal*, *42*(5): 507–525.

Ambrose, M. L., & Cropanzano, R. (2003). A longitudinal analysis of organizational fairness: An examination of reactions to tenure and promotion decisions. *Journal of Applied Psychology*, *88*(2): 266–275.

Barnard, C. I. (1938). *The functions of the executive*. Cambridge, MA: Harvard University Press.

Berman, S. L., Wicks, A. C., Kotha, S., & Jones, T. M. (1999). Does stakeholder orientation matter? The relationship between stakeholder management models and firm financial performance. *Academy of Management Journal*, *42*(5): 488–506.

Bosse, D. A., & Coughlan, R. (2016). Stakeholder relationship bonds. *Journal of Management Studies*, *53*(7): 1197–1222.

Bosse, D. A., & Harrison, J. S. (2011). Stakeholders, entrepreneurial rent and bounded self-interest. In R. A. Phillips, ed., *Stakeholder theory: Impact and prospects*, pp. 193–211. Cheltenham, UK: Edward Elgar.

Bosse, D. A., & Phillips, R. A. (2016). Agency theory and bounded self-interest. *Academy of Management Review*, *41*(2): 276–297.

Bosse, D. A., Phillips, R. A., & Harrison, J. S. (2009). Stakeholders, reciprocity, and firm performance. *Strategic Management Journal*, *30*(4): 447–456.

Brandenburger, A., & Stuart, H. (1996). Value-based business strategy. *Journal of Economic and Management Strategy*, *5*(1): 5–24.

Brickson, S. L. (2007). Organizational identity orientation: The genesis of the role of the firm and distinct forms of social value. *Academy of Management Review*, *32*(3): 864–888.

Bridoux, F., & Stoelhorst, J. W. (2014). Microfoundations for stakeholder theory: Managing stakeholders with heterogeneous motives. *Strategic Management Journal*, *35*(1): 107–125.

Buysse, K., & Verbeke, A. (2003). Proactive environmental strategies: A stakeholder management perspective. *Strategic Management Journal*, *24*(5): 453–470.

Chatterji, A. K., & Toffel, M. W. (2010). How firms respond to being rated. *Strategic Management Journal*, *31*(9): 917–945.

Chen, H., & Rao, A. R. (2002). Close encounters of two kinds: False alarms and dashed hopes. *Marketing Science*, *21*(2): 178–196.

Choi, J., & Wang, H. (2009). Stakeholder relations and the persistence of corporate financial performance. *Strategic Management Journal*, *30*(8): 895–907.

Choi, Y. R., & Shepherd, D. A. (2005). Stakeholder perceptions of age and other dimensions of newness. *Journal of Management*, *31*(4): 573–596.

Coff, R. W. (1999). When competitive advantage doesn't lead to performance: The resource-based view and stakeholder bargaining power. *Organization Science*, *10*(2): 119–133.

Coombs, J. E., & Gilley, K. M. (2005). Stakeholder management as a predictor of CEO compensation: Main effects and interactions with financial performance. *Strategic Management Journal*, *26*(9): 827–840.

Crilly, D. (2013). Recasting enterprise strategy: Towards stakeholder research that matters to general managers. *Journal of Management Studies*, *50*(8): 1427–1447.

Crilly, D., & Sloan, P. (2012). Enterprise logic: Explaining corporate attention to stakeholders from the inside-out. *Strategic Management Journal*, *33*(10): 1174–1193.

Crilly, D., & Sloan, P. (2014). Autonomy or control? Organizational architecture and corporate attention to stakeholders. *Organization Science*, *25*(2): 339–355.

Crilly, D., Zollo, M., & Hansen, M. T. (2012). Faking it or muddling through? Understanding decoupling in response to stakeholder pressures. *Academy of Management Journal*, 55(6): 1429–1448.

Darnall, N., Henriques, I., & Sadorsky, P. (2010). Adopting proactive environmental strategy: The influence of stakeholders and firm size. *Journal of Management Studies*, 47(6): 1072–1094.

David, P., O'Brien, J. P., Yoshikawa, T., & Delios, A. (2010). Do shareholders or stakeholders appropriate the rents from corporate diversification? The influence of ownership structure. *Academy of Management Journal*, 53(3): 636–654.

de Luque, M. S., Washburn, N. T., & Waldman, D. A. (2008). Unrequited profit: How stakeholder and economic values relate to subordinates' perceptions of leadership and firm performance. *Administrative Science Quarterly*, 53(4): 626–654.

Doh, J. P, Lawton, T. C., & Rajwani, T. (2012). Advancing nonmarket strategy research: Institutional perspectives in a changing world. *Academy of Management Perspectives*, 26(3): 22–39.

Donaldson, T., & Preston, L. E. (1995). The stakeholder theory of the corporation: Concepts, evidence, and implications. *Academy of Management Review*, 20(1): 65–91.

Drucker, P. E. (1954). *The practice of management*. New York: Harper & Row.

Eesley, C., & Lenox, M. J. (2006). Firm responses to secondary stakeholder action. *Strategic Management Journal*, 27(8): 765–781.

Evan, W. M., & Freeman, R. E. (1993). A stakeholder theory of the modern corporation: Kantian capitalism. In T. L. Beauchamp & N. E. Bowie, eds., *Ethical theory and business*, pp. 97–106. Englewood Cliffs, NJ: Prentice-Hall.

Fehr, E., & Gächter, S. (2000). Fairness and retaliation: The economics of reciprocity. *Journal of Economic Perspectives*, 14(3): 159–181.

Freeman, R. E. (1984). *Strategic management: A stakeholder approach*. Boston, MA: Pitman Publishing.

Freeman, R. E. (1994). The politics of stakeholder theory: Some future directions. *Business Ethics Quarterly*, 4(4): 409–421.

Freeman, R. E. (1999). Divergent stakeholder theory: Response. *Academy of Management Review*, 24(2): 233–236.

Freeman, R. E., & Gilbert, D. R. (1988). *Corporate strategy and the search for ethics*. Englewood Cliffs, NJ: Prentice-Hall.

Freeman, R. E., Harrison, J. S., Wicks, A. C., Parmar, B. L., & de Colle, S. (2010). *Stakeholder theory: The state of the art*. Cambridge, UK: Cambridge University Press.

Freeman, R. E., & Phillips, R. (2002). Stakeholder theory: A libertarian defense. *Business Ethics Quarterly*, 12(3): 331–350.

Freeman, R. E, Wicks, A. C., & Parmar, B. (2004). Stakeholder theory and "the corporate objective revisited." *Organization Science*, 15 (3): 364–369.

Frooman, J. (1999). Stakeholder influence strategies. *Academy of Management Review*, 24(2): 191–205.

Garcia-Castro, R., & Aguilera, R. V. (2015). Incremental value creation and appropriation in a world with multiple stakeholders. *Strategic Management Journal*, 36(1): 137–147.

Greenley, G. E., & Foxall, G. R. (1997). Multiple stakeholder orientation in UK companies and the implications for company performance. *Journal of Management Studies*, 34(2): 259–284.

Harrison, J. S., & Bosse, D. A. (2013). How much is too much? The limits to generous treatment of stakeholders. *Business Horizons*, 56(3): 313–322.

Harrison, J. S., Bosse, D. A., & Phillips, R. A. (2010). Managing for stakeholders, stakeholder utility functions, and competitive advantage. *Strategic Management Journal*, 31(1): 58–74.

Hart, S. L. (1995). A natural-resource-based view of the firm. *Academy of Management Review*, 20(4): 986–1014.

Henisz, W. J., Dorobantu, S., & Nartey, L. J. (2014). Spinning gold: The financial returns to stakeholder engagement. *Strategic Management Journal*, 35 (12): 1727–1748.

Henriques, I., & Sadorsky, P. (1999). The relationship between environmental commitment and managerial perceptions of stakeholder importance. *Academy of Management Journal*, 42(1): 87–99.

Hill, C. W. L., & Jones, T. M. (1992). Stakeholder-agency theory. *Journal of Management Studies*, 29 (2): 131–154.

Hillman, A. J., & Keim, G. D. (2001). Shareholder value, stakeholder management, and social issues: What's the bottom line? *Strategic Management Journal*, 22(2): 125–139.

Jawahar, I. M., & McLaughlin, G. L. (2001). Toward a descriptive stakeholder theory: An organizational life cycle approach. *Academy of Management Review*, 26(3): 397–414.

Jolls, C., Sunstein, C. R., & Thaler, R. (1998). A behavioral approach to law and economics. *Stanford Law Review*, 50(5): 1471–1550.

Jones, T. M. (1995). Instrumental stakeholder theory – A synthesis of ethics and economics. *Academy of Management Review*, *20*(2): 404–437.

Jones, T. M., & Wicks, A. C. (1999). Convergent stakeholder theory. *Academy of Management Review*, *24*(2): 206–221.

Julian, S. D., Ofori-Dankwa, J. C., & Justis, R. T. (2008). Understanding strategic responses to interest group pressures. *Strategic Management Journal*, *29*(9): 963–984.

Kahneman, D. (1992). Reference points, anchors, norms, and mixed feelings. *Organizational Behavior and Human Decision Processes*, *51*(2): 296–312.

Kahneman, D., Knetsch, J. L., & Thaler, R. (1986). Fairness as a constraint on profit seeking: Entitlements in the market. *American Economic Review*, *76*(4): 728–741.

Kahneman, D., & Tversky, A. (1979). Prospect theory: An analysis of decision under risk. *Econometrica*, *47*(2): 263–292.

Kassinis, G., & Vafeas, N. (2006). Stakeholder pressures and environmental performance. *Academy of Management Journal*, *49*(1): 145–159.

King, B. G., & Soule, S. A. (2007). Social movements as extra-institutional entrepreneurs: The effect of protests on stock price returns. *Administrative Science Quarterly*, *52*(3): 413–442.

Kochan, T. A., & Rubinstein, S. A. (2000). Toward a stakeholder theory of the firm: The Saturn partnership. *Organization Science*, *11*(4): 367–386.

Kock, C. J., Santalo, J., & Diestre, L. (2012). Corporate governance and the environment: What type of governance creates greener companies? *Journal of Management Studies*, *49*(3): 492–514.

Leaf, C. (2017). No margin, no mission. Fortune, September 15: 12.

Lieberman, M. B., Garcia-Castro, R., & Balasubramanian, N. (2017). Measuring value creation and appropriation in firms: The VCA model. *Strategic Management Journal*, *38*(6): 1193–1211.

Luoma, P., & Goodstein, J. (1999). Stakeholders and corporate boards: Institutional influences on board composition and structure. *Academy of Management Journal*, *42*(5): 553–563.

Meznar, M. B., Nigh, D., & Kwok, C. C. Y. (1994). Effect of announcements of withdrawal from South Africa on stockholder wealth. *Academy of Management Journal*, *37*(6): 1633–1648.

Mitchell, R. K., Agle, B. R., & Wood, D. J. (1997). Toward a theory of stakeholder identification and salience: Defining the principle of who and what really counts. *Academy of Management Review*, *22*(4): 853–886.

Murillo-Luna, J. L., Garces-Ayerbe, C., & Rivera-Torres, P. (2008). Why do patterns of environmental response differ? A stakeholders' pressure approach. *Strategic Management Journal*, *29*(11): 1225–1240.

Nag, R., Hambrick, D. C., & Chen, M-J. (2007). What is strategic management, really? Inductive derivation of a consensus definition of the field. *Strategic Management Journal*, *28*(9): 935–955.

North, D. (1990). *Institutions, institutional change and economic performance*. Cambridge, UK: Cambridge University Press.

Ogden, S, & Watson, R. (1999). Corporate performance and stakeholder management: Balancing shareholder and customer interests in the UK privatized water industry. *Academy of Management Journal*, *42*(5): 526–538.

Pajunen, K. (2006). Stakeholder influences in organizational survival. *Journal of Management Studies*, *43*(6): 1261–1288.

Phillips, R. (1997). Stakeholder theory and a principle of fairness. *Business Ethics Quarterly*, *7*(1): 51–66.

Pirson, M., & Malhotra, D. (2011). Foundations of organizational trust: What matters to different stakeholders? *Organization Science*, *22*(4): 1087–1104.

Purnell, L. S., & Freeman, R. E. (2012). Stakeholder theory, fact/value dichotomy, and the normative core: How Wall Street stops the ethics conversation. *Journal of Business Ethics*, *109*: 109–116.

Porter, M. E. (1980). *Competitive strategy*. New York: Free Press.

Rowley, T. J. (1997). Moving beyond dyadic ties: A network theory of stakeholder influences. *Academy of Management Review*, *22*(4): 887–910.

Rowley, T. J., & Moldoveanu, M. (2003). When will stakeholder groups act? An interest- and identity-based model of stakeholder group mobilization. *Academy of Management Review*, *28*(2): 204–219.

Rumelt, R. P. (1987). Theory, strategy, and entrepreneurship. In D. Teece, ed., *The competitive challenge*, pp. 137–158. Cambridge, MA: Ballinger.

Rumelt, R. P., Schendel, D. E., & Teece, D. J. (1994). *Fundamental issues in strategy: A research agenda*. Boston, MA: Harvard Business School Press.

Schendel, D. E., & Hofer, C. W. (1979). *Strategic Management: A New View of Business Policy and Planning*. Boston, MA: Little Brown.

Sharma, S., & Henriques, I. (2005). Stakeholder influences on sustainability practices in the Canadian forest products industry. *Strategic Management Journal*, 26(2): 159–180.

Smith, A. (1776). *An inquiry into the nature and causes of the wealth of nations*. London: George Routledge and Sons.

Smith, N. C., & Rönnegard, D. (2014). Shareholder primacy, corporate social responsibility, and the role of business schools. *Journal of Business Ethics*, 134(3): 463–478.

Stevens, J. M., Steensma, H. K., Harrison, D. A., & Cochran, P. L. (2005). Symbolic or substantive document? The influence of ethics codes on financial executives' decisions. *Strategic Management Journal*, 26(2): 181–195.

Sundaram, A. K., & Inkpen, A. C. (2004). The corporate objective revisited. *Organization Science*, 15(3): 350–363.

Trahms, C. A., Ndofor, H. A., & Sirmon, D. G. (2013). Organizational decline and turnaround: A review and agenda for future research. *Journal of Management*, 39(5): 1277–1307.

Wicks, A. C., Berman, S. L., & Jones, T. M. (1999). The structure of optimal trust: Moral and strategic implications. *Academy of Management Review*, 24 (1): 99–116.

Wicks, A.C., Freeman, R.E., & Gilbert, D.R. (1994). A feminist reinterpretation of the stakeholder concept. *Business Ethics Quarterly*, 4(4): 475–497.

Wolfe, R. A., & Putler, D. S. (2002). How tight are the ties that bind stakeholder groups? *Organization Science*, 13(1): 64–80.

PART IV

Stakeholder Theory in Education and Practice

Stakeholder Theory in Management Education

IRENE HENRIQUES
York University

Introduction

We cannot solve our problems with the same thinking we used when we created them.

Albert Einstein

Should firms care about social issues? What stakeholders should managers listen to? What are the risks associated with such involvement? What role does power play in such relationships? How do we engage stakeholders? Given that firm activity is embedded in a network of stakeholder relations (Darnall, Henriques, & Sadorsky, 2010; Rowley & Moldoveanu, 2003), such questions can be debated in a classroom setting using stakeholder theory. Stakeholders are defined as "any group or individual who can affect or is affected by the achievement of the organization's objectives" (Freeman, 1984: 46). Stakeholders include customers, employees, suppliers, shareholders, government regulators, public interest groups, community organizations, labor unions, and industry associations – just to name a few. Stakeholder theory delves into the "complex web of stakeholders in a context characterized by multiplicity and interdependencies" (Reade, et al., 2008: 821).

The advent of social media has added to this complexity. Social media has not only opened the door to two-way communication but also to worldwide broadcasting. For example, Facebook and Twitter are progressively popular means for stakeholders to voice support for issues or problems of concern and for businesses to advertise products, services, and opportunities (Robson, et al., 2013). People can now associate with issues/groups they value in an instant via Facebook and Twitter. Conflicts between social actors and businesses are now broadcast worldwide.

Although there have been a number of papers written on the importance of teaching ethics (Toft, 2015), sustainability (Banerjee, 2011), corporate social responsibility (Rendtorff, 2015), and global social issues such as poverty (Reade, et al., 2008) to future managers, there has been less written on the methods stakeholder scholars have used to teach this material. There has been even less discussion about how best to teach stakeholder thinking in management courses. This chapter seeks to address this lacuna by focusing on some interesting practices scholars have employed to make stakeholder theory relevant for students and practitioners (e.g., executive education). We have all experienced dismay when our students express little interest in the theoretical or ontological underpinnings of stakeholder theory (Frostenson, 2015). Teaching stakeholder theory and drawing students into the complexity of an issue and the multiplicity of actors and decisions are critical elements in unlocking students' imagination and creativity. This chapter examines teaching methods and techniques for teaching stakeholder theory that can be employed to challenge business students to seek creative solutions or develop a more holistic understanding of contested issues.

This chapter is structured as follows. First, I present some typical teaching methods and materials used in teaching stakeholder theory. Although I focus on strategic management and CSR/Sustainability/Ethics classes to address some of the challenges and opportunities of teaching stakeholder theory, stakeholder theory can be useful in any management course and many of the exercises and examples I discuss can be adapted for use across the management curriculum. Second, I present some novel in-class, experiential stakeholder-focused teaching approaches that have been used to bring the complexity of issues facing the firm to life. Third, I examine some thought-provoking research questions resulting from these experiential teaching methods that still need to be addressed if stakeholder theory is to continue to be not only a vibrant research area, but also an engaging teaching and learning experience. Fourth, rapid changes in communication technologies have created both opportunities and challenges in higher education. How these changes may impact our ability to teach stakeholder theory will be examined. I end the chapter with a discussion of the lessons learned and implications of using a stakeholder perspective for teaching not only ethics, sustainability, corporate social responsibility, and strategic management, but any management course, and make some suggestions about possible future teaching directions.

Teaching Stakeholder Theory

Although stakeholder theory has made significant strides in terms of research output, as observed by the number of published papers in leading academic journals such as the *Academy of Management Review*, the *Academy of Management Journal*, the *Strategic Management Journal*, and the *Administrative Science Quarterly* (Bridoux & Stoelhorst, 2014; Bridoux & Stoelhorst, 2016; Harrison, Bosse, & Phillips, 2010; Henriques & Sadorsky, 1999; Kacperczyk, 2009; Margolis & Walsh, 2003; Rowley, 1997), its insertion into our management teaching toolkit has been slower (Bonnafous-Boucher & Rendtorff, 2015). Stakeholder theory is often introduced in discussions on topics such as ethics, corporate social responsibility, and sustainability (e.g., Hill & Hult, 2017). In other words, it is often employed to help students understand contested concepts and issues in these types of courses.

In comparison to other types of management courses, instructors who teach ethics, sustainability, or corporate social responsibility courses have a relatively easy time introducing stakeholder theory because these courses often challenge students to explore how business can create sustainable value for their key stakeholders using real-life

examples of organizational lapses in ethics, environmental management, or corporate/financial behavior. These lapses have allowed us to lay bare "the complexities involved in understanding the relationship between privately owned organizations and the wider interests of society that CSR and business ethics are about" (Toft, 2015: 78). The outcomes of such lapses include potential financial losses (Alpaslan, 2009), reputational losses (Lange, Lee, & Dai, 2011; Rindova et al. 2005), and possible damage or restrictions to the company's social license to operate (Rooney, Leach, & Ashworth, 2014).

Although Freeman's (1984) classic was actually intended to be a strategic management textbook, adoption of the stakeholder perspective is less common in strategic management courses than in ethics, sustainability, or corporate social responsibility courses. Strategic management textbooks at both the undergraduate and graduate levels are typically founded on two main theoretical foundations, namely industrial organization economics (Porter, 1996) and resource-based theory (Barney, 1991). However, high profile cases such as the Enron scandal, the 2008–2009 financial crisis, global warming, the increase in precarious work and child labor, to name just a few, have encouraged strategy academics and practitioners alike to seek a third theoretical foundation that is not solely based on maximizing financial returns – namely stakeholder theory (Freeman & MacVea, 2005). Together these three theories help the instructor weave an interesting narrative regarding the purpose of the firm with discussions on how an organization can create value for multiple stakeholders. Management textbooks that have embedded stakeholder theory include Harrison and St. John (2014) and Hoskisson et al. (2013). In other words, shareholders are not the sole residual claimants of an organization (Mahoney, 2012).

Contrasting a strategic management class with an ethics class, for example, the role of the instructor in the strategic management class is one of a conductor who is trying to get as many stakeholder "voices" on the table without their necessarily being an ethical crisis or perhaps before such an event arises. If a case being studied only equates resources with economic gain, other intangible resources that stakeholders may value such as respect, identification, and meaningfulness are ignored (Mitchell, et al., 2016). In other words, money may not be the appropriate currency. Various stakeholders may, in fact, be unwilling to trade intangible resources for tangible resources. However, Freeman, Wicks, and Parmar (2004) argue that a strict shareholder wealth maximization approach ignores these ethically relevant considerations thereby creating a dilemma that cannot be solved. The instructor, therefore, tries to help students focus beyond maximizing shareholder wealth and engage in constructive sensemaking (Mitchell, et al., 2016). Bringing stakeholder theory to life in the classroom engages students in this constructive sensemaking (Morsing & Schultz, 2006).

For all types of management courses, there is a great deal of research on stakeholder theory that instructors can use. Research papers, textbooks, videos, and blogs are just a few examples of sources.[1] This Handbook provides yet another excellent resource. In most management courses, it is easy to contrast stakeholder theory with the shareholder value orientation and demonstrate that there may be other values that organizations account for when analyzing their external environment, their internal resource allocation, their strategic direction (mission, vision, and values), their cooperative strategies, their implementation strategies, and their strategic control. What instructors often wrestle with is how to teach stakeholder theory in a way that makes it applicable and useful to business students and, in the case of executive education, practitioners (Frostenson, 2015). We often turn to the case method where students are encouraged to think about the stakeholders that are the most relevant for the case. Having students represent critical stakeholders on cases involving competitive exchange, alliance partnerships, mergers and acquisitions, and corporate governance are activities that some of our colleagues have found to be very enriching for all involved. Nevertheless, we have all experienced times when it is difficult to get students thinking beyond a stereotypical stakeholder need(s). For example, students may focus on a perspective in which employees only want high salaries, consumers

only want low prices or high quality, governments only raise business costs, and suppliers want the best price. In other words, how can we incorporate stakeholders' plurality of needs/values into the classroom? The next section provides some possible answers to this question.

Bringing Stakeholder Theory to Life in the Classroom

While the management of stakeholder demands in an organization is a difficult assignment, it is an activity that our business students will inevitably be exposed to in their careers. Both internal (employees, customers, suppliers, and shareholders) and external (government, community representatives, and media) stakeholders convey their perspectives and concerns in times when critical management decisions are being made. In cases where the stakeholder and the firm are resource interdependent (Frooman, 1999), ignoring such concerns can be very costly to the organization. In cases where the stakeholder is not resource dependent on the firm, the stakeholder can nonetheless exert significant pressure on those stakeholders on whom the firm is resource dependent via mainstream and social media outlets by calling for customer boycotts or investor divestment (Henriques & Sharma, 2005; Sharma & Henriques, 2005). Consequently, there is a need to expose students to situations where they can learn how to listen, empathize, and make sense of the myriad of demands and trade-offs an organization faces that not only affect the organization in the short run but in the long run as well.

In Chapter 6, Ron Mitchell and Jae Lee argue that at the heart of stakeholder theory (Freeman, 1984) is value creation for stakeholders, which requires a better explanation of the "how" and "why" needed to undertake these efforts. They introduce the notion of "stakeholder work." Interestingly, that is what is required when teaching stakeholder theory to future business leaders. Students need to identify, understand, be aware of, prioritize, and engage stakeholders. These are all verbs – actions that can take place in a classroom setting using a combination of multi-media, role playing exercises, invited stakeholder presentations, and cases. In other words, we need to bring stakeholders to life so that our students can empathize with stakeholders, their needs, and the societal issues they bring to the table.

So how do we bring stakeholder theory to life in the classroom? I present four interesting methods: video cases, stakeholder negotiation exercises, social protest novels, and issue-based stakeholder town hall exercises. Below I discuss each method as well as its strengths and weaknesses. A resource list for each of these methods is provided at the end of this chapter.

Video Cases

A typical case consists of a write up of a situation facing a real-life firm and perhaps some associated academic articles that students are required to read. The case is usually accompanied by a teaching note that an instructor uses to guide class discussion. Case teaching is an art where the instructor serves as host, moderator, devil's advocate, and arbiter. A video case has the same elements except that there is also a video component that brings the stakeholders in the case to life. Here company stakeholders work with the case writer to explain their perspectives on the issue. Not only do students read the financial and operational elements of the case but they also witness the human and emotional elements of the case. As an instructor who is familiar with case method teaching, I was intrigued by the prospect of using a video case to see whether the addition of the video element to the case would elicit better learning outcomes insofar as student engagement, empathy, and innovative thinking are concerned.

Michael Russo at the University of Oregon has written a video case with Dan Goldstein on a company named Seventh Generation – a maker of environmentally sensitive household non-durables (Russo & Goldstein, 2007) – that was facing a crisis due to a supplier declining to continue manufacturing the company's natural baby wipes. The authors sent me the case and video. The video was divided into segments: the company, the complaints, the problem, the debate, the meeting, the decision, and the epilogue. Interestingly, the video component, which consisted of interviews with employees in marketing,

operations, and finance and the CEO, brought the written case to life for students by demonstrating how internal stakeholders in a value-driven organization manage sustainability-oriented trade-offs and customer expectations.

The engagement in the case was remarkable. In addition to the visual component of the case, I brought environmentally sensitive and regular household nondurable products to class so that the students could evaluate the products for themselves.[2] Although the students were not experts in green chemistry, they were able to understand which products contained harmful chemicals by using their senses. The hands-on exercise helped students understand the anger customers exhibited when they discovered that the baby wipes they purchased were not "natural." The outcomes of this video case resulted in deeper discussions regarding values – financial, organizational, and ethical – as well as interesting solutions to real-world stakeholder problems and challenges.

Russo and Crooke (2016) have a recent video case entitled "Guayakí: Securing supplies, strengthening the mission" that is available for free online along with a teaching note and VIMEO video.[3] Guayakí is an energy drink company and the video shows the CEO's personal history, the emergence of Guayakí as an energy drink company, and the company's efforts to work with Indigenous people in South America to secure supplies of a key ingredient. The case seeks to get students to understand the complexity and time it takes companies to meet social, environmental, and economic goals when securing long-term supplies. Student engagement is increased by the fact that many students may have deeper knowledge of and strong opinions on energy drinks – the perfect setting for a stakeholder dialogue.

Video cases require the participation of the organization. Acquiring such access is not easy and may explain why (along with the amount of resources needed to undertake such an endeavor) there are so few video cases available. The benefits of such cases to learning, however, are significant in that they allow students to experience multi-objective decision-making within the strategic management context (Mitchell, et al., 2017).

Stakeholder Negotiation Exercises

Experiential teaching methods, such as stakeholder negotiation exercises involving multiple-objective decision-making, allow students to begin to understand what Mitchell, Lee, and Agle (2017: 4) call "stakeholder work," defined as the "purposive processes of organization aimed at being aware of, identifying, understanding, prioritizing and engaging stakeholders." Examples of such exercises include using actual stakeholders as coaches in a negotiation exercise (Ramus, 2003) and undertaking a stakeholder negotiation exercise from an issue-based perspective rather than a firm-centric perspective (Collins & Kearins, 2007). Ramus (2003) provides a fascinating experiential learning exercise combining environmental rule making with learning the skills necessary to manage complex negotiation settings. Here the stakeholders involved in the real world negotiation are invited to be the students' coaches. The instructor develops the case study, confidential role instructions, and identifies and invites an individual from each of the major stakeholder groupings in the case. The stakeholder coaches and the assigned students prepare for the simulation.

Once prepared, the students simulate the regulatory negotiation with the stakeholders silently observing. The simulation ends with the student(s) representing the regulator stating their decision and reasons. There is a debriefing session followed by the stakeholders themselves presenting his/her perspective on the issues of the case. Not only do students get to see where they diverged, the stakeholders also get to see how their message may or may not have been understood by the general public. In other words, this exercise allows all parties – students, invited stakeholders, and instructor – to learn something from the simulation. Any decision that requires the assent of multiple stakeholders can be used as a stakeholder negotiation exercise.

The challenges associated with this approach relate to resources on the part of both the instructor and the stakeholders being called upon. Half a day is required for all parties to fully benefit from this stakeholder-led exercise. Here an intensive MBA or executive MBA class would work. A shortened version could also be applied across several classes. The instructor-developed case must be a complex, multi-issue, and multi-party negotiation where a solution is unobvious and parties have serious differences of opinion (Ramus, 2003). Again, the learning benefits are significant and, according to Ramus (2003), the stakeholders are more than willing to participate in educational exercises where they have the opportunity to communicate their perspectives.

A second option is to use in-class, issue-based stakeholder negotiation exercise whereby students can experience and reflect critically on the potential and risks of engaging stakeholders (Collins & Kearins, 2007; Egri 1999, 2003). Sustainability issues are often chosen because they provide the ideal setting in which the students are asked to understand the complexity and uncertainty of the problem as well as the many differing stakeholder perspectives as to how the problem should or should not be addressed. The instructor needs to choose a local or national issue of significance so as to heighten students' involvement and interest. The instructor must then decide whether the students or the instructor will undertake or provide the required research on the issue. Whichever is chosen, it is imperative that information on the main stakeholders be robust to enable students to take on the specific roles.

The model used by Collins and Kearins (2007), for example, suggests that facilitators research the issue, form the stakeholder groups, schedule the negotiation session, negotiate the rules of interaction, and work with the groups to achieve consensus. Whether consensus is reached or not, all parties are asked to keep a journal on what was achieved, what was missed, how things could have worked differently, and whether the outcome was "beneficial." Once the exercise is completed, a debriefing takes place where students reflect on the process and outcomes – their individual role and risk taking, the group's ability to work together, their perspective of who "won or lost," and learning experience. According to Collins and Kearins (2007: 535), "power differentials, ethical dilemmas, challenges to identity and reputation, and compromises often arise within the exercise."

Stakeholder negotiation exercises are challenging. If the exercise does not interest the students, it becomes very difficult to get a fulsome discussion. One possible solution is to invite one or two key stakeholders of the exercise to speak to your class on their perspectives prior to undertaking the in-class exercise. For example, if an important stakeholder is employees, a union representative may be invited; if the issue is an environmental matter, an environmental non-governmental organization (ENGO) representative is invited. A number of years ago, I was developing a stakeholder negotiation exercise that had Indigenous peoples as a key stakeholder. Realizing that business students are not normally exposed to Indigenous issues or viewpoints, I invited a leader of the Mohawk Council of Akwesasne to speak to my class. The Council's mission states:[4]

> Humans were given the responsibility to speak for all life our Mother Earth sustains. As the Environment Program, we are further charged with gathering and sharing knowledge with Akwesasro:non to ensure that all life is respected, protected, and preserved for the generations to come.

The speaker began his talk with a prayer thanking Mother Earth for everything she has given us. Students immediately understood that negotiating with Indigenous peoples would require a much deeper understanding of their values.

Social Protest Novel

Crane, Henriques, Husted, and Matten (2015) have argued that management scholars need to recapture both the intellectual history as well as the practice of contemporary notions of stakeholder management, corporate governance, political strategy, and corporate social responsibility before these fields emerged. History can be used to inform and guide present research and teaching. Husted (2015), for example, goes back into the nineteenth century to examine CSR practice in the United Kingdom, the United States, Japan, India, and Germany.

But how can we bring a historical stakeholder perspective into the classroom? Westerman and Westerman (2009) suggest a unique idea – namely, the use of social protest novels. Social protest novels were the product of the rapid rise in industrialization and urbanization that led to a host of societal ills.

Westerman and Westerman (2009: 659) argue that a social protest novel provides "a uniquely powerful medium in that it effectively captures student's imagination and interest with an engrossing narrative, personalizes the importance of management issues and decisions through a student's identification with the characters, and utilizes its grounding in real world events to demonstrate the capacity for change." Students are confronted with the historical roots of some of society's greatest social challenges. The novel Westerman and Westerman (2009) use to illustrate the method is *Hawk's Nest* (Skidmore, 1941), which recounts Union Carbide Corporation's development of a hydroelectric dam in West Virginia in the 1930s. The novel tells the story of the social injustices that occurred at the time and how people reacted. Westerman and Westerman (2009) also provide a list of other protest novels including *The Grapes of Wrath* (Steinbeck, 1939), *The Jungle* (Sinclair, 1906), *To Make My Bread* (Lumpkin, 1995), and *Life in the Iron Mills* (Davis, 1861), to name just a few.

In class discussions of the social protest novel, Westerman and Westerman (2009) suggest using both the Friedman (1970) approach (i.e., the social responsibility of business is to increase profits) and the stakeholder management approach (Freeman, 1984). The stakeholder analysis opens students' eyes to how things have changed (or not) across time. Interestingly, it also provides a literary window into how society has addressed social injustices across time and how societal norms and laws have changed. In other words, history matters.

One potential problem with using this approach is getting students to read the novel. A novel requires more input than simply reading a case. Moreover, a novel is not specifically written for a management audience. One possible solution is to introduce a social media component into the analysis by asking students to share their thoughts with the class as they read the novel via Twitter. Not only would the social media buzz entice other classmates to read the novel but it will also provide the instructor with important insights into students' understanding of the novel and their ability to relate complex historical issues to fellow management students novel prior to discussing the novel in class.

Issue-Based Stakeholder Town Hall

Another method that can be used to bring stakeholder theory to life is an issue-based stakeholder town hall exercise. An issue-based stakeholder town hall is a stakeholder exercise that is based on an issue that has yet to be resolved. The ideal issue is in the news, is complex, involves a company or an industry, has multiple stakeholders with differing perspectives, and is contested. Below I describe a stakeholder town hall exercise dealing with the Keystone XL pipeline controversy that I developed and provide some suggestions as to how such an approach can be used when teaching stakeholder management in divisive times.

A Canadian company, TransCanada, is seeking to build a 2,739 km (1,702 mile) pipeline from Alberta, Canada, to refineries in the Gulf coast. This pipeline would pass through Nebraska's Ogallala Aquifer. The Ogallala Aquifer underlies approximately 450,000 square km (174,000 square miles) of eight states.[5] The Ogallala Aquifer provides 78 percent of the water used by Nebraska's residents and industry and 83 per cent of the state's irrigation water. The farming industry represented approximately 18 per cent of Nebraska's gross domestic product in 2009 (Song, 2011). Although the Ogallala Aquifer is responsible for turning the region into America's breadbasket, there are also concerns that it is at risk of depletion (Parker, 2016). Stakeholders are fearful that a pipeline spill will affect an important irreplaceable and depleting natural resource, which would have significant economic implications to not only current stakeholders but future generations as well.

Prior to the exercise, students are asked to read three articles: (1) Song's 2011 *Inside Climate News* article entitled "Keystone XL Primer: How the Pipeline's Route Could Impact the Ogallala Aquifer" (http://insideclimatenews.org/news/20110811/keystone-xl-pipeline-route-ogallala-aquifer-nebraska-sandhills); (2) a CBC news article entitled "Keystone XL pipeline delay disappoints TransCanada" (www.cbc.ca/news/world/story/2011/11/10/keyston-pipeline-route.html); and (3) Mitchell, Agle, and Wood's 1997 *Academy of Management Review*

article entitled "Toward a Theory of Stakeholder Identification and Salience: Defining the Principle of Who and What Really Counts." Students are also asked to watch a video made by the Pembina Institute (an environmental non-governmental organization [ENGO]) regarding the Canadian oil sands (www.pembina.org/pub/1280). Depending on time constraints, this video can be watched in class prior to students forming their stakeholder groups.

The students are asked to take on the role of a specific stakeholder involved in the Keystone XL dilemma. Their objective is to find the arguments that will give their group the most leverage in getting other stakeholders (and not necessarily the most powerful) to see their perspective. They are given thirty minutes to draw up their arguments and one person in each group is chosen to be the spokesperson. Stakeholders include, but are not limited to, oil sand developers, pipeline companies, governments (Alberta, Canada, and US governments), ENGOs, Indigenous peoples, Alberta farmers, Nebraskan farmers, citizens of Fort McMurray, and citizens of Nebraska and Alberta. Sometimes I choose the stakeholder-student combination and other times, I let students choose. Students then get into their groups to develop their arguments as to whether the pipeline should or should not be built as planned. The stakeholder groups can also visit other stakeholders to establish coalitions with other groups that they believe may have similar perspectives. Once the groups have completed their deliberations, everyone returns to class for a town hall meeting where one person from each group addresses the class. There are three ways the exercise can be evaluated:

1. The instructor takes on the role of US President who will, based on what was said in class, make his/her decision regarding the pipeline.
2. You ask the students to vote on the perspective that most convinced them – note that they cannot vote for their own perspective.
3. You can have a couple of colleagues act as a jury (they only need to be present for the presentations).

Whichever method is chosen, students seem to enjoy the experience. The questions students raise after the experiment include: How does management deal with the different value propositions that stakeholders bring to the table? How important are stakeholder coalitions in raising a group's power? What role do social media play in affecting stakeholder influence? Not only are these excellent questions to pursue in subsequent class discussions, they are also excellent research questions that require greater investigation.

Challenges and Research Questions

One of the great challenges arising from stakeholder exercises is, of course, "How do we deal with biases?" Although we all have biases, the purpose of a stakeholder exercise is for the students to not only take up and discover the "value" of the stakeholder perspective or view he/she has been assigned but also to help them learn to identify their own biases, and perhaps challenge them. For example, in the Keystone XL exercise, Indigenous peoples are an important stakeholder who have very differing perspectives on the value of air, land, and water (Convening of Indigenous Peoples for the Healing of Mother Earth, 2008). Snyder, Williams, and Peterson (2003) reason that the failure of institutions – banks, companies and governments – to assess the "culture losses" of Indigenous peoples due to natural resource extraction damage make it difficult for Western society to comprehend that a monetary economic approach is simply not adequate to value the "sense of place" (Kirsch, 2001) of Indigenous peoples. An understanding of such differences can go a long way in helping organizations make sense of stakeholder demands.

Broadening our notion of value, as Thomas Jones and Jeffrey Harrison stress in Chapter 4 of this Handbook, is critical. Building on the notion that what gets measured gets done, Harrison and Wicks (2013) develop a four-factor value perspective focusing on the utility stakeholders receive from a firm – namely stakeholder utility associated with actual goods and services, stakeholder utility associated with organizational justice, stakeholder utility from affiliation, and stakeholder utility associated with perceived opportunity costs. They argue that financial performance is an incomplete measure of firm value as it ignores other more intrinsic benefits that stakeholders seek which engender the continued collaboration and support needed for the business to thrive. They suggest that happiness is one possible construct that could be used to help broaden the measure of value in organizations. A broader notion of value is especially relevant when stakeholders do not cooperate.

The digital age has provided the ideal arena in which stakeholders (powerful or not) use social media to call on companies to address service failures (Grégoire, Salle, & Tripp, 2015). The digital age comprises social media platforms that allow people to connect and interact with each other. Social media (Facebook, YouTube, Twitter, wikis, blogs, Flickr, etc.) are a group of internet-based applications that allow the creation and exchange of user-generated content (Kaplan & Haenlein, 2010). The World Wide Web is the first mass medium that allows streams of information without any gatekeeping or filtering (Pang, Hassan, & Chong, 2013), and social media influencers are emerging as important stakeholders with whom companies need to engage (Freberg, et al., 2011). Many of our students use social media to communicate their dissatisfaction/satisfaction and share their views with an almost limitless number of parties. From a stakeholder perspective, the digital age has opened up a wonderful opportunity for firms to communicate with their stakeholders. With the proliferation of modern information technologies and search engines, accessing and retrieving information from stakeholders has never been easier for organizations. On the other hand, firms are also confronted with the paradox of being inundated with irrelevant or unnecessary information while facing a dangerous dearth of pertinent information (Königer & Janowitz, 1995). The lack of gatekeeping and filtering of the information on the World Wide Web also forces organizations to ask questions, validate assertions, and check sources (Wallace, 2017) before acting on the information; an added burden for which many are unprepared. The teaching methods discussed in this chapter could be easily supplemented with a social media component whereby students are required to ask questions, validate assertions, and check sources.

The advent of social media and, more specifically, social movements (de Bakker, et al., 2013) and their impact on stakeholder influence (Frooman, 1999) is another issue that students, especially those who have significant business experience, are seeking guidance on when taking part in these experiential stakeholder exercises. As so eloquently stated by Margolis and Walsh (2003: 268), "companies are increasingly asked to provide innovative solutions to deep-seated problems of human misery, even as economic theory instructs managers to focus on maximizing their shareholders' wealth." Social movements together with social media have amplified such calls. The two questions business students and executives often ask during stakeholder exercises are: How important are stakeholder coalitions in raising a group's power? and What role do social media play in affecting stakeholder influence and how does one respond? From a teaching perspective, the United Airlines overbooking fiasco (Arco, 2017) and stories of angry passengers being turned away from overbooked Air Canada flights (Harris, 2017) provide excellent examples not only of how an issue can go viral but also of how competitors can employ such an event to gain market share. For example, WestJet, a Canadian airline, took advantage of this fiasco by producing a "WestJet doesn't overbook because #OwnersCare about your business" campaign along with a funny video.[6] More research is needed to understand how companies can involve stakeholders in two-way communication to develop long-lasting stakeholder relationships (Morsing & Schultz, 2006).

Some of the exercises contained in this chapter also give rise to questions initiated by critical management theory scholars (Banerjee, 2011) as to why conflicts between societal actors and corporations seem to continue despite the adoption of CSR practices by corporations (see Greenwood & Mir, Chapter 3 of this Handbook). More research is needed to understand the risks associated with stakeholder engagement as well as the benefits (Crane & Livesey, 2003). Student stakeholder engagement

exercises suggest that action-learning models (Bradbury-Huang, 2010; Coghlan, 2011), which these stakeholder exercises try to mimic, may be a method companies and researchers can use to bring stakeholders together to better understand the power dynamics involved.

Future Prospects for Educational Delivery of the Stakeholder Perspective

Technological changes over the past twenty years have not only changed the way we interact with each other (text, video conferencing, voice over internet protocol [VoIP]), these technologies have also changed how we do business (e.g., on-line shopping). Higher education is not immune to these changes. Web-based technologies have evolved to the point where many students are discovering online business courses and programs to be not only more accessible but desirable especially if faced with significant time and/or geographical constraints.[7] So it should come as no surprise that business schools worldwide are seriously exploring and introducing on-line education options and hybrid options that require some face-to-face contact. At the same time, however, instructors are seeking online teaching methods and learning management systems that can replicate, or perhaps improve upon, face-to-face learning outcomes related to important business skills such as group work, communication skills, strategic thinking and analysis, and collaboration. Using stakeholder theory to challenge business students to seek creative solutions or develop a more holistic understanding of contested issues, however, requires careful planning as to how an instructor can maintain high-level engagement whereby students are required to not only interact with the instructor but each other.

Teaching stakeholder theory requires two-way communication (audio and visual). A customizable, mobile, accessible, and adaptive learning management system is required for the instructor to co-create an engaging learning environment in which the stakeholder exercises described in this chapter can be used. Using multi-media materials, the instructor becomes the curator of the stakeholder exercise providing students access to a virtual classroom in which students, and perhaps even stakeholders themselves, collaborate and share documents, PowerPoint presentations, and/or visual presentations. These activities can be synchronistic (e.g., debates where all students must be present at the same time) or asynchronistic. Social media platforms such as Facebook and Twitter can be used to replicate viral events and "twitterstorms" in an effort to get students to assess whether such events can break through established mindsets and re-establish new mental framing (Hahn, et al., 2014).

Another novel technological advancement that is starting to gain traction in the educational field because of its ability to promote students' motivation and engagement is gamification. An application to stakeholder theory would entail the creation of a "stakeholder game" where students take on different stakeholders' roles in a business case game. The game would be designed with multiple decision points leading to different outcomes depending on the decision each stakeholder makes. Unpredictable stakeholder events such as viral videos depicting poor service or twitterstorms criticizing company behavior can also be introduced into the game to increase it realism. Here the interdependencies between stakeholders can be designed into the game whereby certain decisions can lead to future economic losses/gains, reputational losses/gains, stakeholders withholding or according legitimacy, etc. In other words, the outcomes of the game result in numerous value propositions that students must think through when making decisions throughout the game.

Gamification is a form of participatory and interactive entertainment that has become an innovative learning tool (Dicheva, Dichev, et al., 2015; Hanus & Fox, 2015; Seaborn & Fels, 2015). Gamification is found to affect three behavioral areas: cognitive intelligence, emotional intelligence, and social intelligence. At the cognitive level, active experimentation and discovery are explored by students via challenges developed according to their skill level. The game helps individual students understand, without the influence of others, what they need to do to complete a challenge (Boyatzis & Saatcioglu, 2008; Lee & Hammer, 2011). From a research perspective, issues of information overload can hamper firm response especially when many social media platforms allow anonymity (Bawden & Robinson,

2009). Gamification may be a way to examine, from a cognitive perspective (Barnett, 2014), both stakeholder and business reactions.

At the emotional intelligence level, which is defined as "the ability to monitor one's own and others' feelings and emotions, to discriminate among them and to use this information to guide one's thinking and actions" (Salovey & Mayer, 1990: 189), students experience pride, optimism, and frustration as they play the game. Gamification offers students an opportunity to face their negative emotions, such as failure or frustration, and manage those (Boyatzis & Saatcioglu, 2008). In a stakeholder game, such emotions and their impact on students' decision-making and views would be recorded by students and discussed.

At the social intelligence level, which is defined as the universe of a person's knowledge, abilities, and skills that promote effective behavior specific to the context and in accordance with the social group (Crowne, 2009), the adoption of stakeholder roles during the game allows students to explore social experiences that they may not have experienced previously. Such experiences build a person's social intelligence.

Gamification, however, like any learning method, has its strengths and weaknesses. The educational strengths associated with gamification are that it reinforces knowledge, promotes the development of skills such as problem solving, collaboration, and communication (Dicheva, Dichev, et al., 2015), offers greater autonomy (Dicheva, Irwin, et al., 2014), encourages new incentives besides grades to promote engagement and interest (Lee & Hammer, 2011), increases students' attention span (Bruder, 2015), allows for immediate feedback (Hanus & Fox, 2015), and increases students' academic achievement (Lee & Hammer, 2011). Weaknesses include a lack of a systematic or standardized method to create gamification experiences (Dicheva, Irwin, et al., 2014), the possibility that incentives may provide extrinsic recognition that could demotivate students (Glover, 2013), and the fact that gamification absorbs a great deal of instructional resources to succeed (Lee & Hammer, 2011). For an online or hybrid management course, such a stakeholder game may enable the instructor to achieve his/her teaching goals.

Conclusions

Teaching stakeholder theory has never been as stimulating. Information on business and society developments has never been as accessible. Deciphering all this information and the stakeholders involved, however, is an ongoing challenge for companies and for educators. Paul Adler in his 2015 Presidential Address entitled "Our Teaching Mission" states: "In strategy, firms will need to develop clearer nonmarket strategies and integrate them more rigorously with their market strategies. And they will need to do this amid greater uncertainty about the future state of markets, regulation, and profit prospects and greater pressure from a diverse range of stakeholders for a broader assortment of outcomes" (Adler, 2016: 188). Stakeholder scholars are well placed to incorporate nonmarket strategies into their management, and especially strategic management courses.

Adler (2016: 189) maintains that our foremost challenge as teachers is how to "teach the debates" that are raging within and beyond the workplace. The four actions Adler (2016: 189) suggests instructors need to undertake are precisely the focus of this stakeholder teaching chapter – namely to: (1) help our students develop stronger critical thinking skills to effectively deal with the complex and contentious issues they will face both within and beyond the workplace; (2) help our students develop new skills so that they can imaginatively and bravely advance controversial ideas with confidence; (3) open the walls of our classroom to help students interact effectively with other constituencies and individuals with very diverse values and priorities; and (4) open our teaching repertoire to include more dialogical and experiential methods. These actions, however, should not be limited to management, ethics, sustainability, and CSR courses. Marketing, accounting, and finance must also take up this teaching challenge.

Albert Einstein said: *We cannot solve our problems with the same thinking we used when we created them.* Bringing stakeholder theory to life in the classroom allows our students – our future business leaders – to more effectively work, empathize, and dialogue with stakeholders with different values and priorities so as to develop creative ideas and solutions. In divisive times, our classrooms will become the place where our students can develop such skills. It is our job to meet this challenge.

Resource List

Video Cases

Seventh Generation Case

Russo, M. V. & Goldstein, D. (2007). Seventh Generation: Balancing Customer Expectations with Supply Chain Realities. oikos sustainability case collection. https://oikos-international.org/wp-content/uploads/2013/10/oikos_Cases_2007_Seventh_Generation.pdf

Information on cotton used by Seventh Generation Diapers: www.youtube.com/watch?v=H5U-0ReBMRw

Guayakí Case

Russo, M. V. & Crooke, M. (2016). Guayakí: Securing Supplies, Strengthening the Mission. oikos Case Writing Competition 2016 – Corporate Sustainability Track 1st Prize. https://oikos-international.org/wp-content/uploads/2015/06/2016_CS_free-case_Guayaki_case.pdf

This case is accompanied by a teaching note, available to faculty only. Please send your request to freecase@oikosinternational.org. Access to the Guayakí case video hosted by VIMEO is also free and the password is in the teaching note.

Stakeholder Negotiation Exercises

• For details on how to undertake a stakeholder negotiation exercise with actual stakeholders of a negotiation as coaches see:

Ramus, C. A. (2003). Stakeholders as Coaches: An Experiential Method for Teaching Environmental Regulatory Negotiation. Journal of Management Education, 27(2): 246–270.

• Issue-based stakeholder negotiation exercises where actual stakeholder coaches are not present require instructors to choose a local or national issue of significance so as to heighten students' involvement and interest. The ideal issue is one that is complex and uncertain and has many differing stakeholder perspectives as to how the problem should or should not be addressed.

Examples include (1) a major labor disruption that not only affects the company and its primary stakeholders but the community as well; and (2) controversial capital investments including building on rich agricultural land, pipeline expansion, mining expansion, etc. For details on methods to engage students in an issue-based stakeholder negotiation exercise see:

Collins, E., & Kearins, K. (2007). Exposing students to the potential and risks of stakeholder engagement then teaching sustainability: A classroom exercise. Journal of Management Education, 31(4): 521–540.

Egri, C. P. (1999). The environmental round table role-play exercise: The dynamics of multi-stakeholder decision-making processes. Journal of Management Education, 23(1): 95–103.

Social Protest Novel

- Some examples of historical social protest novels that have led to change include: *The Jungle* by Upton Sinclair (1906) on the terrible treatment of immigrant laborers in food processing facilities in the United States; *The Feminine Mystique* by Betty Friedan (1963) on the dissatisfaction of housewives across America; *Invisible Man* by Ralph Ellison (1947) about societal repression and African American's community's resulting frustrations; and *Silent Spring* by Rachel Carson (1962) on the serious health problems that chemical companies denied. All these novels preceded subsequent changes to the Meat Inspection Act, the Feminist movement, the Civil Rights movement, and the Environmental movement respectively.
- For a discussion on how to introduce historical protest novels into a classroom setting and suggestions of social protest novels for a management classroom see:

Westerman, J. W., & Westerman, J. H. (2009). Social Protest Novels in Management Education: Using Hawk's Nest to Enhance Stakeholder Analysis. Journal of Management Education, 33(6): 659–675.

Issue-Based Stakeholder Town Hall

An issue-based stakeholder town hall is a stakeholder exercise that is based on an issue that has yet to be resolved. The ideal issue is in the news, is complex, involves a company or an industry, has multiple stakeholders with differing perspectives, and is contested. Below I provide a few examples

- Pipeline expansion: Keystone XL Pipeline expansion Resource List

Song's 2011 Inside Climate News article entitled "Keystone XL Primer: How the Pipeline's Route Could Impact the Ogallala Aquifer" http://insideclimatenews.org/news/20110811/keystone-xl-pipeline-route-ogallala-aquifer-nebraska-sandhills

CBC news article entitled "Keystone XL pipeline delay disappoints TransCanada" http://www.cbc.ca/news/world/story/2011/11/10/keyston-pipeline-route.html

Mitchell, R. K., Agle, B. R., & Wood, D. J. (1997). Toward a theory of stakeholder identification and salience: Defining the principle of who and what really counts. Academy of Management Review, 22(4), 853–886.

Students are also asked to watch a video made by the Pembina Institute (an environmental non-governmental organization) regarding the Canadian oil sands which can be found at www.pembina.org/pub/1280.

The Dakota Access Pipeline controversy is another example that can be used. For a synopsis of the issues, see the articles by

Sidder, A. (2016: September 14), Understanding the Controversy Behind the Dakota Access Pipeline, Simthosonian.com. Retrieved from www.smithsonianmag.com/smart-news/understanding-controversy-behind-dakota-access-pipeline-180960450/

and

Kennedy, M. (2017: June 1), Crude Oil Begins to Flow through Controversial Dakota Access Pipeline. The two-way breaking news from NPR. Retrieved from www.npr.org/sections/thetwo-way/2017/06/01/531097758/crude-oil-begins-to-flow-through-controversial-dakota-access-pipeline

- The impact of technology adoption on employment

Concern regarding technology replacing jobs is not news. What is news is the *speed* at which technology is and will replace jobs as artificial intelligence and robotic automation takes hold. Driverless vehicles, automated kiosks, robo-investing are all examples of this radical transition. This is an ideal, although uncomfortable, topic for management students to discuss. Taking on various stakeholder roles related to this issue would allow students to think through the short-term and long-term implications of an issue that may affect their future.

Suggested readings and videos:

The Guardian article provides perceptual and actual data on robotic automation: www.bbc.com/future/story/20150805-will-machines-eventually-take-on-every-job

The Economist (2016: 25 June) "Special report: The return of the machinery question" provides an excellent look at the issue and introduces students to the importance of government as an important stakeholder. www.economist.com/news/special-report/21700758-will-smarter-machines-cause-mass-unemployment-automation-and-anxiety

TED-Talks by Andrew McAfee and Erik Brynjolfsson authors of:

Brynjolfsson, E., & McAfee, A. (2011). *Race against the machine*, Lexington, MA: Digital Frontier Press.

Brynjolfsson, E., & McAfee, A. (2014). *The second machine age*, New York: W.W. Norton & Company.www.ted.com/talks/andrew_mcafee_what_will_future_jobs_look_likewww.ted.com/talks/erik_brynjolfsson_the_key_to_growth_race_em_with_em_the_machines

Notes

1. Examples include seminal papers on the salience of stakeholders – e.g., Mitchell, Agle, & Wood (1997); strategic management textbooks using stakeholder theory as a key theory – e.g., Rothaermel (2017); stakeholder theory videos – e.g., the Darden Business Ethics series www.youtube.com/view_play_list?p=91681CE5A128EBF8; and practitioner blogs on stakeholder management – e.g., https://stakeholdermanagement.wordpress.com/

2. Let's just say that by the time we left the class, we had a spotless classroom.

3. More information on where to access this case can be found in the resource list at the end of this chapter.

4. See www.akwesasne.ca/environment

5. Information collected from the Water Encyclopedia: Science and Issues. www.waterencyclopedia.com/Oc-Po/Ogallala-Aquifer.html.

6. Westjet no overbooking advertisement: www.youtube.com/watch?v=h1ECNvo6DMQ

7. For example, one of the benefits of streaming video services like Netflix is that people can watch their favorite shows when they desire and on any media platform (phone, tablet, personal computer, television). In other words, the asynchronistic aspect of video streaming relative to synchronistic aspect of network programing is being assessed when consumers are deciding which they will purchase.

References

Adler, P. S. (2016). 2015 Presidential Address: Our teaching mission. *Academy of Management Review*, 41(2): 185–195. DOI: 10.5465/amr.2016.0017.

Alpaslan, C. M. (2009). Ethical management of crises: Shareholder value maximisation or stakeholder loss minimisation? *Journal of Corporate Citizenship*, 36: 41–50.

Arco, M. (2017). Christie calls on feds to make big changes after United Airlines fiasco. NJ.com.

de Bakker, F. G. A., den Hond, F., King, B., & Weber, K. (2013). Social movements, civil society and corporations: Taking stock and looking ahead. *Organization Studies*, 34(5–6):573–593. DOI: 10.1177/0170840613479222.

Banerjee, S. B. (2011). Embedding sustainability across the organization: A critical perspective. *Academy of Management Learning and Education*, 10(4): 719–731. DOI: 10.5465/amle.2010.0005.

Barnett, M. L. (2007). Shareholder influence capacity and the variability of financial returns to corporate social responsibility. *Academy of Management Review*, 32(3): 794–816. DOI: 10.5465/amr.2007.25275520.

Barnett, M. L. (2014). Why stakeholders ignore firm misconduct. *Journal of Management*, 40(3): 676–702. DOI: 10.1177/0149206311433854.

Barney, J. (1991). Firm resources and sustained competitive advantage. *Journal of Management*, 17(1): 99–120.

Bawden, D., & Robinson, L. (2009). The dark side of information: Overload, anxiety and other paradoxes and pathologies. *Journal of Information Science*, 35(2): 180–191. DOI: 10.1177/0165551508095781.

Bonnafous-Boucher, M., & Rendtorff, J. D. (2015). Teaching Business Ethics and Stakeholder Theory. *Journal of Business Ethics Education*, 12: 3–4.

Boyatzis, R. E., & Saatcioglu, A. (2008). A 20-year view of trying to develop emotional, social and cognitive intelligence competencies in graduate management education. *Journal of Management Development*, 27(1): 92–108. DOI: 10.1108/02621710810840785.

Bradbury-Huang, H. (2010). What is good action research? Why the resurgent interest?. *Action Research*, 8(1): 93–109. DOI: 10.1177/1476750310362435.

Bridoux, F., & Stoelhorst, J. W. (2014). Microfoundations for stakeholder theory: Managing stakeholders with heterogeneous motives. *Strategic Management Journal*, 35(1): 107–125. DOI: 10.1002/smj.2089.

Bridoux, F., & Stoelhorst, J. W. (2016). Stakeholder Relationships and Social Welfare: A Behavioral Theory of Contributions to Joint Value Creation. *Academy of Management Review*, 41(2): 229–251. DOI: 10.5465/amr.2013.0475.

Bruder, P. (2015). Game on: gamification in the classroom. *Education Digest*, 80(7): 56.

Coghlan, D. (2011). Action research: Exploring perspectives on a philosophy of practical knowing. *The Academy of Management Annals*, 5(1): 53–87. DOI: 10.1080/19416520.2011.571520.

Collins, E., & Kearins, K. (2007). Exposing students to the potential and risks of stakeholder engagement when teaching sustainability: A classroom exercise. *Journal of Management Education*, 31 (4): 521–540. DOI: 10.1177/1052562906291307.

Convening of Indigenous Peoples for the Healing of Mother Earth. (2008). Message of the Living Spirit of the Convening of Indigenous Peoples for the Healing of Mother Earth at the Cultural Territory of the Maya, pp. 1–7. Palenque, Chiapas, Mexico.

Crane, A., Henriques, I., Husted, B., & Matten, D. (2015). Defining the scope of business & society. *Business & Society*, 54(4): 427–434. DOI: 10.1177/0007650315590896.

Crane, A., & Livesey, S. (2003). Are you talking to me? Stakeholder communication and the risks and rewards of dialogue. In J. Andriof, S. Waddock, B. W. Husted, & S. S. Rahmaneds., Unfolding Stakeholder Thinking: Relationships, communication, reporting and performance, pp. 39–52. Sheffield, UK: Greenleaf Publishing.

Crowne, K. A. (2009). The relationships among social intelligence, emotional intelligence and cultural intelligence. *Organization Management Journal*, 6(3): 148–63. DOI: 10.1057/omj.2009.20.

Darnall, N., Henriques, I., & Sadorsky, P. (2010). Adopting proactive environmental strategy: The influence of stakeholders and firm size. *Journal of Management Studies*, 47(6): 1072–94. DOI: 10.1111/j.1467-6486.2009.00873.x.

Davis, R. H. (1861). *Life in the iron mills*. New York: The Feminist Press.

Dicheva, D., Dichev, C., Agre, G., & Angelova, G. (2015). Gamification in education: A systematic mapping study gamification in education. Educational Technology & Society, 18(June): 75–88.

Dicheva, D., Irwin, K., Dichev, C., & Talasila, S. (2014). A course gamification platform supporting student motivation and engagement. *2014 International Conference on Web and Open Access to Learning, ICWOAL 2014*. DOI: 10.1109/ICWOAL.2014.7009214.

Egri, C. P. (1999). The environmental round table role-play exercise: The dynamics of multi-stakeholder decision-making processes. *Journal of Management Education*, 23(1): 95–103.

Egri, C. P. (2003). Teaching about the natural environment in management education: New directions and approaches. *Journal of Management Education*, 27(2): 139–143. DOI: 10.1177/1052562903251409.

Freberg, K., Graham, K., McGaughey, K., & Freberg, L. A. (2011). Who are the social media influencers? A study of public perceptions of personality. *Public Relations Review*, 37(1): 90–92. Elsevier Inc. DOI: 10.1016/j.pubrev.2010.11.001.

Freeman, R. E. (1984). *Strategic management: A stakeholder approach*. Boston: Pitman.

Freeman, R. E., & MacVea, J. (2005). A stakeholder approach to strategic, management. In M. Hitt, R. E. Freeman, & J. Harrison, eds., *Handbook of strategic management*, pp. 189–207. Oxford: Blackwell Publishing. DOI: 10.2139/ssrn.263511.

Freeman, R. E., Wicks, A. C., & Parmar, B. (2004). Stakeholder theory and "The Corporate Objective Revisited." *Organization Science*, 15(3): 364–369. DOI: 10.1287/orsc.1040.0066.

Friedman, M. (1970). The social responsibility of business is to increase its profits. *The New York Times Magazine*, 32: 122–124.

Frooman, J. (1999). Strategies influence. *The Academy of Management Review*, 24(2): 191–205.

Frostenson, M. (2015). Teaching issues-driven stakeholder theory. *Journal of Business Ethics*, 12: 43–52.

Glover, I. (2013). Play as you learn: Gamification as a technique for motivating learners. Proceedings of World Conference on Educational Multimedia, Hypermedia and Telecommunications, 1998–2008.

Grégoire, Y., Salle, A., & Tripp, T. M. (2015). Managing social media crises with your customers: The good, the bad, and the ugly. *Business Horizons*, 58(2): 173–182. DOI: 10.1016/j.bushor.2014.11.001.

Hahn, T., Preuss, L., Pinkse, J., & Figge, F. (2014). cognitive frames in corporate sustainability: Managerial sensemaking with paradoxical and business case frames. *Academy of Management Review*, 39(4): 463–487. DOI: 10.5465/amr.2012.0341.

Hanus, M. D., & Fox, J. (2015). Assessing the effects of gamification in the classroom: A longitudinal study on intrinsic motivation, social comparison, satisfaction, effort, and academic performance. *Computers and Education*, 80: 152–161. DOI: 10.1016/j.compedu.2014.08.019.

Harris, S. (2017). Westjet boasts it doesn't overbook flights in ad targeting airlines that do. CBC News Business.

Harrison, J. S., Bosse, D. A., & Phillips, R. A. (2010). Managing for stakeholders, stakeholder utility functions, and competitive advantage. *Strategic Management Journal*, 31(1): 58–74. DOI: 10.1002/smj.801.

Harrison, J. S., & St. John, C. H. (2014). *Foundations in strategic management*, 6th edn. Independence, KY: Cengage/South-Western.

Harrison, J. S., & Wicks, A. C. (2013). Stakeholder theory, value, and firm performance. *Business Ethics Quarterly*, 23(1): 97–124. DOI: 10.5840/beq20132314.

Henriques, I., & Sadorsky, P. (1999). The relationship between environmental commitment and managerial perceptions of stakeholder importance. *Academy of Management Journal*, 42(1): 87–99.

Henriques, I., & Sharma, S. (2005). Pathways of stakeholder influence in the Canadian forestry industry. *Business Strategy and the Environment*, 14(6): 384–398.

Hill, C. W. L., & Hult, G. T. M. (2017). International business: Competing in the global marketplace, 11th edn. New York: McGraw-Hill Education.

Hoskisson, R. E., Hitt, M. A., Ireland, R. D., & Harrison, J. S. (2013). Competing for advantage, 3rd edn. Independence, KY: Cengage/South-Western.

Husted, B. W. (2015). Corporate social responsibility practice from 1800–1914: Past initiatives and current debates. *Business Ethics Quarterly*, 25(1): 125–141. DOI: 10.1017/beq.2014.1.

Kacperczyk, A. (2009). With greater power comes greater responsibility? Takeover protection and corporate attention to stakeholders. *Strategic Management Journal*, 30: 261–85. DOI: 10.1002/smj.733.

Kaplan, A. M., & Haenlein, M. (2010). Users of the world, unite! The challenges and opportunities of Social Media. *Business Horizons*, 53(1): 59–68. DOI: 10.1016/j.bushor.2009.09.003.

Kirsch, S. (2001). Lost worlds: Environmental disaster, "culture loss," and the law. *Current Anthropology*, 42(2): 167–198.

Königer, P., & Janowitz, K. (1995). Drowning in information, but thirsty for knowledge. *International Journal of Information Management*, 15(1): 5–16. DOI: 10.1016/0268-4012(94)00002-B.

Lange, D., Lee, P. M., & Dai, Y. (2011). Organizational reputation: A review. *Journal of Management*, 37(1): 153–84. DOI: 10.1177/0149206310390963.

Lee, J. J., & Hammer, J. (2011). Gamification in education: What, how, why bother? *Academic Exchange Quarterly*, 15(2): 1–5.

Lumpkin, G. (1995). *To make my bread*. Urbana: University of Illinois Press.

Mahoney, J. T. (2012). Towards a stakeholder theory of strategic management. In J. E. Ricart Costa & J. M. Rosanas Marti, eds., *Towards a new theory of the firm: Humanizing the firm and the management profession*, pp. 153–182. Cambridge, MA: Ballinger Publishing.

Margolis, J., & Walsh, J. P. (2003). Misery loves companies: Rethinking social initiatives by business. *Administrative Science Quarterly*, 48(2): 268–305. DOI: 10.1080/10350339209360349.

Mitchell, R. K., Agle, B. R., & Wood, D. J. (1997). Toward a theory of stakeholder identification and salience: Defining the principle of who and what really counts. *Academy of Management Review*, 22(4): 853–86. DOI: 10.5465/AMR.1997.9711022105.

Mitchell, R. K., Lee, J. H., & Agle, B. R. (2017). Stakeholder prioritization work: The role of stakeholder salience in stakeholder research. In D. Wasieleski & J. Weber, eds., *Stakeholder management: Business & society 360*, vol. 1, pp. 1–45. Bingley, UK: Emerald Group Publishing.

Mitchell, R. K., Weaver, G. R., Agle, B. R., Bailey, A. D., & Carlson, J. (2016). Stakeholder agency and social welfare: Pluralism and decision making in the multi-objective corporation. *Academy of Management Review*, 41(2): 252–275.

Morsing, M., & Schultz, M. (2006). Corporate social responsibility communication: Stakeholder information, response and involvement strategies. *Business Ethics: A European Review*, 15 (October): 323–338. DOI: 10.1111/j.1467-8608.2006.00460.x.

Pang, A., Hassan, N. B. B. A., & Chong, A. C. Y. (2013). Negotiating crisis in the social media environment. *Corporate Communications: An International Journal*, 19(1): 96–118. DOI: 10.1108/CCIJ-09-2012-0064.

Parker, L. (2016). What happens to the U.S. Midwest when the water's gone? National Geographic, (August).

Porter, M. E. (1996). What is strategy?. *Harvard Business Review*, 74(6): 61–78. DOI: 10.1098/rspb.2008.0355.

Ramus, C. A. (2003). Stakeholders as coaches: An experiential method for teaching environmental regulatory negotiation. *Journal of Management Education*, 27(2): 246–270. DOI: 10.1177/1052562903251416.

Reade, C., Todd, a. M., Osland, a., & Osland, J. (2008). Poverty and the multiple stakeholder challenge for global leaders. *Journal of Management Education*, 32(6): 820–840. DOI: 10.1177/1052562908317445.

Rendtorff, J. D. (2015). An interactive method for teaching business ethics, stakeholder theory and corporate social responsibility (CSR). Journal of Business Ethics Education, 12(Special Issue): 93–106.

Rindova, V. P., Williamson, I. O., Petkova, A. P., & Sever, J. M. (2005). Being good or being known: An empirical examination of the dimensions, antecedents, and consequences of organizational reputation. *Academy of Management Journal*, 48(6): 1033–1049. DOI: 10.5465/AMJ.2005.19573108.

Robson, C., Hearst, M., Kau, C., & Pierce, J. (2013). Comparing the Use of Social Networking and Traditional Media Channels for Promoting Citizen Science. *CSCW '13 Proceedings of the 2013 conference on Computer supported cooperative work*, 1463–8. DOI: 10.1145/2441776.2441941.

Rooney, D., Leach, J., & Ashworth, P. (2014). Doing the social in social license. *Social Epistemology*, 28(3–4): 209–218. DOI: 10.1080/02691728.2014.922644.

Rothaermel, F. (2017). *Strategic management.*, 3rd edn. New York: McGraw-Hill Education.

Rowley, T. J. (1997). Moving beyond dyadic ties: A network theory of stakeholder influences. *The Academy of Management Review*, 22(4): 887–910.

Rowley, T. J., & Moldoveanu, M. (2003). When will stakeholder groups act? An interest- and identity-based model of stakeholder group mobilization. *Academy of Management Review*, 28(2): 204–219. DOI: 10.5465/amr.2003.9416080.

Russo, M. V, & Crooke, M. (2016). *Guayakí: Securing supplies, strengthening the Mission. oikos Case Writing Competition 2016 – Corporate Sustainability Track*, pp. 1–30.

Russo, M. V., & Goldstein, D. (2007). *Seventh Generation: Balancing customer expectations with supply chain realities. oikos Sustainability Case Collection*, pp. 1–25.

Salovey, P., & Mayer, J. D. (1990). Emotional intelligence. *Imagination, Cognition, and Personality*, 9(3): 185–211. DOI: 10.1016/S0962-1849(05)80058-7.

Seaborn, K., & Fels, D. I. (2015). Gamification in theory and action: A survey. *International Journal of Human Computer Studies*, 74: 14–31. DOI: 10.1016/j.ijhcs.2014.09.006.

Sharma, S., & Henriques, I. (2005). Stakeholder influences on sustainability practices in the Canadian forest products industry. *Strategic Management Journal*, 26(2): 159–180.

Sinclair, U. (1906). The Jungle. In C. V. Ebyed., *Norton critical editions*. New York: W.W. Norton.

Skidmore, H. (1941). *Hawk's Nest: A Novel.* Knoxville: University of Tennessee Press.

Snyder, R., Williams, D., & Peterson, G. (2003). Culture loss and sense of place in resource valuation: Economics, anthropology, and indigenous cultures. In S. Jentoft, H. Minde, & R. Nilsen, eds., *Indigenous peoples: Resource management and global rights*, pp. 107–23. Chicago: University of Chicago Press.

Song, L. (2011). Keystone XL Primer: How the Pipeline's route could impact the Ogallala Aquifer. *Inside Climate News.*

Steinbeck, J. (1939). *The Grapes of Wrath.* New York: Viking.

Toft, K. H. (2015). Teaching business ethics to critical students: Adopting the stance of political CSR. *Journal of Business Ethics Education*, 12: 77–92.

Wallace, C. (2017). Scarecrows, watchdogs and strange bedfellows. The Toronto Star, IN6-IN7.

Westerman, J. W., & Westerman, J. H. (2009). Social protest novels in management education: Using *Hawk's Nest* to enhance stakeholder analysis. *Journal of Management Education*, 33(6): 659–675. DOI: 10.1177/1052562908329815.

The Practice of Stakeholder Engagement[1]

JOHANNA KUJALA

Tampere University

SYBILLE SACHS

University of Applied Sciences Zurich (HWZ)

Introduction

Stakeholder theory is currently having a broad impact on a variety of topics in organizational research. Since Freeman's (1984) influential work, stakeholder theory has been used to examine multiple phenomena in various fields, such as strategic management (e.g., Haksever, Chaganti, & Cook, 2004; Harrison, Bosse, & Phillips, 2010; Sachs & Rühli, 2011), corporate responsibility (e.g., Kujala, et al., 2017; Sachs & Maurer, 2009; Smith & Rönnegard, 2016; Strand, Freeman, & Hockerts 2015), business ethics (e.g., Phillips, 1997; Purnell & Freeman, 2012; Wicks, 1996), and international business (e.g., Lehtimäki & Kujala, 2017). When the theory was first proposed, stakeholder scholars were interested in who the most important stakeholders are and what their stakes or interests are in organizational settings (e.g., Clarkson, 1995; Mitchell, Agle, & Wood, 1997). More recently, however, the focus has shifted toward stakeholder collaboration, cooperation, and engagement (& Stoelhurst, 2016; Harrison & Wicks, 2013; Tantalo & Priem, 2016).

There is an increasing amount of literature on how organizations are applying these ideas about stakeholders in practice (Freeman, Kujala, & Sachs, 2017; Greenwood, 2007; Jones, Felps, & Bigley, 2007; Harrison, Freeman, & de Abreu, 2015; Heugens, van den Bosch, & van Riel, 2002; Jones et al., 2007). In recent years, stakeholder engagement, or "practicing the ideas of stakeholder theory," has been developed by various public, private, and third-sector organizations. However, "stakeholder engagement" literature is still somewhat fragmented, and few scholars have attempted to develop a general framework for research on this subject (Freeman, et al., 2017). Such a framework would help to identify the relations between work on this subject as well as the topics on which further work should focus.

The purpose of this chapter is to provide a structure for current work on stakeholder engagement based on a general framework as well as to identify work in this area that still must be done. We have organized the rest of this chapter as follows. First, we will structure stakeholder engagement research according to four key themes of stakeholder engagement practices. Then, based on an overview of recent stakeholder engagement literature, we will provide a theoretical guide for investigating stakeholder engagement with those four themes. Elaborating upon that, the chapter will then discuss avenues for future research into stakeholder engagement.

The Structure of Stakeholder Engagement Research

Stakeholder engagement has become the term for practicing stakeholder theory in businesses and other organizations (2002 Freeman et al., 2010; Greenwood, 2007; Harrison, et al., 2015; Heugens et al., 2002; Jones et al., 2007; Post, Preston, & Sachs, 2002). However, stakeholder engagement has been understood in a variety of different ways and from a variety of different theoretical perspectives (Greenwood, 2007). For example, according to Maak (2007), stakeholder engagement concerns the embeddedness of stakeholders' objectives, expectations, actor relations, and actions in the leadership of an organization.

On the other hand, Noland and Phillips (2010: 40) point out that stakeholder engagement has a moral core and, therefore, they see it as "a type of interaction that involves, at minimum, recognition and respect of common humanity and the ways in which the actions of each may affect the other." Moreover, in order to be successful, stakeholder engagement needs to be integrated into the strategy of an organization (Noland & Phillips, 2010). In this chapter, we broadly define stakeholder engagement "as practices the organization undertakes to involve stakeholders in a positive manner in organizational activities" (Greenwood, 2017: 315).

To create a structure for the ample literature on stakeholder engagement practices, we will build upon Freeman et al.'s (2017) framework for grouping cases of stakeholder engagement. This framework allows us to portray stakeholder theory from both *managerial* and *pragmatic* perspectives. In the following, we organize our presentation of the most important works on the practice of stakeholder engagement according to the four themes of this framework: (1) examining stakeholder relations, (2) communicating with stakeholders, (3) learning with and from stakeholders, and (4) integrative stakeholder engagement (Figure 14.1).

The various themes of our framework naturally overlap, and their distinction is superficial to some extent. However, they form a continuum from examining stakeholder relationships through communicating with and learning from stakeholders toward integrative stakeholder engagement that

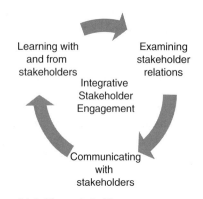

Figure 14.1 The stakeholder engagement framework (Freeman et al., 2017: 5)

incorporates all other aspects of engagement. Like many previous authors, we view stakeholder engagement as a process or a cycle that evolves and progresses over time.

In the next section, we will provide a theoretical guide for examining stakeholder engagement through the four themes based on an overview of recent stakeholder engagement literature. We will describe the themes in more detail and discuss what has been learned about them and how they have affected stakeholder engagement practices. Further, we identify three or four important issues that have been raised by the sub-literature we reviewed. These insights are based on a broad array of different studies and will enable further development of stakeholder engagement practices, which creates economic and social value.

A Theoretical Guide to Work on Stakeholder Engagement Practices

Examining Stakeholder Relations

Stakeholder value creation is an important aspect of many recent studies on stakeholder engagement (e.g., Freeman, et al., 2010; Garcia-Castro & Aguilera, 2015; Garriga, 2014; Harrison & Wicks, 2013; Rühli, et al., 2017; Schneider & Sachs 2017; Tantalo & Priem, 2016). Regarding value creation, the literature examining stakeholder relationships emphasizes value cocreation as both a transactional practice (Garcia-Castro & Aguilera, 2015; Mitchell, et al., 1997) and a relational practice (Maak, 2007; Myllykangas, Kujala, & Lehtimäki, 2010). Stakeholder utility (Harrison & Wicks, 2013; Tantalo & Priem, 2016) and issue-based stakeholder networks (Roloff, 2008; Rühli et al., 2017; Schneider & Sachs, 2017) have also been important issues in the literature.

Transactional Practices in Value Creation. The transactional view of stakeholder engagement is interested in the exchange of value among stakeholders and the focal company, but it often narrows the concept of a stakeholder to entail only shareholders or owners of the company. Mitchell et al. (1997) made an important contribution to the idea of stakeholder engagement by proposing to broaden the vision of business beyond profit maximisation to include the interests and claims of nonstockholding groups. They also identified three attributes of stakeholder relationships that can serve as a basis for stakeholder salience: power, urgency and legitimacy (Mitchell, et al., 1997). While the value of the salience model in understanding stakeholder engagement has been widely acknowledged, the model has also been criticized for its inability to fully understand stakeholder engagement dynamics (Friedman & Miles, 2002; Moir, Kennerley, & Ferguson, 2007) and stakeholder interfaces and networks (Frooman, 1999; Rowley, 1997; Rowley & Moldoveanu, 2003).

A more recent example of the transactional view of stakeholder engagement, Garcia-Castro and Aguilera (2015) presented a conceptual framework of incremental value creation and appropriation, which expands the concept of value and value capture to include all stakeholders of the firm. Their dynamic value creation–appropriation (VCA) model distinguishes between different value creation and appropriation scenarios, enabling depiction of the relationship between the value appropriated by a stakeholder and the total value created during a period of time (Garcia-Castro & Aguilera, 2015). This view broadens the definition of value creation beyond only the economic value gained by shareholders to the total value gained by all the stakeholders of the firm. However, the value creation process in stakeholder engagement is still seen as consisting of more transactional trade-offs than relational cocreation.

Relational Practices in Value Cocreation. Many authors (Maak, 2007; Mitchell, et al., 2016; Myllykangas, et al., 2010) have proposed moving beyond the transactional view and examining stakeholder engagement as a relational process. In his study on responsible leadership and stakeholder engagement, Maak (2007) argued that, in order to address the moral complexity that follows complex stakeholder demands, leaders need to invest in building long-term and jointly valuable relations with their stakeholders. Such relationships result in social capital and the value networks consisting of various stakeholders, which improve both business and social sustainability.

The underlying ideas of the relational view are that stakeholder engagement should aim to incorporate and balance all stakeholder needs over time and that stakeholder engagement is a relational process. To understand this process, we need to understand how relationships are built and managed. Myllykangas et al. (2010) examined relational factors in stakeholder engagement and argued that, instead of asking who and what is important in stakeholder relationships (Mitchell, et al., 1997), we should ask how value is created. Their study suggests that, for successful stakeholder engagement and value creation, it is imperative to follow practices related to the following six elements of stakeholder relationships: (1) stakeholders' targets and (2) learning potential, (3) the history of the collaboration, (4) interaction and (5) information sharing in the relationship, and (6) trust (Myllykangas, et al., 2010). Recently, Mitchell, et al. (2016), following Jones and Felps (2013a; 2013b), rejected the notion of a corporate single-value object when considering the benefits of value creation for social welfare, suggesting instead that "multiple considerations" of stakeholders might be relevant to the value creation process.

Stakeholder Utility. Many examinations of stakeholder engagement begin by asking what stakeholder utilities are. Harrison and Wicks (2013) argued that the drivers of stakeholder engagement should be considered from a more complex perspective than their economic value alone. To do so, they developed a four-factor perspective for stakeholder utility that incorporates both the tangible value stakeholders seek and the process and distribution of stakeholder value (Harrison & Wicks, 2013). Based on theoretical discussion, they suggested that the following four elements are important to stakeholder utility: (1) stakeholder utility associated with actual goods and services, (2) stakeholder utility associated with organizational justice, (3) stakeholder utility from affiliation, and (4) stakeholder utility associated with perceived opportunity costs (Harrison & Wicks, 2013).

Garriga (2014) used the capability approach to move beyond stakeholder utility and identify and measure stakeholders' capabilities in the value creation process. Based on an in-depth case study of one of the leading companies in the agricultural sector of Argentina, she argued that the following attributes are relevant to stakeholder value creation: employability, autonomy, innovativeness, entrepreneurship, responsiveness, social integration, being emphatic, being "green," and health (Garriga, 2014). In contrast to Harrison and Wicks (2013), Garriga (2014) brought environmental concerns to companies' direct attention, although environmentally oriented value was considered indirectly through stakeholders.

Tantalo and Priem (2016) also addressed stakeholder utility by examining the ways in which value can be created simultaneously for multiple stakeholder groups. They argued that stakeholder utility consists of more than just economic utilities and that different stakeholder groups may understand economic utilities in different ways. Therefore, we should understand that the possibilities for value creation related to stakeholder engagement go beyond traditional customer-oriented value creation and include supplier-oriented, employee-oriented and community-oriented value creation.

Issue-Based Stakeholder Networks. Stakeholder engagement literature has been interested in examining stakeholder relations, especially practices for cocreating value in multi-stakeholder settings and in issue-based stakeholder networks (Rühli, et al., 2017). Roloff (2008) differentiated between two types of stakeholder engagement: (1) organization-focused stakeholder engagement, which emphasises the organization's welfare, and (2) issue-focused stakeholder engagement, which emphasises the issues that affect relationships with and the welfare of stakeholders. She argued that issue-focused stakeholder engagement acknowledges the various challenges of the changing global business environment and helps companies to increase the legitimacy of their activities.

Value creation in issue-based stakeholder networks relies on the fact that individual stakeholder identities can be bridged during value creation through the intergroup relationships in an issue-based stakeholder network (Schneider & Sachs, 2017). Trust is highest between stakeholder groups in an issue-based network when there is a superordinate stakeholder identity, while cooperation increases only if specific stakeholder identities become more salient. Participants should thus regain awareness of their specific stakeholder affiliations in the advanced stages of a multi-stakeholder process and in the context of a superordinate identity. When specific stakeholder in-groups become more salient, the participants' cognitive and organizational accessibility to their stakeholder resources and capabilities increases.

Communicating with Stakeholders

Stakeholder communication has become an important topic in stakeholder engagement research, which has shifted its focus from stakeholder management to stakeholder communication and interaction. Today, stakeholder engagement necessitates ongoing stakeholder attentiveness and requires more refined communication than previous decades (Morsing & Schultz, 2006). Stakeholder engagement involves not only communicating *to* stakeholders but also communicating *with* stakeholders, and therefore, moving from stakeholder *debate* to stakeholder *dialogue* is an integral part of stakeholder communication (Kaptein & Van Tulder, 2003; Lehtimäki & Kujala, 2017). In addition to general discussion about stakeholder dialogue, there are many studies that analyze the stakeholder dialogue process (Friedman & Miles, 2002; Golob & Podnar, 2014; O'Riordan & Fairbrass, 2008; Pedersen, 2006). Recently, the idea of respecting the voices of critical, silent, and marginalized stakeholders has gained importance in stakeholder communication research (Dawkins, 2015; Derry, 2012; Joutsenvirta, 2009, 2011). Stakeholder accounting and reporting remain important themes (Brown & Dillard, 2015; Greenwood, 2007; Siltaoja & Onkila, 2013).

Moving from Stakeholder Debate to Stakeholder Dialogue. In general, stakeholder dialogue can be defined as a two-way communication in oral or written form, and it can occur directly (e.g., face-to-face discussion) or indirectly (e.g., corporate reporting or media coverage read by both parties) (Lehtimäki & Kujala, 2017). Kaptein and Van Tulder (2003: 210) define stakeholder dialogue as "a structured interactive and proactive process aimed at creating sustainable strategies." Stakeholder dialogue differs from stakeholder debate in many respects (Kaptein & Van Tulder, 2003): instead of egocentric competition, it focuses on empathetic cooperation; instead of speaking and influencing, it aims to listen and convince; and instead of confrontation and defensiveness, it builds on constructive and vulnerable attitudes. In stakeholder dialogue, "opinions are exchanged, (future) interests and expectations are discussed, and standards are developed with respect to business practice" (Kaptein & Van Tulder, 2003: 208). As preconditions for successful stakeholder dialogue, Kaptein and Van Tulder (2003) presented the following issues: the parties need to be acquainted with each other and understand their common areas of interest; the parties need to trust in the integrity of the other party and value the dialogue; the parties need to agree upon clear rules and structure for the dialogue; the parties should be ready to develop their dialogue skills and understand that dialogue demands a certain communication style; the dialogue should be understood as a process with, preferably, several successive meetings, and the parties should be able to give feedback on the results and outcomes of the dialogue.

As the outcome of the dialogue depends on its organization, it should be conducted in a well-considered manner. Special attention needs to be paid to the dialogic process. Lehtimäki and Kujala (2017: 489) argued that "stakeholder dialogue, to be other than a shouting match, requires not so much arranging for opportunities for more communication between the parties, but rather attention to the ways by which the meaning of the content of dialogue is being ascribed in communication." They further argued that seeing stakeholder relations as discourse advances theories on stakeholder engagement and enables understanding of how language both shapes and reflects dynamic stakeholder relations (Lehtimäki & Kujala, 2017).

Morsing and Schultz (2006: 333) suggested that stakeholder engagement should not inform communication strategies, but respond to them, involve strategies, and provide "pro-active endorsement" of stakeholders. Brownlee, Dmytriyev, and Elias (2017) described the collaborative, dialogue-based stakeholder engagement process that occurred between the Coca Cola Company and the World Wildlife Fund for a freshwater conservation initiative. The study is an example of how the focal company, although substantially influencing its value chain, can demonstrate the stakeholders' mind-set by engaging stakeholders beyond the original partners, including stakeholders across the entire value chain.

Analyzing the Process of Stakeholder Dialogue. According to O'Riordan and Fairbrass (2008: 755), stakeholder dialogue "offers a fruitful approach to managing stakeholder relations." Through the process of stakeholder dialogue, business managers may recognize means to identify, evaluate, address, and balance the expectations, needs, and demands of their stakeholders. Literature on the process of stakeholder dialogue fosters the idea of stakeholder engagement by incorporating stakeholders' interests into firms' decision-making in order to guide the transformation of the theory of stakeholder dialogue into actual practice (Friedman & Miles, 2002). Pedersen (2006) argued that, due to the multifaceted nature of stakeholder dialogue, an analytical framework is needed to evaluate the actual level of stakeholder engagement. In high-engagement processes, all relevant stakeholders are included in dialogue, which is structured around an open set of questions or issues. New critical voices are respected, and thus the dialogue promotes freedom and equality. Moreover, high-engagement stakeholder dialogue results in full access to information about the process and its outcomes.

Effective stakeholder dialogue takes into account the following four elements as a practical framework for responding to stakeholder expectations (O'Riordan & Fairbrass, 2008):

(1) The context in which stakeholders operate, including the political, economic, social, technological, legal, and environmental climate; industrial structure; competitor activity, and media influence.

(2) Identification and prioritization of stake-holders as well as their expectations for inter-nal company factors, such as number of employees, sales revenue, and capital, level of success, business culture and governance.

(3) Recognition of the potential impact of certain events, which allows crisis and issue manage-ment to be incorporated into stakeholder dia-logue management.

(4) Management's response to the relation between stakeholder dialogue and strategy, which can help incorporate stakeholder dialo-gue into strategic plans and action.

Dialogue is often seen as a way for organizations to reply to criticism of their social and environmental activities (Golob & Podnar, 2014). Six central issues are important to the process of stakeholder dialogue: (1) the concept of the dialogue itself, (2) the motives for engaging in the dialogue, (3) the quality of the dialogue, (4) the outcomes of the dialogic process, (5) stakeholders' expectations for the dialogue, and (6) the role of the dialogue in corporate social responsibility implementation and communication.

Respecting Critical and Silent Voices. While the advice for successful stakeholder dialogue pre-sented above is certainly helpful when organiza-tions seek to engage in dialogue with collaborative and affirmative stakeholders, there is little advice regarding how to engage more critical or silent stakeholders. Rather than only seeking shared value, it may be necessary to only pursue solutions to stakeholders' conflicts. To do so, Dawkins (2015) promotes an agonistic perspective of stake-holder relations in which stakeholders can protect their own values and interests.

Third-sector organizations or non-governmental organizations (NGOs) are also important actors in the field of stakeholder engagement (Baur & Palazzo, 2011; Yaziji & Doh, 2009). Engagement with NGO stakeholders can vary from traditional philanthropy to cross-sector multi-stakeholder partnerships like the GAVI Global Alliance on Vaccines and Immunization (www.gavi.org), which brings together the public and private sec-tors in order to provide children in the world's poorest countries access to vaccines. Often,

NGOs are critical of businesses and use a variety of strategies to influence them.

Joutsenvirta (2009, 2011) identified four main discourses in her analysis of environmental debate about the use of forests between a foresting com-pany and Greenpeace: knowledge, responsibility, openness, and the market. Further, she identified five different legitimation strategies used in the debate: scientific, nationalistic, and commercial rationalization, as well as moralization and normal-ization. Her studies showed that paying attention to different parties' use of language enables under-standing of the way in which certain language hinders or facilitates efforts to create a more balanced relationship between business, nature, and society.

Regarding silent and marginal stakeholders, the prevailing firm-centric and manager-oriented per-spectives should be challenged, and new ways to outline stakeholder legitimacy must be developed (Derry, 2012). Derry (2012: 263) argued that, as management scholars, "our ultimate job is to work to understand how business can benefit society, not how society can optimize business." Thus, we should be ready to question the dominant stake-holder frameworks and change the prevailing lan-guage and narratives regarding businesses and stakeholders. Only then can we expand the view of various stakeholders and their expectations beyond those groups that are traditionally consid-ered salient to also respect those groups who are silent or regarded as marginal.

Social and Environmental Accounting and Reporting. In many studies, the reporting process is understood as an important part of the dialogue between the company and its stakeholders (Greenwood, 2007), and therefore it is a significant tool for stakeholder engagement for companies and other organizations. Stakeholder reporting has also been studied as a social practice. The literature has identified two distinctive discursive strategies for responsibility reports: centralizing and decentraliz-ing (Siltaoja & Onkila, 2013). Centralizing strate-gies view businesses as actively participating in reporting instead of merely responding to regula-tions or stakeholder expectations, while decentraliz-ing strategies present businesses as actors that react and respond to the expectations of different stakeholders and perhaps even openly address stakeholders' interests and needs (Siltaoja & Onkila, 2013). Overall, research on stakeholder accounting and reporting challenges the shareholder-based focus of conventional accounting and calls for new approaches to promote participatory stakeholder accountability and engagement (Brown & Dillard, 2015).

Learning with and from Stakeholders

Stakeholder engagement offers companies the opportunity to learn with and from stakeholders. More specifically, companies can use criticism and feedback as opportunities for value creation (Lee, 2015; Mena & Chabowski, 2015) and see stakeholder engagement as a continuous learning process (Post, et al., 2002; Sachs & Rühli, 2011). There is ample literature on the various aspects of organizational learning through stakeholder dialogue (Burchell & Cook, 2006; Calton & Payne, 2004; Payne & Calton, 2003).

Stakeholders' Criticism and Feedback as Opportunities for Value Creation. To learn about their stakeholders' claims (Mena & Chabowski, 2015), firms can seek to acquire knowledge internally or externally (Lee, 2015). Those firms that can establish a high level of organizational memory of accumulated knowledge concerning stakeholder claims and practices will create more value (Mena & Chabowski, 2015).

Stakeholder Engagement as a Learning Process for Firms. Longitudinal case studies have distinguished three stakeholder engagement processes (Post, et al., 2002; Sachs & Rühli, 2011):

(1) Adaptive learning from stakeholder engagement implies that processes and behaviors undergo modification while the structure, strategy, and culture of the firm remain largely unchanged. Most adaptive learning is based on firms' stakeholder orientation and is characterized by many single loops of learning.

(2) Renewal learning is due to relevant stakeholders' expectations for the firm and affects the evaluation of assumptions about the firm's interaction with stakeholders. Fundamental values and objectives can be pursued in new ways, with noticeable strategic and structural changes. It involves both single- and double-loop learning.

(3) Transformational learning is often induced by a wake-up call regarding stakeholder engagement and implies a fundamental change in the firm's strategy, structure, and culture to increase the likelihood of success in a changing environment. Double- or even deutero-loop learning is necessary to implement generative change in all three core elements of a firm.

Organizational Learning through Stakeholder Dialogue. Burchell and Cook (2006) examined stakeholder dialogue as an interactive, developmental, and exploratory sense-making process, arguing that the results of dialogue are improved if the participants understand the implications of the dialogue process and have a long-term perspective on its outcomes. Moreover, Calton and Payne (2003) presented multi-stakeholder learning dialogues as means to cope with challenges in stakeholder networks and suggested that stakeholder dialogue as an interactive, developmental, and exploratory sense-making process may enhance the governance of stakeholder networks.

Payne and Calton (2004) studied multi-stakeholder learning dialogues, stating that assumptions, goals and processes of these dialogues should foster critical thinking, creativity, and learning through relational responsibilities. They argued that, first, special attention should be paid to the antecedents, preconditions, and introductory characteristics of dialogue to improve stakeholder relationships. This means, for example, that the cultural factors, leadership styles, and catalysts of change should be thoroughly understood before engaging in multi-stakeholder dialogue (Payne & Calton, 2004). Second, they argued, dialogic processes, including participants' attitudes and communication styles (verbal and non-verbal), should be examined to understand participants' perceptions of opportunities for relationship building and learning (Payne & Calton, 2004). Third, the potential risks and limitations of stakeholder dialogue should be recognized and acknowledged.

This means, for example, that manipulation and distortion by powerful stakeholders, as well as disappointment and frustration in cases of unsuccessful stakeholder dialogue, should be addressed in a proper manner. Based on their theoretical discussion, Payne and Calton (2004: 77) suggested that multi-stakeholder learning dialogues should be studied from various perspectives and their evaluation should be expanded "beyond the conventional social sciences or purely analytical means" of evaluating their effectiveness or efficiency.

Integrative Stakeholder Engagement

We identified three important themes regarding integrative stakeholder engagement: (1) the phases of stakeholder engagement, (2) firm-, stakeholder- and problem-centric views of stakeholder engagement, and (3) the nature of stakeholder engagement.

Phases of Stakeholder Engagement. In his seminal book, Freeman (1984) presented an integrative view of stakeholder engagement with three levels: (1) the rational stakeholder identification level, (2) the procedural stakeholder communication level, and (3) the transactional stakeholder involvement or dialogue level. This view includes not only stakeholder identification but also stakeholder communication and dialogue as important parts of the stakeholder engagement process. Since then, different models of the phases of stakeholder engagement have been developed (O'Riordan & Fairbrass, 2008; Plaza-Úbeda, et al., 2010; Sachs, Groth, & Schmitt, 2010a).

Firm-, Stakeholder- and Problem-Centric Views. The integrative stakeholder engagement approaches have been debated from the perspective of the firm, of specific stakeholders and of certain networks or issues (Heugens & Boesch, 2002; Sachs & Rühli, 2011). Using the firm-centric approach, Plaza-Úbeda et al. (2010: 419) conceptualized stakeholder integration (SI) as an integrative concept involving an organization's "ability to establish positive collaborative relationships with a wide variety of stakeholders" with three dimensions. The first dimension describes practices to gain and document information about stakeholders and their demands; the second dimension considers the organization's approach to communication, cooperation and consultation with its stakeholders, and the third dimension involves responsiveness to stakeholder concerns.

Using the stakeholder-focused approach, Burchell and Cook (2008) argued that NGOs seek a strategic balance between cooperation and confrontation. Thus, this perspective not only takes into account the direct interaction of NGOs but also the indirect interactions of NGOs that are not willing to cooperate, and emphasises the need for a network-based view of engagement and negotiation.

Using the problem-based approach, Gray and Stites (2013) described the general features of multi-stakeholder settings after systematic review of the literature on collaboration. They argue that multi-stakeholder settings can be described as problem-oriented social interaction between three or more affected actors dealing with conflicts of interest. This interaction occurs in a way that all participants consider fair.

Stakeholder engagement occurs at several levels in practice as well as in theory (Sachs, Rühli, & Meier, 2010b). At the global level, standards such as the Global Compact initiated a dialogue between firms, stakeholders, and policy-makers (Rasche & Waddock, 2014). At the state level, various issues, such as renewable energy or the rising cost of healthcare, are categorized as multi-stakeholder initiatives (Fransen & Kolks, 2007). Furthermore, in public–private partnerships, multi-stakeholder processes can help to reconcile various stakeholders' interests (Rühli, et al., 2017). These firm-centred engagement processes are evaluated according to the Global Reporting Initiative (Boiral, Heras-Saizarbitoria, & Brotherton, 2017).

Nature of Stakeholder Engagement. Stakeholder theory and the practices of stakeholder engagement are based on both strategic and moral arguments (Dawkins, 2015; Donaldson & Preston 1995; Freeman, et al., 2010; Greenwood, 2007; Jones & Wicks, 1999; Kujala, Heikkinen, & Lehtimäki, 2012; Noland & Phillips, 2010; Post, et al., 2002; Scherer & Palazzo, 2007). Since the seminal article written by Donaldson and Preston (1995), there have traditionally been two different views of stakeholder engagement. However, replying to this article, Jones and Wicks (1999) presented an integrative view of stakeholder engagement that considers it to be simultaneously strategic and moral. Freeman et al. (2010: 412) call this integrated view the "ethics of capitalism," and "[v]alue can be created, traded, and sustained because parties to an agreement are willing to accept responsibility for the consequences of their actions."

Similarly, Kujala et al. (2012) elaborated on the strategic and ethical nature of stakeholder engagement by examining the justification for different stakeholder interests. Greenwood (2007) pointed out that stakeholder engagement is neither good nor bad *per se*, but depends on the level of stakeholder engagement and agency. Noland and Phillips (2010) introduced the term "ethical strategist" to describe those who consider the firm to be dependent upon the stakeholders. Thereby, managers re-evaluate the outcomes and means "for including honest, open, respectful engagement of stakeholders as a vital part a firm's strategy" (Noland & Philips, 2010: 49).

Obviously, there are differences in the forms and practices of stakeholder engagement across industries and areas. In the chemical industry, for example, the Responsible Care Initiative, a voluntary commitment to improve global health, safety, and sustainability, has been adopted by over sixty-five countries around the world (www.icca-chem.org/responsible-care/). In addition, large corporations set an example for stakeholder engagement processes, while small- and medium-sized companies take care of their stakeholders in less formal ways through everyday consultation. In other words, stakeholder engagement is often more casual and less structured in small businesses than it is in big corporations.

We can conclude that the literature on stakeholder engagement has evolved significantly over the last decade and has provided insights for various issues in stakeholder engagement practices (see Table 14.1).

Future Avenues of Research

To develop the stakeholder engagement practices further, we emphasize future avenues of research based on the four themes of the stakeholder engagement framework (Freeman, et al., 2017) and make some methodological suggestions.

The first theme involves examination of stakeholder relationships, and the literature emphasises transactional and relational practices in value cocreation, stakeholder utility, participative multi-stakeholder innovation processes, and issue-based stakeholder networks. The underlying idea of this theme is that stakeholder engagement must incorporate and balance all stakeholders' needs. Additionally, this theme emphasises that stakeholder engagement is a relational process, and thus we need to understand how relationships are built and managed. Many authors have noted that the relationship between organizations and their stakeholders fundamentally depends on trust (Burchell & Cook, 2006; Greenwood & Van Buren III, 2010; Myllykangas, et al., 2010; Pirson & Maholtra, 2011; Post, et al., 2002). However, distrust as a distinct construct of (low) trust has received little consideration in stakeholder engagement literature (Kujala, Lehtimäki, & Pučėtaitė, 2016; Palazzo & Richter, 2005). Therefore, in the context of stakeholder engagement practices, the antecedents and consequences of stakeholder distrust require further investigation (Bijlsma-Frankema, Sitkin, & Weibel, 2015).

The second theme addresses stakeholder communication. We found that the shift from stakeholder debate to stakeholder dialogue and analysis of the process of stakeholder dialogue as well as respect of critical and silent voices are important for effective stakeholder communication. Recently, the literature has acknowledged stakeholder accounting and reporting as important forms of participatory stakeholder accountability and engagement processes. However, the relevance of common ground in stakeholder engagement processes needs to be clarified. Stakeholders' specific interests can result in conflict that seems insurmountable through dialogue and, eventually, compromises (Gottschalg & Zollo, 2007; Roloff, 2008). Developing a common ground, defined as a "backdrop of ideas, experiences, values, and information held in common by two or more parties" (Priem & Nystrom, 2014: 767), is especially challenging when facing wicked issues due to these

Table 14.1 A Theoretical Guide of Work on Stakeholder Engagement Practices

Key themes of the stakeholder engagement framework	Issues in stakeholder engagement practices	Authors
Examining stakeholder relations	Transactional practices in value creation	Garcia-Castro & Aguilera, 2015; Mitchell et al., 1997
	Relational practices in value co-creation	Maak, 2007; Mitchell et al., 2016; Myllykangas et al., 2010
	Stakeholder utility	Garriga, 2014; Harrison & Wicks, 2013; Tantalo & Priem, 2016
	Issue-based stakeholder networks	Roloff, 2008; Rühli et al., 2017; Schneider & Sachs, 2017
Communicating with stakeholders	Shift from stakeholder debate to stakeholder dialogue	Brownlee et al., 2017; Kaptein & Van Tulder, 2003; Lehtimäki & Kujala, 2017; Morsing & Schultz, 2006
	Analysis of the process of stakeholder dialogue	Golob & Podnar, 2014; Friedman & Miles, 2007; O'Riordan & Fairbrass, 2008; Pederson, 2006
	Respect of critical and silent voices	Dawkins, 2015; Derry, 2012; Joutsenvirta, 2009, 2011
	Stakeholder accounting and reporting	Brown & Dillard, 2015; Greenwood, 2007; Siltaoja & Onkila, 2013
Learning with and from stakeholders	Stakeholders' criticism and feedback as opportunities for value creation	Lee, 2015; Mena & Chabowski, 2015
	Stakeholder engagement as a learning process for firms	Post et al., 2002; Sachs & Rühli, 2011
	Organizational learning through stakeholder dialogue	Burchell & Cook, 2006; Calton & Payne, 2004; Payne & Calton, 2003
Integrative stakeholder engagement	Phases of stakeholder engagement	Freeman, 1984; O'Riordan & Fairbrass, 2008; Plaza-Úbeda et al., 2010; Sachs et al., 2010a
	Firm-, stakeholder- and problem-centric views	Burchell & Cook, 2013; Gray & Stites, 2013; Heugens & Boesch, 2002; Plaza-Úbeda et al., 2010; Sachs & Rühli, 2011
	Nature of stakeholder engagement	Dawkins, 2015; Donaldson & Preston, 1995; Freeman et al., 2010; Greenwood, 2007; Jones & Wicks, 1999; Kujala et al., 2012; Noland & Phillips, 2010; Post et al., 2002; Scherer & Palazzo, 2007

issues' interconnectedness with sub-issues and different sectors (Camillus, 2008; Rittel, 1972, Rühli, et al., 2017).

The third theme covered different types of learning with and from stakeholders. The literature emphasises that stakeholder engagement involves critical thinking, creativity, and learning through relational responsibilities. From a learning perspective, stakeholder engagement can be seen as an interactive, developmental, and exploratory sense-making process. Additionally, stakeholder engagement enhances the governance of multi-

stakeholder networks. However, stakeholders' decision-making processes must be explored if the outcome of the stakeholder engagement is unknown (Alvarez & Barney, 2005, Alvarez & Sachs, 2017). The role of uncertainty in stakeholder engagement practices is addressed only in stakeholder relationships due to stakeholder pressures (Helmig, Spraul, & Ingenhoff, 2016; Mukundhan & Nandakumar, 2016) and how stakeholders have the power to withhold strategic resources (Herremans, Nazari, & Mahmoudian, 2016). However, uncertainty is a characteristic of decisions that have important economic and social consequences, including decisions about exploiting new and untested technological and market opportunities or social wicked issues (Alvarez & Sachs, 2017).

The fourth theme concentrated on integrative stakeholder engagement. Based on the work of previous authors, we conclude that integrative stakeholder engagement involves models of the phases of stakeholder engagement and firm-, stakeholder- and problem-centric views, and that it addresses the nature of stakeholder engagement. Stakeholder integration involves establishing collaborative relationships with a wide range of stakeholders. These relationships are not only dyadic but also form a network of stakeholder engagement and negotiation. Finally, stakeholder engagement is, by nature, both strategic and moral.

However, to achieve a more developed understanding of integrative stakeholder engagement, we need more empirical examples and case studies on stakeholder engagement. As our chapter shows, stakeholder theory, particularly stakeholder engagement, has been under increased scrutiny in recent years. However, the lack of real examples of stakeholder engagement is evident in the literature. As shown by previous studies, stakeholder engagement is highly dependent on context, and therefore examples from all kinds of organizations and from all over the world are needed to fully understand it. Moreover, despite some efforts to conceptualize the field (Freeman, Kujala, & Sachs, 2017), there is a clear need to develop the concepts and frameworks within it for further analysis of stakeholder engagement practices, which allows conceptualization and framework development.

Furthermore, to achieve a more comprehensive understanding of the various forms, challenges, and benefits of stakeholder engagement practices, a variety of methods must be used for empirical analysis. For example, scholars should be encouraged to use mixed methods (Hurmerinta-Peltomäki & Nummela, 2006) and interdisciplinary research (Repko, 2008) as well as various types of case studies (Stutz & Sachs 2016). Moreover, we should take the linguistic turn in organizational studies seriously (Alvesson & Kärreman, 2000) and increasingly use less traditional organizational analyses, like discourse, or rhetorical or narrative

analysis. Often, this involves acknowledging the social and political interests inherent in language (Vaara, 2010) as well as paying attention to the role of power and power relations (Dawkins, 2015) in the stakeholder engagement processes.

Finally, there is a gap between stakeholder theory and practice. The relationship between organizational theory and business practices in management theory is under constant discussion (Sandberg & Tsoukas, 2011). Additionally, theorizing often relies more on rigor than relevance (Mahoney, 2012). Van de Ven and Johnson (2006) proposed engaged scholarship that explores and integrates different discourses in the scientific and practitioner communities. In this vein, we have to overcome the science–practice gap of stakeholder engagement (Banks, et al., 2016) and be ready to promote and interlink both theoretical advances and practical developments in stakeholder engagement.

Notes

1. The authors gratefully acknowledge the financial support from the Academy of Finland (Decision no. 298663). Both authors contributed equally to this chapter. Some of the ideas contained in this chapter were developed through work with Edward Freeman, found in Freeman, et al., 2017.

References

Alvarez, S. A., & Barney, J. B. (2005). How do entrepreneurs organize firms under conditions of uncertainty? *Journal of Management*, *31*: 776–793.

Alvarez, S., & Sachs, S. (2017). *Stakeholders, Uncertainty, and Value Creation*. Panel Symposium at the 77th Annual Meeting of the Academy of Management, Atlanta, Georgia, United States.

Alvesson, M., & Kärreman, D. (2000). Taking the linguistic turn in organizational research challenges, responses, consequences. *The Journal of Applied Behavioral Science*, *36*(2): 136–158.

Baur, D., & Palazzo, G. (2011). The moral legitimacy of NGOs as partners of corporations. *Business Ethics Quarterly*, *21*(4): 579–604.

Banks, G. C., Pollack, J. M., Bochantin, J. E., Kirkman, B. L., Whelpley, C. E., & O'Boyle, E. H. (2016). Management's science–practice gap: A grand challenge for all stakeholders. *Academy of Management Journal*, *59*(6): 2205–2231.

Bijlsma-Frankema, K., Sitkin, S. B., & Weibel, A. (2015). Distrust in the balance: The emergence and development of intergroup distrust in a court of law. *Organization Science*, *26*(4): 1018–1039.

Boiral, O., Heras-Saizarbitoria, I., & Brotherton, M. C. (2017). Assessing and improving the quality of sustainability reports: The auditors' perspective. *Journal of Business Ethics*. First Online: 27 March 2017.

Bridoux, F., & Stoelhorst, J. W. (2016). Stakeholder relationships and social welfare: A behavioral theory of contributions to joint value creation. *Academy of Management Review*, *41*(2): 229–251.

Brown, J., & Dillard, J. (2015). Dialogic accountings for stakeholders: On opening up and closing down participatory governance. *Journal of Management Studies*, *52*(7): 961–985.

Brownlee, E. R., Dmytriyev, S., & Elias, A. (2017). Integrative stakeholder engagement: Stakeholder-oriented partnership between the Coca-Cola Company and World Wildlife Fund. In R. E. Freeman, J. Kujala, & S. Sachs, eds., *Stakeholder engagement: Clinical research cases*, pp. 339–364. Switzerland: Springer.

Burchell, J., & Cook, J. (2006). It's good to talk? Examining attitudes towards corporate social responsibility dialogue and engagement processes. *Business Ethics: A European Review*, *15*(2): 154–170.

Burchell, J., & Cook, J. (2008). Stakeholder dialogue and organisational learning: Changing relationships between companies and NGOs. *Business Ethics: A European Review*, *17*: 35–46.

Burchell, J., & Cook, J. (2013). Sleeping with the enemy? Strategic transformations in business-NGO relationships through stakeholder dialogue. *Journal of Business Ethics*, *113*(3): 505–518.

Calton, J. M., & Payne, S. L. (2003). Coping with paradox: Multistakeholder learning dialogue as a pluralist sensemaking process for addressing messy problems. *Business & Society*, *42*(1): 7–42.

Camillus, J. C. (2008). Strategy as a wicked problem. *Harvard Business Review*, May: 98–106.

Clarkson, M. B. E. (1995). A stakeholder framework for analyzing and evaluating corporate social performance. *Academy of Management Review*, *20*(1): 92–117.

Dawkins, C. (2015). Agonistic pluralism and stakeholder engagement. *Business Ethics Quarterly*, *25* (01): 1–28.

Derry, R. (2012). Reclaiming marginalized stakeholders. *Journal of Business Ethics*, *111*: 253–264.

Donaldson, T., & Preston, L. E. (1995). The stakeholder theory of the corporation: Concepts, evidence, and implications. *Academy of Management Review*, *20*(1): 65–91.

Fransen, L. W., & Kolk, A. (2007). Global rule-setting for business: A critical analysis of multi-stakeholder standards. *Organization*, *14*(5): 667–684.

Friedman, A. L., & Miles, S. (2002). Developing stakeholder theory. *Journal of Management Studies*, *39*: 1–21.

Freeman R. E., Kujala, J., & Sachs, S. (2017). *Stakeholder engagement: Clinical research cases*. Switzerland: Springer.

Freeman, R. E. (1984). *Strategic management: A stakeholder approach*. Marshfield, MA: Pitman.

Freeman, R. E., Harrison, J. S., Wicks, A. C., Parmar, B. L., & De Colle, S. (2010). *Stakeholder theory: The state of the art*. Cambridge: Cambridge University Press.

Frooman, J. (1999). Stakeholder influence strategies. *Academy of Management Review*, *24*(2): 191–205.

Garcia-Castro, R., & Aguilera, R. V. (2015). Incremental value creation and appropriation in a world with multiple stakeholders. *Strategic Management Journal*, *36*(1): 137–147.

Garriga, E. (2014). Beyond stakeholder utility function: Stakeholder capability in the value creation process. *Journal of Business Ethics*, *120*(4): 489–507.

Golob, U., & Podnar, K. (2014). Critical points of CSR-related stakeholder dialogue in practice. *Business Ethics: A European Review*, *23*(3): 248–257.

Gottschalg, O., & Zollo, M. (2007). Interest alignment and competitive advantage. *Academy of Management Review*, *32*, 418–437.

Gray, B., & Stites, J. P. (2013). Sustainability through partnerships. Retrieved January 15. 2015, from http://nbs.net/wp-content/uploads/NBS-Systematic-Review-Partnerships.pdf.

Greenwood, M. (2007). Stakeholder engagement: Beyond the myth of corporate responsibility. *Journal of Business Ethics*, *74*(4): 315–327.

Greenwood, M., & van Buren III, H. J. (2010). Trust and stakeholder theory: Trustworthiness in the organisation–stakeholder relationship. *Journal of Business Ethics*, *95*(3): 425–438.

Haksever, C., Chaganti, R., & Cook, R. G. (2004). A model of value creation: Strategic view. *Journal of Business Ethics*, *49*(3): 295–307.

Harrison, J. S., Bosse, D. A., & Phillips, R. A. (2010). Managing for stakeholders, stakeholder utility functions, and competitive advantage. *Strategic Management Journal, 31*: 58–74.

Harrison, J. S., Freeman, R. E., & de Abreu, M. C. S. (2015). Stakeholder theory as an ethical approach to effective management: Applying the theory to multiple contexts. *Revista Brasileira de Gestão de Negócios, 17*(55): 858–869.

Harrison, J. S., & Wicks A. C. (2013). Stakeholder theory, value, and firm performance. *Business Ethics Quarterly, 23*(1): 97–124.

Helmig, B., Spraul, K., & Ingenhoff, D. (2016). Under positive pressure how stakeholder pressure affects corporate social responsibility implementation. *Business & Society, 55*(2): 151–187.

Herremans, I. M., Nazari, J. A., & Mahmoudian, F. (2016). Stakeholder relationships, engagement, and sustainability reporting. *Journal of Business Ethics, 138*(3): 417–435.

Heugens, P. P. M. A. R., van den Bosch, F. A. J., & van Riel, C. B. M. (2002). Stakeholder integration: Building mutually enforcing relationships. *Business & Society, 41*(1): 36–60.

Hurmerinta-Peltomäki, L., & Nummela, N. (2006). Mixed methods in international business research: A value-added perspective. *Management International Review, 46*(4): 439–459.

Jones, T. M., Felps, W., & Bigley, G. A. (2007). Ethical theory and stakeholder-related decisions: The role of stakeholder culture. *Academy of Management Review, 32*(1): 137–155.

Jones, T. M., & Felps, W. (2013a). Shareholder wealth maximization and social welfare: A utilitarian critique. *Business Ethics Quarterly, 23*(2): 207–238.

Jones, T. M., & Felps, W. (2013b). Stakeholder happiness enhancement: A neo-utilitarian objective for the modern corporation. *Business Ethics Quarterly, 23*(3): 349–379.

Jones, T. M., & Wicks, A. C. (1999). Convergent stakeholder theory. *Academy of Management Review, 24*(2): 206–221.

Joutsenvirta, M. (2009). A language perspective to environmental management and corporate responsibility. *Business Strategy and the Environment, 18*(4): 240–253.

Joutsenvirta, M. (2011). Setting boundaries for corporate social responsibility: Firm–NGO relationship as discursive legitimation struggle. *Journal of Business Ethics, 102*(1): 57–75.

Kaptein, M., & Van Tulder, R. (2003). Toward effective stakeholder dialogue. *Business and Society Review, 108*(2): 203–224.

Kujala, J., Heikkinen, A., & Lehtimäki, H. (2012). Understanding the nature of stakeholder relationships: An empirical examination of a conflict situation. *Journal of Business Ethics, 109*(1): 53–65.

Kujala, J., Lämsä, A-M., Riivari, E., & Riivari, E. (2017). Company stakeholder responsibility: An empirical investigation of top managers' attitudinal change. *Baltic Journal of Management, 12*(2): 114–138.

Kujala, J., Lehtimäki, H., & Pučėtaitė, R. (2016). Trust and distrust constructing unity and fragmentation of organisational culture. *Journal of Business Ethics, 139*: 701–716.

Lee, J. H. (2015). *Stakeholder work and value creation stakeholder engagement: An integrative framework.* Lubbock: Texas Tech University.

Lehtimäki, H., & Kujala, J. (2017). Framing dynamically changing firm–stakeholder relationships in an international dispute over a foreign investment. A discursive analysis approach. *Business & Society, 56*(3): 487–523.

Maak, T. (2007). Responsible leadership, stakeholder engagement, and the emergence of social capital. *Journal of Business Ethics, 74*(4): 329–343.

Mahoney, J. T. (2012). Towards a Stakeholder Theory of Strategic Management. College of Business Working Paper.

Mukundhan, K. V., & Nandakumar, M. K. (2016). Stakeholder influences on the choice and performance of FDI-based market entry modes: A conceptual model. *International Studies of Management & Organization, 46*(1): 63–74.

Mitchell, R. K., Agle, B. R., & Wood, D. J. (1997). Toward a theory of stakeholder identification and salience: Defining the principle of who and what really counts. *Academy of Management Review, 22*(4): 853–886.

Mitchell, R. K., Weaver, G. R., Agle, B. R., Bailey, A. D., & Carlson, J. (2016). Stakeholder agency and social welfare: Pluralism and decision making in the multi-objective corporation. *Academy of Management Review, 41*(2): 252–275.

Mena, J. A., & Chabowski, B. R. (2015). The role of organizational learning in stakeholder marketing. *Journal of the Academy of Marketing Science, 43*, 1–24.

Moir, L., Kennerley, M., & Ferguson, D. (2007). Measuring the business case: Linking stakeholder and shareholder value. *Corporate Governance, 7*(4): 388–400.

Morsing, M., & Schultz, M. (2006). Corporate social responsibility communication: stakeholder information, response and involvement strategies. *Business Ethics: A European Review*, *15*(4): 323–338.

Myllykangas, P., Kujala, J., & Lehtimäki, H. (2010). Analyzing the essence of stakeholder relationships: What do we need in addition to power, legitimacy and urgency? *Journal of Business Ethics*, *96*(1): 65–72.

Noland, J., & Phillips, R. (2010). Stakeholder engagement, discourse ethics and strategic management. *International Journal of Management Reviews*, *12* (1): 39–49.

O'Riordan, L., & Fairbrass, J. (2008). Corporate social responsibility (CSR): Models and theories in stakeholder dialogue. *Journal of Business Ethics*, *83*: 745–758.

Palazzo, G., & Richter, U. (2005). CSR business as usual? The case of the tobacco industry. *Journal of Business Ethics*, *61*(4): 387–401.

Payne, S. L., & Calton, J. M. (2004). Exploring research potentials and applications for multi-stakeholder learning dialogues. *Journal of Business Ethics*, *55*: 71–78.

Pedersen, E. R. (2006). Making corporate social responsibility (CSR) operable: How companies translate stakeholder dialogue into practice. *Business and Society Review*, *111*: 137–163.

Phillips, R. A. (1997). Stakeholder theory and a principle of fairness. *Business Ethics Quarterly*, *7*(1): 51–66.

Pirson, M., & Malhotra, D. (2011). Foundations of organizational trust: What matters to different stakeholders? *Organization Science*, *22*(4): 1087–1104.

Plaza-Úbeda, J. A., de Burgos-Jiménez, J., & Carmona-Moreno, E. (2010). Measuring stakeholder integration: Knowledge, interaction and adaptational behavior dimensions. *Journal of Business Ethics*, *93*(3): 419–442.

Post, J. E., Preston, L. E., & Sachs, S. 2002. *Redefining the corporation: Stakeholder management and organizational wealth*. Stanford, CA: Stanford University Press.

Priem, R. L., & Nystrom, P. C. (2014). Exploring the dynamics of workgroup fracture common ground, trust-with-trepidation, and warranted distrust. *Journal of Management*, *40*(3): 764–795.

Purnell, L. S.,& Freeman, R. E. (2012). Stakeholder theory, fact/value dichotomy, and the normative core: How Wall Street stops the ethics conversation. *Journal of Business Ethics*, *109*(1): 109–116.

Rasche, A., & Waddock, S. (2014). Global sustainability governance and the UN Global Compact: A rejoinder to critics. *Journal of Business Ethics*, *122*(2): 209–216.

Repko, A. F. (2008). *Interdisciplinary research: Process and theory*. Los Angeles: Sage.

Rittel, H. (1972). On the planning crisis: System analysis of the "First and Second Generations." *Bedriftsøkonomen*, *8*: 390–396.

Roloff, J. (2008). Learning from multi-stakeholder networks: Issue-focused stakeholder management. *Journal of Business Ethics*, *82*: 233–250.

Rowley, T. J. (1997). Moving beyond dyadic ties: A network theory of stakeholder influences. *Academy of Management Review*, *22*(4): 887–910.

Rowley, T. J., & Moldoveanu, M. (2003). When will stakeholder groups act? An interest- and identity-based model of stakeholder group mobilization. *Academy of Management Review*, *28*(2): 204–219.

Rühli, E., Sachs, S., Schmitt, R., & Schneider, T. (2017). Innovation in multistakeholder settings: The case of a wicked issue in health care. *Journal of Business Ethics*, *143*(2): 289–305.

Sachs, S., Groth, H., & Schmitt, R. (2010a). The 'stakeholder view' approach: An untapped opportunity to manage corporate performance and wealth. *Strategic Change*, *19*(3–4): 147–162.

Sachs, S., Rühli, E., & Meier, C. (2010b). Stakeholder governance as a response to wicked issues. *Journal of Business Ethics*, *96*(S1): 57–64.

Sachs, S., & Maurer, M. (2009). Toward dynamic corporate stakeholder responsibility. *Journal of Business Ethics*, *85*(3): 535–544.

Sachs, S., & Rühli, E. (2011). *Stakeholders matter: A new paradigm for strategy in society*. Cambridge: Cambridge University Press.

Sandberg, J., & Tsoukas, H. (2011). Grasping the logic of practice: Theorizing through practical rationality. *Academy of Management Review*, *36* (2): 338–360.

Scherer, A. G., & Palazzo, G. (2007). Toward a political conception of corporate responsibility: Business and society seen from a Habermasian perspective. *Academy of Management Review*, *32* (4): 1096–1120.

Schneider, T., & Sachs, S. (2017). The impact of stakeholder identities on value creation in issue-based stakeholder networks. *Journal of Business Ethics*, *144*(1): 41–57.

Siltaoja, M. E., & Onkila, T. J. (2013). Business in society: the construction of business-society relations in responsibility reports from a critical discursive perspective. *Business Ethics: A European Review*, *22*(4): 357–373.

Smith, N. C., & Rönnegard, D. (2016). Shareholder primacy, corporate social responsibility, and the role of business schools. *Journal of Business Ethics*, *134*(3): 463–478.

Strand, R., Freeman, R. E.,& Hockerts, K. (2015). Corporate social responsibility and sustainability in Scandinavia: An overview. *Journal of Business Ethics*, *127*(1): 1–15.

Stutz, C., & Sachs, S. 2016. Facing the normative challenges: The potential of reflexive historical research. *Business & Society*, pp. 1–33. Advance online publication. doi:10.1177/0007650316681989.

Tantalo, C., & Priem, R. L. (2016). Value creation through stakeholder synergy. *Strategic Management Journal*, *37*(2): 314–329.

Vaara, E. (2010). Taking the linguistic turn seriously: Strategy as a multifaceted interdiscursive phenomenon. *Advances in Strategic Management*, *27*: 29–50.

Van De Ven, A. H., & Johnson, P. E. (2006). Knowledge for theory and practice. *Academy of Management Review*, *31*(4): 802–821.

Wicks, A. C. (1996). Overcoming the separation thesis. The need for a reconsideration of business and society research. *Business & Society*, *35*(1): 89–118.

Yaziji, M., & Doh, J. (2009). *NGOs and corporations: Conflict and collaboration*. Cambridge: Cambridge University Press.

Internet Sources

www.icca-chem.org/responsible-care/
www.gavi.org

PART V
New Voices in Stakeholder Thinking

Considering a Behavioral View of Stakeholders

JONATHAN BUNDY

Arizona State University

My first appreciation for the ideas underlying stakeholder theory came long before I knew a theory existed. It happened early in my first career. I was an economic development manager charged with facilitating job growth in my hometown. We were working on a deal to help a *Fortune 100* technology firm expand its local manufacturing operations, which would add at least several hundred new jobs. The expansion and associated government incentives had widespread support from city and state decision-makers, including the mayor, city council, county commission, and the governor. Also proclaiming support were several local newspapers, employee groups, and a wide range of community leaders. In the economic development world, it was a slam dunk; all parties seemed ready and willing to get the deal done.

But there was one exception. A small group of local activists worried that the expansion would lead to environmental and health concerns, particularly for those living adjacent to the facility. This group had been fighting the company for years, and its concerns were, for the most part, dismissed by other members of the community. On the verge of a major professional victory, and bolstered by my youth and inexperience, I quickly joined the chorus of dismissers. I saw the activist group as nothing more than an annoying gadfly. As such, I was rather surprised when the regional manager invited me to a last-minute meeting to consider how the company might respond to the activists.

In that meeting, I learned that the company was deeply committed to its local communities – as a matter of self-identity – and that it was sincerely concerned about addressing the activists' anxieties. Indeed, several local managers lived in the same communities as the activists, knew their names and faces, and interacted with them on a semi-regular basis. They were connected to these activists on an

individual level, despite having considerably different interests and beliefs. What followed was a significant investment of time, energy, and capital in an attempt to assuage the resolute concerns of these stakeholders. What struck me was the authentic and genuine nature of the company's response; for various reasons, the managers representing the company (including many from outside the immediate area) truly wanted to resolve the issue.

This experience remained with me throughout my time in economic development, and became a touchstone as I entered academia and familiarized myself with the nature and nuances of stakeholder theory. For example, I came to realize that these activists had very little power (it truly was only a handful of individuals), almost no legitimacy (hampered by the fact that several technical studies largely discredited their claims), and no real urgency (they had been active for nearly two decades). As such, traditional notions in stakeholder theory suggested that the group should receive very little managerial attention (e.g., Mitchell, Agle, & Wood, 1997).

Of course, this was not the case, and I was inspired to understand why. Puzzling this out led my coauthors and me to rekindle the concept of issue salience and to consider how certain stakeholder concerns (in this case, accusations of community harm) could resonate with managers in different ways (see Bundy, Shropshire, & Buchholtz, 2013). Our theory detailed a cognitive process of interpretation and action, and thus contributed to a better understanding of the psychological and behavioral "microfoundations" of stakeholder theory (Bridoux & Stoelhorst, 2014; Felin & Foss, 2005; Greve, 2013; Keevil, 2014; McVea & Freeman, 2005; Powell, Lovallo, & Fox, 2011).

Such a behavioral approach – focused on the role of individual cognition, emotion, and behavior in managing stakeholders (Powell, et al., 2011) – helped me to better understand my own professional experience, which was somewhat at odds with extant theory. When I consider the future of stakeholder theory, I believe that such a behavioral approach offers an incredible array of additional opportunities for research in the field.

A Behavioral View of Stakeholder Theory

In reflecting on the tenants of stakeholder theory, Freeman (2011: 215) noted that, "modern schools of business have come to be schools of economics and economic reason, often narrowly construed . . . This runs the risk of ignoring the fact that businesses are *populated by human beings in all their complexity*, and have been so since the dawn of commerce" (emphasis added). At its core, stakeholder theory recognizes the inherent value and standing of those human beings that compose organizations. While often focused on more macro topics or abstract ideals and principles, stakeholder-centered research has also long considered the "complexity" of human nature on organization outcomes.

For example, different micro or behavioral foundations of stakeholder theory appear throughout Freeman's seminal 1984 text, including the notion of values "fit" between organizations and stakeholders (reflecting micro ideas of person-organization fit; also see Bundy, Vogel, & Zachary, 2018), and notions of individual roles and role conflict (reflecting ideas from behavioral role theory). Additional behavioral concepts have appeared in numerous studies since. To name but a few, stakeholder researchers have considered the behavioral nature of identity and identification (Brickson, 2005; Scott & Lane, 2000), trust and fairness (Bosse, Phillips, & Harrison, 2009; Bridoux & Stoelhorst, 2014; Harrison, Bosse, & Phillips, 2010; Keevil, 2014), and social expectations (Bundy et al., 2013; Crilly, Hansen, & Zollo, 2016). McVea and Freeman's (2005) appeal for a "names-and-faces" approach to stakeholder management also acknowledges the critical importance of a behavioral approach by simply emphasizing the individuals behind the stakeholder labels.

Building on this base, Keevil (2014: 4) recently argued, "there is an enormous opportunity for an approach that considers how stakeholders *actually behave* . . . " (emphasis added). As Keevil recognized, numerous avenues for scholarship are opened as we consider the motivations, values, and ultimately the actions of individual stakeholders and managers that work to foster value-creating relationships. As such, a behavioral approach to stakeholder theory offers a compelling path forward for stakeholder researchers, particularly those interested in stakeholder engagement. In the following section, I describe a few possibilities.

Areas to Consider

One area for potential expansion is to consider the individual attributes of firm and stakeholder leaders. Indeed, such an expansion has already begun, with several recent studies from the upper-echelons tradition considering how CEO attributes – including political ideology (Chin, Hambrick, & Trevino, 2013), commitment to ethics (Muller & Kolk, 2010), and narcissistic tendencies (Petrenko, et al., 2016) – influence engagement with stakeholders. A focus on CEO attributes informs us about the managerial mind-set (Freeman, et al., 2010) and helps to explain why different leaders prioritize different stakeholders and how they view the purpose of the firm.

Researchers could extend this work by considering any number of additional CEO attributes. Perhaps more importantly, however, would be an attempt to uncover how such attributes influence the leaders of stakeholder groups, whose "stakeholder mind-sets" may fundamentally differ from the classic managerial mind-set, particularly in defining the purpose of the firm. As part of this effort, researchers could consider how such managerial and stakeholder mind-sets might clash, or which individual attributes might encourage cooperative versus competitive relationships.

Additionally, future research might consider how different attributes and characteristics of the dyadic relationships between managers and stakeholders may influence critical outcomes. Recent research in stakeholder theory has set a strong foundation for such an approach. For example, drawing from behavioral tenants of justice and fairness, Bosse, Phillips, and Harrison (Bosse, et al., 2009; Harrison, et al., 2010) recognized that stakeholders are boundedly self-interested such that their desire to maximize value in a relationship is constrained by fairness norms. Building on this logic, Bridoux and Stoelhorst (2014, 2016) recognized that individual stakeholders may also have heterogeneous preferences for fairness, with some stakeholders approaching their relationships from a self-regarding, transactional point-of-view, and other stakeholders approaching their relationships from an other-regarding, reciprocating point-of-view. By challenging our assumptions and unpacking the motives of individual stakeholders – particularly as related to trust and fairness – these authors were able to advance our understanding of stakeholder relationships.

Future research could consider additional norms and motivations that guide individual stakeholder relationships. Of particular interest to me are the relational expectations associated with stakeholders' social evaluations, including image, reputation, and status judgments (for reviews of these and related concepts, see Bundy & Pfarrer, 2015; Devers et al., 2009; Logsdon & Wood, 2002; Rindvoa, Pollock, & Hayward, 2006). For example, reputation is often defined as a perception of firm value or quality, and stakeholders use reputation as an important signal to define expectations in a relationship (Rindova, et al., 2005). When a high-reputation firm violates these expectations – such as delivering poor quality products or services – the impact on individual relationships is quite varied. A number of behavioral factors may influence this variation, including stakeholders' level of identification with the violating firm (Zavyalova et al., 2016), how they perceive the violation and attribute blame (Coombs, 2007; Lange & Washburn, 2012), and the way in which the firm responds (Bundy & Pfarrer, 2015).

Despite this recent attention, much is left to be considered. For example, in the wake of an expectancy violation, it may be important to consider not only how stakeholders are influenced by their own expectations (based on prior perceptions and experiences with the firm), but also how they are influenced by other stakeholders' expectations (based on how other stakeholders react to the violation). Consider that after an employee accident or death, numerous stakeholders are negatively affected. How might each stakeholder's willingness to forgive depend on the actions of one another? It is not hard to envision that a public statement of forgiveness (or non-forgiveness) from the affected employee's family would move the thoughts and minds of others to similar conclusions. Considering such factors not only extends our behavioral understanding of firm–stakeholder relationships, but also considers the role of social context.

Finally, a critical behavioral topic for researchers to consider is the role of affect and emotions in stakeholder relationships. In my personal experience with the technology company, it seems clear that strong emotional reactions influenced the company's engagement efforts. In their review of stakeholder theory, Laplume, Sonpar, and Litz (2008) called for additional research to elaborate on the idea of stakeholder emotions. However, only a handful of studies seem to have materialized. For example, Muller, Pfarrer, and Little (2014) recently considered how collective empathy coming from the bottom-level of organizations can bubble up to influence firm-level philanthropic decisions.

Future research might address how the degree of emotional arousal (so called "hot" versus "cold" emotions) influences stakeholder reactions, perhaps in response to issues of fairness and trust. For example, whether or not a violation of trust evokes anger versus sadness is likely to have important implications on the trust repair process. Research might also consider how firm leaders' emotional intelligence might influence the depth and breadth of their stakeholder engagement.

Conclusion

As I learned early in my adult life, stakeholders and managers are indeed people, and people vary in their motivations, beliefs, and behavioral tendencies. What I naïvely categorized as a non-issue was to my counterparts an important and critical issue of self-definition. A behavioral approach to stakeholder theory helps us see such issues more clearly and to understand the resulting behaviors and outcomes more completely. I believe that an ongoing emphasis in a behavioral direction will continue to reveal interesting nuances that underlie stakeholder theory. I am excited to be a part of it and I am excited to see what we collectively discover.

References

Bosse, D. A., Phillips, R. A., & Harrison, J. S. (2009). Stakeholders, reciprocity, and firm performance. *Strategic Management Journal, 30*(4): 447–456.

Brickson, S. L. (2005). Organizational identity orientation: Forging a link between organizational identity and organizations' relations with stakeholders. *Administrative Science Quarterly, 50*(4): 576–609.

Bridoux, F., & Stoelhorst, J. (2014). Microfoundations for stakeholder theory: Managing stakeholders with heterogeneous motives. *Strategic Management Journal, 35*(1): 107–125.

Bridoux, F., & Stoelhorst, J. (2016). Stakeholder relationships and social welfare: A behavioral theory of contributions to joint value creation. *Academy of Management Review, 41*(2): 229–251.

Bundy, J., & Pfarrer, M. D. (2015). A burden of responsibility: The role of social approval at the onset of a crisis. *Academy of Management Review, 40*(3): 345–369.

Bundy, J., Shropshire, C., & Buchholtz, A. K. (2013). Strategic cognition and issue salience: Toward an explanation of firm responsiveness to stakeholder concerns. *Academy of Management Review, 38*(3): 352–376.

Bundy, J., Vogel, R. M., & Zachary, M. A. (2018). Organization-stakeholder fit: A dynamic theory of cooperation, compromise, and conflict between an organization and its stakeholders. *Strategic Management Journal, 39*(2): 476–501.

Chin, M., Hambrick, D. C., & Treviño, L. K. (2013). Political ideologies of CEOs: The influence of executives' values on corporate social responsibility. *Administrative Science Quarterly, 58*(2): 197–232.

Coombs, W. T. (2007). Attribution theory as a guide for post-crisis communication research. *Public Relations Review, 33*(2): 135–139.

Crilly, D., Hansen, M., & Zollo, M. (2016). The grammar of decoupling: A cognitive-linguistic perspective on firms' sustainability

claims and stakeholders' interpretation. *Academy of Management Journal, 59*(2): 705–729.

Devers, C. E., Dewett, T., Mishina, Y., & Belsito, C. A. (2009). A general theory of organizational stigma. *Organization Science, 20*(1): 154–171.

Felin, T., & Foss, N. J. (2005). Strategic organization: A field in search of micro-foundations. *Strategic Organization, 3*(4): 441–455.

Freeman, R. E. (1984). *Strategic management: A stakeholder approach.* Cambridge, MA: Cambridge University Press.

Freeman, R. E. (2011). Some thoughts on the development of stakeholder theory. In R. A. Phillips, ed., *Stakeholder theory: Impact and prospects,* pp. 212–233. Cheltenham, UK: Edward Elgar.

Freeman, R. E., Harrison, J. S., Wicks, A. C., Parmar, B. L., & De Colle, S. (2010). *Stakeholder theory: The state of the art.* Cambridge, UK: Cambridge University Press.

Greve, H. R. (2013). Microfoundations of management: Behavioral strategies and levels of rationality in organizational action. *Academy of Management Perspectives, 27*(2): 103–119.

Harrison, J. S., Bosse, D. A., & Phillips, R. A. (2010). Managing for stakeholders, stakeholder utility functions, and competitive advantage. *Strategic Management Journal, 31*(1): 58–74.

Keevil, A. A. C. (2014). Behavioral stakeholder theory. Unpublished dissertation, University of Virginia.

Lange, D., & Washburn, N. T. (2012). Understanding Attributions of Corporate Social Irresponsibility. *Academy of Management Review, 37*(2): 300–326.

Laplume, A. O., Sonpar, K., & Litz, R. A. (2008). Stakeholder theory: Reviewing a theory that moves us. *Journal of Management, 34*(6): 1152–1189.

Logsdon, J. M., & Wood, D. J. (2002). Reputation as an emerging construct in the business and society field: An introduction. *Business & Society, 41*(4): 365–370.

McVea, J. F., & Freeman, R. E. (2005). A Names-and-faces approach to stakeholder management how focusing on stakeholders as individuals can bring ethics and entrepreneurial strategy together. *Journal of Management Inquiry, 14*(1): 57–69.

Mitchell, R. K., Agle, B. R., & Wood, D. J. (1997). Toward a theory of stakeholder identification and salience: Defining the principle of who and what really counts. *Academy of Management Review, 22*(4): 853–886.

Muller, A., & Kolk, A. (2010). Extrinsic and intrinsic drivers of corporate social performance: Evidence from foreign and domestic firms in Mexico. *Journal of Management Studies, 47*(1): 1–26.

Muller, A. R., Pfarrer, M. D., & Little, L. M. (2014). A Theory of Collective Empathy in Corporate Philanthropy Decisions. *Academy of Management Review, 39*(1): 1–21.

Petrenko, O. V., Aime, F., Ridge, J., & Hill, A. (2016). Corporate social responsibility or CEO narcissism? CSR motivations and organizational performance. *Strategic Management Journal, 37*(2): 262–279.

Powell, T. C., Lovallo, D., & Fox, C. R. (2011). Behavioral strategy. *Strategic Management Journal, 32*(12): 1369–1386.

Rindova, V. P., Williamson, I. O., Petkova, A. P., & Sever, J. M. (2005). Being good or being known: An empirical examination of the dimensions, antecedents, and consequences of organizational reputation. *Academy of Management Journal, 48* (6): 1033–1049.

Scott, S., & Lane, V. (2000). A stakeholder approach to organizational identity. *Academy of Management Review, 25*(1): 43–62.

Zavyalova, A., Pfarrer, M. D., Reger, R. K., & Hubbard, T. D. (2016). Reputation as a Benefit and a Burden? How Stakeholders' Organizational Identification Affects the Role of Reputation Following a Negative Event. *Academy of Management Journal, 59*(1): 253–276.

Behavioral Stakeholder Theory

DONAL CRILLY

London Business School

In this essay, I address the potential of using a behavioral lens to understand how firms engage with their stakeholders. Much existing stakeholder research focuses on macro-level explanations that emphasize the importance of the external environment in shaping firm–stakeholder relations. In contrast, a behaviorally informed perspective looks inside firms and stakeholder organizations alike to understand better the drivers, and consequences, of the relations between firms and their stakeholders. I outline a possible research program and describe the questions it is equipped to answer.

Introduction

Behavioral research "aims to bring realistic assumptions about human cognition, emotions, and social behavior to the strategic management of organizations" (Powell, Lovallo, & Fox, 2011: 1371). What is the need for a behavioral stakeholder theory? The simple answer is that scholars have to account better for why firms in the same context vary in how they address similar stakeholder pressures. Understanding how executives and managers individually and collectively make sense of, and respond to, stakeholder pressures is indispensable in this regard. The Strategic Management Society's Stakeholder Strategy Interest Group explicitly recognizes the central role that individuals play in building their firms' stakeholder strategies: "How do individuals and their shared values, emotions and cognitions influence firms' stakeholder orientation and engagement strategies, sustainability oriented change processes, and, ultimately, the firm's economic, social and environmental performance?" (Strategic Management Society, 2017).

But, behavioral stakeholder strategy goes beyond understanding the psychological attributes of managers to encompass those of stakeholders as well. Notably, though stakeholders' decision-making has been largely neglected in the literature, even stakeholders that apparently pursue similar objectives – for example, Greenpeace and the Rainforest Alliance – routinely react differently to the same corporate initiative. Stakeholders vary in their motives. Whereas some stakeholders are squarely focused on their own economic benefit, others are equally (or even more so) interested in how firms treat other actors (Bridoux & Stoelhorst, 2014). Crucially, stakeholder interests are not given *a priori* and are instead "crafted and shaped by the way in which stakeholders and managers make sense of their situation and the available alternatives" (Freeman, et al., 2010: 246–247). The premise of a behavioral approach lies in recognizing that corporate responses to stakeholder pressures and stakeholders' subsequent reactions are not wholly determined by the environment. Rather, executives' perceptions mediate the influence of the environment on their responses, and, similarly, stakeholders interpret corporate action before deciding to reward or sanction firms.

Thus, behavioral stakeholder research advances a micro-foundational explanation of stakeholder strategy by taking account of the social and cognitive factors that shape firms' actions *and* stakeholders' reactions. This dual focus contributes to resolving two outstanding issues in the literature. First, a broad stakeholder orientation – engaging with numerous stakeholders in the social-political environment – is associated with positive outcomes for firms in the form of increased collaboration and reduced conflict with actors in their socio-political environments (Henisz, Dorobantu, & Nartey, 2014). Nonetheless, a recent review highlights the complexity in managing the "multiple dimensions involving stakeholder groups while companies are constrained with limited resources" (Wang, et al., 2016: 535). Looking *inside* the firm, particularly at how interdependencies and trade-offs across stakeholders are viewed and managed, helps to explain why some firms attend to the interests of more stakeholders than others. Second, efforts to appeal to some stakeholders often fail to create value for firms (Hillman & Keim, 2001). Whilst one explanation is that firms misallocate shareholder funds to inappropriate projects, it may be that the intended beneficiaries do not evaluate corporate initiatives as expected. This shifts the focus to how firms communicate their initiatives and how stakeholders perceive the same initiatives.

Consistent with the above, behavioral research in stakeholder theory can address two overarching themes. The first theme concerns how executives interpret their environment and devise appropriate responses (thus, accounting for heterogeneity across firms). The second theme concerns how stakeholders make sense of corporate data and difficult-to-observe corporate practices (thus, accounting for heterogeneity across outcomes).

Cognitive Foundations of Responses to Stakeholder Pressures

What explains why firms in the same context differ in the pattern and extent of their stakeholder engagement? Freeman and colleagues (2010: 288) declare: "We need a richer description of one of the most fundamental topics in the stakeholder literature – identification of stakeholders and their interests [. . .] How do executives make sense of who is or is not a stakeholder?" The dominant way to explain stakeholder salience is to use the attributes of stakeholders as the point of departure: Stakeholders that have power and legitimacy and make urgent claims are likely to be attended to (Mitchell, Agle, & Wood, 1997). Yet, as Mitchell and colleagues acknowledge, executives – within the same firm, or across firms – will not necessarily agree about the power, legitimacy, and urgency of a given stakeholder's claims.

Seminal work in stakeholder theory has already recognized a role for values in determining "who matters to CEOs" (Agle, Mitchell, & Sonnenfeld, 1999: 507). But, apart from values, other psychological attributes matter, including emotion (e.g.,

Weitzner & Deutsch, 2015) and identity (Brickson, 2005). Crucially, behavioral research does not only consider how executives individually come to form their impressions but also considers how these impressions are constructed organizationally. Organizations are composed of multiple individuals, units, and/or departments. By enabling individual units to specialize through the division of labor, organizations achieve more complex tasks than do individuals working by themselves. From the view of stakeholder theory, one of the most complex problems facing organizations concerns how to address multiple, potentially conflicting, stakeholder demands. Just as effective organizations enable a division of labor, attending successfully to multiple stakeholders requires a cognitive division of labor within the firm (Crilly & Sloan, 2012), whereby managers can focus their attention on understanding a few stakeholder groups. Management teams that successfully engage with a diverse range of stakeholders may construe their firms' relationships with society in broad terms, but their executives focus their attention on a small number of distinct stakeholders rather than pay attention to a large number of stakeholder concerns.

The notion of specialized attention comes to the fore in recent research which addresses the role of organization design in distributing attention across middle managers who interact with customers, suppliers, community representatives, and government agencies, etc. Crilly & Sloan (2014) draw on survey data to show how design decisions surrounding incentives and training shape managerial attention to stakeholders. Though firms routinely claim in public that all stakeholders are important, such discourse is counterproductive if it leads to a lack of prioritization and a duplication of effort.[1] Rather, allowing front-line managers to focus their attention on the needs of a specific stakeholder group produces benefits from specialization. Executives must strike a balance between directing subordinates and leaving them to respond appropriately to their immediate context. This line of research stands to benefit from many of the insights of the Carnegie School (e.g., March, 1962). Indeed, recent work in the Carnegie tradition, that explicitly recognizes organizations as embedded in larger social contexts (Gavetti, Levinthal, & Ocasio, 2007), speaks directly to the interests of stakeholder scholars and offers them a useful point of departure.

Stakeholders' Interpretive Work

How do stakeholders perceive firms' social and environmental initiatives? The flip side in a micro-foundational explanation of firm-stakeholder relations is the need to understand how stakeholders perceive corporate initiatives. This, too, is a critical issue for stakeholder theory: Many mechanisms, such as reputation and enhanced stakeholder support, that translate firms' engagement with non-shareholding stakeholders into competitive advantage require stakeholders to be aware of, and to welcome, firms' efforts. A behavioral perspective shifts the focus to the kinds of biases – such as overly attending to negative information – that lead stakeholders to be overly cynical about firms and also to the conditions under which stakeholders are misled by firms.

Recent studies have begun to shed light on the psychological mechanisms that underlie exchanges between firms and their stakeholders. Stakeholders, especially external stakeholders, often attribute beliefs and intentions to firms and their executives (Love & Kraatz, 2017). Because stakeholders are liable to interpret firms' conduct negatively, firms that communicate their initiatives ineffectively can fail to benefit from their stakeholder engagement. Policy capturing studies involving non-governmental organization leaders reveal how two systematic biases – attribution error and insider preference – affect stakeholders when evaluating firms' social performance and, ultimately, when deciding whether to collaborate with firms (Crilly, Ni, & Jiang, 2016). How firms communicate their engagement initiatives is important. Stakeholders react negatively toward multinational enterprises when they focus their engagement message on mitigating negative externalities, such as reducing pollution, rather than on contributing to positive externalities, such as improving the local skills base. The critical insight is that stakeholders are sensitive to the ways in which social and environmental policies are communicated. Behavioral

research is apt for identifying other biases that influence stakeholder perception and, ultimately, organizational success.

The biases that shape stakeholders' impressions of, and reactions to, corporations place an onus on stakeholders who are charged with monitoring corporate conduct. Critically, stakeholders bear their own responsibility to ensure that the kinds of corporate policies and practices they desire are actually implemented. An important question for the literature is: How accurately do stakeholders monitor how seriously a given firm takes its public commitments? Some insights from research are discouraging insofar as they suggest that, despite the prevalence of external metrics, stakeholders are largely unaware of the state of corporate practice. One reason may be that stakeholders' close involvement with firms hampers their impartiality (Kivleniece & Quelin, 2012).

An implication of this line of research is that research must take seriously stakeholders' ability and motivation to penetrate beyond superficial corporate communications. As firms report ever more data that could be relevant to stakeholders (Harrison & van der Laan Smith, 2015), there is a growing need to study both how firms present data and how stakeholders interpret such data.

Taking the Agenda Forward: Cognitive Science and Methods

The behavioral lens has implications for the disciplines and methods that stakeholder scholars are likely to use in the future. Most notably, whereas stakeholder theory has largely been developed on the basis of economics with important insights from ethics and sociology, the cognitive sciences can inform work on the micro-foundations that underlie firm–stakeholder interactions. Working with new disciplines raises challenges and opportunities for stakeholder scholars. It is notable that most journals publishing applied psychology research, such as *Organizational Behavior and Human Decision Processes* and the *Journal of Applied Psychology*, have a strong tradition of featuring research on ethics, values, and prosocial behavior. Yet, with few exceptions (e.g., Burke,

Borucki, & Hurley, 1992; Carter & Mossholder, 2015), very little research in these journals directly addresses stakeholder themes other than employee-related topics.

It is noteworthy that research into the psychology of decision-making can directly inform stakeholder theory. Many psychological theories map managerial psychology to the targets of organizational action and thus help to explain actions for stakeholders. For example, threat rigidity theory specifies that labelling issues as threats prompts attention to internal processes, restricting managers' foci to a narrow range of actors and their concerns (Dutton & Jackson, 1987). In contrast, labelling issues as opportunities prompts externally directed and proactive responses. Thus, there remains ample scope to identify how framing outcomes in different ways (for instance, in terms of gains or losses) influences how managers address stakeholders' concerns and how stakeholders evaluate corporate action. One important idea is that stakeholders' evaluations of corporate action are inherently subjective and do not only depend on firms' amount of engagement but also on the yardstick to which it is compared. Firms often have the choice between gain and loss frames in communicating the same action. As Lankoski, Smith, and Van Wassenhove (2016) argue, this choice is likely to shape stakeholder evaluations.

Investigating the language that executives use helps to advance empirical work in stakeholder theory. Language provides insight into how executives come to prioritize the stakeholders they do, and firms' use of language influences how stakeholders respond to firms' initiatives. Recently, text analysis has been applied to take advantage of the availability of textual data and to understand stakeholder reactions to firms' initiatives (e.g., Henisz, et al., 2014). But, there are also other ways of using language, including topic modeling (Jaworska & Nanda, 2017), latent semantic analysis (Crilly & Sloan, 2014), and grammatical analysis (Ireland & Pennebaker, 2010). Cognitive approaches to analyzing language recognize that language – not only content, but also latent features such as grammatical structure and figures of speech – provides insight into how actors construe the world around them. For example, firms' deception – such as when firms espouse stakeholder-friendly policies without implementing them – does not appear in the content of their communication but in subtle linguistic cues, which derive from how managers construe their external environments (Crilly, Hansen, & Zollo, 2016).

Language is therefore useful for understanding why executives take the action they do. But, language is also performative: Corporate discourse influences other actors, including subordinates and external stakeholders. Any initiative can be communicated in different ways, with implications for directing subordinate attention and gaining stakeholder support. Hence, linguistic analysis is apt for assessing why stakeholders react to corporate initiatives in the ways they do. There is the potential to use linguistic analysis to understand interaction amongst stakeholders and firms, in the way that it has been applied to shed light on communicative success in coordination (Selten & Warglien, 2007). Here, too, grammar helps to explain how even actors with divergent interests coordinate (Ireland & Pennebaker, 2010), which is a central issue for stakeholder theory.

Similarly, behavioral stakeholder theory shifts the focus toward methods that are less conventional in current stakeholder research. At present, much empirical work involves the use of archival data. Nonetheless, there is a role for experiments to identify the mechanisms through which choices are made and impressions are formed. Field experiments, which have already become established in the discipline of development economics (Duflo, Dupas, & Kremer, 2015), should be particularly encouraged, but laboratory studies are also useful both in developing new insight and in testing the causal claims in the existing stakeholder literature. In laboratory experiments, the selection of appropriate samples is crucial if scholars are less interested in general psychological mechanisms than in understanding how actual stakeholders react to specific corporate initiatives. After all, undergraduate students are unlikely to evaluate corporate initiatives in the same way as actors with a direct stake in the outcomes of such initiatives. Correspondingly, laboratory studies may have to involve samples of actual stakeholders. Panel survey organizations with access to specialized populations offer one potential solution here (Crilly, et al., 2016). Similarly, there is a role for formal theory, too, in advancing understanding of how firms address multiple, potentially conflicting, stakeholder pressures. The advantage of formal theory for behavioral stakeholder theory lies in modeling the complex interactions that arise between multiple stakeholders which may be difficult to encompass in experiments.

Conclusion

The overarching goal of adopting a behavioral perspective in advancing stakeholder theory is to understand why firms respond to stakeholder pressures in different ways and with what consequences. Behavioral research suggests some novel perspectives as to why firms address stakeholder pressures in different ways. The stakeholder problem is as much one of managing attention *within* the firm as it is one of managing external demands upon the firm. Second, recognizing that stakeholders interpret corporate action, the behavioral perspective shifts the focus to important roles for communication and language in explaining why firms may fail to benefit from their stakeholder engagement. Linguistic analysis and experimental work are promising tools for stakeholder scholars to equip themselves with.

Notes

1. It is surprisingly common to find in corporations' external and internal documents statements to this effect that do not indicate potential trade-offs and that do not prioritize stakeholders: for example, "This will continue to drive strong returns for all stakeholders" (Amcor annual report, 2016); "We create value for all stakeholders," (Carillon annual report, 2015: 18). Stakeholder theory, of course, does not imply that all stakeholders are equally important.

References

Agle, B. R., Mitchell, R. K., & Sonnenfeld, J. A. (1999). Who matters to CEOs? An investigation of stakeholder attributions and salience, corporate performance, and CEO values. *Academy of Management Journal*, 42: 507–525.

Amcor. (2016). Annual report 2016. Retrieved from www.amcor.com/investors/financial-information/annual-reports.

Brickson, S. L. (2005). Organizational identity orientation: Forging a link between organizational identity and organizations' relations with stakeholders. *Administrative Science Quarterly*, 50(4): 576–609.

Bridoux, F., & Stoelhorst, J. W. (2014). Microfoundations for stakeholder theory: Managing stakeholders with heterogenous motives. *Strategic Management Journal*, 35(1): 107–125.

Burke, M. J., Borucki, C. C., & Hurley, A. E. (1992). Reconceptualizing psychological climate in a retail service environment: A multiple-stakeholder perspective. *Journal of Applied Psychology*, 77 (5): 717–729.

Carillion. (2015). Annual report and accounts 2015. Retrieved from www.annualreports.co.uk/Company/carillion-plc.

Carter, M. Z., & Mossholder, K. W. (2015). Are we on the same page? The effects of congruence between supervisor and group trust. *Journal of Applied Psychology*, 100(5): 1349–1363.

Crilly, D., Hansen, M. & Zollo, M. (2016). The grammar of decoupling: A cognitive-linguistic perspective on firms' sustainability claims and stakeholders' interpretation. *Academy of Management Journal*, 59(2): 705–729.

Crilly, D., Ni, N., & Jiang, Y. (2016). Do no harm versus do good social responsibility. Attributional thinking and the liability of foreignness. *Strategic Management Journal*, 37(7): 1316–1329.

Crilly, D., & Sloan, P. (2012). Corporate attention to stakeholders: Enterprise logic and an inside-out explanation. *Strategic Management Journal*, 33 (10): 1174–1193.

Crilly, D., & Sloan, P. (2014). Autonomy or control? Organizational architecture and corporate attention to stakeholders. *Organization Science*, 25(2): 339–355.

Duflo, E., Dupas, P., & Kremer, M. (2015). Education, HIV, and early fertility: Experimental evidence from Kenya. *American Economic Review*, 105(9): 2757–2797.

Dutton, J. E., & Jackson, S. E. (1987). Categorizing strategic issues: Links to organizational action. *Academy of Management Review*, 12(1): 76–90.

Freeman, R. E., Harrison, J. S., Wicks, A. C., Parmar, B. L., & De Colle, S. (2010). *Stakeholder theory. The state of the art*. Cambridge University Press.

Gavetti, G., Levinthal, D., & Ocasio, W. (2007). Perspective – Neo-Carnegie: The Carnegie School's past, present, and reconstructing for the future. *Organization Science, 18*(3): 523–536.

Harrison, J. S., & van der Laan Smith, J. (2015). Responsible accounting for stakeholders. *Journal of Management Studies, 52*(7): 935–960.

Henisz, W. J., Dorobantu, S., & Nartey, L. (2014). Spinning gold: The financial returns to external stakeholder engagement. Strategic Management Journal, *35*: 1727–1748.

Hillman, A. J., & Keim, G. D. (2001). Shareholder value, stakeholder management, and social issues: What's the bottom line? *Strategic Management Journal, 22*: 125–139.

Ireland, M. E., & Pennebaker, J. W. (2010). Language style matching in writing: Synchrony in essays, correspondence, and poetry. *Journal of Personality and Social Psychology, 99*: 549–571.

Jaworska, S., & Nanda, A. (2017). Doing well by talking good: A topic-modelling assisted discourse study of corporate social responsibility. *Applied Linguistics, 39*(3): 373–399.

Kivleniece, I., & Quelin, B. V. (2012). Creating and capturing value in public-private ties: A private actor's perspective. *Academy of Management Review, 37*: 272–299.

Lankoski, L., Smith, C. S., & Van Wassenhove, L. (2016). Stakeholder judgments of value. *Business Ethics Quarterly, 26*(2): 227–256.

Love, E. G., & Kraatz, M. (2017). Failed stakeholder exchanges and corporate reputation: The case of earnings misses. Academy of Management Journal, *60*(3): 880–903.

March, J. G. (1962). The business firm as a political coalition. *Journal of Politics, 24*(4): 662–678.

Mitchell R. K., Agle B. R., & Wood D. J. (1997). Toward a theory of stakeholder identification and salience: Defining the principle of who and what really counts. *Academy of Management Review, 22*: 853–886.

Powell, T. C., Lovallo, D., & Fox, C. R. (2011). Behavioral strategy. *Strategic Management Journal, 32*: 1369–1386.

Selten, R., & Warglien, M. (2007). The emergence of simple languages in an experimental coordination game. *Proceedings of the National Academy of Sciences of the United States of America, 104*(18): 7361–7366.

Strategic Management Society. (2017). Stakeholder strategy. Retrieved from www.strategicmanagement.net/ig/stakeholder_strategy.php.

Wang, H., Tong, L., Takeuchi, R., & George, G. (2016). Corporate social responsibility: An overview and new research directions. *Academy of Management Journal, 59*(2): 534–544.

Weitzner, D., & Deutsch, Y. (2015). Understanding motivation and social influence in stakeholder prioritization. *Organization Studies, 36*(10): 1337–1360.

Sketches of New and Future Research on Stakeholder Management

SINZIANA DOROBANTU

New York University

Rarely a day goes by without a headline to remind managers and investors of the importance of stakeholder management. "Uber to repay millions to drivers, who could be owed far more," reads a recent headline from *The New York Times* (Scheiber, 2017). "Volkswagen among most criticized companies by NGOs," writes the BBC (BBC News, 2016). The list of examples goes on, and, if I were to venture a guess, will grow even faster going forward. Diminishing costs of information sharing have dramatically increased transparency across the corporate, political, and social domains, while growing concerns about social and economic inequality are drawing more attention to corporate practices that are perceived to accentuate it. Phrases like "corporate social responsibility" or CSR, "sustainability," and "shared value" are present reminders that firms and stakeholders are continuously renegotiating the terms that define how economic value is created and distributed in today's markets.

Academic research is similarly paying increasing attention to the role played by various stakeholders in the process of value creation and to the managerial practices for stakeholder engagement. Yet, as it is often the case with growing areas of research, the work completed thus far has opened up an even wider range of questions that are yet to be answered. Far from aiming to provide an exhaustive list, I highlight some questions that can be broadly grouped into three areas: (1) What mechanisms of governance are available to manage the relationships between a firm and its stakeholders? (2) How do the interactions between the stakeholders themselves and the differences among them influence strategies of stakeholder management and their effectiveness? (3) How does stakeholder management differ across institutional and physical environments? In the present chapter, I discuss some recent studies that begin to address these questions and sketch the outlines of future research that could probe even deeper. The order of these questions also suggests a need to broaden the scope of stakeholder research beyond its traditional focus on the firm–stakeholder relationship as the primary unit of analysis to examine interactions among the stakeholder groups and the broader environment that influences both firm–stakeholder and stakeholder–stakeholder relationships.

(1) *Stakeholder Governance: Mechanisms, Arrangements and Time Horizons.* Since its inception (Freeman, 1984; Freeman & Reed, 1983), stakeholder theory has stressed the merits of creating value for stakeholders. Emphasizing a "managing for stakeholders" approach, research in this tradition has highlighted that to successfully create value, firms must engage their stakeholders (Freeman, et al., 2010). Thus, relationships between managers and stakeholders have been critical to understanding how value is created, how value is distributed, and when the process of value creation breaks down. Yet, despite the centrality of firm–stakeholder relationships to the development of stakeholder theory, empirical research that focuses on understanding how these relationships are governed is just beginning to emerge. In practice, important differences exist in this regard. First, while relationships between firms and some stakeholders (e.g., employees, shareholders, suppliers) are governed by *contractual* agreements, relationships with other stakeholders (e.g., local communities, civil society groups) are largely *relational*, relying on some combination of shared norms, aligned incentives, reciprocity, credibility, and trust (Bosse, Phillips, & Harrison, 2009; Harrison, Bosse, & Phillips, 2010). Second, while some relationships are strictly *dyadic*, between managers and a well-defined type of stakeholder (e.g., an employee's relationship with the firm), others are *collective*, involving one or more firms and multiple stakeholder groups (so-called multi-stakeholder initiatives). Lastly, while relationships between firms and some stakeholders (e.g., full-time employees, long-term suppliers) are developed over a long time and with a long future time horizon in mind, relationships with other stakeholders (e.g., day workers, one-time suppliers) are sporadic and shortsighted (i.e., myopic).

These three dimensions – the mechanism of governance (contractual vs. relational), the relational arrangement (dyadic vs. collective), and the time horizon defining the stakeholder relationship (long vs. short-term) – have important implications for the management of stakeholder relations. Empirical research is starting to unpack the strategic decisions involved along these dimensions and their financial implications, but many questions are still in the realm of future research. In a recent article, my co-author and I focused on the rise of contractual agreements between firms and local communities and examined their financial value (Dorobantu & Odziemkowska 2017). We argued that these contracts (known as community benefits agreements, or CBAs) reduce the probability of conflict between firms and local communities, and are perceived as particularly valuable by investors when they are signed with communities that have strong property rights and a history of extra-institutional mobilization through protests and blockades. Future research can further examine when such contracts are more likely to be signed – specifically, under what conditions do both a firm and a local community perceive a contractual agreement (which is costly to negotiate, invariably incomplete, yet constraining for future behavior) as a better option than a relational arrangement unconstrained by a legally binding agreement.

Similarly, the antecedents and implications of different relational arrangements (dyadic vs. collective) are important to understand in stakeholder research. Stakeholder theory has largely assumed that firms' relationships with their stakeholders are dyadic in nature. Yet, firm–stakeholder relations are often defined by and developed within the confines of collective institutional arrangements that involve multiple stakeholders and sometimes multiple firms in an industry or a geographic location. Collective bargaining agreements for employees are clear historical examples; more recent ones include global, industry-wide programs involving industry, governments, nongovernmental organizations, and intergovernmental organizations (e.g., Extractive Industries Transparency Initiative) and local development initiatives that similarly involve a wide range of stakeholders within a specific geographical area (e.g., Niger Delta Partnership Initiative). Collective arrangements are likely to differ in fundamental ways from dyadic ones both in their evolution and in their effects (Dorobantu, Kaul, & Zelner, 2017). Some of these differences might be understood using existing frameworks developed to analyze multi-stakeholder institutions for governing common resources (Ostrom 1990, 2010; Ostrom, Gardner, & Walker, 1994) and industry self-regulatory agreements (Barnett & King, 2008; King & Lenox, 2000; Lenox, 2006), while others might need additional theoretical probing.

Finally, differences in the time horizon (i.e., the expectation of repeated interaction) governing firm–stakeholder relations are also important. Norms that sustain cooperation among individuals (e.g., fairness, reciprocity) are less likely to emerge in limited (one-time) interactions (Bosse, et al., 2009). With the increase in global communication and trade that enabled supplier relations across continents (Gereffi, 1999) and technological developments that are accelerating the growth of contingent work (i.e., task-specific, short-duration work relationships; Barley, Bechky, & Milliken, 2017), expectations of long-term, repeated interactions between firms and stakeholders are also weakening. Firms that already struggle to manage their long-term stakeholder relationships are likely to encounter even greater challenges in their management of short-term relationships. The changing nature of work and supplier relations underscores the importance of thinking more closely about whether and how the first principles of stakeholder management might change as time horizons shorten in the decades ahead and how stakeholder cooperation can be sustained even in the absence of repeated, long-term interactions.

Most likely, firms will pay attention to "short-term stakeholders" only when facing pressures from activists concerned with firms' social and environmental sustainability. For detached observers, the interplay between diminishing incentives to invest in stakeholder relationships because of shortening time horizons and increased socio-political pressures to enhance a firm's attention to its long-term impact will be fascinating to study. For managers having to balance these seemingly opposing forces, getting this right is likely to be a matter of corporate survival and success. The lens of stakeholder research can provide practical guidance in this area through future research that considers more closely how time horizons and temporal dynamics affect stakeholder relationships.

(2) Understanding the Stakeholder Landscape: Relationships between Stakeholders and Differences among Them. Research on stakeholder management assumes a firm-centered perspective; indeed, one of the main contributions of stakeholder theory to the field of strategic management is its focus on the relationships that exist between firms and their various stakeholders (Freeman 1984; Freeman, et al., 2010). The firm is represented at the center of visual schemas portraying these relationships (see, for example, Freeman, Harrison, & Wicks, 2007). While perfectly appropriate for emphasizing that managers need to consider and engage different stakeholder groups, this perspective downplays the relationships that exist among the stakeholders themselves. But stakeholders are part of a broader ecosystem, defined by a wide set of relationships. In the political world, for instance, both the local and the central governments are important stakeholders that can affect a firm's operations through decisions on permitting, inspections, and taxation. The two are clearly related to each other: they

interact in the political system and their relationship is defined by various interactions that predate and go beyond their interactions with the firm.

The relationships that exist between stakeholders directly influence a firm's relationship with them. Imagine the oversimplified example of a firm with only two local stakeholders – say, two village communities adjacent to a mine. How the managers of this mine engage the two communities will likely depend (1) on whether the communities are connected or not (Are they on the same side or on different sides of a mountain or of a national border? Are they neighbors connected by a road? Have they worked together in the past?); (2) on whether they get along (Are they from the same or different ethnic groups? Do they share a history of cooperation or conflict?); (3) on whether they can influence each other (Does one community follow the lead of the other?); (4) on whether they perceive each other as rivals (Is engaging one stakeholder likely to alienate the other or trigger a race among them?); and so on. The effectiveness of stakeholder engagement will vary with many of these factors, so awareness of the relational landscape among stakeholders is necessary both in practice and in the research that seeks to understand and guide it.

Even in the absence of connections or coordination mechanisms between stakeholders, the relationship between the firm and one stakeholder can influence or be influenced by the relationship between the firm and a different stakeholder. Recently, my co-authors and I showed empirically how some stakeholders' reactions to critical events (e.g., a court decision or a critical report by a nongovernmental organization) affect other stakeholders' reactions to the same event (Dorobantu, Henisz, & Nartey, 2017a). Our paper demonstrated that when firms fail to build good stakeholder relationships, a critical event can easily escalate into a crisis with significant reputational and performance implications for the firm. When, by contrast, the firm has good relationships with most stakeholders, a similar event will have less of an impact because stakeholders rely more on their own information about the firm (their *priors*) and less on the information provided by the critical event and by other stakeholders' reactions. While similar in emphasis to prior research highlighting the insurance value of CSR (Godfrey, 2005; Godfrey, Merrill, & Hansen, 2009; Minor & Morgan, 2011), this paper spells out the mechanisms that trigger or prevent cascades of stakeholder mobilization and provides stakeholder-level empirical evidence of how stakeholders' reactions feed onto each other even in the absence of pre-existing networks or coordination channels. The paper also contributes to research on the impact of social movements in markets (Davis, et al., 2008) by showing that stakeholder reactions provide essential information not only to managers (Ingram, Yue, & Rao, 2010), analysts (Vasi & King 2012), and investors (King & Soule 2007), but also to other stakeholders assessing their own position toward a firm as they decide whether or not to mobilize to oppose or support a firm.

In addition to considering how the relationships and interactions between stakeholders themselves influence a firm's engagement with its stakeholders, research and practice must also acknowledge that stakeholders differ along many dimensions. They have different utility functions (Harrison, et al., 2010) and different preferences for fair treatment and reciprocity (Bridoux & Stoelhorst, 2014). As a result, they are likely to respond very differently to similar efforts by a firm to engage them. A meeting with a political stakeholder might be enough to reach some common understanding of a project's costs and benefits, and to obtain their backing. Obtaining the support of a local community, by contrast, may require repeated rounds of engagement that include meetings, donations, and collaborative endeavors to benefit local development. Even engaging with a local political stakeholder (say, a mayor or a tribal council) may be a very different experience than working with a minister in the central government or a provincial governor.

Part of the explanation for this variation is the differences in stakeholders' norms and values.[1] That is, important cultural differences exist among stakeholders. After decades of suffering affront when being approached by various corporate representatives, Indigenous communities in Canada have resorted to publishing protocols of engagement – documents outlining how Western managers should communicate with tribal leaders and members of tribal council. Such efforts are clear signals that Indigenous communities care greatly about others respecting their rules and traditions. Across the world, land and various natural resources such as forests, rivers, and lakes, can vary tremendously in their value to different people or communities. To some, a piece of land is simply a resource that can be productively employed toward agriculture, industry, or real estate. To others, it is a sacred ancient territory, the land that belonged to their family for generations, or just "home"; efforts to repurpose it or represent it by a monetary amount in an economic transaction are perceived as insulting. Similarly, when firms interact with civil society organizations, one of the most challenging parts of the interaction is recognizing that they are driven by different values and norms.

But stakeholders also differ in terms of their knowledge, which can be further differentiated into information (i.e., how much they know about a certain issue or project) and skills (i.e., what models they use to assess the information). Ministers have experience dealing with companies, understand what large projects entail, and know how to evaluate them. Their decision-making process is largely based on the evaluation of net impact – whether, on average, most citizens are better off with the new project than without it.[2] By contrast, leaders of local communities might have never interacted with a large firm in the past and a project like the one under consideration is completely new to them; they have to be informed about the project's benefits and costs and also trained on how to evaluate them. Such asymmetries greatly affect stakeholder relationships and engagement. In the example above, there are fewer information and skill asymmetries between the firm and the minister than between the firm and the local community, and many managers would perceive the latter to play to their advantage. In most instances, however, efforts to reduce information and skill asymmetries in the early phases of engagement (i.e., through proactive engagement) are likely to enhance stakeholder cooperation (Dorobantu, Henisz, & Nartley, 2017b) and enable the creation of value through trust building and additional exchange of information (Harrison, et al., 2010).

Information and skill asymmetries work both ways. While the firm knows more about its project's potential benefits and costs, stakeholders have a better understanding of the local institutional and physical environment. Government representatives know more about the regulatory process, while local communities have a considerable advantage in their knowledge about the local environment, which could be critical in discovering ways to minimize the project's negative impact. For decades, international business research has employed the construct of "liability of foreignness" (Hymer, 1976; Zaheer, 1995) to represent these two types of information asymmetries – that multinational firms have only a limited understanding of how things work in the host country and that host-country stakeholders have only a limited understanding of the multinational's operations – and to study its implications for firms' performance abroad (Wu & Salomon, 2016; Zaheer 1995). More recently, scholars have focused on defining the "distance" between the cultural, political and economic conditions in a multinational's home and host countries (Berry, Guillén, & Zhou, 2010; Ghemawat 2001). A parallel construct of firm–stakeholder distance might prove useful in stakeholder research to highlight that distance between a firm and its stakeholders varies across the different stakeholders, with important implications for strategies of stakeholder engagement and their effectiveness.

One possibility is to build upon stakeholder theory's initial differentiation among many types of stakeholders – employees, suppliers, customers, communities, governments, civil society groups, and others – and additional differentiations between primary and secondary stakeholders, to recognize that stakeholders also belong to different domains: economic, social, and political. Stakeholders within the firm and within the value chain are *economic* stakeholders; those occupying formal (elected or appointed) roles within political institutions (e.g., parliamentarians, ministers, mayors, party leaders) are *political* stakeholders; and stakeholders representing various interest groups (e.g., ethnic or religious groups, environmental activists) are *social* stakeholders. While the

differences within each category should not be downplayed, stakeholder research might be able to pin down important distinctions between the roles they play in the value creation process, their values and norms, and their access to information and skills. Distinctions between economic, political, and social stakeholders are particularly important as stakeholder research studies the effects of the institutional environment on stakeholder management in different settings – the topic to which I turn next.

(3) *Stakeholder Engagement in Different Institutional Environments.* Over the course of its development, stakeholder research has emphasized variations across stakeholders and across firms' engagement strategies. While the broader institutional environment – the rules and norms that govern interactions in the marketplace and beyond (North, 1990: 3; Ostrom, 1990: 51) – has not been part of the development of stakeholder theory, institutional variations across locations (countries or regions within a country) and across industries necessarily influence how firms and stakeholders interact. For example, in a distinct but related literature on the varieties of capitalism, scholars have described and sought to explain why different market economies have evolved toward different equilibria in which stakeholders play different roles in the process of economic value creation. In an influential book, Hall and Soskice (2001) propose a typology that differentiates between liberal market economies, such as the United Kingdom and the United States, and coordinated market economies like Germany, Sweden, and Italy. In liberal market economies, most relationships between companies and their stakeholders, including employees, financiers, and regulators, are defined and developed through arms-length transactions. Employees have strong disincentives to invest in firm-specific skills and prefer investing in general skills that are easily transferable across firms and across industries; financiers diversify across industries with only a limited understanding of long-term trends within them; and regulators are slow to adapt, and do so mostly in response to pressures from interest

groups. By contrast, in coordinated market economies, there is much more emphasis on long-term
relationships and joint decision-making – for
example, through corporate boards that ensure the
representation of both employees and banks
(Aguilera & Jackson, 2003). A strong supporting
set of government institutions – including an educational system that provides vocational training
within many domains, regulations that encourage
long employee tenure, and a strong welfare state
that buffers against downturns in specialized
industries – has coevolved to sustain "coordination" across multiple stakeholders who participate
in the process of value creation within an industry.
As this literature has shown, the institutional background plays a critical role in defining and influencing firm–stakeholder relations.

An immediate corollary of these ideas is that
stakeholder relationships and engagement strategies are likely to vary even within the boundaries
of the same firm if the firm operates in multiple
countries. Anecdotal evidence from large energy
firms that tend to span multiple geographical borders suggests important differences across subsidiaries. As a top manager for local community
relations for a large oil and gas firm mentioned to
me in a recent personal conversation, "our company may be doing great things in one location and
be years behind in another." Recent research by
Durand and Jacqueminet (2015) identifies similar
variations in the implementation of CSR strategies
across subsidiaries of multinational firms.
The authors suggest that these variations can be
largely explained by pressures from local external
stakeholders.

Finally, I suggest that in addition to considering
how the institutional environment might affect
firm–stakeholder relationships, scholars of stakeholder theory might also want to think about geography and man-made infrastructure that connects
or divides firms and their stakeholders, and the
stakeholders themselves. Here, again, the insights
provided by Elinor Ostrom's (1990, 2005) work on
the emergence of local institutions for the management of common pool resources (e.g., fisheries,
water bodies, irrigation systems, open pastures,
and clean air) in different physical environments

can inspire new stakeholder research. Among the
many insights provided throughout her work, a few
seem particularly relevant to stakeholder research:
(1) matching the governance mechanisms to local
(physical, social, and economic) conditions; (2)
enabling stakeholders to participate in defining
and modifying the governance of their relationship
with the firm; (3) ensuring that firm–stakeholder
governance mechanisms are compatible with existing institutions and respected by outside authorities
(e.g., governments); (4) establishing clear mechanisms for monitoring, feedback, and adjustment;
and (5) allowing for accessible, low-cost mechanisms for conflict resolution. A nuanced understanding of these aspects in the context of
firm–stakeholder relations can further advance
research on the factors that enable or constrain
the development of cooperative firm–stakeholder
relations.

***

Stakeholder research has come a long way over
recent decades. Insightful theoretical pieces highlight the role played by various market and nonmarket stakeholders in the process of value creation.
The collection of work in this tradition offers
a compelling theory of management that brings to
the forefront relationships between the firm's managers and its stakeholders. As stakeholder theory
continues to develop, future research has the potential to further both scholarship and practice. Among
the many questions that can guide research going
forward, I suggest that future work could provide
additional insight into how firm–stakeholder relationships are governed – through contractual or
relational agreements, in a dyadic or collective
arrangement, over long or short time horizons; into
how firm–stakeholder relationships are affected by
interactions among the stakeholders themselves as
well as by differences between them in terms of
values, norms and access to information and skills;
and into how the broader institutional environment
might enable or constrain firm–stakeholder interactions. There are many other questions, of course;
their totality offers an incredibly exciting area for
scholarship that contributes to both management
theory and practice.

Notes

1. Stakeholders' norms and values play directly into their utility functions. Stakeholder utility functions include the factors that drive utility for stakeholders and the weights they assign to each factor (Harrison, et al., 2010: 59). These weights are a function of stakeholders' values (Do they care more about economic benefits, social impacts or environmental preservation?) and their norms (How much do they care about reciprocity and equal treatment relative to other stakeholders?).
2. Such calculations assume no corruption in the process. In the last section, I suggest that different institutional settings – including corruption and captured institutions – also affect stakeholder relations and engagement.

References

Aguilera, R. V., & Jackson, G. (2003). The cross-national diversity of corporate governance: Dimensions and determinants. *Academy of Management Review, 28*(3): 447–465.

Barley, S. R., Bechky, B. A., & Milliken, F. J. (2017). The changing nature of work: Careers, identities, and work lives in the 21st century. *Academy of Management Discoveries, 3*(2): 111–115.

Barnett, M. L., & King, A. A. (2008). Good fences make good neighbors: A longitudinal analysis of an industry self-regulatory institution. *The Academy of Management Journal, 51*(6): 1150–1170.

BBC News. (2016, January 17). Volkswagen among most criticised companies by NGOs. *BBC News.* Retrieved from www.bbc.com/news/business-35337891.

Berry, H., Guillén, M. F., & Zhou, N. (2010). An institutional approach to cross-national distance. *Journal of International Business Studies, 41*(9): 1460–1480.

Bosse, D. A., Phillips, R. A., & Harrison, J. S. (2009). Stakeholders, reciprocity, and firm performance. *Strategic Management Journal, 30*(4): 447–456.

Bridoux, F., & Stoelhorst, J. W. (2014). Microfoundations for stakeholder theory: Managing stakeholders with heterogeneous motives. *Strategic Management Journal, 35*(1): 107–125.

Davis, G. F., Morrill, C., Rao, H., & Soule, S. A. (2008). Introduction: Social movements in organizations and markets. *Administrative Science Quarterly, 53*(3): 389–394.

Dorobantu, S., Henisz, W. J., & Nartey, L. (2017a). Not all sparks light a fire: Stakeholder and shareholder reactions to critical events in contested markets. *Administrative Science Quarterly, 62*(3): 561–597.

Dorobantu, S., Henisz, W. J., & Nartey, L. J. (2017b). Proactive stakeholder engagement and the formation of stakeholder preferences for firm investments. Working Paper, New York University.

Dorobantu, S., Kaul, A., & Zelner, B. A. (2017). Nonmarket strategy through the lens of new institutional economics: A review and future directions. *Strategic Management Journal, 38*(1): 114–140.

Dorobantu, S., & Odziemkowska, K. (2017). Valuing stakeholder governance: Property rights, community mobilization, and firm value. Strategic Management Journal, *38*(13): 2682–2703. doi:10.1002/smj.2675

Durand, R., & Jacqueminet, A. (2015). Peer conformity, attention, and heterogeneous implementation of practices in MNEs. *Journal of International Business Studies, 46*(8): 917–937.

Freeman, R. E. (1984). *Strategic management: A stakeholder approach,* Boston: Pitman.

Freeman, R. E., Harrison, J. S., & Wicks, A. C. (2007). *Managing for stakeholders: Survival, reputation, and success.* New Haven: Yale University Press.

Freeman, R. E., Harrison, J. S., Wicks, A. C., Parmar, B. L., & Colle, S. de. (2010). *Stakeholder theory: The state of the art.* Cambridge; New York: Cambridge University Press.

Freeman, R. E., & Reed, D. L. (1983). Stockholders and stakeholders: A new perspective on corporate governance. *California Management Review, 25*(3): 88–106.

Gereffi, G. (1999). International trade and industrial upgrading in the apparel commodity chain. *Journal of International Economics, 48*: 37–70.

Ghemawat, P. (2001). Distance still matters: The hard reality of global expansion. *Harvard Business Review, 79*(8): 137–147.

Godfrey, P. C. (2005). The relationship between corporate philanthropy and shareholder wealth: A risk management perspective. *The Academy of Management Review, 30*(4): 777–798.

Godfrey, P. C., Merrill, C. B., & Hansen, J. M. (2009). The relationship between corporate social responsibility and shareholder value: an empirical test of the risk management hypothesis. *Strategic Management Journal, 30*(4): 425–445.

Hall, P. A., & Soskice, D., eds. (2001). *Varieties of capitalism: The institutional foundations of comparative advantage*. Oxford, UK; New York: Oxford University Press.

Harrison, J. S., Bosse, D. A., & Phillips, R. A. (2010). Managing for stakeholders, stakeholder utility functions, and competitive advantage. *Strategic Management Journal*, *31*(1): 58–74.

Hymer, S. H. (1976). *The international operations of national firms: a study of direct foreign investment*. Cambridge, MA: The MIT Press.

Ingram, P., Yue, L. Q., & Rao, H. (2010). Trouble in store: Probes, protests, and store openings by Wal-Mart, 1998–2007. *American Journal of Sociology*, *116*(1): 53–92.

King, A. A., & Lenox, M. J. (2000). Industry self-regulation without sanctions: The chemical industry's responsible care program. *Academy of Management Journal*, *43*(4): 698–716.

King, B. G., & Soule, S. A. (2007). Social movements as extra-institutional entrepreneurs: The effect of protests on stock price returns. *Administrative Science Quarterly*, *52*(3): 413–442.

Lenox, M. J. (2006). The Role of Private Decentralized Institutions in Sustaining Industry Self-Regulation. *Organization Science*, *17*(6): 677–690.

Minor, D., & Morgan, J. (2011). CSR as Reputation Insurance: Primum Non Nocere. *California Management Review*, *53*(3): 40–59.

North, D. C. (1990). *Institutions, institutional change, and economic performance*. Cambridge: Cambridge University Press.

Ostrom, E. (1990). *Governing the commons: The evolution of institutions for collective action*. Cambridge; New York: Cambridge University Press.

Ostrom, E. (2005). *Understanding institutional diversity*. Princeton: Princeton University Press.

Ostrom, E. (2010). Beyond markets and states: Polycentric governance of complex economic systems. *The American Economic Review*, *100*(3): 641–672.

Ostrom, E., Gardner, R., & Walker, J. (1994). *Rules, games, and common-pool resources*, Ann Arbor: University of Michigan Press.

Scheiber, N. (2017, May 23). Uber to repay millions to drivers, who could be owed far more. The New York Times. Retrieved from www.nytimes.com/2017/05/23/business/economy/uber-drivers-tax.html.

Vasi, I. B., & King, B. G. (2012). Social movements, risk perceptions, and economic outcomes: The effect of primary and secondary stakeholder activism on firms' perceived environmental risk and financial performance. *American Sociological Review*, *77*(4): 573–596.

Wu, Z., & Salomon, R. (2016). Does imitation reduce the liability of foreignness? Linking distance, isomorphism, and performance. Strategic Management Journal, *37*(12): 2441–2462.

Zaheer, S. (1995). Overcoming the liability of foreignness. *The Academy of Management Journal*, *38*(2): 341–363.

Contextual Richness at the Core of New Stakeholder Research

LITE J. NARTEY

University of South Carolina

Stakeholder theory is "best regarded practically or pragmatically" and aims to create, trade and sustain value by providing tools for managers, constituents and theorists to understand, leverage and manage the value creation process and outcomes (Freeman, et al., 2012: 1). To truly conceptually grasp value creation that has theoretical, practical and policy relevance, context – "that amorphous concept capturing theory-relevant, surrounding phenomena or temporal conditions" (Bamberger, 2008: 839) – is important (Blair & Hunt, 1986; Cappelli & Sherer, 1991; Johns, 2006; Rousseau & Fried, 2001; Tsui, 2006). Stakeholder theory must be understood as inherently contextual in that stakeholders differ within diverse environments and espouse, as well as are driven by, different values, motivations, legacies and histories. Because context shapes and defines who stakeholders are, contextual factors may shape or drive key questions of stakeholder theory including stakeholder engagement, identification, morality, corporate social responsibility, as well as large socially based and stakeholder-driven problems such as environmental sustainability, poverty or development. Contextual factors inherently shape the ability of firms to not only understand the actions of stakeholders, but critically, for firms to engage with and thereby create value with and for stakeholders.

While context is based inherently on richness – i.e., a nuanced and deep understanding of the stakeholders themselves and the environments in which they live and interact –, conversely, current academic research approaches seek to identify generalizable outcomes and lessons. Thus, the question of contextual richness versus generalizable scope is an important tradeoff for new work in stakeholder theory. Extant stakeholder theory leverages generalizable theoretical models and

large sample data for empirical model development. These approaches, especially the theoretical work, have laid the foundations for seminal work within stakeholder theory (Donaldson & Preston, 1995; Harrison & Freeman, 1999; Jones, 1995; Mitchell, Agle & Wood, 1997) and of course, the development of stakeholder theory itself (Freeman, 1984; Freeman, et al., 2010). To move stakeholder theory forward, however, a change in research philosophy and approach to a focus on narrower research questions driven by richer data and a deeper more nuanced understanding of the stakeholders and the environments in which they operate, may be needed.

Finding the balance between the advantages and disadvantages of richness and generalizable scope in research on stakeholder theory is difficult, but the loss of generalizability to gain the valuable nuance and understanding offered through narrow context-based research is important, at least for some research questions, particularly those of managerial relevance. In this chapter, I focus on the area of stakeholder engagement work and highlight my lessons from extensive fieldwork and interviews with extractive firms and their stakeholders in large-scale investment projects in the developing world. Through three vignettes, I highlight the importance of understanding contextual nuances in the management of stakeholders, identifying new, and often contradictory, questions and outcomes of research interest that arise from the attempts of these firms to successfully engage with their diverse stakeholders. I also briefly explore how these stories may inform our approach to extant and future stakeholder engagement theorizing, and share research designs of ongoing work seeking to capture context for managerially relevant stakeholder engagement work.

Context and Unexpected Consequences

Marching to the Stakeholder Tune

An extractive company seeks to engage with a poor local community occupied by only a few thousand inhabitants living under dire conditions. The local school is dilapidated, there are no health facilities and people have to travel, often through dense forest, to a local clinic over one hundred miles away. The road system is nonexistent, and the single bridge, which serves as the primary means of exiting the community, is rickety and dangerous to cross. Given the level of poverty and poor infrastructure, the primary means of transport for these inhabitants is on foot, by wheelbarrow or bicycle. There is no government support system or welfare system for the community to rely upon. How does the extractive company engage with the inhabitants of such a community?

Stakeholder engagement theory would argue that the firm should win the hearts and minds of these local community members by creating value for them by engaging in development. A key question however is: in this particular environment, what constitutes value creation in development? A generally understood approach is to automatically fix what we (as scholars and practitioners) see as something that the people will "need." Does the firm start with the school? Or build a small clinic? And, of course, how does the firm address the need for supporting educational or medical personnel or equipment? Repairing the bridge seems feasible and easily executed, especially as extractive firms build infrastructure as a standard means of developing their assets. Clearing some of the forest to facilitate road access is also a quick means of engagement which also lies within the scope of firm expertise. Based on this particular context, what is "needed" first may not always be easily identifiable; and, even defining the correct engagement approach may be context-driven.

Confounded by where to start, firm executives chose to ask the community what they wanted or needed. The surprising answer was – a marching band! At first blush, this response, especially in the face of the lack of infrastructure and extreme poverty, makes little rational sense. However, instead of dismissing this request, and focusing on the generally understood multinational approach to development, i.e., build or fix some physical structure, the firm asked more questions and found a purely rational need for the marching band. The neighboring community, similarly poor and similarly dilapidated, had a marching band and every weekend and sometimes into the week, the youth of the focal community traveled to the neighboring community to enjoy the nightlife offered by the presence of the marching band. The rational fear of the community dying due to the lack of young people was the primary focus of community leaders. By respecting this wish for a marching band, the firm created value for stakeholders in the community and was subsequently able to execute more sustainable development-based engagement strategies in partnership with the community! The lesson here is that stakeholder rationality is contextual and thus the ability, or indeed opportunity, to engage is contingent on the firm fully understanding, respecting, and working with(in) these contextual factors.

Scholars and practitioners may take the example above as simply a lesson where "listening" to stakeholders, which is of course an important aspect of stakeholder engagement work especially in the development arena, provides a means for value creation for the firm and for stakeholders. But the lessons from a different community proved otherwise.

Dangerous Catch

An extractive firm operating off-shore oil assets close to several local fishing communities used a floating production and storage vessel. This massive vessel is the size of 3 football fields put together (over 200 feet by over 1,000 feet), has a maximum storage capacity of 1.6 million barrels of oil and is a temporary home to hundreds of personnel. To protect local fishermen and the vessel, the firm enforced a safety perimeter of 500 meters (approximately 550 yards) around the vessel, and yet the number of local fishermen incursions into the safety perimeter kept increasing annually! The firm's response, per accepted best practice in stakeholder engagement, was to educate first (as the assumption was: the fishermen did not understand the dangers associated with operating close to the vessel), and provide alternatives (as the assumption was: the fishermen would "obviously" prefer an easier means of obtaining their liveli-hoods). The firm therefore embarked on numerous educational "safety campaigns," and created sev-eral on-shore subsistence livelihood projects to help facilitate new sources of income for fishermen and their families. These attempts at re-tooling the fishermen were met with strong protests, as stated by the leader: "we are fishermen: we live and die by the sea." The firm also leveraged a means of enfor-cement by working with the national navy and marine police to seize local ships (large canoes carrying over 30 fishermen) that ventured into the safety perimeter. Despite these measures, the num-ber of fishermen incursions close to the vessel continued to increase!

Finally, in meetings with the local fishermen, the firm learned that the fishermen firmly believed that the oil vessel not only harbored fish but that it also created a shady environment that enabled fish to grow larger than in open waters. Therefore, from the perspective of local fishermen, beneath the vessel was the best place to fish. Seeking to create shared value for the firm and local fishermen, an independent auditor for the firm's primary devel-opment partner suggested a scheduled time every week for local fishermen to fish within the safety perimeter. At first this seemed to be a reasonable solution for shared value, yet further interviews with the fishermen revealed an alarming fact – the local fishermen, for expediency, sometimes fished with dynamite! Given over 1 million barrels of oil in the vessel, there can of course be no opportu-nities for shared scheduling of the waters close to the vessel!

In such a context, when the firm has employed not only best practice but also theoretically sound engagement strategies, has listened to the stake-holders and can find no opportunities to involve or provide stakeholders access, in what further ways can the firm create value for stakeholders while protecting its own assets? The firm in ques-tion is still exploring new onshore livelihood pro-jects in an attempt to entice the fishermen to

abandon their pursuit of the fish beneath the storage vessel. But, firm managers have also accepted that incursions by local fishermen will never stop regardless of the level of engagement.

The Price of Engagement Success

Listening to stakeholder demands is a critical aspect of engaging with stakeholders, especially in the context of development. And, for many firms, enga-ging with these actors through large-scale projects is an aspect of firm responsibility due to the lack of political will and resource constraints of local and central governments. While numerous engagement cases by extractive firms have left "white elephants" scattered across the developing world (Frynas, 2005, 2008), there are some exceptional engage-ment successes. An extractive firm working off an island in the Niger Delta listened to the needs of the community, worked with the community, engaged local managers who understood the context of the communities, and devised – from our scholarly the-ory and notions of practitioner best practice – ideal "needed" engagement strategies, including: electri-fied all focal communities, built a technical school, provided excellent hospital (not clinic) facilities, as well as offered numerous scholarships. Although current theoretical and empirical research still seeks to identify "good stakeholder engagement," from field trips and interviews, these projects could certainly be described as meeting (if not exceeding) any reasonable conceptual standard of good engagement.

But, can stakeholder engagement be done "too well"? What would engagement that is "too good" look like? What are the consequences for the firm (and stakeholders) when it comes to engagement that is too good?

While various consequences are possible, the firm in question faced growing stakeholder demands, not only from the true island local popu-lation (97 communities along the pipeline route), but additional new demands driven by an influx of people from the mainland who also wanted to benefit from the electricity, good school, excellent health facilities and scholarships offered by the firm. In response, the firm substantially increased its level of engagement: in education, from an initial graduating class of 24 students in 2010 to an accredited technical school catering to over 1,500 students by 2015 due to intense interest (over 1,400 applicants for 100 spots in 2013); electrification for over 11,000 inhabitants by 2013 with an increase in over 1,000 new customers every year; and health facilities that now catered for up to 200 hospital beds from an initial capacity of 32 beds, outpatient services covering around 3,000 patients a month up from 600 patients a month, and an additional five primary health centers scattered about the island. In interviews, the firm's primary stakeholder engagement concern changed from how best to engage to how to *reduce* stakeholder engagement without causing a backlash from its diverse stakeholders! One "obvious" solution to this dilemma would be to involve other actors who could take up some of these engagement responsibilities (i.e., managing the school or the hospital), such as international NGOs and multilateral development partners. After many attempts by the firm however, no development partners would take over these projects because the firm, as an extractive company, was perceived to have ample and endless resources by these potential development partners.

Despite this runaway best-practice engagement dilemma, the firm should have been able to take solace in the fact that it is indeed winning the hearts and minds of (and creating value for) stakeholders, especially given the well-documented hostility and violence among firms, communities and governments in the Niger Delta. However, in spite of best practice, listening to and addressing stakeholder needs and demands, in a meeting with stakeholders, the general sentiment and expressed stakeholder statement was that there is "absolutely nothing the firm can do now or ever to make up for the lost heritage and traditions (specifically, fishing and marine wildlife which, given a legacy of decades of oil and gas exploration and spillage, was never ecologically returning)!" This stakeholder statement contradicts a fundamental basis of the engagement strategy used by firms to win hearts and minds and create shared value, essentially: demonstrate commitment to and create value for stakeholders through development projects and the firm will win appreciation, loyalty and the social license to operate

(Gunningham, Kagan, & Thornton, 2004) from stakeholders. The surprising stakeholder sentiment may have been driven by another unexpected contextual factor in this particular environment – who the stakeholders were in this community. Although a relatively poor community, the stakeholders were unexpectedly diverse with many having flown in from the United States, United Kingdom and other European or developed country environments to make demands upon the firm. This unique mix of stakeholders further complicated what and whether stakeholder engagement activities by the firm not only created value for stakeholders, but were appreciated by the communities.

The lessons in this third example are complex – our theoretical (and practitioner) understanding of engagement and responsibility has long moved well beyond the questions of do we engage with stakeholders to how to engage. But little to no research has explored contextually relevant factors such as how to manage the short, medium and especially long-term consequences of "good" engagement. How and when do we engage development partners? Does strategically aiming to execute "best practice" provide only limited (inverted U-shaped) performance benefits and therefore, should firms seek to engage only "enough," with stakeholders? What does "enough" look like in each context? Do stakeholder wins or value gains in fact mean firm losses, even when engagement is executed as best practice? How can scholars help practitioners to identify and manage a balance of win-win outcomes in the long-term? What do contextual win-wins look like? How do managers know when they are winning the hearts and minds of stakeholders? How do executives identify early in the scope of engagement that their engagement is being done "too well"? And, is there a difference between value creation for stakeholders and appreciation of that value by stakeholders and how can firms ensure that value creation results in stakeholder appreciation?

Unfortunately, the firm in question is, several years later, still trying to understand how to manage this best practice scenario. In the meantime, to keep stakeholders mollified – especially given the ongoing volatility of communities in their engagement with another, albeit differently owned and operated, asset nearby, the firm continues to simply expand engagement as demanded by stakeholders.

Informing Extant and Future Stakeholder Theoretic Research

The stories clearly demonstrate the importance of context for managing diverse and unique stakeholder engagement situations. For scholars, however, the key question remains: how may these stories inform our approach to extant and future stakeholder engagement theorizing? Consider three areas of engagement scholarly work, raised from the vignettes, where context is especially important – heterogeneous value creation, dynamic stakeholder identification, and boundaries of stakeholder rationality – and the situational, temporal or actor-level variables across various levels of analysis (Hitt, et al., 2007; Kozlowski & Klein 2000) that may capture contextual variability.

Contextual value creation for stakeholders is inherently heterogenous. A marching band, access to larger fish, return of lost heritage – the vignettes only touch at the surface of value sought by diverse stakeholders, especially in the developing world context. Value creation is arguably "the" primary outcome sought from stakeholder engagement strategies by firms and a diverse set of other actors, such as governments, multilaterals and nonprofit organizations. In addition to variation by actor type, the *value created or sought by stakeholders will differ based on political, social, economic and cultural situational and temporal factors*. Value gained or created must also be shared among diverse stakeholders and how that value is shared (e.g., equitably, equally, by actor attribute) will also differ by actor type and situational and temporal factors. Value created may have a different shelf-life in the short, medium and long timeframes; may fundamentally change over time; or, there may be some sequencing of value types (e.g., marching band before "real" engagement), based on situational factors. Additionally, the destruction of value may also depend on time and place.

Contextual stakeholder identification is dynamic. Intra- vs. inter-community identity; fishermen vs. farmers (the firm sought to change the livelihoods of the fishermen; the fishermen viewed the firm as wanting to change their identify from fishermen to farmers); local (poor) vs. international (highly educated, western-based, wealthy) stakeholders. Understanding *who the actors are based on their context* is critical to understanding how to engage these actors for the creation of value, e.g., engaging poor stakeholders may be fundamentally different from engaging wealthy, educated stakeholders. Mitchell et al. (1997) argue that power, urgency and legitimacy attributes of stakeholders define which stakeholders receive managerial attention; however, which stakeholder is powerful (or whose claim is legitimate or urgent) is also based on the attributes and situational and temporal factors of the stakeholder *as well as* the manager. How stakeholders identify themselves, particularly with regard to context (e.g., we are fishermen: we live and die by the sea) may shape not only the value they seek (i.e., the outcome) but also the type of engagement they may be receptive to (i.e., the process). Additionally, the time-dependent "strength" of that stakeholder's identity may impact the firm's ability to engage as well as the type of value created. For example, stakeholders who have lived and died in a particular environment for generations may be more difficult (or easier) to dissuade, change or influence, compared with stakeholders who have held a particular identity for a shorter period of time.

Contextual stakeholder rationality is also bounded by "*complexity* [in] environmental constraints" (Simon 1972: 164; emphasis in original). We want a marching band to prevent the emigration of youth from the community; we are not deterred by using dynamite near large oil vessels because it is our heritage; we will never be satisfied with any level of engagement but we demand more engagement. *Stakeholders rationalize their expectations and perceptions based on situational, temporal or other boundary conditions affecting them.* Further, stakeholder expectations and perceptions may not reflect situational and temporal realities. Firms and stakeholders often begin their interactions based on divergent rationale. While the rationale for engagement with stakeholders in extant research is considered primarily from a Western viewpoint largely based on market logic, this market-based view is often not the viewpoint of local stakeholders, especially in diverse international environments. Even among local stakeholders, rationality is diverse and might not be limited by only education and wealth – the socioeconomic variables usually considered in scholarly work – but also by more complex situational and temporal factors such as culture, history or legacy.

Although the contextual factors of value creation, identification and rationality have been touched upon separately, managerially relevant stakeholder engagement is so complex that important questions of how and when to engage may be contingent on interactions across these, and other, areas including important firm attributes and characteristics at various levels (e.g., employees, firms, multinationals, etc.). For example, the type(s) of value sought by particular firms, with particular stakeholders, in particular environments, may be contingent on the identity and the rationality (real and perceived) of different types of stakeholders, under specific situational and temporal conditions.

The Need for Context-Driven Research Designs

To develop new practice- and policy-relevant stakeholder engagement scholarly work, careful integration of contextual factors within scholarly research design is critical. Whether in large sample research or in qualitative case-study research (Eisenhardt 1989; Welch, et al., 2011; Yin 2002), finding contextually rich data is necessarily the starting point.

In my own work with Henisz and Dorobantu (Dorobantu, Henisz, & Nartey 2017; Henisz, Dorobantu, & Nartey 2014; Nartey, Dorobantu, & Henisz 2017; Nartey, Henisz & Dorobantu, 2017), using a unique sample of twenty-six mining companies around the world located primarily in developing country contexts, we create a data set comprising over 50,000 stakeholder interactionships and use this data to map the stakeholder networks defined by these stakeholder interactions. We capture variables of interest at the firm and

stakeholder levels, as well as relevant country, culture (language), location, source, and relationship variables. Collecting rich and contextual data for such a large dataset was not straightforward. We leveraged a team of twenty-two undergrads over a three-year period to read thoroughly over 24,000 news articles pertaining to these twenty-six firms. This allowed us to identify variables such as engagement strategy, or degree of cooperation and conflict, that leverage the richness of the specific interactions to help us better understand the context in which these firms operate, and define appropriate engagement strategies firms in similar environments can leverage.

In ongoing work with Teegen (Nartey & Teegen 2017), we take this contextual approach further and specifically seek to explore context as it applies to value creation, trade-offs and synergies across large-scale infrastructure projects in which the private sector development wing of the World Bank Group – The International Finance Corporation (IFC) – invests. We seek to understand specifically how contextual relationships and factors shape the outcomes of these projects and define project value across seven different value categories pertaining to different stakeholder types and contexts. To delve more deeply into project contexts, we focus initially on five global investment projects where we go beyond the use of news articles and, in addition, utilize proprietary access to all IFC project data and documentation (which, for some projects, is well over 5,000 documents). We have also conducted hours of interviews/meetings with project managers in Washington DC, and have spent months in the field conducting field based assessments and stakeholder interviews with in-country firm personnel, community leaders and lay people, international and local NGOs, government personnel, and have even accompanied consultants on their independent auditing trips. Through these diverse approaches we seek to understand what the relevant contextual variables are. Ongoing work will leverage these field-based insights to build richer datasets to answer the key question of what creates stakeholder value and how this value can be maximized across projects while being equitably shared by the numerous and diverse stakeholders affected by the firm's large-scale investment project.

In sum, context is fundamental to new work in stakeholder theory, especially in the area of stakeholder engagement. The three vignettes outlined above all speak to the diversity and importance of context in stakeholder engagement scholarship and practice. Despite the fact that these examples all refer to firms operating in the extractives industry in the developing world, we cannot generalize the lessons learned or the questions raised. Each environment has contextual factors which idiosyncratically shape the environment in which the firm must operate and also determine the firm's possible stakeholder engagement options and outcomes. To effectively understand how (and critically, which) contextual factors drive or impact stakeholder engagement, we need better and richer qualitative and empirical data, better empirical instruments, and better understandings of what contextual variables to look for prior to our ability to theorize and empirically model; only then can we begin to try to effectively generalize lessons and findings. Much of what we currently focus on within the stakeholder literature does not delve deeply enough into the context, especially within complex developing country environments where our current theories and assumptions (from my field-based research experience) often do not hold. New questions must be driven by the richness of context. If not, by excluding serious explorations of context within our work, we run the real risk that our theory and the lessons learned from our research are less relevant for practitioners and policy makers and provide limited understanding and management of value creation for, by, and with stakeholders.

References

Bamberger, P. (2008). From the editors beyond contextualization: Using context theories to narrow the micro-macro gap in management research. *Academy of Management Journal*, 51(5): 839–846.

Blair, J. D. & Hunt, J. G. (1986). Getting inside the head of the management researcher one more time: Context-free and context-specific orientations in research. *Journal of Management*, 12(2): 147–166.

Cappelli, P. & Sherer, P. D. (1991). The missing role of context in OB: The need for a meso-level approach. In L. L. Cummings & B. M. Staw, eds., *Research in organizational behavior*, pp. 55–110. Greenwich, CT: JAI Press.

Donaldson, T., & Preston, L. E. (1995). The stakeholder theory of the corporation: Concepts, evidence, and implications. *Academy of Management Review*, 20(1): 65–91.

Dorobantu, S., Henisz, W. J., & Nartey, L. (2017). Not all sparks light a fire: Stakeholder and shareholder reactions to critical events in contested markets. *Administrative Science Quarterly*, 62(3): 561–597.

Eisenhardt, K. M. (1989). Building theories from case study research. *Academy of Management Review*, 14(4): 532–550.

Freeman, R. E. (1984). *Strategic management: A stakeholder approach*. Boston: Pitman Publishing.

Freeman, R. E., Harrison, J.S., Wicks, A.C., Parmar, B.L., & de Colle, S. (2010). *Stakeholder theory: The state of the art*. Cambridge, UK: Cambridge University Press.

Freeman, R. E., Rusconi, G., Signori, S., & Strudler, A. (2012). Stakeholder theory(ies): Ethical ideas and managerial action. *Journal of Business Ethics*, 109(1): 1–2.

Frynas, J. G. (2005). The false developmental promise of corporate social responsibility: Evidence from multinational oil companies. *International Affairs*, 81(3): 581–598.

Frynas, J. G. (2008). Corporate social responsibility and international development: Critical assessment. *Corporate Governance: An International Review*, 16(4): 274–281.

Gunningham, N., Kagan, R. A., & Thornton, D. (2004). Social license and environmental protection: Why businesses go beyond compliance. *Law and Social Inquiry*, 29: 307–341.

Harrison, J. S., & Freeman, R. E. (1999). Stakeholders, social responsibility, and performance: Empirical evidence and theoretical perspectives. *Academy of Management Journal*, 42(5): 479–485.

Henisz, W. J., Dorobantu, S., & Nartey, L. J. (2014). Spinning gold: The financial returns to stakeholder engagement. *Strategic Management Journal*, 35(12): 1727–1748.

Hitt, M. A., Beamish, P. W., Jackson, S. E., & Mathieu, J. E. (2007). Building theoretical and empirical bridges across levels: Multilevel research in management. *Academy of Management Journal*, 50(6): 1385–1399.

Johns, G. (2006). The essential impact of context on organizational behavior. *Academy of Management Review*, 31(2): 386–408.

Jones, T. M. (1995). Instrumental stakeholder theory: A synthesis of ethics and economics. *The Academy of Management Review*, 20(2): 404–437.

Kozlowski, S. J., & Klein, K. J. (2000). A multilevel approach to theory and research in organizations: Contextual, temporal and emergent processes. In K. J. Kleine & S. J. Kozlowski, eds., *Multilevel theory, research, and methods in organizations: Foundations, extensions and new directions*, pp. 3–90. San Francisco, CA: Jossey-Bass.

Mitchell, R. K., Agle, B. R., & Wood, D. J. (1997. Toward a theory of stakeholder identification and salience: Defining the principle of who and what really counts. *Academy of Management Review*, 22 (4): 853–886.

Nartey, L., Dorobantu, S., & Henisz, W. J. (2017). A participatory approach to stakeholder engagement: Defining a hierarchy of strategic action. Working paper, University of South Carolina.

Nartey, L., Henisz, W. J., & Dorobantu, S. (2017). Status climbing versus bridging: Multinational stakeholder engagement strategies. *Strategy Science*, 3(2): 367–392.

Nartey, L., & Teegen, H. (2017). A convening model to enhance value creation and pluralistic appropriation in large-scale investment projects. Working paper, University of South Carolina.

Rousseau, D. M., & Fried, Y. (2001). Editorial: Location, location, location: Contextualizing organizational research. *Journal of Organizational Behavior*, 22(1): 1–13.

Simon, H.A. (1972). Theories of bounded rationality. In C. McGuire & R. Radner, eds., *Decision and organization*. Amsterdam: North-Holland.

Tsui, A. S. (2006). Contextualization in Chinese management research. *Management and Organization Review*, 2(1): 1–13.

Welch, C., Piekkari, R., Plakoyiannaki, E., & Paavilainen-Mäntymäki, E. (2011). Theorising from case studies: Towards a pluralist future for international business research. *Journal of International Business Studies*, 42(5): 740–762.

Yin, R. K. (2002). *Applications of case study research*, 2nd edn. Thousand Oaks, CA: Sage.

Index